W9-CUA-081

Macroeconomics

Fourth Edition

Copyright © by Houghton Mifflin Company. All rights reserved.

Due 3/17.

Macroeconomics

Fourth Edition

William Boyes

Arizona State University

Michael Melvin

Arizona State University

Copyright © by Houghton Mifflin Company. All rights reserved.

HOUGHTON MIFFLIN COMPANY   Boston   New York

WITHDRAWN

To our families
W. B.   M. M.

Senior Sponsoring Editor: Bonnie Binkert
Associate Project Editor: Rachel D'Angelo Wimberly
Senior Production/Design Coordinator: Carol Merrigan
Senior Manufacturing Coordinator: Marie Barnes
Marketing Manager: Juli Bliss

CREDITS

Cover designer: Cathy Hawkes, Cat and Mouse Design
Cover image: illustration by Ken McMillan

Chapter photos: p. 3 © Dean Abramson/Stock Boston; p. 8 © Robert Frerck/Odyssey/Chicago; p. 31 © Amy C. Etra/Photo Edit; p. 41 © Cameramann/The Image Works; p. 49 © Marc Romanelli/The Image Bank; p. 50 © Ron McMillan/Gamma-Liaison; p. 50 © David R. Frazier Photolibrary; p. 66 © Robert Frerck/Odyssey/Chicago; p. 81 © Matthew Neil McVay/Stock Boston; p. 97 © Paul Chesley/Tony Stone Images; p. 97 © Cameramann International, Ltd.; p. 109 © Porter Gifford/Liaison International; p. 119 © Najlah Feanny/Stock Boston; p. 124 © Richemond/The Image Works; p. 133 © Paul Chesley/Tony Stone Images; p. 143 © Mark E. Gibson; p. 157 © Visual Departures, Ltd./Photo Researchers; p. 164 © Jean Pragen/Tony Stone Images; p. 173 © Bob Daemmrich/The Image Works; p. 176 Margaret Bourke-White, Life Magazine © Time Warner; p. 180 © Gilles Mingasson/Gamma-Liaison; p. 201 © F. Carter Smith/Sygma; p. 216 © David R. Frazier Photolibrary; p. 229 © Bob Krist/Tony Stone Images; p. 232 © Richard Bradbury/Tony Stone Images; p. 244 © Richard Pasley/Stock Boston; p. 261 © Larry Mayer/Gamma-Liaison; p. 289 © Sandra Baker/Gamma-Liaison; p. 293 © Suzanne & Nick Geary/Tony Stone Images; p. 317 © F. Lochon/Gamma-Liaison; p. 341 © Patrick Aventurier/Gamma-Liaison; p. 346

Bettmann Newsphotos; p. 369 © William S. Helsel/Tony Stone Images; p. 388 © Owen Franken/Stock Boston; p. 390 © Patrick Robert/Sygma; p. 397 © Bill Nation/Sygma; p. 413 © Glen Allison/Tony Stone Images; p. 425 © Cameramann International; p. 439 © Alain Le Garsmeur/Tony Stone Images; p. 447 © David Austen/Stock Boston; p. 454 © Robert Fried; p. 461 © David R. Frazier Photolibrary; p. 472 © Paul Chesley/Tony Stone Images; p. 476 © Dilip Mehta/Contact Press; p. 479 © Chris Niedenthal/Black Star; p. 481 © David Kampfner/Liaison International; p. 495 © Charles Gupton/Tony Stone Images; p. 499 © Jean-Leo Dugast/Sygma; p. 517 © Fred R. Palmer/Stock Boston; p. 530 © David R. Frazier Photolibrary; p. 539 © Andy Freeberg.

Copyright © 1999 by Houghton Mifflin Company. All rights reserved.

No part of this work may be reproduced or transmitted in any form or by any means, electronic or mechanical, including photocopying and recording, or by any information storage or retrieval system without the prior written permission of Houghton Mifflin Company unless such copying is expressly permitted by federal copyright law. Address inquiries to College Permissions, Houghton Mifflin Company, 222 Berkeley Street, Boston, MA 02116-3764.

Printed in the U.S.A.

Library of Congress Catalog Card Number: 98-71995

ISBN: 0-395-90806-X

2 3 4 5 6 7 8 9 —VH— 02 01 00 99

Copyright © by Houghton Mifflin Company. All rights reserved.

Preface

In the first edition of *Macroeconomics* we integrated the global perspective with the traditional economic principles to give students a framework to understand the globally developing economic world. Events since then have made this approach even more imperative. The Soviet Union has disintegrated, newly independent nations have emerged, and markets have been established where none had existed before. Students and instructors embraced the idea that the economies of countries are interrelated and that this should be made clear in the study of economics. *Macroeconomics* gives students the tools they need to make connections between the economic principles they learn and the now-global world they live in.

Current users of *Macroeconomics* report that their students find the book "very interesting," "really easy to understand," and "easy to learn from." We have also discovered that this book has well served students from many different backgrounds and with varying future plans—from those who major in business, psychology, education, engineering, English, and other fields to those who choose to pursue economics.

Now, in the fourth edition, we continue to refine and improve the text as a teaching and learning instrument while expanding its international base by updating and adding examples related to global economics throughout.

CHANGES IN THE FOURTH EDITION

The fourth edition of *Macroeconomics* has been streamlined and thoroughly updated and refined. Streamlining was primarily achieved by eliminating or combining several chapters as outlined in the sections following. A detailed account of all the additions, deletions, and modifications is in the Transition Guide in the *Instructor's Resource Manual* and on the web site at http://www.hmco.com/college.

Revised Macroeconomic Coverage

The macroeconomic chapters have been updated to include the latest available economic statistics, in most instances up through 1998. In many chapters, numerical examples have been revised to provide greater clarity in the graphical presentations. These chapters stress one model—aggregate demand and aggregate supply. The Keynesian aggregate expenditures material is available

and thoroughly covered in Chapters 10 and 11 and then is integrated into the aggregate demand model at the end of Chapter 11. The last chapter of the Third Edition, "The Transition From Socialism to Capitalism" has now been integrated into Chapter 19, "Development Economics."

New Features Throughout

Each chapter contains approximately 15 exercises that challenge students, test their retention and understanding of the material, and extend their knowledge. New to the fourth edition are Internet Exercises, one per chapter, which allow interested students to participate in activities that require accessing data from the Internet. For example, in Chapter 1, students can access our web site and examine statistics of people attending college in the United States. Students are then asked several questions about the data. Additional web-based assignments, at least one per chapter, are also available on the supporting web site at http://www.hmco.com/college.

SUCCESSFUL FEATURES RETAINED FROM THE THIRD EDITION

In addition to the considerable updating and revising we've done for the fourth edition, there are several features preserved from the previous edition that we think instructors will find interesting.

Enhanced Student Relevance

With all the demands on today's students, it's no wonder that they resist spending time on a subject unless they see how the material relates to them and how they will benefit from mastering it. We incorporate features throughout the text that show economics as the relevant and necessary subject we know it to be.

Real-World Examples Students are rarely intrigued by unknown manufacturers or service companies. Our text talks about people and firms that students recognize. We describe business decisions made by McDonald's and Pizza Hut, by Kodak and Fuji, and by the local video store or café. We discuss the policies of Bill Clinton and other world leaders. These examples grab students' interest. Reviewers have repeatedly praised the use of novel examples to convey economic concepts.

Copyright © by Houghton Mifflin Company. All rights reserved.

Economic Insight Boxes   These brief boxes bring in contemporary material from current periodicals and journals to illustrate or extend the discussion in the chapter. By reserving interesting but more technical sidelights for boxes, we lessen the likelihood that students will be confused or distracted by issues that are not critical to understanding the chapter. By including excerpts from articles, we help students learn to move from theory to real-world examples. And by including plenty of contemporary issues, we guarantee that students will see how economics relates to their own lives.

Economically Speaking Boxes   The objective of the principles course is to teach students how to translate the predictions that come out of economic models to the real world and to translate real-world events into an economic model in order to analyze and understand what lies behind the events. The Economically Speaking boxes present students with examples of this kind of analysis. Students read an article that appears on the left-hand page of a two-page spread at the end of each chapter. The commentary on the right-hand page shows how the facts and events in the article translate into a specific economic model or idea, thereby demonstrating the relevance of theory.

An Effective and Proven System of Teaching and Learning Aids

This text is designed to make teaching easier by enhancing student learning. Tested pedagogy motivates students, emphasizes clarity, reinforces relationships, simplifies review, and fosters critical thinking. And, as we have discovered from reviewer and user feedback, this pedagogy works.

In-Text Referencing System   Sections are numbered for easy reference and to reinforce hierarchies of ideas. Numbered section heads serve as an outline of the chapter, allowing instructors flexibility in assigning reading, and making it easy for students to find topics to review. Each item in the key terms list and summary at the end of the chapter refers students back to the appropriate section's number.

The section numbering system appears throughout the Boyes/Melvin ancillary package; the *Test Banks, Study Guides,* and *Instructor's Resource Manual* are organized according to the same system.

Fundamental Questions   These questions help to organize the chapter and highlight those issues that are critical to understanding. Students can then read the chapter with these questions in mind; this active participation enhances understanding and retention. Each fundamental

question also appears in the margin by the text discussion that helps students to answer the question. Fundamental questions are also used to organize the chapter summaries. Brief paragraphs answering each of these questions are found in the *Study Guides* available as supplements to this text. The fundamental questions also serve as one of several criteria used to categorize questions in the *Test Banks.*

Preview   This motivating lead-in sets the stage for the chapter. Much more than a road map, it helps students identify real-world issues that relate to the concepts that will be presented.

Recaps   Briefly listing the main points covered, a recap appears at the end of each major section within a chapter. Students are able to quickly review what they have just read before going on to the next section.

Summary   The summary at the end of each chapter is organized along two dimensions. The primary organizational device is the list of fundamental questions. A brief synopsis of the discussion that helps students to answer those questions is arranged by section below each of the questions. Students are encouraged to create their own links among topics as they keep in mind the connections between the big picture and the details that make it up.

Comments   Found in the text margins, these comments highlight especially important concepts, point out common mistakes, and warn students of common pitfalls. They alert students to parts of the discussion that they should read with particular care.

Key Terms   Key terms appear in bold type in the text. They also appear with their definition in the margin and are listed at the end of the chapter for easy review. All key terms are included in the Glossary at the end of the text.

Friendly Appearance

Economics can be intimidating; this is why we've striven to keep *Macroeconomics* looking friendly and inviting. The one-column design and ample white space in this text provide an accessible backdrop. Over 150 figures rely on well-developed pedagogy and consistent use of color to reinforce understanding. Striking colors were chosen to enhance readability and provide visual interest. Specific curves were assigned specific colors, and families of curves were assigned related colors.

Annotations on the art point out areas of particular concern or importance. Students can see exactly which part of a graph illustrates a shortage or a surplus, a change in consumption or consumer surplus. Tables that

Copyright © by Houghton Mifflin Company. All rights reserved.

provide data from which graphs are plotted are paired with their graphs. Where appropriate, color is used to show correlations between the art and the table, and captions clearly explain what is shown in the figures and link them to the text discussion.

The color photographs not only provide visual images but make the text appealing. These vibrant photos tell stories as well as illustrate concepts, and often lengthy captions explain what is in the photos, again to draw connections between the images and the text discussion.

Thoroughly International Coverage

Students understand that they live in a global economy; they can hardly shop, watch the news, or read a newspaper without stumbling on this basic fact. International examples are presented in every chapter but are not merely added on, as is the case with many other texts. By introducing international effects on demand and supply in Chapter 3 and then describing in a nontechnical manner the basics of the foreign exchange market and the balance of payments in Chapter 7, we are able to incorporate the international sector into the economic models and applications wherever appropriate thereafter. Because the international content is incorporated from the beginning, students develop a far more realistic picture of the national economy; as a result they don't have to alter their thinking to allow for international factors later on. The three chapters that focus on international topics at the end of the text allow those instructors who desire to delve much more deeply into international issues to do so.

The global applicability of economics is emphasized by *using traditional economic concepts to explain international economic events and using international events to illustrate economic concepts that have traditionally been illustrated with domestic examples.* Instructors need not know the international institutions to introduce international examples since the topics through which they are addressed are familiar, for example, price ceilings, price discrimination, expenditures on resources, marginal productivity theory, and others.

Uniquely international elements of the macroeconomic coverage in the text include:

- The treatment of the international sector as one of the economic participants and the inclusion of net exports as early as Chapter 4

- The early description of the foreign exchange market and the balance of payments in Chapter 7

- International elements in the development of aggregate demand and supply

- An extended treatment of macroeconomic links between countries in Chapter 17

Modern Macroeconomic Organization and Content

Macroeconomics is changing and textbooks must reflect that change. We begin with the basics—GDP, unemployment, and inflation. These are the ongoing concerns of any economy, for they have a significant influence on how people feel. These are the issues that don't go away. Added to these core topics is an easy-to-understand, descriptive introduction to the foreign exchange market and the balance of payments. We provide a critical alternative for those instructors who believe that it is no longer reasonable to relegate this material to the final chapters, where coverage may be rushed.

Armed with these basics, students are ready to delve into the richness of macroeconomic thought. Macro models and approaches have evolved over the years, and they continue to invite exciting theoretical and policy debates. The majority of instructors we asked voiced frustration with the challenge of pulling this rich and varied material together in class and stressed that a coherent picture of the aggregate demand and supply model was critical. We have structured the macro portion to allow for many teaching preferences while assuring a clear delineation of the aggregate demand/aggregate supply model.

To help instructors successfully present a single coherent model, we present aggregate demand and aggregate supply first, in Chapter 9, immediately following the chapter on inflation and unemployment. This sequence allows for the smooth transition from business cycle fluctuations to aggregate demand/aggregate supply *(AD/AS)*. The Keynesian income and expenditures model is presented in full in Chapters 10 and 11 as the fixed-price version of the *AD/AS* model (with a horizontal aggregate supply curve). Those who want to use the *AD/AS* model exclusively will have no problem moving from the Chapter 9 presentation of it to the fiscal policy material in Chapter 12. The policy chapters rely on the *AD/AS* model for analysis.

The macroeconomic policy chapters begin with a thorough presentation of fiscal policy, money and banking, and monetary policy, with international elements included. Chapter 15 covers contemporary policy issues, and various schools of thought are treated in Chapter 16, when students are ready to appreciate the differences and can benefit from a discussion of new Keynesian and new classical models as well as of their precursors. Chapter 17 develops macroeconomic links between countries. This chapter helps students understand why economies cannot function in isolation from each other and clearly

Copyright © by Houghton Mifflin Company. All rights reserved.

demonstrates why policy actions undertaken by one government affect not only that government's citizens but citizens and businesses of other countries as well.

Part IV, "Economic Growth and Development," brings together the concepts and issues presented in the core macro chapters to explain how economies grow and what factors encourage or discourage growth. Most of the world's population live in poor countries. Growth and development are critical to those people. The material in these chapters also addresses issues of importance to industrial countries, such as the slowdown of productivity growth in the United States.

A COMPLETE TEACHING AND LEARNING PACKAGE

In today's market no book is complete without a full complement of ancillaries. Those instructors who face huge classes find good transparencies (acetates) to be critical instructional tools. Others may find that computer simulations and tutorials are invaluable. Still others use projection technology and want *PowerPoint* slides. All of these are available. And to foster the development of consistent teaching and study strategies, the ancillaries pick up pedagogical features of the text—like the fundamental questions—wherever appropriate.

Transparencies Available to adopters are over 100 color acetates showing the most important figures in the text. Over 10 percent of these figures have one to three overlays, which in addition to adding clarity and flexibility to the discussion, allow instructors to visually demonstrate the dynamic nature of economics.

Instructor's Resource Manual (**IRM**) Patricia Diane Nipper has produced a manual that will streamline preparation for both new and experienced faculty. Preliminary sections cover class administration, alternative syllabi, and a guide to the use of cooperative learning in teaching the principles of economics.

The *IRM* also contains a detailed chapter-by-chapter review of all the changes made in the fourth edition. This Transition Guide should help instructors more easily move from the use of the third edition to this new edition.

Each chapter of the *IRM* contains:

- Teaching objectives *that address (1) critical points to cover if your students are to succeed with later chapters, (2) concepts traditionally difficult for students to master, and (3) the unique features of the chapter*

- The fundamental questions
- The key terms
- A lecture outline with *teaching strategies*—general techniques and guidelines, essay topics, and other hints to enliven your classes
- Opportunities for discussion
- Answers to every end-of-chapter exercise
- Answers to *Study Guide* homework questions

Study Guides Janet L. Wolcutt and James E. Clark of the Center for Economic Education at Wichita State University have revised the *Macroeconomics* and *Microeconomics Study Guides* to give students the practice they need to master this course. Initially received by students and instructors with great enthusiasm, the guides maintain their warm and lively style to keep students on the right track. For each chapter:

- Fundamental questions are answered in one or several paragraphs. For students who have trouble formulating their own answers to these questions after reading the text, the *Study Guides* provide an invaluable model.
- Key terms are listed.
- A Quick Check Quiz is organized by section, so any wrong answers send the student directly to the relevant material in the text.
- Practice Questions and Problems, which is also organized by section, includes a variety of question formats—multiple choice, true/false, matching, and fill in the blank. They test understanding of the concepts and ask students to construct or perform computations.
- Thinking About and Applying . . . uses newspaper headlines or some other real-life applications to test students' ability to reason in economic terms.
- A Homework page at the end of each chapter contains five (two factual, two applied, and one synthesis/analysis) questions that can be answered on the sheet and turned in for grading. Answers are included in the *IRM*.
- Sample tests appear at the end of each *Study Guide* part and consist of 25 to 50 questions similar to *Test Bank* questions. Taking the sample tests helps students determine whether they are prepared for exams.
- Answers are provided to all but Homework questions. Students are referred back to the relevant pages in the main text.

Copyright © by Houghton Mifflin Company. All rights reserved.

Test Banks   *Test Banks* for both *Macroeconomics* and *Microeconomics* are available. Nearly 8,000 test items, many of them new to this edition, provide a wealth of material for classroom testing. Features include:

- Multiple choice, true/false, and essay questions in every chapter

- Nearly 1,000 questions new to this edition, marked for easy identification

- An increased number of analytical, applied, and graphical questions

- The identification of all test items according to topic, question type (factual, interpretive, or applied), level of difficulty, and applicable fundamental question

- A *Study Guide* section of the test that includes five test items taken directly from the *Study Guide* and five test items that parallel *Study Guide* questions, for the instructor who is interested in rewarding students for working through the *Study Guide*

Computerized Test Bank

This innovative test-assembly program, revised for this edition, renders precise, preprogrammed graphs on the computer quickly, easily, and accurately. You can select from among more than 7,000 questions, edit nongraphic items, peruse items in order, add your own questions to customize tests, and print out alternative versions using a number of variables. Individual items or tests in their entirety can be previewed before printing. The sophisticated data retrieval capabilities of the computerized test bank allow instructors to generate multiple versions of a test automatically and assure compatability of tests consisting of different test items. This program also allows the importation of files from ASCII, WordStar, and WordPerfect. It is available for IBM-PC®, PS/2, and compatible microcomputers.

New Tutorial/Simulation Software   This software provides the opportunity for students to review and apply the most important concepts covered in the text. It consists of two major components—tutorial and simulation—either of which can be used for independent study and practice, in small group work in a computer lab, or as part of a classroom demonstration. The instructor could also assign specific modules as homework, since students can print the graphs they generate.

- The tutorial portion of the program consists of modules, one per chapter, tied to the major topics of the text (e.g., "Supply and Demand," "Consumer Theory and Utility," "The Role of Government," and "Monetary Policy"). Each module is broken up into several major sections, with a self-test offered at the end of each section to reinforce what has been covered.

Working at their own pace, students experiment with the curves by entering and changing the values of discrete variables in order to see the results played out in the corresponding graph window. Narrating text prompts the student to make changes to variables and, with reinforcing explanation, encourages the student to reflect on what has happened in the graph window. A View menu allows students to view the graphs with or without a background grid (in a variety of styles) or with thin or thick curves. (This feature is also handy for classroom demonstrations.) An extensive Help menu enables students to access the Boyes/Melvin Glossary whenever they need to refresh their memories on the meaning of a particular term.

- In the simulation component of the Courseware, the structured sequence of the tutorial is replaced by more open-ended problem-solving. Students begin by choosing one of several scenarios, which range from "Effects of a Tariff" to "A Pollution Policy for Denver." But, instead of being presented with graphs linked to text screens, the student is encouraged to pull up his or her choices of data from a rich library of data, choose a relevant time period, and construct a meaningful graph or table. Here the student must not only choose and assemble the data but also begin the process of interpretation. With over 20 complete sets of data which include such information as nominal GDP, inflation rate, and unemployment rate, the possibilities for analysis of data are almost endless. All data are provided in both annual and quarterly figures from 1930 to 1998 where those years are available.

The simulation scenarios also offer a kind of exploration that is not possible in other software programs. When the student is interested in doing some independent exploring, the screen is cleared and all the micro and macro data sets become accessible. Students can plot up to three data series against time or choose from among the data series to plot variables against each other. This is an ideal vehicle around which professors can build substantive student assignments.

Copyright © by Houghton Mifflin Company. All rights reserved.

PowerPoint Slides Figures, tables, key equations from the text, and other resources that extend the text are provided on electronic slides created for Microsoft's popular *PowerPoint* presentation software. *PowerPoint* allows instructors to create customized lecture presentations that can be displayed on computer-based projection systems. The slides are produced as a complete presentation, but using *PowerPoint*, presenters can also insert their own slides into the presentation or use specific slides in sets that they create themselves. These slides ship with a copy of the *PowerPoint* Viewer, which allows presenters who don't own a copy of *PowerPoint* to use the presentation, but not to change or add to the slides.

Web Site The web site used in this edition (**http://www.hmco.com/college**) provides an extended learning environment for students and a rich store of teaching resources for instructors. Included are key economic links for every chapter, extended web-based assignments, and on-line tests—all intended to help students test their mastery of the chapter content. Also included for instructors are economic and teaching resource links, teaching tips, and access to demonstrations of other components of the teaching package.

ACKNOWLEDGMENTS

Writing a text of this scope is a challenge that requires the expertise and efforts of many. We are grateful to our friends and colleagues who have so generously given their time, creativity, and insight to help us create a text that best meets the needs of today's students.

We'd like to thank members of an advisory board of adopters and nonadopters who responded to an extensive survey. Their comments were invaluable in planning the fourth edition. Members of the advisory board were: **David Black,** University of Toledo; **Gary Bogner,** Baker College of Muskegon; **Bradley Braun,** University of Central Florida; **Bill Brewer,** Genesee Community College; **Greg Brown,** Martin Community College; **Kristin Carrico,** Umpaqua Community College; **Jill L. Caviglia,** Carson Newman College; **Kenny Christianson,** Ithaca College; **Valerie Collins,** Colorado Mountain College; **Wilfrid W. Csaplar, Jr.,** Southside Virginia Community College; **Stephen Davis,** Valley City State University; **Ray Egan,** Pierce College; **Martha K. Field,** Greenfield Community College; **Fred Fisher,** Colorado Mountain College; **Bradley Garton,** Laramie County Community College; **Omer Gokcekus,** North Carolina

Central University; **Rik Hafer,** Southern Illinois University, Edwardsville; **Michael Harsh,** Randolph-Macon College; **Arleen Hoag,** Owens Community College; **James G. Ibe,** Morris College; **James Johnson,** Black Hawk College; **F. Jeffrey Keil,** J. Sargent Reynolds Community College; **Donna M. Kish-Goodling,** Muhlenberg College; **Ali Kutan,** Southern Illinois University, Edwardsville; **Nick Laopodis,** Villa Julie College; **Paul Lockard,** Black Hawk College; **Glenna Lunday,** Western Oklahoma State College; **Les Manns,** Doane College; **Milton Miller,** Carteret Community College; **Diane Nipper,** Southside Virginia Community College; **Robert Payne,** Baker College of Port Huron; **Lynne Pierson Doti,** Chapman University; **Kojo A. Quartey,** Talladega College; **Richard M. Risinit,** Reading Area Community College; **J. Richard Sealscott,** Northwest State Community College; **Steve Seteroff,** Chapman University; **Richard Skolnik,** Tiffin University; **John Somers,** Portland Community College; **Rob Verner,** Ursuline College; **Mark Wohar,** University of Nebraska-Omaha; and **Girma Zelleke,** Kutztown University.

Unsolicited feedback from current users has also been greatly appreciated. We'd like to thank Nancy Roberts and Elmer Gooding of Arizona State University, Arthur Gibb from the U.S. Naval Academy, Peter C. Garlick at the State University of New York at New Paltz, and Neil Reznik of the Community College of Philadelphia for their very useful feedback.

Thanks go to Eugenio Dante Suarez and Melissa Hardison for their work on the *Test Banks* for this edition. The important contributions of Bettina Peiers and Karen Thomas-Brandt of Arizona State University on the second edition *Test Bank* and Michael Couvillion of Plymouth State College on the first edition *Test Bank* must also be acknowledged. Thanks, too, go to Paul S. Estenson of Gustavus Adolphus College and Edward T. Merkel of Troy State University for their tremendous contribution in preparing the second edition *Instructor's Resource Manual*.

We want to thank the many people at Houghton Mifflin Company who devoted countless hours to making this text the best it could be, including Bonnie Binkert, Joanne White, Bernadette Walsh, Rachel D'Angelo Wimberly, Tezeta Tulloch, and Carol Merrigan. We are grateful for their enthusiasm, expertise, and energy.

Finally, we wish to thank our families and friends. The inspiration they provided through the conception and development of this book cannot be measured but certainly was essential.

Copyright © by Houghton Mifflin Company. All rights reserved.

Our students at Arizona State University continue to help us improve the text through each edition; their many questions have given us invaluable insight into how best to present this intriguing subject. It is our hope that this textbook will bring a clear understanding of economic thought to many other students as well. We welcome any feedback for improvements.

W. B.   M. M.

Copyright © by Houghton Mifflin Company. All rights reserved.

ADVISORY BOARD REVIEWERS

David Black
University of Toledo
Toledo, OH

Gary Bogner
Baker College-Muskegon
Muskegon, MI

Bradley Braun
University of Central Florida
Orlando, FL

William S. Brewer
Genesee Community College
Batavia, NY

Gregory Brown
Martin Community College
Williamston, NC

Kristin Carrico
Umpqua Community College
Roseburg, OR

Jill L. Caviglia
Salisbury State University
Salisbury, MD

Kenneth W. Christianson, Jr.
Ithaca College
Ithaca, NY

Valerie A. Collins
Colorado Mountain College
Glenwood Springs, CO

Wilfrid W. Csaplar, Jr.
Southside Virginia Community College
Keysville, VA

Stephen B. Davis
Valley City State University
Valley City, ND

Lynne Pierson Doti
Chapman University
Orange, CA

Raymond J. Egan
WA
(Retired, formerly at Pierce College)

Martha Field
Greenfield Community College
Greenfield, MA

Fred Fisher
Colorado Mountain College, CO

Bradley Garton
Laramie County Community College
Laramie, Wyoming

Omer Gokcekus
North Carolina Central University
Durham, NC

R.W. Hafer
Southern Illinois University–
Edwardsville
Edwardsville, IL

Michael Harsh
Randolph-Macon College

Arleen Hoag
Owens Community College
Toledo, OH

James Johnson
Black Hawk College
Moline, IL

Jeff Keil
J. Sargent Reynolds
Community College

Donna Kish-Goodling
Muhlenburg College
Allentown, PA

Ali Kutan
SIUE
Edwardsville, IL

Nikiforos Laopodis
Villa Julie College, MD

Paul Lockard
Black Hawk College
Moline, IL

Glenna Lunday
Western Oklahoma State College

Les Manns
Doane College

Dan Marburger
Arkansas State University
Jonesborough, AK

Buddy Miller
Carteret Community College
Morehead City, NC

Charles Okeke
Community College of Southern
Nevada
Las Vegas, NV

Robert Payne
Baher College
Port Huron, MI

Dick Risinit
Reading Area Community College

Robert S. Rycroft
Mary Washington College
Fredericksburg, VA

Charles Saccardo
Bentley College, MA

Charles Sackrey
Bucknell University
Lewisburg, PA

J. Richard Sealscott
Northwest State Community College

Steve Seteroff
Chapman University Bangor Academic
Center, WA
City University, WA

Richard Skolnik
SUNY-Oswego
Oswego, NY

Scott F. Smith
University at Albany
Albany, NY

John Somers
Portland Community College–Sylvania
Portland, Oregon

John J. Spitzer
State University of New York
College at Brockport
Brockport, NY

Rob Verner
Ursuline College
Pepper Pike, OH

Mark E. Wohar
University of Nebraska
Omaha, NE

Darrel A. Young
University of Texas
Austin, TX

Girma Zelleke
Kutztown University
Kutztown, PA

Copyright © by Houghton Mifflin Company. All rights reserved.

Brief Contents

Copyright © by Houghton Mifflin Company. All rights reserved.

Copyright © by Houghton Mifflin Company. All rights reserved.

Contents

Copyright © by Houghton Mifflin Company. All rights reserved.

Copyright © by Houghton Mifflin Company. All rights reserved.

Copyright © by Houghton Mifflin Company. All rights reserved.

Copyright © by Houghton Mifflin Company. All rights reserved.

Copyright © by Houghton Mifflin Company. All rights reserved.

Macroeconomics

Fourth Edition

Copyright © by Houghton Mifflin Company. All rights reserved.

Copyright © by Houghton Mifflin Company. All rights reserved.

I

Introduction to the Price System

Copyright © by Houghton Mifflin Company. All rights reserved.

1

Economics: The World Around You

1. What is economics?

2. What is the economic way of thinking?

Copyright © by Houghton Mifflin Company. All rights reserved.

Copyright © by Houghton Mifflin Company. All rights reserved.

You are a member of a very select group: you are attending college. Only about 19 percent of the American population has a college degree (bachelor's or associate's), and about 50 percent of people between the ages of 18 and 22 are currently attending college.

Why aren't more people attending college? Part of the reason may be the increased costs of college; during the 1980s and 1990s, the direct expenses associated with college rose much more rapidly than average income. Yet, attending college and acquiring an education is more valuable today than it was during the 1970s and early 1980s. Technological change and increased international trade have placed a premium on a college education; more and more jobs require the skills acquired in college. As a result, the wage disparity between college-educated and non-college-educated workers is rising fairly rapidly. Over their lifetimes, college-educated people earn nearly twice as much as people without college degrees.

Why are you attending college? Perhaps you've never really given it a great deal of thought—your family always just assumed that college was a

necessary step after high school; perhaps you analyzed the situation and decided that college was better than the alternatives. Whichever approach you took, you were practicing economics. You, or your family, were examining alternatives and making choices. This is what economics is about.

The objective of economics is to understand why the real world is what it is. This is not an easy proposition, for the real world is very complex. After all, what happens in the real world is the result of human behavior, and humans are not simple creatures. Nonetheless, there are some fundamental regularities of human behavior that can help to explain the world we observe.

One such regularity is that people behave in ways that make themselves and those they care about better off and happier. Even without knowing that having a college education means your income will be higher than if you do not earn a college degree, you and your family knew or suspected that the college degree would mean a better lifestyle and a more secure or more prestigious job for you. However, what makes one person happy may not make others happy.

Knowing that it is the person without a college degree who is first laid off or unemployed during a recession, that the riskier jobs are held by those without a college degree, and that a person without a college degree is six times more likely to fall into poverty than a person with a college degree, we might be inclined to argue that the 75 percent of young people not attending college are making the wrong choice. But we can't say that. We don't know their circumstances; we don't know what makes them and their families happy. We only know that they do not believe the benefits of college outweigh the costs; otherwise they would be in college.

Knowing that most people behave in ways that make themselves better off and that most people compare costs and benefits in coming to a decision is powerful stuff. It allows us to explain much of the real world and to predict how that world might change if certain events occur.

This knowledge of human behavior is the subject matter of economics. To study economics is to seek answers not only for why people choose to go to college but also for why economies go through cycles, at times expanding and creating new jobs and at other times dipping into recessions; for why some people are thrown out of jobs to join the ranks of the unemployed while others are drawn out of the ranks of the unemployed into new jobs; for why some people live on welfare; for why some nations are richer than others; for why the illegal drug trade is so difficult to stop; for why health care is so expensive; or, in general, for why the world is what it is.

This chapter is the introduction to our study of economics. In it we present some of the terminology commonly used in economics and outline what the study of economics is. ■

1. THE DEFINITION OF ECONOMICS

People have unlimited wants—they always want more goods and services than they have or can purchase with their incomes. Whether they are wealthy or poor, what they have is never enough. Since people do not have everything they want, they must use their limited time and income to select those things they want most and forgo, or relinquish, the rest. The choices they make and the manner in which the choices are made explain much of why the real world is what it is.

1.a. Scarcity

scarcity:
when less of something is available than is wanted at the zero price.

economic good:
any item that is scarce

free good:
a good for which there is no scarcity

Neither the poor nor the wealthy have unlimited time, income, or wealth, and both must make choices to use these limited items in away that best satisfies their wants. Because wants are unlimited and incomes, time, and other items are not, scarcity exists everywhere. **Scarcity** of something means that there is not enough of that item to satisfy everyone who wants it; it means that if a good has no cost, that is, at a zero price, the amount of the good that people want is greater than the amount that is available. Anything for which this condition holds is called an **economic good**. An economic good refers to *goods and services*—where goods are physical products, such as books or food, and services are nonphysical products, such as haircuts or golf lessons.

If there is enough of an item to satisfy wants, even at a zero price, the item is said to be a **free good**. It is difficult to think of examples of free goods. At one time people referred to air as free, but with air pollution control devices

Copyright © by Houghton Mifflin Company. All rights reserved.

ECONOMIC INSIGHT

"Free" Air?

Although air might be what we describe as a free good, quality, breathable air is not free in many places in the world. One of the most successful new business ventures in Mexico City, in fact, is providing clean, breathable air. In this city of 19 million people and 3 million cars, dust, lead, and chemicals make the air unsafe to breathe more than 300 days a year. Private companies are now operating oxygen booths in local parks and malls. Breathable air, which costs more than $1.60 per minute, has become a popular product.

No city in the United States has resorted to oxygen boutiques, but there are large costs for air pollution abatement in many cities. It has been estimated that the cost of meeting federal air quality standards in Los Angeles will soon exceed $1,200 per year for every resident of the Los Angeles metropolitan area.

Sources: "Breathable Air for Swap or Sale," Peter Passell, *New York Times*, Jan. 30, 1992, p. D2; "Best Things in Life Aren't Always Free," Matt Moffett, *The Wall Street Journal*, May 8, 1992, p. A1.

and other costly activities directed toward the maintenance of air quality standards, "clean" air, at least, is not a free good, as noted in the Economic Insight "'Free' Air?"

If people would pay to have less of an item, that item is called an **economic bad**. It is not so hard to think of examples of bads: pollution, garbage, and disease fit the description.

Some goods are used to produce other goods. For instance, to make chocolate chip cookies we need flour, sugar, chocolate chips, butter, our own labor, and an oven. To distinguish between the ingredients of a good and the good itself, we call the ingredients **resources**. (Resources are also called **factors of production** and **inputs**; the terms are interchangeable.) The ingredients of the cookies are the resources, and the cookies are the goods.

As illustrated in Figure 1(a), economists have classified resources into three categories: land, labor and capital.

1. **Land** includes all natural resources, such as minerals, timber, and water, as well as the land itself.

2. **Labor** refers to the physical and intellectual services of people, including the training, education, and abilities of the individuals in a society.

3. **Capital** refers to products such as machinery and equipment that are used in production. Capital is a manufactured or created product used solely for the production of the goods and services that are consumed by individuals. You will often hear the term *capital* used to describe the financial backing for some project or the stocks and bonds used to finance some business. This common usage is not incorrect but should be distinguished from the physical entity—the machinery and equipment and the buildings, warehouses, and factories. Thus we refer to the stocks and bonds as *financial capital* and to the physical entity as capital.

People obtain income by selling their resources or the use of their resources, as illustrated in Figure 1(b). Owners of land receive *rent*; people who provide labor services are paid *wages*; and owners of capital receive *interest*.

economic bad:
any item for which we would pay to have less

resources, factors of production, or **inputs:**
goods used to produce other goods, i.e., land, labor and capital

land:
all natural resources, such as minerals, timber, and water, as well as the land itself

labor:
the physical and intellectual services of people, including the training, education, and abilities of the individuals in a society

capital:
products such as machinery and equipment that are used in production

Copyright © by Houghton Mifflin Company. All rights reserved.

Figure 1
Flow of Resources and Income
Three types of resources are used to produce goods and services: land, labor and capital. See 1(a). The owners of resources are provided income for selling their services. Landowners are paid rent; laborers receive wages; and capital receives interest. See 1(b). Figure 1(c) links

Figures 1(a) and 1(b). People use their resources to acquire income with which they purchase the goods they want. Producers use the money received from selling the goods to pay for the use of the resources in making goods. Resources and income flow between certain firms and certain resource owners as people allocate their scarce resources to best satisfy their wants.

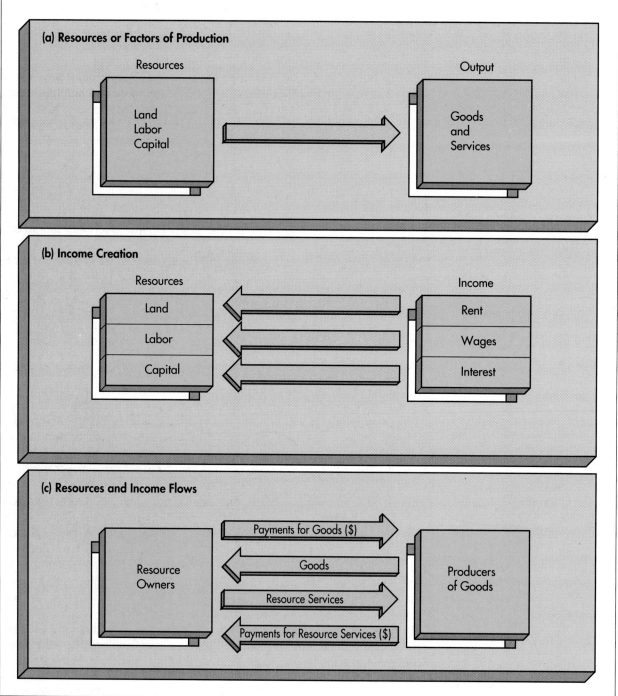

Copyright © by Houghton Mifflin Company. All rights reserved.

Figures 1(a) and 1(b) are linked because the income that resource owners acquire from selling the use of their resources provides them the ability to buy goods and services. And producers use the money received from selling their goods to pay for the resource services. In Figure 1(c), the flows of money are indicated along the outside arrows, and the flows of goods or resource services are indicated along the inside arrows. The resource services flow from resource owners to producers of goods in return for income; the flows of goods go from the producers of the goods to resource owners in return for the money payment for these goods.

1.b. Choices

What is economics?

Scarcity means that people have to make choices. People don't have everything they want; they do not have the time or the money to purchase everything they want. When people choose some things, they have to give up, or forgo, other things. *Economics is the study of how people choose to use their scarce resources to attempt to satisfy their unlimited wants.*

1.c. Rational Self-Interest

rational self-interest:
how people choose the options that give them the greatest amount of satisfaction

Rational self-interest is the term economists use to describe how people make choices. It means that people will make the choices that, at the time and with the information they have at their disposal, will give them the greatest amount of satisfaction.

You chose to attend college although 50 percent of those in your age group chose not to attend. All of you made rational choices based on what you perceived was in your best interest. How could it be in your best interest to do one thing and in another person's best interest to do exactly the opposite? Each person has unique goals and attitudes and faces different costs. Although your weighing of the alternatives came down on the side of attending college, another person weighed similar alternatives and came down on the side of not attending college. Both decisions were rational because in both cases the individual compared alternatives and selected the option that the *individual* thought was in his or her best interest.

It is important to note that rational self-interest depends on the information at hand and the individual's perception of what is in his or her best interest. People will make different choices even when facing the same information. Even though the probability of death in an accident is nearly 20 percent less if seat belts are worn, many people choose not to use them. Are these people rational? The answer is yes. Perhaps they do not want their clothes wrinkled or perhaps seat belts are just too inconvenient or perhaps they think the odds of getting in an accident are just too small to worry about. Whatever the reason, these people are choosing the option that at the time gives them the greatest satisfaction. *This is rational self-interest.* Economists sometimes use the term *bounded rationality* to emphasize the point that people do not have perfect knowledge or perfect insight. In this book we simply use the term *rational* to refer to the comparison of costs and benefits.

If we told those people choosing not to wear seat belts that they definitely would have an accident and would suffer very serious injuries unless they wore the seat belts, their choice would probably be different. But because *we* think wearing seat belts is smart does not mean that others who choose not to wear seat belts are irrational or any less smart. Similarly, the expense of

Copyright © by Houghton Mifflin Company. All rights reserved.

Having only a few minutes before his economics class begins, and having to reach the building located on the lower peninsula, the student grabs his hang glider and prepares to jump off the cliff. The student knows that instead of attending class, he might continue hang gliding, hike in the Guatemalan mountains, or sail in the beautiful waters. However, he has compared benefits and costs of attending class versus not attending; he decided to attend class.

college and the commitment of four or more years of time might not make college seem like such a good choice to many people. Because some people choose not to attend college does not make them irrational. They are rational because they are comparing alternatives in order to select the option that *they* think will make them better off.

Economists think that most of the time most human beings are weighing alternatives, looking at costs and benefits, and making decisions in a way that they believe makes them better off. This is not to say that economists look upon human beings as androids lacking feelings and able only to carry out complex calculations like a computer. Rather, economists believe that the feelings and attitudes of human beings enter into people's comparisons of alternatives and help determine how people decide something is in their best interest.

Human beings are self-interested, *not selfish*. People do contribute to charitable organizations and help others; people do make individual sacrifices because those sacrifices benefit their families or people they care about; soldiers do risk their lives to defend their country. All these acts are made in the name of rational self-interest.

Relying on the idea that most people, most of the time, are rationally self-interested allows economists to explain many real-world observations that otherwise might be inexplicable. Why, for instance, has the number of driver deaths from automobile accidents declined while the number of pedestrian deaths has risen since the introduction of safety devices such as seat belts, air bags, antilock brakes, and reinforced passenger cages? One possible explanation, based on self-interest, is that because they now feel safer, drivers have become more reckless. They drive faster, run more red lights, and take more chances. In fact, research has shown that since the introduction of these safety devices there have been more accidents but fewer driver deaths per accident, and more pedestrians have been killed. As we will see throughout the book, rational self-interest provides a valuable first step in analyzing issues and answering questions.

Copyright © by Houghton Mifflin Company. All rights reserved.

RECAP

1. Scarcity exists when people want more of an item than exists at a zero price.

2. Goods are produced with resources (also called factors of production and inputs). Economists have classified resources into three categories: land, labor, and capital.

3. Choices have to be made because of scarcity. People cannot have or do everything they desire all the time.

4. People make choices in a manner known as rational self-interest; people make the choices that at the time and with the information they have at their disposal will give them the greatest satisfaction.

2. THE ECONOMIC APPROACH

What is the economic way of thinking?

Economists often refer to the "economic approach" or to "economic thinking." By this, they mean that the principles of scarcity and rational self-interest are used in a specific way to search out answers to questions about the real world.

2.a. Positive and Normative Analysis

positive analysis:
analysis of what is

normative analysis:
analysis of what ought to be

Conclusions based on opinion or value judgments do not advance one's understanding of events.

In applying the principles of economics to questions about the real world, it is important to avoid imposing your opinions or value judgments on others. Analysis that does not impose the value judgments of one individual on the decisions of others is called **positive analysis**. If you demonstrate that unemployment in the automobile industry in the United States rises when people purchase cars produced in other countries instead of cars produced in the United States, you are undertaking positive analysis. However, if you claim that there ought to be a law to stop people from buying foreign-made cars, you are imposing your value judgments on the decisions and desires of others. That is not positive analysis. It is, instead, **normative analysis**. *Normative means "what ought to be"; positive means "what is."* If you demonstrate that the probability of death in an automobile accident is 20 percent higher if seat belts are not worn, you are using positive analysis. If you argue that there should be a law requiring seat belts to be worn, you are using normative analysis.

2.b. Scientific Method

scientific method:
a manner of analyzing issues that involves five steps: recognizing the problem, making assumptions, building a model, making predictions, and testing the model

As stated before, economists want to understand the real world and to be able to predict the results of certain events. These goals are hardly unique to economics—they are the same goals most scientists strive toward. A chemist may want to predict the results of combining certain chemicals, and an astronomer may want to predict the results of black holes on galaxy behavior. Similarly, an economist may want to predict the result of an increase in the tuition and fees of college or the result of an increase in taxes. The economist uses much the same methodology as the chemist and astronomer to examine the real world—the **scientific method**. There are five steps in the

Copyright © by Houghton Mifflin Company. All rights reserved.

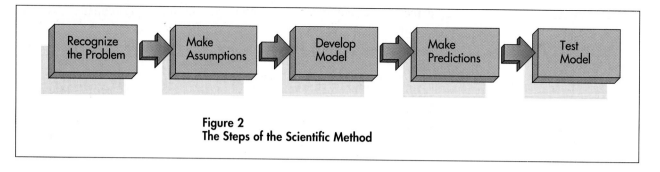

Figure 2
The Steps of the Scientific Method

scientific method, as noted in Figure 2: (1) recognize the problem or issue, (2) cut away unnecessary detail by making assumptions, (3) develop a model or story of the problem or issue, (4) make predictions, and (5) test the model.

The first step in the scientific method, the recognition of the problem, means that an issue is identified—rise in unemployment, accelerated inflation, failure of a business, growth of social security taxes, increased cocaine addiction, the AIDS epidemic, the purchase of one cereal over another, the choice of one job over another, and on and on. Once the issue is identified, the next step is to explain it. This step may seem simple enough, but often it is not. Each problem in economics is so complex that the task of explaining it seems impossible. Thousands, even hundreds of thousands, of details are involved in something as apparently straightforward as deciding why people choose one college over another. The location of the college relative to the home, the appearance of the college, the friendliness of the admissions officers, the reputation of the football team, the occupations of parents, whether friends are attending college, the weather during the day the college was visited, and whether the student was feeling well the day applications were submitted are all details involved in the decision. Economists, like sociologists, political scientists, and paleontologists, cannot often take into account all the details surrounding an event they want to study. They have to reduce the complexity of the real world to manageable proportions using models and assumptions.

theory or model:
a simplification or abstraction of the real world that enables scientists to organize their thoughts

A **theory**, or **model**, is merely a simplification, or abstraction, of the real world that enables scientists to organize their thoughts. A paper airplane is a model of a real airplane; a computer simulation of space is a model of the galaxies. Each model can illustrate certain aspects of the real world but is not intended to capture every aspect of the real world. Good economic models are those that explain or predict well; poor models are those that do not explain or predict well.

assumptions:
statements accepted as true without proof

An economic model uses assumptions to simplify the problem at hand. **Assumptions** are statements taken for granted or accepted as true without proof. One of the most commonly used assumptions is *everything else held constant,* referred to quite often in its Latin form, ***ceteris paribus***.

ceteris paribus:
other things being equal, or everything else held constant

We might say that fewer people attend college as the tuition of college rises, *ceteris paribus*. This means that if only the tuition and number of people attending college are allowed to change, then a higher tuition means fewer people attend college. If we did not make the assumption of everything else held constant, then the statement could be grossly in error. If, for instance, incomes quadrupled while tuition rose a mere

Copyright © by Houghton Mifflin Company. All rights reserved.

5 percent, we could observe more people attending college even as the tuition rose. Similarly, if the income-earning potential of those with a college degree increased significantly, we might observe that more people attended college even as the tuition rose. Assumptions allow us to focus on the relationship between the variables in which we are interested, in this case tuition and the number of people attending college.

An economic model (or theory) is a tool used in the attempt to understand the real world. As with any theory, it must undergo **tests** to see whether it is consistent with the facts—whether it can be used to make accurate predictions.

tests:
trials or measurements used to determine whether a theory is consistent with the facts

2.c. Common Mistakes

Why are so many items sold for $2.99 rather than $3? Most people attribute this practice to ignorance on the part of others: "People look at the first number and round to it—they see $2.99 but think $2." Although this reasoning may be correct, no one admits to such behavior when asked. A common error in the attempt to understand human behavior is to argue that other people do not understand something or are stupid. Instead of relying on rational self-interest to explain human behavior, ignorance or stupidity is called on.

Another common mistake in economic analysis, called the **fallacy of composition**, is the error of attributing what applies in the case of one to the case of many. If one person in a theater realizes a fire has begun and races to the exit, that one person is better off. If we assume that a thousand people in a crowded theater would be better off behaving exactly like the single individual, we would be committing the mistake known as the fallacy of composition.

The mistaken interpretation of **association as causation** occurs when unrelated or coincidental events that occur at about the same time are believed to have a cause-and-effect relationship. For example, the result of the football Super Bowl game is sometimes said to predict how the stock market will perform. According to this "theory," if the NFC team wins, the stock market will rise in the new year, but if the AFC team wins, the market will fall. This bit of folklore is a clear example of confusion between causation and association. Simply because two events seem to occur together does not mean that one causes the other. Clearly, a football game cannot cause the stock market to rise or fall.

fallacy of composition:
the mistaken assumption that what applies in the case of one applies to the case of many

association as causation:
the mistaken assumption that because two events seem to occur together, one causes the other

2.d. Microeconomics and Macroeconomics

Economics is the study of how people choose to allocate their scarce resources among their unlimited wants and involves the application of certain principles—scarcity, choice, rational self-interest—in a consistent manner using the scientific method. The study of economics is usually separated into two general areas, microeconomics and macroeconomics. **Microeconomics** is the study of economics at the level of the individual economic entity: the individual firm, the individual consumer, and the individual workers. In **macroeconomics**, rather than analyzing the behavior of an individual consumer, we look at the sum of the behaviors of all consumers, which is called the consumer sector, or household sector. Similarly, instead of examining the behavior of an individual firm, in macroeconomics we examine the sum of the behaviors of all firms, called the business sector.

microeconomics:
the study of economics at the level of the individual

macroeconomics:
the study of the economy as a whole

Copyright © by Houghton Mifflin Company. All rights reserved.

RECAP

1. The objective of economics is to understand why the real world is what it is.
2. Positive analysis refers to what is, while normative analysis refers to what ought to be.
3. The scientific method consists of five steps: recognition of the problem, assumptions, model, predictions, and tests of the model.
4. Assumptions are a means of simplifying the analysis; they are statements accepted as true without proof.
5. Assuming that others are ignorant, the fallacy of composition, and interpreting association as causation are three commonly made errors in economic analysis.
6. The study of economics is typically divided into two parts, macroeconomics and microeconomics.

SUMMARY

■■ What is economics?

1. The objective of economics is to understand why the real world is what it is. Preview
2. The resources that go into the production of goods are land, labor and capital. §1.a
3. Economics is the study of how people choose to allocate scarce resources to satisfy their unlimited wants. §1.b
4. Scarcity is universal; it applies to anything people would like more of than is available at a zero price. Because of scarcity, choices must be made, and choices are made in a way that is in the decision-maker's rational self-interest. §1.a, 1.b, 1.c
5. People make choices that, at the time and with the information at hand, will give them the greatest satisfaction. §1.c

■■ What is the economic way of thinking?

6. Positive analysis is analysis of what is; normative analysis is analysis of what ought to be. §2.a
7. The scientific method consists of five steps: recognition of the problem, assumptions, model, predictions, and tests of the model. §2.b
8. Assumptions are a means of simplifying the analysis. §2.b
9. Assuming that others are ignorant, the fallacy of composition, and interpreting association as causation are three commonly made errors in economic analysis. §2.c
10. The study of economics is typically divided into two parts, macroeconomics and microeconomics. §2.d

KEY TERMS

scarcity §1.a

economic good §1.a

free good §1.a

economic bad §1.a

Copyright © by Houghton Mifflin Company. All rights reserved.

resources, factors of production, or inputs §1.a

land §1.a

labor §1.a

capital §1.a

rational self-interest §1.c

positive analysis §2.a

normative analysis §2.a

scientific method §2.b

theory or model §2.b

assumptions §2.b

ceteris paribus §2.b

tests §2.b

fallacy of composition §2.c

association as causation §2.c

microeconomics §2.d

macroeconomics §2.d

EXERCISES

1. Which of the following are economic goods? Explain why each is or is not an economic good.

    a. Steaks

    b. Houses

    c. Cars

    d. Garbage

    e. T-shirts

2. Many people go to a medical doctor every time they are ill; others never visit a doctor. Explain how a "model" of human behavior can include such opposite behaviors.

3. Erin has purchased a $35 ticket to a "Grateful Dead" concert. She is invited to a sendoff party for a friend who is moving to another part of the country. The party is scheduled for the same day as the concert. If she had known about the party before she bought the concert ticket, she would have chosen to attend the party. Will Erin choose to attend the concert? Explain.

4. It is well documented in scientific research that smoking is harmful to our health. Smokers have higher incidences of coronary disease, cancer, and other catastrophic illnesses. Knowing this, about 30 percent of young people begin smoking and about 25 percent of the U.S. population smokes. Are the people who choose to smoke irrational? What do you think of the argument that we should ban smoking in order to protect these people from themselves?

5. Indicate which of the following statements is true or false. If the statement is false, change it to make it true.

    a. Positive analysis imposes the value judgments of one individual on the decisions of others.

    b. *Ceteris paribus* is Latin for "let the buyer beware."

    c. Rational self-interest is the same thing as selfishness.

    d. An economic good is scarce if it has a positive price.

    e. An economic bad is an item that has a positive price.

    f. A resource is the ingredient used to make factors of production.

6. Are the following statements normative or positive? If a statement is normative, change it to a positive statement.

    a. The government should provide free tuition to all college students.

    b. An effective way to increase the skills of the work force is to provide free tuition to all college students.

    c. The government must provide job training if we are to compete with other countries.

Copyright © by Houghton Mifflin Company. All rights reserved.

7. In the *New York Times Magazine* in 1970, Milton Friedman, a Nobel Prize–winning economist, argued that "the social responsibility of business is to increase profits." How would Friedman's argument fit with the basic economic model that people behave in ways they believe are in their best self-interest?

8. Two economists crossed the street one day when one spied a twenty-dollar bill on the sidewalk. The first economist pointed out to the second economist that there was a twenty-dollar bill on the sidewalk. The second said, "No, there isn't a twenty-dollar bill there. If it were a twenty-dollar bill, somebody would have picked it up." In what sense does this joke describe the scientific methodology used by economists?

9. Use economics to explain why men's and women's restrooms tend to be located near each other in airports and other public buildings.

10. Use economics to explain why diamonds are more expensive than water, when water is necessary for survival and diamonds are not.

11. Use economics to explain why people leave tips in the following two cases: (a) at a restaurant they visit often; (b) at a restaurant they visit only once.

12. Use economics to explain why people contribute to charities.

13. Use economics to explain this statement: "Increasing the speed limit has, to some degree, compromised highway safety on interstate roads but enhanced safety on non-interstate roads."

Copyright © by Houghton Mifflin Company. All rights reserved.

INTERNET EXERCISE

The Preview discusses the choice of going to college or not. Use the internet to examine the number of people who choose to attend college. Go to the Boyes/Melvin web site at **http://www.hmco.com/** **college/** and click on the internet exercise link for this chapter. Now answer the questions that appear on the web page.

Copyright © by Houghton Mifflin Company. All rights reserved.

Pumped Up Over Cheap Gas

Two women duked it out. Two men crashed their cars. Another woman wrote a letter to her grandmother, read 150 pages in a paperback and sat for 3 and one-half hours. Why? Cheap gas.

Circle K sold 49-cent gas for two hours Saturday at two new stores at Priest Drive and Elliot Road in south Tempe and Chandler Boulevard and Desert Foothills Parkway in Phoenix.

The stores are Circle K's first to open in the Valley in five years, an event the corporation celebrated by dropping gasoline prices lower than they've been since Gerald Ford was president.

"I remember when I was little going with my mom when there were gasoline wars. That's what it reminds me of," said Ann Vry, spokeswoman for Circle K. "People would get very excited about filling up their tanks." Whitney Hamilton of Gilbert knows the feeling. She got in the Tempe line at 6:30 a.m.; the special began at 10. "I was in line before there was a line," said Hamilton, who read and wrote her grandmother. "I've never seen them (gas prices) this low. I don't think I'll ever see them this low again."

Vera Lujan drove the 15 or so miles from her central Phoenix home to Tempe, arriving at 8 a.m. Seven cars were ahead of her. "I was already on empty, so I put in $1 and drove over," Lujan said. "I know. It's weird."

About 300 cars were in line at the Tempe store when the cheap gas began. Crowds were lighter in Phoenix, where only about 25 cars waited at any given time.

Circle K officials estimated that they filled up at least 12 cars every five minutes. A 15-gallon limit on the fill-ups was enforced.

"I think I burned more gas than I'm going to get," Ben Valdez of Tempe said as he approached the pumps after waiting 90 minutes.

Some of those waiting could have used a lesson in patience.

"There've been a few little temper raises," Tempe police Officer Dick Steely said, including a fistfight that broke out when one woman tried to cut in front of another.

John Fecther of Tempe came for the gas but saw the long lines and tried to make a U-turn away from the area. He was hit by another vehicle.

"I was going to get the heck out of here," he said as he filled out a police report. "People are crazy. What are you going to save? $4 or $5? I guess to some people that's a lot of money."

Source: "Pumped Up Over Cheap Gas," from *The Arizona Republic,* January 22, 1995, p. B1. Used with permission. Permission does not imply endorsement.

Copyright © by Houghton Mifflin Company. All rights reserved.

*The Arizona Republic/***January 22, 1995**

COMMENTARY

Economics is the study of human behavior. How then does economics explain the rush to purchase cheap gas? Economists claim that decisions are the process of comparing costs and benefits. In this article, people have chosen to drive to the Circle K store and spend time in line in order to purchase 15 gallons of gasoline at a price of $.49. Thus, people looked at their costs of driving to the station and spending time in line and decided that these costs were less than the benefits they derived from the cheap gas. So let's look at this decision.

The usual price for gasoline at this time in this market was $1.09 a gallon. Thus, each gallon purchased at the cheap price, $.49, means a savings of $.60. Since 15 gallons could be purchased, the most one could save on the gas purchase would be $9.00.

Did the savings outweigh the costs?

At one station, 300 cars were in line. Since 12 cars were served each five minutes, the wait at that station was about 2 hours and 5 minutes. If one gallon of gas was consumed waiting in line and another gallon driving to and from the station, then the savings would be 13 gallons at $.60 or $7.80. Thus, it would seem that those people choosing to purchase the gas believed that more than 2 hours of their time was worth less than $7.80.

However, the time waiting was not the only possible cost of purchasing the gas. The story indicates that some people got into fights and another was in an accident. The possibility of a mishap could also be considered a cost. In addition, the wear and tear on the car from starting and stopping or idling could be considered. The frustration of waiting and in observing other people attempting to crowd or cheat in line could also be a cost. And, whatever else a person could have been doing for that 2 to 3 hours is a cost.

There might be benefits we haven't considered yet. For some people, the joy of being in a large group might be a benefit. These same people might drive anywhere that large groups form. For other people, the demonstration of how important cheap gas is, is the important point, not the money savings. These people are price shoppers—always on the lookout for the best price. For still others, getting out of the house with a good excuse and having some time for reading or reflection might be a benefit.

Whatever factors go into the calculation of costs and benefits, it seems that for many people, the benefits of the cheap gas outweighed the costs. John Fecther said that he was attempting to get out of there after seeing the long lines. John had made a comparison of costs and benefits, apparently assuming that there would be shorter lines. Once he altered his calculation of costs, he changed his mind. He said, "People are crazy. What are you going to save—$4 or $5? I guess that's a lot of money for some people." Is Mr. Fecther right? Was it the $4 or $5 savings that enticed people? Would Mr. Fecther have driven to another appliance store a mile or two away if he was shopping for a dishwasher and learned that he could save $4 or $5 at the other store? Probably not. Why then did he decide to go purchase the cheap gas, even thinking the lines would be shorter?

Copyright © by Houghton Mifflin Company. All rights reserved.

Working with Graphs

According to the old saying, one picture is worth a thousand words. If that maxim is correct, and, in addition, if producing a thousand words takes more time and effort than producing one picture, it is no wonder that economists rely so extensively on pictures. The pictures that economists use to explain concepts are called *graphs*. The purpose of this appendix is to explain how graphs are constructed and how to interpret them.

1. READING GRAPHS

The three kinds of graphs used by economists are shown in Figures 1, 2, and 3. Figure 1 is a *line graph*. It is the most commonly used type of graph in

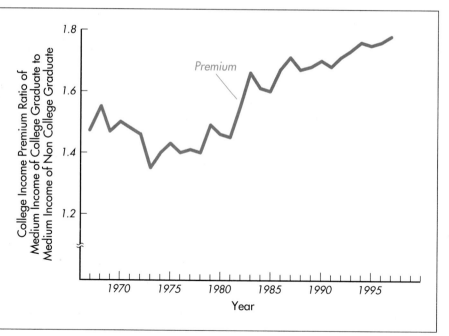

Figure 1
Ratio of Median Incomes of College- to High School- Educated Workers
Figure 1 is a line graph showing the ratio of the median income of people who have completed four or more years of college to the median income of those who completed four years of high school. The line shows the income premium for educational attainment, or the value of a college education in terms of income from year to year. The rise in the line since about 1979 shows that the premium for completing college has risen. Source: *Statistical Abstract of the United States, 1996* (Washington, D.C.: U.S. Government Printing Office).

Copyright © by Houghton Mifflin Company. All rights reserved.

Figure 2
Unemployment and Education
Figure 2 is a bar graph indicating the unemployment rate by educational attainment. The blue refers to high school dropouts, the red refers to those with four years of high school, and the green refers to those with four or more years of college. One set of bars is presented for males and one set for females. The bars are arranged in order, with the highest incidence of unemployment shown first, the next highest second, and the lowest located third. This arrangement is made only for ease in reading and interpretation. The bars could be arranged in any order. Sources: *Economic Report of the President, 1997. Statistical Abstract of the United States, 1996* (Washington, D.C.: U.S. Government Printing Office).

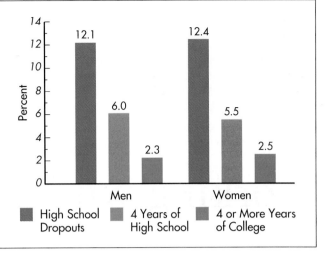

economics. Figure 2 is a *bar graph*. It is probably used more often in popular magazines than any other kind of graph. Figure 3 is a *pie graph*, or *pie chart*. Although it is less popular than the bar and line graphs, it appears often enough that you need to be familiar with it.

1.a. Relationships Between Variables

Figure 1 is a line graph showing the ratio of the median income of people who have completed four or more years of college to the median income of those who have completed just four years of high school. The line shows the value of a college education in terms of the additional income earned relative to the income earned without a college degree on a year-to-year basis. You can see that the premium for completing college has risen in recent years.

Figure 2 is a bar graph indicating the unemployment rate by educational attainment. The blue refers to high school dropouts, the red refers to those with four years of high school, and the green refers to those with four or more years of college. One set of bars is presented for males and one set for females. The bars are arranged in order, with the highest incidence of unemployment depicted first, the next highest second, and the lowest located third. This arrangement is made only for ease in reading and interpretation. The bars could be arranged in any order. The graph illustrates that unemployment strikes those with less education more than it does those with more education.

Figure 3 is a pie chart showing the percentage of the U.S. population completing various years of schooling. Unlike line and bar graphs, a pie chart is not actually a picture of a relationship between two variables. Instead, the pie represents the whole, 100 percent of the U.S. population, and the pieces of the pie represent parts of the whole—the percentage of the population completing one to four years of elementary school only, five to seven years of elementary school, and so on up to four or more years of college.

Copyright © by Houghton Mifflin Company. All rights reserved.

Figure 3
Educational Attainment

Figure 3 is a pie chart showing the percentage of the U.S. population completing various years of schooling. Unlike line and bar graphs, a pie chart is not actually a picture of a relationship between two variables. Instead, the pie represents the whole, 100 percent of the U.S. population, and the pieces of the pie represent parts of the whole—the percentage of the population completing one to four years of elementary school only, five to seven years of elementary school, and so on up to four or more years of college. Source: *Statistical Abstract of the United States, 1996* (Washington, D.C.: U.S. Government Printing Office).

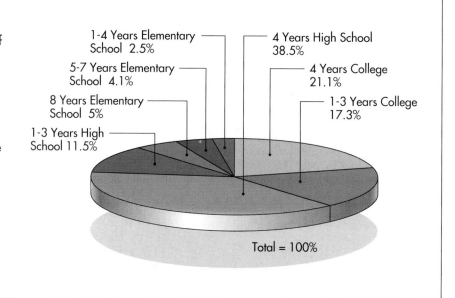

1-4 Years Elementary School 2.5%

5-7 Years Elementary School 4.1%

8 Years Elementary School 5%

1-3 Years High School 11.5%

4 Years High School 38.5%

4 Years College 21.1%

1-3 Years College 17.3%

Total = 100%

Because a pie chart does not show the relationship between variables, it is not as useful for explaining economic concepts as line and bar graphs. Line graphs are used more often than bar graphs to explain economic concepts.

1.b. Independent and Dependent Variables

independent variable:
the variable whose value does not depend on the value of other variables

dependent variable:
the variable whose value depends on the value of the independent variable

Most line and bar graphs involve just two variables, an **independent variable** and a **dependent variable**. An independent variable is one whose value does not depend on the values of other variables; a dependent variable, on the other hand, is one whose value does depend on the values of other variables. The value of the dependent variable is determined after the value of the independent variable is determined.

In Figure 2, the *independent* variable is the educational status of the man or woman, and the *dependent* variable is the incidence of unemployment (percentage of group that is unemployed). The incidence of unemployment depends on the educational attainment of the man or woman.

1.c. Direct and Inverse Relationships

direct or positive relationship:
the relationship that exists when the values of related variables move in the same direction

inverse or negative relationship:
the relationship that exists when the values of related variables move in opposite directions

If the value of the dependent variable increases as the value of the independent variable increases, the relationship between the two types of variables is called a **direct**, or **positive**, **relationship**. If the value of the dependent variable decreases as the value of the independent variable increases, the relationship between the two types of variables is called an **inverse**, or **negative**, **relationship**.

In Figure 2, unemployment and educational attainment are inversely, or negatively, related: as people acquire more education, they are less likely to be unemployed.

Copyright © by Houghton Mifflin Company. All rights reserved.

2. CONSTRUCTING A GRAPH

Let's now construct a graph. We will begin with a consideration of the horizontal and vertical axes, or lines, and then we will put the axes together. We are going to construct a *straight-line curve*. This sounds contradictory, but it is common terminology. Economists often refer to the demand or supply *curve*, and that curve may be a straight line.

2.a. The Axes

It is important to understand how the *axes* (the horizontal and vertical lines) are used and what they measure. Let's begin with the horizontal axis, the line running across the page in a horizontal direction. Notice in Figure 4(a) that the line is divided into equal segments. Each point on the line represents a quantity, or the value of the variables being measured. For example, each segment could represent one year or 10,000 pounds of diamonds or some other value. Whatever is measured, the value increases from left to right,

---

Figure 4
The Axes, the Coordinate System, and the Positive Quadrant
Figure 4(a) shows the vertical and horizontal axes. The horizontal axis has an origin, measured as zero, in the middle. Negative numbers are to the left of zero, positive numbers to the right. The vertical axis also has an origin in the middle. Positive numbers are above the origin, negative numbers below. The horizontal and vertical

axes together show the entire coordinate system. Positive numbers are in quadrant I, negative numbers in quadrant III, and combinations of negative and positive numbers in quadrants II and IV.

Figure 4(b) shows only the positive quadrant. Because most economic data are positive, often only the upper right quadrant, the positive quadrant, of the coordinate system is used.

(a) The Coordinate System

(b) The Positive Quadrant

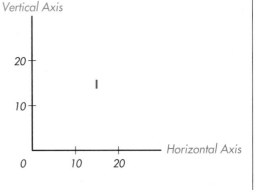

Copyright © by Houghton Mifflin Company. All rights reserved.

beginning with negative values, going on to zero, which is called the *origin*, and then moving on to positive numbers.

A number line in the vertical direction can be constructed as well, also shown in Figure 4(a). Zero is the origin, and the numbers increase from bottom to top. Like the horizontal axis, the vertical axis is divided into equal segments; the distance between 0 and 10 is the same as the distance between 0 and –10, between 10 and 20, and so on.

In most cases, the variable measured along the horizontal axis is the independent variable. This isn't always true in economics, however. Economists often measure the independent variable on the vertical axis. Do not assume that the variable on the horizontal axis is independent and the variable on the vertical axis is dependent.

Putting the horizontal and vertical lines together lets us express relationships between two variables graphically. The axes cross, or intersect, at their origins, as shown in Figure 4(a). From the common origin, movements to the right and up, in the area—called a quadrant—marked I, are combinations of positive numbers; movements to the left and down, in quadrant III, are combinations of negative numbers; movements to the right and down, in quadrant IV, are negative values on the vertical axis and positive values on the horizontal axis; and movements to the left and up, in quadrant II, are positive values on the vertical axis and negative values on the horizontal axis.

Economic data are typically positive numbers: the unemployment rate, the inflation rate, the price of something, the quantity of something produced or sold, and so on. Because economic data are usually positive numbers, the only part of the coordinate system that usually comes into play in economics is the upper right portion, quadrant I. That is why economists may simply sketch a vertical line down to the origin and then extend a horizontal line out to the right, as shown in Figure 4(b). Once in a while, economic data are negative—for instance, profit is negative when costs exceed revenues. When data are negative, quadrants II, III, and IV of the coordinate system could be used.

2.b. Constructing a Graph from a Table

Now that you are familiar with the axes, that is, the coordinate system, you are ready to construct a graph using the data in the table in Figure 5. The table lists a series of possible price levels for a personal computer (PC) and the corresponding number of PCs people choose to purchase. The data are only hypothetical; they are not drawn from actual cases.

The information given in the table is graphed in Figure 5. We begin by marking off and labeling the axes. The vertical axis is the list of possible price levels. We begin at zero and move up the axis at equal increments of $1,000. The horizontal axis is the number of PCs sold. We begin at zero and move out the axis at equal increments of 1,000 PCs. According to the information presented in the table, if the price is $10,000, no one buys a PC. The combination of $10,000 and 0 PCs is point *A* on the graph. To plot this point, find the quantity zero on the horizontal axis (it is at the origin), and then move up the vertical axis from zero to a price level of $10,000. (Note that we have measured the units in the table and on the graph in thousands.) At a price of $9,000, there are 1,000 PCs purchased. To plot the combination

Copyright © by Houghton Mifflin Company. All rights reserved.

Figure 5
Personal Computer Prices and Purchases

The information given in the table is graphed below. We begin by marking off and labeling the axes. The vertical axis is the list of possible price levels. The horizontal axis is the number of PCs purchased. Beginning at zero, the axes are marked at equal increments of 1,000. According to the information presented in the table, if the price level is $10,000, no PCs are purchased. The combination of $10,000 and 0 PCs is point A on the graph. At a price of $9,000, there are 1,000 PCs purchased. This is point B. The final step in constructing a line graph is to connect the points that are plotted. When the points are connected, the straight line slanting downward shows the relationship between the price of PCs and the number of PCs purchased.

Point	Price per PC (thousands of dollars)	Number of PCs Purchased (thousands)
A	$10	0
B	9	1
C	8	2
D	7	3
E	6	4
F	5	5
G	4	6
H	3	7
I	2	8
J	1	9
K	0	10

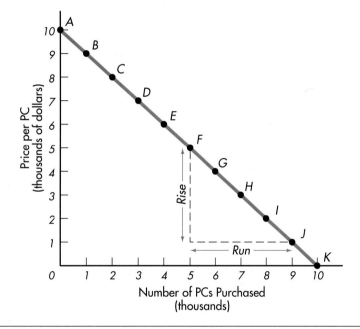

of $9,000 and 1,000 PCs, find 1,000 units on the horizontal axis and then measure up from there to a price of $9,000. This is point B. Point C represents a price of $8,000 and 2,000 PCs. Point D represents a price of $7,000 and 3,000 PCs. Each combination of price and PCs purchased listed in the table is plotted in Figure 5.

The final step in constructing a line graph is to connect the points that are plotted. When the points are connected, the straight line slanting downward

Copyright © by Houghton Mifflin Company. All rights reserved.

from left to right in Figure 5 is obtained. It shows the relationship between the price of PCs and the number of PCs purchased.

2.c. Interpreting Points on a Graph

Let's use Figure 5 to demonstrate how points on a graph may be interpreted. Suppose the current price of a PC is $6,000. Are you able to tell how many PCs are being purchased at this price? By tracing that price level from the vertical axis over to the curve and then down to the horizontal axis, you find that 4,000 PCs are purchased. You can also find what happens to the number purchased if the price falls from $6,000 to $5,000. By tracing the price from $5,000 to the curve and then down to the horizontal axis, you discover that 5,000 PCs are purchased. Thus, according to the graph, a decrease in the price from $6,000 to $5,000 results in 1,000 more PCs being purchased.

2.d. Shifts of Curves

Graphs can be used to illustrate the effects of a change in a variable not represented on the graph. For instance, the curve drawn in Figure 5 shows the relationship between the price of PCs and the number of PCs purchased. When this curve was drawn, the only two variables that were allowed to change were the price and the number of computers. However, it is likely that people's incomes determine their reaction to the price of computers as well. An increase in income would enable more people to purchase computers. Thus, at every price more computers would be purchased. How would this be represented? As an outward shift of the curve, from points A, B, C, etc. to A', B', C', etc. as shown in Figure 6.

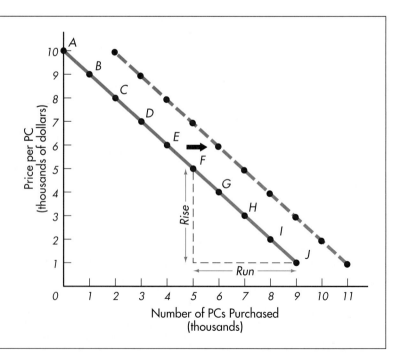

Figure 6
Shift of Curve
An increase in income allows more people to purchase PCs at each price. At a price of $8,000, for instance, 4,000 PCs are purchased rather than 2,000.

Copyright © by Houghton Mifflin Company. All rights reserved.

Following the shift of the curve, we can see that more PCs are purchased at each price than was the case prior to the income increase. For instance, at a price of $8,000 the increased income allows 4,000 PCs to be purchased rather than 2,000. The important point to note is that if some variable that influences the relationship shown in a curve or line graph changes, then the entire curve or line changes—that is, it shifts.

3. SLOPES

A curve may represent an inverse, or negative, relationship or a direct, or positive, relationship. The slope of the curve reveals the kind of relationship that exists between two variables.

3.a. Positive and Negative Slopes

slope:
the steepness of a curve, measured as the ratio of the rise to the run

The **slope** of a curve is its steepness, the rate at which the value of a variable measured on the vertical axis changes with respect to a given change in the value of the variable measured on the horizontal axis. If the value of a variable measured on one axis goes up when the value of the variable measured on the other axis goes down, the variables have an inverse (or negative) relationship. If the values of the variables rise or fall together, the variables have a direct (or positive) relationship. Inverse relationships are represented by curves that run downward from left to right; direct relationships by curves that run upward from left to right.

Slope is calculated by measuring the amount by which the variable on the vertical axis changes and dividing that figure by the amount by which the variable on the horizontal axis changes. The vertical change is called the *rise,* and the horizontal change is called the *run.* Slope is referred to as the *rise over the run*:

$$\text{Slope} = \frac{\text{rise}}{\text{run}}$$

The slope of any inverse relationship is negative. The slope of any direct relationship is positive.

Let's calculate the slope of the curve in Figure 5. Price (*P*) is measured on the vertical axis, and quantity of PCs purchased (*Q*) is measured on the horizontal axis. The rise is the change in price (ΔP), the change in the value of the variable measured on the vertical axis. The run is the change in quantity of PCs purchased (ΔQ), the change in the value of the variable measured on the horizontal axis. The symbol Δ means "change in"; it is the Greek letter delta, so ΔP means "change in *P*" and ΔQ means "change in *Q*." Remember that slope equals the rise over the run. Thus the equation for the slope of the straight-line curve running downward from left to right in Figure 5 is

$$\text{Slope} = \frac{\Delta P}{\Delta Q}$$

As the price (*P*) declines, the number of PCs purchased (*Q*) increases. The rise is negative, and the run is positive. Thus, the slope is a negative value.

Copyright © by Houghton Mifflin Company. All rights reserved.

The slope is the same anywhere along a straight line. Thus, it does not matter where we calculate the changes along the vertical and horizontal axes. For instance, from 0 to 9,000 on the horizontal axis—a change of 9,000—the vertical change is a negative $9,000 (from $10,000 down to $1,000). Thus, the rise over the run is –9,000/9,000, or –1. Similarly, from 5,000 to 9,000 in the horizontal direction, the corresponding rise is $5,000 to $1,000, or –$4,000, so that the rise over the run is –4,000/4,000, or –1.

Remember that direct, or positive, relationships between variables are represented by lines that run upward from left to right. These lines have positive slopes. Figure 7 is a graph showing the number of PCs that producers offer for sale at various price levels. The curve represents the relationship between the two variables, number of PCs offered for sale and price. It shows that as price rises, so does the number of PCs offered for sale. The slope of the curve is positive. The change in the rise (the vertical direction) that comes with an increase in the run (the horizontal direction) is positive. Because the graph is a straight line, you can measure the rise and run using any two points along the curve and the slope will be the same. We find the slope by calculating the rise that accompanies the run. Moving from 0 to 4,000 PCs gives us a run of 4,000. Looking at the curve, we see that the corresponding rise is 2,000. Thus, the rise over the run is 2,000/4,000, or .50.

3.b. Equations

Graphs and equations can be used to illustrate the same topics. Some people prefer to use equations rather than graphs, or both equations and graphs, to explain a concept. Since a few equations are used in this book, we need to briefly discuss how they demonstrate the same things as a graph.

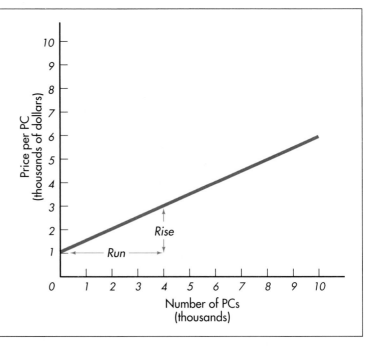

Figure 7
Personal Computers Offered for Sale and Price
Figure 7 is a graph showing the number of PCs offered for sale at various price levels. The curve shows that as price rises, so does the number of PCs purchased. We move from 0 to 4,000, giving us a run of 4,000. The corresponding rise is 2,000. Thus, the rise over the run is 2,000/4,000 or .50.

Copyright © by Houghton Mifflin Company. All rights reserved.

The general equation of a straight line has the form: $Y = a + bX$, where Y is the dependent variable, X is the independent variable, a defines the intercept (the value of Y when $X = 0$), and b is the slope. If b is negative, the line slopes downward. If b is positive, the line slopes upward. In the case of Figure 5, the price, P, is the independent variable, and the number of PCs purchased, Q, is the dependent variable. The number of PCs purchased depends on the price. In equation form, substituting Q for Y and P for X, the relationship between price and PCs purchased is $Q = a + bP$. We already know that the slope, b, is negative. For each \$1,000 decline in price, 1,000 more PCs are purchased. The slope, b, is -1. The value of a represents the value of Q when P is zero. When the price is zero, 10,000 PCs are purchased. Thus, $a = 10,000$. The equation of Figure 5 is $Q = 10,000 - 1P$.

The equation can be used to tell us how many PCs will be purchased at any given price. Suppose the price is $P = \$4,000$. Substituting \$4,000 for P in the equation yields:

$$Q = 10,000 - 1(4,000)$$
$$= 6,000$$

SUMMARY

1. There are three commonly used types of graphs: the line graph, the bar graph, and the pie chart. §1.a

2. An independent variable is a variable whose value does not depend on the values of other variables. The values of a dependent variable do depend on the values of other variables. §1.b

3. A direct, or positive, relationship occurs when the value of the dependent variable increases as the value of the independent variable increases. An indirect, or negative, relationship occurs when the value of the dependent variable decreases as the value of the independent variable increases. §1.c

4. Most economic data are positive numbers, so often only the upper right quadrant of the coordinate system is used in economics. §2.a

5. A curve shifts when a variable that affects the dependent variable and is not measured on the axes changes.

6. The slope of a curve is the rise over the run: the change in the variable measured on the vertical axis that corresponds to a change in the variable measured on the horizontal axis. §3.a

7. The slope of a straight-line curve is the same at all points along the curve. §3.a

8. The equation of a straight line has the general form: $Y = a + bX$, where Y is the dependent variable, X the independent variable, a the value of Y when X equals zero, and b the slope. §3.b

Copyright © by Houghton Mifflin Company. All rights reserved.

KEY TERMS

independent variable §1.b

dependent variable §1.b

direct or positive relationship §1.c

inverse or negative relationship §1.c

slope §3.a

EXERCISES

1. Listed below are two sets of figures: the total quantity of Mexican pesos (new pesos) in circulation (the total amount of Mexican money available) and the peso price of a dollar (how many pesos are needed to purchase one dollar). Values are given for the years 1987 through 1996 for each variable.

   a. Plot each variable by measuring time (years) on the horizontal axis and, in the first graph, pesos in circulation on the vertical axis and, in the second graph, peso price of a dollar on the vertical axis.

   b. Plot the combinations of variables by measuring pesos in circulation on the horizontal axis and peso prices of a dollar on the vertical axis.

   c. In each of the graphs in parts a and b, what are the dependent and independent variables?

   d. In each of the graphs in parts a and b, indicate whether the relationship between the dependent and independent variables is direct or inverse.

Year	Pesos in Circulation (billions)	Peso Price of a Dollar
1987	12,627	1.3782
1988	21,191	2.2731
1989	29,087	2.4615
1990	47,439	2.8126
1991	106,227	3.0184
1992	122,220	3.0949
1993	143,902	3.1156
1994	145,429	3.3751
1995	150,572	6.4194
1996	206,180	7.5994

Copyright © by Houghton Mifflin Company. All rights reserved.

2. Plot the data listed in the following table.

Price	Quantity Sold	Total Revenue
$1,000	200	200,000
900	400	360,000
800	600	480,000
700	800	560,000
600	1,000	600,000
500	1,200	600,000
400	1,400	560,000
300	1,600	480,000
200	1,800	360,000
100	2,000	200,000

a. Use price as the vertical axis and quantity as the horizontal axis and plot the first two columns.

b. Show what quantity is sold when the price is $550.

c. Directly below the graph in part a, plot the data in columns 2 and 3. Use quantity as the horizontal axis and total revenue as the vertical axis.

d. What is total revenue when the price is $550? Will total revenue increase or decrease when the price is lowered?

Copyright © by Houghton Mifflin Company. All rights reserved.

2

Choice, Opportunity Costs, and Specialization

FUNDAMENTAL QUESTIONS

1. What are opportunity costs? Are they part of the economic way of thinking?

2. What is a production possibilities curve?

3. Why does specialization occur?

4. What are the benefits of trade?

Copyright © by Houghton Mifflin Company. All rights reserved.

I n the previous chapter we learned that scarcity forces people to make choices. There are costs involved in any choice. As the old saying goes, "There is no free lunch." In every choice, alternatives are forgone, or sacrificed. Having nearly 4 million people in the armed forces, as the United States did in 1969, meant that these 4 million people were not employed in producing automobiles, health care, or other nondefense-related items. The nondefense goods and services not produced—forgone—during that period are part of the costs of choosing to focus on military activities. However, reducing the numbers employed in the military and in military-related activities, as occurred in the early 1990s, is not free either. The equipment and the skills people had acquired that were useful in the production of military goods sometimes had little value in other industries.

All choices, then, have both costs and benefits. This chapter explains how to calculate these costs and benefits from the perspective of both the individual and society as a whole. ■

Copyright © by Houghton Mifflin Company. All rights reserved.

What are opportunity costs? Are they part of the economic way of thinking?

opportunity costs:
the highest-valued alternative that must be forgone when a choice is made

The cost of any item or activity includes the opportunity cost involved in its purchase.

1. OPPORTUNITY COSTS

A choice is simply a comparison of alternatives: to attend college or not to attend college, to change jobs or not to change jobs, to purchase a new car or to keep the old one. An individual compares the costs and benefits of each option and chooses the option expected to provide the most happiness or net benefit. Of course, when one option is chosen, the benefits of the alternatives are forgone. You choose not to attend college and you forgo the benefits of attending college; you buy a new car and forgo the benefits of having the money to use in other ways. *Economists refer to the forgone opportunities or forgone benefits of the next best alternative as* **opportunity costs**—the highest-valued alternative that must be forgone when a choice is made.

Opportunity costs are part of every decision and activity. Your opportunity costs of reading this book are whatever else you could be doing—perhaps watching TV, talking with friends, working, or listening to music. Your opportunity costs of attending college are whatever else you could be doing— perhaps working full time or traveling around the world. Each choice means giving up something else.

1.a. The Opportunity Cost of Going to College

Suppose you decided to attend a college where the tuition and other expenses add up to $4,290 per year. Are these your total costs of attending college? If you answer yes, you are ignoring opportunity costs. Remember that you must account for forgone opportunities. If instead of going to college you could have worked full time, then the benefits of full-time employment are your opportunity costs. If you could have obtained a position with an annual income of $20,800, the actual cost of college is the $4,290 of direct expenses plus the $20,800 of forgone salary, or $25,090. This calculation assumes you would not work part-time or during the summer.

1.b. Tradeoffs and Decisions at the Margin

tradeoff:
the giving up of one good or activity in order to obtain some other good or activity

Life is a continuous sequence of decisions, and every single decision involves choosing one thing over another or trading off something for something else. A **tradeoff** means giving up one good or activity in order to obtain some other good or activity. Each term you must decide whether to register for college or not. You could work full time and not attend college, attend college and not work, or work part time and attend college. The time you devote to college will decrease as you devote more time to work. You trade off hours spent at work for hours spent in college; in other words, you compare the benefits you think you will get from going to college this term with the costs of college this term. Once you decide to go to college, you must decide how much to study. Once you sit down and begin studying, you are deciding whether to continue studying or to do something else. "What should I do for the next hour, study or watch TV?" The "next" hour is the additional, or what economists call the marginal, hour. Making choices involves comparing the **marginal costs** and the **marginal benefits**. *Marginal* means "change," so a decision involves the comparison of a change in benefits and a change in costs.

marginal cost:
additional cost

marginal benefit:
additional benefit

1.c. The Production Possibilities Curve

What is a production possibilities curve?

production possibilities curve (PPC):
a graphical representation showing the maximum quantity of goods and services that can be produced using limited resources to the fullest extent possible

Societies, like individuals, face scarcities and must make choices. And societies, like individuals, forgo opportunities each time they make a particular choice and must compare the marginal costs and marginal benefits of each alternative.

The tradeoffs facing a society can be illustrated in a graph known as the **production possibilities curve (PPC)**. The production possibilities curve shows the maximum quantity of goods and services that can be produced using limited resources to the fullest extent possible. Figure 1 shows a production possibilities curve based on the information (see table) about the production of defense goods and services and nondefense goods and services by a nation such as the United States. Defense goods and services include guns, ships, bombs, personnel, and so forth, that are used for national defense. Nondefense goods and services include education, housing, and food that are not used for national defense. All societies allocate their scarce resources in order to produce some combination of defense and nondefense goods and services. Because resources are scarce, a nation cannot produce as much of everything as it wants. When it produces more health care, it must forgo the production of education or automobiles; when it devotes more of its resources to the military area, fewer are available to devote to health care.

Copyright © by Houghton Mifflin Company. All rights reserved.

Combination	Defense Goods and Services (millions of units)	Nondefense Goods and Services (millions of units)
A_1	200	0
B_1	175	75
C_1	130	125
D_1	70	150
E_1	0	160
F_1	130	25
G_1	200	75

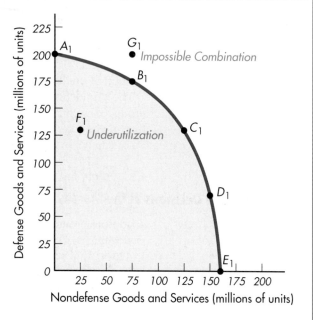

Figure 1
The Production Possibilities Curve
With a limited amount of resources, only certain combinations of defense and nondefense goods and services can be produced. The maximum amounts that can be produced, given various tradeoffs, are represented by points A_1 through E_1. Point F_1 lies inside the curve and represents the underutilization of resources. More of one type of goods and less of another could be produced, or more of both types could be produced. Point G_1 represents an impossible combination. There are insufficient resources to produce quantities lying beyond the curve.

If we could draw or even visualize many dimensions, we could draw a PPC that has a specific good measured along the axis in each dimension. Since we can't, we typically just draw a two-dimensional graph and thus can have just two classes of goods. In Figure 1 the two classes are defense-type goods and nondefense-type goods. But we could just as easily draw a PPC for health care and all other goods or for education and all other goods. These PPCs would look like Figure 1 except that the axes would measure units of health care and other goods or units of education and other goods.

A production possibilities curve shows that more of one type of good can be produced only by reducing the quantity of other types of goods that are produced; it shows that a society has scarce resources; and it shows what the marginal costs and marginal benefits of alternative decisions are. In what way does the PPC show these things? We can answer that question by looking more carefully at Figure 1. In this figure, units of defense goods and services are measured on the vertical axis; units of nondefense goods and services on the horizontal axis. If all resources are allocated to producing defense goods and services, then 200 million units can be produced, but the production of nondefense goods and services will cease. The combination of 200 million units of defense goods and services and 0 units of nondefense goods and services is point A_1, a point on the vertical axis. At 175 million units of defense goods and services, 75 million units of nondefense goods and services can be

Copyright © by Houghton Mifflin Company. All rights reserved.

produced (point B_1). Point C_1 represents 125 million units of nondefense goods and services and 130 million units of defense goods. Point D_1 represents 150 million units of nondefense goods and services and 70 million units of defense goods and services. Point E_1, a point on the horizontal axis, shows the combination of no production of defense goods and services and total production of nondefense goods and services.

The production possibilities curve represents the maximum, or the outer limit, of what can be produced.

The production possibilities curve shows the *maximum* output that can be produced with a limited quantity and quality of resources. The PPC is a picture of the tradeoffs facing society. Only one combination of goods and services can be produced at any one time. All other combinations are forgone.

1.c.1. Points Inside the Production Possibilities Curve
Suppose a nation produces 130 million units of defense goods and services and 25 million units of nondefense goods and services. That combination, Point F_1 in Figure 1, lies inside the production possibilities curve. A point lying inside the production possibilities curve indicates that resources are not being fully or efficiently used. If the existing work force is employed only 20 hours per week, it is not being fully used. If two workers are used when one would be sufficient—say, two people in each Domino's Pizza delivery car—then resources are not being used efficiently. If there are resources available for use, society can move from point F_1 to a point on the PPC, such as point C_1. The move would gain 100 million units of nondefense goods and services with no loss of defense goods and services.

1.c.2. Points Outside the Production Possibilities Curve
Point G_1 in Figure 1 represents the production of 200 million units of defense goods and services and 75 units of nondefense goods and services. Point G_1, however, represents the use of more resources than are available—it lies outside the production possibilities curve. Unless more resources can be obtained and/or the quality of resources improved so that the nation can produce more with the same quantity of resources, there is no way the society can currently produce 200 million units of defense goods and 75 million units of nondefense goods.

1.c.3. Shifts of the Production Possibilities Curve
If a nation obtains more resources, points outside its current production possibilities curve become attainable. Suppose a country discovers new sources of oil within its borders and is able to greatly increase its production of oil. Greater oil supplies would enable the country to increase production of all types of goods and services.

Figure 2 shows the production possibilities curve before (PPC_1) and after (PPC_2) the discovery of oil. PPC_1 is based on the data given in Figure 1. PPC_2 is based on the data given in Figure 2 (see table), which shows the increase in production of goods and services that results from the increase in oil supplies. The first combination of goods and services on PPC_2, point A_2, is 220 million units of defense goods and 0 units of nondefense goods. The second point, B_2, is a combination of 200 million units of defense goods and 75 million units of nondefense goods. C_2 through F_2 are the combinations shown in the table of Figure 2. Connecting these points yields the bowed-out curve, PPC_2. Because of the availability of new supplies of oil, the nation is able to increase production of all goods, as shown by the *shift* from PPC_1 to PPC_2. A comparison of the two curves shows that more goods and services for both defense and nondefense are possible along PPC_2 than along PPC_1.

The outward shift of the PPC can be the result of an increase in the quantity of resources, but it also can occur because the quality of resources improves.

Copyright © by Houghton Mifflin Company. All rights reserved.

Combination	Defense Goods and Services (millions of units)	Nondefense Goods and Services (millions of units)
A_2	220	0
B_2	200	75
C_2	175	125
D_2	130	150
E_2	70	160
F_2	0	165

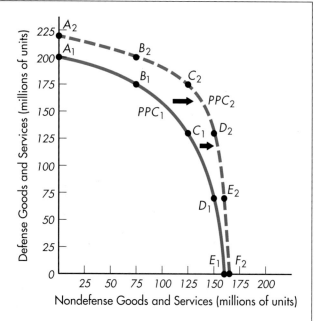

Figure 2
A Shift of the Production Possibilities Curve
Whenever everything else is not constant, the curve shifts. In this case, an increase in the quantity of a resource enables the society to produce more of both types of goods. The curve shifts out, away from the origin.

For instance, a technological breakthrough could conceivably improve the way that communication occurs, thereby requiring fewer people and machines and less time to produce the same quantity and quality of goods. The work force could become more literate, thereby requiring less time to produce the same quantity and quality of goods. Each of these quality improvements in resources could lead to an outward shift of the PPC.

The outward shift of the PPC illustrates that the capacity, or potential, of the economy has grown. However, being able to produce more of all goods doesn't mean that a society will do that. A society might produce at a point on the PPC, inside the PPC, or even attempt to produce at a point outside the PPC.

Knowing that the opportunity costs include the entire PPC plus the forgone production of those resources not fully or efficiently used, why would a society produce at a point inside the PPC? Almost as puzzling is why a society might try to produce beyond its capacity, something it cannot sustain, when the opportunity costs include not only the entire PPC but the possible damage to the society's "internal organs" due to overheating. The answers to these questions are far from straightforward; in fact, a significant part of macroeconomics is devoted to answering them.

RECAP

1. Opportunity costs are the benefits that are forgone due to a choice. When you choose one thing you must give up—forgo—others.

Copyright © by Houghton Mifflin Company. All rights reserved.

2. Opportunity costs are an individual concept but can be used to demonstrate scarcity and choice for a society as a whole.

3. The production possibilities curve represents all combinations of goods and services that can be produced using limited resources efficiently to their full capabilities.

4. Points inside the production possibilities curve represent the underutilization or inefficient use of resources—more goods and services could be produced by using the limited resources more fully or efficiently.

5. Points outside the production possibilities curve represent combinations of goods and services that are unattainable given the limitation of resources. More resources would have to be obtained, or a more efficient means of production through the development of technology or innovative management techniques would have to be discovered, to produce quantities of goods and services outside the current production possibilities curve.

2. SPECIALIZATION AND TRADE

No matter which combination of goods and services a society chooses to produce, other combinations of goods are forgone. The PPC illustrates what these forgone combinations are. The PPC also illustrates how easily a society can transfer resources from one activity to another. If someone is equally productive making either rocket launchers or medical equipment, total output will not change as that person moves from producing one type of product to producing the other type. However, a specialist in the design of rocket launchers might not be very good at designing medical equipment. By taking that specialist from the production of defense goods and placing her into the health-care industry, many rocket launchers may have to be forgone with little additional production in the health-care industry. We describe how specialization affects the shape of the PPC curve in the following section.

2.a. Marginal Opportunity Cost

The shape of the PPC illustrates the ease with which resources can be transferred from one activity to another. If it becomes increasingly more difficult or costly to move resources from one activity to another, the PPC will have the bowed-out shape of Figure 1. With each successive increase in the production of nondefense goods, we see that some amount of defense goods has to be given up. The incremental amounts of defense production given up with each increase in the production of nondefense goods are known as marginal opportunity costs. **Marginal opportunity cost** is the amount of one good or service that must be given up to obtain one additional unit of another good or service, no matter how many units are being produced.

marginal opportunity cost:
the amount of one good or service that must be given up to obtain one additional unit of another good or service, no matter how many units are being produced

The bowed-out shape shows that for each additional nondefense good, more and more defense goods have to be forgone. According to the table and graph in Figure 3, we see that moving from point A to point B on the PPC means increasing nondefense production from 0 to 25 million units and decreasing defense production from 200 million to 195 million units, resulting in a marginal opportunity cost of 5 million units of defense goods and services for

Copyright © by Houghton Mifflin Company. All rights reserved.

Figure 3
The Production Possibilities Curve and Marginal Opportunity Costs

With a limited amount of resources, only certain combinations of defense and nondefense goods and services can be produced. The maximum amounts that can be produced are represented by points A through H. With each increase of non-defense production, marginal opportunity costs increase. This occurs as a result of specialization. The first resources switched from defense to nondefense production are those that are least specialized in the production of defense goods. But as more and more nondefense goods are produced, the more specialized resources have to be switched as well. This means higher opportunity costs; increasing amounts of defense goods have to be forgone.

Combination	Defense Goods and Services (millions of units)	Marginal Opportunity Costs (defense units forgone per 25 units of nondefense units gained)	Nondefense Goods and Services (millions of units)
A	200		0
		5	
B	195		25
		7	
C	188		50
		13	
D	175		75
		20	
E	155		100
		30	
F	125		125
		50	
G	75		150
		75	
H	0		160

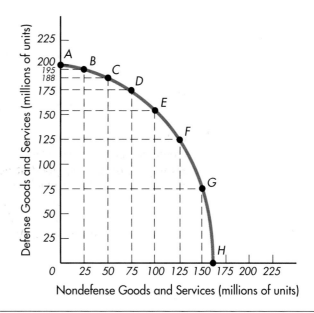

each 25 million units of nondefense goods and services. Moving from point B to point C means increasing nondefense production from 25 to 50 million units, decreasing defense production from 195 to 188 million units and creating a marginal opportunity cost of 7 million units. Moving from point C to point D causes nondefense production to increase from 50 to 75 million units, a decrease in defense production from 188 million to 175 million units and a marginal opportunity cost of 13 million units. As you can see from the table for Figure 3, marginal opportunity costs increase with each successive increase of nondefense production. In other words, it gets more and more costly to produce nondefense goods. The increased marginal opportunity costs occur as a result of specialization. The first resources switched from defense to nondefense production are those that are least specialized in the

Copyright © by Houghton Mifflin Company. All rights reserved.

production of defense goods. Switching these resources is less costly (less has to be given up) than switching the specialists. An accountant can do accounting in either defense- or nondefense-related industries equally well; an expert rocket physicist cannot work as efficiently in health care as in the defense area. But as more and more nondefense goods are produced, the more specialized resources have to be switched as well. This means higher opportunity costs, and increasing amounts of defense goods have to be forgone.

2.b. Specialize Where Opportunity Costs Are Lowest

Why does specialization occur?

Individuals, firms, and nations select the option with the lowest opportunity costs.

Few of us are jacks-of-all-trades. Nations, similarly, have limited amounts of resources and must choose where to devote those resources. How do we decide where to devote our energies? The answer is to *specialize in those activities that require us to give up the smallest amount of other things*; in other words, specialize where costs are lowest. A plumber does plumbing and leaves teaching to the teachers. The teacher teaches and leaves electrical work to the electrician. A country such as Grenada, which has abundant rich land suitable for the cultivation and production of nutmeg and other spices, specializes in spice production. If we specialize, however, how do we get the other things we want? The answer is that we trade, or exchange goods and services.

2.b.1. Trade   By specializing in activities in which opportunity costs are lowest and then trading, each country or individual will end up with more than if each tried to produce everything. Consider a simple hypothetical example, as given in Figure 4, which concerns two countries, Haiti and the Dominican Republic, that share an island. Assume Haiti and the Dominican Republic must decide how to allocate their resources between food production and health care. Haiti's daily production possibilities curve is plotted using the data in columns 2 and 3 of the table. If Haiti devotes all of its resources to health care, then it would be able to provide 1,000 people adequate care each day but would have no resources with which to produce food. If it devotes half of its available resources to each activity, then it would provide 500 people adequate health care and produce 7 tons of food. Devoting all of its resources to food production would mean that Haiti could produce 10 tons of food but would have no health care. The Dominican Republic's production possibilities curve is plotted using the data in columns 4 and 5 of the table. If the Dominican Republic devotes all of its resources to health care, it could provide adequate care to 500 people daily but would be unable to produce any food. If it devotes half of its resources to each activity then it could provide 300 people health care and produce 5 tons of food; and if it devotes all of its resources to food production, it could produce 10 tons of food but no health care.

Suppose that Haiti and the Dominican Republic each want 500 people per day provided adequate health care. By itself, the Dominican Republic would be unable to grow any food if it devoted resources to health care for 500 people. However, if the Dominican Republic and Haiti could agree to some type of exchange, perhaps the Dominican Republic could get some food and give the 500 people the health care. But who produces what? The answer depends on opportunity costs. If the Dominican Republic decides to provide health care to 500 people, it must forgo 10 tons of food; Haiti, on the other hand, must forgo only 3 tons of food if it decides to provide health care to 500 people. Haiti's opportunity cost for devoting its resources to providing

Copyright © by Houghton Mifflin Company. All rights reserved.

500 people health care, 3 tons of food, is lower than the Dominican Republic's, 10 tons. Conversely, if the Dominican Republic produces 10 tons of food, it forgoes providing health care for only 500 people while Haiti forgoes health care for 1,000 people. Clearly, the Dominican Republic's opportunity costs of producing food are lower than Haiti's.

Given the differences in opportunity costs, it would make sense for Haiti to devote its resources to health care and for the Dominican Republic to devote its resources to food production. In this case, Haiti would provide 1,000 people health care and produce no food and the Dominican Republic would produce 10 tons of food but no health care. The two nations would then trade. The Dominican Republic might give 8 tons of food to Haiti in exchange for health care for 500 people. Under this scheme, where each country gets health care for 500 people, the Dominican Republic would be better off by the 2 tons of food it would also get, while Haiti would be better off by the 8 rather than 7 tons of food it would get if it provided the 500 people health care using its own resources. Each is made better off by specialization and trade.

Specialization and trade enable nations to acquire combinations of goods that lie beyond their own resource capabilities. This is shown in Figure 4: the trade point of 500 people being provided health care and 2 tons of food is beyond the Dominican Republic's PPC. Similarly, the trade point of 500 people being provided health care and 8 tons of food is beyond Haiti's PPC. The same result applies to individuals and firms. Even though one person, one firm, or one nation is limited to the combinations of goods it can produce using its own resources along or inside its own PPC, through specialization and trade more goods can be acquired. This is why people, firms, and nations trade; this is why there are buyers and sellers.

2.c. Comparative Advantage

comparative advantage:
the ability to produce a good or service at a lower opportunity cost than someone else

We have seen that the choice of which area or activity to specialize in is made on the basis of opportunity costs. Economists refer to the ability of one person or nation to do something with a lower opportunity cost than another as **comparative advantage**. In the example shown in Figure 4, the Dominican Republic had a comparative advantage in food production and Haiti had a comparative advantage in health-care provision. Devoting all resources to health care, Haiti can provide 1,000 people health care while the Dominican Republic can provide only 500 people health care. Devoting all resources to food production, both Haiti and the Dominican Republic can produce 10 tons of food. Clearly, Haiti is better at health care and no worse at food production. Yet, each country has a comparative advantage. Haiti's comparative advantage is in producing health care—it gives up three tons of food for providing 500 people health care while the Dominican Republic gives up ten tons of food for providing 500 people health care. Conversely, the Dominican Republic has a comparative advantage in food production. It gives up providing 500 people health care if it produces ten tons of food while Haiti gives up providing 1,000 people health care if it produces ten tons of food. Haiti has a *comparative advantage* in health care and the Dominican Republic has a *comparative advantage* in food production. It is the relative amount given up not the absolute amount that can be produced that determines comparative advantage. Even if Haiti could produce eleven tons of food while the Dominican Republic could produce only ten, the Dominican Republic's comparative advantage would be in food production.

Copyright © by Houghton Mifflin Company. All rights reserved.

Figure 4
The Benefits of Trade
The trade point of providing health care to 500 people and 2 tons of food is beyond the Dominican Republic's PPC; similarly, the trade point of providing health care to 500 people and 8 tons of food is beyond Haiti's PPC. However, through specialization and trade, these points are achieved by the two nations.

	Haiti		Dominican Republic	
Allocation of Resources to Health Care	Health Care (no. of people provided care)	Food (tons)	Health Care (no. of people provided care)	Food (tons)
100%	1,000	0	500	0
50	500	7	300	5
0	0	10	0	10

(a) Haiti

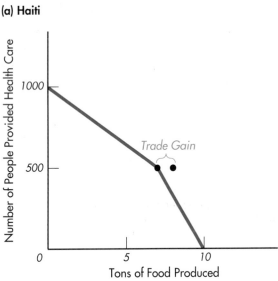

(b) Dominican Republic

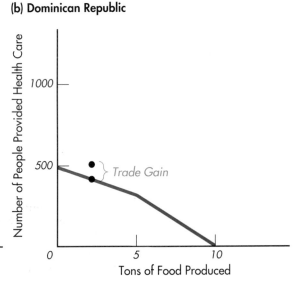

Comparative advantage applies to every case of trade or exchange. You may be better at both computer programming and literature than your roommate, but you may be much better at computer programming and only slightly better at literature. You, then, have a comparative advantage in computers. Your roommate has a comparative advantage as well, in literature. Remember, comparative advantage depends on opportunity costs. Just because you are better than your roommate at both activities, you do not have the same opportunity costs in both. Like Haiti and the Dominican Republic, you and your roommate are better off specializing and then trading (helping each other) than if both of you do all the studying all by yourselves. You both get better grades and have more time to devote to other activities.

2.d. Specialization and Trade Occur Everywhere

Each of us will specialize in some activity, earn an income, and then trade our output (or income) for other goods and services we want. Specialization and trade ensure that we are better off than doing everything ourselves.

Copyright © by Houghton Mifflin Company. All rights reserved.

The fruit of the prickly pear cactus is popular in salads and drinks. Recently, the extract from the cactus leaves has been found to relieve some of the symptoms of diabetes. Physicians in Mexico and Japan prescribe the extract as a substitute for insulin in some cases and as an enhancement to insulin in others. Though the prickly pear cactus grows in southwestern United States as well, the harvesting of the cacti occurs mainly in Mexico because most of the prickly pear cactus forests are in Mexico, and the labor-intensive harvesting process is less costly in Mexico than it would be in the United States. Mexico has a comparative advantage in the harvesting of the cacti.

Copyright © by Houghton Mifflin Company. All rights reserved.

What are the benefits of trade?

Individuals specialize in the activity in which their opportunity costs are lowest.

Specialization according to comparative advantage followed by trade allows everyone to acquire more of the goods they want.

We have now explored the basics of economics. We know that scarcity means that choices must be made. We have learned that choices are made according to rational self-interest. And we just discovered that specialization according to comparative advantage followed by trade ensures that people are as well off as they can possibly be. Trade usually refers to the exchange of goods and services by nations, but trade is also what we do when we purchase goods and services. We trade money for goods and services. We acquired money as a payment for the resource services we provided—working, owning land, or providing funds for capital. Thus, we are, in essence, trading our resource services for the goods and services others provide.

RECAP

1. Marginal opportunity cost is the amount of one good or service that must be given up to obtain one additional unit of another good or service.

2. The rule of specialization is: the individual (firm, region, or nation) will specialize in the production of the good or service that has the lowest opportunity cost.

3. Comparative advantage exists whenever one person (firm, nation) can do something with fewer opportunity costs than some other individual (firm, nation) can.

4. Specialization and trade enable individuals, firms, and nations to get more than they could without specialization and trade.

SUMMARY

▬▬▬ What are opportunity costs? Are they part of the economic way of thinking?

1. Opportunity costs are the forgone opportunities of the next best alternative. Choice means both gaining something and giving up something. When you choose one option you forgo all others. The benefits of the next best alternative are the opportunity costs of your choice. §1

▬▬▬ What is a production possibilities curve?

2. A production possibilities curve represents the tradeoffs involved in the allocation of scarce resources. It shows the maximum quantity of goods and services that can be produced using limited resources to the fullest extent possible. §1.c

3. The bowed-out shape of the PPC occurs because of specialization and increasing marginal opportunity costs. §2.a

▬▬▬ Why does specialization occur?

4. Comparative advantage accounts for specialization. We specialize in the activities in which we have the lowest opportunity costs, that is, in which we have a comparative advantage. §2.c

▬▬▬ What are the benefits of trade?

5. Specialization and trade enable those involved to acquire more than they could by not specializing and engaging in trade. §2.d

KEY TERMS

opportunity costs §1
tradeoff §1.b
marginal cost §1.b
marginal benefit §1.b

production possibilities curve (PPC) §1.c
marginal opportunity cost §2.a
comparative advantage §2.c

EXERCISES

1. In most presidential campaigns, candidates promise more than they can deliver. Clinton and Gore promised more and better health care, a better environment, only minor reductions in defense, better education, and a better and improved system of roads, bridges, sewer systems, water systems, and so on. What economic concept were the candidates ignoring?

2. Janine is an accountant who makes $30,000 a year. Robert is a college student who makes $8,000 a year. All other things being equal, who is more likely to stand in a long line to get a concert ticket?

3. Back in the 1960s, President Lyndon Johnson passed legislation that increased expenditures for both the Vietnam War and social problems in the United States. Since the U.S. economy was operating at its full employment level when President Johnson did this, he appeared to be ignoring what economic concept?

Copyright © by Houghton Mifflin Company. All rights reserved.

4. The following numbers measure the tradeoff between grades and income.

Total Hours	Hours Studying	GPA	Hours Working	Income
60	60	4.0	0	$ 0
60	40	3.0	20	100
60	30	2.0	30	150
60	10	1.0	50	250
60	0	0.0	60	300

a. Calculate the opportunity cost of an increase in the number of hours spent studying in order to earn a 3.0 grade point average (GPA) rather than a 2.0 GPA.

b. Is the opportunity cost the same for a move from a 0.0 GPA to a 1.0 GPA as it is for a move from a 1.0 GPA to a 2.0 GPA?

c. What is the opportunity cost of an increase in salary from $100 to $150?

5. Suppose a second individual has the following tradeoffs between income and grades:

Total Hours	Hours Studying	GPA	Hours Working	Income
60	50	4.0	10	$ 60
60	40	3.0	20	120
60	20	2.0	40	240
60	10	1.0	50	300
60	0	0.0	60	360

a. Define comparative advantage.

b. Does either individual (the one in question 4 or the one in question 5) have a comparative advantage in both activities?

c. Who should specialize in studying and who should specialize in working?

6. A doctor earns $250,000 per year while a professor earns $40,000. They play tennis against each other each Saturday morning, each giving up a morning of relaxing, reading the paper, and playing with their children.

They could each decide to work a few extra hours on Saturday and earn more income. But they choose to play tennis or to relax around the house. Are their opportunity costs of playing tennis different?

7. Plot the PPC given by the following data.

Combination	Health Care	All Other Goods
A	0	100
B	25	90
C	50	70
D	75	40
E	100	0

a. Calculate the marginal opportunity cost of each combination.

b. What is the opportunity cost of combination C?

c. Suppose a second nation has the following PPC. Plot the PPC and then determine which nation has the comparative advantage in which activity. Show whether the two nations can gain from specialization and trade.

Combination	Health Care	All Other Goods
A	0	50
B	20	40
C	40	25
D	60	5
E	65	0

8. A doctor earns $200 per hour, a plumber $40 per hour, and a professor $20 per hour. Everything else the same, which one will devote more hours to negotiating the price of a new car?

9. Perhaps you've heard of the old saying "There is no such thing as a free lunch." What does it mean? If someone invites you to a lunch and offers to pay for it, is it free to you?

10. You have waited 30 minutes in a line for the Star Tours ride at Disneyland. You see a sign

Copyright © by Houghton Mifflin Company. All rights reserved.

that says, "From this point on your wait is 45 minutes." You must decide whether to continue in line or to move elsewhere. On what basis do you make the decision? Do the 30 minutes you've already stood in line come into play?

11. The university is deciding between two meal plans. One plan charges a fixed fee of $600 per semester and allows students to eat as much as they want. The other plan charges a fee based on the quantity of food consumed. Under which plan will students eat the most?

12. Evaluate this statement: "You are a natural athlete, an attractive person who learns easily and communicates well. Clearly, you can do everything better than your friends and acquaintances. As a result, the term *specialization* has no meaning for you. Specialization would cost you rather than benefit you."

13. During China's Cultural Revolution in the late 1960s and early 1970s, many people with a high school or college education were forced to move to farms and work in the fields. Some were common laborers for eight or more years. What does this policy say about specialization and the PPC? Would you predict that the policy would lead to an increase in output?

14. In elementary school and through middle school most students have the same teacher throughout the day and for the entire school year. Then, beginning in high school different subjects are taught by different teachers. In college, the same subject is often taught at different levels—freshman, sophomore, junior-senior, or graduate—by different faculty. Is education taking advantage of specialization only from high school on? Comment on the differences between elementary school and college and the use of specialization.

15. The top officials in federal government and high-ranking officers of large corporations often have chauffeurs to drive them around the city or from meeting to meeting. Is this simply one of the perquisites of their position, or is the use of chauffeurs justifiable on the basis of comparative advantage?

Copyright © by Houghton Mifflin Company. All rights reserved.

 **INTERNET EXERCISE**

This chapter focuses on specialization and trade. Use the internet to examine international trade across countries. Go to the Boyes/Melvin web site at **http://www.hmco.com/college/** and click on the internet exercise link for this chapter. Now answer the questions that appear on the web page.

Copyright © by Houghton Mifflin Company. All rights reserved.

The Naked Truth: 'Full Monty's' Blue-Collar Chippendales Gently Reveal the Trauma of Open Borders and Shuttered Mills

Remember when Pat Buchanan "discovered" unemployment in New Hampshire, during the 1992 presidential campaign? And shocked George Bush and the political press by flirting with 40 percent of the GOP primary vote?

Outside shuttered shoe factories in the snow, he suddenly understood the political blind spot among cocooned journalists and free-trade intellectuals both liberal and conservative back in Washington. In a governmental capital that manufactures nothing heavier than hot air, many seldom if ever encountered discarded assembly-line workers. . . .

Coincidentally or not, the biggest surprise of the fall movie season has been "The Full Monty," a bittersweet tale of British steelworkers left for scrap when their steel mill in England's blighted industrial north closes. Those mandarins surprised by the failure of fast track might want to catch up with this word-of-mouth British movie smash. Sometimes it takes an imported movie with a cast speaking barely recognizable English to explain the pockets of dread and distress scattered through their own backyards.

Rich in serious themes handled with the deftest of comic touches, "The Full Monty" has surpassed "Four Weddings and a Funeral" in England as the top-grossing British movie ever and become a very profitable film. Made for $3.5 million, it has grossed more than $133 million worldwide, $31 million of that in America. And that's before a planned Oscar promotional blitz for the film, directed by Peter Cattaneo and written by Simon Beaufoy. Not bad for six welders and a funeral for British heavy industry.

When the steel mill in de-industrializing Sheffield shuts down, Gaz and his newly unemployed mates learn that losing a job means losing more than a paycheck. Gaz, unable to maintain child-support payments to his ex-wife, faces the loss of visitation rights to his son. His overweight friend Dave becomes impotent.

Plant foreman Gerald exudes pride in his petit-bourgeois superiority to the working class boys on the shop floor. He confronts unemployment with such a stiff upper lip that he is unable to tell his wife the bad news for six months. . . .

In a city where the working-class ideal of masculinity is dying along with the steel industry, the women are flocking to a nightclub offering a travesty of masculinity, a revue of Chippendale-style male strippers. At first, Gaz is contemptuous of the spectacle: "Some poof gettin' his kit off." Then he learns the revue's nightly take is 10,000 pounds. Soon he is assembling his own chorus line of male strippers out of Sheffield's reserve army of the unemployed.

One problem: Gaz and his friends aren't built like Chippendale dancers. Okay, two problems: They can't dance either—except for the man named Horse, who knows the Funky Chicken but has a "dodgy hip." If they want to top the sculpted pros, they'll have to go "the full monty" (British for "the whole nine yards"). In other words, they will have to bare all caboodle and kit, too. In a way, they have learned Adam Smith's secret of comparative advantage. . . .

Source: "Six Welders and a Funeral," by Daniel Wattenberg, from *The Weekly Standard,* December 15, 1997. Reprinted by permission.

Copyright © by Houghton Mifflin Company. All rights reserved.

COMMENTARY

I first ran across the movie *The Full Monty* as did most others, by word of mouth. I overheard people talking about what a great movie it was. I initially thought it must be a Monty Python comedy but was quickly disabused of this notion. It is a movie about unemployment—steel workers in Britain thrown out of their jobs when the mill closes down. To many, the movie reinforces the idea that free trade simply causes unemployment.

According to many people there are no gains, only losses, from free trade. As a result, these people argue, governments should protect their industries by restricting trade. Rather than free trade arrangements like the North American Free Trade Agreement (NAFTA), governments should place restrictions on the amounts that other nations can ship to the United States.

Although *The Full Monty* seems to be an argument against free trade, it is actually an argument for free trade. The stars of the movie struggle through their unemployment; all have some problems, some personal problems, others marital problems. They learn that the male strippers at nearby clubs are earning huge incomes—10,000 pounds or about $17,000—for a night's work. Soon the unemployed steel workers have organized their own chorus line and are working in the strip joints.

Free trade can be difficult for some. For whom? For those working in an industry that has no comparative advantage. If another nation can produce steel more efficiently than Britain can, then free trade will drive the British steel industry out of business. Those employed in the British steel industry will have to switch to other industries. This switch, or transition, to other industries is difficult and costly for those involved. But, the result is economic growth, more income, and the ability to purchase more than could be produced just by Britain.

We learned in this chapter that nations could gain by specializing where their opportunity costs are lowest and then trading. Trade allows a society to acquire goods and services beyond its own PPC. Suppose that the following figure represents Britain's PPC. With trade, Britain could gain some amount, say *A* to *B*. Not allowing trade means consumers can consume less than they could with trade. British consumers would be restricted to the nation's own PPC, represented by point *A* or any point on or inside the PPC. Trade restrictions would mean that British consumers have an opportunity cost of amount *A* to *B*; they forgo the additional amount of goods and services that trade would allow. There is no doubt that free trade will benefit British consumers. But, the transition from a restricted trade to free trade, from *A* to *B*, may involve the loss of jobs in one area of the economy and the increase in jobs in another area of the economy. The people employed in the losing area will feel the effect of trade negatively while those employed in the gaining area will feel the benefits of trade.

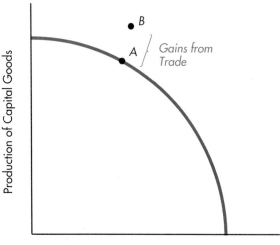

Copyright © by Houghton Mifflin Company. All rights reserved.

3

Markets, Demand and Supply, and the Price System

FUNDAMENTAL QUESTIONS

1. What is a market?

2. What is demand?

3. What is supply?

4. How is price determined by demand and supply?

5. What causes price to change?

6. What happens when price is not allowed to change with market forces?

Copyright © by Houghton Mifflin Company. All rights reserved.

P eople (and firms and nations) can get more if they specialize in certain activities and then trade with one another to acquire the goods and services they desire. But how are the specialized producers to get together or to know who specializes in what? We could allow the government to decide, or we could rely on first-come, first-served, or even simply luck. Typically it is the market mechanism—buyers and sellers interacting via prices—we rely on to ensure that gains from trade occur. To see why, consider the following situation and then carry out the exercise.

I. At a sightseeing point, reachable only after a strenuous hike, a firm has established a stand where bottled water is sold. The water, carried in by the employees of the firm, is sold to thirsty hikers in 6-ounce bottles. The price is $1 per bottle. Typically only 100 bottles of the water are sold each day. On a particularly hot day, 200 hikers each want to buy at least one bottle of water. Indicate what you think of each of the following means of distributing the water to the hikers by responding to each allocation approach with one of the following five responses:

a. Completely fair

b. Acceptable

c. Unfair

d. Very unfair

e. Totally unfair

1. Increasing the price until the quantity of water bottles hikers are willing and able to purchase exactly equals the number of water bottles available for sale

2. Selling the water for $1 per bottle on a first-come, first-served basis

3. Having the local authority (government) buy the water for $1 per bottle and distribute it according to its own judgment

4. Selling the water at $1 per bottle following a random selection procedure or lottery

The following is a similar situation but involves a different product.

II. A physician has been providing medical services at a fee of $100 per patient and typically sees thirty patients per day. One day the flu bug has been so vicious that the number of patients attempting to visit the physician exceeds sixty. Indicate what you think of each of the following means of distributing the physician's services to the sick patients by responding with one of the following five answers:

Copyright © by Houghton Mifflin Company. All rights reserved.

Preview

a. Completely fair

b. Acceptable

c. Unfair

d. Very unfair

e. Totally unfair

1. Raising the price until the number of patients the doctor sees is exactly equal to those patients willing and able to pay the doctor's fee

2. Selling the services at $100 per patient on a first-come, first-served basis

3. Having the local authority (government) pay the physician $100 per patient and choose who is to receive the services according to its own judgment

4. Selling the physician's services for $100 per patient following a random selection procedure or lottery

How did you answer the exercises? Did you notice that in fact, each allocation mechanism is unfair in the sense that someone gets the good or service and someone does not? With the market system, it is those without income or wealth who must do without. Under the first-come, first-served system it is those who arrive later who do without. Under the government scheme it is those not in favor or those who do not match up with the government's rules who do without. And, with a random procedure, it is those who do not have the lucky ticket or correct number who are left out.

Since each allocation mechanism is in a sense unfair, how do we decide which to use? One way might be by the incentives each creates.

With the first-come, first-served allocation scheme, the incentive is to be first. You have no reason to improve the quality of your products or to increase the value of your resources. Your only incentive is to be first. Supply will not increase. Why would anyone produce when all everyone wants is to be first? As a result, growth will not occur and standards of living will not rise. A society based on first-come, first-served would die a quick death.

Copyright © by Houghton Mifflin Company. All rights reserved.

A market arises when buyers and sellers exchange a well-defined good or service. In stock markets, buyers and sellers exchange their "goods," or stocks, solely through electronic connections. Shoppers at a fish market can examine the day's catch and make their choices.

A government scheme provides an incentive either to be a member of government and thus help determine the allocation rules or to perform according to government dictates. There are no incentives to improve production and efficiency, to improve quantities supplied, and thus no reason for the economy to grow. We have seen how this system fared with the collapse of the Soviet Union.

The random allocation provides no incentives at all; simply hope that manna from heaven falls on you.

With the market system, the incentive is to acquire purchasing ability—to obtain income and wealth. This means you must provide goods that have high value to others and provide resources that have high value to producers—to enhance your worth as an employee by acquiring education or training and to enhance the value of the resources you own.

The market system also provides incentives for quantities of scarce goods to increase. In the case of the water stand in scenario I, if the price of the water increases and the owner of the water stand is earning significant profits, others may carry or truck water to the top of the hill and sell it to thirsty hikers; the amount of water available thus increases. In the case of the doctor in scenario II, other doctors may think that opening an office near the first might be a way to earn more; the amount of physician services available increases. Since the market system creates the incentive for the amount supplied to increase, economies grow and expand and standards of living improve. The market system also ensures that resources are allocated to where they are most highly valued. If the price of an item rises, consumers may switch over to another item, or another good or service, that can serve about the same purpose. When consumers switch, production of the alternative good rises and thus resources used in its production must increase as well. The resources then are reallocated from lower-valued uses to higher-valued uses. ∎

1. MARKETS

Copyright © by Houghton Mifflin Company. All rights reserved.

What is a market?

The supermarket, the stock market, the market for foreign exchange, and all other markets are similar in that well-defined goods and services are exchanged. A market may be a specific location, such as the supermarket or the stock market, or it may be the exchange of particular goods or services at many different locations, such as the foreign exchange market.

1.a. Market Definition

market:
a place or service that enables buyers and sellers to exchange goods and services

A **market** makes possible the exchange of goods and services. Food, shares of stock, and various national monies are bought and sold in, respectively, the supermarket, the stock market, and the foreign exchange market.

A market may be a formally organized exchange, such as the New York Stock Exchange, or it may be loosely organized like the market for used bicycles or automobiles. A market may be confined to one location, as in the case of a supermarket or the stock market, or it may encompass a city, a state, a country, or the entire world. The market for agricultural products, for instance, is international, but the market for labor services is mostly local or national.

1.b. Barter and Money Exchanges

barter:
the direct exchange of goods and services without the use of money

double coincidence of wants:
the situation that exists when A has what B wants and B has what A wants

transaction costs:
the cost involved in making an exchange

The purpose of markets is to facilitate the exchange of goods and services between buyers and sellers. In some cases money changes hands; in others only goods and services are exchanged. The exchange of goods and services directly, without money, is called **barter.** Barter occurs when a plumber fixes a leaky pipe for a lawyer in exchange for the lawyer's work on a will, and when a Chinese citizen provides fresh vegetables to an American visitor in exchange for a pack of American cigarettes.

Most markets involve money because goods and services can be exchanged more easily with money than without it. When IBM purchases microchips from Yakamoto of Japan, IBM and Yakamoto don't exchange goods directly. Neither firm may have what the other wants. Barter requires a **double coincidence of wants**: IBM must have what Yakamoto wants, and Yakamoto must have what IBM wants. The **transaction costs** (the costs associated with making an exchange) of finding a double coincidence of wants for barter transactions are typically very high. Money reduces these transaction costs. To obtain the microchips, all IBM has to do is provide dollars to Yakamoto. Yakamoto is willing to accept the money since it can spend it to obtain the goods that it wants.

1.c. Relative Price

relative price:
the price of one good expressed in terms of the price of another good

The relative price is the price that affects economic decision making.

When people agree to trade or exchange, they must agree on the rate of exchange, or the price. The price of an exchange is a **relative price**—the price of one good expressed in terms of the price of another good. In a barter exchange a relative price is established between the goods traded. When the lawyer exchanges 2 hours of work for 1 hour of the plumber's work, the relative price established is 2/1. In a money exchange the relative price is more implicit. You pay a money price of $1 for a carton of milk. But, with that purchase you are forgoing everything else you could get for that dollar. Thus, the carton of milk is worth 1/3 of a $3 box of Quaker Oats 100% Natural cereal, 1/200 of a $200 used Diamond Back mountain bike, 20 sticks of $.05/stick Trident gum, and so on. These are the relative prices of the milk. Relative prices are a measure of what you must give up to get one unit of a good or service and are, therefore, a measure of opportunity costs. Since opportunity costs are what decisions are based on, when economists refer to the price of something, it is the relative price they have in mind.

RECAP

1. A market is not necessarily a specific location or store. Instead, the term *market* refers to buyers and sellers communicating with each other regarding the quality and quantity of a well-defined product, what buyers are willing and able to pay for a product, and what sellers must receive in order to produce and sell a product.

2. Barter refers to exchanges made without the use of money.

3. Money makes it easier and less expensive to exchange goods and services.

4. The price of a good or service is a measure of what you must give up to get one unit of that good or service.

Copyright © by Houghton Mifflin Company. All rights reserved.

2. DEMAND

Demand and supply determine the price of any good or service. To understand how a price level is determined and why a price rises or falls, it is necessary to know how demand and supply function. We begin by considering demand alone, then supply, and then we put the two together. Before we begin, we discuss some economic terminology that is often confusing.

Economists distinguish between the terms **demand** and **quantity demanded**. When they refer to the *quantity demanded* they are talking about the amount of a product that people are willing and able to purchase at a *specific* price. When they refer to *demand* they are talking about the amount that people would be willing and able to purchase at *every possible* price. Demand is the quantities demanded at every price. Thus, the statement that "the demand for U.S. white wine rose after a 300 percent tariff was applied to French white wine" means that at each price for U.S. white wine, more people were willing and able to purchase U.S. white wine. And the statement that "the quantity demanded of white wine fell as the price of white wine rose" means that people were willing and able to purchase less white wine because the price of the wine rose.

What is demand?

demand:
the amount of a product that people are willing and able to purchase at every possible price

quantity demanded:
the amount of a product that people are willing and able to purchase at a specific price

2.a. The Law of Demand

law of demand:
as the price of a good or service rises (falls), the quantity of that good or service that people are willing and able to purchase during a particular period of time falls (rises), everything else held constant

Consumers and merchants know that if you lower the price of a good or service without altering its quality or quantity, people will beat a path to your doorway. This simple truth is referred to as the **law of demand**.

According to the law of demand, people purchase more of something when the price of that item falls. More formally, the law of demand states that the quantity of some item that people are willing and able to purchase, during a particular period of time, decreases as the price rises, and vice versa.

The more formal definition of the law of demand can be broken down into five phrases:

1. the quantity of a well-defined good or service that
2. people are willing and able to purchase
3. during a particular period of time
4. decreases as the price of that good or service rises and increases as the price falls
5. everything else held constant

The first phrase ensures that we are referring to the same item, that we are not mixing different goods. A watch is a commodity defined and distinguished from other goods by several characteristics: quality, color, and design of the watch face, to name a few. The law of demand applies to the well-defined good, in this case, a watch. If one of the characteristics should change, the good would no longer be well-defined—in fact, it would be a different good. A Rolex watch is different from a Timex watch; Polo brand golf shirts are different goods than generic brand golf shirts; Mercedes-Benz automobiles are different goods than Yugo automobiles.

The second phrase indicates that people must not only *want* to purchase some good, they must be *able* to purchase that good in order for their wants to be counted as part of demand. For example, Sue would love to buy a

Copyright © by Houghton Mifflin Company. All rights reserved.

membership to the Paradise Valley Country Club, but because the membership costs $35,000, she is not able to purchase the membership. Though willing, she is not able. At a price of $5,000, however, she is willing and able to purchase the membership.

The third phrase points out that the demand for any good is defined for a specific period of time. Without reference to a time period, a demand relationship would not make any sense. For instance, the statement that "at a price of $3 per Happy Meal, 13 million Happy Meals are demanded" provides no useful information. Are the 13 million meals sold in one week or one year? Think of demand as a rate of purchase at each possible price over a period of time—2 per month, 1 per day, and so on.

The fourth phrase points out that price and quantity demanded move in opposite directions; that is, as the price rises, the quantity demanded falls, and as the price falls, the quantity demanded rises.

Demand is a measure of the relationship between the price and quantity demanded of a particular good or service, when the determinants of demand do not change. The **determinants of demand** are income, tastes, prices of related goods and services, expectations, and the number of buyers. If any one of these items changes, demand changes. The final phrase, everything else held constant, ensures that the determinants of demand do not change.

determinants of demand:
factors other than the price of the good that influence demand—income, tastes, prices of related goods and services, expectations, and number of buyers

2.b. The Demand Schedule

demand schedule:
a table or list of the prices and the corresponding quantities demanded of a particular good or service

A **demand schedule** is a table or list of the prices and the corresponding quantities demanded of a particular good or service. The table in Figure 1 is a demand schedule for video rentals (movies). It shows the number of videos that a consumer named Bob would be willing and able to rent at each price during the year, everything else held constant. As the rental price of the videos gets higher relative to the prices of other goods, Bob would be willing and able to rent fewer videos.

At the high price of $5 per video, Bob indicates that he will rent only 10 videos during the year. At a price of $4 per video, Bob tells us that he will rent 20 videos during the year. As the price drops from $5 to $4 to $3 to $2 and to $1, Bob is willing and able to rent more videos. At a price of $1, Bob would rent 50 videos during the year, nearly 1 per week.

2.c. The Demand Curve

demand curve:
a graph of a demand schedule that measures price on the vertical axis and quantity demanded on the horizontal axis

When speaking of the demand curve or demand schedule, we are using constant-quality units. The quality of a good does not change as the price changes along a demand curve.

A **demand curve** is a graph of the demand schedule. The demand curve shown in Figure 1 is plotted from the information given in the demand schedule. Price is measured on the vertical axis, quantity per unit of time on the horizontal axis. The demand curve slopes downward because of the inverse relationship between the rental price of the videos and the quantity an individual is willing and able to purchase (rent). Point A in Figure 1 corresponds to combination A in the table: a price of $5 and 10 videos demanded. Similarly, points B, C, D, and E in Figure 1 represent the corresponding combinations in the table. The line connecting these points is Bob's demand curve for videos.

All demand curves slope down because of the law of demand: as price falls, quantity demanded increases. The demand curves for bread, electricity, automobiles, colleges, labor services, and any other good or service you can think of slope down. You might be saying to yourself, "That's not true. What

Copyright © by Houghton Mifflin Company. All rights reserved.

Copyright © by Houghton Mifflin Company. All rights reserved.

Figure 1
Bob's Demand Schedule and Demand Curve for Videos

The number of videos that Bob is willing and able to rent at each price during the year is listed in the table, or demand schedule. The demand curve is derived from the combinations given in the demand schedule. The price-quantity combination of $5 per video and 10 videos is point A. The combination of $4 per video and 20 videos is point B. Each combination is plotted, and the points are connected to form the demand curve.

Combination	Price per Video (constant-quality units)	Quantity Demanded per Year (constant-quality units)
A	$5	10
B	4	20
C	3	30
D	2	40
E	1	50

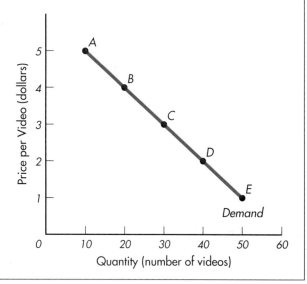

about the demand for Mercedes-Benz cars or Gucci bags? As their price goes up, they become more prestigious and the quantity demanded actually rises." To avoid confusion in such circumstances, we say "everything else held constant." With this statement we are assuming that tastes don't change and that, therefore, the goods *cannot* become more prestigious as the price changes. Similarly, we do not allow the quality or the brand name of a product to change as we define the demand schedule or demand curve. We concentrate on the one quality or the one brand; so when we say that the price of a good has risen, we are talking about a good that is identical at all prices.

2.d. From Individual Demand Curves to a Market Curve

Bob's demand curve for video rentals is plotted in Figure 1. Unless Bob is the only renter of the videos, his demand curve is not the total, or market demand, curve. Market demand is the sum of all individual demands. To derive the market demand curve, then, the individual demand curves of all consumers in the market must be added together. The table in Figure 2 lists the demand schedules of three individuals, Bob, Helen, and Art. Because in this example the market consists only of Bob, Helen, and Art, their individual demands are added together to derive the market demand. The market demand is the last column of the table.

Bob's, Helen's, and Art's demand schedules are plotted as individual demand curves in Figure 2(a). In Figure 2(b) their individual demand curves have been added together to obtain the market demand curve. (Notice that we

Figure 2

The Market Demand Schedule and Curve for Videos

The market is defined to consist of three individuals: Bob, Helen, and Art. Their demand schedules are listed in the table and plotted as the individual demand curves shown in Figure 2(a). By adding the quantities that each demands at every price, we obtain the market demand curve shown in Figure 2(b). At a price of $1 we add Bob's quantity demanded of 50 to Helen's quantity demanded of 25 to Art's quantity demanded of 27 to obtain the market quantity demanded of 102. At a price of $2 we add Bob's 40 to Helen's 20 to Art's 24 to obtain the market quantity demanded of 84. To obtain the market demand curve, for every price we sum the quantities demanded by each market participant.

Price per Video	Quantities Demanded per Year by			Market Demand
	Bob	Helen	Art	
$5	10 +	5 +	15 =	30
4	20	10	18	48
3	30	15	21	66
2	40	20	24	84
1	50	25	27	102

(a) Individual Demand Curves

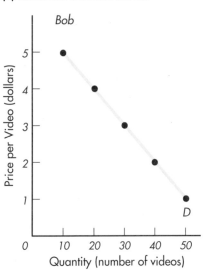

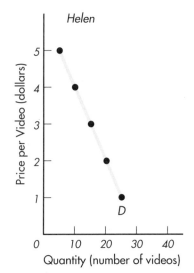

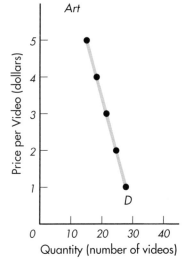

(b) Market Demand Curve

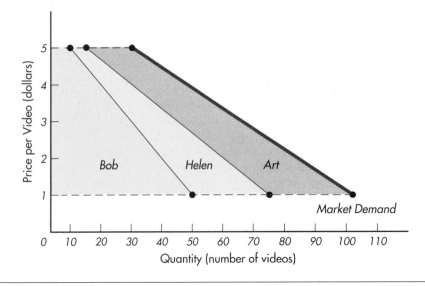

Copyright © by Houghton Mifflin Company. All rights reserved.

add in a horizontal direction—that is, we add quantities at each price, not the prices at each quantity.) At a price of $5, we add the quantity Bob would buy, 10, to the quantity Helen would buy, 5, to the quantity Art would buy, 15, to get the market demand of 30. At a price of $4, we add the quantities each of the consumers is willing and able to buy to get the total quantity demanded of 48. At all prices, then, we add the quantities demanded by each individual consumer to get the total, or market quantity, demanded.

2.e. Changes in Demand and Changes in Quantity Demanded

When one of the determinants of demand—income, tastes, prices of related goods, expectations, or number of buyers—is allowed to change, the demand for a good or service changes as well. What does it mean to say that demand changes? Demand is the entire demand schedule, or demand curve. When we say that demand changes, we are referring to a change in the quantities demanded at each and every price.

For example, if Bob's income rises, then his demand for video rentals rises. At each and every price, the number of videos Bob is willing and able to rent each year rises. This increase is shown in the last column of the table in Figure 3. A change in demand is represented by a shift of the demand curve, as shown in Figure 3(a). The shift to the right, from D_1 to D_2, indicates that Bob is willing and able to rent more videos at every price.

When the price of a good or service is the only factor that changes, the quantity demanded changes but the demand curve does not shift. Instead, as the price of the rentals is decreased (increased), everything else held constant, the quantity that people are willing and able to purchase increases (decreases). This change is merely a movement from one point on the demand curve to another point on the same demand curve, not a shift of the demand curve. *Change in the quantity demanded* is the phrase economists use to describe the change in the quantities of a particular good or service that people are willing and able to purchase as the price of that good or service changes. A change in the quantity demanded, from point A to point B on the demand curve, is shown in Figure 3(b).

The demand curve shifts when income, tastes, prices of related goods, expectations, or the number of buyers changes. Let's consider how each of these determinants of demand affects the demand curve.

Income   The demand for any good or service depends on income. The higher someone's income is, the more goods and services that person can purchase at any given price. The increase in Bob's income causes his demand to increase. This change is shown in Figure 3(a) by the shift to the right from the curve labeled D_1 to the curve labeled D_2. Increased income means a greater ability to purchase goods and services. At every price, more videos are demanded along curve D_2 than along curve D_1.

Tastes   The demand for any good or service depends on individuals' tastes and preferences. For decades, the destination of choice for college students in the East and Midwest during spring break was Fort Lauderdale, Florida. In the early 1990s, many students decided that Mexico offered a more exciting destination than Fort Lauderdale. Regardless of the prices of the Fort Lauderdale and Mexican vacations, tastes changed so that more students went to Mexico. The demand curve for the Mexican vacation shifted to the right while that for the Fort Lauderdale vacation shifted to the left.

Copyright © by Houghton Mifflin Company. All rights reserved.

Figure 3
A Change in Demand and a Change in the Quantity Demanded
According to the table, Bob's demand for videos has increased by 5 videos at each price level. In Figure 3(a), this change is shown as a shift of the demand curve from D_1 to D_2. Figure 3(b) shows a change in the quantity demanded. The change is an increase in the quantity that consumers are willing and able to purchase at a lower price. It is shown as a movement along the demand curve from point A to point B.

Price per Video	Quantity Demanded per Year	
	Before	After
$5	10	15
4	20	25
3	30	35
2	40	45
1	50	55

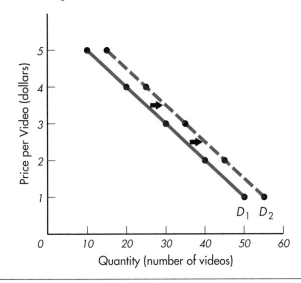

(a) Change in Demand

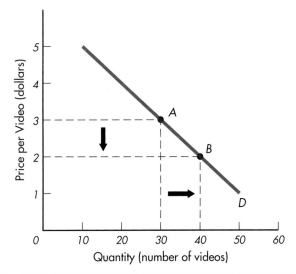

(b) Change in Quantity Demanded

substitute goods:
goods that can be used in place of each other; as the price of one rises, the demand for the other rises

complementary goods:
goods that are used together; as the price of one rises, the demand for the other falls

A change in demand is represented by a shift of the demand curve.

Prices of Related Goods and Services   Goods and services may be related in two ways. **Substitute goods** can be used for each other, so that as the price of one rises, the demand for the other rises. Bread and crackers, BMWs and Acuras, video rentals and theater movies, universities and community colleges, electricity and natural gas are, more or less, pairs of substitutes. As the price of cassette tapes rises, everything else held constant, the demand for CDs will rise and the demand curve for CDs will shift to the right. As the price of theater movies increases, the demand for video rentals will rise and the demand curve for the videos will shift to the right.

Complementary goods are used together, and as the price of one rises, the demand for the other falls. Bread and margarine, beer and peanuts, cameras and film, shoes and socks, CDs and CD players, video rentals and VCRs are examples of pairs of complementary goods. As the price of cameras rises, people tend to purchase fewer cameras, but they also tend to purchase less film. As the price of VCRs rises, people tend to purchase fewer VCRs, but they also demand fewer video rentals. The demand curve for a complementary good shifts to the left when the price of the related good increases.

Copyright © by Houghton Mifflin Company. All rights reserved.

Expectations   Expectations about future events can have an effect on demand today. People make purchases today because they expect their income level to be a certain amount in the future, or they expect the price of certain items to be higher in the future. A change in expected income or expected prices can have an effect on today's expenditures. For instance, you might be planning to purchase a car, some furniture, or a house today thinking that your income will be a certain amount next year. If for some reason you change your expectation of next year's income, you may also change your current expenditures. In November 1992, the United States threatened to impose a 300 percent tariff on French white wine beginning in December 1992. The tariff would have increased white wine prices in the United States from about $8 a bottle to $24. Expecting the higher prices in December, U.S. consumers immediately went out and stockpiled French white wine. The effect of changed expectations on demand is represented by a shift of the demand curve. The demand for a good or service may rise (fall) and the demand curve may shift to the right (left) because of a change in expectations.

Number of Buyers   Market demand consists of the sum of the demands of all individuals. The more individuals there are with income to spend, the greater the market demand is likely to be. For example, the populations of Florida and Arizona are much larger during the winter than they are during the summer. The demand for any particular good or service in Arizona and Florida rises (the demand curve shifts to the right) during the winter and falls (the demand curve shifts to the left) during the summer.

2.f. International Effects

exchange rate:
the rate at which monies of different countries are exchanged

The law of demand says the amount of a good or service that people are willing and able to purchase during a particular period of time falls as the price rises and rises as the price falls. It does not indicate whether those people are residents of the United States or some other country. The demand for a product that is available to residents of other countries as well as to residents of the United States will consist of the sum of the demands by U.S. and foreign residents. However, because nations use different monies or currencies, the demand will be affected by the rate at which the different currencies are exchanged. As pointed out in the Economic Insight "The Foreign Exchange Market," an **exchange rate** is the rate at which monies of different countries are exchanged. If the exchange rate changes, then the foreign price of a good produced in the United States will change. To illustrate this, let's consider an example using Levi's blue jeans sold to both U.S. and Japanese customers. The Japanese currency is the yen (¥). In January 1998, it took 130 yen to purchase one dollar. Suppose that a pair of Levi's blue jeans is priced at $20 in the United States. That dollar price in terms of yen is ¥2,600. The exchange rate between the yen and the dollar means that ¥2,600 converts to $20; ¥2,600 = $20 × 130¥/$. In July of 1997 the exchange rate was ¥124 per dollar. If the U.S. price of the blue jeans was $20, in Japan, the yen value of the blue jeans would be $20 × ¥124/$ = ¥2,480. The blue jeans were more expensive in Japan because of the exchange rate change, even though the U.S. price of blue jeans did not change. The demand for U.S. blue jeans would have declined from July 1997 to January 1998 simply because of the exchange rate change. Thus, changes in exchange rates can affect the demand

Copyright © by Houghton Mifflin Company. All rights reserved.

The Foreign Exchange Market

Most countries have their own national currency. Germany has the deutsche mark, France the franc, England the pound sterling, Japan the yen, the United States the dollar, and so on. The citizens of each country use their national currency to carry out transactions. For transactions among nations to occur, however, some exchange of foreign currencies is necessary.

Americans buy Toyotas and Nissans from Japan, while American computer companies sell pocket calculators to businesses in Mexico. Some Americans open bank accounts in Switzerland, while American real estate companies sell property to citizens in England. These transactions require the acquisition of a foreign currency. An English businessman who wants to buy property in the United States will have to exchange his money, pounds sterling, for dollars. An American car distributor who imports Toyotas will have to exchange dollars for yen in order to pay the Toyota manufacturer.

The exchange of currency and the determination of the value of national currencies occur in the foreign exchange market. This is not a tightly organized market operating in a building in New York. Usually, the term *foreign exchange market* refers to the trading that occurs among large international banks. Such trading is global and is done largely through telephone and computer communication systems. If, for example, a foreign exchange trader at First Chicago Bank calls a trader at Bank of Tokyo to buy $1 million worth of Japanese yen, that is a foreign exchange market transaction. Banks buy and sell currencies according to the needs and demands of their customers. Business firms and individuals rely largely on banks to buy and sell foreign exchange for them.

The price of one currency expressed in terms of another currency is called a *foreign exchange rate,* or just *exchange rate.* You can think of an exchange rate as the number of dollars it costs to purchase one unit of another country's currency. For instance, how many dollars does it take to purchase one unit of Japan's currency, the yen? One yen (¥) costs about $.008, or eight-tenths of a cent. The list that follows shows the number of U.S. dollars it took to purchase one unit of several different nations' currencies in January 1998.

Number of U.S. Dollars Needed to Purchase One

Australian dollar	.6503
Belgian franc	.0269
Canadian dollar	.6999
French franc	.1663
German mark	.5562
Italian lira	.00056
Japanese yen	.0076
Dutch guilder	.4935
Spanish peseta	.00656
Swedish krona	.1259
Swiss franc	.6843
United Kingdom pound	1.6508

Copyright © by Houghton Mifflin Company. All rights reserved.

for goods. At constant U.S. prices, demand curves for U.S. goods will shift around as exchange rates change and foreign purchases fluctuate.

RECAP

1. According to the law of demand, as the price of any good or service rises (falls), the quantity demanded of that good or service falls (rises), during a specific period of time, everything else held constant.

2. A demand schedule is a listing of the quantity demanded at each price.

3. The demand curve is a downward-sloping line plotted using the values of the demand schedule.

4. Market demand is the sum of all individual demands.

5. Demand changes when one of the determinants of demand changes. A demand change is a shift of the demand curve.

6. The quantity demanded changes when the price of the good or service changes. This is a change from one point on the demand curve to another point on the same demand curve.

7. The determinants of demand are income, tastes, prices of related goods and services, expectations, and number of buyers.

8. The exchange rate also is a determinant of demand when a good is sold in both the United States and other countries.

3. SUPPLY

Why is the price of hotel accommodations higher in Phoenix in the winter than in the summer? Demand AND supply. Why is the price of beef higher in Japan than in the United States? Demand AND supply. Why did the price of the dollar in terms of the Japanese yen rise in 1997? Demand AND supply. Both demand and supply determine price; neither demand nor supply alone determine price. We now discuss supply.

3.a. The Law of Supply

What is supply?

supply:
the amount of a good or service that producers are willing and able to offer for sale at each possible price during a period of time, everything else held constant

quantity supplied:
the amount sellers are willing to offer at a given price, during a particular period of time, everything else held constant

law of supply:
as the price of a good or service that producers are willing and able to offer for sale at each possible price during a particular period of time rises (falls), the quantity of that good or service rises (falls), everything else held constant

determinants of supply:
factors other than the price of the good that influence supply—prices of resources, technology and productivity, expectations of producers, number of producers, and the prices of related good and services

Just as demand is the relation between the price and the quantity demanded of a good or service, supply is the relation between price and quantity supplied. **Supply** is the amount of the good or service producers are willing and able to offer for sale at each possible price during a period of time, everything else held constant. **Quantity supplied** is the amount of the good or service producers are willing and able to offer for sale at a *specific* price, during a period of time, everything else held constant. According to the **law of supply**, as the price of a good or service rises, the quantity supplied rises, and vice versa.

The formal statement of the law of supply consists of five phrases:

1. the quantity of a well-defined good or service that
2. producers are willing and able to offer for sale
3. during a particular period of time
4. increases as the price of the good or service increases and decreases as the price decreases
5. everything else held constant

The first phrase is the same as the first phrase in the law of demand. The second phrase indicates that producers must not only *want* to offer the product for sale but must be *able* to offer the product. The third phrase points out that the quantities producers will offer for sale depend on the period of time being considered. For instance, the prices at which producers of personal computers would sell their products in January 1998 may be significantly different than in January 2000. The fourth phrase points out that more will be supplied at higher than at lower prices. The final phrase ensures that the **determinants of supply** do not change. The determinants of supply are those factors that influence the willingness and ability of producers to offer their goods and services for sale other than the price of the good or service—the prices of resources used to produce the product, technology and productivity, expectations of

Copyright © by Houghton Mifflin Company. All rights reserved.

producers, the number of producers in the market, and the prices of related goods and services. If any one of these should change, supply changes.

3.b. The Supply Schedule and Supply Curve

supply schedule:
a table or list of prices and corresponding quantities supplied of a particular good or service

supply curve:
a graph of a supply schedule that measures price on the vertical axis and quantity supplied on the horizontal axis

A **supply schedule** is a table or list of the prices and the corresponding quantities supplied of a good or service. The table in Figure 4 presents MGA's supply schedule of videos. The schedule lists the quantities that MGA is willing and able to supply at each price, everything else held constant. As the price increases, MGA is willing and able to offer more videos for rent.

A **supply curve** is a graph of the supply schedule. Figure 4 shows MGA's supply curve of videos. The price and quantity combinations given in the supply schedule correspond to the points on the curve. For instance, combination A in the table corresponds to point *A* on the curve; combination B in the table corresponds to point *B* on the curve, and so on for each price-quantity combination.

MGA's supply curve slopes upward. This means that MGA is willing and able to supply more at higher prices than it is at lower prices. Recall from Chapter 2 that as society puts more and more resources into the production of any specific item, the opportunity cost of each additional unit of production rises because more specialized resources are transferred to activities in which they are relatively less productive. MGA, too, finds that as it increases production, the opportunity costs of additional production rise. Hence, the only way that MGA, or any producer, is willing and able to produce more is if the price rises sufficiently to cover these increasing opportunity costs.

Figure 4
MGA's Supply Schedule and Supply Curve for Videos
The quantity that MGA is willing and able to offer for sale at each price is listed in the supply schedule and shown on the supply curve. At point *A*, the price is $5 per video and the quantity supplied is 60 videos. The combination of $4 per video and 50 videos is point *B*. Each price-quantity combination is plotted, and the points are connected to form the supply curve.

Combination	Price per Video (constant-quality units)	Quantity Supplied per Year (constant-quality units)
A	$5	60
B	4	50
C	3	40
D	2	30
E	1	20

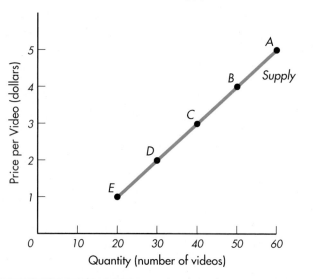

Copyright © by Houghton Mifflin Company. All rights reserved.

3.c. From Individual Supply Curves to the Market Supply

To derive market supply, the quantities that each producer supplies at each price are added together, just as the quantities demanded by each consumer are added together to get market demand. The table in Figure 5 lists the supply schedules of three video rental stores: MGA, Motown, and Blockmaster. For our example, we assume that these three are the only video rental stores. (We are also assuming that the brand names are not associated with quality or any other differences.)

The supply schedule of each producer is plotted in Figure 5(a). Then in Figure 5(b) the individual supply curves have been added together to obtain the market supply curve. At a price of $5, the quantity supplied by MGA is 60, the quantity supplied by Motown is 30, and the quantity supplied by Blockmaster is 12. This means a total quantity supplied in the market of 102. At a price of $4, the quantities supplied are 50 by MGA, 25 by Motown, and 9 by Blockmaster for a total market quantity supplied of 84. The market supply schedule is the last column in the table. The plot of the price and quantity combinations listed in this column is the market supply curve. The market supply curve slopes up because each of the individual supply curves has a positive slope. The market supply curve tells us that the quantity supplied in the market increases as the price rises.

3.d. Changes in Supply and Changes in Quantity Supplied

A change in the quantity supplied is a movement along the supply curve. A change in the supply is a shift of the supply curve.

When we draw the supply curve, we allow only the price and quantity supplied of the good or service we are discussing to change. Everything else that might affect supply is assumed not to change. If any of the determinants of supply—the prices of resources used to produce the product, technology and productivity, expectations of producers, the number of producers in the market, and the prices of related goods and services—changes, the supply schedule changes and the supply curve shifts.

Prices of Resources   If labor costs—one of the resources used to produce video rentals—rise, higher rental prices will be necessary to induce each store to offer as many videos as it did before the cost of the resource rose. The higher cost of resources causes a decrease in supply, meaning a leftward shift of the supply curve, from S_1 to S_2 in Figure 6(a).

Two interpretations of a leftward shift of the supply curve are possible. One comes from comparing the old and new curves in a horizontal direction; the other comes from comparing the curves in a vertical direction. In the vertical direction, the decrease in supply informs us that sellers want a higher price to produce any given quantity. Compare, for example, point A on curve S_1 with C on curve S_2. A and C represent the same quantity but different prices. Sellers will offer 66 videos at a price of $3 per video according to supply curve S_1. But if the supply curve shifts to the left, then the sellers want more ($3.50) for 66 units.

In the horizontal direction, the decrease in supply means that sellers will offer less for sale at any given price. This can be seen by comparing point B on curve S_2 with A on curve S_1. Both points correspond to a price of $3, but along curve S_1, sellers are willing to offer 66 units for rent, while curve S_2 indicates that sellers will offer only 57 videos for rent.

Copyright © by Houghton Mifflin Company. All rights reserved.

Figure 5
The Market Supply Schedule and Curve for Videos

The market supply is derived by summing the quantities that each producer is willing and able to offer for sale at each price. In this example, there are three producers: MGA, Motown, and Blockmaster. The supply schedules of each are listed in the table and plotted as the individual supply curves shown in Figure 5(a). By adding the quantities supplied at each price, we obtain the market supply curve shown in Figure 5(b). For instance, at a price of $5, MGA offers 60 units, Motown 30 units, and Blockmaster 12 units, for a market supply quantity of 102. The market supply curve reflects the quantities that each producer is able and willing to supply at each price.

Price per Video	Quantities Supplied per Year by			Market Supply
	MGA	Motown	Blockmaster	
$5	60 +	30 +	12 =	102
4	50	25	9	84
3	40	20	6	66
2	30	15	3	48
1	20	10	0	30

(a) Individual Supply Curves

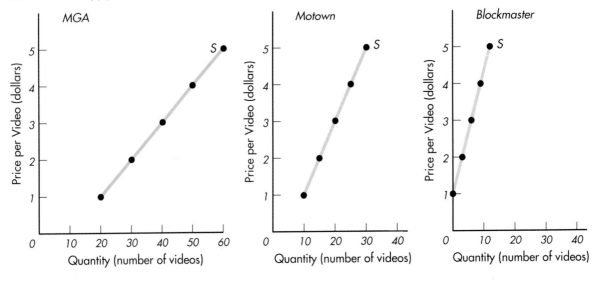

(b) Market Supply Curve

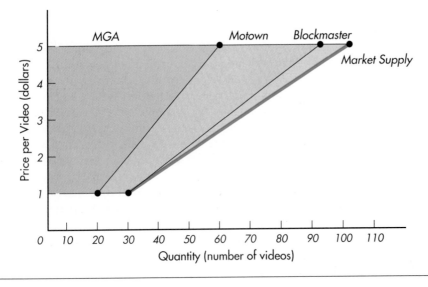

Copyright © by Houghton Mifflin Company. All rights reserved.

Figure 6
A Shift of the Supply Curve
Figure 6(a) shows a decrease in supply and the shift of the supply curve to the left, from S_1 to S_2. The decrease is caused by a change in one of the determinants of video supply—an increase in the price of labor. Because of the increased price of labor, producers are willing and able to offer fewer videos for rent at each price than they were before the price of labor rose. Supply curve S_2 shows that at a price of $3 per video, suppliers will offer 57 videos. That is 9 units less than the 66 videos at $3 per video indicated by supply curve S_1. Conversely, to offer a given quantity, producers must receive a higher price per video than they previously were getting: $3.50 per video for 66 videos (on supply curve S_2) instead of $3 per video (on supply curve S_1).

Figure 6(b) shows an increase in supply. A technological improvement or an increase in productivity causes the supply curve to shift to the right, from S_1 to S_2. At each price, a higher quantity is offered for sale. At a price of $3, 66 units were offered, but with the shift of the supply curve, the quantity of units for sale at $3 apiece increases to 84. Conversely, producers can reduce prices for a given quantity—for example, charging $2 per video for 66 units.

Copyright © by Houghton Mifflin Company. All rights reserved.

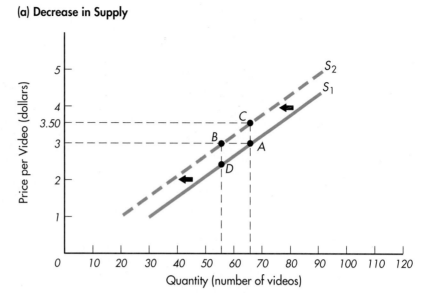

(a) Decrease in Supply

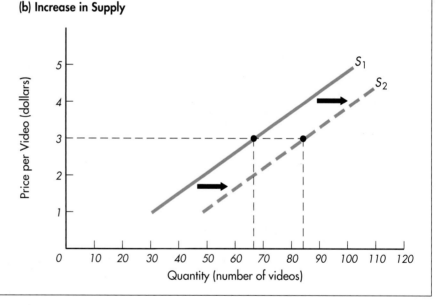

(b) Increase in Supply

If resource prices declined, then supply would increase. That combination would be illustrated by a rightward shift of the supply curve. If a firm purchases supplies from other nations, exchange rate changes can affect the firm's costs and thus, its supply curve. For instance, suppose a U.S. firm purchases lumber from Canada. At an exchange rate of 1 Canadian dollar per 1 U.S. dollar, 1,000 Canadian dollars worth of supplies costs 1,000 U.S. dollars. In 1998, with the Canadian dollar worth only .6992 U.S. dollars, the supplies worth 1,000 Canadian dollars cost only 699.20 U.S. dollars. Since the cost of supplies has declined for the U.S. firm, its supply curve shifts out.

Before computers and x-ray fluorescence equipment were invented, curators of museums and authenticators of art had to destroy portions of art to determine the age and components of the art. Now, as shown in the Prada Museum in Madrid, the hi-tech equipment is used to study the inorganic pigments in paint and determine when, where, and how the art was created, all without damaging any aspect of the art.

Technology and Productivity   If resources are used more efficiently in the production of a good or service, more of that good or service can be produced for the same cost, or the original quantity can be produced for a lower cost. As a result, the supply curve shifts to the right, as in Figure 6(b).

The move from horse-drawn plows to tractors or from mainframe computers to personal computers meant that each worker was able to produce more. The increase in output produced by each unit of a resource is called a *productivity increase.* **Productivity** is defined as the quantity of output produced per unit of resource. Improvements in technology cause productivity increases, which lead to an increase in supply.

productivity:
the quantity of output produced per unit of resource

Expectations of Producers   Sellers may choose to alter the quantity offered for sale today because of a change in expectations regarding the determinants of supply. A supply curve illustrates the quantities that suppliers are willing and able to supply at every possible price level. If suppliers expect something to occur to resource supplies or technology, then suppliers may alter the quantities they are willing and able to supply at every possible price. The key point is that the supply curve will shift if producers expect something to occur that will alter the anticipated profits at every possible price level, not just a change in one price. For instance, the expectation that demand will decline in the future does not lead to a shift of the supply curve; it leads instead to a decline in quantity supplied as the new demand curve intersects the supply curve at a lower level of prices and output.

Number of Producers   When more people decide to produce a good or service, the market supply increases. More is offered for sale at each and every price, causing a rightward shift of the supply curve.

Copyright © by Houghton Mifflin Company. All rights reserved.

Prices of Related Goods or Services The opportunity cost of producing and selling any good or service is the forgone opportunity to produce any other good or service. If the price of an alternative good changes, then the opportunity cost of producing a particular good changes. This could cause the supply curve to change. For instance, if the video store can offer videos or arcade games with equal ease, an increase in the price of the arcade games could induce the store owner to offer more arcade games and fewer videos. The supply curve of videos would then shift to the left.

3.e. International Effects

Many firms purchase supplies from other nations or even locate factories and produce in other nations. Events in other parts of the world can influence their costs and thus the amounts they are willing to supply. Nike purchases its shoes from manufacturers in other parts of the world, particularly Asia. The exchange rate between the United States and Malaysia in December 1997 was .2570 U.S. dollar to the ringgit. If the Nike shoes cost 78 ringgit to produce in Malaysia, in dollar terms that is $20.05. In July 1997 the exchange rate was .3150 ringgit to the U.S. dollar, so manufacturing costs were 78 ringgit, or $24.57. The costs to Nike rose without any changes in production. This means the supply curve of Nike shoes would shift in from 1996 to 1997. Then, by April 1998, the ringgit was worth .289 U.S. dollar, so that manufacturing costs of 78 ringgit meant dollar costs of $22.45. The change from 1997 to 1998 would be represented by an inward shift of Nike's supply curve.

A *change in supply* occurs when the quantity supplied at each and every price changes or there is a shift in the supply curve—like the shift from S_1 to S_2 in Figure 7(a). A change in one of the determinants of supply brings about a change in supply.

When only the price changes, a greater or smaller quantity is supplied. This is shown as a movement along the supply curve, not as a shift of the curve. A change in price is said to cause a *change in the quantity supplied*. An increase in quantity supplied is shown in the move from point A to point B on the supply curve of Figure 7(b).

RECAP

1. According to the law of supply, the quantity supplied of any good or service is directly related to the price of the good or service, during a specific period of time, everything else held constant.

2. Market supply is found by adding together the quantities supplied at each price by every producer in the market.

3. Supply changes if the prices of relevant resources change, if technology or productivity changes, if producers' expectations change, if the number of producers changes, or if the prices of related goods and services change.

4. Changes in supply are reflected in shifts of the supply curve. Changes in the quantity supplied are reflected in movements along the supply curve.

Copyright © by Houghton Mifflin Company. All rights reserved.

Figure 7
A Change in Supply and a Change in the Quantity Supplied
In Figure 7(a), the quantities that producers are willing and able to offer for sale at every price decrease, caus-

ing a leftward shift of the supply curve from S_1 to S_2. In Figure 7(b), the quantities that producers are willing and able to offer for sale increase, due to an increase in the price of the good, causing a movement along the supply curve from point A to point B.

(a) Change in Supply

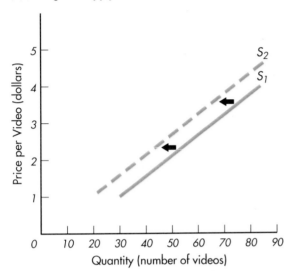

(b) Change in Quantity Supplied

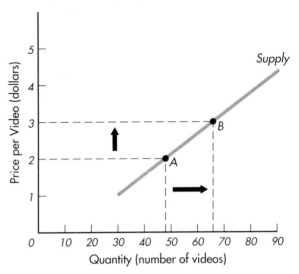

4. EQUILIBRIUM: PUTTING DEMAND AND SUPPLY TOGETHER

The demand curve shows the quantity of a good or service that buyers are willing and able to purchase at each price. The supply curve shows the quantity that producers are willing and able to offer for sale at each price. Only where the two curves intersect is the quantity supplied equal to the quantity demanded. This intersection is the point of **equilibrium.**

equilibrium:
the price and quantity at which quantity demanded and quantity supplied are equal

4.a. Determination of Equilibrium

How is price determined by demand and supply?

Figure 8 brings together the market demand and market supply curves for video rentals. The supply and demand schedules are listed in the table and the curves are plotted in the graph in Figure 8. Notice that the curves intersect at only one point, labeled *e*, a price of $3 and a quantity of 66. The intersection point is the equilibrium price, the only price at which the quantity demanded and quantity supplied are the same. You can see that at any other price the quantity demanded and quantity supplied are not the same. These are called **disequilibrium** points.

disequilibrium:
a point at which quantity demanded and quantity supplied are not equal at a particular price

Whenever the price is greater than the equilibrium price, a **surplus** arises. For example, at $4, the quantity of videos demanded is 48 and the quantity supplied is 84. Thus, at $4 per video there is a surplus of 36 videos—that is, 36 videos are not rented. Conversely, whenever the price is below the

Copyright © by Houghton Mifflin Company. All rights reserved.

Figure 8
Equilibrium
Equilibrium is established at the point where the quantity that suppliers are willing and able to offer for sale is the same as the quantity that buyers are willing and able to purchase. Here, equilibrium occurs at the price of $3 per video and the quantity of 66 videos. It is shown as point e at the intersection of the demand and supply curves. At prices above $3, the quantity supplied is greater than the quantity demanded, and the result is a surplus. At prices below $3, the quantity supplied is less than the quantity demanded, and the result is a shortage. The area shaded brown shows all prices at which there is a surplus—where quantity supplied is greater than the quantity demanded. The surplus is measured in horizontal direction at each price. The area shaded blue represents all prices at which a shortage exists—where the quantity demanded is greater than the quantity supplied. The shortage is measured in a horizontal direction at each price.

Price per Video	Quantity Demanded per Year	Quantity Supplied per Year	Status
$5	30	102	Surplus of 72
4	48	84	Surplus of 36
3	66	66	Equilibrium
2	84	48	Shortage of 36
1	102	30	Shortage of 72

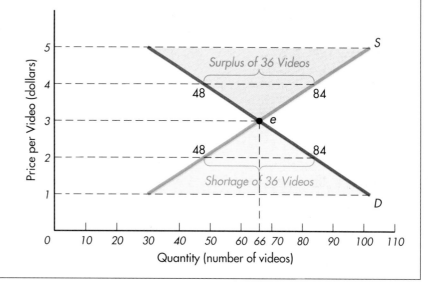

surplus:
a quantity supplied that is larger than the quantity demanded at a given price; it occurs whenever the price is greater than the equilibrium price

shortage:
a quantity supplied that is smaller than the quantity demanded at a given price; it occurs whenever the price is less than the equilibrium price

equilibrium price, the quantity demanded is greater than the quantity supplied and there is a **shortage.** For instance, if the price is $2 per video, consumers will want and be able to pay for more videos than are available. As shown in the table in Figure 8, the quantity demanded at a price of $2 is 84 but the quantity supplied is only 48. There is a shortage of 36 videos at the price of $2.

Neither a surplus nor a shortage exists for long if the price of the product is free to change. Producers who are stuck with videos sitting on the shelves getting brittle and out of style will lower the price and reduce the quantities they are offering for rent in order to eliminate a surplus. Conversely, producers whose shelves are empty even as consumers demand videos will acquire more videos and raise the rental price to eliminate a shortage. Surpluses lead to decreases in the price and the quantity supplied and increases in the quantity demanded. Shortages lead to increases in the price and the quantity supplied and decreases in the quantity demanded.

Note that a shortage is not the same thing as scarcity. A shortage exists only when the quantity that people are willing and able to purchase at a particular price is more than the quantity supplied *at that price.* Scarcity occurs when more is wanted at a zero price than is available.

Copyright © by Houghton Mifflin Company. All rights reserved.

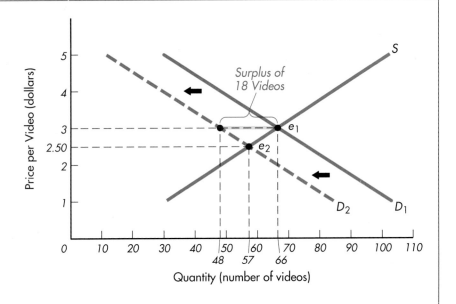

Figure 9
The Effects of a Shift of the Demand Curve
The initial equilibrium price ($3 per video) and quantity (66 videos) are established at point e_1, where the initial demand and supply curves intersect. A change in the tastes for videos causes demand to decrease, and the demand curve shifts to the left. At $3 per video, the initial quantity supplied, 66 videos, is now greater than the quantity demanded, 48 videos. The surplus of 18 units causes producers to reduce production and lower the price. The market reaches a new equilibrium, at point e_2, $2.50 per video and 57 videos.

✳ 4.b. Changes in the Equilibrium Price: Demand Shifts

What causes price to change?

Equilibrium is the combination of price and quantity at which the quantities demanded and supplied are the same. Once an equilibrium is achieved, there is no incentive for producers or consumers to move away from it. An equilibrium price changes only when demand and/or supply changes—that is, when the determinants of demand or determinants of supply change.

Let's consider a change in demand and what it means for the equilibrium price. Suppose that experiments on rats show that watching videos causes brain damage. As a result, a large segment of the human population decides not to rent videos. Stores find that the demand for videos has decreased, as shown in Figure 9 by a leftward shift of the demand curve, from curve D_1 to curve D_2.

Once the demand curve has shifted, the original equilibrium price of $3 per video at point e_1 is no longer equilibrium. At a price of $3, the quantity supplied is still 66, but the quantity demanded has declined to 48 (look at the demand curve D_2 at a price of $3). There is, therefore, a surplus of 18 videos at the price of $3.

With a surplus comes downward pressure on the price. This downward pressure occurs because producers acquire fewer videos to offer for rent and reduce the rental price in an attempt to rent the videos sitting on the shelves. Producers continue reducing the price and the quantity available until consumers rent all copies of the videos that the sellers have available, or until a new equilibrium is established. That new equilibrium occurs at point e_2 with a price of $2.50 and a quantity of 57.

The decrease in demand is represented by the leftward shift of the demand curve. A decrease in demand results in a lower equilibrium price and a lower equilibrium quantity as long as there is no change in supply. Conversely, an increase in demand would be represented as a rightward shift of the demand curve and would result in a higher equilibrium price and a higher equilibrium quantity as long as there is no change in supply.

Copyright © by Houghton Mifflin Company. All rights reserved.

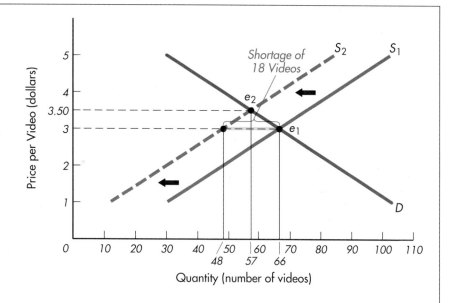

Figure 10
The Effects of a Shift of the Supply Curve
The initial equilibrium price and quantity are $3 and 66 units, at point e_1. When the price of labor increases, suppliers are willing and able to offer fewer videos for rent at each price. The result is a leftward (upward) shift of the supply curve, from S_1 to S_2. At the old price of $3, the quantity demanded is still 66, but the quantity supplied falls to 48. The shortage is 18 videos. The shortage causes suppliers to acquire more videos to offer for rent and to raise the rental price. The new equilibrium, e_2, the intersection between curves S_2 and D, is $3.50 per video and 57 videos.

Copyright © by Houghton Mifflin Company. All rights reserved.

4.c. Changes in Equilibrium Price: Supply Shifts

The equilibrium price and quantity may be altered by a change in supply as well. If the price of relevant resources, technology and productivity, expectations of producers, the number of producers, or the price of related products change, supply changes.

Let's consider an example. Petroleum is a key ingredient in videotapes. Suppose the quantity of oil available is reduced by 40 percent, causing the price of oil to rise. Every video manufacturer has to pay more for oil, which means that the rental stores must pay more for each videotape. To purchase the videos and offer them for rent, the rental stores must receive a higher rental price in order to cover their higher costs. This is represented by a leftward shift of the supply curve in Figure 10.

The leftward shift of the supply curve, from curve S_1 to curve S_2, leads to a new equilibrium price and quantity. At the original equilibrium price of $3 at point e_1, 66 videos are supplied. After the shift in the supply curve, 48 videos are offered for rent at a price of $3 apiece, and there is a shortage of 18 videos. The shortage puts upward pressure on price. As the price rises, consumers decrease the quantities that they are willing and able to rent, and sellers increase the quantities that they are willing and able to supply. Eventually, a new equilibrium price and quantity is established at $3.50 and 57 videos at point e_2.

The decrease in supply is represented by the leftward shift of the supply curve. A decrease in supply with no change in demand results in a higher price and a lower quantity. Conversely, an increase in supply would be represented as a rightward shift of the supply curve. An increase in supply with no change in demand would result in a lower price and a higher quantity.

4.d. Equilibrium in Reality

What happens when price is
not allowed to change with
market forces?

We have examined a hypothetical (imaginary) market for video rentals in order to represent what goes on in real markets. We have established that the price of a good or service is defined by equilibrium between demand and supply. We noted that an equilibrium could be disturbed by a change in demand or a change in supply and the equilibrium could also be disturbed by simultaneous changes in demand and supply. The important point of this discussion is to demonstrate that when not in equilibrium, the price and the quantities demanded and/or supplied change until equilibrium is established. The market is always attempting to reach equilibrium.

Looking at last year's sweaters piled up on the sale racks, waiting over an hour for a table at a restaurant, finding that the VCR rental store never has a copy of the movie you want to rent in stock, or hearing that 5 or 6 percent of people willing and able to work are unemployed may make you wonder whether equilibrium is ever established. In fact, it is not uncommon to observe situations where quantities demanded and supplied are not equal. But this observation does not cast doubt on the usefulness of the equilibrium concept. Even if all markets do not clear, or reach equilibrium, all the time, we can be reasonably assured that market forces are operating so that the market is moving toward an equilibrium. The market forces exist even when the price is not allowed to change, as illustrated in the following section.

price floor:
a situation where the price is not allowed to decrease below a certain level

4.d.1. Price Ceilings and Price Floors

A **price floor** is the situation where the price is not allowed to decrease below a certain level. Consider Figure 11 representing the market for sugar. The equilibrium price of sugar is $.10 a pound, but because the government has set a price floor of $.20 a pound, as shown by the solid yellow line, the price is not allowed to move to its equilibrium level. A surplus of 250,000 pounds of sugar results from the price floor. Sugar growers produce 1 million pounds of sugar and consumers purchase 750,000 pounds of sugar.

We saw previously that whenever the price is above the equilibrium price, market forces work to decrease the price. The price floor interferes with the functioning of the market; a surplus exists because the government will not allow the price to drop. How does the government ensure that the price floor remains in force? It has to purchase the excess sugar. The government must purchase the surplus so that its price floor of $.20 per pound remains in force.

What would occur if the government had set the price floor at $.09 a pound? Since at $.09 a pound a shortage of sugar would result, the price would rise. A price floor only keeps the price from falling, not rising. So the price rises to its equilibrium level of $.10. Only if the price floor is set above the equilibrium price is it an effective price floor.

price ceiling:
a situation where the price is not allowed to rise above a certain level

A **price ceiling** is the situation where a price is not allowed to rise to its equilibrium level. Los Angeles, San Francisco, and New York are among over 125 U.S. cities that have *rent controls*. A rent control law places a ceiling on the rents that landlords can charge for apartments. Figure 12 is a demand and supply graph representing the market for apartments in New York. The equilibrium price is $3,000 a month. The government has set a price of $1,500 a month as the maximum that can be charged. The price ceiling is shown by the solid yellow line. At the rent control price of $1,500 per month, 3,000 apartments are available but consumers want 6,000 apartments. There is a shortage of 3,000 apartments.

Copyright © by Houghton Mifflin Company. All rights reserved.

Copyright © by Houghton Mifflin Company. All rights reserved.

Figure 11
A Price Floor
The equilibrium price of sugar is $.10 a pound, but because the government has set a price floor of $.20 a pound, as shown by the solid yellow line, the price is not allowed to move to its equilibrium level. A surplus of 250,000 pounds of sugar results from the price floor. Sugar growers produce 1 million pounds of sugar and consumers purchase 750,000 pounds of sugar.

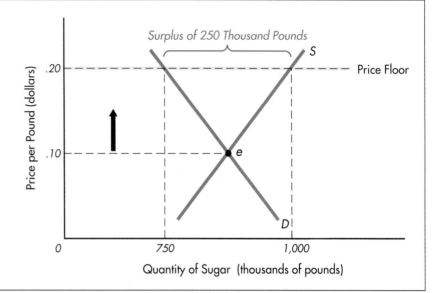

The shortage means that not everyone willing and able to purchase the apartment will be allowed to. Since the price is not allowed to ration the apartments, something else will have to. It may be that those willing and able to stand in line the longest get the apartments. Perhaps bribing an important official might be the way to get an apartment. Perhaps relatives of officials or important citizens will get the apartments. Whenever a price ceiling exists, a shortage results and some rationing device other than price will arise.

Had the government set the rent control price at $4,000 per month, the price ceiling would not have had an effect. Since the equilibrium is $3,000 a month, the price would not have risen to $4,000. Only if the price ceiling is below the equilibrium price will it be an effective price ceiling.

Figure 12
Rent Controls
A demand and supply graph representing the market for apartments in New York City is shown. The equilibrium price is $3,000 a month. The government has set a price of $1,500 a month. The government's price ceiling is shown by the solid yellow line. At the government's price, 3,000 apartments are available but consumers want 6,000. There is a shortage of 3,000 apartments.

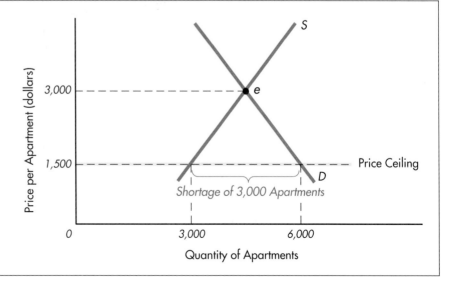

Price ceilings are not uncommon features in the United States or in other economies. China had a severe housing shortage for thirty years because the price of housing was kept below equilibrium. Faced with unhappy citizens and realizing the cause of the shortage, officials began to lift the restrictions on housing prices in 1985. The shortage has diminished. In the former Soviet Union, prices on all goods and services were defined by the government. For most consumer items, the price was set below equilibrium; shortages existed. The long lines of people waiting to purchase food or clothing were the result of the price ceilings on all goods and services. In the United States, price ceilings on all goods and services have been imposed at times. During the first and second world wars and during the Nixon administration of the early 1970s, wage and price controls were imposed. These were price ceilings on all goods and services. As a result of the ceilings, people were unable to purchase many of the products they desired. The Organization of Petroleum Exporting Countries (OPEC) restricted the quantity of oil in the early 1970s and drove its price up considerably. The United States government responded by placing a price ceiling on gasoline. The result was long lines at gas stations—shortages of gasoline.

Price floors are quite common features in economies as well. The agricultural policies of most of the developed nations are founded on price floors—the government guarantees that the price of an agricultural product will not fall below some level. Price floors result in surpluses, and this has been the case with agricultural products as well. The surpluses in agricultural products in the United States have resulted in cases where dairy farmers dumped milk in the river, where grain was given to other nations at taxpayer expense, and where citrus ranchers picked and then discarded thousands of tons of citrus, all to reduce huge surpluses.

There are many reasons other than price ceilings and price floors why we observe excess supplies or demands in the real world. In most cases, the excess demands or supplies are due to the difficulty of changing prices rapidly or to the desires of either the demanders or suppliers not to have prices change rapidly. We shall consider many such cases in the text. The important part of the discussion in this chapter is to keep in mind that unless the price is not allowed to change, surpluses and shortages will put pressure on the price to move to its equilibrium level.

RECAP

1. Equilibrium occurs when quantity demanded and quantity supplied are equal: it is the price-quantity combination where the demand and supply curves intersect.

2. A price that is above the equilibrium price creates a surplus. Producers are willing and able to offer more for sale than buyers are willing and able to purchase.

3. A price that is below the equilibrium price leads to a shortage, because buyers are willing and able to purchase more than producers are willing and able to offer for sale.

4. When demand changes, price and quantity change in the same direction—both rise as demand increases and both fall as demand decreases.

Copyright © by Houghton Mifflin Company. All rights reserved.

5. When supply changes, price and quantity change but not in the same direction. When supply increases, price falls and quantity rises. When supply decreases, price rises and quantity falls.

6. When both demand and supply change, the direction of the change in price and quantity depends on the relative sizes of the changes of demand and supply.

7. A price floor is a situation where a price is set above the equilibrium price. This creates a surplus.

8. A price ceiling is a case where a price is set below the equilibrium price. This creates a shortage.

SUMMARY

▬▬ What is a market?

1. A market is where buyers and sellers trade a well-defined good or service. §1

▬▬ What is demand?

2. Demand is the quantities that buyers are willing and able to buy at alternative prices. §2

3. The quantity demanded is a specific amount at one price. §2

4. The law of demand states that as the price of a well-defined commodity rises (falls), the quantity demanded during a given period of time will fall (rise), everything else held constant. §2.a

5. Demand will change when one of the determinants of demand changes, that is, when income, tastes, prices of related goods and services, expectations, or number of buyers change. In addition, the demand may change when exchange rates change. A demand change is illustrated as a shift of the demand curve. §2.e, 2.f

▬▬ What is supply?

6. Supply is the quantities that sellers will offer for sale at alternative prices. §3.a

7. The quantity supplied is the amount sellers offer for sale at one price. §3.a

8. The law of supply states that as the price of a well-defined commodity rises (falls), the quantity supplied during a given period of time will rise (fall), everything else held constant. §3.a

9. Supply changes when one of the determinants of supply changes, that is, when prices of resources, technology and productivity, expectations of producers, the number of producers, or the prices of related goods or services change. A supply change is illustrated as a shift of the supply curve. §3.d

▬▬ How is price determined by demand and supply?

10. Together, demand and supply determine the equilibrium price and quantity. §4

▬▬ What causes price to change?

11. A price that is above equilibrium creates a surplus, which leads to a lower price. A price that is below equilibrium creates a shortage, which leads to a higher price. §4.a

12. A change in demand or a change in supply (a shift of either curve) will cause the equilibrium price and quantity to change. §4.b, 4.c

13. Markets are not always in equilibrium, but forces work to move them toward equilibrium. §4.d

▬▬ What happens when price is not allowed to change with market forces?

14. A price floor is a situation where a price is not allowed to decrease below a certain level—it is set above the equilibrium price. This creates a surplus. A price ceiling is a case where a price is not allowed to rise—it is set below the equilibrium price. This creates a shortage. §4.d

Copyright © by Houghton Mifflin Company. All rights reserved.

KEY TERMS

market §1.a

barter §1.b

double coincidence of wants §1.b

transaction costs §1.b

relative price §1.c

demand §2

quantity demanded §2

law of demand §2.a

determinants of demand §2.a

demand schedule §2.b

demand curve §2.c

substitute goods §2.e

complementary goods §2.e

exchange rate §2.f

supply §3.a

quantity supplied §3.a

law of supply §3.a

determinants of supply §3.a

supply schedule §3.b

supply curve §3.b

productivity §3.d

equilibrium §4

disequilibrium, §4.a

surplus §4.a

shortage §4.a

price floor §4.d

price ceiling §4.d

EXERCISES

1. Illustrate each of the following events using a demand and supply diagram for bananas.

   a. Reports surface that imported bananas are infected with a deadly virus.

   b. Consumers' incomes drop.

   c. The price of bananas rises.

   d. The price of oranges falls.

   e. Consumers expect the price of bananas to decrease in the future.

2. Answer true or false and if the statement is false, change it to make it true. Illustrate your answers on a demand and supply graph.

   a. An increase in demand is represented by a movement up the demand curve.

   b. An increase in supply is represented by a movement up the supply curve.

   c. An increase in demand without any changes in supply will cause the price to rise.

   d. An increase in supply without any changes in demand will cause the price to rise.

3. Using the following schedule, define the equilibrium price and quantity. Describe the situation at a price of $10. What will occur? Describe the situation at a price of $2. What will occur?

Price	Quantity Demanded	Quantity Supplied
$ 1	500	100
2	400	120
3	350	150
4	320	200
5	300	300
6	275	410
7	260	500
8	230	650
9	200	800
10	150	975

4. Suppose the government imposed a minimum price of $7 in the schedule of question 3. What would occur? Illustrate.

5. In question 3, indicate what the price would have to be to represent an effective price ceiling. Point out the surplus or shortage that results. Illustrate a price floor and provide an example of a price floor.

6. A common feature of skiing is waiting in lift lines. Does the existence of lift lines mean that the price is not working to allocate the scarce resource? If so, what should be done about it?

Copyright © by Houghton Mifflin Company. All rights reserved.

7. Why don't we observe barter systems as often as we observe the use of currency?

8. A severe drought in California has resulted in a nearly 30 percent reduction in the quantity of citrus grown and produced in California. Explain what effect this event might have on the Florida citrus market.

9. The prices of the Ralph Lauren "Polo" line of clothing are considerably higher than comparable quality lines. Yet, it sells more than a J. C. Penney brand line of clothing. Does this violate the law of demand?

10. In December, the price of Christmas trees rises and the quantity of trees sold rises. Is this a violation of the law of demand?

11. In recent years, the price of artificial Christmas trees has fallen while the quality has risen. What impact has this event had on the price of cut Christmas trees?

12. Many restaurants don't take reservations. You simply arrive and wait your turn. If you arrive at 7:30 in the evening, you have at least an hour wait. Notwithstanding that fact, a few people arrive, speak quietly with the maitre d', hand him some money, and are promptly seated. At some restaurants that do take reservations, there is a month wait for a Saturday evening, three weeks for a Friday evening, two weeks for Tuesday through Thursday, and virtually no wait for Sunday or Monday evening. How do you explain these events using demand and supply?

13. Evaluate the following statement: "The demand for U.S. oranges has increased because the quantity of U.S. oranges demanded in Japan has risen."

14. In December 1992, the federal government began requiring that all foods display information about fat content and other ingredients on food packages. The displays had to be verified by independent laboratories. The price of an evaluation of a food product could run as much as $20,000. What impact do you think this law had on the market for meat?

15. Draw a PPC. Which combination shown by the PPC will be produced? Does the combination that is produced depend on how goods and services are allocated?

⌨ INTERNET EXERCISE

This chapter focuses on demand and supply. Use the internet to examine the demand for Coca-Cola. Go to the Boyes/Melvin web site at http://www.hmco.com/college/ and click on the internet exercise link for this chapter. Now answer the questions that appear on the web page.

Copyright © by Houghton Mifflin Company. All rights reserved.

Letters to the Editor: Feeling the Pain of San Francisco Landlords

I suffered a major heart attack six months ago, but that's nothing to the heart pain I'm supposed to feel for landlords in San Francisco. Poor things, they bought property so that they could have tenants to pay their mortgage, interest, taxes, maintenance and repairs. When it comes to a future sale of their property, because of inflation, landlords would pocket handsome capital gains on their investment.

My heart bleeds especially for those landlords who threaten to keep their rental units off the market rather than deal with city restrictions. Many of them are quoted in news articles that "it's not worth the hassle" and "they don't need the money." If that's true, why should I feel sorry for them? That's their choice.

As a renter I don't feel an obligation to make a guaranteed profit for landlords. If they don't like being fair to renters, they can put their money in other investments.

Landlords always bristle at the term "rent control." To them it's a red flag of government control. Let's call it what it is, "Guaranteed Income Plan for Landlords, A Fair Shake for Renters to be Able to Afford to Live in San Francisco and Purchase Goods and Services."

NAT RESTIVO
San Francisco

Source: From *The San Francisco Chronicle,* December 30, 1997, p. A18.

Copyright © by Houghton Mifflin Company. All rights reserved.

COMMENTARY

Copyright © by Houghton Mifflin Company. All rights reserved.

Rent control—the attempt to make housing available to more people by controlling its cost—is among the most hotly contested local political issues in America. Since 1960, the number of jurisdictions with rent-control ordinances has swelled to more than 125, and the decision to adopt such laws is being debated in still more communities.

Rent controls, at their simplest, can be represented as a price ceiling (see figure, below left). A rent control could be represented as a maximum, or ceiling price, of P_m, which is less than the equilibrium price P_1. This price ceiling creates a shortage: At the rent-control price P_m, the quantity of housing units demanded is Q_d while the quantity of housing units supplied is only Q_s. The difference, $Q_d - Q_s$, is the number of families willing and able to rent a house at price P_m but for whom there are no homes available.

How is this excess demand resolved? Two things occur. One is that something other than price serves as the allocater. Common replacements for price are: first-come, first-served; preferences of the landlord; or black market or under-the-table payoffs. The second is that the landlord decreases the maintenance on the existing rentals, and new rental units are not brought to the market. As the landlord experiences a lower return on the rental housing, he or she has a lower incentive to devote resources to the upkeep of the unit. As a result, the quality of the housing deteriorates.

This is what the author of the letter to the editor fails to recognize. Unable to secure what he or she considers a fair return, the landlord has no incentive to make improvements or maintain the property.

Not only does rent control lead to deterioration but the lower return on the rental housing means that some landlords may convert their units to condominiums or to commercial properties and sell them. Over time, the supply of rental housing declines. The supply curve shifts in, to S_2 in the figure, below right, creating greater excess demand.

If rent control provides the same return as the free market would, there is no rent control. If the law provides a lower return, then the benefits to tenants rise, but the incentives for deterioration of the housing market also rise.

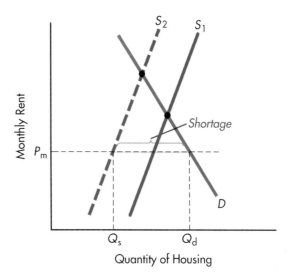

4

The Market System and the Private Sector

FUNDAMENTAL QUESTIONS

1. In a market system, who decides what goods and services are produced and how they are produced, and who obtains the goods and services that are produced?

2. What is a household, and what is household income and spending?

3. What is a business firm, and what is business spending?

4. How does the international sector affect the economy?

5. How do the three private sectors—households, businesses, and the international sector—interact in the economy?

Copyright © by Houghton Mifflin Company. All rights reserved.

Copyright © by Houghton Mifflin Company. All rights reserved.

Preview

You decide to buy a new Toyota, so you go to a Toyota dealer and exchange money for the car. The Toyota dealer has rented land and buildings and hired workers in order to make cars available to you and other members of the public. The employees earn incomes paid by the Toyota dealer and then use their incomes to buy food from the grocery store. This transaction generates revenue for the grocery store, which hires workers and pays them incomes that they then use to buy groceries and Toyotas. Your expenditure for the Toyota is part of a circular flow. Revenue is received by the Toyota dealer, who pays employees, who, in turn, buy goods and services.

Of course, the story is complicated by the fact that the Toyota is originally manufactured and purchased in Japan and then shipped to the United States before it can be sold by the local Toyota dealer. Your purchase of the Toyota creates revenue for the local dealer as well as for the manufacturer in Japan, who pays Japanese autoworkers to produce Toyotas. Furthermore, when you

buy your Toyota, you must pay a tax to the government, which uses tax revenues to pay for police protection, national defense, the legal system, and other services. Many people in different areas of the economy are involved.

An economy is made up of individual buyers and sellers. Economists could discuss the neighborhood economy that surrounds your university, the economy of the city of Chicago, or the economy of the state of Massachusetts. But typically it is the national economy, the economy of the

In a market system, who decides what goods and services are produced and how they are produced, and who obtains the goods and services that are produced?

United States, that is the center of their attention. To clarify the operation of the national economy, economists usually group individual buyers and sellers into three sectors: households, businesses, and government. Omitted from this grouping, however, is an important source of activity, the international sector. Since the U.S. economy affects, and is affected by, the rest of the world, to understand how the economy functions we must include the international sector.

We begin this chapter by examining the way that buyers and sellers interact in a market system. The impersonal forces of supply and demand operate to answer the following questions: Who determines what is produced and how they are produced? Who gets the output that is produced? The answers are given by the market system and involve the private-sector participants: households, business firms, and the international sector. Government also plays a major role in answering these questions, but we leave government and its role for the next chapter.

Following the discussion of the market system, we examine basic data and information on each individual sector with the objective of answering some general questions: What is a household, and how do households spend their incomes? What is a business firm, and how does a corporation differ from a partnership? What does it mean if the United States has a trade deficit?

After describing the three sectors that make up the private sector of the national economy, we present a simple economic model to illustrate the interrelationships linking all the individual sectors into the national economy. ■

1. THE MARKET SYSTEM

As we learned in Chapter 2, the production possibilities curve represents all possible combinations of goods and services that a society can produce if its resources are used fully and efficiently. Which combination, that is, which point on the PPC, will society choose? In a price or market system, the answer is given by demand and supply.

1.a. Consumer Sovereignty

In recent years, time-starved Americans spent about as much time eating out as they did eating at home. In the 1950s and 1960s, this trend was just beginning. Consumers wanted more and more restaurants and fast-food outlets. As a result, McDonald's, Wendy's, Big Boy, White Castle, Pizza Hut, Godfather's Pizza, and other fast-food outlets flourished. The trend toward eating away from home reached fever pitch in the late 1970s, when the average number of meals per person eaten out (excluding brown-bag lunches and other meals prepared at home but eaten elsewhere) exceeded one per day.

In the 1980s, people wanted the fast food but didn't want to go get it. By emphasizing delivery, Domino's Pizza and a few other fast-food outlets became very successful. In the 1990s, the takeout taxi business—where restaurant food is delivered to homes—grew ten percent per year. However, the star of this story is not Domino's, Pizza Hut, or other restaurants. It is the consumer. In a market system, if consumers are willing and able to pay for more restaurant meals, more restaurants appear. If consumers are willing and able to pay for food delivered to their homes, food is delivered to their homes.

Why does the consumer wield such power? The name of the game for business is profit, and the only way business can make a profit is by satisfying consumer wants. The consumer, not the politician or the business firm, ultimately determines what is to be produced. A firm that produces something that no consumers want will not remain in business very long. **Consumer**

consumer sovereignty:
the authority of consumers to determine what is produced through their purchases of goods and services

sovereignty—the authority of consumers to determine what is produced through their purchases of goods and services—dictates what goods and services will be produced. Supermarkets and grocery stores are responding to the consumer as well, by putting fast-food restaurants, like Pizza Hut and Taco Bell, inside their stores.

1.b. Profit and the Allocation of Resources

When a good or service seems to have the potential to generate a profit, someone with entrepreneurial ability will put together the resources needed to produce that good or service. An individual with entrepreneurial ability

Copyright © by Houghton Mifflin Company. All rights reserved.

aims to earn a profit by renting land, hiring labor, and using capital to produce a good or service that can be sold for more than the sum of rent, wages, and interest. If the potential profit turns into a loss, the entrepreneur may stop buying resources and turn to some other occupation or project. The resources used in the losing operation would then be available for use in an activity where they would be more highly valued.

To illustrate how resources get allocated in the market system, let's look at the market for fast foods. Figure 1 shows a change in demand for meals eaten in restaurants. The initial demand curve, D_1, and supply curve, S, are shown in Figure 1(a). With these demand and supply curves, the equilibrium price (P_1) is $8, and the equilibrium quantity (Q_1) is 100 units (meals). At this price-quantity combination, the number of meals demanded equals the number of meals sold; equilibrium is reached, so we say the market clears (there is no shortage or surplus).

The second part of the figure shows what happened when consumer tastes changed, and people preferred to have food delivered to their homes. This change in tastes caused the demand for restaurants to decline and is represented by a leftward shift of the demand curve, from D_1 to D_2, in Figure 1(b). The demand curve shifted to the left because fewer in-restaurant meals were demanded at each price. Consumer tastes, not the price of in-restaurant meals, changed first. (A price change would have led to a change in the quantity demanded and would be represented by a move *along* demand curve D_1.) The

Copyright © by Houghton Mifflin Company. All rights reserved.

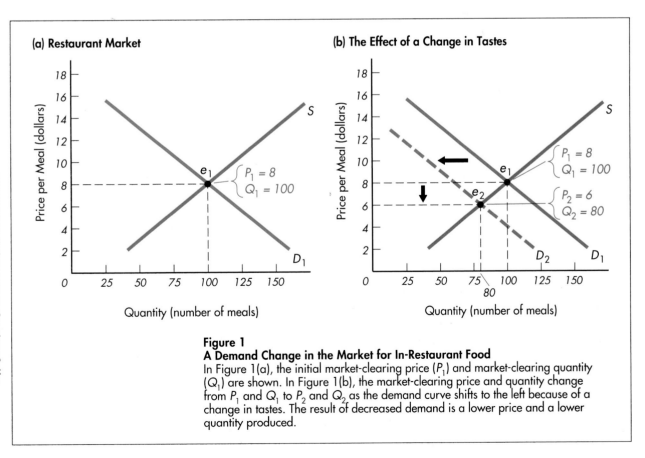

Figure 1
A Demand Change in the Market for In-Restaurant Food
In Figure 1(a), the initial market-clearing price (P_1) and market-clearing quantity (Q_1) are shown. In Figure 1(b), the market-clearing price and quantity change from P_1 and Q_1 to P_2 and Q_2 as the demand curve shifts to the left because of a change in tastes. The result of decreased demand is a lower price and a lower quantity produced.

change in tastes caused a change in demand and a leftward shift of the demand curve. The shift from D_1 to D_2 created a new equilibrium point. The equilibrium price (P_2) decreased to $6, and the equilibrium quantity (Q_2) decreased to 80 units (meals).

While the market for in-restaurant food was changing, so was the market for delivered food. People substituted meals delivered to their homes for meals eaten in restaurants. Figure 2(a) shows the original demand for food delivered to the home. Figure 2(b) shows a rightward shift of the demand curve, from D_1 to D_2, representing increased demand for home delivery. This demand change resulted in a higher market-clearing price for food delivered to the home, from $10 to $12.

The changing profit potential of the two markets induced existing firms to switch from in-restaurant service to home delivery and for new firms to offer delivery from the start. Domino's Pizza, which is a delivery-only firm, grew from a one-store operation to become the second largest pizza chain in the United States, with sales exceeding $2 billion per year. Little Caesar's, another takeout chain, grew from $63.6 million in sales in 1980 to nearly $1 billion in 1987. Pizza Hut, which at first did not offer home delivery, had to play catch-up; and by 1992, about two-thirds of Pizza Hut's more than 5,000 restaurants were delivering pizza. In 1994, many non-fast-food restaurants began offering delivery.

As the market-clearing price of in-restaurant fast food fell (from $8 to $6 in Figure 1), the quantity of in-restaurant meals sold also declined (from 100 to 80) because the decreased demand, lower price, and resulting lower profit

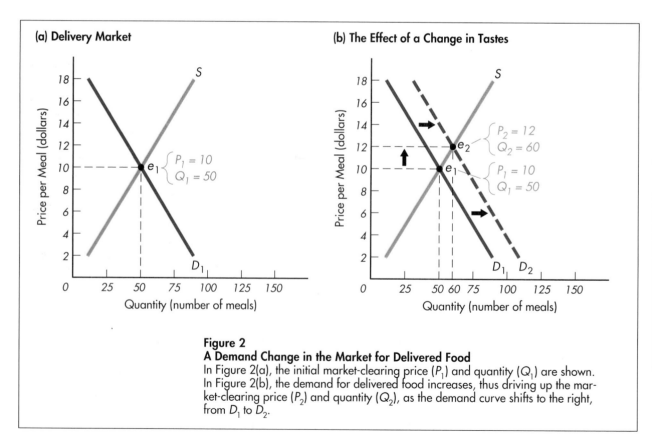

Figure 2
A Demand Change in the Market for Delivered Food
In Figure 2(a), the initial market-clearing price (P_1) and quantity (Q_1) are shown. In Figure 2(b), the demand for delivered food increases, thus driving up the market-clearing price (P_2) and quantity (Q_2), as the demand curve shifts to the right, from D_1 to D_2.

Copyright © by Houghton Mifflin Company. All rights reserved.

induced some firms to decrease production. In the delivery business, the opposite occurred. As the market-clearing price rose (from $10 to $12 in Figure 2[b]), the number of meals delivered also rose (from 50 to 60). The increased demand, higher price, and resulting higher profit induced firms to increase production.

Why did the production of delivered foods increase while the production of meals at restaurants decreased? Not because of government decree. Not because of the desires of the business sector, especially the owners of restaurants. The consumer—consumer sovereignty—made all this happen. Businesses that failed to respond to consumer desires and failed to provide the desired good at the lowest price failed to survive.

1.c. The Flow of Resources

After demand shifted to home-delivered food, the resources that had been used in the restaurants were available for use elsewhere. A few former waiters, waitresses, and cooks were able to get jobs in the delivery firms. Some of the equipment used in eat-in restaurants—ovens, pots, and pans—was purchased by the delivery firms; and some of the ingredients that previously would have gone to the eat-in restaurants were bought by the delivery firms. A few former employees of the eat-in restaurants became employed at department stores, at local pubs, and at hotels. Some of the equipment was sold as scrap; other equipment was sold to other restaurants. In other words, the resources moved from an activity where their value was relatively low to an activity where they were more highly valued. No one commanded the resources to move. They moved because they could earn more in some other activity.

Adam Smith described this phenomenon in his 1776 treatise *The Wealth of Nations,* saying it was as if an invisible hand reached out and guided the resources to their most-valued use. That invisible hand is the self-interest that drives firms to provide what consumers want to buy, leads consumers to use their limited incomes to buy the goods and services that bring them the greatest satisfaction, and induces resource owners to supply resource services where they are most highly valued. (There is more about Smith in the Economic Insight "Adam Smith.")

Competitive firms produce in the manner that minimizes costs and maximizes profits.

Firms produce the goods and services and use the resources that enable them to generate the highest profits. If one firm does this better than others, then that firm earns a greater profit than others. Seeing that success, other firms copy or mimic the first firm. If a firm cannot be as profitable as the others, it will eventually go out of business or move to another line of business where it can be successful. In the process of firms always seeking to lower costs and make higher profits, society finds that the goods and services buyers want are produced in the least costly manner. Consumers not only get the goods and services they want and will pay for, but they get these products at the lowest possible price.

1.d. The Determination of Income

Consumer demands dictate *what* is produced, and the search for profit defines *how* goods and services are produced. *For whom* are the goods and services produced, that is, who gets the goods and services? In a price or market system, those who have the ability to pay for the products get the products. Your income determines your ability to pay, but where does income come from? Income is obtained by selling the services of resources. When you sell your

Copyright © by Houghton Mifflin Company. All rights reserved.

Adam Smith

Adam Smith was born in 1723 and reared in Kirkcaldy, Scotland, near Edinburgh. He went to the University of Glasgow when he was fourteen, and three years later began studies at Oxford, where he stayed for six years. In 1751, Smith became professor of logic and then moral philosophy at Glasgow. From 1764 to 1766, he tutored the future duke of Buccleuch in France, and then he was given a pension for the remainder of his life. Between 1766 and 1776, Smith completed *The Wealth of Nations*. He became commissioner of customs for Scotland and spent his remaining years in Edinburgh. He died in 1790.

Economists date the beginning of their discipline from the publication of *The Wealth of Nations* in 1776. In this major treatise, Smith emphasizes the role of self-interest in the functioning of markets, specialization, and division of labor.

According to Smith, the fundamental explanation of human behavior is found in the rational pursuit of self-interest. Smith uses it to explain how men choose occupations, how farmers till their lands, and how leaders of the American Revolution were led by it to rebellion. Smith did not equate self-interest with selfishness but broadened the definition of self-interest, believing that a person is interested "in the fortune of others and renders their happiness necessary to him, though he derives nothing from it, except the pleasure of seeing it." On the basis of self-interest, Smith constructed a theory of how markets work: how goods, once produced, are sold to the highest bidders, and how the quantities of the goods that are produced are governed by their costs and selling prices. But Smith's insight showed that this self-interest resulted in the best situation for society as a whole. In a celebrated and often-quoted passage from the treatise Smith says:

But man has almost constant occasion for the help of his brethren, and it is in vain for him to expect it from their benevolence only. He will be more likely to prevail if he can interest their self-love in his favour, and show them that it is for their own advantage to do for him what he requires of them. . . . It is not from the benevolence of the butcher, the brewer, or the baker, that we can expect our dinner, but from their regard to their own interest.

Source: *An Inquiry into the Nature and Causes of the Wealth of Nations*, edited and with an introduction, notes, marginal summary, and index by Edwin Cannan. (Chicago: University of Chicago Press, 1976). Reprinted by permission of the University of Chicago Press.

Ownership of resources determines who gets what goods and services in a market system.

private sector
households, businesses, and the international sector

public sector
the government

labor services, your money income reflects your wage rate or salary level. When you sell the services of the capital you own, you receive interest; and when you sell the services of the land you own, you receive rent. A person with entrepreneurial ability earns profit as a payment for services. Thus, we see that buyers and sellers of goods and services and resource owners are linked together in an economy: the more one buys, the more income or revenue the other receives. In the remainder of this chapter, we learn more about the linkages among the sectors of the economy. We classify the buyers and the resource owners into the household sector; the sellers or business firms are the business sector; households and firms in other countries, who may also be buyers and sellers of this country's goods and services, are the international sector. These three sectors—households, business firms, and the international sector—constitute the **private sector** of the economy. In this chapter we focus on the interaction among the components of the private sector. In the next chapter we focus on the **public sector,** government, and examine its role in the economy.

Copyright © by Houghton Mifflin Company. All rights reserved.

RECAP

1. In a market system, consumers are sovereign and decide by means of their purchases what goods and services will be produced.

2. In a market system, firms decide how to produce the goods and services that consumers want. In order to earn maximum profits, firms use the least-cost combinations of resources.

3. Income and prices determine who gets what in a market system. Income is determined by the ownership of resources.

2. HOUSEHOLDS

What is a household, and what is household income and spending?

household:
one or more persons who occupy a unit of housing

A **household** consists of one or more persons who occupy a unit of housing. The unit of housing may be a house, an apartment, or even a single room, as long as it constitutes separate living quarters. A household may consist of related family members, like a father, mother, and children, or it may comprise unrelated individuals, like three college students sharing an apartment. The person in whose name the house or apartment is owned or rented is called the *householder.*

2.a. Number of Households and Household Income

In 1996, there were more than 99 million households in the United States. The breakdown of households by age of householder is shown in Figure 3. Householders between 35 and 44 years old make up the largest number of households. Householders between 45 and 54 years old have the largest median income. The *median* is the middle value—half of the households in an age group have an income higher than the median and half have an income lower than the median. Figure 3 shows that households in which the householder is between 45 and 54 years old have a median income of about

Copyright © by Houghton Mifflin Company. All rights reserved.

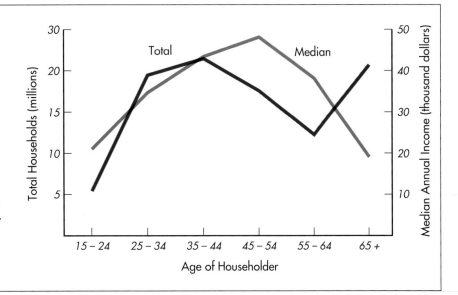

Figure 3
Age of Householder, Number of Households, and Median Household Income in the United States
The graph reveals that householders aged 35 to 44 make up the largest number of households, and householders aged 45 to 54 earn the highest median annual income. Source: U.S. Department of Commerce, *Statistical Abstract of the United States, 1997* (Washington, D.C.: U.S. Government Printing Office, 1997).

$48,000, substantially higher than the median incomes of other age groups. Typically, workers in this age group are at the peak of their earning power. Younger households are gaining experience and training; older households include retired workers.

The size distribution of households in the United States is shown in Figure 4. Thirty-two percent of all households, or 31,880,000 are two-person households. The stereotypical household of husband, wife, and two children accounts for only 16 percent of all households. There are relatively few large households in the United States. Of the more than 99 million households in the country, only 996,000 (1 percent) have seven or more persons.

2.b. Household Spending

consumption:
household spending

Household spending is called **consumption.** Householders consume housing, transportation, food, entertainment, and other goods and services. Household spending (also called *consumer spending*) per year in the United States is shown in Figure 5, along with household income. The pattern is one of steady increase. Spending by the household sector is the largest component of total spending in the economy—rising to over $4 trillion in 1994.

RECAP

1. A household consists of one or more persons who occupy a unit of housing.
2. An apartment or house is rented or owned by a householder.
3. As a group, householders between the ages of 45 and 54 have the highest median incomes.
4. Household spending is called *consumption*.

Copyright © by Houghton Mifflin Company. All rights reserved.

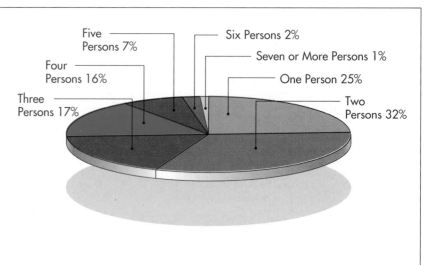

Figure 4
Size Distribution of Households in the United States
As the pie chart illustrates, two-person households make up a larger percentage of the total number of households than any other group, a total of 32 percent. Large households with seven or more persons are becoming a rarity, accounting for only 1 percent of the total number of households. Source: *Statistical Abstract of the United States, 1997* (Washington, D.C.: U.S. Government Printing Office, 1997).

Five Persons 7%
Six Persons 2%
Four Persons 16%
Seven or More Persons 1%
One Person 25%
Three Persons 17%
Two Persons 32%

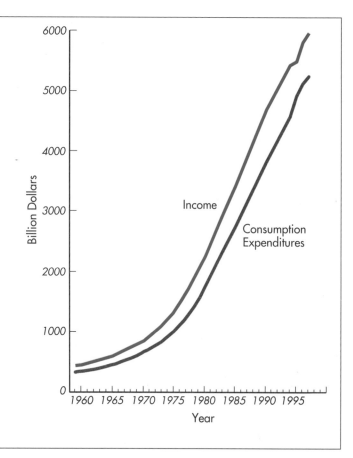

Figure 5
Household Spending and Income
Household spending (consumption) and income each year from 1959 to 1997 are shown. Both show a pattern of steady increase.

3. BUSINESS FIRMS

business firm:
a business organization controlled by a single management

A **business firm** is a business organization controlled by a single management. The firm's business may be conducted at more than one location. The terms *company, enterprise,* and *business* are used interchangeably with *firm*.

3.a. Forms of Business Organizations

What is a business firm, and what is business spending?

sole proprietorship:
a business owned by one person who receives all the profits and is responsible for all the debts incurred by the business

partnership:
a business with two or more owners who share the firm's profits and losses

Firms are organized as sole proprietorships, partnerships, or corporations. A **sole proprietorship** is a business owned by one person. This type of firm may be a one-person operation or a large enterprise with many employees. In either case, the owner receives all the profits and is responsible for all the debts incurred by the business.

A **partnership** is a business owned by two or more partners who share both the profits of the business and responsibility for the firm's losses. The partners could be individuals, estates, or other businesses.

A **corporation** is a business whose identity in the eyes of the law is distinct from the identity of its owners. State law allows the formation of corporations. A corporation is an economic entity that, like a person, can own property and borrow money in its own name. The owners of a corporation are shareholders. If a corporation cannot pay its debts, creditors cannot seek payment from the shareholders' personal wealth. The corporation itself is

Copyright © by Houghton Mifflin Company. All rights reserved.

corporation:
a legal entity owned by share-holders whose liability for the firm's losses is limited to the value of the stock they own

multinational business:
a firm that owns and operates producing units in foreign countries

responsible for all its actions. The shareholders' liability is limited to the value of the stock they own.

Many firms are global in their operations even though they may have been founded and may be owned by residents of a single country. Firms typically first enter the international market by selling products to foreign countries. As revenues from these sales increase, the firms realize advantages by locating subsidiaries in foreign countries. A **multinational business** is a firm that owns and operates producing units in foreign countries. The best-known U.S. corporations are multinational firms. Ford, IBM, PepsiCo, and McDonald's all own operating units in many different countries. Ford Motor Company, for instance, is the parent firm of sales organizations and assembly plants located around the world. As transportation and communication technologies progress, multinational business activity will grow.

Figure 6
Number and Revenue of Business Firms
As Figure 6(a) illustrates, most sole proprietorships and partnerships are small firms, with nearly 70 percent of all proprietorships falling into the less-than-$25,000 revenue category, and over 60 percent of all partnerships falling into the same lowest revenue category. Corporations are more likely to be larger—17 percent have revenues exceeding $1 million. Figure 6(b) shows that

most sole proprietorship revenues are earned by the larger proprietorships, those in the $100,000 to $499,000 category. By contrast, the small number of partnerships in the top revenue category is enough to account for 79 percent of all partnership revenues.
Source: *Statistical Abstract of the United States, 1997* (Washington, D.C.: U.S. Government Printing Office, 1997).

(a) Number of Business Firms by Revenue Amount

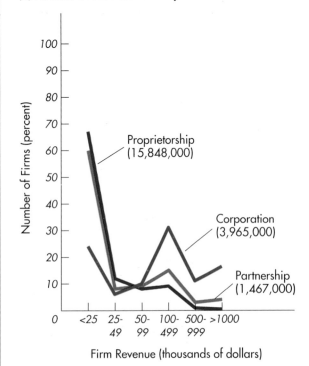

(b) Percent of Total Business Type by Revenue Amount

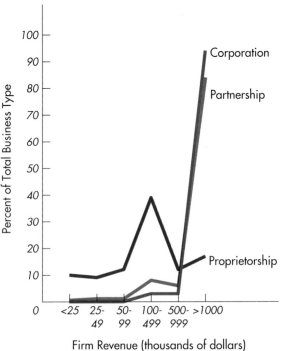

Copyright © by Houghton Mifflin Company. All rights reserved.

3.b. Business Statistics

Figure 6(a) shows that in the United States there are far more sole proprietorships than partnerships or corporations. Figure 6(a) also compares the revenues earned by each type of business. The great majority of sole proprietorships are small businesses, with revenues under $25,000 a year. Similarly, over half of all partnerships also have revenues under $25,000 a year, but only 24 percent of the corporations are in this category.

Figure 6(b) shows that the 67 percent of sole proprietorships that earn less than $25,000 a year account for only 10 percent of the revenue earned by proprietorships. The 0.4 percent of proprietorships with revenue of $1 million or more account for 17 percent. Even more striking are the figures for partnerships and corporations. The 60 percent of partnerships with the smallest revenue account for only 0.5 percent of the total revenue earned by partnerships. At the other extreme, the 4 percent of partnerships with the largest revenue account for 84 percent of total partnership revenue. The 24 percent of corporations in the smallest range account for less than 0.1 percent of total corporate revenue, while the 17 percent of corporations in the largest range account for 94 percent of corporate revenue.

The message of Figure 6 is that big business is important in the United States. There are many small firms, but large firms and corporations account for the greatest share of business revenue. Although there are only about one-third as many corporations as sole proprietorships, corporations have more than fifteen times the revenue of sole proprietorships.

3.c. Firms Around the World

Big business is a dominant force in the United States. Many people believe that because the United States is the world's largest economy, U.S. firms are the largest in the world. Figure 7 shows that this is not true. Of the ten largest

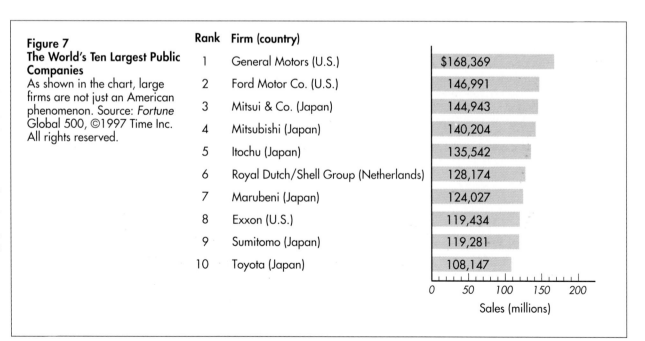

Figure 7
The World's Ten Largest Public Companies
As shown in the chart, large firms are not just an American phenomenon. Source: *Fortune Global 500*, ©1997 Time Inc. All rights reserved.

Rank	Firm (country)	Sales (millions)
1	General Motors (U.S.)	$168,369
2	Ford Motor Co. (U.S.)	146,991
3	Mitsui & Co. (Japan)	144,943
4	Mitsubishi (Japan)	140,204
5	Itochu (Japan)	135,542
6	Royal Dutch/Shell Group (Netherlands)	128,174
7	Marubeni (Japan)	124,027
8	Exxon (U.S.)	119,434
9	Sumitomo (Japan)	119,281
10	Toyota (Japan)	108,147

Copyright © by Houghton Mifflin Company. All rights reserved.

The Successful Entrepreneur (Sometimes It's Better to Be Lucky Than Good)

Entrepreneurs do not always develop an abstract idea into reality when starting a new firm. Sometimes people stumble onto a good thing by accident and then are clever enough and willing to take the necessary risk to turn their lucky find into a commercial success.

In 1875, a Philadelphia pharmacist on his honeymoon tasted tea made from an innkeeper's old family recipe. The tea, made from sixteen wild roots and berries, was so delicious that the pharmacist asked the innkeeper's wife for the recipe. When he returned to his pharmacy, he created a solid concentrate of the drink that could be sold for home consumption.

The pharmacist was Charles Hires, a devout Quaker, who intended to sell "Hires Herb Tea" to hard-drinking Pennsylvania coal miners as a nonalcoholic alternative to beer and whiskey. A friend of Hires suggested that miners would not drink anything called "tea" and recommended that he call his drink "root beer."

The initial response to Hires Root Beer was so enthusiastic that Hires soon began nationwide distribution. The yellow box of root beer extract was a familiar sight in homes and drugstore fountains across America. By 1895, Hires, who started with a $3,000 loan, was operating a business valued at half a million dollars (a lot of money in 1895) and bottling ready-to-drink root beer across the country.

Hires, of course, is not the only entrepreneur clever enough to turn a lucky discovery into a business success. In 1894, in Battle Creek, Michigan, a sanitarium handyman named Will Kellogg was helping his older brother prepare wheat meal to serve to patients in the sanitarium's dining room. The two men would boil wheat dough and then run it through rollers to produce thin sheets of meal. One day they left a batch of the dough out overnight. The next day, when the dough was run through the rollers, it broke up into flakes instead of forming a sheet.

By letting the dough stand overnight, the Kelloggs had allowed moisture to be distributed evenly to each individual wheat berry. When the dough went through the rollers, the berries formed separate flakes instead of binding together. The Kelloggs toasted the wheat flakes and served them to the patients. They were an immediate success. In fact, the brothers had to start a mail-order flaked-cereal business because patients wanted flaked cereal for their households.

Kellogg saw the market potential for the discovery and started his own cereal company (his brother refused to join him in the business). He was a great promoter who used innovations like four-color magazine ads and free-sample promotions. In New York City, he offered a free box of corn flakes to every woman who winked at her grocer on a specified day. The promotion was considered risqué, but Kellogg's sales in New York increased from two railroad cars of cereal a month to one car a day.

Will Kellogg, a poorly paid sanitarium worker in his mid-forties, became a daring entrepreneur after his mistake with wheat flour led to the discovery of a way to produce flaked cereal. He became one of the richest men in America because of his entrepreneurial ability.

Source: *Entrepreneurs* by Joseph and Suzy Fucini. Hall and Company, 1985.

corporations in the world (measured by sales), six are Japanese. Big business is not just an American phenomenon.

3.d. Entrepreneurial Ability

The emphasis on bigness should not hide the fact that many new firms are started each year. Businesses are typically begun as small sole proprietorships. Many of them are forced to go out of business within a year or two. Businesses survive in the long run only if they provide a good or service that people want enough to yield a profit for the entrepreneur. Although there are

Copyright © by Houghton Mifflin Company. All rights reserved.

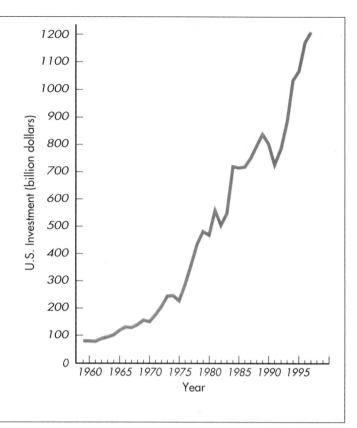

Figure 8
U.S. Investment Spending,
1959–1997
Business expenditures on capital goods have been increasing erratically since 1959. Source: *Economic Report of the President, 1997* (Washington, D.C.: U.S. Government Printing Office, 1997).

fabulous success stories, the failure rate among new firms is high. Thorough research of the market and careful planning play a large part in determining whether or not a new business succeeds but so can luck, as the Economic Insight "The Successful Entrepreneur" confirms.

That many new businesses fail is a fact of economic life. In the U.S. economy, anyone with an idea and sufficient resources has the freedom to open a business. However, if buyers do not respond to the new offering, the business fails. Only firms that satisfy this "market test" survive. Entrepreneurs thus try to ensure that as wants change, goods and services are produced to satisfy those wants.

3.e. Business Spending

investment:
spending on capital goods to be used in producing goods and services

Investment is the expenditure by business firms for capital goods—machines, tools, and buildings—that will be used to produce goods and services. The economic meaning of *investment* is different from the everyday meaning, "a financial transaction such as buying bonds or stocks." In economics, the term *investment* refers to business spending for capital goods.

Investment spending in 1997 was $1,205 billion, an amount equal to roughly one-fifth of consumption, or household spending. Investment spending between 1959 and 1997 is shown in Figure 8. Compare Figures 5 and 8 and notice the different patterns of spending. Investment increases unevenly, actually falling at times and then rising very rapidly. Even though investment spending is much smaller than consumption, the wide swings in investment spending mean that business expenditures are an important factor in determining the economic health of the nation.

Copyright © by Houghton Mifflin Company. All rights reserved.

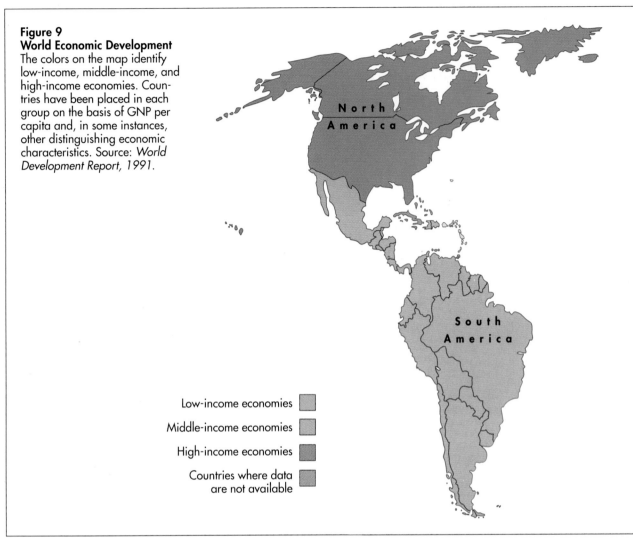

Figure 9
World Economic Development
The colors on the map identify low-income, middle-income, and high-income economies. Countries have been placed in each group on the basis of GNP per capita and, in some instances, other distinguishing economic characteristics. Source: *World Development Report, 1991.*

Low-income economies
Middle-income economies
High-income economies
Countries where data are not available

RECAP

1. Business firms may be organized as sole proprietorships, partnerships, or corporations.
2. Large corporations account for the largest fraction of total business revenue.
3. Many new firms are started each year, but the failure rate is high.
4. Business investment spending fluctuates widely over time.

4. THE INTERNATIONAL SECTOR

How does the international sector affect the economy?

Today, foreign buyers and sellers have a significant effect on economic conditions in the United States, and developments in the rest of the world often influence U.S. buyers and sellers. We saw in Chapter 3, for instance, how exchange rate changes can affect the demand for U.S. goods and services.

Copyright © by Houghton Mifflin Company. All rights reserved.

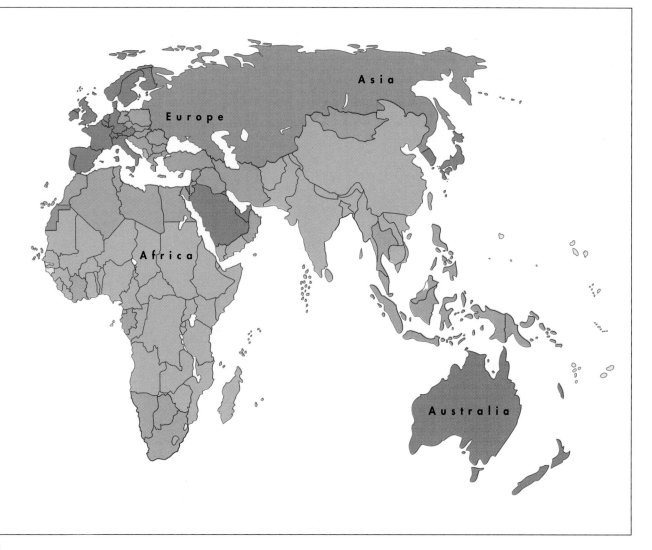

Copyright © by Houghton Mifflin Company. All rights reserved.

4.a. Types of Countries

The nations of the world may be divided into two categories: industrial countries and developing countries. Developing countries greatly outnumber industrial countries (see Figure 9). The World Bank (an international organization that makes loans to developing countries) groups countries according to per capita income (income per person). Low-income economies are those with per capita incomes of $750 or less. Middle-income economies have per capita incomes of $750 to $8,260. High-income economies—oil exporters and industrial market economies—are distinguished from the middle-income economies and have per capita incomes of greater than $8,260. Some countries are not members of the World Bank and so are not categorized, and information about a few small countries is so limited that the World Bank is unable to classify them.

It is readily apparent from Figure 9 that low-income economies are heavily concentrated in Africa and Asia. Countries in these regions have a low profile in U.S. trade, although they may receive aid from the United States.

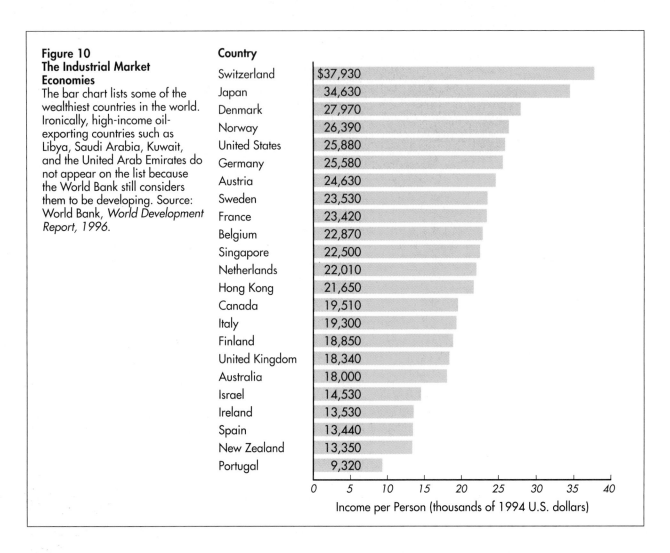

Figure 10
The Industrial Market Economies
The bar chart lists some of the wealthiest countries in the world. Ironically, high-income oil-exporting countries such as Libya, Saudi Arabia, Kuwait, and the United Arab Emirates do not appear on the list because the World Bank still considers them to be developing. Source: World Bank, *World Development Report, 1996.*

Country

Switzerland	$37,930
Japan	34,630
Denmark	27,970
Norway	26,390
United States	25,880
Germany	25,580
Austria	24,630
Sweden	23,530
France	23,420
Belgium	22,870
Singapore	22,500
Netherlands	22,010
Hong Kong	21,650
Canada	19,510
Italy	19,300
Finland	18,850
United Kingdom	18,340
Australia	18,000
Israel	14,530
Ireland	13,530
Spain	13,440
New Zealand	13,350
Portugal	9,320

Income per Person (thousands of 1994 U.S. dollars)

U.S. trade is concentrated with its neighbors Canada and Mexico, along with the major industrial powers. Nations in each group present different economic challenges to the United States.

4.a.1. The Industrial Countries   The World Bank uses per capita income to classify twenty-three countries as "industrial market economies." They are listed in the bar chart in Figure 10. The twenty-three countries listed in Figure 10 are among the wealthiest countries in the world. Not appearing on the list are the high-income oil-exporting nations like Libya, Saudi Arabia, Kuwait, and the United Arab Emirates. The World Bank considers those countries to be "still developing."

The economies of the industrial nations are highly interdependent. As conditions change in one nation, business firms and individuals looking for the best return or interest rate on their funds may shift large sums of money between countries. As the funds flow from one country to another, economic conditions in one country spread to other countries. As a result, the industrial countries, particularly the major economic powers like the United States, Germany, and Japan, are forced to pay close attention to each other's economic policies.

Copyright © by Houghton Mifflin Company. All rights reserved.

Copyright © by Houghton Mifflin Company. All rights reserved.

4.a.2. The Developing Countries The developing countries (sometimes referred to as *less developed countries,* or *LDCs*) provide a different set of problems for the United States than do the industrial countries. In the 1980s, the debts of the developing countries to the developed nations reached tremendous heights. For instance, at the end of 1989, Brazil owed foreign creditors $111.3 billion, Mexico owed $95.6 billion, and Argentina owed $64.7 billion. In each case, the amounts owed were more than several times the annual sales of goods and services by those countries to the rest of the world. The United States had to arrange loans at special terms and establish special trade arrangements in order for those countries to be able to buy U.S. goods.

The United States tends to buy, or *import,* primary products such as agricultural produce and minerals from the developing countries. Products that a country buys from another country are called **imports.** The United States tends to sell, or *export,* manufactured goods to developing countries. Products that a country sells to another country are called **exports.** The United States is the largest producer and exporter of grains and other agricultural output in the world. The efficiency of U.S. farming relative to farming in much of the rest of the world gives the United States a comparative advantage in many agricultural products.

imports:
products that a country buys from other countries

exports:
products that a country sells to other countries

4.b. International Sector Spending

U.S. economic activity with the rest of the world includes U.S. spending on foreign goods and foreign spending on U.S. goods. Figure 11 shows how U.S. exports and imports are spread over different countries. Notice that two countries, Canada and Japan, account for roughly one-third of U.S. exports and

Trade between the United States and the Asian nations has been growing for several years even though some of the Asian nations attempt to restrict the sale of foreign goods in their country or to otherwise limit trade. In the photos shown here, it is clear that Coca Cola has been able to enter the Korean market, dominating its soft drink industry. In contrast, the United States has been relatively open to foreign goods. Although threatening trade sanctions against Japan or China at times, citizens of the United States clamor for the goods made in other nations. Here, seamstresses in Korea prepare clothes for major distributors in the United States.

more than one-third of U.S. imports. Trade with the industrial countries is approximately twice as large as trade with the developing countries, and U.S. trade with Eastern Europe is trivial.

When exports exceed imports, a **trade surplus** exists. When imports exceed exports, a **trade deficit** exists. Figure 11 shows that the United States is importing much more than it exports.

The term **net exports** refers to the difference between the value of exports and the value of imports: net exports equals exports minus imports. Figure 12 traces U.S. net exports over time. Positive net exports represent trade surpluses; negative net exports represent trade deficits. The trade deficits (indicated by negative net exports) of the 1980s were unprecedented. Reasons for this pattern of international trade are discussed in later chapters.

trade surplus:
the situation that exists when imports are less than exports

trade deficit:
the situation that exists when imports exceed exports

net exports:
the difference between the value of exports and the value of imports

RECAP

1. The majority of U.S. trade is with the industrial market economies.
2. Exports are products sold to foreign countries; imports are products bought from foreign countries.
3. Exports minus imports equals net exports.
4. Positive net exports signal a trade surplus; negative net exports signal a trade deficit.

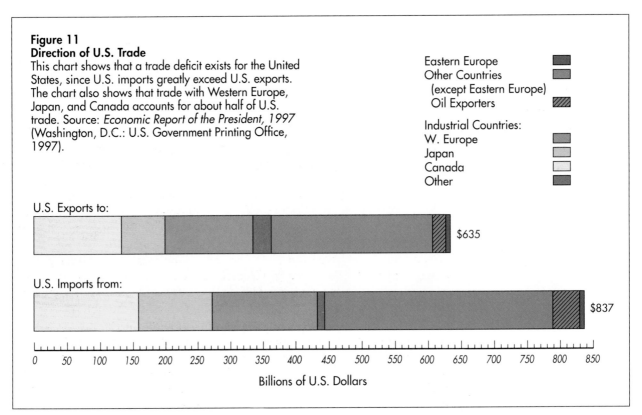

Figure 11
Direction of U.S. Trade
This chart shows that a trade deficit exists for the United States, since U.S. imports greatly exceed U.S. exports. The chart also shows that trade with Western Europe, Japan, and Canada accounts for about half of U.S. trade. Source: *Economic Report of the President, 1997* (Washington, D.C.: U.S. Government Printing Office, 1997).

Eastern Europe
Other Countries
 (except Eastern Europe)
Oil Exporters

Industrial Countries:
W. Europe
Japan
Canada
Other

U.S. Exports to:
$635

U.S. Imports from:
$837

0   50   100   150   200   250   300   350   400   450   500   550   600   650   700   750   800   850

Billions of U.S. Dollars

Copyright © by Houghton Mifflin Company. All rights reserved.

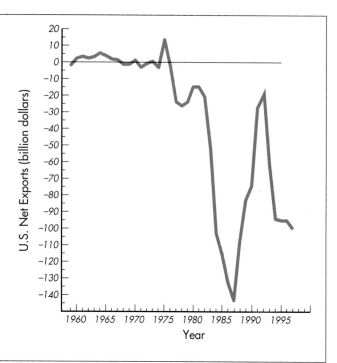

Figure 12
U.S. Net Exports
Prior to the late 1960s, the United States generally exported more than it imported and had a trade surplus. Since 1976, net exports have been negative, and the United States has had a trade deficit. Source: *Economic Report of the President, 1997* (Washington, D.C.: U.S. Government Printing Office, 1997).

5. LINKING THE SECTORS

Now that we have an idea of the size and structure of each of the private sectors—households, businesses, and international—let's discuss how the sectors interact.

5.a. Households and Firms

How do the three private sectors—households, businesses, and the international sector—interact in the economy?

Households own all the basic resources, or factors of production, in the economy. Household members own land and provide labor, and they are the entrepreneurs, stockholders, proprietors, and partners who own business firms.

Households and businesses interact with each other by means of buying and selling. Businesses employ the services of resources in order to produce goods and services. Business firms pay households for their services of resources.

Households sell their resource services to businesses in exchange for money payments. The flow of resource services from households to businesses is shown by the blue-green line at the bottom of Figure 13. The flow of money payments from firms to households is shown by the gold line at the bottom of Figure 13. Households use the money payments to buy goods and services from firms. These money payments are the firms' revenues. The flow of money payments from households to firms is shown by the gold line at the top of the diagram. The flow of goods and services from firms to households is shown by the blue-green line at the top of Figure 13. There is, therefore, a flow of money and goods and services from one sector to the other. The pay-

Copyright © by Houghton Mifflin Company. All rights reserved.

ments made by one sector are the receipts taken in by the other sector. Money, goods, and services flow from households to firms and back to households in a circular flow.

Households do not spend all of the money they receive. They save some fraction of their income. In Figure 13, we see that household saving is deposited in **financial intermediaries** like banks, credit unions, and saving and loan firms. A financial intermediary accepts deposits from savers and makes loans to borrowers. The money that is saved by the households reenters the economy in the form of investment spending as business firms borrow for expansion of their productive capacity.

financial intermediaries:
institutions that accept deposits from savers and make loans to borrowers

Figure 13
The Circular Flow: Households and Firms
The diagram indicates that income is equal to the value of output. Firms hire resources from households. The payments for these resources represent household income. Households spend their income for goods and services produced by the firms. Household spending represents revenue for firms. Households save some of their income. This income reenters the circular flow as investment spending. Financial intermediaries like banks take in the saving of households and then lend this money to business firms for investment spending.

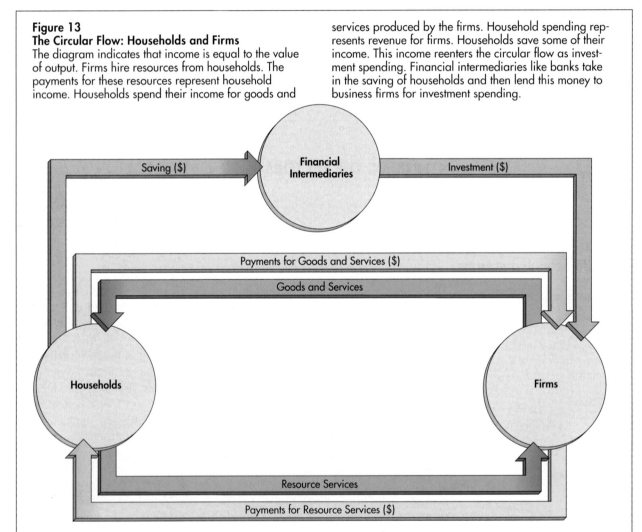

Copyright © by Houghton Mifflin Company. All rights reserved.

circular flow diagram:
a model showing the flow of output and income from one sector of the economy to another

The **circular flow diagram** represented in Figure 13 indicates that income is equal to the value of output. Money flows to the household sector are the sum of the payments to the resource owners, including the payments to entrepreneurs. Money flows to firms are the revenue that firms receive when they sell the goods and services they produce. Revenue minus the costs of land, labor, and capital is profit. Profit represents the payment to entrepreneurs and other owners of corporations, partnerships, and sole proprietorships. In this simple economy, household income is equal to business revenue—the value of goods and services produced.

5.b. Households, Firms, and the International Sector

Figure 14 includes foreign countries in the circular flow. To simplify the circular flow diagram, let's assume that households are not directly engaged in international trade and that only business firms are buying and selling goods and services across international borders. This assumption is not far from the truth for the industrial countries and for many developing countries. We typically buy a foreign-made product from a local business firm rather than directly from the foreign producer.

A line labeled "net exports" connects firms and foreign countries in Figure 14, as well as a line labeled "payments for net exports." Notice that neither line has an arrow indicating the direction of flow as do the other lines in the diagram. The reason is that net exports of the home country may be either positive (a trade surplus) or negative (a trade deficit). When net exports are positive, there is a net flow of goods from the firms of the home country to foreign countries and a net flow of money from foreign countries to the firms of the home country. When net exports are negative, the opposite occurs. A trade deficit involves net flows of goods from foreign countries to the firms of the home country and net money flows from the domestic firms to the foreign countries. If exports and imports are equal, net exports are zero because the value of exports is offset by the value of imports.

Figure 14 shows the circular flow linking the private sectors of the economy. This model is a simplified view of the world, but it highlights the important interrelationships. The value of output equals income, as always; but spending may be for foreign as well as domestic goods. Domestic firms may produce for foreign as well as domestic consumption.

RECAP

1. The circular flow diagram illustrates how the main sectors of the economy fit together.
2. The circular flow diagram shows that the value of output is equal to income.

Copyright © by Houghton Mifflin Company. All rights reserved.

Figure 14
The Circular Flow: Households, Firms, and Foreign Countries

The diagram assumes that households are not directly engaged in international trade. The flow of goods and services between countries is represented by the line labeled "net exports." Neither the net exports line nor the line labeled "payments for net exports" has an arrow indicating the direction of the flow because the flow can go from the home country to foreign countries or vice versa. When the domestic economy has positive net exports (a trade surplus), goods and services flow out of the domestic firms toward foreign countries and money payments flow from the foreign countries to the domestic firms. With negative net exports (a trade deficit), the reverse is true.

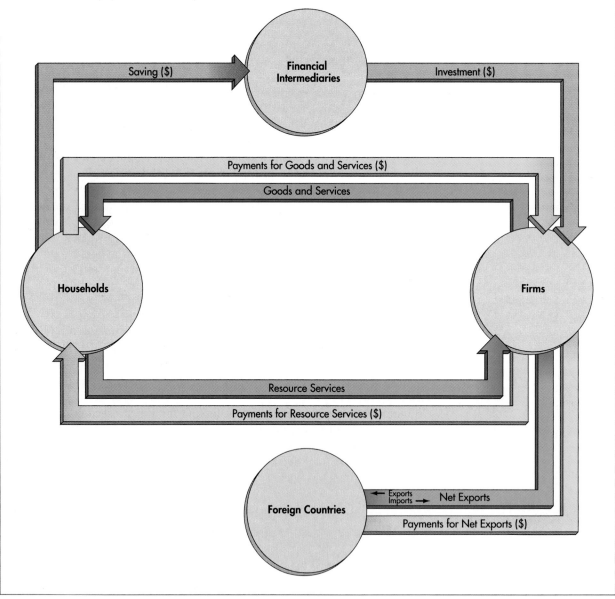

Copyright © by Houghton Mifflin Company. All rights reserved.

SUMMARY

Copyright © by Houghton Mifflin Company. All rights reserved.

▰▰▰ In a market system, who decides what goods and services are produced?

1. In a market system, consumers are sovereign and decide by means of their purchases what goods and services will be produced. §1.a

▰▰▰ How are goods and services produced?

2. In a market system, firms decide how to produce the goods and services that consumers want. In order to earn maximum profits, firms use the least-cost combinations of resources. §1.c

▰▰▰ Who obtains the goods and services that are produced?

3. Income and prices determine who gets what in a market system. Income is determined by the ownership of resources. §1.d

▰▰▰ What is a household, and what is household income and spending?

4. A household consists of one or more persons who occupy a unit of housing. §2

5. Household spending is called *consumption* and is the largest component of spending in the economy. §2.b

▰▰▰ What is a business firm, and what is business spending?

6. A business firm is a business organization controlled by a single management. §3

7. Businesses may be organized as sole proprietorships, partnerships, or corporations. §3.a

8. Business investment spending—the expenditure by business firms for capital goods—fluctuates a great deal over time. §3.e

▰▰▰ How does the international sector affect the economy?

9. The international trade of the United States occurs predominantly with the other industrial economies. §4.a

10. Exports are products sold to the rest of the world. Imports are products bought from the rest of the world. §4.a.2

11. Exports minus imports equals net exports. Positive net exports mean that exports are greater than imports and a trade surplus exists. Negative net exports mean that imports exceed exports and a trade deficit exists. §4.b

▰▰▰ How do the three private sectors—households, businesses, and the international sector—interact in the economy?

12. The resources combined to produce goods and services are also known as factors of production. They consist of land, labor, capital, and entrepreneurial ability. §5.a

13. The total value of output produced by the factors of production is equal to the income received by the owners of the factors of production. §5.a

KEY TERMS

consumer sovereignty §1.a

private sector §1.d

public sector §1.d

household §2

consumption §2.b

business firm §3

sole proprietorship §3.a

partnership §3.a

corporation §3.a

multinational business §3.a

investment §3.e

imports §4.a.2

exports §4.a.2

trade surplus §4.b

trade deficit §4.b

net exports §4.b

financial intermediaries §5.a

circular flow diagram §5.a

EXERCISES

1. What is consumer sovereignty? What does it have to do with determining what goods and services are produced? Who determines how goods and services are produced? Who receives the goods and services in a market system?

2. Is a family a household? Is a household a family?

3. What is the median value of the following series?
4, 6, 8, 3, 9, 10, 10, 1, 5, 7, 12

4. Which sector (households, business, or international) spends the most? Which sector spends the least? Which sector, because of volatility, has importance greater than is warranted by its size?

5. What does it mean if net exports are negative?

6. Why does the value of output always equal the income received by the resources that produced the output?

7. Total spending in the economy is equal to consumption plus investment plus government spending plus net exports. If households want to save and thus do not use all of their income for consumption, what will happen to total spending? Because total spending in the economy is equal to total income and output, what will happen to the output of goods and services if households want to save more?

8. People sometimes argue that imports should be limited by government policy. Suppose a government quota on the quantity of imports causes net exports to rise. Using the circular flow diagram as a guide, explain why total expenditures and national output may rise after the quota is imposed. Who is likely to benefit from the quota? Who will be hurt?

9. Draw the circular flow diagram linking households, business firms, and the international sector. Use the diagram to explain the effects of a decision by the household sector to increase saving.

10. Suppose there are three countries in the world. Country A exports $11 million worth of goods to country B and $5 million worth of goods to country C; country B exports $3 million worth of goods to country A and $6 million worth of goods to country C; and country C exports $4 million worth of goods to country A and $1 million worth of goods to country B.

    a. What are the net exports of countries A, B, and C?

    b. Which country is running a trade deficit? A trade surplus?

11. Over time, there has been a shift away from outdoor drive-in movie theaters to indoor movie theaters. Use supply and demand curves to illustrate and explain how consumers can bring about such change when tastes change.

12. Figure 3 indicates that the youngest and the oldest households have the lowest household incomes. Why should middle-aged households have higher incomes than the youngest and oldest?

13. The chapter provides data indicating that there are many more sole proprietorships than corporations or partnerships. Why are there so many sole proprietorships? Why is the revenue of the average sole proprietorship less than that of the typical corporation?

14. List the four sectors of the economy along with the type of spending associated with each sector. Order the types of spending in terms of magnitude and give an example of each kind of spending.

15. The circular flow diagram of Figure 14 excludes the government sector. Draw a new version of the figure that includes this sector with government spending and taxes added to the diagram. Label your new figure and be sure to include arrows to illustrate the direction of flows.

Copyright © by Houghton Mifflin Company. All rights reserved.

 **INTERNET EXERCISE**

Figure 11 in this chapter showed how U.S. international trade is distributed across countries. Use the internet to update the information in the figure. Go to the Boyes/Melvin web site at **http://** **www.hmco.com/college/** and click on the internet exercise link for this chapter. Now answer the questions that appear on the web page.

Copyright © by Houghton Mifflin Company. All rights reserved.

Public Pressure on Tabloids Rises

LONDON—Britain's press watchdog commission is investigating the behavior of international photographers accused of playing a role in the crash that killed Princess Diana and whose intrusive pictures of her filled Fleet Street tabloids for years.

John Wakeham, chairman of the commission, said he has begun "urgent discussions with editors across the industry."

Meanwhile, PressWise, a media ethics group based in Bristol, England, called for a boycott of the national newspapers Saturday as a symbolic protest against invasive tactics by the press.

"It's a way of directing people's outrage, rather than passing new laws, because you usually get bad law in those circumstances," said Mike Jempson, executive director of the group, which advises people who think they've been harassed by the press.

Editors of London newspapers aren't talking publicly about the attack on the press. "We don't believe the issue of the industry is the correct subject to chew over before the princess is buried," says Nick Fullagar, spokesman for the Mirror Group, which owns the Mirror, a Diana-obsessed tabloid with a daily circulation of 2.3 million copies.

In their editorials, most of the big newspapers have urged caution in assigning blame for the crash. And they're playing up the details coming out of Paris that indicated the princess's driver was drunk and may have taunted pursuing photographers. The Sun, criticized for running intrusive photos of Diana in the past, filled its front page Tuesday with the giant headline "Drunk at 121MPH" and a picture of the princess's wrecked car.

Meanwhile, the face that launched a thousand front pages continues to sell papers and is likely to do so until long after her funeral on Saturday.

Monday's Sun, featuring a dignity-drenched color shot of her royal standard-draped coffin on the shoulders of uniformed pallbearers, sold 1 million more copies than its usual 4 million press run, press-watchers said. The Mirror and the Daily Mail also sold 25% to 30% more than their usual 2 million-plus, according to reports.

PressWise called on the papers to give up their profits from the extra sales. "They would do much to improve their standing in the public's eyes if they donated their extra profits to the (newly created) Princess Diana Fund," Jempson says.

The consensus of politicians and pundits here seems to be that the press should restrain itself by refusing to buy invasive photos of the rich and royal—such as those taken of the wreckage with the dying Diana still inside.

Says Jempson, "I think there will be rather more judicious coverage for the time being—or at least until the next sensation."

Source: Copyright © 1997, *USA Today*. Reprinted with permission.

Copyright © by Houghton Mifflin Company. All rights reserved.

USA Today/September 3, 1997

COMMENTARY

Standing in line at the grocery store you notice the headlines on the tabloid, "Aliens take body of Roseanne" and you wonder how anyone could pay for these tabloids. Some people not only wonder about that but, as this article notes, think that these tabloids are invading the privacy of citizens. As the article states, media ethics organizations are actively lobbying for change in the aftermath of Princess Diana's death. Who determines whether these newspapers and magazines are appropriate or not? Who defines whether the tabloids are pulling us into the sewer?

In a market system, it is consumers who determine whether the magazines and newspapers exist. If the producers of the newspapers and magazines can not cover their costs with their revenues from sales and advertisements, then the producers will change what they do. They will either alter the coverage or presentation of stories or they will get out of the business altogether.

In a market system, products are provided if they result in a profit to producers. This means the customer must be willing and able to pay for them. If stories about baseball have no interest to readers, then consumers will not purchase magazines that focus on baseball. As a result, magazines will have to alter what they do present in order to attempt to retain their sales. *Sports Illustrated* has to have stories about other sports, swimsuits, and other topics instead of baseball. If sports magazines can not write about baseball because major league baseball does not exist, then those consumers who want to read primarily about baseball will not purchase the magazines.

If people do not want to read tabloids and they are unwilling to purchase the newspapers, then the tabloids will not exist. Only if people are willing and able to pay the price sufficient for the newspaper publishers to make a profit will the newspapers be published. No one is forcing anyone to read the tabloids.

Suppose that the market for tabloids is represented in the demand and supply diagram shown below. Suppose that for some reason, perhaps the tragedy of Princess Diana's death, that the willingness to purchase tabloids decreases. This is illustrated by an inward shift of the demand curve, from D_1 to D_2. The magazine and newspaper prices will decline, from P_1 to P_2. In addition, fewer magazines and newspapers are purchased—quantity sold falls from Q_1 to Q_2.

A decline in sales of the tabloids is not necessarily a good or a bad thing. All it really is, is a change in tastes and preferences and a shift of the demand curve. For some reason, people are not willing and able to purchase as many of the tabloids as they did before. There is no "good" or "bad" to this fact. It is simply a positive statement.

The lesson here is that the consumer does reign supreme in a market system. No profit-maximizing firm will ignore customer desires. Firms may try new cost-reducing approaches or revenue enhancing techniques, but whether the tabloids are published depends on whether customers are willing and able to buy them.

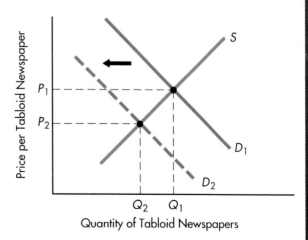

Copyright © by Houghton Mifflin Company. All rights reserved.

5

The Public Sector

Copyright © by Houghton Mifflin Company. All rights reserved.

FUNDAMENTAL QUESTIONS

1. How does the government interact with the other sectors of the economy?

2. What is the economic role of government?

3. Why is the public sector such a large part of a market economy?

4. What does the government do?

5. How do the sizes of public sectors in various countries compare?

Copyright © by Houghton Mifflin Company. All rights reserved.

From conception to death, we are affected by the activities of the government. Many mothers receive prenatal care through government programs. We are born in hospitals that are subsidized or run by the government. We are delivered by doctors who received training in subsidized colleges. Our births are recorded on certificates filed with the government. Ninety percent of us attend public schools. Many of us live in housing that is directly subsidized by the government or whose mortgages are insured by the government. Most of us at one time or another put savings into accounts that are insured by the government. Virtually all of us, at some time in our lives, receive money from the government—from student loan programs, unemployment compensation, disability insurance, social security, or Medicare. Twenty percent of the work force is employed by the government. The prices of wheat, corn, sugar, and dairy products are controlled or strongly influenced by the government. The prices we pay for cigarettes, alcohol, automobiles, utilities, water, gas, and a multitude of other goods are directly or indirectly influenced by the government. We travel on

public roads and publicly subsidized or controlled airlines, airports, trains, and ships. Our legal structure provides a framework in which we all live and act; the national defense ensures our rights of citizenship and protects our private property. By law, the government is responsible for employment and the general health of the economy.

According to virtually any measure, government in the United States has been a growth industry since 1930. The number of people employed by the local, state, and federal governments combined grew from 3 million in 1930 to over 19 million today; there are now more people employed in government than there are in manufacturing. Annual expenditures by the federal government rose from $3 billion in 1930 to approximately $1.7 trillion today, and total government (federal, state, and local) expenditures now equal about $2.3 trillion annually. In 1929, government spending constituted less than 2.5 percent of total spending in the economy. Today, it is around 20 percent. The number of rules and regulations created by the government is so large that it is measured by the number of telephone-book-sized pages needed just to list them, and that number is more than 67,000. The cost of all federal rules and regulations is estimated to be somewhere between $4,000 and $17,000 per U.S. household each year, and the number of federal employees required to police these rules is about 125,000.

There is no doubt that the government (often referred to as the *public sector*) is a major player in the United States economy. But in the last few chapters we have been learning about the market system and how well it works. If the market system works so well, why is the public sector such a large part of the economy? In this chapter we discuss the public sector and the role government plays in a market economy. ■

1. THE CIRCULAR FLOW

How does the government interact with the other sectors of the economy?

Government in the United States exists at the federal, state, and local levels. Local government includes county, regional, and municipal units. Economic discussions tend to focus on the federal government because national economic policy is set at that level. Nevertheless, each level affects us through its taxing and spending decisions, and laws regulating behavior.

To illustrate how the government sector affects the economy, let's add government to the circular flow model presented in the previous chapter. Government at the federal, state, and local levels interacts with both households and firms. Because the government employs factors of production to produce government services, households receive payments from the government in exchange for the services of the factors of production. The flow of resource services from households to government is illustrated by the blue-green line flowing from the households to government in Figure 1. The flow of money from government to households is shown by the gold line flowing from government to households. We assume that government, like a household, does not trade directly with foreign countries but obtains foreign goods from domestic firms who do trade with the rest of the world.

Households pay taxes to support the provision of government services, such as national defense, education, and police and fire protection. In a sense, then, the household sector is purchasing goods and services from the government as well as from private businesses. The flow of tax payments from households and businesses to government is illustrated by the gold lines flowing from households and businesses to government, and the flow of government services to households and businesses is illustrated by the purple lines flowing from government.

The addition of government brings significant changes to the model. Households have an additional place to sell their resources for income, and businesses have an additional market for goods and services. The value of *private* production no longer equals the value of household income. Households receive income from government in exchange for providing resource services to government. The total value of output in the economy is equal to the total income received, but government is included as a source of income and a producer of services.

RECAP

1. The circular flow diagram illustrates how the main sectors of the economy fit together.

2. Government interacts with both households and firms. Households get government services and pay taxes; they provide resource services and receive income. Firms sell goods and services to government and receive income.

Copyright © by Houghton Mifflin Company. All rights reserved.

Copyright © by Houghton Mifflin Company. All rights reserved.

Figure 1
The Circular Flow: Households, Firms, Government, and Foreign Countries
The diagram assumes that households and government are not directly engaged in international trade. Domestic firms trade with firms in foreign countries. The government sector buys resource services from households and goods and services from firms. This government spending represents income for the households and revenue for the firms. The government uses the resource services and goods and services to provide government services for households and firms. Households and firms pay taxes to the government to finance government expenditures.

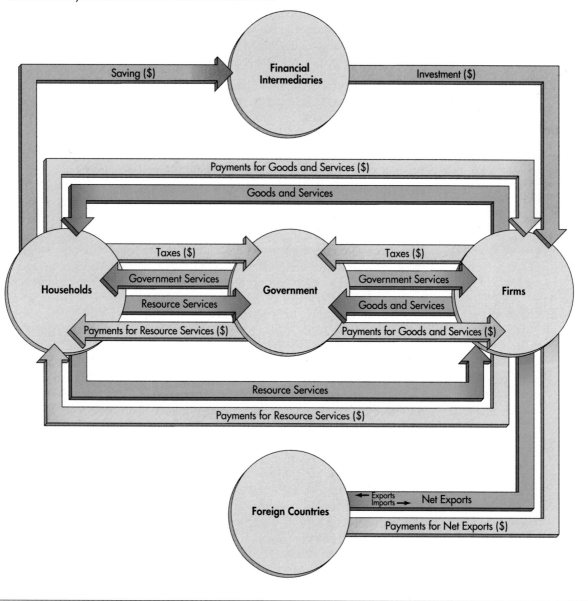

2. THE ROLE OF GOVERNMENT IN THE MARKET SYSTEM

We have learned that consumers use their limited incomes to buy the goods and services that give them the greatest satisfaction; that resource owners offer the services of their resources to the highest bidder; and that firms produce the

What is the economic role of government?

goods and services and use the resources that enable them to generate the highest profits. In other words, everyone—consumers, firms, resource suppliers—attempts to get the most benefits for the least cost.

This apparently narrow, self-interested behavior is converted by the market into a social outcome in which no one can be made better off without making someone else worse off. Any resource allocation that could make someone better off and no one any worse off would increase efficiency. When all such allocations have been realized, so that the *only* way to make one person better off would harm someone else, then we have realized the best allocation society can achieve. As Adam Smith noted in 1776, self-interested individuals, wholly unaware of the effects of their actions, act as if driven by an *invisible hand* to produce the greatest social good.

2.a. Government as the Guardian of Efficiency

economic efficiency:
a situation where no one in society can be made better off without making someone else worse off

technical efficiency:
producing at a point on the PPC

Economic efficiency is the name given to the events described by Adam Smith. Efficiency can mean many things to many different people. Even within economics there are different definitions of efficiency. We have already talked about the production possibilities curve and efficiency; operating at a point on the PPC is called **productive** or **technical efficiency**. A firm is said to be operating efficiently when it produces a given quantity and quality of goods at the lowest possible cost. Consumers are said to be efficient when they are getting the greatest bang for the buck, using their scarce resources to get the greatest benefits. *Economic efficiency* encompasses all of these definitions of efficiency. When *one person cannot be made better off without harming someone else*, then we say economic efficiency prevails.

Somewhat amazingly, economic efficiency occurs in a market system simply through the self-interested individual actions of participants in that system. Efficiency is not the result of some despot controlling the economy and telling people what they can and cannot do. The market system results in efficiency because people own their resources and goods and will exchange their goods or resources for others only if the exchange makes them better off. The higher profits go, the more income is earned by people with entrepreneurial ability. In order to earn profits, entrepreneurs have to provide, at the lowest possible cost, the goods and services that consumers want and are able to buy. This means that the least-cost combination of resources is used by each firm, but it also means that resources are employed in their most highly valued uses. Any reallocation of resources results in a situation that is worse—some resources will not be used where they are most highly valued, and some consumers will be less satisfied with the goods and services they can purchase.

As we saw in the Preview, the government plays a significant role in the U.S. economy; governmental influence is even larger in other market economies and is especially large in a socialist economy like Cuba. Why, if the actions of individuals in the market system results in the best social outcome, does the government play such a large role?

Why is the public sector such a large part of a market economy?

There are two justifications given for the government's role in a market economy beyond ensuring private property rights. One is based on cases where the market may not always result in economic efficiency. The second is based on the idea that people who do not like the market outcome use the government to change the outcome. Sections 2.b through 2.f are brief discus-

Copyright © by Houghton Mifflin Company. All rights reserved.

sions of some cases where the market system may fail to achieve economic efficiency. Section 2.g is a brief discussion of cases where people manipulate the market outcome.

2.b. Information and the Price System

As you learned in Chapters 3 and 4, a market is a place or service that allows buyers and sellers to exchange information on what they know about a product, what buyers are willing and able to pay for a product, and what sellers want to receive in order to produce and sell a product. A market price is a signal indicating when more or less of a good is desired. When the market price rises, buyers know that the quantity demanded at the prior equilibrium price exceeded the quantity supplied.

A market price is only as good an indicator as the information that exists in the market. It takes time for people to gather information about a product. It takes time to go to a market and purchase an item. It takes time for producers to learn what people want and bring together the resources necessary to produce that product. Thus, people are not likely to be perfectly informed, nor will everyone have the same information. This means that not all markets will adjust instantaneously or even at the same speed to a change in demand or supply. It also means that some people may pay higher prices for a product than others pay. Some people may be swindled by a sharp operator, and some firms may fail to collect debts owed them.

market imperfection:
a lack of efficiency that results from imperfect information in the marketplace

When information is not perfect, **market imperfections** may result. As a result of market imperfections, least-cost combinations of resources may not be used, or resources may not be used where they have the highest value. Often in such cases, people have argued for the government to step in with rules and regulations concerning the amount of information that must be provided. The government requires, for example, that specific information be provided on the labels of food products, that warning labels be placed on cigarettes and alcohol products, and that statements about the condition of a used car be made available to buyers. The government also declares certain actions by firms or consumers to be fraudulent or illegal. It also tests and licenses pharmaceuticals and members of many professions—medical doctors, lawyers, beauticians, barbers, nurses, and others.

2.c. Externalities

The market system works efficiently only if the market price reflects the full costs and benefits of producing and consuming a particular good or service. Recall that people make decisions on the basis of their opportunity costs and the market price is a measure of what must be forgone to acquire some good or service. If the market price does not reflect the full costs, then decisions cannot reflect opportunity costs. For instance, when you use air conditioners, you contaminate the ozone layer with Freon but you don't pay the costs of that contamination. When you drive, you don't pay for all of the pollution created by your car. When you have a loud, late-night party, you don't pay for the distractions you impose on your neighbors. When firms dump wastes or create radioactive by-products, they don't pay the costs. When homeowners allow their properties to become rundown, they reduce the value of neighboring properties but they don't pay for the loss of value. When society is educated, it costs

Copyright © by Houghton Mifflin Company. All rights reserved.

less to produce signs, ballots, tax forms, and other information tools. Literacy enables a democracy to function effectively, and higher education may stimulate scientific discoveries that improve the welfare of society. When you acquire an education, however, you do not get a check in the amount of savings your education will create for society. All these side effects—some negative and some positive—which are not covered by the market price are called **externalities.**

externalities:
costs or benefits of a transaction that are borne by someone not directly involved in the transaction

Externalities are the costs or benefits of a market activity borne by someone who is not a direct party to the market transaction. When you drive, you pay only for gasoline and car maintenance. You don't pay for the noise and pollutants that your car emits. You also don't pay for the added congestion and delays that you impose on other drivers. Thus, the *market* price of driving understates the *full* cost of driving to society; as a result, people drive more frequently than they would if they had to pay the full cost.

The government is often called upon to intervene in the market to resolve externality problems. Government agencies, such as the Environmental Protection Agency, are established to set and enforce air quality standards, and taxes are imposed to obtain funds to pay for external costs or subsidize external benefits. Thus, the government provides education to society at below-market prices because the positive externality of education benefits everyone.

2.d. Public Goods

The market system works efficiently only if the benefits derived from consuming a particular good or service are available only to the consumer who buys the good or service. You buy a pizza, and only you receive the benefits of eating that pizza. What would happen if you weren't allowed to enjoy that pizza all by yourself? Suppose your neighbors have the right to come to your home when you have a pizza delivered and share your pizza. How often would you buy a pizza? There is no way to exclude others from enjoying the benefits of some of the goods you purchase. These types of goods are called **public goods,** and they create a problem for the market system.

public goods:
goods whose consumption cannot be limited only to the person who purchased the good

Radio broadcasts are public goods. Everyone who tunes in a station enjoys the benefits. National defense is also a public good. You could buy a missile to protect your house, but your neighbors, as well as you, would benefit from the protection it provided. A pizza, however, is not a public good. If you pay for it, only you get to enjoy the benefits. Thus, you have an incentive to purchase pizza. You don't have that incentive to purchase public goods. If you and I both benefit from the public good, who will buy it? I'd prefer that you buy it so that I receive its benefits at no cost. Conversely, you'd prefer that I buy it. The result may be that no one will buy it.

Fire protection provides a good example of the problem that occurs with public goods. Suppose that as a homeowner you have the choice of subscribing to fire protection services from a private firm or having no fire protection. If you subscribe and your house catches fire, the fire engines will arrive as soon as possible and your house may be saved. If you do not subscribe, your house will burn. Do you choose to subscribe? You might say to yourself that as long as your neighbors subscribe, you need not do so. The fact that your neighbors subscribe means that fires in their houses won't cause a fire in yours, and you do not expect a fire to begin in your house. If many people made decisions in this way, fire protection services would not be available because not enough people would subscribe to make the services profitable.

Copyright © by Houghton Mifflin Company. All rights reserved.

Government Creates a Market for Fishing Rights

There is no practical way to establish ownership rights of ocean fish stocks. Traditionally, fish have been free for the taking—a common pool resource. Theory teaches that such underpricing leads to overconsumption. In the halibut fisheries off Alaska, fishing fleets caught so many halibut that the survival of the stock was threatened. No single fishing boat had an incentive to harvest fewer fish since the impact on its own future catch would be minimal and others would only increase their take. This is an example of what is known as "the tragedy of the commons."

Officials tried limiting the length of the fishing season. But this effort only encouraged new capital investment such as larger and faster boats with more effective (and expensive) fishing equipment. In order to control the number of fish caught, the season was shortened in some areas from 4 months to 2 days by the early 1990s. Most of the halibut caught had to be frozen rather than marketed fresh, and halibut caught out of season had to be discarded.

In late 1992, the federal government proposed a new approach: assigning each fisherman a permit to catch a certain number of fish. The total number of fish for which permits are issued will reflect scientific estimates of the number of fish that can be caught without endangering the survival of the species. Also, the permits will be transferable—they can be bought and sold. By making the permits transferable, the system in effect creates a market where one did not exist previously. The proposed system will encourage the most profitable and efficient boats to operate at full capacity by buying permits from less successful boats, ensuring a fishing fleet that uses labor and equipment efficiently. Moreover, the transferable permits system establishes a market price for the opportunity to fish—a price that better reflects the true social cost of using this common resource.

Source: *Economic Report of the President*, 1993 (Washington, D.C.: U.S. Government Printing Office, 1993), p. 207.

private property right:
the limitation of ownership to an individual

free ride:
the enjoyment of the benefits of a good by a producer or consumer without having to pay for it

The problem with a public good is the communal nature of the good. No one has a **private property right** to a public good. If you buy a car, you must pay the seller an acceptable price. Once this price is paid, the car is all yours and no one else can use it without your permission. The car is your private property, and you make the decisions about its use. In other words, you have the private property right to the car. Public goods are available to all because no one individual owns them or has property rights to them.

When goods are public, people have an incentive to try to obtain a **free ride**—the enjoyment of the benefits of a good without paying for the good. Your neighbors would free-ride on your purchases of pizza if you didn't have the private property rights to the pizza. People who enjoy public radio and public television stations without donating money to them are getting free rides from those people who do donate to them. People who benefit from the provision of a good whether they pay for it or not have an incentive not to pay for it.

Typically, in the absence of private property rights to a good, people call on the government to claim ownership and provide the good. For instance, governments act as owners of police departments and specify how police services are used. The Economic Insight "Government Creates a Market for Fishing Rights" provides one example of government specifying private property rights.

Copyright © by Houghton Mifflin Company. All rights reserved.

2.e. Monopoly

monopoly:
a situation where there is only
one producer of a good

If only one firm produces a good that is desired by consumers, then that firm might produce a smaller amount of the good in order to charge a higher price. In this case, resources might not be used in their most highly valued manner and consumers might not be able to purchase the goods they desire. A situation where there is only one producer of a good is called a **monopoly**. The existence of a monopoly can imply the lack of economic efficiency. The government is often called on to regulate the behavior of firms that are monopolies or even to run the monopolies as government enterprises.

2.f. Business Cycles

business cycles:
fluctuations in the economy
between growth and stagnation

People are made better off by economic growth. Economic growth increases the number of jobs and draws people out of poverty and into the mainstream of economic progress. Economic stagnation, on the other hand, throws the relatively poor out of their jobs and into poverty. These fluctuations in the economy are called **business cycles**. People call on the government to protect them against the periods of economic ill health and to minimize the damaging effects of business cycles. Government agencies are established to control the money supply and other important parts of the economy, and government-financed programs are implemented to offset some of the losses that result during bad economic times. The U.S. Congress requires that the government provide economic growth and minimize unemployment. History has shown that this is easier said than done.

2.g. The Public Choice Theory of Government

The efficiency basis for government intervention in the economy discussed in sections 2.b through 2.f implies that the government is a cohesive organization functioning in much the same way that a benevolent dictator would. This organization intervenes in the market system only to correct the ills created by the market. Not all economists agree with this view of government. Many claim that the government is not a benevolent dictator looking out for the best interests of society, but is instead merely a collection of individuals who respond to the same economic impulses we all do—that is, the desire to satisfy our own interests.

Economic efficiency does not mean that everyone is as well off as he or she desires. Economic efficiency merely means that someone or some group cannot be made better off without harming some other person or group of people. People always have an incentive to attempt to make themselves better off. If their attempts result in the transfer of benefits to themselves and away from others, however, economic efficiency has not increased. Moreover, the resources devoted to enacting the transfer of benefits are not productive; they do not create new income and benefits but merely transfer income and benefits. Such activity is called **rent seeking**. Rent seeking refers to cases where people devote resources to attempting to create income transfers to themselves. Rent seeking includes the expenditures on lobbyists in Congress, the time and expenses that health-care professionals devote to fighting nationalized health care, the time and expenses farmers devote to improving their subsidies, and millions of other examples.

rent seeking:
the use of resources to transfer
income from one sector to
another

Copyright © by Houghton Mifflin Company. All rights reserved.

Copyright © by Houghton Mifflin Company. All rights reserved.

public choice:
the study of how government actions result from the self-interested behaviors of voters and politicians

A group of economists, referred to as **public choice** economists, argue that government is more the result of rent seeking than it is market failure. The study of public choice focuses on how government actions result from the self-interested behaviors of voters and politicians. Whereas the efficiency justification of government argues that it is only in cases where the market does not work that the government steps in, the public choice theory says that the government may be brought into the market system whenever someone or some group can benefit, even if efficiency is not served.

According to the public choice economists, price ceilings or price floors may be enacted for political gain rather than market failure; government spending or taxing policies may be enacted not to resolve a market failure but instead to implement an income redistribution from one group to another; government agencies such as the Food and Drug Administration may exist not to improve the functioning of the market but to enact a wealth transfer from one group to another. Each such instance of manipulation leads to a larger role for government in a market economy. Moreover, government employees have the incentive to increase their role and importance in the economy and therefore transfer income or other benefits to themselves.

The government sector is far from a trivial part of the market system. Whether the government's role is one of improving economic efficiency or the result of rent seeking is a topic for debate, and in later chapters we discuss this debate in more detail. For now, it is satisfactory just to recognize how important the public sector is in the market system and what the possible reasons for its prevalence are.

RECAP

1. The government's role in the economy may stem from the inefficiencies that exist in a market system.

2. The market system does not result in economic efficiency when there are market imperfections such as imperfect information or when the costs or benefits of the transaction are borne by parties not directly involved in the transaction. Such cases are called externalities. Also, the market system may not be efficient when private ownership rights are not well defined. The government is called upon to resolve these inefficiencies that exist in the market system.

3. The government is asked to minimize the problems that result from business cycles.

4. The public choice school of economics maintains that the government's role in the market system is more the result of rent seeking than of reducing market inefficiencies.

3. OVERVIEW OF THE UNITED STATES GOVERNMENT

What does the government do?

When Americans think of government policies, rules, and regulations, they typically think of Washington, D.C., because their economic lives are regulated and shaped more by policies made there than by policies made at the local and

TABLE 1
U.S. Government Economic Policymakers and Related Agencies

Institution	Role
Fiscal policymakers	
President	Provides leadership in formulating fiscal policy
Congress	Sets government spending and taxes and passes laws related to economic conduct
Monetary policymaker	
Federal Reserve	Controls money supply and credit conditions
Related agencies	
Council of Economic Advisers	Monitors the economy and advises the president
Office of Management and Budget	Prepares and analyzes the federal budget
Treasury Department	Administers the financial affairs of the federal government
Commerce Department	Administers federal policy regulating industry
Justice Department	Enforces legal setting of business
Comptroller of the Currency	Oversees national banks
International Trade Commission	Investigates unfair international trade practices
Federal Trade Commission	Administers laws related to fair business practices and competition

Copyright © by Houghton Mifflin Company. All rights reserved.

state levels. Who actually is involved in economic policymaking? Important government institutions that shape U.S. economic policy are listed in Table 1. This list is far from inclusive, but it includes the agencies with the broadest powers and greatest influence.

Economic policy involves macroeconomic issues like government spending and control of the money supply and microeconomic issues aimed at providing public goods like police and military protection, correcting externalities like pollution, and maintaining a competitive economy.

3.a. Microeconomic Policy

Government provides public goods to avoid the free-rider problem that would occur if private firms provided the goods.

One reason for government's microeconomic role is the free-rider problem associated with the provision of public goods. If an army makes all citizens safer, then all citizens should pay for it. But even if one person does not pay taxes, the army still protects this citizen from foreign attack. To minimize free riding, the government collects mandatory taxes to finance public goods.

The United States Congress plays an active role in setting U.S. fiscal policy through its power to control government spending and taxes.

Congress and the president determine the level of public goods needed and how to finance them.

Microeconomic policy also deals with externalities. Activities that cause air or water pollution impose costs on everyone. For instance, a steel mill may generate air pollutants that have a negative effect on the surrounding population. A microeconomic function of government is to internalize the externality—that is, to force the steelmaker to bear the full cost to society of producing steel. In addition to assuming the costs of hiring land, labor, and capital, the mill should bear the costs associated with polluting the air. Congress and the president determine which externalities to address and the best way of taxing or subsidizing each activity in order to ensure that the amount of the good produced and its price reflect the true value to society.

Government taxes or subsidizes some activities that create externalities.

Another of government's microeconomic roles is to promote competition. Laws to restrict the ability of business firms to engage in practices that limit competition exist and are monitored by the Justice Department and the Federal Trade Commission. Some firms, such as public utilities, are monopolies and face no competition. The government defines the output, prices, and profits of many monopolies. In some cases, the monopolies are government-run enterprises.

Government regulates industries where free market competition may not exist and polices other industries to promote competition.

3.b. Macroeconomic Policy

monetary policy:
policy directed toward control of money and credit

Federal Reserve:
the central bank of the United States

The focus of the government's macroeconomic policy is monetary and fiscal policy. **Monetary policy** is policy directed toward control of money and credit. The major player in this policy arena is the Federal Reserve, commonly called "the Fed." The **Federal Reserve** is the central bank of the United States. It serves as a banker for the U.S. government and regulates the U.S. money supply.

Copyright © by Houghton Mifflin Company. All rights reserved.

The Federal Reserve System is run by a seven-member Board of Governors. The most important member of the Board is the chairman, who is appointed by the president for a term of four years. The Board meets regularly (from ten to twelve times a year) with a group of high-level officials to review the current economic situation and set policy for the growth of U.S. money and credit. The Federal Reserve exercises a great deal of influence on U.S. economic policy.

fiscal policy:
policy directed toward government spending and taxation

Government has the responsibility of minimizing the damage from business cycles.

Fiscal policy, the other area of macroeconomic policy, is policy directed toward government spending and taxation. In the United States, fiscal policy is determined by laws that are passed by Congress and signed by the president. The relative roles of the legislative and executive branches in shaping fiscal policy vary with the political climate, but usually it is the president who initiates major policy changes. Presidents rely on key advisers for fiscal policy information. These advisers include Cabinet officers such as the secretary of the treasury and the secretary of state as well as the director of the Office of Management and Budget. In addition, the president has a Council of Economic Advisers made up of three economists—usually a chair, a macroeconomist, and a microeconomist—who, together with their staff, monitor and interpret economic developments for the president. The degree of influence wielded by these advisers depends on their personal relationship with the president.

3.c. Government Spending

Federal, state, and local government spending for goods and services is shown in Figure 2. Except during times of war in the 1940s and 1950s, federal expen-

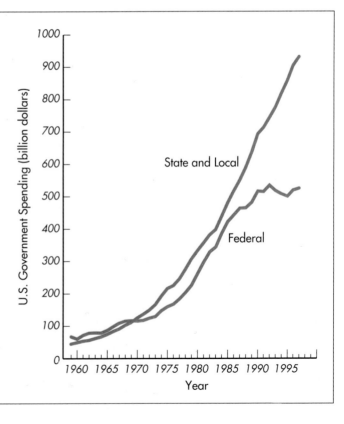

Figure 2
Federal, State, and Local Government Expenditures for Goods and Services
In the 1950s and early 1960s, federal government spending was above state and local government spending. In 1969, state and local expenditures rose above federal spending and have remained higher ever since. Source: Data are from the *Economic Report of the President, 1997* (Washington, D.C.: U.S. Government Printing Office, 1997).

Copyright © by Houghton Mifflin Company. All rights reserved.

ditures were roughly similar in size to state and local expenditures until 1969. Since 1969, state and local spending has been growing more rapidly than federal spending.

Combined government spending on goods and services is larger than investment spending but much smaller than consumption. In 1996, combined government spending was about $1,400 billion, investment spending was about $1,200 billion, and consumption was about $5,200 billion.

Besides government expenditures on goods and services, government also serves as an intermediary, taking money from some taxpayers and transferring this income to others. Such **transfer payments** are a part of total government expenditures, so that the total government budget is much larger than the expenditures on goods and services reported in Figure 2. In 1996, total expenditures of federal, state, and local government for goods and services was about $1,400 billion. In this same year, transfer payments paid by all levels of government were about $1,000 billion.

The magnitude of federal government spending relative to federal government revenue from taxes has become an important issue in recent years. Figure 3 shows that the federal budget was roughly balanced until the early 1970s. The budget is a measure of spending and revenue. A balanced budget occurs when federal spending is approximately equal to federal revenue. This was the case through the 1950s and 1960s. If federal government spending is less than tax revenue, a **budget surplus** exists. The U.S. government last had a budget surplus in 1969. By the early 1980s, federal government spending was much larger than revenue, so a large **budget deficit** existed. The federal budget deficit grew very rapidly to almost $280 billion by the early 1990s before beginning to drop.

transfer payments:
income transferred from a citizen, who is earning income, to another citizen by the government

budget surplus:
the excess that results when government spending is less than revenue

budget deficit:
the shortage that results when government spending is greater than revenue

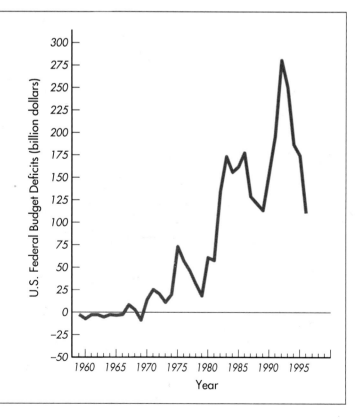

Figure 3
U.S. Federal Budget Deficits
The budget deficit is equal to the excess of government spending over tax revenue. If taxes are greater than government spending, a budget surplus (shown as a negative deficit) exists. The United States has run a budget deficit for all but two years in the period since 1959. Source: Data are from the *Economic Report of the President, 1997* (Washington, D.C.: U.S. Government Printing Office, 1997).

Copyright © by Houghton Mifflin Company. All rights reserved.

When spending is greater than revenue, the excess spending must be covered by borrowing, and this borrowing can have effects on investment and consumption as well as on economic relationships with other countries.

RECAP

1. The microeconomic functions of government include correcting externalities, redistributing income from high-income groups to lower-income groups, enforcing a competitive economy, and providing public goods.
2. Macroeconomic policy attempts to control the economy through monetary and fiscal policy.
3. The Federal Reserve conducts monetary policy. Congress and the president formulate fiscal policy.
4. Government spending is larger than investment spending but much smaller than consumption spending.
5. When government spending exceeds tax revenue, a budget deficit exists. When government spending is less than tax revenue, a budget surplus exists.

4. GOVERNMENT IN OTHER ECONOMIES

How do the sizes of public sectors in various countries compare?

centrally planned economy: an economic system in which the government determines what goods and services are produced and the prices at which they are sold

The government plays a role in every economy, and in most the public sector is a much larger part of the economy than it is in the United States. In some economies, referred to as **centrally planned,** or nonmarket, economies, the public sector is the principal component of the economy. There are significant differences between the market system and the centrally planned systems. In market economies, people can own businesses, be private owners of land, start new businesses, and purchase what they want as long as they can pay the price. They may see their jobs disappear as business conditions worsen, but they are free to take business risks and to reap the rewards if taking these risks pays off. Under centrally planned systems, people are not free to own property other than a house, a car, and personal belongings. They are not free to start a business. They work as employees of the state. Their jobs are guaranteed regardless of whether their employer is making the right or wrong decisions and regardless of how much effort they expend on the job. Even though they might have money in their pockets, they may not be able to buy many of the things they want. Money prices are often not used to ration goods and services, so people may spend much of their time standing in lines to buy the products available on the shelves of government stores. Waiting in line is a result of charging a money price lower than equilibrium and imposing a quantity limit on how much a person can buy. The time costs, along with the money price required to buy goods, will ration the limited supply.

The Soviet Union implemented a centrally planned economy in the 1920s, following its October 1917 revolution. During, and especially following, World War II, the Soviet system expanded into Eastern Europe, China, North Korea, and Vietnam. At the peak of Soviet influence, about one-third of the world's population lived in countries generally described as having centrally planned economic systems. The 1980s and 1990s ushered in a new world order, however. The Soviet Union's economy failed and ultimately led to the fall of the communist governments in Eastern Europe, the disintegration of the Soviet Union, the end of the Cold War, and the reunification of West and East Germany.

4.a. Overview of Major Market Economies

Figure 4 shows the size of government and the type of economy for several countries. The United States is representative of nations that are market economies with relatively small public sectors. Cuba is representative of nations that are primarily centrally planned. Germany, Japan, and the United Kingdom are market economies but the public sector plays a larger role than it does in the United States.

4.a.1. France
The public sector in France is much larger than it is in the United States. France is a market economy in which a national economic plan has been used to influence resource allocation. The French plan, however, does not order firms to do things. The plan is indicative; it offers suggested targets. The state uses its budget and its ownership of firms to attempt to further the implementation of the plan. Government ownership is concentrated in banking, coal, gas and electricity, transportation, and auto and aircraft production. The government-sector share of the economy is quite large; total government expenditures were nearly 50 percent of total output in 1996.

4.a.2. United Kingdom
The role of the public sector in the United Kingdom is significant but not exceptional by European standards. Great Britain is an island economy with a land area slightly greater than that of the state of Minnesota and a population of just over 58 million persons. The resource base of the economy is quite limited, and the British economy is tied very closely to other economies. The British concept of an appropriate role for the public sector in economic affairs is more limited than that prevailing in France.

Copyright © by Houghton Mifflin Company. All rights reserved.

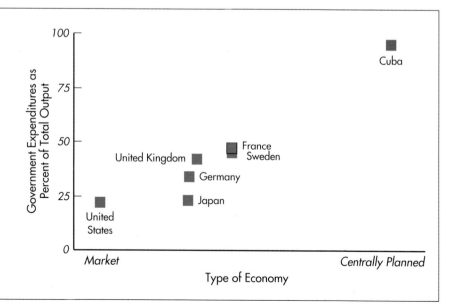

Figure 4
The Economic Systems
The closer a country is to a market economy without a public sector, the closer to the lower-left area of the diagram it is placed. Conversely, the more the country is a centrally planned economy, the closer to the upper-right area of the diagram it is placed.

The extent of government involvement in the economy varies from country to country. The government's role in the European economies is larger than it is in the United States. For instance, the French government owns Aerospatiale Usine Airbus, the Toulouse, France, firm that helps produce the airbus. The airbus is a direct competitor to private firms in the United States, Boeing and McDonnell-Douglas. As a result, many U.S. politicians and others associated with the aerospace industry have called on the U.S. government to provide some protection to the private firms in the U.S. that compete with the government enterprises or government-subsidized firms of other nations.

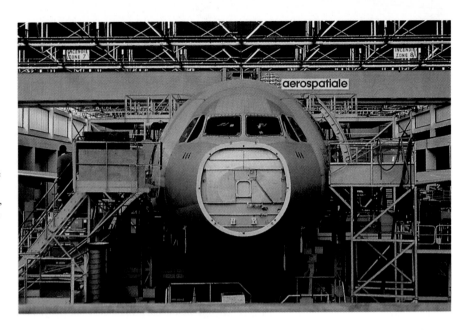

Government spending in 1996 was about 42 percent of total output in the United Kingdom.

4.a.3. Germany   There is no significant planning apparatus in Germany, and the public sector owns few businesses, but the public sector intervenes a great deal to foster social programs. For instance, the government regulates business hours, supports minimum prices for brand-name articles, imposes rent controls, regulates the hiring and firing of employees, regulates vacations, and has a series of other laws protecting workers and renters. State expenditures were about 34 percent of total output in 1996. The unification of the East and West German economies and the merging of two different types of systems has led to additional government intervention.

4.a.4. Japan   Japan is a capitalist economy whose postwar rate of economic growth is the highest among the major industrialized countries. Japan is a small country with adequate labor but generally limited supplies of natural resources and land. Like Great Britain, Japan is an island economy. With a population of approximately 126 million and a land area slightly smaller than that of the state of California, Japan is densely populated. The public sector appears on the surface to have a relatively small role in the Japanese economy: government spending as a percent of total output was only about 23 percent in 1996. But this statistic understates the reality. The public sector plays a very important role through the Japanese industrial families known as *keiretsu*. The government wields its influence on the keiretsu through various ministries. For example, the Ministry of International Trade and Industry (MITI) is responsible for international trade, domestic production, and domestic industrial structure. MITI guides and influences economic decisions by promoting key sectors of the economy and carefully phasing out other, low-productivity sectors. MITI uses government funds for research and development and to provide assistance for organizational change, such as mergers. Economic planning has not been an important element in the Japanese economy. Japan has had a planning agency since the late 1940s

Copyright © by Houghton Mifflin Company. All rights reserved.

and has assembled numerous plans, but the plans are neither binding nor involuntarily implemented.

4.a.5. Sweden The Swedish economic system and its performance are of interest because Sweden is viewed as a system that has been able, over an extended period of time, to sustain economic progress through the efficiency of the market while at the same time ensuring that incomes are equally distributed. Sweden is a relatively small but highly industrialized country. It has a total area of roughly 450,000 square kilometers (somewhat larger than the state of California) and a population of just over 8.8 million. Foreign trade is of vital importance to Sweden, accounting for more than 70 percent of its total output. The Swedish economy looks like a market economy in the production of goods and services, but the government accounts for nearly 45 percent of total purchases in Sweden.

RECAP

1. No economy is purely private. The public sector plays a role in every economy.

2. A market economy relies on prices and individual actions to solve economic problems. In centrally planned economies, the government decides what is produced, how it is produced, and who gets what.

SUMMARY

▰ How does the government interact with the other sectors of the economy?

1. The circular flow diagram illustrates the interaction among all sectors of the economy—households, businesses, the international sector, and the public sector. §1

▰ What is the economic role of government?

2. The market system results in economic efficiency. Economic efficiency means that in an economy one person cannot be made better off without harming someone else. §2.a

3. The market system does not result in economic efficiency when there are market imperfections, externalities, or public goods. Market imperfections occur when information is imperfect. §2.b–2.g

▰ Why is the public sector such a large part of a market economy?

4. Two general reasons are given for the government's participation in the economy: the government may resolve the inefficiencies that

occur in a market system, or the government may be the result of rent seeking. §2.b–2.g

5. Economic efficiency means that some people cannot be made better off without others being made worse off. Some people do not like the result of the market outcome and want to alter it. In such cases, resources are devoted to creating a transfer of income. This is called rent seeking. §2.g

▰ What does the government do?

6. The government carries out microeconomic and macroeconomic activities. The microeconomic activities include resolving market imperfections, externalities, and public goods problems. The macroeconomic activities are directed toward monetary and fiscal policy and minimizing disruptions due to business cycles. §3

7. Governments often provide public goods and services such as fire protection, police protection, and national defense. Governments place limits on what firms and consumers can do in

Copyright © by Houghton Mifflin Company. All rights reserved.

certain types of situations. Governments tax externalities or otherwise attempt to make price reflect the full cost of production and consumption. §3.a

8. Governments carry out monetary and fiscal policy to attempt to control business cycles. In the United States, monetary policy is the province of the Federal Reserve, and fiscal policy is up to the Congress and the president. §3.b

▭▭▭ How do the sizes of public sectors in various countries compare?

9. Market systems rely on the decisions of individuals. Centrally planned systems rely on the government to answer economic questions for all individuals. §4

10. The size and influence of the public sector ranges from the market economies of the United States and Canada to the centrally planned economy of Cuba. §4.a

KEY TERMS

economic efficiency §2.a

technical efficiency §2.a

market imperfection §2.b

externalities §2.c

public goods §2.d

private property right §2.d

free ride §2.d

monopoly §2.e

business cycles §2.f

rent seeking §2.g

public choice §2.g

monetary policy §3.b

Federal Reserve §3.b

fiscal policy §3.b

transfer payments §3.c

budget surplus §3.c

budget deficit §3.c

centrally planned economy §4

EXERCISES

1. Illustrate productive or technical efficiency using a production possibilities curve. Can you illustrate economic efficiency? Are you able to show the exact point where economic efficiency would occur?

2. Why would an externality be referred to as a market failure? Explain how your driving on a highway imposes costs on other drivers. Why is this an externality? How might the externality be resolved or internalized?

3. What is the difference between a compact disk recording of a rock concert and a radio broadcast of that rock concert? Why would you spend $12 on the CD but refuse to provide any support to the radio station?

4. "The American buffalo disappeared because they were not privately owned." Evaluate this statement.

5. Which of the following economic policies are the responsibility of the Federal Reserve? Congress and the president?

a. An increase in the rate of growth of the money supply

b. A decrease in the rate of interest

c. An increase in taxes on the richest 2 percent of Americans

d. A reduction in taxes on the middle class

e. An increase in the rate of growth of spending on health care

6. "The Department of Justice plans to file a lawsuit against major airlines, claiming they violated price-fixing laws by sharing plans for fare changes through a computer system, officials said Friday." This statement was reported in newspapers on December 12, 1992. Is this a microeconomic or macroeconomic policy?

7. People sometimes argue that imports should be limited by government policy. Suppose a government quota on the quantity of imports causes net exports to rise. Using the circular flow diagram as a guide, explain why total expenditures and national output may rise after

Copyright © by Houghton Mifflin Company. All rights reserved.

the quota is imposed. Who is likely to benefit from the quota? Who will be hurt? Explain why the government would become involved in the economy through its imposition of quotas.

8. Most highways are "free" ways: there is no toll charge for using them. What problem does free access create? How would you solve this?

9. Explain why the suggested government action may or may not make sense in each of the following scenarios.

a. People purchase a VCR with a guarantee provided by its maker, only to find that within a year the company has gone out of business. Consumers demand that the government provide the guarantee.

b. Korean microchip producers are selling the microchips at a price that is below the cost of making the microchips in the United States. The U.S. government must impose taxes on the Korean microchips imported into the United States.

c. The economy has slowed down, unemployment has risen, and interest rates are high. The government should provide jobs and force interest rates down.

d. Fully 15 percent of all United States citizens are without health insurance. The government must provide health care for all Americans.

e. The rising value of the dollar is making it nearly impossible for U.S. manufacturers to sell their products to other nations. The government must decrease the value of the dollar.

f. The rich got richer at a faster rate than the poor got richer during the 1990s. The government must increase the tax rate on the rich to equalize the income distribution.

g. The AIDS epidemic has placed such a state of emergency on health care that the only solution is to provide some pharmaceutical firm with a monopoly on any drugs or solutions discovered for HIV or AIDS.

10. Many nations of Eastern Europe are undergoing a transition from a centrally planned to a market economic system. An important step in the process is to define private property rights in countries where they did not exist before. What does this mean? Why is it necessary to have private property rights?

11. Using the circular flow diagram, illustrate the effects of an increase in taxes imposed on the household sector.

12. Using the circular flow diagram, explain how the government can continually run budget deficits, that is, spend more than it receives in revenue from taxes.

13. Suppose you believe that government is the problem, not the solution. How would you explain the rapid growth of government during the past few decades?

14. The government intervenes in the private sector by imposing laws that ban smoking in all publicly used buildings. As a result, smoking is illegal in bars, restaurants, hotels, dance clubs, and other establishments. Is such a ban justified by economics?

15. In reference to question 14, we could say that before a ban is imposed, the owners of businesses owned the private property right to the air in their establishments. As owners of this valuable asset they would ensure it is used to earn them the greatest return. Thus, if their customers desired nonsmoking, then they would provide nonsmoking environments. How then does the ban on smoking improve things? Doesn't it merely transfer ownership of the air from the business owners to the nonsmokers?

🖥 INTERNET EXERCISE

In section 3 of this chapter we learned about government budget deficits and surpluses. Use the internet to determine the current state of the federal and state and local government budgets. Go to the Boyes/Melvin web site at http://www.hmco. com/college/ and click on the internet exercise link for this chapter. Now answer the questions that appear on the web page.

Copyright © by Houghton Mifflin Company. All rights reserved.

The Cutting Edge: Breaking the Speed Barrier with the Regular Internet Congested, Research Scientists Are Busy Building Special Routes for Their Own Private Data Flow

When a flash flood of Mars Pathfinder enthusiasts threatened to overwhelm the Internet on the Fourth of July, a network manager at NASA's Ames Research Center in Silicon Valley quickly channeled the traffic off the regular Internet and onto a special, high-speed research network.

There the river of digital bits instantly swelled to 20 megabits per second—more than triple the capacity of the normal network connection to the Mars Web site at the Jet Propulsion Laboratory in Pasadena, though still only a fraction of what the experimental network could carry. In the days that followed, JPL's Web site attracted more than 400 million "hits," and 1 million people downloaded images, audio and video.

Few people had any reason to know their timely connections were made possible by advanced Internet technology normally reserved for a select group of university researchers and supercomputer users. But NASA's experimental Research and Education Network, or NREN, is just one of a series of projects supporting continued innovation in Internet technology—and assuring that the scientific community has access to the high-speed networks it needs.

The Internet, of course, was originally built for scientists and engineers. But the explosion in the commercial use of the network over the last several years has created congestion so severe that the Internet today is useless for much advanced research. And the private sector, which took over operation of the Internet "backbone" from the National Science Foundation in 1994, has not done a good job of pushing network technology forward, federal officials say. . . .

The new push for advanced networking research and development efforts reflects a surprising change of heart about the relationship between the federal government and the Internet. When the Internet backbone was first privatized, it was thought that commercial providers could handle the technological challenges by themselves, under the spur of market competition.

Now, though, any thought that industry on its own will develop the next wave of Internet-networking technology has been abandoned, federal officials say.

Moreover, they acknowledge that privatization of the Internet caused a slip in the development of new technology.

"There were research applications that were going begging for the lack of high-performance networks," said George Strawn, the National Science Foundation's division director for networking and communications research and infrastructure. "So we find ourselves developing high-performance networking and a new set of technologies for which it is not clear yet there is a business case." . . .

Source: "The Cutting Edge: Breaking the Speed Barrier: With regular Internet congested, research scientists are busy building special routes for their own private data flow," by Robert Lee Hotz. From *Los Angeles Times*, August 25, 1997, p. D1. Copyright © 1997, Los Angeles Times. Reprinted by permission.

Copyright © by Houghton Mifflin Company. All rights reserved.

The Los Angeles Times/August 25, 1997

COMMENTARY

The Internet is a world-wide communication system allowing computer users to transmit messages and information. As stated in the article, the Internet was started by the government and has been heavily subsidized by taxpayers since its inception. In 1994, the "backbone" of the Internet was "privatized," or turned over to business firms. There are two questions related to this article that seem particularly relevant in the context of this chapter: (1) Why was the Internet originally started by government rather than private enterprise? (2) What are the implications of privatization for Internet users and why is government funding now behind the development of new technology?

The answer to the first question may be found in several sections of this chaper. Section 2.b informs us that a well-functioning market economy depends on well-informed participants. The lower the cost of information, the more rapidly prices reflect changes in supply and demand and the better decisions firms and households are able to make. The Internet may be thought of as one way in which government has tried to improve the flow of information in the economy. Other ways that government has intervened in the marketplace to improve information includes requiring truthful advertising or labeling ingredients on food products.

Information is only part of the answer in building a case for government provision of the Internet. Section 2.c discusses the role of government in addressing externalities. The Internet was originally developed to allow researchers in academic institutions and government organizations to more efficiently communicate. Research and development provides beneficial externalities as new technologies are created that offer benefits to the economy at large. The provision of the Internet speeds the transmission of research efforts and allows researchers to accelerate the pace of discovery.

With the reasons just discussed for the government provision of the Internet, why was the Internet partially privatized? Section 2.d of this chapter discussed the difference between public goods and private goods. If there was no way to exclude potential Internet users from participating in the communication network, then we would consider the Internet a public good. However, it is not difficult to establish private property rights in the computer communication system; it is much like what occurs with the telephone. Given the ease of establishing private property rights and then charging user fees, the existence of a private Internet system is not difficult to establish. The reason why this privatization occurs is to increase the efficiency of the system and improve the quality of service. Service providers will compete for subscribers on the basis of price and quality of service. The end result is expected to be a more user friendly communication system.

The article informs us that privatization slowed the development of new Internet technology. This was probably a result of private business's not being able to capture the externalities generated by research and development expenditures. The "information superhighway" may be somewhat analogous to roads, which are better provided by government. In the United States, government has used taxpayer dollars to fund the construction of an interstate highway system along with local freeways and streets. The argument for the government provision of the roads is that everyone benefits from a more efficient transportation network so everyone should pay. A system of privately operated toll roads might not connect as easily and could isolate some would-be travelers. Similarly some argue that government should continue to operate the Internet as it has continued to operate the interstate highway system.

This article serves to remind us that there are few areas of government involvement in economic life that are not controversial.

Copyright © by Houghton Mifflin Company. All rights reserved.

Copyright © by Houghton Mifflin Company. All rights reserved.

II

Macroeconomic Basics

Copyright © by Houghton Mifflin Company. All rights reserved.

6

National Income Accounting

FUNDAMENTAL QUESTIONS

1. How is the total output of an economy measured?

2. Who produces the nation's goods and services?

3. Who purchases the goods and services produced?

4. Who receives the income from the production of goods and services?

5. What is the difference between nominal and real GDP?

6. What is a price index?

Copyright © by Houghton Mifflin Company. All rights reserved.

The Korean economy grew at an average rate of 8 percent per year from 1970 to 1996. This compares with an average rate of 2.5 percent per year in the United States over the same period. Still, the U.S. economy is much larger than the Korean economy and larger than the economies of the fifty largest developing countries combined. The *size* of an economy cannot be compared across countries without common standards of measurement. National income accounting provides these standards. Economists use this system to evaluate the economic condition of a country and to compare conditions across time and countries.

A national economy is a complex arrangement of many different buyers and sellers—of households, businesses, and government units—and of their interactions with the rest of the world. To assess the economic health of a country or to compare the performance of an economy from year to year, economists must be able to measure national output and real GDP. Without these data, policymakers cannot evaluate their economic policies. For instance, real GDP fell in the United States in 1980, 1981, 1982, and again in 1990–1991. This drop in real GDP was accompanied by widespread job loss and a general decline in the economic health of the country. As this information became known, political and economic debate centered on economic policies, on what should be done to stimulate the economy. Without real GDP statistics, policymakers would not have known there were problems, let alone how to go about fixing them. ■

1. MEASURES OF OUTPUT AND INCOME

How is the total output of an economy measured?

national income accounting: the framework that summarizes and categorizes productive activity in an economy over a specific period of time, typically a year

In this chapter we discuss gross domestic product, real GDP, and other measures of national productive activity by making use of the **national income accounting** system used by all countries. National income accounting provides a framework for discussing macroeconomics. Figure 1 reproduces the circular flow diagram you saw in Chapter 5. The lines connecting the various sectors of the economy represent flows of goods and services, and money expenditures (income). National income accounting is the process of counting the value of the flows between sectors and then summing them to find the total value of economic activity in an economy. National income accounting fills in the dollar values in the circular flow.

Copyright © by Houghton Mifflin Company. All rights reserved.

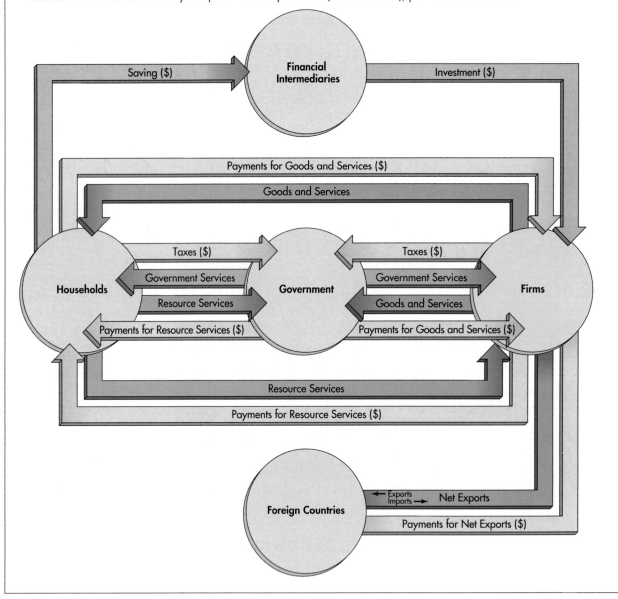

Figure 1
The Circular Flow: Households, Firms, Government, and Foreign Countries
The value of national output equals expenditures and income. If the domestic economy has positive net exports (a trade surplus), goods and services flow out of the domestic firms toward the foreign countries and money payments flow from the foreign countries to the domestic firms. If the domestic economy has negative net exports (a trade deficit), just the reverse is true.

National income accounting measures the output of an entire economy as well as the flows between sectors. It summarizes the level of production in an economy over a specific period of time, typically a year. In practice, the process *estimates* the amount of activity that occurs. It is beyond the capability of government officials to count every transaction that takes place in a modern economy. Still, national income accounting generates useful and fairly accurate measures of economic activity in most countries, especially wealthy industrial countries that have comprehensive accounting systems.

Copyright © by Houghton Mifflin Company. All rights reserved.

1.a. Gross Domestic Product

Copyright © by Houghton Mifflin Company. All rights reserved.

The most common measure of a nation's output is GDP.

Modern economies produce an amazing variety of goods and services. To measure an economy's total production, economists combine the quantities of oranges, golf balls, automobiles, and all the other goods and services produced, into a single measure of output. Of course, simply adding up the number of things produced—the number of oranges, golf balls, and automobiles—does not reveal the *value* of what is being produced. If a nation produces 1 million more oranges and 1 million fewer automobiles this year than it did last year, the total number of things produced remains the same. But because automobiles are much more valuable than oranges, the value of output has dropped substantially. Prices reflect the value of goods and services in the market, so economists use the money value of things to create a measure of total output, a measure that is more meaningful than the sum of units produced.

The most common measure of a nation's output is gross domestic product. **Gross domestic product (GDP)** is the market value of all final goods and services produced in a year within a country's borders. A closer look at three parts of this definition—*market value, final goods and services,* and *produced in a year*—will make clear what the GDP does and does not include.

gross domestic product (GDP):
the market value of all final goods and services produced in a year within a country

Market value   The *market value* of final goods and services is their value at market price. The process of determining market value is straightforward where prices are known and transactions are observable. However, there are cases where prices are not known and transactions are not observable. For instance, illegal drug transactions are not reported to the government, which means they are not included in GDP statistics. In fact, almost any activity that is not traded in a market is not included. For example, production that takes place in households, such as homemakers' services (as discussed in the Economic Insight "The Value of Homemaker Services"), is not counted, nor are unreported barter and cash transactions. For instance, if a lawyer has a sick dog and a veterinarian needs some legal advice, by trading services and not reporting the activity to the tax authorities, each can avoid taxation on the income that would have been reported had they sold their services to each other. If the value of a transaction is not recorded as taxable income, it generally does not appear in the GDP. There are some exceptions, however. Contributions toward GDP are estimated for *in-kind wages,* nonmonetary compensation like room and board. GDP values also are assigned to the output consumed by a producer—for example, the home consumption of crops by a farmer.

Final goods and services   The second part of the definition of GDP limits the measure to *final goods and services,* the goods and services available to the ultimate consumer. This limitation avoids double-counting. Suppose a retail store sells a shirt to a consumer for $20. The value of the shirt in the GDP is $20. But the shirt is made of cotton that has been grown by a farmer, woven at a mill, and cut and sewn by a manufacturer. What would happen if we counted the value of the shirt at each of these stages of the production process? We would overstate the market value of the shirt.

intermediate good:
a good that is used as an input in the production of final goods and services

Intermediate goods are goods that are used in the production of a final product. For instance, the ingredients for a meal are intermediate goods to a restaurant. Similarly, the cotton and the cloth are intermediate goods in the production of the shirt. The stages of production of the $20 shirt are shown in

ECONOMIC INSIGHT

The Value of Homemaker Services

One way GDP underestimates the total value of a nation's output is by failing to record nonmarket production. A prime example is the work homemakers do. Of course, people are not paid for their work around the house, so it is difficult to measure the value of their output. But notice that we say *difficult,* not impossible. Economists can use several methods to assign value to homemaker services.

One is an opportunity cost approach. This approach measures the value of a homemaker's services by the forgone market salary the homemaker could have earned if he or she worked full time outside the home. The rationale is that society loses the output the homemaker would have produced in the market job in order to gain the output the homemaker produces in the home.

Another alternative is to estimate what it would cost to hire workers to produce the goods and services that the homemaker produces. For example, what would it cost to hire someone to prepare meals, iron, clean, and take care of the household? It has been estimated that the average homemaker spends almost 8 hours a day, 7 days a week, on household work. This amounts to over 50 hours a week. At a rate of $10 an hour, the value of the homemaker's services is over $500 a week.

Whichever method we use, two things are clear. The value of homemaker services to the household and the economy is substantial. And by failing to account for those services, the GDP substantially underestimates the value of the nation's output.

value added:
the difference between the value of output and the value of the intermediate goods used in the production of that output

Figure 2. The value-of-output axis measures the value of the product at each stage. The cotton produced by the farmer sells for $1. The cloth woven by the textile mill sells for $5. The shirt manufacturer sells the shirt wholesale to the retail store for $12. The retail store sells the shirt—the final good—to the ultimate consumer for $20.

Remember that GDP is based on the market value of final goods and services. In our example, the market value of the shirt is $20. That price already includes the value of the intermediate goods that were used to produce the shirt. If we add to it the value of output at every stage of production, we would be counting the value of the intermediate goods twice, and we would be overstating the GDP.

It is possible to compute GDP by computing the **value added** at each stage of production. Value added is the difference between the value of output and the value of the intermediate goods used in the production of that output. In Figure 2, the value added by each stage of production is listed at the right. The farmer adds $1 to the value of the shirt. The mill takes the cotton worth $1 and produces cloth worth $5, adding $4 to the value of the shirt. The manufacturer uses $5 worth of cloth to produce a shirt it sells for $12, so the manufacturer adds $7 to the shirt's value. Finally, the retail store adds $8 to the value of the shirt: it pays the manufacturer $12 for the shirt and sells it to the consumer for $20. The sum of the value added at each stage of production is $20. The total value added, then, is equal to the market value of the final product.

Economists can compute GDP using two methods: the final goods and services method uses the market value of the final good or service; the value-added method uses the value added at each stage of production. Both methods count the value of intermediate goods only once. This is an important distinction: GDP is not based on the market value of *all* goods and services, but on the market value of all *final* goods and services.

Copyright © by Houghton Mifflin Company. All rights reserved.

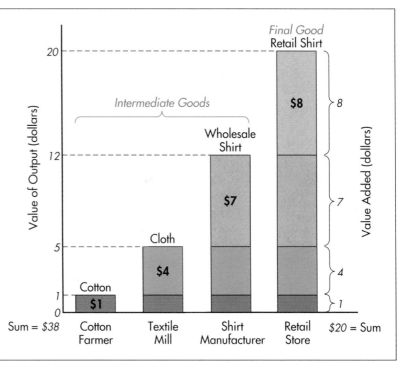

Figure 2
Stages of Production and Value Added in Shirt Manufacturing
A cotton farmer sells cotton to a textile mill for $1, adding $1 to the value of the final shirt. The textile mill sells cloth to a shirt manufacturer for $5, adding $4 to the value of the final shirt. The manufacturer sells the shirt wholesale to the retail store for $12, adding $7 to the value of the final shirt. The retail store sells the final shirt to a consumer for $20, adding $8 to the value of the final shirt. The sum of the prices received at each stage of production equals $38, which is greater than the price of the final shirt. The sum of the value added at each stage of production equals $20, which equals the market value of the shirt.

Copyright © by Houghton Mifflin Company. All rights reserved.

inventory:
the stock of unsold goods held by a firm

Produced in a year   GDP measures the value of output *produced in a year.* The value of goods produced last year is counted in last year's GDP; the value of goods produced this year is counted in this year's GDP. The year of production, not the year of sale, determines allocation to GDP. Although the value of last year's goods is not counted in this year's GDP, the value of services involved in the sale is. This year's GDP does not include the value of a house built last year, but it does include the value of the real estate broker's fee; it does not include the value of a used car, but it does include the income earned by the used-car dealer in the sale of that car.

To determine the value of goods produced in a year but not sold in that year, economists calculate changes in inventory. **Inventory** is a firm's stock of unsold goods. If a shirt that is produced this year remains on the retail store's shelf at the end of the year, it increases the value of the store's inventory. A $20 shirt increases that value by $20. Changes in inventory allow economists to count goods in the year in which they are produced whether or not they are sold.

Changes in inventory can be planned or unplanned. A store may want a cushion above expected sales (*planned inventory changes*), or it may not be able to sell all the goods it expected to sell when it placed the order (*unplanned inventory changes*). For instance, suppose Jeremy owns a surfboard shop, and he always wants to keep 10 surfboards above what he expects to sell. This is done so that in case business is surprisingly good, he does not have to turn away customers to his competitors and lose those sales. At the beginning of the year, Jeremy has 10 surfboards and then builds as many new boards during the year as he expects to sell. Jeremy *plans* on having an inventory at the end of the year of 10 surfboards. Suppose Jeremy expects to sell 100 surfboards during the year, so he builds 100 new boards. If business is surprisingly poor so that Jeremy sells only 80 surfboards, how do we count the 20 new boards that he made but did not sell? We count the change in his inventory. He started the year with 10 surfboards and ends the year with 20 more unsold boards for a year-end inventory of 30. The change in inventory of 20 (equal to the ending inventory of 30 minus the starting inventory of 10) represents output that is counted in GDP. In Jeremy's case, the inventory change is unplanned since he expected to sell the 20 extra surfboards that he has in his shop at the end of the year. But whether the inventory change is planned or unplanned, changes in inventory will count output that is produced but not sold in a given year.

1.a.1. GDP as Output

GDP is a measure of the market value of a nation's total output in a year. Remember that economists divide the economy into four sectors: households, businesses, government, and the international sector. Figure 1 shows how the total value of economic activity equals the sum of the output produced in each sector. Figure 3 indicates where the U.S. GDP is actually produced.[1] Since GDP counts the output produced in the United States, U.S. GDP is produced in business firms, households, and government located within the boundaries of the United States.

Not unexpectedly in a capitalist country, privately owned businesses account for the largest percentage of output: in the United States, 84 percent of the GDP is produced by private firms. Government produces 11 percent of the GDP, and households 5 percent.

Figure 3 defines GDP in terms of output: GDP is the value of final goods and services produced by domestic households, businesses, and government units. If some of the firms producing in the United States are foreign-owned, their output produced in the United States is counted in U.S. GDP.

1.a.2. GDP as Expenditures

The circular flow in Figure 1 shows not only the output of goods and services from each sector, but also the payment for goods and services. Here we look at GDP in terms of what each sector pays for the goods and services it purchases.

The dollar value of total expenditures—the sum of the amount each sector spends on final goods and services—equals the dollar value of output. In Chapter 4 you learned that household spending is called *consumption*. Households spend their income on goods and services to be consumed. Business spending is called *investment*. Investment is spending on capital goods that will be used to produce other goods and services. The two other components of total spending are *government spending* and *net exports*. Net exports are the value of *exports* (goods and services sold to the rest of the world) minus the value of *imports* (goods and services bought from the rest of the world).

GDP = consumption + investment + government spending + net exports

Or, in the shorter form commonly used by economists

$$GDP = C + I + G + X$$

where X is net exports.

---

[1] Due to rounding, percentages and dollar amounts in the next three figures will not add exactly to the totals given.

Who produces the nation's goods and services?

GDP is the value of final goods and services produced by domestic households, businesses, and government.

Who purchases the goods and services produced?

GDP = C + I + G + X

Copyright © by Houghton Mifflin Company. All rights reserved.

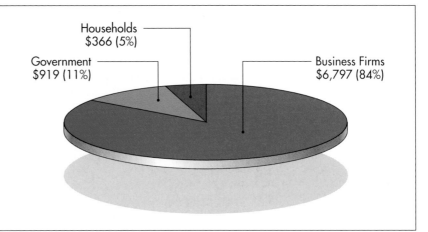

Figure 3
U.S. Gross Domestic Product by Sector, 1996 (billion dollars)
Business firms produce 84 percent of the U.S. GDP. Government produces 11 percent; households, 5 percent. Source: Data from Bureau of Economic Analysis.

Households
$366 (5%)

Government
$919 (11%)

Business Firms
$6,797 (84%)

Figure 4 shows the U.S. GDP in terms of total expenditures. Consumption, or household spending, accounts for 68 percent of national expenditures. Government spending represents 18 percent of expenditures, and business investment, 15 percent. Net exports are negative (-1 percent), which means that imports exceeded exports. To determine total national expenditures on *domestic* output, the value of imports, spending on foreign output, are subtracted from total expenditures.

1.a.3. GDP as Income   The total value of output can be calculated by adding up the expenditures of each sector. And because one sector's expenditures are another's income, the total value of output also can be computed by adding up the income of all sectors.

Business firms use factors of production to produce goods and services. Remember that the income earned by factors of production is classified as wages, interest, rent, and profits. *Wages* are payments to labor, including fringe benefits, social security contributions, and retirement payments. *Interest* is the net interest paid by businesses to households plus the net interest received from foreigners (the interest they pay us minus the interest we pay them). *Rent* is income earned from selling the use of real property (houses, shops, farms). Finally, *profits* are the sum of corporate profits plus proprietors' income (income from sole proprietorships and partnerships).

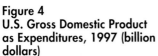

Who receives the income from the production of goods and services?

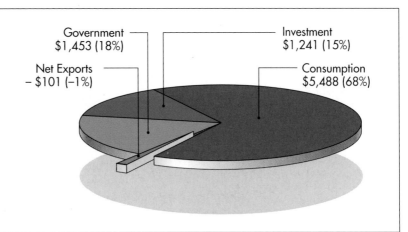

Figure 4
U.S. Gross Domestic Product as Expenditures, 1997 (billion dollars)
Consumption by households accounts for 68 percent of the GDP, followed by government spending of 18 percent, investment by business firms of 15 percent, and net exports of -1 percent. Source: Data from Bureau of Economic Analysis.

Government
$1,453 (18%)

Net Exports
$-$101 ($-1%$)

Investment
$1,241 (15%)

Consumption
$5,488 (68%)

Copyright © by Houghton Mifflin Company. All rights reserved.

Figure 5 shows the U.S. GDP in terms of income. Notice that wages account for 58 percent of the GDP. Interest and profits account for 5 percent and 10 percent of the GDP, respectively. Proprietors' income accounts for 7 percent. Rent (2 percent) is very small in comparison. *Net factor income from abroad* is income received from U.S.-owned resources located in other countries minus income paid to foreign-owned resources located in the United States. Since U.S. GDP refers only to income earned within U.S. borders, we must deduct this kind of income to arrive at GDP (−.2 percent).

Figure 5 includes two income categories that we have not discussed: capital consumption allowance and indirect business taxes. **Capital consumption allowance** is not a money payment to a factor of production; it is the estimated value of capital goods used up or worn out in production plus the value of accidental damage to capital goods. The value of accidental damage is relatively small, so it is common to hear economists refer to capital consumption allowance as **depreciation**. Machines and other capital goods wear out over time. The reduction in the value of capital stock due to its being used up or worn out over time is called depreciation. A depreciating capital good loses value each year of its useful life until its value is zero.

Even though capital consumption allowance does not represent income received by a factor of production, it must be accounted for in GDP as income. Otherwise the value of GDP measured as output would be higher than the value of the GDP as income. Depreciation is a kind of resource payment, part of the total payment to the owners of capital. All of the income categories—wages, interest, rent, profits, and capital consumption allowance—are expenses incurred in the production of output.

The last item in Figure 5 is indirect business taxes. **Indirect business taxes**, like capital consumption allowances, are not payments to a factor of production. They are taxes collected by businesses that then are turned over to the government. Both excise taxes and sales taxes are forms of indirect business taxes.

capital consumption allowance:
the estimated value of depreciation plus the value of accidental damage to capital stock

depreciation:
a reduction in the value of capital goods over time due to their use in production

indirect business tax:
a tax that is collected by businesses for a government agency

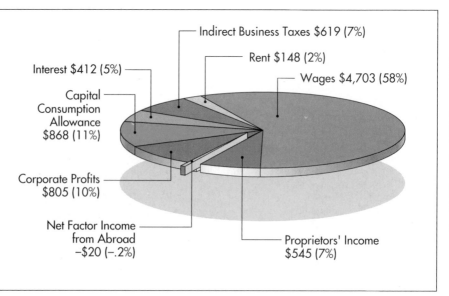

Figure 5
U.S. Gross Domestic Product as Income Received, 1997 (billion dollars)
The largest component of income is wages, at 58 percent of the GDP. Profits represent 10 percent, interest 5 percent, proprietors' income 7 percent, and rent 2 percent. Capital consumption allowance (11 percent) and indirect business taxes (7 percent) are not income received but still must be added; net factor income from abroad must be subtracted (−.2 percent). Source: Data from Bureau of Economic Analysis.

Indirect Business Taxes $619 (7%)
Rent $148 (2%)
Wages $4,703 (58%)
Interest $412 (5%)
Capital Consumption Allowance $868 (11%)
Corporate Profits $805 (10%)
Net Factor Income from Abroad −$20 (−.2%)
Proprietors' Income $545 (7%)

Copyright © by Houghton Mifflin Company. All rights reserved.

For example, suppose a motel room in Florida costs $80 a night. A consumer would be charged $90. Of that $90, the motel receives $80 as the value of the service sold; the other $10 is an excise tax. The motel cannot keep the $10; it must turn it over to the state government. (In effect, the motel is acting as the government's tax collector.) The consumer spends $90; the motel earns $80. To balance expenditures and income, we have to allocate the $10 difference to indirect business taxes.

GDP as income is equal to the sum of wages, interest, rent, profits, less net factor income from abroad, plus capital consumption allowance and indirect business taxes.

To summarize, GDP measured as income includes the four payments to the factors of production: wages, interest, rent, and profits. These income items represent expenses incurred in the production of GDP. To these we must subtract net factor income from abroad in order for the total to sum to GDP. Along with these payments are two nonincome items: capital consumption allowance and indirect business taxes.

GDP = wages + interest + rent + profits − net factor income from abroad + capital consumption allowance + indirect business taxes

GDP is the total value of output produced in a year, the total value of expenditures made to purchase that output, and the total value of income received by the factors of production. Because all three are measures of the same thing—GDP—all must be equal.

1.b. Other Measures of Output and Income

GDP is the most common measure of a nation's output, but it is not the only measure. Economists rely on a number of others in analyzing the performance of components of an economy.

gross national product (GNP):
gross domestic product plus receipts of factor income from the rest of the world minus payments of factor income to the rest of the world

1.b.1. Gross National Product Gross national product (GNP) equals GDP plus receipts of factor income from the rest of the world minus payments of factor income to the rest of the world. If we add to GDP the value of income earned by U.S. residents from factors of production located outside the United States and subtract the value of income earned by foreign residents from factors of production located inside the United States, we have a measure of the value of output produced by U.S.-owned resources—GNP.

Figure 6 shows the national income accounts in the United States. The figure begins with the GDP and then shows the calculations necessary to obtain the GNP and other measures of national output. In 1997, the U.S. GNP was $8,060.1 billion.

net national product (NNP):
gross national product minus capital consumption allowance

1.b.2. Net National Product Net national product (NNP) equals GNP minus capital consumption allowance. NNP measures the value of goods and services produced in a year less the value of capital goods that became obsolete or were used up during the year. Because NNP includes only net additions to a nation's capital, it is a better measure of the expansion or contraction of current output than is GNP. Remember how we defined GDP in terms of expenditures in section 1.a.2:

GDP = consumption + investment + government spending + net exports

gross investment:
total investment, including investment expenditures required to replace capital goods consumed in current production

The investment measure in GDP (and GNP) is called **gross investment**. Gross investment is total investment, which includes investment expenditures required to replace capital goods consumed in current production. NNP does not include investment expenditures required to replace worn-out capital

Copyright © by Houghton Mifflin Company. All rights reserved.

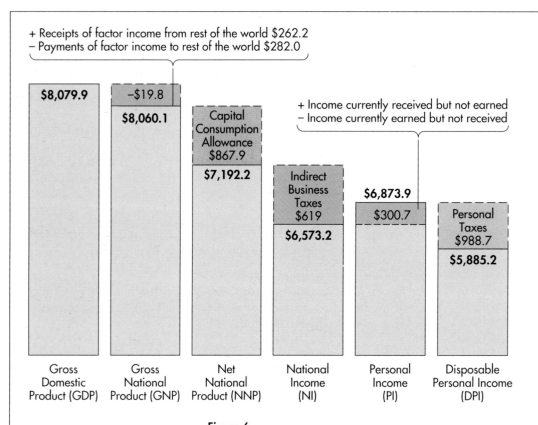

Figure 6
U.S. National Income Accounts, 1997 (billion dollars)
Gross domestic product plus receipts of factor income from the rest of the world minus payments of factor income to the rest of the world equals gross national product. Gross national product minus capital consumption allowance equals net national product. Net national product minus indirect business taxes equals national income. National income plus income currently received but not earned (transfer payments, personal interest, dividend income) minus income currently earned but not received (corporate profits, net interest, social security taxes) equals personal income. Personal income minus personal taxes equals disposable personal income. Source: Data from Bureau of Economic Analysis.

Copyright © by Houghton Mifflin Company. All rights reserved.

net investment:
gross investment minus capital consumption allowance

goods; it includes only net investment. **Net investment** is equal to gross investment minus capital consumption allowance. Net investment measures business spending over and above that required to replace worn-out capital goods.

Figure 6 shows that in 1997, the U.S. NNP was $7,192.2 billion. This means that the U.S. economy produced well over $7 trillion worth of goods and services above those required to replace capital stock that had depreciated. Over $867 billion in capital was "worn out" in 1997.

national income:
net national product minus indirect business taxes

1.b.3. National Income National income (NI) equals the NNP minus indirect business taxes, plus or minus a couple of other small adjustments. NI captures the costs of the factors of production used in producing output. Remember that GDP includes two nonincome expense items: capital consumption allowance

All final goods and services produced in a year are counted in GDP. For instance, the value of a rafting trip down the Colorado River through the Grand Canyon is part of the national output of the United States. The value of the rafting trip would be equal to the amount that travelers would have to pay the guide company in order to take the trip. This price would reflect the value of the personnel, equipment, and food provided by the guide company.

Copyright © by Houghton Mifflin Company. All rights reserved.

and indirect business taxes (section 1.a.3). Subtracting both of these items from the GDP leaves the income payments that actually go to resources.

Because the NNP equals the GNP minus capital consumption allowance, we can subtract indirect business taxes from the NNP to find NI, as shown in Figure 6. This measure helps economists analyze how the costs of (or payments received by) resources change.

personal income (PI):
national income plus income currently received but not earned, minus income currently earned but not received

transfer payment:
income transferred from one citizen, who is earning income, to another citizen, who may not be

1.b.4. Personal Income Personal income (PI) is national income adjusted for income that is received but not earned in the current year and income that is earned but not received in the current year. Social security and welfare benefits are examples of income that is received but not earned in the current year. As you learned in Chapter 5, they are called **transfer payments**. Transfer payments represent income transferred from one citizen, who is earning income, to another citizen, who may not be. The government transfers income by taxing one group of citizens and using the tax payments to fund the income for another group. An example of income that is currently earned but not received is profits that are retained by a corporation to finance current needs rather than paid out to stockholders. Another is social security (FICA) taxes, which are deducted from workers' paychecks.

disposable personal income (DPI):
personal income minus personal taxes

1.b.5. Disposable Personal Income Disposable personal income (DPI) equals personal income minus personal taxes—income taxes, excise and real estate taxes on personal property, and other personal taxes. DPI is the income that individuals have at their disposal for spending or saving. The sum of consumption spending plus saving must equal disposable personal income.

RECAP

1. Gross domestic product (GDP) is the market value of all final goods and services produced in an economy in a year.

2. GDP can be calculated by summing the market value of all final goods and services produced in a year, by summing the value added at each stage of production, by adding total expenditures on goods and services (GDP = consumption + investment + government spending + net exports), and by using the total income earned in the production of goods and services (GDP = wages + interest + rent + profits) and subtracting net factor income from abroad, and adding depreciation, and indirect business taxes.

3. Other measures of output and income include gross national product (GNP), net national product (NNP), national income (NI), personal income (PI), and disposable personal income (DPI).

National Income Accounts

GDP = consumption + investment + government spending + net exports

GNP = GDP + receipts of factor income from the rest of the world − payments of factor income to the rest of the world

NNP = GNP − capital consumption allowance

NI = NNP − indirect business taxes

PI = NI − income earned but not received + income received but not earned

DPI = PI − personal taxes

2. NOMINAL AND REAL MEASURES

What is the difference between nominal and real GDP?

GDP is the market value of all final goods and services produced within a country in a year. Value is measured in money terms, so the U.S. GDP is reported in dollars, the German GDP in marks, the Mexican GDP in pesos, and so on. Market value is the product of two elements: the money price and the quantity produced.

2.a. Nominal and Real GDP

nominal GDP:
a measure of national output based on the current prices of goods and services

real GDP:
a measure of the quantity of final goods and services produced, obtained by eliminating the influence of price changes from the nominal GDP statistics

Nominal GDP measures output in terms of its current dollar value. **Real GDP** is adjusted for changing price levels. In 1980, the U.S. GDP was $2,784 billion; in 1997, it was $8,079.9 billion—an increase of 190 percent. Does this mean that the United States produced 190 percent more goods and services in 1997 than it did in 1980? If the numbers reported are for nominal GDP, we cannot be sure. Nominal GDP cannot tell us whether the economy produced more goods and services, because nominal GDP changes when prices change *and* when quantity changes.

Real GDP measures output in constant prices. This allows economists to identify the changes in actual production of final goods and services: real GDP measures the quantity of goods and services produced after eliminating

Copyright © by Houghton Mifflin Company. All rights reserved.

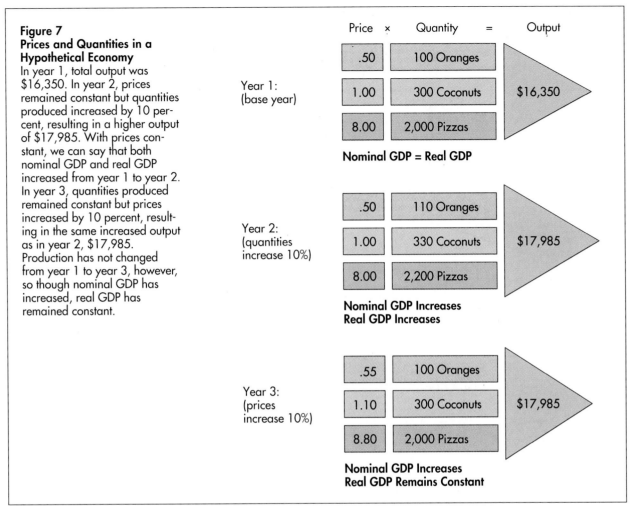

Figure 7
Prices and Quantities in a Hypothetical Economy
In year 1, total output was $16,350. In year 2, prices remained constant but quantities produced increased by 10 percent, resulting in a higher output of $17,985. With prices constant, we can say that both nominal GDP and real GDP increased from year 1 to year 2. In year 3, quantities produced remained constant but prices increased by 10 percent, resulting in the same increased output as in year 2, $17,985. Production has not changed from year 1 to year 3, however, so though nominal GDP has increased, real GDP has remained constant.

Price	×	Quantity	=	Output

Year 1:
(base year)

.50	100 Oranges	
1.00	300 Coconuts	$16,350
8.00	2,000 Pizzas	

Nominal GDP = Real GDP

Year 2:
(quantities increase 10%)

.50	110 Oranges	
1.00	330 Coconuts	$17,985
8.00	2,200 Pizzas	

Nominal GDP Increases
Real GDP Increases

Year 3:
(prices increase 10%)

.55	100 Oranges	
1.10	300 Coconuts	$17,985
8.80	2,000 Pizzas	

Nominal GDP Increases
Real GDP Remains Constant

the influence of price changes contained in nominal GDP. In 1980, real GDP in the United States was $4,612 billion; in 1997, it was $7,188.8 billion, an increase of just 56 percent. The 190 percent increase in nominal GDP in large part reflects increased prices, not increased output.

Since we prefer more goods and services to higher prices, it is better to have nominal GDP rise because of higher output than higher prices. We want nominal GDP to increase as a result of an increase in real GDP.

Consider a simple example that illustrates the difference between nominal GDP and real GDP. Suppose a hypothetical economy produces just three goods: oranges, coconuts, and pizzas. The dollar value of output in three different years is listed in the table in Figure 7.

As shown in Figure 7, in year 1, 100 oranges were produced at $.50 per orange, 300 coconuts at $1 per coconut, and 2,000 pizzas at $8 per pizza. The total dollar value of output in year 1 is $16,350. In year 2, prices are constant at the year 1 values, but the quantity of each good has increased by 10 percent. The dollar value of output in year 2 is $17,985, 10 percent higher than the value of output in year 1. In year 3, the quantity of each good is back at the year 1 level, but prices have increased by 10 percent. Oranges now cost $.55, coconuts $1.10, and pizzas $8.80. The dollar value of output in year 3 is $17,985.

Copyright © by Houghton Mifflin Company. All rights reserved.

Notice that in years 2 and 3, the dollar value of output ($17,985) is 10 percent higher than it was in year 1. But there is a difference here. In year 2, the increase in output is due entirely to an increase in the production of the three goods. In year 3, the increase is due entirely to an increase in the prices of the goods.

Because prices did not change between years 1 and 2, the increase in nominal GDP is entirely accounted for by an increase in real output, or real GDP. In years 1 and 3, the actual quantities produced did not change, which means that real GDP was constant; only nominal GDP was higher, a product only of higher prices.

2.b. Price Indexes

What is a price index?

price index:
a measure of the average price level in an economy

base year:
the year against which other years are measured

The value of the price index in any particular year indicates how prices have changed relative to the base year.

The total dollar value of output or income is equal to price multiplied by the quantity of goods and services produced:

$$\text{Dollar value of output} = \text{price} \times \text{quantity}$$

By dividing the dollar value of output by price, you can determine the quantity of goods and services produced:

$$\text{Quantity} = \frac{\text{dollar value of output}}{\text{price}}$$

In macroeconomics, a **price index** measures the average level of prices in an economy and shows how prices, on average, have changed. Prices of individual goods can rise and fall relative to one another, but a price index shows the general trend in prices across the economy.

2.b.1. Base Year   The example in Figure 7 provides a simple introduction to price indexes. The first step is to pick a **base year**, the year against which other years are measured. Any year can serve as the base year. Suppose we pick year 1 in Figure 7. The value of the price index in year 1, the base year, is defined to be 100. This simply means that prices in year 1 are 100 percent of prices in year 1 (100 percent of 1 is 1). In the example, year 2 prices are equal to year 1 prices, so the price index also is equal to 100 in year 2. In year 3, every price has risen 10 percent relative to the base-year (year 1) prices, so the price index is 10 percent higher in year 3, or 110. The value of the price index in any particular year indicates how prices have changed relative to the base year. A value of 110 indicates that prices are 110 percent of base-year prices, or that the average price level has increased 10 percent.

Price index in any year = 100 + (or −) percentage change in prices from the base year

Beginning in 1995, the U.S. Department of Commerce is calculating the growth of real GDP using a "chain-type" price series instead of the old method of calculating a "constant dollar" real GDP.

The old constant dollar real GDP was calculated by picking a base year and then using prices in the base year to value output in all years. Over time, a constant dollar real GDP will suffer from "substitution bias." This bias occurs because as prices of some goods rise faster than other goods, buyers will substitute away from the higher-priced goods and buy more of the lower priced goods. Such substitutions will cause output to grow faster in the industries with relatively low price increases. Because prices in these industries were relatively high in the base year, their growth will be overstated and constant-dollar real GDP will overestimate the true growth in the economy.

Copyright © by Houghton Mifflin Company. All rights reserved.

Copyright © by Houghton Mifflin Company. All rights reserved.

The computer industry provides a good example of substitution bias at work. Prices of computers have fallen since the 1992 base year used for estimating constant-dollar real GDP. By using the 1992 prices of computers in calculating real GDP, the substantial increase in the output of computer equipment is given too much weight. If evaluated at the falling prices actually occurring, the growth of both the computer industry and the overall economy would be lower.

chain-type real GDP growth: the geometric mean of the growth rates found using beginning and ending year prices

Chain-type indexes of real GDP correct for this bias that is included in constant-dollar real GDP. A chain-type real GDP index utilizes prices in two years to calculate the percentage change in real GDP between the two years. Then an index of real GDP is created based on the estimated percentage growth. Table 1 illustrates the creation of a chain-type real GDP index compared to a constant-dollar index.

Table 1 illustrates a simple economy that only produces two goods: apples and bread. Note that total spending on food is $500 in year 1 and $900 in year 2. How should we compute real GDP to best measure how real output of goods has changed? First, let's see what a constant dollar measure would yield and then compare this to a chain-type index measure as now being used to measure output in the United States. Using Year 1 as the base year, we would construct real GDP in each year using Year 1 prices associated with quantities. Valuing the quantities purchased in each year at Year 1 prices results in a ratio of Year 2 expenditures to Year 1 expenditures of 1.2. This gives us a 20 percent increase in real GDP. Alternatively, we use Year 2 prices to value quantities in each year. Valuing the quantities purchased each year at Year 2 prices results in a ratio of Year 2 expenditures to Year 1 expenditures of 1.06. This gives us a 6 percent increase in real GDP. Moving the base year forward in time has (and actually had) the impact of reducing the estimated growth of constant-dollar real GDP because the goods whose quantities increased the most are those whose prices increased, relatively, the least. So using the old prices gives too much weight to the rapidly growing sectors of the economy where prices are growing relatively slowly.

The chain-type index is calculated by taking an average of the growth rates found with the beginning and ending year prices. The actual average used by the Department of Commerce is a *geometric mean*. The geometric mean is found by multiplying the two expenditures ratios together, taking the square root, and then subtracting 1: $1.2 \times 1.06 = 1.272$, and the square root of 1.272 equals 1.13. So the growth of real GDP measured by the chain-type index is 13 percent. The term "chain-type index" indicates that the growth rate from one year to another is being estimated by "chaining together" the growth rates estimated using both the first and second year prices to value quantities rather than arbitrarily picking one period's prices.

Once the percentage changes in real GDP are estimated, then an index number for real GDP is created by picking some arbitrary year to equal 100 (1992 is the year currently used in the United States) and then increasing or decreasing the real GDP index for every other year by the percentage change found from the chain-type measure. We should note that the level of such a real GDP index has no meaning or interpretation apart from the percentage changes from year to year. The value of nominal GDP has a clear interpretation since it is the observable dollar value of expenditures on output. But to say that the level of the chain-type real GDP index equals 116.1 in 1994 gives no meaning other than with comparison to other years. If the real GDP index equals 112.2 in 1993, then we can find the growth rate of real GDP from 1993 to 1994 of 3.5 percent ($[116.1/112.2] - 1 = .035$ or 3.5%).

TABLE 1
Constant Dollar and Chain-Type Real GDP Growth

Year 1

	Quantity	Price	Expenditures
Apples	300	$1	$300
Bread	100	2	200
			$500

Year 2

	Quantity	Price	Expenditures
Apples	200	$2	$400
Bread	200	2.50	500
			$900

Constant Dollar Real GDP Growth Using Year 1 as Base Year:

(expenditures in Year 2 using Year 1 prices)/(expenditures in Year 1 using Year 1 prices) $- 1 =$

$$\frac{(200 \text{ apples} \times \$1) + (200 \text{ bread} \times \$2)}{(300 \text{ apples} \times \$1) + (100 \text{ bread} \times \$2)} = \frac{\$600}{\$500} = 1.2,$$

$$1.2 - 1.0 = .2 \text{ or } 20\%$$

Constant Dollar Real GDP Growth Using Year 2 as Base Year:

(expenditures in Year 2 using Year 2 prices)/(expenditures in Year 1 using Year 2 prices) $- 1 =$

$$\frac{(200 \text{ apples} \times \$2) + (200 \text{ bread} \times \$2.50)}{(300 \text{ apples} \times \$2) + (100 \text{ bread} \times \$2.50)} = \frac{\$900}{\$850} = 1.06,$$

$$1.06 - 1.00 = .06 \text{ or } 6\%$$

Chain-Type Real GDP Growth:

Square root of (expenditures ratio with Year 1 base year $\times$ expenditures ratio with Year 2 base year) $- 1 =$
Square root of $(1.2 \times 1.06) - 1 =$ Square root of $1.272 - 1 = 1.13 - 1 =$
.13 or 13%

2.b.2. Types of Price Indexes The price of a single good is easy to determine. But how do economists determine a single measure of the prices of the millions of goods and services produced in an economy? They have constructed price indexes to measure the price level; there are several different price indexes used to measure the price level in any economy. Not all prices rise or fall at the same time or by the same amount. This is why there are several measures of the price level in an economy.

The price index used to estimate constant dollar real GDP is the **GDP price index (GDPPI)**, a measure of prices across the economy that reflects

GDP price index:
a broad measure of the prices of goods and services included in the gross domestic product

Copyright © by Houghton Mifflin Company. All rights reserved.

Copyright © by Houghton Mifflin Company. All rights reserved.

The Consumer Price Index

The CPI is calculated by the Department of Labor using price surveys taken in 91 American cities. Although the CPI often is called a *cost of living index,* it is not. The CPI represents the cost of a fixed market basket of goods purchased by a hypothetical household, not a real one.

In fact, no household consumes the market basket used to estimate the CPI. As relative prices change, households alter their spending patterns. But the CPI market basket changes only every 10 years. This is due in part to the high cost of surveying the public to determine spending patterns. Then, too, individual households have different tastes and spend a different portion of their budgets on the various components of household spending (housing, food, clothing, transportation, medical care). Only a household that spends exactly the same portion of its income on each item counted in the CPI would find the CPI representative of its cost of living.

The current CPI market basket is based on spending patterns in the period between 1993 and 1995. The Department of Labor surveys spending in eight major areas. The figure shows the areas and the

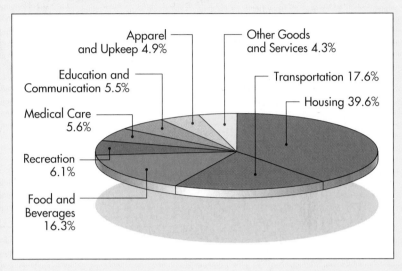

percentage of the typical household budget devoted to each area. If you kept track of your spending over the course of several months, you probably would find that you spend much more than the "typical" household on some items and much less on others. In other words, the CPI is not a very good measure of *your* cost of living.

Recently, the CPI has been criticized as overestimating the true inflation rate by about 1 percentage point mainly because it does not take into account the improved quality of many goods and services.

For instance, new automobiles are now more reliable than they were a few years ago, but the CPI does not adjust for this in counting auto prices. If prices rise due to higher-quality goods, then the price increase should not be counted the same as price increases for goods with constant quality. This "bias" in the CPI has provoked much discussion and will probably be addressed in the near future by the Department of Labor.

Source: Data from Bureau of Labor Statistics

---

all of the categories of goods and services included in GDP. The GDP price index is a very broad measure. Economists use other price indexes to analyze how prices change in more specific categories of goods and services.

consumer price index (CPI): a measure of the average price of goods and services purchased by the typical household

Probably the best-known price index is the **consumer price index (CPI)**. The CPI measures the average price of consumer goods and services that a typical household purchases. (See the Economic Insight "The Consumer Price Index.") The CPI is a narrower measure than the GDPPI because it includes fewer items. However, because of the relevance of consumer prices to the standard of living, news reports on price changes in the economy typically focus

Figure 8
The GDP Price Index, the CPI, and the PPI

The graph plots the annual percentage change in the GDP price index (GDPPI), the consumer price index (CPI), and the producer price index (PPI). The GDPPI is used to construct constant-dollar real GDP. The CPI measures the average price of consumer goods and services that a typical household purchases. The PPI measures the average price received by producers; it is the most variable of the three because fluctuations in equilibrium prices of intermediate goods are much greater than for final goods. Source: *Economic Report of the President, 1997* (Washington, D.C.: U.S. Government Printing Office, 1997).

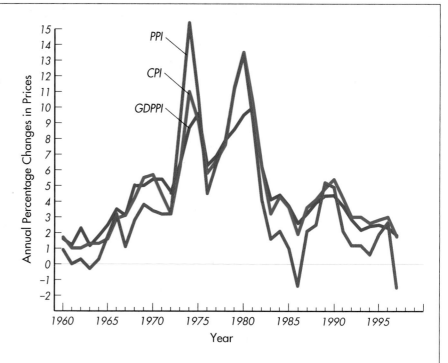

cost of living adjustment (COLA):
an increase in wages that is designed to match increases in prices of items purchased by the typical household

producer price index (PPI):
a measure of average prices received by producers

on consumer price changes. In addition, labor contracts sometimes include provisions that raise wages as the CPI goes up. Social security payments also are tied to increases in the CPI. These increases are called **cost of living adjustments (COLAs)**, because they are supposed to keep nominal income rising along with the cost of items purchased by the typical household.

The **producer price index (PPI)** measures average prices received by producers. At one time this price index was known as the *wholesale price index* (WPI). Because the PPI measures price changes at an earlier stage of production than the CPI, it can indicate a coming change in the CPI. If producer input costs are rising, we can expect the price of goods produced to go up as well.

Figure 8 illustrates how the three different measures of prices changed between 1960 and 1997. Notice that the PPI is more volatile than the GDPPI or the CPI. This is because there are smaller fluctuations in the equilibrium prices of final goods than intermediate goods.

RECAP

1. Nominal GDP is measured using current dollars.
2. Real GDP measures output with price effects removed.
3. Chain-type real GDP growth equals the geometric mean of the growth rates found with beginning and ending year prices.
4. The GDP price index, the consumer price index, and the producer price index are all measures of the level of prices in an economy.

Copyright © by Houghton Mifflin Company. All rights reserved.

3. FLOWS OF INCOME AND EXPENDITURES

GDP is both a measure of total expenditures on final goods and services and a measure of the total income earned in the production of those goods and services. The idea that total expenditures equal total income is clearly illustrated in Figure 1.

The figure links the four sectors of the economy: households, firms, government, and foreign countries. The arrows between the sectors indicate the direction of the flows. Gold arrows with dollar signs represent money flows; blue-green arrows without dollar signs represent flows of real goods and services. The money flows are both income and expenditures. For instance, household expenditures for goods and services from business firms are represented by the gold arrow at the top of the diagram. Household income from firms is represented by the gold arrow flowing from firms to households at the bottom of the diagram. Because one sector's expenditures represent another sector's income, the total expenditures on goods and services must be the same as the total income from selling goods and services, and those must both be equal to the total value of the goods and services produced.

RECAP

1. Total spending on final goods and services equals the total income received in producing those goods and services.

2. The circular flow model shows that one sector's expenditures represent the income of other sectors.

SUMMARY

■■■ **How is the total output of an economy measured?**

1. National income accounting is the system economists use to measure both the output of an economy and the flows between sectors of that economy. §1

2. Gross domestic product (GDP) is the market value of all final goods and services produced in a year in a country. §1.a

3. GDP also equals the value added at each stage of production. §1.a

■■■ **Who produces the nation's goods and services?**

4. GDP as output equals the sum of the output of households, business firms, and government within the country. Business firms produce 85 percent of the U.S. GDP. §1.a.1

■■■ **Who purchases the goods and services produced?**

5. GDP as expenditures equals the sum of consumption plus investment plus government spending plus net exports. In the United States, consumption accounts for roughly two-thirds of total expenditures. §1.a.2

■■■ **Who receives the income from the production of goods and services?**

6. GDP as income equals the sum of wages, interest, rent, profits, proprietors' income, capital consumption allowance, and indirect business taxes less net factor income from abroad. Wages account for about 60 percent of the total. §1.a.3

7. Capital consumption allowance is the estimated value of depreciation plus the value of accidental damage to capital stock. §1.a.3

Copyright © by Houghton Mifflin Company. All rights reserved.

8. Other measures of national output include gross national product (GNP), net national product (NNP), national income (NI), personal income (PI), and disposable personal income (DPI). §1.b

What is the difference between nominal and real GDP?

9. Nominal GDP measures output in terms of its current dollar value including the effects of price changes; real GDP measures output after eliminating the effects of price changes. §2.a

What is a price index?

10. A price index measures the average level of prices across an economy. §2.b

11. The GDP price index is a measure of the prices of all the goods and services included in the GDP. §2.b.2

12. The consumer price index (CPI) measures the average price of goods and services consumed by the typical household. §2.b.2

13. The producer price index (PPI) measures average prices received by producers (wholesale prices). §2.b.2

14. Total expenditures on final goods and services equal total income. §3

KEY TERMS

national income accounting §1

gross domestic product (GDP) §1.a

intermediate good §1.a

value added §1.a

inventory §1.a

capital consumption allowance §1.a.3

depreciation §1.a.3

indirect business tax §1.a.3

gross national product (GNP) §1.b.1

net national product (NNP) §1.b.2

gross investment §1.b.2

net investment §1.b.2

national income (NI) §1.b.3

personal income (PI) §1.b.4

transfer payment §1.b.4

disposable personal income (DPI) §1.b.5

nominal GDP §2.a

real GDP §2.a

price index §2.b

base year §2.b.1

chain-type real GDP §2.b.1

GDP price index §2.b.2

consumer price index (CPI) §2.b.2

cost of living adjustment (COLA) §2.b.2

producer price index (PPI) §2.b.2

EXERCISES

1. The following table lists the stages required in the production of a personal computer. What is the value of the computer in the GDP?

Stage	Value Added
Components manufacture	$ 50
Assembly	250
Wholesaler	500
Retailer	1,500

2. What is the difference between GDP and each of the following?
   a. Gross national product
   b. Net national product
   c. National income
   d. Personal income
   e. Disposable personal income

Copyright © by Houghton Mifflin Company. All rights reserved.

3.

	Year I		Year 2	
	Quantity	Price	Quantity	Price
Oranges	100	$3	150	$3
Pears	100	3	75	4

a. What is the growth rate of constant-dollar real GDP using Year 1 as the base year?

b. What is the growth rate of constant-dollar real GDP using Year 2 as the base year?

c. What is the chain-type real GDP growth rate between Years 1 and 2?

4. Why do total expenditures on final goods and services equal total income in the economy?

5. Why don't we measure national output by simply counting the total number of goods and services produced each year?

6. Why isn't the CPI a useful measure of *your* cost of living?

Use the following national income accounting information to answer questions 7–11:

Consumption	$400
Imports	10
Net investment	20
Government purchases	100
Exports	20
Capital consumption allowance	20
Indirect business taxes	5
Receipts of factor income from the rest of the world	12
Payments of factor income to the rest of the world	10

7. What is the GDP for this economy?

8. What is the GNP for this economy?

9. What is the NNP for this economy?

10. What is the national income for this economy?

11. What is the gross investment in this economy?

12. Indirect business taxes and capital consumption allowance are not income, yet they are included in order to find GDP as income received. Why do we add these two non-income components to the other components of income (like wages, rent, interest, profits, and net factor income from abroad) to find GDP?

13. Why has nominal GDP increased faster than real GDP in the United States over time? What would it mean if an economy had real GDP increasing faster than nominal GDP?

14. We usually discuss GDP in terms of what is included in the definition. What is *not* included in GDP? Why are these things excluded?

15. If a surfboard is produced this year but not sold until next year, how is it counted in this year's GDP and not next year's?

🖥 INTERNET EXERCISE

In section 2.b of this chapter we learned about price indexes. Suppose you work for an employer who offers to give you a cost-of-living raise each year based on how much prices have changed over the past year. Your boss will let you pick the price index to use in determining the rate of inflation over the year. To see how different price indexes have recently behaved, go to the Boyes/Melvin web site at http://www.hmco.com/college/. Now answer the questions that appear on the web page.

Copyright © by Houghton Mifflin Company. All rights reserved.

Brussels Sets Out on Road to Green GDP

European environment ministers will today discuss for the first time an alternative model of national accounting, the first step to a "green GDP" which would balance economic growth against pollution, adding up the real social and environmental costs of trade.

The results could be politically depressing. An early academic attempt to establish an "Index of Sustainable Economic Welfare" estimated that Britain's "real" social wealth per capita rose in the 1950s and 1960s, and then collapsed. Published three years ago by the Stockholm Environmental Institute, it claimed that when unemployment, crime and pollution were included, Britain's index of social welfare had by 1990 fallen back to 1950s levels.

Alternative accounting and a green GDP remain controversial. Opponents argue that too many of the costs are notional or impossible to measure. But even critics admit that conventional GDP figures are flawed. They can, for example, count road accidents as growth because of the activity they generate in insurance, replacement cars, demand on the health sector and undertakers.

The EU commissioner for the environment, Denmark's Ritt Bjerregaard, will present a brief progress report on "environmental indicators and green national accounting" to today's council of environmental ministers in Luxembourg, pending a full discussion in December. A footnote to today's meeting, which will focus on big issues such as the EU stance at the Kyoto summit on global warming, it represents a breakthrough for environmental activists.

"This will be the first time that a massive economy like Europe begins to assess its real profits and losses," the European director of the World Wide Fund for Nature, Tony Long, said yesterday.

"Now that it is on the agenda, we can look forward to figures which start to put a real cost on pollution and carbon dioxide emissions, and demonstrate the real savings green policies can bring."

The EU commission first tackled the statistical challenge of putting green issues into national accounts two years ago. The WWF and Keele University are working on a draft model of a green GDP for Britain.

It is hoped that this new model will be seen as less influenced by political factors—such as income distribution—than the initial models of ISEW (Index of Sustainable Economic Welfare) first devised in 1989 by Herman Daly and John Cobb in their groundbreaking book, *For the Common Good*. But even when modified, the ISEW models have suggested that while conventional GDP in Britain more than doubled from pounds 2,900 to pounds 6,000 per capita between 1950 and 1990, the alternative index showed an overall zero growth in real social wealth.

A survey using the ISEW model by the Stockholm Environmental Institute in 1994 showed Britain's social GDP per head rising steadily from pounds 1,100 in 1950, and peaking at just over pounds 2,000 in 1974, then falling back to pounds 1,100 in 1990.

The ISEW index is based on personal consumption adjusted by income distribution patterns, to penalise societies where there is a wide or growing gap between rich and poor. It factors in non-market labour (such as household work), government spending that promotes social welfare, stocks of private goods and public infrastructure. It then subtracts the estimated costs of unemployment, commuting, car accidents and water, air and noise pollution.

The EU's own stab at alternative accounting is expected to be far more conventional. But with deadlock looming at next month's Kyoto summit on global warming, green accounting could offer a compromise.

Source: "Brussels Sets Out on Road to Green GDP," from *The Guardian,* October 16, 1997, p. 14. Copyright © 1997 by *The Guardian.* Reprinted by permission.

The Guardian/October 16, 1997

Copyright © by Houghton Mifflin Company. All rights reserved.

COMMENTARY

I n this chapter we learn about different measures of the performance of the economy. The actual compilation of these statistics is a formidable task, especially in a country with an economy as large and complex as that of the United States. The article discusses how a "green GDP" may be estimated and provides some insight into the manner in which government economists and statisticians attempt to interpret what is occurring. The impression we are left with is that the collection and reporting of economic data, at least in terms of presenting a picture of recent performance, is somewhat arbitrary and imprecise.

Most macroeconomic data are estimates. It is simply impossible to count every new final good and service produced in a year to measure GDP exactly. Instead, government economists attempt to construct reasonable estimates of GDP by counting small amounts of output in the many different sectors of the economy. For example, veterinary services and pet services provided by pet stores are included in GDP. However, the government does not know the exact number and value of services actually provided by every veterinarian and pet store in a given year. The value of pet services is estimated by the number of purebred dogs reported to be in the United States by the American Kennel Club multiplied by a consumer price index for pet services. As the number of dogs increases, the value of pet services in GDP also increases.

Measuring the value of environmental goods and bads sounds reasonable and desirable, yet it presents a new challenge to government economists charged with gathering national income data. When goods are sold in a market, we observe the price and quantity so that value is fairly easy to estimate. However, placing an annual value on forests or air and water pollution is a much different problem. If such property is not privately owned, we might still assess its "market" value if it were to be sold. However, this would miss the value to society at large in terms of cleaning the air and water. Since no one owns the air and water, it is very difficult to place a monetary value on these benefits to all.

Although there are major practical problems in incorporating environmental costs and benefits in GDP, critics of the current system remind us that not addressing these problems may result in misleading estimates of our well-being.

Copyright © by Houghton Mifflin Company. All rights reserved.

7

An Introduction to the Foreign Exchange Market and the Balance of Payments

---

FUNDAMENTAL QUESTIONS

1. How do individuals of one nation trade money with individuals of another nation?

2. How do changes in exchange rates affect international trade?

3. How do nations record their transactions with the rest of the world?

Copyright © by Houghton Mifflin Company. All rights reserved.

n Chapter 6, you learned that gross domestic product equals the sum of consumption, investment, government spending, and net exports (GDP = $C + I + G + X$). Net exports (X) are one key measure of a nation's transactions with other countries, a principal link between a nation's GDP and developments in the rest of the world. In this chapter, we extend the macroeconomic accounting framework to include more detail on a nation's international transactions. This extension is known as balance of payments accounting.

International transactions have grown rapidly in recent years as the economies of the world have become increasingly interrelated. Improvements in transportation and communication, and global markets for goods and services, have created a community of world economies. Products made in one country sell in the world market, where they compete against products from other nations. Europeans purchase stocks listed on the New York Stock Exchange; Americans purchase bonds issued in Japan.

Different countries use different monies. When goods and services are exchanged across international borders, national monies also are traded. To make buying and selling decisions in the global marketplace, people must be able to compare prices across countries, to compare prices quoted in Japanese yen with those quoted in Mexican pesos. This chapter begins with a look at how national monies are priced and traded in the foreign exchange market. ■

Copyright © by Houghton Mifflin Company. All rights reserved.

1. THE FOREIGN EXCHANGE MARKET

How do individuals of one nation trade money with individuals of another nation?

foreign exchange:
currency and bank deposits that are denominated in foreign money

foreign exchange market:
a global market in which people trade one currency for another

Foreign exchange is foreign money, including paper money and bank deposits like checking accounts that are denominated in foreign currency. When someone with U.S. dollars wants to trade those dollars for Japanese yen, the trade takes place in the **foreign exchange market**, a global market in which people trade one currency for another. Many financial markets are located in a specific geographic location. For instance, the New York Stock Exchange is a specific location in New York City where stocks are bought and sold. The Commodity Exchange is a specific location in New York City where contracts to deliver agricultural and metal commodities are bought and sold. The foreign exchange market is not in a single geographic location, however. Trading occurs all over the world electronically and by telephone. Most of the activity involves large banks in New York, London, and other financial centers. A foreign exchange trader at Morgan Guaranty Bank in New York can buy or sell currencies with a trader at Barclays Bank in London by calling the other trader on the telephone or exchanging computer messages.

Only tourism and a few other transactions in the foreign exchange market involve the actual movement of currency. The great majority of transactions involve the buying and selling of bank deposits denominated in foreign currency. A bank deposit can be a checking account that a firm or individual writes checks against to make payments to others, or it may be an interest-earning savings account with no check-writing privileges. Currency notes, like dollar bills, are used in a relatively small fraction of transactions. When a large corporation or a government buys foreign currency, it buys a bank deposit denominated in the foreign currency. Still, all exchanges in the market require that monies have a price.

1.a. Exchange Rates

exchange rate:
the rate at which monies of different countries are exchanged

An **exchange rate** is the price of one country's money in terms of another country's money. Exchange rates are needed to compare prices quoted in two different currencies. Suppose a shirt that has been manufactured in Canada sells for 20 U.S. dollars in Seattle, Washington, and for 25 Canadian dollars in Vancouver, British Columbia. Where would you get the better buy? Unless you know the exchange rate between U.S. and Canadian dollars, you can't tell. The exchange rate allows you to convert the foreign currency price into its domestic currency equivalent, which then can be compared to the domestic price.

Figure 1 lists exchange rates for January 9, 1998. The rates are quoted in U.S. dollars per unit of foreign currency in the second column, and units of foreign currency per U.S. dollar in the last column. For instance, the Canadian dollar was selling for $.6992, or a little more than 69 U.S. cents. The same day, the U.S. dollar was selling for 1.4303 Canadian dollars (1 U.S. dollar would buy 1.4303 Canadian dollars).

Find the reciprocal of a number by writing it as a fraction and then turning the fraction upside down. In other words, make the numerator the denominator and the denominator the numerator.

If you know the price in U.S. dollars of a currency, you can find the price of the U.S. dollar in that currency by taking the reciprocal. To find the reciprocal of a number, write it as a fraction and then turn the fraction upside down. Let's say that 1 British pound sells for 2 U.S. dollars. In fraction form, 2 is 2/1. The reciprocal of 2/1 is 1/2, or .5. So 1 U.S. dollar sells for .5 British pounds. The figure shows that the actual dollar price of the pound was 1.6130. The *reciprocal exchange rate*—the number of pounds per dollar—is .6200 (1/1.6130), which was the pound price of 1 dollar that day.

Let's go back to comparing the price of the Canadian shirt in Seattle and Vancouver. The symbol for the U.S. dollar is $. The symbol for the Canadian dollar is C$. (Table 1 lists the symbols for a number of currencies.) The shirt sells for $20 in Seattle and C$25 in Vancouver. Suppose the exchange rate between the U.S. dollar and the Canadian dollar is .8. This means that C$1 costs .8 U.S. dollars, or 80 U.S. cents. To find the domestic currency value of

Copyright © by Houghton Mifflin Company. All rights reserved.

Figure 1
Exchange Rates

The second column lists U.S. dollars per foreign currency, or how much one unit of foreign currency is worth in U.S. dollars. On January 9 you could get about 70 U.S. cents for 1 Canadian dollar. The third column lists foreign currency per U.S. dollar, or how much 1 U.S. dollar is worth in foreign currency. On the same day, you could get about 1.43 Canadian dollars for 1 U.S. dollar.

EXCHANGE RATES
January 9, 1998

COUNTRY	U.S.$ PER CURRENCY	CURRENCY PER U.S.$
Argentina (peso)	1.0001	.99999
Australia (dollar)	.6444	1.5518
Britain (pound)	1.6130	.6200
Canada (dollar)	.6992	1.4303
China (renminbi)	.1203	8.3100
France (franc)	.1639	6.0995
Germany (mark)	.5487	1.8225
Israel (shekel)	.2806	3.5632
Italy (lira)	.00055	1,792.0
Japan (yen)	.00757	132.12
Mexico (peso)	.1222	8.1800
New Zealand (dollar)	.5709	1.7516
Russia (ruble)	.1674	5.9740
Singapore (dollar)	.5616	1.7805
Switzerland (franc)	.6770	1.4770

a foreign currency price, multiply the foreign currency price by the exchange rate:

Domestic currency value = foreign currency price $\times$ exchange rate

In our example, the U.S. dollar is the domestic currency:

U.S. dollar value = C$25 $\times$ .8 = $20

If we multiply the price of the shirt in Canadian dollars (C$25) by the exchange rate (.8), we find the U.S. dollar value ($20). After adjusting for the exchange rate, then, we can see that the shirt sells for the same price when the price is measured in a single currency.

1.b. Exchange Rate Changes and International Trade

How do changes in exchange rates affect international trade?

A currency appreciates in value when its value rises in relation to another currency.

Because exchange rates determine the domestic currency value of foreign goods, changes in those rates affect the demand for and supply of goods traded internationally. Suppose the price of the shirt in Seattle and in Vancouver remains the same, but the exchange rate changes from .8 to .9 U.S. dollars per Canadian dollar. What happens? The U.S. dollar price of the shirt in Vancouver increases. At the new rate, the shirt that sells for C$25 in Vancouver costs a U.S. buyer $22.50 (C$25 $\times$ .9).

A rise in the value of a currency is called *appreciation*. In our example, as the exchange rate moves from $.8 = C$1 to $.9 = C$1, the Canadian dollar appreciates against the U.S. dollar. As a country's currency appreciates, international demand for its products falls, other things equal.

Copyright © by Houghton Mifflin Company. All rights reserved.

TABLE 1
International Currency Symbols, Selected Countries

Country	Currency	Symbol
Australia	Dollar	A$
Austria	Schilling	Sch
Belgium	Franc	BF
Canada	Dollar	C$
China	Yuan	Y
Denmark	Krone	DKr
Finland	Markka	FM
France	Franc	FF
Germany	Deutsche mark	DM
Greece	Drachma	Dr
India	Rupee	Rs
Iran	Rial	Rl
Italy	Lira	Lit
Japan	Yen	¥
Kuwait	Dinar	KD
Mexico	Peso	Ps
Netherlands	Guilder	FL
Norway	Krone	NKr
Russia	Ruble	Rub
Saudi Arabia	Riyal	SR
Singapore	Dollar	S$
South Africa	Rand	R
Spain	Peseta	Pts
Sweden	Krona	SKr
Switzerland	Franc	SF
United Kingdom	Pound	£
United States	Dollar	$
Venezuela	Bolivar	B

A currency depreciates in value when its value falls in relation to another currency.

Suppose the exchange rate in our example moves from $.8 = C$1 to $.7 = C$1. Now the shirt that sells for C$25 in Vancouver costs a U.S. buyer $17.50 (C$25 × .7). In this case the Canadian dollar has *depreciated* in value relative to the U.S. dollar. As a country's currency depreciates, its goods sell for lower prices in other countries and the demand for its products increases, other things equal.

When the Canadian dollar is appreciating against the U.S. dollar, the U.S. dollar must be depreciating against the Canadian dollar. For instance, when the exchange rate between the U.S. dollar and the Canadian dollar moves from $.8 = C$1 to $.9 = C$1, the reciprocal exchange rate—the rate between the Canadian dollar and the U.S. dollar—moves from C$1.25 = $1 (1/.8 = 1.25) to C$1.11 = $1 (1/.9 = 1.11). At the same time that Canadian goods are becoming more expensive to U.S. buyers, U.S. goods are becoming cheaper to Canadian buyers.

In later chapters we look more closely at how changes in exchange rates affect international trade and at how governments use exchange rates to change their net exports. Often when governments restrict trading in the for-

Copyright © by Houghton Mifflin Company. All rights reserved.

Copyright © by Houghton Mifflin Company. All rights reserved.

ECONOMIC INSIGHT

Black Markets in Foreign Exchange

Many developing countries impose restrictions on foreign currency transactions. These restrictions can take the form of government licensing requirements, under which only the government is allowed to exchange foreign currency for domestic currency; quotas on the amount of foreign currency that can be purchased; or even prohibitions on the use of foreign currency by private concerns. One product of these restrictions is illegal markets, or *black markets,* in foreign exchange. In many countries, the black market exists openly with little or no government intervention. In other countries, foreign exchange laws are strictly enforced.

Government policy creates the black market. The demand stems from the legal restrictions on buying foreign exchange; the supply stems from government-mandated exchange rates that offer less than the free market. Ironically, governments cite the need for controls to conserve scarce foreign exchange

for high-priority uses. But controls actually reduce the flow of foreign exchange to the government, as traders turn to the black market instead.

During periods of economic hardship, illegal markets allow normal economic activities to continue through a steady supply of foreign exchange. Some governments unofficially acknowledge the benefits of the black market by allowing the market to exist openly. For instance, Guatemala had an artificially low official exchange rate of 1 quetzal per U.S. dollar for more than three decades. But the government allowed a black market to operate openly in front of the country's main post office. There the exchange rate fluctuated daily with market conditions. In many Latin American countries, the post office is a center for black market trading because relatives living in the United States send millions of dollars in checks and money orders home. This sort of government-tolerated alternative to the

official exchange market often is called a *parallel market* rather than a black market.

Mexico has had a thriving parallel market whenever the official exchange rate between the peso and the U.S. dollar has diverged greatly from the market rate. For example, in August 1982 the Mexican government banned the sale of U.S. dollars by Mexican banks. The parallel market immediately responded. The official exchange rate was 69.5 pesos per 1 U.S. dollar; the rate on the street ranged from 120 to 150. Private currency trades flourished at the Mexico City airport and other public places.

Black markets or parallel markets are common in developing countries where foreign exchange transactions are restricted. In many countries the official exchange rate bears no relation to current economic reality. Economists often look to the black market to see how the supply of and demand for foreign exchange are changing.

eign exchange market illegal trading results. An example is given in the Economic Insight "Black Markets in Foreign Exchange".

RECAP

1. The foreign exchange market is a global market in which foreign money, largely bank deposits, is bought and sold.

2. An exchange rate is the price of one money in terms of another.

3. Foreign demand for domestic goods decreases as the domestic currency appreciates and increases as the domestic currency depreciates.

2. THE BALANCE OF PAYMENTS

The U.S. economy does not operate in a vacuum. It affects and is affected by the economies of other nations. This point was brought home to Americans in the 1980s and 1990s as newspaper headlines announced the latest trade deficit

How do nations record their
transactions with the rest of
the world?

balance of payments:
a record of a country's trade in
goods, services, and financial
assets with the rest of the world

and politicians denounced foreign countries for running trade surpluses against the United States. It seemed as if everywhere there was talk of the balance of payments.

The **balance of payments** is a record of a country's trade in goods, services, and financial assets with the rest of the world. This record is divided into categories, or accounts, that summarize the nation's international economic transactions. For example, one category measures transactions in merchandise; another measures transactions involving financial assets (bank deposits, bonds, stocks, loans). These accounts distinguish between private transactions (by individuals and businesses) and official transactions (by governments). Balance of payments data are reported quarterly for most developed countries.

2.a. Accounting for International Transactions

double-entry bookkeeping:
a system of accounting in which
every transaction is recorded
in at least two accounts and in
which the debit total must
equal the credit total for the
transaction as a whole

The balance of payments is an accounting statement based on **double-entry bookkeeping,** a system in which every transaction is recorded in at least two accounts. Suppose a U.S. tractor manufacturer sells a $50,000 tractor to a resident of France. The transaction is recorded twice: once as the tractor going from the United States to France, and then again as the payment of $50,000 going from France to the United States.

Double-entry bookkeeping means that for each transaction there is a credit entry and a debit entry. *Credits* record activities that bring payments into a country; *debits* record activities that involve payments to the rest of the world. Table 2 shows the entries in the U.S. balance of payments to record the sale of a $50,000 U.S. tractor to a French importer. The sale of the tractor represents a $50,000 credit entry in the balance of payments because U.S. exports earn foreign exchange for U.S. residents. To complete the record of this transaction, we must know how payment was made for the tractor. Let's assume that the French buyer paid with a $50,000 check drawn on a U.S. bank. Money that is withdrawn from a foreign-owned bank account in the United States is treated as foreign exchange moved out of the country. So we record the payment as a debit entry in the balance of payments. In fact, the money did not leave the country; its ownership was transferred from the French buyer to the U.S. seller.

The sum of total credits must equal the sum of total debits so that the two columns of the balance of payments always balance.

The tractor sale is recorded on both sides of the balance of payments. There is a credit entry, and there is a debit entry. For every international transaction,

TABLE 2
Balance of Payments Entries for the Sale of a
U.S. Tractor to a French Buyer

Activity	Credit	Debit
U.S. firm exports tractor and receives $50,000 from French buyer	$50,000	
French buyer imports tractor and transfers $50,000 from U.S. bank account to U.S. firm		$50,000
	$50,000	$50,000

Copyright © by Houghton Mifflin Company. All rights reserved.

there must be both a credit entry and a debit entry. This means that the sum of total credits and the sum of total debits must be equal. Credits always offset, or balance, debits.

2.b. Balance of Payments Accounts

current account:
the sum of the merchandise, services, investment income, and unilateral transfers accounts in the balance of payments

The balance of payments uses several different accounts to classify transactions (Table 3). The **current account** is the sum of the balances in the merchandise, services, investment income, and unilateral transfers accounts.

Merchandise This account records all transactions involving goods. U.S. exports of goods are merchandise credits; U.S. imports of foreign goods are merchandise debits. When exports (or credits) exceed imports (or debits), the merchandise account shows a **surplus.** When imports exceed exports, the account shows a **deficit.** The balance on the merchandise account is frequently referred to as the **balance of trade.**

surplus:
in a balance of payments account, the amount by which credits exceed debits

deficit:
in a balance of payments account, the amount by which debits exceed credits

In the first quarter of 1997, the merchandise account in the U.S. balance of payments showed a deficit of $49,787 million. This means that the merchandise credits of $162,527 million created by U.S. exports were $49,787 million less than the merchandise debits of $212,314 million created by U.S. imports. In other words, the United States bought more goods from other nations than it sold to them.

balance of trade:
the balance on the merchandise account in a nation's balance of payments

Services This account measures trade involving services. It includes travel and tourism, royalties, transportation costs, and insurance premiums. In Table 3, the balance on the services account was a $20,487 million surplus.

Investment Income The income earned from investments in foreign countries is a credit; the income paid on foreign-owned investments in the United States is a debit. Investment income is the return on a special kind of service: it is the value of services provided by capital in foreign countries. In Table 3, there is a deficit of $1,990 million in the investment income account.

Unilateral Transfers In a unilateral transfer, one party gives something but gets nothing in return. Gifts and retirement pensions are forms of unilateral transfers. For instance, if a farmworker in El Centro, California, sends money to his family in Guaymas, Mexico, this is a unilateral transfer from the United

Copyright © by Houghton Mifflin Company. All rights reserved.

TABLE 3
Simplified U.S. Balance of Payments, 1997 First Quarter (million dollars)

Account	Credit	Debit	Net Balance
Merchandise	$162,527	$212,314	−$49,787
Services	$ 61,725	$ 41,238	$20,487
Investment income	$ 55,269	$ 57,259	−$ 1,990
Unilateral transfers			−$ 8,682
Current account			**−$39,972**
Capital account	**$182,238**	**$127,969**	**$54,269**
Statistical discrepancy			−$14,297

Source: Data from Bureau of Economic Analysis.

Every nation uses its own currency: dollars in the United States, pesetas in Spain, kroner in Norway, and pounds in England. Trade between countries must involve buying and selling national currencies. Since U.S. exporters ultimately want U.S. dollars for their products, if they export goods to England, pounds must be exchanged for dollars. The foreign exchange market is where national currencies are bought and sold.

capital account:
the record in the balance of payments of the flow of financial assets into and out of a country

States to Mexico. Only the net balance on unilateral transfers is reported. In Table 3, that balance was a deficit of $8,682 million.

The current account is a useful measure of international transactions because it contains all of the activities involving goods and services. The **capital account** is where trade involving financial assets and international investment is recorded. In the first quarter of 1997, the current account showed a deficit of $39,972 million. This means that U.S. imports of merchandise, services, investment income, and unilateral transfers were $39,972 million greater than exports of these items.

If we draw a line in the balance of payments under the current account, then all entries below the line relate to financing the movement of merchandise, services, investment income, and unilateral transfers into and out of the country. In the terminology of the balance of payments, *capital* refers to financial and investment flows—bank deposits, purchases of stocks and bonds, loans, land purchases, and purchases of business firms—not simply the factories and equipment that are defined as capital in the macroeconomic sense of the word. Credits to the capital account reflect foreign purchases of U.S. financial assets or real property like land and buildings, and debits reflect U.S. purchases of foreign financial assets and real property. In Table 3, the U.S. capital account showed a surplus of $54,269 million.

The *statistical discrepancy* account, the last account listed in Table 3, could be called *omissions and errors*. Government cannot accurately measure all transactions that take place. Some international shipments of goods and services go uncounted or are miscounted, as are some international flows of cap-

Copyright © by Houghton Mifflin Company. All rights reserved.

ital. The statistical discrepancy account is used to correct for these omissions and errors. In Table 3, measured debits were less than measured credits, so the statistical discrepancy was –$14,297 million.

Over all of the balance of payments accounts, the sum of credits must equal the sum of debits. The bottom line—the *net balance*—must be zero. It cannot show a surplus or a deficit. When people talk about a surplus or a deficit in the balance of payments, they actually are talking about a surplus or a deficit in one of the balance of payments accounts. The balance of payments itself by definition is always in balance, a function of double-entry bookkeeping.

2.c. The Current Account and the Capital Account

The current account reflects the movement of goods and services into and out of a country. The capital account reflects the flow of financial assets into and out of a country. In Table 3, the current account shows a deficit balance of $39,972 million. Remember that the balance of payments must *balance*. If there is a deficit in the current account, there must be a surplus in the capital account that exactly offsets that deficit.

What is important here is not the bookkeeping process, the concept that the balance of payments must balance, but rather the meaning of deficits and surpluses in the current and capital accounts. These deficits and surpluses tell us whether a country is a net borrower from or lender to the rest of the world. A deficit in the current account means that a country is running a net surplus in its capital account. And it signals that a country is a net borrower from the rest of the world. A country that is running a current account deficit must borrow from abroad an amount sufficient to finance that deficit. A capital account surplus is achieved by selling more bonds and other debts of the domestic country to the rest of the world than the country buys from the rest of the world.

Copyright © by Houghton Mifflin Company. All rights reserved.

A net debtor owes more to the rest of the world than it is owed; a net creditor is owed more than it owes.

Figure 2 shows the annual current account balance in the United States. The United States experienced large current account deficits in the 1980s and then again in the mid-1990s. Such deficits indicate that the United States consumed more than it produced. This means that the United States sold financial assets and borrowed large amounts of money from foreign residents to finance its current account deficits. This large foreign borrowing made the United States the largest debtor in the world. A *net debtor* owes more to the rest of the world than it is owed; a *net creditor* is owed more than it owes. The United States was an international net creditor from the end of World War I until the mid-1980s. The country financed its large current account deficits in the 1980s by borrowing from the rest of the world. As a result of this accumulated borrowing, in 1985 the United States became an international net debtor for the first time in almost 70 years. Since that time, the net debtor status of the United States has grown steadily.

RECAP

1. The balance of payments is a record of a nation's international transactions.

2. Double-entry bookkeeping requires that every transaction be entered in at least two accounts, so that credits and debits are balanced.

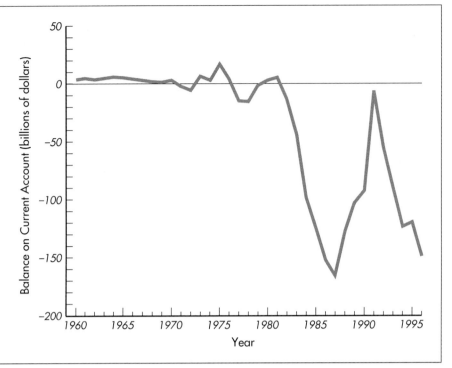

Figure 2
The U.S. Current Account Balance
The current account of the balance of payments is the sum of the balances in the merchandise, services, investment income, and unilateral transfers accounts. The United States experienced very large current account deficits in the 1980s. Source: From *International Financial Statistics,* December 1997. Reprinted courtesy of International Monetary Fund.

3. In the balance of payments, credits record activities that represent payments into the country, and debits record activities that represent payments out of the country.

4. The current account is the sum of the balances in the merchandise, services, investment income, and unilateral transfers accounts.

5. A surplus exists when credits exceed debits; a deficit exists when credits are less than debits.

6. The capital account is where the transactions necessary to finance the movement of merchandise, services, investment income, and unilateral transfers into and out of the country are recorded.

7. The net balance in the balance of payments must be zero.

8. A deficit in the current account must be offset by a surplus in the capital account. It also indicates that the nation is a net borrower.

SUMMARY

How do individuals of one nation trade money with individuals of another nation?

1. Foreign exchange is currency and bank deposits that are denominated in foreign currency. §1

2. The foreign exchange market is a global market in which people trade one currency for another. §1

3. Exchange rates, the price of one country's money in terms of another country's money, are necessary to compare prices quoted in different currencies. §1.a

4. The value of a good in a domestic currency equals the foreign currency price times the exchange rate. §1.a

Copyright © by Houghton Mifflin Company. All rights reserved.

How do changes in exchange rates affect international trade?

5. When a domestic currency appreciates, domestic goods become more expensive to foreigners and foreign goods become cheaper to domestic residents. §1.b

6. When a domestic currency depreciates, domestic goods become cheaper to foreigners and foreign goods become more expensive to domestic residents. §1.b

How do nations record their transactions with the rest of the world?

7. The balance of payments is a record of a nation's transactions with the rest of the world. §2

8. The balance of payments is based on double-entry bookkeeping. §2.a

9. Credits record activities that bring payments into a country; debits record activities that take payments out of a country. §2.a

10. In the balance of payments, the sum of total credits and the sum of total debits must be equal. §2.a

11. The current account is the sum of the balances in the merchandise, services, investment income, and unilateral transfers accounts. §2.b

12. In a balance of payments account, a surplus is the amount by which credits exceed debits, and a deficit is the amount by which debits exceed credits. §2.b

13. The capital account reflects the transactions necessary to finance the movement of merchandise, services, investment income, and unilateral transfers into and out of the country. §2.b

14. The net balance in the balance of payments must be zero. §2.b

15. A deficit in the current account must be offset by a surplus in the capital account. §2.c

16. A country that shows a deficit in its current account (or a surplus in its capital account) is a net borrower. §2.c

KEY TERMS

foreign exchange §1

foreign exchange market §1

exchange rate §1.a

balance of payments §2

double-entry
  bookkeeping §2.a

current account §2.b

surplus §2.b

deficit §2.b

balance of trade §2.b

capital account §2.b

EXERCISES

1. What is the price of 1 U.S. dollar in terms of each of the following currencies, given the following exchange rates?

   a. 1 Austrian schilling = $.10

   b. 1 Chinese yuan = $.12

   c. 1 Israeli shekel = $.30

   d. 1 Kuwaiti dinar = $3.20

2. A bicycle manufactured in the United States costs $100. Using the exchange rates listed in Figure 1, what would the bicycle cost in each of the following countries?

   a. Argentina

   b. Britain

   c. Canada

Copyright © by Houghton Mifflin Company. All rights reserved.

3. The U.S. dollar price of a Swedish krona changes from $.1572 to $.1730.

a. Has the dollar depreciated or appreciated against the krona?

b. Has the krona appreciated or depreciated against the dollar?

Use the information in the following table on Mexico's 1996 international transactions to answer questions 4–6 (the amounts are the U.S. dollar values in millions):

Merchandise imports	$96,000
Merchandise exports	$89,469
Services exports	$10,901
Services imports	$10,819
Investment income receipts	$ 4,032
Investment income payments	$17,099
Unilateral transfers	$ 4,531

4. What is the balance of trade?

5. What is the current account?

6. Did Mexico become a larger international net debtor during 1996?

7. How reasonable is it for every country to follow policies aimed at increasing net exports?

8. How did the United States become the world's largest debtor nation in the 1980s?

9. If the U.S. dollar appreciated against the German mark, what would you expect to happen to U.S. net exports with Germany?

10. Suppose the U.S. dollar price of a British pound is $1.50; the dollar price of a German mark is $.60; a hotel room in London, England, costs 120 British pounds; and a comparable hotel room in Hanover, Germany, costs 220 German marks.

a. Which hotel room is cheaper to a U.S. tourist?

b. What is the exchange rate between the German mark and the British pound?

11. Many residents of the United States send money to relatives living in other countries. For instance, a Salvadoran farmworker who is temporarily working in San Diego, California, sends money back to his family in El Salvador. How are such transactions recorded in the balance of payments? Are they debits or credits?

12. Suppose the U.S. dollar price of the Canadian dollar is $.75. How many Canadian dollars will it take to buy a set of dishes selling for $60 in Detroit, Michigan?

13. Why is it true that if the dollar depreciates against the yen, the yen must appreciate against the dollar?

14. Why does the balance of payments contain an account called "statistical discrepancy"?

Copyright © by Houghton Mifflin Company. All rights reserved.

INTERNET EXERCISE

In section 1 of this chapter we learned about exchange rates and how exchange rate changes can affect the prices of goods and services traded internationally. Go to the Boyes/Melvin web site at http://www.hmco.com/college/ and click on the internet exercise link for this chapter. Now answer the questions that appear on the web page.

Copyright © by Houghton Mifflin Company. All rights reserved.

Surge from the South—Mexican Shoppers Come Back to Texas

The Gianni Versace store didn't exactly suit Miguel Reyes.

Neither did the price tags in the Mondo Collections clothing shop.

So Mr. Reyes continued sauntering the polished pathways of the Dallas Galleria, searching stacks and racks for ways to spend the $2,000 safely.

It was the Mexico City resident's first foray to the Southwest's golden shopping arcade since the collapse of the peso two years ago severely hurt his family's business. But as the Mexican economy improved, so did Mr. Reyes' ability to shop at the Galleria, attend a Dallas Cowboys' game, stay in a downtown hotel, dine at eateries, Macarena at a few nightclubs and transform that roll of U.S. cash into a gain for the Texas economy.

"Because of the devaluation, that prevented me from coming over to the States," Mr. Reyes said as a Mexican couple entered the Gianni Versace store. "Now that it's getting back up there, it's allowed me to come here for five days."

When the peso was devalued two years ago, it set off months of economic crisis in Mexico, causing a drop in tourism to Texas and a fall in Lone Star exports to Mexico. Business with the state's southern neighbor deteriorated.

Now that Mexico's economy is improving, merchants have noticed a return of Mexican shoppers. That's one reason most economists agree the holiday shopping season will be better in Texas then elsewhere in the nation.

At the same time, Texas companies are exporting more goods to Mexico, and more Mexicans are venturing to Texas for medical and other services, economists said.

"It's pretty clear that Mexico's economy has begun its recovery from the peso devaluation," said Jon Hockenyos, a private economist in Austin. "Texas is exporting more goods and services to Mexico than we were a year or two ago. Mexican shoppers are beginning to come back to Texas. That's having a very positive effect on several Texas markets." . . .

From clothing bought at the Galleria to petrochemicals from the gulf coast, Texas' business relationship with Mexico is unique. In fact, Texas does more business with Mexico than it does with any state in its homeland.

Once a part of Mexico, Texas remains entwined by political and cultural influences south of the border. Business ties are tight.

Nearly half of U.S. exports to Mexico are from Texas. Texas' exports to Mexico constitute 5 percent of the state's overall economy.

Added to that is more than $1 billion in expenditures by Mexican tourists, economists said.

Exports to Mexico

On the export front, increased sales to Mexico this year have played a major role in boosting the state's overall exports to foreign nations, said the Texas Department of Commerce.

For the first six months this year, Texas' shipment of goods to Mexico was $12.9 billion, an increase of 21.5 percent over the same time last year. Nearly half of the state's $7.5 billion in exports of electronic equipment and components were shipped to Mexico.

Nearly 20 percent of industrial machinery and computer equipment to foreign countries went to Mexico. Some businesses have felt the difference.

"Our growth rate has been about double this year over last year" for notebooks, desktops and servers shipped to Mexico, said Cathie Hargett, a spokeswoman for Dell Computer Corp. in Austin. "Our growth rate of exports to Mexico this year over last year is over 100 percent, which is four times faster than the overall growth in the Mexico PC market." . . .

Source: Reprinted with permission of *The Dallas Morning News.*

Copyright © by Houghton Mifflin Company. All rights reserved.

The Dallas Morning News/December 8, 1996

COMMENTARY

There are two components involved in determining the price of an internationally traded good: the price in terms of the home currency of the country where the good is produced and the exchange rate. With constant dollar prices of U.S. goods, if the Mexican peso depreciates in value against the dollar, U.S. goods will become more expensive to Mexican buyers, as emphasized in the article.

In December 1994, a financial crisis which saw the peso/dollar exchange rate change from around 3.5 pesos per dollar to around 8 pesos over a two-year period began in Mexico. More dramatically, in the two-month period from November 1994 to January 1995, the peso depreciated from about 3.5 per dollar to about 5.6 per dollar—a fall of more than 60 percent. This means that even if U.S. dollar prices were unchanged in this period, U.S. goods became 60 percent more expensive to Mexicans in just two months! A Mexican resident who wanted to travel north to Texas for a shopping trip found that buying $100 worth of goods at the Galleria shopping center increased in peso terms from 350 pesos to 560 pesos. As a result, Mexicans made fewer shopping trips north of the border and U.S. firms, in general, found their sales to Mexico falling. Over time, as the Mexican economy recovered and the peso/dollar exchange rate stabilized, Mexicans increased their purchases from U.S. suppliers and resumed shopping trips to Dallas, San Antonio, Houston, Phoenix, San Diego, and other favorite cities. The article explains how important the Mexican recovery was to the Texas economy, as well as to individual firms like Dell Computers.

This article reminds us how interdependent countries are. When one nation undergoes economic problems, they spill over to trading partners. The story of the Mexican financial crisis serves as a good example of how the exchange rate between two currencies is one of the key variables linking countries together.

Copyright © by Houghton Mifflin Company. All rights reserved.

8

Unemployment and Inflation

FUNDAMENTAL QUESTIONS

1. What is a business cycle?

2. How is the unemployment rate defined and measured?

3. What is the cost of unemployed resources?

4. What is inflation?

5. Why is inflation a problem?

Copyright © by Houghton Mifflin Company. All rights reserved.

Copyright © by Houghton Mifflin Company. All rights reserved.

I f you were graduating from college today, what would your job prospects be? In 1932, they would have been bleak. A large number of people were out of work (about one in four workers), and a large number of firms had laid off workers or gone out of business. At any time, job opportunities depend not only on the individual's ability and experience, but also on the current state of the economy.

Economies follow cycles of activity: periods of expansion, where output and employment increase, are followed by periods of contraction, where output and employment decrease. For instance, during the expansionary period of the 1990s, less than 5 percent of U.S. workers had no job by 1997. But during the period of contraction of 1981–1982, 9.5 percent of U.S. workers had no job. When the economy is growing, the demand for goods and services tends to increase. To produce those goods and services, firms hire more workers. Economic expansion also has an impact on inflation. As the demand for goods and services goes up, the prices of those

goods and services also tend to rise. By the late 1990s, following several years of economic growth, consumer prices in the United States were rising by about 3 percent a year. During periods of contraction, as more people are out of work, demand for goods and services tends to fall and there is less pressure for rising prices. During the period of the Great Depression in the 1930s in the United States, consumer prices fell by more than 5 percent in 1933. Both price increases and the fraction of workers without jobs are affected by business cycles in fairly regular ways. But their effects on individual standards of living, income, and purchasing power are much less predictable.

Why do certain events move in tandem? What are the links between unemployment and inflation? What causes the business cycle to behave as it does? What effect does government activity have on the business cycle— and on unemployment and inflation? Who is harmed by rising unemployment and inflation? Who benefits? Macroeconomics attempts to answer all of these questions. ■

1. BUSINESS CYCLES

In this chapter we describe the business cycle and examine measures of unemployment and inflation. We talk about the ways in which the business cycle, unemployment, and inflation are related. And we describe their effects on the participants in the economy.

The most widely used measure of a nation's output is gross domestic product. When we examine the value of real GDP over time, we find periods in which it rises and other periods in which it falls.

1.a. Definitions

What is a business cycle?

business cycle:
pattern of rising real GDP followed by falling real GDP

recession:
a period in which real GDP falls

This pattern—real GDP rising, then falling—is called a **business cycle.** The pattern occurs over and over again, but as Figure 1 shows, the pattern over time is anything but regular. Historically the duration of business cycles and the rate at which real GDP rises or falls (indicated by the steepness of the line in Figure 1) vary considerably.

Looking at Figure 1, it is clear that the U.S. economy has experienced up-and-down swings in the years since 1959. Still, real GDP has grown at an average rate of approximately 3 percent per year. While it is important to recognize that periods of economic growth, or prosperity, are followed by periods of contraction, or **recession,** it is also important to recognize the presence of long-term economic growth—despite the presence of periodic recessions, in the long run the economy produces more goods and services. The long-run growth in the economy depends on the growth in productive resources, like land, labor, and capital, along with technological advance.

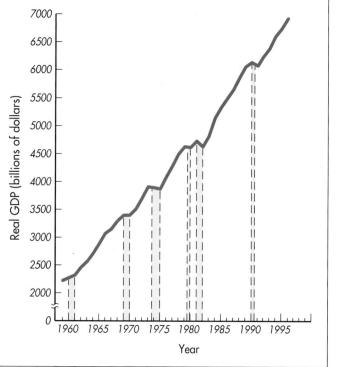

Figure 1
U.S. Real GDP
The shaded areas represent periods of economic contraction (recession). The table lists the dates of business-cycle peaks and troughs. The peak dates indicate when contractions began; the trough dates, when expansions began. Source: Data from *Economic Report of the President, 1997* (Washington, D.C.: U.S. Government Printing Office, 1997).

Peaks	Troughs
April 1960	February 1961
December 1969	November 1970
November 1973	March 1975
January 1980	July 1980
July 1981	November 1982
July 1990	March 1991

Copyright © by Houghton Mifflin Company. All rights reserved.

Technological change increases the productivity of resources so that output increases even with a fixed amount of inputs. In recent years there has been concern about the growth rate of U.S. productivity and its effect on the long-run growth potential of the economy.

Figure 2 shows how real GDP behaves over a hypothetical business cycle and identifies the stages of the cycle. The vertical axis on the graph measures the level of real GDP; the horizontal axis measures time in years. In year 1, real GDP is growing; the economy is in the *expansion* phase, or *boom* period, of the business cycle. Growth continues until the *peak* is reached, in year 2. Real GDP begins to fall during the *contraction* phase of the cycle, which continues until year 4. The *trough* marks the end of the contraction and the start of a new expansion. Even though the economy is subject to periodic ups and downs, real GDP, the measure of a nation's output, has risen over the long term, as illustrated by the upward-sloping line labeled *trend*.

If an economy is growing over time, why do economists worry about business cycles? Economists try to understand the causes of business cycles so that they can learn to moderate or avoid recessions and their harmful effects on standards of living.

1.b. Historical Record

depression:

a severe, prolonged economic contraction

The official dating of recessions in the United States is the responsibility of the National Bureau of Economic Research (NBER), an independent research organization. The NBER has identified the shaded areas in the graph in Figure 1 as recessions, the unshaded areas as expansions. Recessions are periods between cyclical peaks and the troughs that follow them. Expansions are periods between cyclical troughs and the peaks that follow them. There have been twelve recessions since 1929. The most severe was the Great Depression. Between 1929 and 1933, national output fell by 25 percent; this period is called the Great Depression. A **depression** is a prolonged period of severe economic contraction. The fact that people refer to "the Depression" when speaking about the recession that began in 1929 indicates the severity of that contraction relative to others in recent experience. There was widespread suffering during the Depression. Many people were jobless and homeless, and many firms went bankrupt.

Copyright © by Houghton Mifflin Company. All rights reserved.

Figure 2
The Business Cycle
The business cycle contains four phases: the expansion (boom), when real GDP is increasing; the peak, which marks the end of an expansion and the beginning of a contraction; the contraction (recession), when real GDP is falling; and the trough, which marks the end of a contraction and the beginning of an expansion.

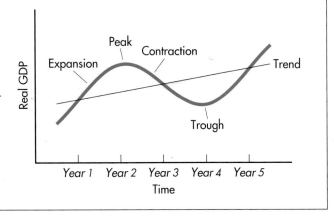

1.c. Indicators

leading indicator:
a variable that changes before real output changes

We have been talking about the business cycle in terms of real GDP. There are a number of other variables that move in a fairly regular manner over the business cycle. The Department of Commerce classifies these variables in three categories—leading indicators, coincident indicators, and lagging indicators—depending on whether they move up or down before, at the same time as, or following a change in real GDP (see Table 1).

Leading indicators generally change before real GDP changes. As a result, economists use them to forecast changes in output. Looking at Table 1, it is easy to see how some of these leading indicators could be used to forecast future output. For instance, new building permits signal new construction. If the number of new permits issued goes up, economists can expect the amount of new construction to increase. Similarly, if manufacturers receive more new orders, economists can expect more goods to be produced.

Leading indicators are not infallible, however. The link between them and future output can be tenuous. For example, leading indicators may fall one month and then rise the next, while real output rises steadily. Economists want to see several consecutive months of a new direction in the leading indicators before forecasting a change in output. Short-run movements in the indicators can be very misleading.

coincident indicator:
a variable that changes at the same time that real output changes

Coincident indicators are economic variables that tend to change at the same time real output changes. For example, as real output increases, economists expect to see employment and sales rise. The coincident indicators listed in Table 1 have demonstrated a strong tendency over time to change along with changes in real GDP.

lagging indicator:
a variable that changes after real output changes

The final group of variables listed in Table 1, **lagging indicators**, do not change their value until after the value of real GDP has changed. For instance, as output increases, jobs are created and more workers are hired. It

As real income falls, living standards go down. This 1937 photo of a depression-era breadline indicates the paradox of the world's richest nation, as emphasized on the billboard in the background, having to offer public support to feed able-bodied workers who are out of work due to the severity of the business-cycle downturn.

Copyright © by Houghton Mifflin Company. All rights reserved.

TABLE 1
Indicators of the Business Cycle

Leading Indicators

Average workweek	New building permits
Unemployment claims	Delivery times of goods
Manufacturers' new orders	Interest rate spread
Stock prices	Money supply
New plant and equipment orders	Consumer expectations

Coincident Indicators   Lagging Indicators

Coincident Indicators	Lagging Indicators
Payroll employment	Labor cost per unit of output
Industrial production	Inventories to sales ratio
Personal income	Unemployment duration
Manufacturing and trade sales	Consumer credit to personal income ratio
	Outstanding commercial loans
	Prime interest rate
	Inflation rate for services

---

makes sense, then, to expect the duration of unemployment (the average time workers are unemployed) to fall. The duration of unemployment is a lagging indicator. Similarly, the inflation rate for services (which measures how prices change for things like dry cleaners, veterinarians, and other services) tends to change after real GDP changes. Lagging indicators are used along with leading and coincident indicators to identify the peaks and troughs in business cycles.

RECAP

1. The business cycle is a recurring pattern of rising and falling real GDP.
2. Although all economies move through periods of expansion and contraction, the duration of expansion and recession varies.
3. Real GDP is not the only variable affected by business cycles; leading, lagging, and coincident indicators also show the effects of economic expansion and contraction.

2. UNEMPLOYMENT

How is the unemployment rate defined and measured?

Recurring periods of prosperity and recession are reflected in the nation's labor markets. In fact, this is what makes understanding the business cycle so important. If business cycles signified only a little more or a little less profit for businesses, governments would not be so anxious to forecast or to control their swings. It is the human costs of lost jobs and incomes—the inability to maintain standards of living—that make an understanding of business cycles and of the factors that affect unemployment so important.

Copyright © by Houghton Mifflin Company. All rights reserved.

2.a. Definition and Measurement

unemployment rate:
the percentage of the labor force that is not working

The **unemployment rate** is the percentage of the labor force that is not working. The rate is calculated by dividing the number of people who are unemployed by the number of people in the labor force:

$$\text{Unemployment rate} = \frac{\text{number unemployed}}{\text{number in labor force}}$$

This ratio seems simple enough, but there are several subtle issues at work here. First, the unemployment rate does not measure the percentage of the total population that is not working; it measures the percentage of the *labor force* that is not working. Who is in the labor force? Obviously, everybody who is employed is part of the labor force. But only some of those who are not currently employed are counted in the labor force.

You are in the labor force if you are working or actively seeking work.

The Bureau of Labor Statistics of the Department of Labor compiles labor data each month based on an extensive survey of U.S. households. All U.S. residents are potential members of the labor force. The Labor Department arrives at the size of the actual labor force by using this formula:

$$\text{Labor force} = \text{all U.S. residents} - \text{residents under 16 years}$$
$$\text{of age} - \text{institutionalized adults} - \text{adults}$$
$$\text{not looking for work}$$

So the labor force includes those adults (an adult being 16 or older) currently employed or actively seeking work. It is relatively simple to see to it that children and institutionalized adults (for instance, those in prison or long-term care facilities) are not counted in the labor force. It is more difficult to identify and accurately measure adults who are not actively looking for work.

A person is actively seeking work if he or she is available to work, has looked for work in the past four weeks, is waiting for a recall after being laid off, or is starting a job within 30 days. Those who are not working and who meet these criteria are considered unemployed.

2.b. Interpreting the Unemployment Rate

Is the unemployment rate an accurate measure? The fact that the rate does not include those who are not actively looking for work is not necessarily a failing. Many people who are not actively looking for work—homemakers, older citizens, and students, for example—have made a decision to do housework, to retire, or to stay in school. These people rightly are not counted among the unemployed.

discouraged workers:
workers who have stopped looking for work because they believe no one will offer them a job

But there are people missing from the unemployment statistics who are not working and are not looking for work, yet would take a job if one were offered. **Discouraged workers** have looked for work in the past year but have given up looking for work because they believe that no one will hire them. These individuals are ignored by the official unemployment rate even though they are able to work and may have spent a long time looking for work. Estimates of the number of discouraged workers indicate that in 1996, 1.5 million people were not counted in the labor force yet claimed that they were available for work. Of this group, 23 percent, or 345 thousand people, were considered to be discouraged workers. It is clear that the reported unemployment rate underestimates the true burden of unemployment in the economy because it ignores discouraged workers.

Copyright © by Houghton Mifflin Company. All rights reserved.

The Underground Economy

Official unemployment data, like national income data, do not include activity in the underground economy. Obviously, drug dealers and prostitutes do not report their earnings. Nor do many of the people who supplement their unemployment benefits with part-time jobs. In addition, people like the waiter who reports a small fraction of his actual tips and the house-cleaning person who requests payment in cash in order to avoid reporting taxable income are also part of the underground economy.

Because activity in the underground economy goes unreported, there is no exact way to determine its size. Estimates range from 5 to 33 percent of the gross domestic product. With the GDP at $7 trillion, this places the value of underground activity between $350 billion and $2.31 trillion.

We will never know the true size of the underground economy, but evidence suggests that it is growing. That evidence has to do with cash. The vast majority of people working in the underground economy are paid in cash. One indicator of the growth of that economy, then, is the rise in currency over time relative to checking accounts. Also, per capita holdings of $100 bills have increased substantially. Certainly, much of the demand for $100 bills is a product of inflation (as the prices of goods and services go up, it is easier to pay for them in larger-denomination bills). But there is also a substantial rise in real holdings of $100 bills as well.

The underground economy forces us to interpret government statistics carefully. We must remember that:

- Official income statistics understate the true national income.
- Official unemployment data overestimate true unemployment.
- When the underground economy grows more rapidly than the rest of the economy, the true rate of growth is higher than reported.

underemployment:
the employment of workers in jobs that do not utilize their productive potential

Activity in the underground economy is not included in official statistics

Discouraged workers are one source of hidden unemployment; underemployment is another. **Underemployment** is the underutilization of workers—employment in tasks that do not fully utilize their productive potential—including part-time workers who prefer full-time employment. Even if every worker has a job, substantial underemployment leaves the economy producing less than its potential GDP.

The effect of discouraged workers and underemployment is an unemployment rate that understates actual unemployment. In contrast, the effect of the *underground economy* is a rate that overstates actual unemployment. A sizable component of the officially unemployed is actually working. The unemployed construction worker who plays in a band at night may not report that activity because he or she wants to avoid paying taxes on his or her earnings as a musician. This person is officially unemployed but has a source of income. Many officially unemployed individuals have an alternate source of income. This means that official statistics overstate the true magnitude of unemployment. The larger the underground economy, the greater this overstatement. (See the Economic Insight "The Underground Economy.")

We have identified two factors, discouraged workers and underemployment, that cause the official unemployment rate to underestimate true unemployment. Another factor, the underground economy, causes the official rate to overestimate the true rate of unemployment. There is no reason to expect these factors to cancel one another out, and there is no way to know for sure which is most important. The point is to remember what the official data on unemployment do and do not measure.

Copyright © by Houghton Mifflin Company. All rights reserved.

2.c. Types of Unemployment

Economists have identified four basic types of unemployment:

Seasonal unemployment A product of regular, recurring changes in the hiring needs of certain industries on a monthly or seasonal basis.

Frictional unemployment A product of the short-term movement of workers between jobs and of first-time job seekers.

Structural unemployment A product of technological change and other changes in the structure of the economy.

Cyclical unemployment A product of business-cycle fluctuations.

In certain industries, labor needs fluctuate throughout the year. When local crops are harvested, farms need lots of workers; the rest of the year, they do not. (Migrant farmworkers move from one region to another, following the harvests, to avoid seasonal unemployment.) Ski resort towns like Park City, Utah, are booming during the ski season, when employment peaks, but need fewer workers during the rest of the year. In the nation as a whole, the Christmas season is a time of peak employment and low unemployment rates. To avoid confusing seasonal fluctuations in unemployment with other sources of unemployment, unemployment data are seasonally adjusted.

Frictional and structural unemployment are always present in a dynamic economy.

Frictional and structural unemployment exist in any dynamic economy. In terms of individual workers, frictional unemployment is short term in nature. Workers quit one job and soon find another; students graduate and soon find a job. This kind of unemployment cannot be eliminated in a free society. In fact, it is a sign of efficiency in an economy when workers try to increase their income or improve their working conditions by leaving one job for another. Frictional unemployment is often called *search unemployment* because workers take time to search for a job after quitting a job or leaving school.

Frictional unemployment is short term; structural unemployment, on the other hand, can be long term. Workers who are displaced by technological

Seasonal unemployment is unemployment that fluctuates with the seasons of the year. For instance, these Santas in training will be employed from fall through Christmas. After Christmas they will be unemployed and must seek new positions. Other examples of seasonal unemployment include farmworkers who migrate to follow the harvest of crops, experiencing unemployment between harvests.

Copyright © by Houghton Mifflin Company. All rights reserved.

change (assembly line workers who have been replaced by machines, for example) or by a permanent reduction in the demand for an industry's output (cigar makers who have been laid off because of a decrease in demand for tobacco) may not have the necessary skills to maintain their level of income in another industry. Rather than accept a much lower salary, these workers tend to prolong their job search. Eventually they adjust their expectations to the realities of the job market, or they enter the pool of discouraged workers.

Structural unemployment is very difficult for those who are unemployed. But for society as a whole, the technological advances that cause structural unemployment raise living standards by giving consumers a greater variety of goods at lower cost.

Cyclical unemployment is a product of recession.

Cyclical unemployment is a result of the business cycle. As a recession occurs, cyclical unemployment increases, and as growth occurs, cyclical unemployment decreases. It is also a primary focus of macroeconomic policy. Economists believe that a greater understanding of business cycles and their causes may enable them to find ways to smooth out those cycles and swings in unemployment. Much of the analysis in future chapters is related to macroeconomic policy aimed at minimizing business-cycle fluctuations. In addition to macroeconomic policy aimed at moderating cyclical unemployment, other policy measures—for example, job training and counseling—are being used to reduce frictional and structural unemployment.

2.d. Costs of Unemployment

What is the cost of unemployed resources?

The cost of being unemployed is more than the obvious loss of income and status suffered by the individual who is not working. In a broader sense, society as a whole loses when resources are unemployed. Unemployed workers produce no output. So an economy with unemployment will operate inside its production possibilities curve rather than on the curve. Economists measure this lost output in terms of the *GDP gap:*

$$\text{GDP gap} = \text{potential real GDP} - \text{actual real GDP}$$

potential real GDP:
the output produced at the natural rate of unemployment

natural rate of unemployment:
the unemployment rate that would exist in the absence of

Potential real GDP is the level of output produced when nonlabor resources are fully utilized and unemployment is at its natural rate. The **natural rate of unemployment** is the unemployment rate that would exist in the absence of cyclical unemployment, so it includes seasonal, frictional, and structural unemployment. The natural rate of unemployment is not fixed; it can change over time. For instance, some economists believe that the natural rate of unemployment has risen in recent decades, a product of the influx of baby boomers and women into the labor force. As more workers move into the labor force (begin looking for jobs), frictional unemployment increases, raising the natural rate of unemployment. The natural rate of unemployment is sometimes called the "nonaccelerating inflation rate of unemployment" or NAIRU. The idea is that there would be upward pressure on wages and prices in a "tight" labor market in which the unemployment rate fell below the NAIRU. We will see macroeconomic models of this phenomenon in later chapters.

Potential real GDP measures what we are capable of producing at the natural rate of unemployment. If we compute potential real GDP and then subtract actual real GDP, we have a measure of the output lost as a result of unemployment, or the cost of unemployment.

Copyright © by Houghton Mifflin Company. All rights reserved.

Figure 3
The GDP Gap

The GDP gap is the difference between what the economy can produce at the natural rate of unemployment
(potential GDP) and actual output (actual GDP). When
the unemployment rate is higher than the natural rate,
actual GDP is less than potential GDP. The gap between
potential and actual real GDP is a cost associated with
unemployment. Recession years are shaded to highlight
how the gap widens around recessions.

(a) Potential and Real GDP

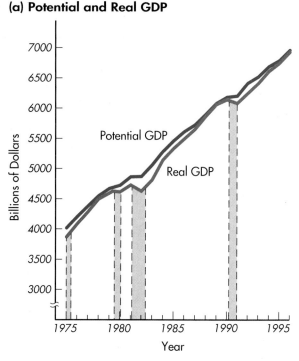

(b) A Graph of the GDP Gap

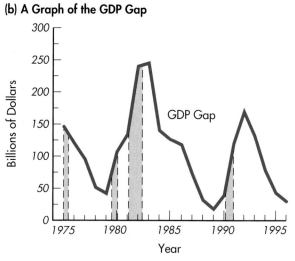

*Because frictional and structural
unemployment are always present,
the term* full employment *is misleading. Today economists use
the term* natural rate of unemployment instead.

The GDP gap in the United States from 1975 to 1996 is shown in Figure 3.
The gap widens during recessions and narrows during expansions. As the gap
widens (as the output not produced increases), there are fewer goods and
services available, and living standards are lower than they would be at the
natural rate of unemployment. Figure 3(b) is a graph of the gap between
potential and real GDP, taken from Figure 3(a).

Until recently economists used the term *full employment* instead of *natural
rate of unemployment*. Today the term *full employment* is rarely used because
it may be interpreted as implying a zero unemployment rate. If frictional and
structural unemployment are always present, zero unemployment is impossible; there must always be unemployed resources in an economy. *Natural rate*

Copyright © by Houghton Mifflin Company. All rights reserved.

of unemployment describes the labor market when the economy is producing what it realistically can produce in the absence of cyclical unemployment.

What is the value of the natural rate of unemployment in the United States? In the 1950s and 1960s, economists generally agreed on 4 percent. By the 1970s, that agreed-on rate had gone up to 5 percent. In the early 1980s, many economists placed the natural rate of unemployment in the United States at 6 to 7 percent. By the late 1980s, some had revised their thinking, placing the rate back at 5 percent. In fact, economists do not know exactly what the natural rate of unemployment is. Over time it varies within a range from around 4 percent to around 7 percent. It will also vary across countries, as labor markets and macroeconomic policies differ.

2.e. The Record of Unemployment

Unemployment rates in the United States from 1951 to 1997 are listed in Table 2. Over this period, the unemployment rate for all workers reached a low of 2.8 percent in 1953 and a high of 9.5 percent in 1982 and 1983. The table shows some general trends in the incidence of unemployment across different demographic groups:

In most years, the unemployment rate for women is higher than it is for men. Several factors may be at work here. First, during this period, a large number of women entered the labor force for the first time. Second, discrimination against women in the workplace limited job opportunities for them, particularly early in this period. Finally, a large number of women move out of the labor force on temporary maternity leaves.

Teenagers have the highest unemployment rates in the economy. This makes sense because teenagers are the least-skilled segment of the labor force.

Whites have lower unemployment rates than nonwhites. Discrimination plays a role here. To the extent that discrimination extends beyond hiring practices and job opportunities for minority workers to the education that is necessary to prepare students to enter the work force, minority workers will have fewer opportunities for employment. The quality of education provided in many schools with large minority populations may not be as good as that provided in schools with large white populations. Equal opportunity programs and legislation are aimed at rectifying this inequality.

Although exact comparisons across countries are difficult to make because countries measure unemployment in different ways, it is interesting to look at the reported unemployment rates of different countries. Table 3 lists unemployment rates for seven major industrial nations. The rates have been adjusted to match as closely as possible the U.S. definition of unemployment. For instance, the official Italian unemployment data include people who have not looked for work in the past 30 days. The data for Italy in Table 3 have been adjusted to remove these people. If the data had not been adjusted, the Italian unemployment rates would be roughly twice as high as those listed.

Countries not only define unemployment differently, they also use different methods to count the unemployed. All major European countries except Sweden use a national unemployment register to identify the unemployed. Only those people who register for unemployment benefits are considered unemployed. A problem with this method is that it excludes those who have not registered because they are not entitled to benefits and it includes those

Copyright © by Houghton Mifflin Company. All rights reserved.

TABLE 2
Unemployment Rates in the United States

	Unemployment Rate, Civilian Workers[1]					
Year	All Civilian Workers	Males	Females	Both Sexes 16–19 Years	White	Black and Other
1951	3.3	2.8	4.4	8.2	3.1	5.3
1953	2.9	2.8	3.3	7.6	2.7	4.5
1955	4.4	4.2	4.9	11.0	3.9	8.7
1957	4.3	4.1	4.7	11.6	3.8	7.9
1959	5.5	5.2	5.9	14.6	4.8	10.7
1961	6.7	6.4	7.2	16.8	6.0	12.4
1963	5.7	5.2	6.5	17.2	5.0	10.8
1965	4.5	4.0	5.5	14.8	4.1	8.1
1967	3.8	3.1	5.2	12.9	3.4	7.4
1969	3.5	2.8	4.7	12.2	3.1	6.4
1971	5.9	5.3	6.9	16.9	5.4	9.9
1973	4.9	4.2	6.0	14.5	4.3	9.0
1975	8.5	7.9	9.3	19.9	7.8	13.8
1977	7.1	6.3	8.2	17.8	6.2	13.1
1979	5.8	5.1	6.8	16.1	5.1	11.3
1980	7.1	6.9	7.4	17.8	6.3	13.1
1981	7.6	7.4	7.9	19.6	6.7	14.2
1982	9.7	9.9	9.4	23.2	8.6	17.3
1983	9.6	9.9	9.2	22.4	8.4	17.8
1984	7.5	7.4	7.6	18.9	6.5	14.4
1985	7.2	7.0	7.4	18.6	6.2	13.7
1986	7.0	6.9	7.1	18.3	6.0	13.1
1987	6.2	6.2	6.2	16.9	5.3	11.6
1988	5.5	5.5	5.6	15.3	4.7	10.4
1989	5.3	5.2	5.4	15.0	4.5	10.0
1990	5.5	5.6	5.4	15.5	4.7	10.1
1991	6.7	7.0	6.3	18.6	6.0	11.1
1992	7.4	7.8	6.9	20.0	6.5	12.7
1993	6.8	7.1	6.5	19.0	6.0	11.7
1994	6.1	6.2	6.0	17.6	5.3	10.5
1995	5.6	5.6	5.6	17.3	4.9	9.6
1996	5.4	5.4	5.4	16.7	4.7	9.3
1997	5.0	4.2	4.4	16.0	4.2	8.8

[1]Unemployed as a percentage of the civilian labor force in the group specified.
Source: *Economic Report of the President, 1997* (Washington, D.C.: U.S. Government Printing Office, 1997).

Copyright © by Houghton Mifflin Company. All rights reserved.

TABLE 3
Unemployment Rates in Major Industrial Countries

	Civilian Unemployment Rate (percent)						
Year	United States	Canada	France	Italy	Japan	United Kingdom	Germany
1960	5.5	6.5	1.5	3.7	1.7	2.2	1.1
1962	5.5	5.5	1.4	2.8	1.3	2.7	.6
1964	5.2	4.4	1.2	2.7	1.2	2.5	.4
1966	3.8	3.4	1.6	3.7	1.4	2.3	.3
1968	3.6	4.5	2.7	3.5	1.2	3.2	1.1
1970	4.9	5.7	2.5	3.2	1.2	3.1	.5
1972	5.6	6.2	2.9	3.8	1.4	4.2	.7
1974	5.6	5.3	2.9	3.1	1.4	3.1	1.6
1976	7.7	7.1	4.5	3.9	2.0	5.9	3.4
1978	6.1	8.3	5.3	4.1	2.3	6.3	3.3
1980	7.1	7.5	6.4	4.4	2.0	7.0	2.9
1981	7.6	7.5	7.6	4.9	2.2	10.5	4.1
1982	9.7	11.0	8.3	5.4	2.4	11.2	5.8
1983	9.6	11.8	8.5	5.9	2.7	11.7	7.1
1984	7.5	11.2	10.0	5.9	2.8	11.7	7.4
1985	7.2	10.5	10.4	6.0	2.6	11.2	7.5
1986	7.0	9.5	10.6	7.5	2.8	11.2	6.9
1987	6.2	8.8	10.8	7.9	2.9	10.2	6.4
1988	5.5	7.8	10.4	7.9	2.5	8.3	6.3
1989	5.3	7.5	9.6	7.8	2.3	6.4	5.7
1990	5.5	8.1	9.2	7.0	2.1	6.9	5.0
1991	6.7	10.3	9.4	6.9	2.1	8.8	4.3
1992	7.4	11.3	10.4	7.3	2.2	10.0	4.6
1993	6.8	11.2	11.8	10.5	2.5	10.4	5.8
1994	6.1	10.4	12.3	11.3	2.9	9.6	6.5
1995	5.6	9.5	11.7	12.0	3.2	8.8	6.5
1996	5.4	9.7	12.7	11.9	3.4	8.1	7.2

Source: *Economic Report of the President, 1997* (Washington, D.C.: U.S. Government Printing Office, 1997), p. 401.

who receive benefits but would not take a job if one was offered. Other countries—among them the United States, Canada, Sweden, and Japan—conduct monthly surveys of households to estimate the unemployment rate. Surveys allow more comprehensive analysis of unemployment and its causes than does the use of a register. The Organization for Economic Cooperation and Development, an organization created to foster international economic cooperation, compared annual surveys of the labor force in Europe with the official register of unemployment data and found that only 80 to 85 percent of those surveyed as unemployed were registered in Germany, France, and the United Kingdom. In Italy, only 63 percent of those surveyed as unemployed were registered.

Knowing their limitations, we can still identify some important trends from the data in Table 3. Through the 1960s and early 1970s, European unemployment

Copyright © by Houghton Mifflin Company. All rights reserved.

rates generally were lower than U.S. and Canadian rates. Over the next decade, European unemployment rates increased substantially, as did the rates in North America. But in the mid-1980s, while U.S. unemployment began to fall, European unemployment remained high. The issue of high unemployment rates in Europe has become a major topic of discussion at international summit meetings. Japanese unemployment rates, like those in Europe, were much lower than U.S. and Canadian rates in the 1960s and 1970s. However, unlike European rates, Japanese rates remained much lower in the 1980s and 1990s.

RECAP

1. The unemployment rate is the number of people unemployed as a percentage of the labor force.
2. To be in the labor force, one must either have or be looking for a job.
3. By its failure to include discouraged workers and the output lost because of underemployment, the unemployment rate understates real unemployment in the United States.
4. By its failure to include activity in the underground economy, the U.S. unemployment rate overstates actual unemployment.
5. Unemployment data are adjusted to eliminate seasonal fluctuations.
6. Frictional and structural unemployment are always present in a dynamic economy.
7. Cyclical unemployment is a product of recession; it can be moderated by controlling the period of contraction in the business cycle.
8. Economists measure the cost of unemployment in terms of lost output.
9. Unemployment data show that women generally have higher unemployment rates than men, that teenagers have the highest unemployment rates in the economy, and that blacks and other minority groups have higher unemployment rates than whites.

3. INFLATION

What is inflation ?

inflation:
a sustained rise in the average level of prices

Inflation is a sustained rise in the average level of prices. Notice the word *sustained*. Inflation does not mean a short-term increase in prices; it means prices are rising over a prolonged period of time. Inflation is measured by the percentage change in price level. The inflation rate in the United States was 1.7 percent in 1997. This means that the level of prices increased 1.7 percent over the year.

3.a. Absolute Versus Relative Price Changes

In the modern economy, over any given period, some prices rise faster than others. To evaluate the rate of inflation in a country, then, economists must know what is happening to prices on average. Here it is important to distinguish between *absolute* and *relative* price changes.

Copyright © by Houghton Mifflin Company. All rights reserved.

Let's look at an example using the prices of fish and beef:

	Year 1	Year 2
1 pound of fish	$1	$2
1 pound of beef	$2	$4

In year 1, beef is twice as expensive as fish. This is the price of beef *relative* to fish. In year 2, beef is still twice as expensive as fish. The relative prices have not changed between years 1 and 2. What has changed? The prices of both beef and fish have doubled. The *absolute* levels of all prices have gone up, but because they have increased by the same percentage, the relative prices are unchanged.

Inflation measures changes in absolute prices. In our example, all prices doubled, so the inflation rate is 100 percent. There was a 100 percent increase in the prices of beef and fish. Inflation does not proceed evenly through the economy. Prices of some goods rise faster than others, which means that relative prices are changing at the same time that absolute prices are rising. The measured inflation rate records the *average* change in absolute prices.

3.b. Effects of Inflation

To understand the effects of inflation, you have to understand what happens to the value of money in an inflationary period. The real value of money is what it can buy, its *purchasing power*:

$$\text{Real value of } \$1 = \frac{\$1}{\text{price level}}$$

The higher the price level, the lower the real value (or *purchasing power*) of the dollar. For instance, suppose an economy had only one good—milk. If a glass of milk sold for $.50, then one dollar would buy two glasses of milk. If the price of milk rose to $1, then a dollar would only buy one glass of milk. The purchasing power, or real value, of money falls as prices rise.

Table 4 lists the real value of the dollar in selected years from 1946 to 1997. The price level in each year is measured relative to the average level of prices over the 1982–1984 period. For instance, the 1946 value, .195, means that prices in 1946 were, on average, only 19.5 percent of prices in the 1982–1984 period. Notice that as prices go up, the purchasing power of the dollar falls. In 1946 a dollar bought five times more than a dollar bought in the early 1980s. The value 5.13 means that one could buy 5.13 times more goods and services with a dollar in 1946 than one could in 1982–1984.

Prices have risen steadily in recent decades. By 1997, they had gone up more than 61 percent above the average level of prices in the 1982–1984 period. Consequently, the purchasing power of a 1997 dollar was lower. In 1997, $1 bought just 62 percent of the goods and services that one could buy with a dollar in 1982–1984.

If prices and nominal income rise by the same percentage, it might seem that inflation is not a problem. It doesn't matter if it takes twice as many dollars now to buy fish and beef than it did before, if we have twice as many dollars in income available to buy the products. Obviously, inflation is very much a problem when a household's nominal income rises at a slower rate than prices. Inflation hurts those households whose income does not keep up with the prices of the goods they buy.

Why is inflation a problem?

The purchasing power of a dollar is the amount of goods and services it can buy.

Copyright © by Houghton Mifflin Company. All rights reserved.

TABLE 4
The Real Value of a Dollar

Year	Average Price Level[1]	Purchasing Power of a Dollar[2]
1946	.195	5.13
1950	.241	4.15
1954	.269	3.72
1958	.289	3.46
1962	.302	3.31
1966	.324	3.09
1970	.388	2.58
1974	.493	2.03
1978	.652	1.53
1982	.965	1.04
1986	1.096	.91
1990	1.307	.77
1994	1.482	.67
1995	1.524	.66
1996	1.569	.64
1997	1.613	.62

[1]Measured by the consumer price index as given in the *Economic Report of the President, 1997* (Washington, D.C.: U.S. Government Printing Office, 1997).

[2]Found by taking the reciprocal of the consumer price index (1/CPI).

In the 1970s in the United States, the rate of inflation rose to near-record levels. Many workers believed that their incomes were lagging behind the rate of inflation, so they negotiated cost-of-living raises in their wage contracts. The typical cost-of-living raise ties salary to changes in the consumer price index. If the CPI rises 8 percent over a year, workers receive an 8 percent raise plus compensation for experience or productivity increases. As the U.S. rate of inflation fell during the 1980s, concern about cost-of-living raises subsided as well.

It is important to distinguish between expected and unexpected inflation. *Unexpectedly high inflation* redistributes income away from those who receive fixed incomes (like creditors who receive debt repayments of a fixed amount of dollars per month) toward those who make fixed expenditures (like debtors who make fixed debt repayments per month). For example, consider a simple loan agreement:

Maria borrows $100 from Ali, promising to repay the loan in one year at 10 percent interest. In one year, Maria will pay Ali $110—principal of $100 plus interest of $10 (10 percent of $100, or $10).

When Maria and Ali agree to the terms of the loan, they do so with some expected rate of inflation in mind. Suppose they both expect 5 percent inflation over the year. In one year it will take 5 percent more money to buy goods than it does now. Ali will need $105 to buy what $100 buys today. Because Ali will receive $110 for the principal and interest on the loan, he will gain purchasing power. However, if the inflation rate over the year turns out to be

Unexpectedly high inflation redistributes income away from those who receive fixed incomes toward those who make fixed expenditures.

Copyright © by Houghton Mifflin Company. All rights reserved.

Part II / Macroeconomic Basics

surprisingly high—say, 15 percent—then Ali will need $115 to buy what $100 buys today. He will lose purchasing power if he makes a loan at a 10 percent rate of interest.

Economists distinguish between nominal and real interest rates when analyzing economic behavior. The **nominal interest rate** is the observed interest rate in the market and includes the effect of inflation. The **real interest rate** is the nominal interest rate minus the rate of inflation:

Copyright © by Houghton Mifflin Company. All rights reserved.

nominal interest rate:
the observed interest rate in the market

real interest rate:
the nominal interest rate minus the rate of inflation

Real interest rates are lower than expected when inflation is higher than expected.

$$\text{Real interest rate} = \text{nominal interest rate} - \text{rate of inflation}$$

If Ali charges Maria 10 percent nominal interest and the inflation rate is 5 percent, the real interest rate is 5 percent (10% − 5% = 5%). This means that Ali will earn a positive real return from the loan. However, if the inflation rate is 10 percent, the real return from a nominal interest rate of 10 percent is zero (10% − 10% = 0). The interest Ali will receive from the loan will just compensate him for the rise in prices; he will not realize an increase in purchasing power. If the inflation rate is higher than the nominal interest rate, then the real interest rate is negative—the lender will lose purchasing power by making the loan.

Now you can see how unexpected inflation redistributes income. Borrowers and creditors agree to loan terms based on what they *expect* the rate of inflation to be over the period of the loan. If the *actual* rate of inflation turns out to be different from what was expected, then the real interest rate paid by the borrower and received by the lender will be different from what was expected. If Ali and Maria both expect a 5 percent inflation rate and agree to a 10 percent nominal interest rate for the loan, then they both expect a real interest rate of 5 percent (10% − 5% = 5%) to be paid on the loan. If the actual inflation rate turns out to be greater than 5 percent, then the real interest rate will be less than expected. Maria will get to borrow Ali's money at a lower real cost than she expected, and Ali will earn a lower real return than he expected. Unexpectedly high inflation hurts creditors and benefits borrowers because it lowers real interest rates.

Figure 4 shows the real interest rates on U.S. Treasury bills from 1970 through 1997. You can see a pronounced pattern in the graph. In the late 1970s, there was a period of negative real interest rates, followed by high positive real rates in the 1980s. The evidence suggests that nominal interest rates did not rise fast enough in the 1970s to offset high inflation. This was a time of severe strain on many creditors, including savings and loan associations and banks. These firms had lent funds at fixed nominal rates of interest. When those rates of interest turned out to be lower than the rate of inflation, the financial institutions suffered significant losses. In the early 1980s, the inflation rate dropped sharply. Because nominal interest rates did not drop nearly as fast as the rate of inflation, real interest rates were high. In this period many debtors were hurt by the high costs of borrowing to finance business or household expenditures.

Unexpected inflation affects more than the two parties to a loan. Any contract calling for fixed payments over some long-term period changes in value as the rate of inflation changes. For instance, a long-term contract that provides union members with 5 percent raises each year for five years gives the workers more purchasing power if inflation is low than if it is high. Similarly, a contract that sells a product at a fixed price over a long-term period will change in value as inflation changes. Suppose a lumber company promises to

Figure 4
The Real Interest Rate on U.S. Treasury Bills
The real interest rate is the difference between the nominal rate (the rate actually observed) and the rate of inflation over the life of the bond. The figure shows the real interest rate in June and December for each year. For instance, in the first observation for June 1970, a six-month Treasury bill paid the holder 6.91 percent interest. This is the nominal rate of interest. To find the real rate of interest on the bond, we subtract the rate of inflation that existed over the six months of the bond's life (June to December 1970), which was 5.17 percent. The difference between the nominal interest rate (6.91 percent) and the rate of inflation (5.17 percent) is the real interest rate, 1.74 percent. Notice that real interest rates were negative during most of the 1970s and then turned highly positive (by historical standards) in the early 1980s.

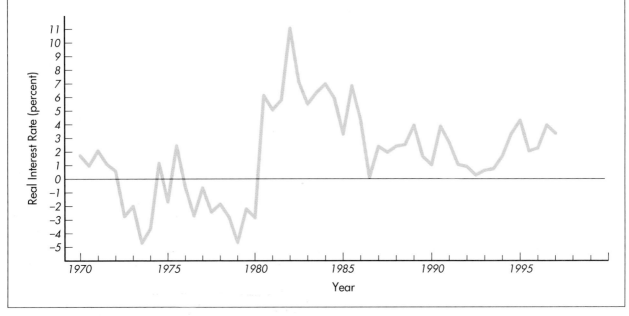

supply a builder with lumber at a fixed price for a two-year period. If the rate of inflation in one year turns out to be higher than expected, the lumber company will end up selling the lumber for less profit than it had planned. Inflation raises costs to the lumber company. Usually the company would raise its prices to compensate for higher costs. Because the company contracted to sell its goods at a fixed price to the builder, however, the builder benefits at the lumber company's expense. Again, unexpectedly high inflation redistributes real income or purchasing power away from those receiving fixed payments to those making fixed payments.

One response to the effects of unexpected inflation is to allow prices, wages, or interest rates to vary with the rate of inflation. Labor sometimes negotiates cost-of-living adjustments as part of new wage contracts. Financial institutions offer variable interest rates on home mortgages to reflect current market conditions. Any contract can be written to adjust dollar amounts over time as the rate of inflation changes.

3.c. Types of Inflation

Economists often classify inflation according to the source of the inflationary pressure. The most straightforward method defines inflation in terms of pressure from the demand side of the market or the supply side of the market:

Copyright © by Houghton Mifflin Company. All rights reserved.

Part II / Macroeconomic Basics

Demand-pull inflation Increases in total spending that are not offset by increases in the supply of goods and services cause the average level of prices to rise.

Cost-push inflation Increases in production costs cause firms to raise prices to avoid losses.

Sometimes inflation is blamed on "too many dollars chasing too few goods." This is a roundabout way of saying that the inflation stems from demand pressures. Because demand-pull inflation is a product of increased spending, it is more likely to occur in an economy that is producing at maximum capacity. If resources are fully employed, in the short run it may not be possible to increase output to meet increased demand. The result: existing goods and services are rationed by rising prices.

Some economists claim that rising prices in the late 1960s were a product of demand-pull inflation. They believe that increased government spending for the Vietnam War caused the level of U.S. prices to rise.

Cost-push inflation can occur in any economy, whatever its output. If prices go up because the costs of resources are rising, the rate of inflation can go up regardless of demand.

For example, some economists argue that the inflation in the United States in the 1970s was largely due to rising oil prices. This means that decreases in the oil supply (a shift to the left in the supply curve) brought about higher oil prices. Because oil is so important in the production of many goods, higher oil prices led to increases in prices throughout the economy. Cost-push inflation stems from changes in the supply side of the market.

Cost-push inflation is sometimes attributed to profit-push or wage-push pressures. *Profit-push pressures* are created by suppliers who want to increase their profit margins by raising prices faster than their costs increase. *Wage-push pressures* are created by labor unions and workers who are able to increase their wages faster than their productivity. There have been times when "greedy" businesses and unions have been blamed for periods of inflation in the United States. The problem with these "theories" is that people have always wanted to improve their economic status and always will. In this sense, people have always been greedy. But inflation has not always been a problem. Were people less greedy in the early 1980s when inflation was low than they were in the late 1970s when inflation was high? Obviously, we have to look to other reasons to explain inflation. We discuss some of those reasons in later chapters.

3.d. The Inflationary Record

Many of our students, having always lived with inflation, are surprised to learn that inflation is a relatively new problem for the United States. From 1789, when the U.S. Constitution was ratified, until 1940, there was no particular trend in the general price level. At times prices rose, and at times they fell. The average level of prices in 1940 was approximately the same as it was in the late eighteenth century.

Since 1940, prices in the United States have gone up markedly. The price level today is eight times what it was in 1940. But the rate of growth has

Copyright © by Houghton Mifflin Company. All rights reserved.

Figure 5
U.S. Consumer Prices
Prices rose relatively rapidly after World War II, then at a slow rate from the late 1940s until the late 1960s. Prices again rose at a fairly rapid rate through the 1970s. In the early 1980s, price increases moderated. Source: *Economic Report of the President, 1997* (Washington, D.C.: U.S. Government Printing Office, 1997).

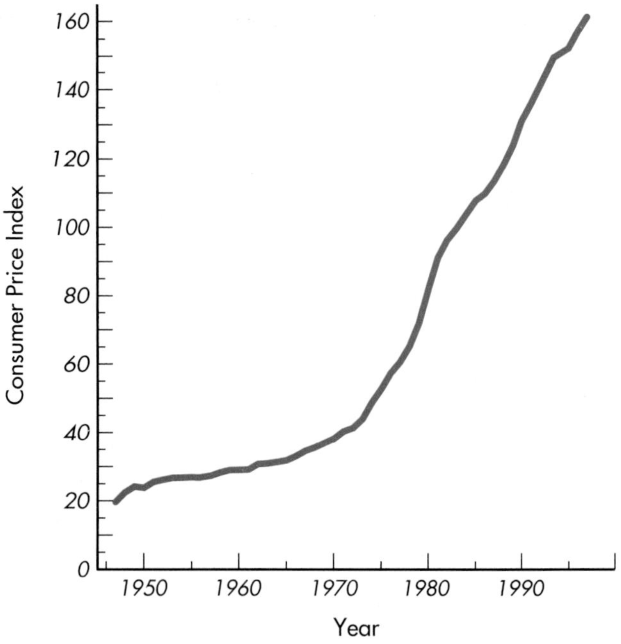

varied. Figure 5 plots the path of consumer prices in the United States in the post–World War II period. Notice that prices rose rapidly for the first couple of years following the war, and then grew at a relatively slow rate through the 1950s and 1960s. In the early 1970s, the rate of inflation began to accelerate. Prices climbed quickly until the early 1980s, when inflation slowed.

Annual rates of inflation for several industrial and developing nations are shown in Table 5. In 1996, the average rate of inflation across all industrial countries was 2.3 percent; the average across all developing countries was 15.7 percent. Look at the diversity across countries: rates range from 0.1 percent in Japan to 659 percent in the Congo.

hyperinflation:
an extremely high rate of inflation

Hyperinflation is an extremely high rate of inflation. In most cases hyperinflation eventually makes a country's currency worthless and leads to the introduction of a new money. Argentina experienced hyperinflation in the 1980s. People had to carry large stacks of currency for small purchases. Cash registers and calculators ran out of digits as prices reached ridiculously high levels. After years of high inflation, Argentina replaced the old peso with the peso Argentino in June 1983. The government set the value of 1 peso Argentino equal to 10,000 old pesos (striking four zeros from all prices). A product that sold for 10,000 old pesos before the reform sold for 1 new peso after. But Argentina did not follow up its monetary reform with a noninflationary change in economic policy. In 1984 and 1985, the inflation rate exceeded 600 percent each year. As a result, in June 1985, the government again introduced a new currency, the austral, setting its value at 1,000 pesos Argentino. However, the economic policy associated with the introduction of the austral only lowered the inflation rate temporarily. By 1988, the inflation rate was over 300 percent, and in 1989 the inflation rate was over 3,000 percent. The rapid rise in prices associated with the austral resulted in the intro-

Copyright © by Houghton Mifflin Company. All rights reserved.

TABLE 5
Rates of Inflation for Selected Countries, 1996

Country	Inflation Rate (percent)
All industrial	2.3
All developing	15.7
Selected industrial:	
Canada	1.6
Germany	1.5
Italy	4.0
Japan	0.1
United Kingdom	2.4
United States	2.9
Selected developing:	
Botswana	10
Brazil	16
Chile	7
Congo	659
Egypt	7
Hong Kong, China	6
India	9
Israel	11
Mexico	34
Philippines	8
Poland	20
South Africa	7

Source: From *International Financial Statistics*, December 1997. Reprinted courtesy of International Monetary fund.

Copyright © by Houghton Mifflin Company. All rights reserved.

duction of yet another currency, again named peso Argentino, in January 1992 with a value equal to 10,000 australes.

The most dramatic hyperinflation in modern times occurred in Europe after World War I. Table 6 shows how the price level rose in Germany between 1914 and 1924 in relation to prices in 1914. For instance, the value in 1915, 126, indicates that prices were 26 percent higher that year than in 1914. The value in 1919, 262, indicates that prices were 162 percent higher that year than in 1914. By 1924, German prices were more than 100 trillion times higher than they had been in 1914. At the height of the inflation, the mark was virtually worthless.

In later chapters, we will see how high rates of inflation generally are caused by rapid growth of the money supply. When a central government wants to spend more than it is capable of funding through taxation or borrowing, it simply issues money to finance its budget deficit. As the money supply increases faster than the demand to hold it, spending increases and prices go up.

TABLE 6
German Wholesale Prices, 1914–1924

Year	Price Index
1914	100
1915	126
1916	150
1917	156
1918	204
1919	262
1920	1,260
1921	1,440
1922	3,670
1923	278,500
1924	117,320,000,000,000

Source: J. P. Young, *European Currency and Finance*
(Washington, D.C.: U.S. Government Printing Office, 1925).

RECAP

1. Inflation is a sustained rise in the average level of prices.
2. The higher the price level, the lower the real value (purchasing power) of money.
3. Unexpectedly high inflation redistributes income away from those who receive fixed-dollar payments (like creditors) toward those who make fixed-dollar payments (like debtors).
4. The real interest rate is the nominal interest rate minus the rate of inflation.
5. Demand-pull inflation is a product of increased spending; cost-push inflation reflects increased production costs.
6. Hyperinflation is a very high rate of inflation that often results in the introduction of a new currency.

SUMMARY

▬ What is a business cycle?

1. Business cycles are recurring changes in real GDP, in which expansion is followed by contraction. §1.a
2. The four stages of the business cycle are expansion (boom), peak, contraction (recession), and trough. §1.a
3. Leading, coincident, and lagging indicators are variables that change in relation to changes in output. §1.c

▬ How is the unemployment rate defined and measured?

4. The unemployment rate is the percentage of the labor force that is not working. §2.a
5. To be in the U.S. labor force, an individual must be working or actively seeking work. §2.a
6. Unemployment can be classified as seasonal, frictional, structural, or cyclical. §2.c

Copyright © by Houghton Mifflin Company. All rights reserved.

7. Frictional and structural unemployment are always present in a dynamic economy; cyclical unemployment is a product of recession. §2.c

What is the cost of unemployed resources?

8. The GDP gap measures the output lost because of unemployment. §2.d

What is inflation?

9. Inflation is a sustained rise in the average level of prices. §3

10. The higher the level of prices, the lower the purchasing power of money. §3.b

Why is inflation a problem?

11. Inflation becomes a problem when income rises at a slower rate than prices. §3.b

12. Unexpectedly high inflation hurts those who receive fixed-dollar payments (like creditors) and benefits those who make fixed-dollar payments (like debtors). §3.b

13. Inflation can stem from demand-pull or cost-push pressures. §3.c

14. Hyperinflation—an extremely high rate of inflation—can force a country to introduce a new currency. §3.d

KEY TERMS

business cycle §1.a

recession §1.a

depression §1.b

leading indicator §1.c

coincident indicator §1.c

lagging indicator §1.c

unemployment rate §2.a

discouraged workers §2.b

underemployment §2.b

potential real GDP §2.d

natural rate of unemployment §2.d

inflation §3

nominal interest rate §3.b

real interest rate §3.b

hyperinflation §3.d

EXERCISES

1. What is the labor force? Do you believe that the U.S. government's definition of the labor force is a good one—that it includes all the people it should include? Explain your answer.

2. List the reasons why the official unemployment rate may not reflect the true social burden of unemployment. Explain whether the official numbers overstate or understate *true* unemployment in light of each reason you discuss.

3. Suppose you are able-bodied and intelligent, but lazy. You'd rather sit home and watch television than work, even though you know you could find an acceptable job if you looked.

   a. Are you officially unemployed?

   b. Are you a discouraged worker?

4. Can government do anything to reduce the number of people in the following categories? If so, what?

   a. Frictionally unemployed

   b. Structurally unemployed

   c. Cyclically unemployed

5. Does the GDP gap measure all of the costs of unemployment? Why or why not?

6. Why do teenagers have the highest unemployment rate in the economy?

7. Suppose you are currently earning $10 an hour. If the inflation rate over the current year is 10% and your firm provides a cost-of-living raise based on the rate of inflation, what would you expect to earn after your raise? If the cost-of-living raise is always granted based on the past year's inflation, is your nominal income really keeping up with the cost of living?

Copyright © by Houghton Mifflin Company. All rights reserved.

8. Write an equation that defines the real interest rate. Use the equation to explain why unexpectedly high inflation redistributes income from creditors to debtors.

9. Many home mortgages in recent years have been made with variable interest rates. Typically, the interest rate is adjusted once a year based on current interest rates on government bonds. How do variable interest rate loans protect creditors from the effects of unexpected inflation?

10. The word *cycle* suggests a regular, recurring pattern of activity. Is there a regular pattern in the business cycle? Support your answer by examining the duration (number of months) of each expansion and contraction in Figure 1.

11. Using the list of leading indicators in Table 1, write a brief paragraph explaining why each variable changes before real output changes. In other words, provide an economic reason why each indicator is expected to lead the business cycle.

12. Suppose 500 people were surveyed, and of those 500, 450 were working full time. Of the 50 not working, 10 were full-time college students, 20 were retired, 5 were under sixteen years of age, 5 had stopped looking for work because they believed there were no jobs for them, and 10 were actively looking for work.

    a. How many of the 500 surveyed are in the labor force?

    b. What is the unemployment rate among the 500 surveyed people?

13. Consider the following price information:

	Year 1	Year 2
Cup of coffee	$ .50	$1.00
Glass of milk	$1.00	$2.00

    a. Based on the information given, what was the inflation rate between year 1 and year 2?

    b. What happened to the price of coffee relative to that of milk between year 1 and year 2?

14. Use a supply and demand diagram to illustrate:

    a. Cost-push inflation caused by a labor union successfully negotiating for a higher wage.

    b. Demand-pull inflation caused by an increase in demand for domestic products from foreign buyers.

15. During the Bolivian hyperinflation in the 1980s, Bolivians used U.S. dollars as a substitute for the domestic currency (the peso) for many transactions. Explain how the value of money is affected by hyperinflation and the incentives to use a low-inflation currency like the dollar as a substitute for a high-inflation currency like the Bolivian peso.

Copyright © by Houghton Mifflin Company. All rights reserved.

 **INTERNET EXERCISE**

In section 3.b of this chapter we learned that the real interest rate is equal to the nominal interest rate minus the rate of inflation. Your friend tells you that interest rates are so low in recent years that you might as well just stuff your money in a can and bury it in the backyard. You want to convince him how one could buy riskless U.S. government securities and still be way ahead of burying money in the backyard. In order to build your argument, you want to compute the real interest rate on buying one-year U.S. Treasury bills in January of 1996 and 1997 that would mature in December of each year. To do so, go to the Boyes/Melvin web site at **http://www. hmco.com/college/** and click on the internet exercise link for this chapter. Now answer the questions that appear on the web page.

Copyright © by Houghton Mifflin Company. All rights reserved.

Though Layoffs Make Headlines, Economy Quietly Creates Jobs

To gauge where the economy is headed, just follow Beverly Davidson's mercurial career.

She was laid off by an oil and gas company in 1986 and a bank in 1990. Ms. Davidson found more work—but was laid off again last August. Now the 34-year-old college graduate is working for a small computer firm.

How long that job will last is any economist's guess. "Everybody has to be fast on their feet," said her new boss, Robert Porter of Altai Inc.

Despite a healthy economy and a declining jobless rate, layoffs are still in the news. Last month Halliburton Co. said it would cut 1,200 employees and Delta Airlines said it would slash up to 15,000 jobs.

But Ms. Davidson seems to have a good chance of surviving these uncertain times, especially in Texas. Economists say that many small companies—in industries such as technology, telecommunications and health care—are adding jobs that more than make up for the layoffs.

And some companies are cutting jobs while hiring workers whose technical skills can improve efficiency.

"Either you upgrade your workers or you hire people instead. IBM laid off thousands, but they're still hiring," said Travis Tullos, an analyst with *Texas Perspectives* newsletter.

Mr. Tullos said there is still a lot of restructuring within companies. He cites the high volume of help-wanted ads and the high unemployment claims as evidence that companies are still laying off workers. Jared Hazelton, a Texas A&M economist said: "Most people laid off find other jobs. It's bad for the people involved, but layoffs are a way of becoming more competitive."

At Altai, manufacturing takes place in sleek offices where workers wear jeans and open-necked shirts, sit with their legs propped on desks and invent software that makes computers work more efficiently.

The number of employees at Altai has doubled to 120 in the past four years, said Mr. Porter, vice president of client services.

Recently, he was trying to hire three employees—one to develop new software and two to replace two employees in support services.

Altai's revenue has grown from $4.7 million in 1989 to $12.0 million last year. It is in stiff competition with similar companies, hence the need to add a new software developer.

The job typically pays between $35,000 and $60,000 annually, Mr. Porter said.

In Ms. Davidson's case, her new job of assisting clients with technical problems pays less than her other jobs did, but she wanted a career change. Ms. Davidson wouldn't discuss her salary.

In the past year, Altai has hired 10 new employees and has had no layoffs, Mr. Porter said. He said he gets calls from people laid off from other businesses every week and has hired some of them.

Many of the larger computer companies are downsizing, he said, because the efficiency of advanced computer systems is making some jobs obsolete. Although there are many jobs around, Mr. Porter said applicants have to be highly qualified to get one.

"Other companies have data processing layoffs because they're taking advantage of new technologies," Mr. Porter said. "We are creating those new technologies."

Source: "Though Layoffs Make Headlines, Economy Quietly Creates Jobs," by Jane Seaberry, *The Dallas Morning News*, June 5, 1994, p. 141. Reprinted by permission of *The Dallas Morning News*.

The Dallas Morning News/June 5, 1994

Copyright © by Houghton Mifflin Company. All rights reserved.

COMMENTARY

Structural change in an economy forces difficult adjustments like structural unemployment. Some of the most dramatic examples of this kind of change have occurred in the so-called Rust Belt of the United States—the industrial region of the Northeast and the Midwest, where well-paying factory jobs are disappearing in the face of foreign competition and new production techniques. Many workers in this region who once had jobs in automobile manufacturing and steel production have recently been left with fewer job prospects and uncertain futures.

Many newly unemployed workers have worked for many years and earned higher salaries than they can expect to earn in other jobs. This, of course, is the problem. If they could simply find another job that offers them comparable pay, they would not be so devastated by the prospect of losing their jobs. This raises an interesting question: If someone is highly valued at one firm and paid accordingly, why aren't they as valuable to other companies who could now hire them? In fact, it is often the case that laid-off workers with successful job histories at one firm are unable to meet entry-level requirements at other jobs.

We can better understand the causes of the plight of many laid-off industrial workers if we consider the determinants of people's wages. Economic theory suggests that people's wages are tied to the amount they contribute to their firm, which implies that wages increase with people's skills. We can think of two broad categories of skills: general skills that make people valuable to any firm and more specialized skills that make people valuable to certain firms. Examples of general skills include welding, bookkeeping, and an ability to manage people. Skills that are useful to only one firm are those that are specifically tied to the product or structure of that firm. Specific knowledge of this second type is not transferable to other firms.

People who work in a particular firm for an extended period learn both general skills that make them valuable to any similar company and specific skills that make them valuable to their company only. For example, the article mentions Beverly Davidson, who had been laid off by a bank prior to her current job. The knowledge she acquired while employed by the bank may not be transferable to her current technical support position at the computer firm.

This distinction between general skills and firm-specific skills begins to explain why retraining has not been very successful for individuals who must move to another line of work. To the extent that retraining enhances abilities that new employers value, it will help the workers earn more. But it is difficult to provide workers with firm-specific skills for new jobs. These skills can only be learned on the job.

The distinction between general and firm-specific skills also suggests why workers least likely to benefit from retraining are those within a few years of retirement. Older workers who must undergo on-the-job training will not be able to use their new firm-specific skills for as many years as younger workers. It is not worthwhile for firms to hire and train workers who are near retirement.

Structural change is an integral part of a dynamic, growing economy. Dislocations are probably inevitable when large-scale structural change occurs, and these dislocations benefit some people while hurting others. Although retraining helps mitigate some of the effects of the upheaval that accompanies structural change, unfortunately it cannot solve all the problems that arise. For the economy as a whole, such change is necessary. As Jared Hazelton said in the article: "Most people laid off find other jobs. It's bad for the people involved, but layoffs are a way of becoming more competitive."

Copyright © by Houghton Mifflin Company. All rights reserved.

9

Macroeconomic Equilibrium: Aggregate Demand and Supply

FUNDAMENTAL QUESTIONS

1. What factors affect aggregate demand?

2. What causes the aggregate demand curve to shift?

3. What factors affect aggregate supply?

4. Why does the short-run aggregate supply curve become steeper as real GDP increases?

5. Why is the long-run aggregate supply curve vertical?

6. What causes the aggregate supply curve to shift?

7. What determines the equilibrium price level and real GDP?

Copyright © by Houghton Mifflin Company. All rights reserved.

Total output and income in the United States have grown over time. Each generation has experienced a higher living standard than the previous generation. Yet, as we learned in Chapter 8, economic growth has not been steady. Economies go through periods of expansion followed by periods of contraction or recession, and such business cycles have major impacts on people's lives, incomes, and living standards.

Economic stagnation and recession throw many, often those who are already relatively poor, out of their jobs and into real poverty. Economic growth increases the number of jobs and draws people out of poverty and into the mainstream of economic progress. To understand why economies grow and why they go through cycles, we must discover why firms decide to produce more or less and why buyers decide to buy more or less. The approach we take is similar to the approach we followed in the first five chapters of the text using demand and supply curves. In Chapters 3, 4, and 5, demand and supply curves were derived and used to examine questions involving the equilibrium price and quantities demanded and supplied of a single good or service. This simple yet powerful microeconomic technique of analysis has a macroeconomic counterpart—aggregate demand and aggregate supply, which are used to determine an equilibrium price level and quantity of goods and services produced for the *entire economy*. In this chapter we shall use aggregate demand and supply curves to illustrate the causes of business cycles and economic growth. ■

Copyright © by Houghton Mifflin Company. All rights reserved.

1. AGGREGATE DEMAND, AGGREGATE SUPPLY, AND BUSINESS CYCLES

What causes economic growth and business cycles? We can provide some answers to this important question using aggregate demand (*AD*) and aggregate supply (*AS*) curves. Suppose we represent the economy in a simple demand and supply diagram, as shown in Figure 1. Aggregate demand represents the total spending in the economy at alternative price levels. Aggregate supply represents the total output of the economy at alternative

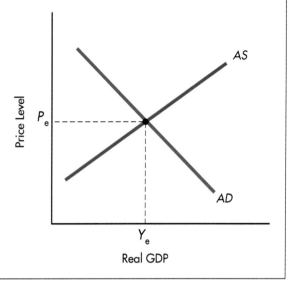

Figure 1
Aggregate Demand and Aggregate Supply Equilibrium
The equilibrium price level and real GDP are determined by the intersection of the *AD* and *AS* curves.

price levels. To understand the causes of business cycles and inflation, we must understand how aggregate demand and supply cause the equilibrium price level and real GDP, the nation's output of goods and services, to change. The intersection between the *AD* and *AS* curves defines the equilibrium level of real GDP and level of prices. The equilibrium price level is P_e and the equilibrium level of real GDP is Y_e. This price and output level represents the level of prices and output for some particular period of time, say 1998. Once that equilibrium is established, there is no tendency for prices and output to change until changes occur in either the aggregate demand curve or the aggregate supply curve. Let's first consider a change in aggregate demand and then look at a change in aggregate supply.

1.a. Aggregate Demand and Business Cycles

An increase in aggregate demand is illustrated by a shift of the *AD* curve to the right, like the shift from AD_1 to AD_2 in Figure 2. This represents a situation in which buyers are buying more at every price level. The shift causes the equilibrium level of real GDP to rise from Y_{e1} to Y_{e2}, illustrating the expansionary phase of the business cycle. As output rises, unemployment decreases. The increase in aggregate demand also leads to a higher price level, as shown by the change in the price level from P_{e1} to P_{e2}. The increase in the price level represents an example of **demand-pull inflation**, which is inflation caused by increasing demand for output.

demand-pull inflation:
inflation caused by increasing demand for output

If aggregate demand falls, like the shift from AD_1 to AD_3, then there is a lower equilibrium level of real GDP, Y_{e3}. In this case, buyers are buying *less* at every price level. The drop in real GDP caused by lower demand would represent an economic slowdown or a recession, when output falls and unemployment rises.

Copyright © by Houghton Mifflin Company. All rights reserved.

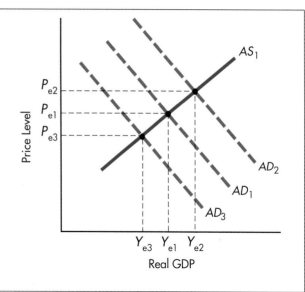

Figure 2
Effects of a Change in Aggregate Demand
If aggregate demand increases from AD_1 to AD_2, the equilibrium price level increases to P_{e2} and the equilibrium level of real GDP rises to Y_{e2}. If aggregate demand decreases from AD_1 to AD_3, the equilibrium price level falls to P_{e3} and the equilibrium level of real GDP drops to Y_{e3}.

1.b. Aggregate Supply and Business Cycles

Changes in aggregate supply can also cause business cycles. Figure 3 illustrates what happens when aggregate supply changes. An increase in aggregate supply is illustrated by the shift from AS_1 to AS_2, leading to an increase in the equilibrium level of real GDP from Y_{e1} to Y_{e2}. An increase in aggregate supply comes about when firms produce more at every price level. Such an increase could result from an improvement in technology or a decrease in costs of production.

If aggregate supply decreased, as in the shift from AS_1 to AS_3, then the equilibrium level of real GDP would fall to Y_{e3} and the equilibrium price level would increase from P_{e1} to P_{e3}. A decrease in aggregate supply could be caused by higher production costs that lead producers to raise their prices. This is an example of **cost-push inflation**—where the price level rises due to increased costs of production and the associated decrease in aggregate supply.

cost-push inflation:
inflation caused by rising costs of production

1.c. A Look Ahead

Business cycles result from changes in aggregate demand, from changes in aggregate supply, and from changes in both *AD* and *AS*. The degree to which real GDP declines during a recession or increases during an expansion depends on the amount by which the *AD* and/or *AS* curves shift. The degree to which an expansion involves output growth or increased inflation depends on the shapes of the *AD* and *AS* curves. We need to consider why the curves have the shapes they do, and what causes them to shift.

The comparison we made earlier, between aggregate demand, aggregate supply, and their microeconomic counterparts, the supply and demand curves, is only superficial. As we examine the aggregate demand and supply curves, you will see that the reasons underlying the shapes and movements of *AD* and *AS* are in fact quite different from those explaining the shapes and movements of the supply and demand curves.

Copyright © by Houghton Mifflin Company. All rights reserved.

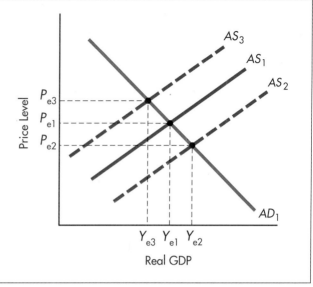

Figure 3
Effects of a Change in Aggregate Supply
If aggregate supply increases from AS_1 to AS_2, the equilibrium price level falls from P_{e1} to P_{e2} and the equilibrium level of real GDP rises to Y_{e2}. If aggregate supply decreases from AS_1 to AS_3, the equilibrium price level rises to P_{e3} and the equilibrium level of real GDP falls to Y_{e3}.

RECAP

1. Aggregate demand (*AD*) represents the total spending in the economy at alternative price levels.
2. Aggregate supply (*AS*) represents the total output of the economy at alternative price levels.
3. The intersection between the *AD* and *AS* curves defines the equilibrium level of real GDP and the level of prices.
4. Business cycles result from changes in *AD* and/or *AS*.

2. FACTORS THAT INFLUENCE AGGREGATE DEMAND

What factors affect aggregate demand?

Aggregate demand is the relation between aggregate expenditures, or total spending, and the price level. Aggregate expenditures are the sum of expenditures of each sector of the economy: households (consumption), business firms (investment), government, and the rest of the world (net exports). Each sector of the economy has different reasons for spending; for instance, household spending depends heavily on household income, while business spending depends on the profits businesses expect to earn. Because each sector of the economy has a different reason for the amount of spending it undertakes, aggregate spending depends on all of these reasons. To understand aggregate demand, therefore, requires that we look at those factors that influence the expenditures of each sector of the economy.

2.a. Consumption

How much households spend depends on their income, wealth, expectations about future prices and incomes, demographics like the age distribution of the population, and taxes.

Copyright © by Houghton Mifflin Company. All rights reserved.

- Income: If current income rises, households purchase more goods and services.

- Wealth: Wealth is different from income. It is the value of assets owned by a household, including homes, cars, bank deposits, stocks, and bonds. An increase in household wealth will increase consumption.

- Expectations: Expectations regarding future changes in income or wealth can affect consumption today. If households expect a recession and worry about job loss, consumption tends to fall. On the other hand, if households become more optimistic regarding future increases in income and wealth, consumption rises today.

- Demographics: Demographic change can affect consumption in several different ways. Population growth is generally associated with higher consumption for an economy. Younger households and older households generally consume more and save less than middle-aged households. Therefore, as the age distribution of a nation changes, so will consumption.

- Taxes: Higher taxes will lower the disposable income of households and decrease consumption, while lower taxes will raise disposable income and increase consumption. Government policy may change taxes and thereby bring about a change in consumption.

2.b. Investment

Investment is business spending on capital goods and inventories. In general, investment depends on the expected profitability of such spending, so any factor that could affect the profitability will be a determinant of investment. Factors affecting the expected profitability of business projects include the interest rate, technology, the cost of capital goods, and capacity utilization.

- Interest rate: Investment is negatively related to the interest rate. The interest rate is the cost of borrowed funds. The greater the cost of borrowing, other things being equal, the fewer investment projects that offer sufficient profit to be undertaken. As the interest rate falls, investment is stimulated as the cost of financing the investment is lowered.

- Technology: New production technology stimulates investment spending as firms are forced to adopt new production methods to stay competitive.

- Cost of capital goods: If machines and equipment purchased by firms rise in price, then the higher costs associated with investment will lower profitability and investment will fall.

- Capacity utilization: The more excess capacity (unused capital goods) is available, the more firms can expand production without purchasing new capital goods, and the lower investment is. As firms approach full capacity, more investment spending is required to expand output further.

2.c. Government Spending

Government spending may be set by government authorities independent of current income or other determinants of aggregate expenditures.

2.d. Net Exports

Net exports are equal to exports minus imports. We assume exports are determined by conditions in the rest of the world, like foreign income, tastes,

Copyright © by Houghton Mifflin Company. All rights reserved.

prices, exchange rates, and government policy. Imports are determined by similar domestic factors.

Income   As domestic income rises and consumption rises, some of this consumption includes goods produced in other countries. Therefore, as domestic income rises, imports rise and net exports fall. Similarly, as foreign income rises, foreign residents buy more domestic goods, and net exports rise.

Prices   Other things being equal, higher (lower) foreign prices make domestic goods relatively cheaper (more expensive) and increase (decrease) net exports. Higher (lower) domestic prices make domestic goods relatively more expensive (cheaper) and decrease (increase) net exports.

Exchange rates   Other things being equal, a depreciation of the domestic currency on the foreign exchange market will make domestic goods cheaper to foreign buyers and make foreign goods more expensive to domestic residents so that net exports will rise. An appreciation of the domestic currency will have just the opposite effects.

Government policy   Net exports may fall if foreign governments restrict the entry of domestic goods into their countries, reducing domestic exports. If the domestic government restricts imports into the domestic economy, net exports may rise.

2.e. Aggregate Expenditures

You can see how aggregate expenditures, the sum of all spending on U.S. goods and services, must depend on prices, income, and all of the other determinants discussed in the previous sections. As with the demand curve for a specific good or service, with the aggregate demand curve we want to classify the factors that influence spending into the price and the nonprice determinants for the aggregate demand curves as well. The components of aggregate expenditures that change as the price level changes will lead to movements along the aggregate demand curve—changes in quantity demanded—while changes in aggregate expenditures caused by nonprice effects will cause shifts of the aggregate demand curve—changes in aggregate demand. In the following section we look first at the price effects, or movements along an aggregate demand curve. Following that discussion, we focus on the nonprice determinants of aggregate demand.

RECAP

1. Aggregate expenditures are the sum of consumption, investment, government spending, and net exports.
2. Consumption depends on household income, wealth, expectations, demographics, and taxation.
3. Investment depends on the interest rate, technology, the cost of capital goods, and capacity utilization.
4. Government spending is determined independent of current income.
5. Net exports depend on foreign and domestic incomes, prices, government policies, and exchange rates.

Copyright © by Houghton Mifflin Company. All rights reserved.

3. THE AGGREGATE DEMAND CURVE

When we examined the demand curves in Chapter 3, we divided our study into two parts: the movement along the curves—changes in quantity demanded—and the shifts of the curve—changes in demand. We take the same approach here in examining aggregate demand. We first look at the movements along the aggregate demand curve caused by changes in the price level. We then turn to the nonprice determinants of aggregate demand that cause shifts in the curve.

3.a. Changes in Aggregate Quantity Demanded: Price-Level Effects

Aggregate demand curves are downward-sloping just like the demand curves for individual goods that were shown in Chapter 3, although for different reasons. Along the demand curve for an individual good, the price of that good changes while the prices of all other goods remain constant. This means that the good in question becomes relatively more or less expensive compared to all other goods in the economy. Consumers tend to substitute a less expensive good for a more expensive good. The effect of this substitution is an inverse relationship between price and quantity demanded. As the price of a good rises, quantity demanded falls. For the economy as a whole, however, it is not a substitution of a less expensive good for a more expensive good that causes the demand curve to slope down. Instead, aggregate quantity demanded, or total spending, will change as the price level changes due to the wealth effect, the interest rate effect, and the international trade effect of a price-level change on aggregate expenditures. We will discuss each of these effects in turn.

3.a.1. The Wealth Effect Individuals and businesses own money, bonds, and other financial assets. The purchasing power of these assets is the quantity of goods and services the assets can be exchanged for. When the level of prices falls, the purchasing power of these assets increases, allowing households and businesses to purchase more. When prices go up, the purchasing power of financial assets falls, which causes households and businesses to spend less. This is the **wealth effect** (sometimes called the *real-balance effect*) of a price change: a change in the real value of wealth that causes spending to change when the level of prices changes. *Real values* are values that have been adjusted for price-level changes. Here *real value* means "purchasing power." When the price level changes, the purchasing power of financial assets also changes. When prices rise, the real value of assets and wealth falls, and aggregate expenditures tend to fall. When prices fall, the real value of assets and wealth rises, and aggregate expenditures tend to rise.

wealth effect:
a change in the real value of wealth that causes spending to change when the level of prices changes

When the price level changes, the purchasing power of financial assets changes.

3.a.2. The Interest Rate Effect When the price level rises, the purchasing power of each dollar falls, which means more money is required to buy any particular quantity of goods and services (see Figure 4). Suppose that a family of three needs $100 each week to buy food. If the price level doubles, the same quantity of food costs $200. The household must have twice as much money to buy the same amount of food. Conversely, when prices fall, the family needs less money to buy food because the purchasing power of each dollar is greater.

When prices go up, people need more money. So they sell their other financial assets, like bonds, to get that money. The increase in supply of bonds lowers bond prices and raises interest rates. Since bonds typically pay

Copyright © by Houghton Mifflin Company. All rights reserved.

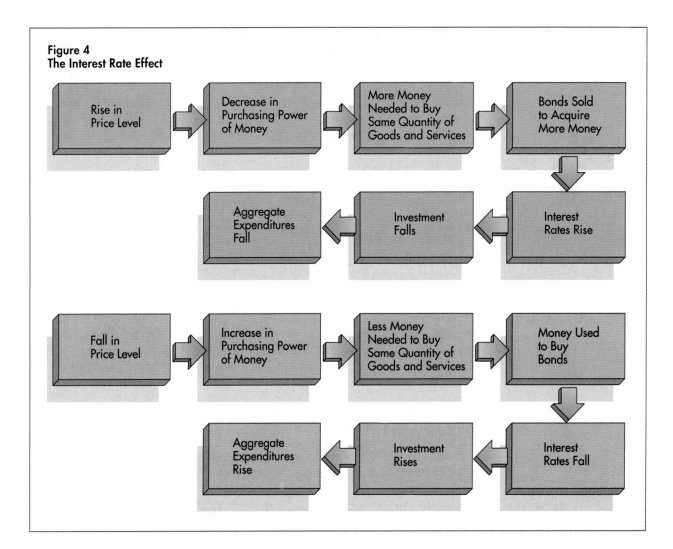

Figure 4
The Interest Rate Effect

fixed-dollar interest payments each year, as the price of a bond varies, the interest rate (or yield) will change. For instance, suppose you pay $1,000 for a bond that pays $100 a year in interest. The interest rate on this bond is found by dividing the annual interest payment by the bond price, or $100/$1,000 5 10 percent. If the price of the bond falls to $900, then the interest rate is equal to the annual interest payment (which remains fixed at $100 for the life of the bond) divided by the new price of $900: $100/$900 5 11 percent. When bond prices fall, interest rates rise, and when bond prices rise, interest rates fall.

If people want more money and they sell some of their bond holdings to raise the money, bond prices will fall and interest rates will rise. The rise in interest rates is necessary to sell the larger quantity of bonds, but it causes investment expenditures to fall, which causes aggregate expenditures to fall.

When prices fall, people need less money to purchase the same quantity of goods. So they use their money holdings to buy bonds and other financial assets. The increased demand for bonds increases bond prices and causes interest rates to fall. Lower interest rates increase investment expenditures, thereby pushing aggregate expenditures up.

Copyright © by Houghton Mifflin Company. All rights reserved.

interest rate effect:
a change in interest rates that causes investment and therefore aggregate expenditures to change as the level of prices changes

Figure 4 shows the **interest rate effect**, the relationship among the price level, interest rates, and aggregate expenditures. As the price level rises, interest rates rise and aggregate expenditures fall. As the price level falls, interest rates fall and aggregate expenditures rise.

3.a.3. The International Trade Effect

The third channel through which a price-level change affects the quantity of goods and services demanded is called the **international trade effect.** A change in the level of domestic prices can cause net exports to change. If domestic prices rise while foreign prices and the foreign exchange rate remain constant, domestic goods become more expensive in relation to foreign goods.

international trade effect:
a change in aggregate expenditures resulting from a change in the domestic price level that changes the price of domestic goods in relation to foreign goods

Suppose the United States sells oranges to Japan. If the oranges sell for $1 per pound and the yen-dollar exchange rate is 100 yen 5 $1, a pound of U.S. oranges costs a Japanese buyer 100 yen. What happens if the level of prices in the United States goes up 10 percent? All prices, including the price of oranges, increase 10 percent. U.S. oranges sell for $1.10 a pound after the price increase. If the exchange rate is still 100 yen 5 $1, a pound of oranges now costs the Japanese buyer 110 yen (100 3 1.10). If orange prices in other countries do not change, some Japanese buyers may buy oranges from those countries. The increase in the level of U.S. prices makes U.S. goods more expensive relative to foreign goods and causes U.S. net exports to fall; a decrease in the level of U.S. prices makes U.S. goods cheaper in relation to foreign goods, which increases U.S. net exports.

When the price of domestic goods increases in relation to the price of foreign goods, net exports fall, causing aggregate expenditures to fall. When the price of domestic goods falls in relation to the price of foreign goods, net exports rise, causing aggregate expenditures to rise. The international trade effect of a change in the level of domestic prices causes aggregate expenditures to change in the opposite direction.

3.a.4. The Sum of the Price-Level Effects

The **aggregate demand curve** (AD) shows how the equilibrium level of expenditures for the economy's output changes as the price level changes. In other words, the curve shows the amount people spend at different price levels.

aggregate demand curve:
a curve that shows the different levels of expenditures on domestic output at different levels of prices

Figure 5 displays the typical shape of the AD curve. The price level is plotted on the vertical axis and real GDP is plotted on the horizontal axis. Suppose that initially the economy is at point A with prices at P_0. At this point, spending equals $500. If prices fall to P_1, expenditures equal $700 and the economy is at point C. If prices rise from P_0 to P_2, expenditures equal $300 at point B.

Because aggregate expenditures increase when the price level decreases, and decrease when the price level increases, the aggregate demand curve slopes down. The aggregate demand curve is drawn with the price level for the *entire economy* on the vertical axis. A price-level change here means that, on average, *all prices in the economy change*; there is no relative price change among domestic goods. The negative slope of the aggregate demand curve is a product of the wealth effect, the interest rate effect, and the international trade effect.

A lower domestic price level increases consumption (the wealth effect), investment (the interest rate effect), and net exports (the international trade effect). As the price level drops, aggregate expenditures rise.

Copyright © by Houghton Mifflin Company. All rights reserved.

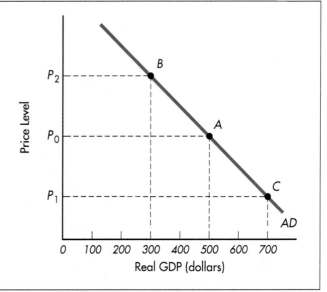

Figure 5
The Aggregate Demand Curve
The aggregate demand curve (AD) shows the level of expenditures at different price levels. At price level P_0, expenditures are $500; at P_1, $700; and at P_2, $300.

A higher domestic price reduces consumption (the wealth effect), investment (the interest rate effect), and net exports (the international trade effect). As prices rise, aggregate expenditures fall. These price effects are summarized in Figure 6.

3.b. Changes in Aggregate Demand: Nonprice Determinants

What causes the aggregate demand curve to shift?

The aggregate demand curve shows the level of aggregate expenditures at alternative price levels. We draw the curve by varying the price level and finding out what the resulting total expenditures are, holding all other things constant. As those "other things"—the nonprice determinants of aggregate demand—change, the aggregate demand curve shifts. The nonprice determinants of aggregate demand include all of the factors covered in the discussion of the components of expenditures—income, wealth, demographics, expectations, taxes, the interest rate (interest rates can change for reasons other than price-level changes), the cost of capital goods, capacity utilization, foreign income and price levels, exchange rates, and government policy. A change in any one of these can cause the *AD* curve to shift. In the discussions that follow, we will focus particularly on the effect of expectations, foreign income and price levels, and will also mention government policy, which will be examined in detail in Chapter 12. Figure 7 summarizes these effects, which are discussed next.

3.b.1. Expectations Consumption and business spending are affected by expectations. Consumption is sensitive to people's expectations of future income, prices, and wealth. For example, when people expect the economy to do well in the future, they increase consumption today at every price level. This is reflected in a shift of the aggregate demand curve to the right, from AD_0 to AD_1, as shown in Figure 8. When aggregate demand increases, aggregate expenditures increase at every price level.

Copyright © by Houghton Mifflin Company. All rights reserved.

Copyright © by Houghton Mifflin Company. All rights reserved.

Figure 6
Why the Aggregate Demand Curve Slopes Down

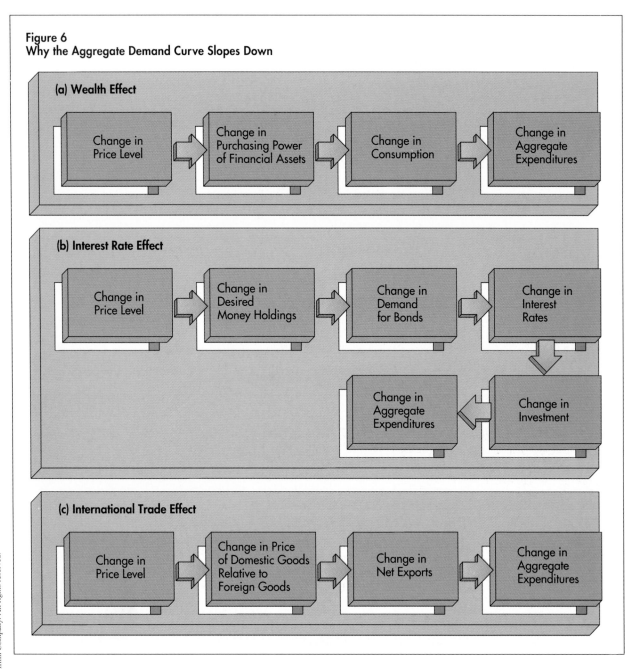

(a) Wealth Effect

Change in Price Level → Change in Purchasing Power of Financial Assets → Change in Consumption → Change in Aggregate Expenditures

(b) Interest Rate Effect

Change in Price Level → Change in Desired Money Holdings → Change in Demand for Bonds → Change in Interest Rates → Change in Investment → Change in Aggregate Expenditures

(c) International Trade Effect

Change in Price Level → Change in Price of Domestic Goods Relative to Foreign Goods → Change in Net Exports → Change in Aggregate Expenditures

On the other hand, if people expect a recession in the near future, they tend to reduce consumption and increase saving in order to protect themselves against a greater likelihood of losing a job or a forced cutback in hours worked. As consumption drops, aggregate demand decreases. The AD curve shifts to the left, from AD_0 to AD_2. At every price level along AD_2, planned expenditures are less than they are along AD_0.

Expectations also play an important role in investment decisions. Before undertaking a particular project, businesses forecast the likely revenues and

Figure 7
Nonprice Determinants: Changes in Aggregate Demand

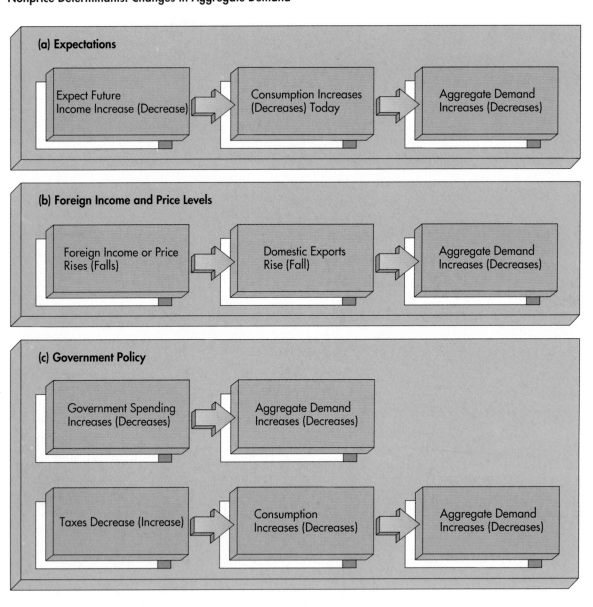

(a) Expectations

Expect Future Income Increase (Decrease) → Consumption Increases (Decreases) Today → Aggregate Demand Increases (Decreases)

(b) Foreign Income and Price Levels

Foreign Income or Price Rises (Falls) → Domestic Exports Rise (Fall) → Aggregate Demand Increases (Decreases)

(c) Government Policy

Government Spending Increases (Decreases) → Aggregate Demand Increases (Decreases)

Taxes Decrease (Increase) → Consumption Increases (Decreases) → Aggregate Demand Increases (Decreases)

Copyright © by Houghton Mifflin Company. All rights reserved.

costs associated with that project. When the profit outlook is good—say, a tax cut is on the horizon—investment and therefore aggregate demand increase. When profits are expected to fall, investment and aggregate demand decrease.

Higher foreign income increases net exports and aggregate demand; lower foreign income reduces net exports and aggregate demand.

3.b.2. Foreign Income and Price Levels   When foreign income increases, so does foreign spending. Some of this increased spending is for goods produced in the domestic economy. As domestic exports increase, aggregate demand rises. Lower foreign income has just the opposite effect. As foreign income falls, foreign spending falls, including foreign spending on the exports of the

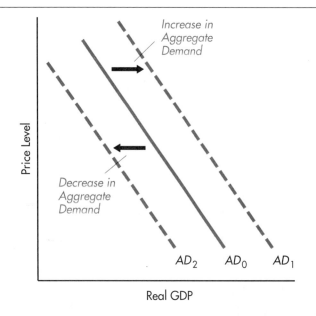

Figure 8
Shifting the Aggregate Demand Curve
As aggregate demand increases, the *AD* curve shifts to the right, like the shift from AD_0 to AD_1. At every price level, the quantity of output demanded increases. As aggregate demand falls, the *AD* curve shifts to the left, like the shift from AD_0 to AD_2. At every price level, the quantity of output demanded falls.

Copyright © by Houghton Mifflin Company. All rights reserved.

Change in the level of foreign prices changes domestic net exports and aggregate demand in the same direction.

domestic economy. Lower foreign income, then, causes domestic net exports and domestic aggregate demand to fall.

If foreign prices rise in relation to domestic prices, domestic goods become less expensive relative to foreign goods, and domestic net exports increase. This means that aggregate demand rises, or the aggregate demand curve shifts up, as the level of foreign prices rises. Conversely, when the level of foreign prices falls, domestic goods become more expensive relative to foreign goods, causing domestic net exports and aggregate demand to fall.

Let's go back to the market for oranges. Suppose U.S. growers compete with Brazilian growers for the Japanese orange market. If the level of prices in Brazil rises while the level of prices in the United States remains stable, the price of Brazilian oranges to the Japanese buyer rises in relation to the price of U.S. oranges. What happens? U.S. exports of oranges to Japan should rise while Brazilian exports of oranges to Japan fall.[1]

3.b.3. Government Policy   One of the goals of macroeconomic policy is to achieve economic growth without inflation. For GDP to increase, either *AD* or *AS* would have to change. Government economic policy can cause the aggregate demand curve to shift. An increase in government spending or a decrease in taxes will increase aggregate demand; a decrease in government spending or an increase in taxes will decrease aggregate demand. We devote an entire chapter on fiscal policy to an examination of the effect of taxes and government spending on aggregate demand. In another chapter, on monetary policy, we describe how changes in the money supply can cause the aggregate demand curve to shift.

---

[1]This assumes no change in exchange rates. We consider the link between price levels and exchange rates in the chapter "Macroeconomic Links Between Countries."

RECAP

1. The aggregate demand curve shows the level of aggregate expenditures at different levels of price.

2. Aggregate expenditures are the sum of consumption, investment, government spending, and net exports.

3. The wealth effect, the interest rate effect, and the international trade effect are three reasons why aggregate demand slopes down. These effects explain movements along a given *AD* curve.

4. The aggregate demand curve shifts with changes in the nonprice determinants of aggregate demand: expectations, foreign income and price levels, and government policy.

4. AGGREGATE SUPPLY

aggregate supply curve:
a curve that shows the amount of real GDP produced at different price levels

---

What factors affect aggregate supply?

The **aggregate supply curve** shows the quantity of real GDP produced at different price levels. The aggregate supply curve (*AS*) looks like the supply curve for an individual good, but, as with aggregate demand and the microeconomic demand curve, different factors are at work. The positive relationship between price and quantity supplied of an individual good is based on the price of that good changing in relation to the prices of all other goods. As the price of a single good rises relative to the prices of other goods, sellers are willing to offer more of the good for sale. With aggregate supply, on the other hand, we are analyzing how the amount of all goods and services produced changes as the level of prices changes. The direct relationship between prices and national output is explained by the effect of changing prices on profits, not by relative price changes.

4.a. Changes in Aggregate Quantity Supplied: Price-Level Effects

Along the aggregate supply curve, everything is held fixed except the price level and output. The price level is the price of output. The prices of resources, that is, the costs of production—wages, rent, and interest—are assumed to be constant, at least for a short time following a change in the price level.

If the price level rises while the costs of production remain fixed, business profits go up. As profits rise, firms are willing to produce more output. As the price level rises, then, the quantity of output firms are willing to supply increases. The result is the positively sloped aggregate supply curve shown in Figure 9.

As the price level rises from P_0 to P_1 in Figure 9, real GDP increases from \$300 to \$500. The higher the price level, the higher are profits, everything else held constant, and the greater is the quantity of output produced in the economy. Conversely, as the price level falls, the quantity of output produced falls.

4.b. Short-Run Versus Long-Run Aggregate Supply

The curve in Figure 9 is a *short-run* aggregate supply curve because the costs of production are held constant. Although production costs may not rise immediately when the price level rises, eventually they will. Labor will

Copyright © by Houghton Mifflin Company. All rights reserved.

Figure 9
Aggregate Supply
The aggregate supply curve shows the amount of real
GDP produced at different price levels. The *AS* curve
slopes up, indicating that the higher the price level, the
greater the quantity of output produced.

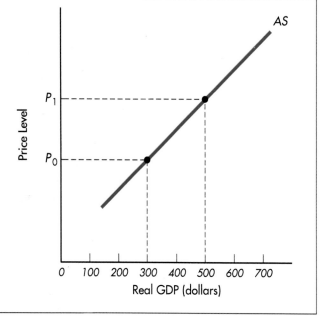

demand higher wages to compensate for the higher cost of living; suppliers
will charge more for materials. The positive slope of the *AS* curve, then, is a
short-run phenomenon. How short is the short run? It is the period of time
over which production costs remain constant. (In the long run, all costs
change or are variable.) For the economy as a whole, the short run can be
months or, at most, a few years.

4.b.1. Short-Run Aggregate Supply Curve   Figure 9 represents the general
shape of the short-run aggregate supply curve. In Figure 10 you see a more

Figure 10
The Shape of the Short-Run Aggregate Supply Curve
The upward-sloping aggregate supply curve occurs when
the price level must rise to induce further increases in
output. The curve gets steeper as real GDP increases,
since the closer the economy comes to the capacity level
of output, the less output will rise in response to higher
prices as more and more firms reach their maximum
level of output in the short run.

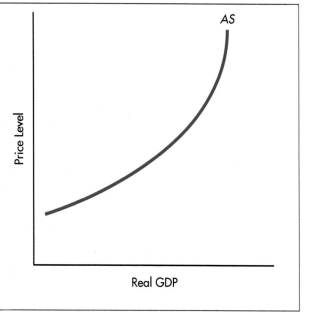

Copyright © by Houghton Mifflin Company. All rights reserved.

Copyright © by Houghton Mifflin Company. All rights reserved.

Why does the short-run aggregate supply curve become steeper as real GDP increases?

realistic version of the same curve—its steepness varies. The steepness of the aggregate supply curve depends on the ability and willingness of producers to respond to price-level changes in the short run. Figure 10 shows the typical shape of the short-run aggregate supply curve.

Notice that as the level of real GDP increases in Figure 10, the *AS* curve becomes steeper. This is because each increase in output requires firms to hire more and more resources, until eventually full capacity is reached in some areas of the economy, resources are fully employed, and some firms reach maximum output. At this point, increases in the price level bring about smaller and smaller increases in output from firms as a whole. The short-run aggregate supply curve becomes increasingly steep as the economy approaches maximum output.

4.b.2. Long-Run Aggregate Supply Curve

Aggregate supply in the short run is different from aggregate supply in the long run (see Figure 11). That difference stems from the fact that quantities and costs of resources are not fixed in the long run. Over time, contracts expire and wages and other resource costs adjust to current conditions. The increased flexibility of resource costs in the long run has costs rising and falling with the price level and changes the shape of the aggregate supply curve. Lack of information about economic conditions in the short run also contributes to the inflexibility of resource prices as compared to the long run. The Economic Insight "How Lack of Information in the Short Run Affects Wages in the Long Run" shows why this is true for labor, as well as for other resources.

long-run aggregate supply curve (*LRAS*):
a vertical line at the potential level of national income

The **long-run aggregate supply curve (*LRAS*)** is viewed by most economists to be a vertical line at the potential level of real GDP or output (Y_p), as shown in Figure 11. Remember that the potential level of real GDP is the income level that is produced in the absence of any cyclical unemployment, or when the natural rate of unemployment exists. In the long run, wages and other resource costs fully adjust to price changes. The short-run *AS* curve slopes up because we assume that the costs of production, particularly wages, do not change to offset changing prices. In the short run, then, higher prices increase producers' profits and stimulate production. In the long run, because the costs of production adjust completely to the change in prices, neither

Why is the long-run aggregate supply curve vertical?

Technological advance shifts the aggregate supply curve outward and increases output. An example of a technological advance that has increased efficiency in banking is the automated teller machine (or ATM). The photo shows an ATM in Brazil that allows the bank to offer the public a lower-cost way to make withdrawals and deposits than dealing with a bank employee. Such innovations can be important determinants of aggregate supply.

Copyright © by Houghton Mifflin Company. All rights reserved.

ECONOMIC INSIGHT

How Lack of Information in the Short Run Affects Wages in the Long Run

Workers do not have perfect information. In other words, they do not know everything that occurs. This lack of information includes information about the price level. If workers form incorrect expectations regarding the price level in the short run, they may be willing to work for a different wage in the short run than in the long run. For example, if workers thought that the inflation rate would be 3 percent over the next year, they would want a smaller wage raise than if they believed that the inflation rate would be 6 percent. If, in fact, they base their wage negotiations on 3 percent inflation and accept a

wage based on that inflation rate, but it turns out that the price level has increased by 6 percent, workers will then seek higher wages. In the long run, wages will reflect price-level changes.

If it cost nothing to obtain information, everyone who was interested would always know the current economic conditions. However, since there are costs of obtaining and understanding information about the economy, people will make mistakes in the short run. Both managers and employees make mistakes due to lack of information. Such mistakes are not due to stupidity but to ignorance—

ignorance of future as well as of current economic conditions. In the long run, mistakes about the price level are realized and wages adjust to the known price level.

We now have two reasons why wages will be more flexible in the long run than in the short run: long-term contracts and lack of information in the short run. The same arguments could be made for other resources as well. Because of these two reasons, the short-run aggregate supply curve is generally upward-sloping due to resource prices being relatively fixed in the short run.

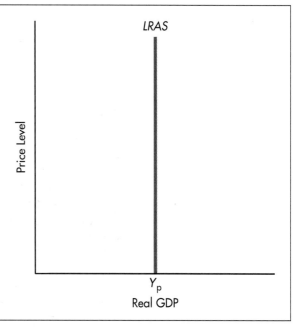

Figure 11
The Shape of the Long-Run Aggregate Supply Curve
In the long run, the *AS* curve is a vertical line at the potential level of real GDP, which indicates that there is no relationship between price-level changes and the quantity of output produced.

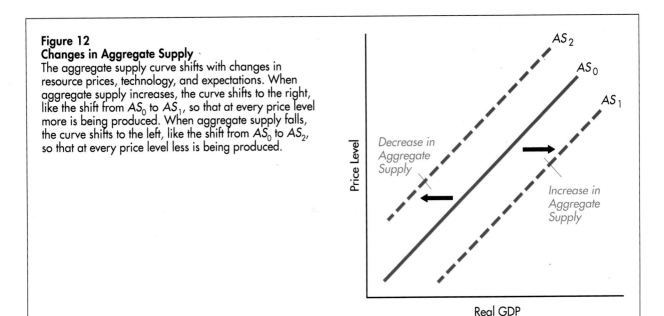

Figure 12
Changes in Aggregate Supply
The aggregate supply curve shifts with changes in resource prices, technology, and expectations. When aggregate supply increases, the curve shifts to the right, like the shift from AS_0 to AS_1, so that at every price level more is being produced. When aggregate supply falls, the curve shifts to the left, like the shift from AS_0 to AS_2, so that at every price level less is being produced.

profits nor production increase. What we find here are higher wages and other costs of production to match the higher level of prices.

4.c. Changes in Aggregate Supply: Nonprice Determinants

What causes the aggregate supply curve to shift?

The aggregate supply curve shifts in response to changes in the price of resources, in technology, and in expectations.

The aggregate supply curve is drawn with everything but the price level and real GDP held constant. There are several things that can change and cause the aggregate supply curve to shift. The shift from AS_0 to AS_1 in Figure 12 represents an increase in aggregate supply. AS_1 lies to the right of AS_0, which means that at every price level, production is higher on AS_1 than on AS_0. The shift from AS_0 to AS_2 represents a decrease in aggregate supply. AS_2 lies to the left of AS_0, which means that at every price level, production along AS_2 is less than along AS_0. The nonprice determinants of aggregate supply are resource prices, technology, and expectations. Figure 13 summarizes the nonprice determinants of aggregate supply, discussed in detail next.

4.c.1. Resource Prices When the price of output changes, the costs of production do not change immediately. At first, then, a change in profits induces a change in production. Costs eventually change in response to the change in prices and production, and when they do, the aggregate supply curve shifts. When the cost of resources—labor, capital goods, materials—falls, the aggregate supply curve shifts to the right, from AS_0 to AS_1 in Figure 12. This means firms are willing to produce more output at any given price level. When the cost of resources goes up, profits fall and the aggregate supply curve shifts to the left, from AS_0 to AS_2. Here, at any given level of price, firms produce less output.

Remember that the vertical axis of the aggregate supply graph plots the price level for all goods and services produced in the economy. Only those changes in resource prices that raise the costs of production across the economy have an impact on the aggregate supply curve. For example, oil is an important raw

Copyright © by Houghton Mifflin Company. All rights reserved.

Copyright © by Houghton Mifflin Company. All rights reserved.

Figure 13
Determinants of Aggregate Supply

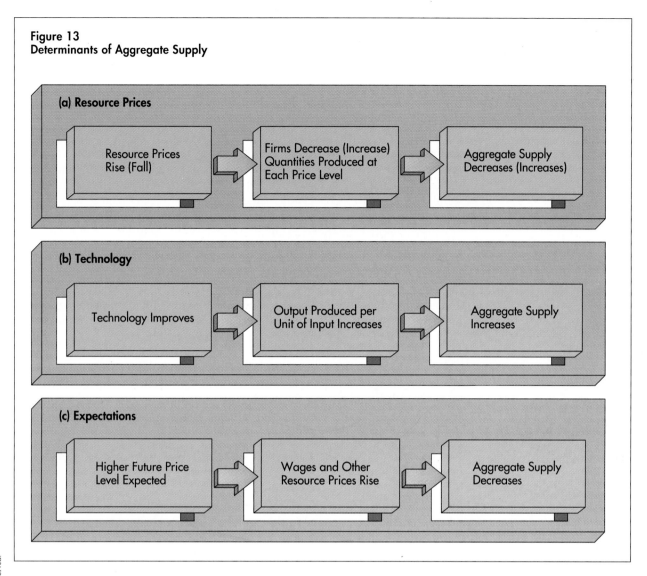

(a) Resource Prices

Resource Prices Rise (Fall) → Firms Decrease (Increase) Quantities Produced at Each Price Level → Aggregate Supply Decreases (Increases)

(b) Technology

Technology Improves → Output Produced per Unit of Input Increases → Aggregate Supply Increases

(c) Expectations

Higher Future Price Level Expected → Wages and Other Resource Prices Rise → Aggregate Supply Decreases

material. If a new source of oil is discovered, the price of oil falls and aggregate supply increases. However, if oil-exporting countries restrict oil supplies and the price of oil increases substantially, aggregate supply decreases, a situation that occurred when OPEC reduced the supply of oil in the 1970s (see the Economic Insight "OPEC and Aggregate Supply"). If the price of only one minor resource changed, then aggregate supply would be unlikely to change. For instance, if the price of land increased in Las Cruces, New Mexico, we would not expect the U.S. aggregate supply curve to be affected.

4.c.2. Technology Technological innovations allow businesses to increase the productivity of their existing resources. As new technology is adopted, the amount of output that can be produced by each unit of input increases, moving the aggregate supply curve to the right. For example, personal computers and word-processing software have allowed secretaries to produce much more output in a day than typewriters allowed.

4.c.3. Expectations

To understand how expectations can affect aggregate supply, consider the case of labor contracts. Manufacturing workers typically contract for a nominal wage based on what they and their employers expect the future level of prices to be. Because wages typically are set for at least a year, any unexpected increase in the price level during the year lowers real wages. Firms receive higher prices for their output, but the cost of labor stays the same. So profits and production go up.

If wages rise in anticipation of higher prices but prices do not go up, the cost of labor rises. Higher real wages caused by expectations of higher prices reduce current profits and production, moving the aggregate supply curve to the left. Other things being equal, anticipated higher prices cause aggregate supply to decrease; conversely, anticipated lower prices cause aggregate supply to increase. In this sense, expectations of price-level changes that shift aggregate supply actually bring about price-level changes.

4.c.4. Economic Growth: Long-Run Aggregate Supply Shifts

The vertical long-run aggregate supply curve, as shown in Figure 11, does not mean that the economy is forever fixed at the current level of potential real gross domestic product. Over time, as new technologies are developed and the quantity and quality of resources increase, potential output also increases, shifting both the short- and long-run aggregate supply curves to the right. Figure 14 shows long-run economic growth by the shift in the aggregate supply curve from $LRAS$ to $LRAS_1$. The movement of the long-run aggregate supply curve to the right reflects the increase in potential real GDP from Y_p to Y_{p1}. Even though the price level has no effect on the level of output in the long run, changes in the determinants of the supply of real output in the economy do.

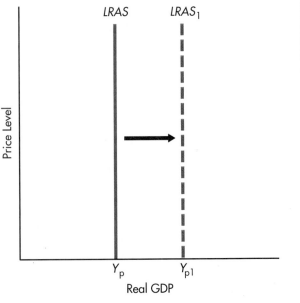

Figure 14
Shifting the Long-Run Aggregate Supply Curve
Changes in technology and the availability and quality of resources can shift the $LRAS$ curve. For instance, a new technology that increases productivity would move the curve to the right, from $LRAS$ to $LRAS_1$.

Copyright © by Houghton Mifflin Company. All rights reserved.

RECAP

1. The aggregate supply curve shows the quantity of output (real GDP) produced at different price levels.

2. The aggregate supply curve slopes up because, everything else held constant, higher prices increase producers' profits, creating an incentive to increase output.

3. The aggregate supply curve shifts with changes in resource prices, technology, and expectations. These are nonprice determinants of aggregate supply.

4. The short-run aggregate supply curve is upward-sloping, showing that increases in production are accompanied by higher prices.

5. The long-run aggregate supply curve is vertical at potential real GDP because, eventually, wages and the costs of other resources adjust fully to price-level changes.

5. AGGREGATE DEMAND AND SUPPLY EQUILIBRIUM

What determines the equilibrium price level and real GDP?

Now that we have defined the aggregate demand and aggregate supply curves separately, we can put them together to determine the equilibrium level of price and real GDP.

5.a. Short-Run Equilibrium

Figure 15 shows the level of equilibrium in a hypothetical economy. Initially the economy is in equilibrium at point 1, where AD_1 and AS_1 intersect. At this point, the equilibrium price is P_1 and the equilibrium real GDP is $500. At price P_1, the amount of output demanded is equal to the amount supplied.

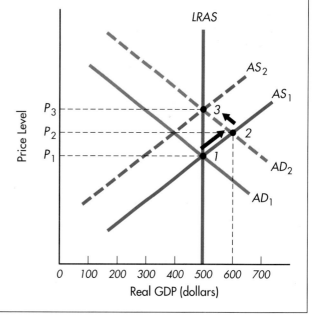

Figure 15
Aggregate Demand and Supply Equilibrium
The equilibrium level of price and real GDP is at the intersection of the AD and AS curves. Initially equilibrium occurs at point 1, where the AD_1 and AS_1 curves intersect. Here the price level is P_1 and real GDP is $500. If aggregate demand increases, moving from AD_1 to AD_2, in the short run there is a new equilibrium at point 2, where AD_2 intersects AS_1. The price level rises to P_2, and the equilibrium level of real GDP increases to $600. Over time, as the costs of wages and other resources rise in response to higher prices, aggregate supply falls, moving AS_1 to AS_2. Final equilibrium occurs at point 3, where the AS_2 curve intersects the AD_2 curve. The price level rises to P_3, but the equilibrium level of real GDP returns to its initial level, $500. In the long run, there is no relationship between prices and the equilibrium level of real GDP because the costs of resources adjust to changes in the level of prices.

Copyright © by Houghton Mifflin Company. All rights reserved.

OPEC and Aggregate Supply

In 1973 and 1974, and again in 1979 and 1980, the Organization of Petroleum Exporting Countries (OPEC) reduced the supply of oil, driving the price of oil up dramatically. For example, the price of Saudi Arabian crude oil more than tripled between 1973 and 1974, and more than doubled between 1979 and 1980. Researchers estimate that the rapid jump in oil prices reduced output by 17 percent in Japan, by 7 percent in the United States, and by 1.9 percent in Germany.*

Oil is an important resource in many industries. When the price of oil increases due to restricted oil output, aggregate supply falls. You can see this in the graph. When the price of oil goes up, the aggregate supply curve falls from AS_1 to AS_2. When aggregate supply falls, the equilibrium level of real GDP (the intersection of the AS curve and the AD curve) falls from Y_1 to Y_2.

Higher oil prices due to restricted oil output would not only decrease short-run aggregate supply and current equilibrium real

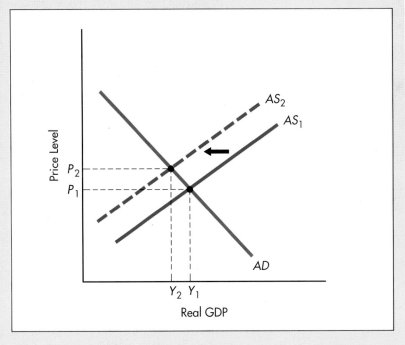

GDP, as shown in the figure, but also potential equilibrium income at the natural rate of unemployment. Unless other factors change to contribute to economic growth, the higher resource (oil) price reduces the productive capacity of the economy.

*These estimates were taken from "Energy Price Shocks, Aggregate Supply, and Monetary Policy: The Theory and the International Evidence," Robert H. Rasche and John A. Tatom, in Karl Brunner and Allan H. Meltzer, eds., *Carnegie-Rochester Conference Series on Public Policy 14* (Spring 1981): pp. 9–93.

Suppose aggregate demand increases from AD_1 to AD_2. In the short run, aggregate supply does not change, so the new equilibrium is at the intersection of the new aggregate demand curve, AD_2, and the same aggregate supply curve, AS_1, at point 2. The new equilibrium price is P_2, and the new equilibrium real GDP is $600. Note that in the short run, the equilibrium point on the short-run aggregate supply curve can lie to the right of the long-run aggregate supply curve (*LRAS*). This is because the *LRAS* represents the potential level of real GDP, not the capacity level. It is possible to produce more than the potential level of real GDP in the short run when the unemployment rate falls below the natural rate of unemployment.

5.b. Long-Run Equilibrium

Point 2 is not a permanent equilibrium because aggregate supply decreases to AS_2 once the costs of production rise in response to higher prices. Final equi-

Copyright © by Houghton Mifflin Company. All rights reserved.

librium is at point 3, where the price level is P_3 and real GDP is $500. Notice that equilibrium here is the same as the initial equilibrium at point 1. Points 1 and 3 both lie along the long-run aggregate supply curve (*LRAS*). The initial shock to or change in the economy was an increase in aggregate demand. The change in aggregate expenditures initially led to higher output and higher prices. Over time, however, as resource costs rise and profit falls, output falls back to its original value.

We are not saying that the level of output never changes. The long-run aggregate supply curve shifts as technology changes and new supplies of resources are obtained. But the output change that results from a change in aggregate demand is a temporary, or short-run, phenomenon. The price level eventually adjusts, and output eventually returns to the potential level.

An increase in aggregate demand increases real GDP only temporarily.

RECAP

1. The equilibrium level of price and real GDP is at the point where the aggregate demand and aggregate supply curves intersect.

2. In the short run, a shift in aggregate demand establishes a temporary equilibrium along the short-run aggregate supply curve.

3. In the long run, the short-run aggregate supply curve shifts so that changes in aggregate demand only affect the price level, not the equilibrium level of output or real GDP.

SUMMARY

▨ What factors affect aggregate demand?

1. Aggregate demand is the relation between aggregate expenditures and the price level. §2

2. Aggregate demand is the sum of consumption, investment, government spending, and net exports at alternative price levels. §2.a, 2.b, 2.c, 2.d

3. Aggregate expenditures change with changes in the price level because of the wealth effect, the interest rate effect, and the international trade effect. These cause a movement along the *AD* curve. §3.a.1, 3.a.2, 3.a.3

▨ What causes the aggregate demand curve to shift?

4. The aggregate demand (*AD*) curve shows the level of expenditures for real GDP at different price levels. §3.a.4

5. Because expenditures and prices move in opposite directions, the *AD* curve is negatively sloped. §3.a.4

6. The nonprice determinants of aggregate demand include expectations, foreign income and price levels, and government policy. §3.b.1, 3.b.2, 3.b.3

▨ What factors affect aggregate supply?

7. The aggregate supply curve shows the quantity of real GDP produced at different price levels. §4

▨ Why does the short-run aggregate supply curve become steeper as real GDP increases?

8. As real GDP rises and the economy pushes closer to capacity output, the level of prices must rise to induce increased production. §4.b.1

▨ Why is the long-run aggregate supply curve vertical?

9. The long-run aggregate supply curve is a vertical line at the potential level of real GDP. The shape of the curve indicates that there is

Copyright © by Houghton Mifflin Company. All rights reserved.

no effect of higher prices on output when an economy is producing at potential real GDP. §4.b.2

■■■ **What causes the aggregate supply curve to shift?**

10. The nonprice determinants of aggregate supply are resource prices, technology, and expectations. §4.c.1, 4.c.2, 4.c.3

■■■ **What determines the equilibrium price level and real GDP?**

11. The equilibrium level of price and real GDP is at the intersection of the aggregate demand and aggregate supply curves. §5.a

12. In the short run, a shift in aggregate demand establishes a new, but temporary, equilibrium along the short-run aggregate supply curve. §5.a

13. In the long run, the short-run aggregate supply curve shifts so that changes in aggregate demand determine the price level, not the equilibrium level of output or real GDP. §5.b

KEY TERMS

demand-pull inflation §1.a
cost-push inflation §1.b
wealth effect §3.a.1
interest rate effect §3.a.2

international trade effect §3.a.3
aggregate demand curve §3.a.4
aggregate supply curve §4
long-run aggregate supply curve (*LRAS*) §4.b.2

EXERCISES

1. How is the aggregate demand curve different from the demand curve for a single good, like hamburgers?

2. Why does the aggregate demand curve slope down? Give real-world examples of the three effects that explain the slope of the curve.

3. How does an increase in foreign income affect domestic aggregate expenditures and demand? Draw a diagram to illustrate your answer.

4. How does a decrease in foreign price levels affect domestic aggregate expenditures and demand? Draw a diagram to illustrate your answer.

5. How is the aggregate supply curve different from the supply curve for a single good, like pizza?

6. There are several determinants of aggregate supply that can cause the aggregate supply curve to shift.

   a. Describe those determinants and give an example of a change in each.

   b. Draw and label an aggregate supply diagram that illustrates the effect of the change in each determinant.

7. Draw a short-run aggregate supply curve that gets steeper as real GDP rises.

   a. Explain why the curve has this shape.

   b. Now draw a long-run aggregate supply curve that intersects a short-run *AS* curve. What is the relationship between short-run *AS* and long-run *AS*?

8. Draw and carefully label an aggregate demand and supply diagram with initial equilibrium at P_0 and Y_0.

   a. Using the diagram, explain what happens when aggregate demand falls.

   b. How is the short run different from the long run?

9. Draw an aggregate demand and supply diagram for Japan. In the diagram, show how each of the following affects aggregate demand and supply.

Copyright © by Houghton Mifflin Company. All rights reserved.

a. U.S. gross domestic product falls.

b. The level of prices in Korea falls.

c. Labor receives a large wage increase.

d. Economists predict higher prices next year.

10. If the long-run aggregate supply curve gives the level of potential real GDP, how can the short-run aggregate supply curve ever lie to the right of the long-run aggregate supply curve?

11. What will happen to the equilibrium price level and real GDP if:

a. aggregate demand and aggregate supply both increase?

b. aggregate demand increases and aggregate supply decreases?

c. aggregate demand and aggregate supply both decrease?

d. aggregate demand decreases and aggregate supply increases?

12. During the Great Depression, the U.S. economy experienced a falling price level and declining real GDP. Using an aggregate demand and aggregate supply diagram, illustrate and explain how this could occur.

13. Suppose aggregate demand increases, causing an increase in real GDP but no change in the price level. Using an aggregate demand and aggregate supply diagram, illustrate and explain how this could occur.

14. Suppose aggregate demand increases, causing an increase in the price level but no change in real GDP. Using an aggregate demand and aggregate supply diagram, illustrate and explain how this could occur.

15. Use an aggregate demand and aggregate supply diagram to illustrate and explain how each of the following will affect the equilibrium price level and real GDP:

a. Consumers expect a recession.

b. Foreign income rises.

c. Foreign price levels fall.

d. Government spending increases.

e. Workers expect higher future inflation and negotiate higher wages now.

f. Technological improvements increase productivity.

🖥 INTERNET EXERCISE

In sections 1.a and 1.b of this chapter we learned how changes in aggregate demand (*AD*) and aggregate supply (*AS*) are associated with business cycle fluctuations. An increase (decrease) in *AD* should be expansionary (contractionary) with rising (falling) GDP and prices. An increase (decrease) in *AS* should be expansionary (contractionary) with rising (falling) GDP and (falling) rising prices. The length of expansions and contractions is determined by the size and duration of shifts in *AD* and *AS*. We can see the history of U.S. business cycle fluctuations by going to the Boyes/Melvin web site at http://www.hmco.com/college/ and clicking on the internet exercise link for this chapter. Now answer the questions that appear on the web page.

Copyright © by Houghton Mifflin Company. All rights reserved.

Opinions Differ in Consumer Confidence Polls

Within one week, two national polls were released gauging consumer confidence: one showing it at a 28-year high and the other disclosing waning sentiment among consumers concerned about the nation's long-term prosperity.

How do consumers really feel about the state of the economy?

"They expect strong economic conditions to continue for the short term," said Lynn Franco, an economist for the Conference Board, a private research group in New York. But, when consumers were asked if that optimism will continue five years from now, Franco said, "They're saying they doubt that."

Franco said short-term optimism, coupled with consumers' long-term doubt, may be to blame for different results from such seemingly similar polls.

The Conference Board asks consumers to rate "general business conditions" and the availability of jobs in their areas. Respondents also are asked to gauge conditions "six months from now."

Its index, released last week, showed that Americans haven't felt this good about their financial well-being since 1969.

Conversely, the Index of Consumer Sentiment compiled by the University of Michigan asks consumers to rate financial conditions in one year and five years. The index fell to 102.1 last month from its record level of 107.2 in November.

The Conference Board "is tapping into a very immediate situation," said Lucia Dunn, an economist at Ohio State University.

Dunn helps compile the Ohio Consumer Confidence Index, measuring consumer sentiment in the state. It changed little during December, rising to 96.4 from a November level of 96.0.

"We focus more on consumer psychology—how they are feeling about long-term conditions," Dunn said of the polls conducted by OSU and the University of Michigan. "The Conference Board is a good short-term assessment, but it doesn't capture that latent uneasiness that is there."

For example, Dunn said, nearly 40 percent of the questions the Conference Board asks are related to employment. With unemployment rates low throughout the country, Dunn said, it's no surprise that consumers' response was positive.

Franco said that even though the two indexes use different polling methods, results tend to mirror one another.

Source: "Opinions Differ in Consumer Confidence Polls," by Jennifer Scott, *The Columbus Dispatch*, January 8, 1998, p. 1B.

Copyright © by Houghton Mifflin Company. All rights reserved.

COMMENTARY

Why would a business firm want to receive reports regarding consumer confidence in the U.S. economy? The answer lies in the role of expectations as a determinant of consumption spending and therefore aggregate demand. If households are confident that incomes will rise and prosperous times are ahead, they are much more likely to spend more than if they expect a recession. By monitoring consumer confidence in the economy, we can better understand consumer spending. Since consumption accounts for about two-thirds of GDP, changes in household spending can play a big role in business-cycle fluctuations.

In terms of aggregate demand and supply analysis, if households are more optimistic about the economy's performance, then the aggregate demand should shift to the right, like the shift from AD_0 to AD_1 in the accompanying figure. This would increase the equilibrium level of real GDP from Y_0 to Y_1. If households are less optimistic about the economy's performance, then the aggregate demand curve should shift to the left, like the shift from AD_0 to AD_2. This would decrease the equilibrium level of real GDP from Y_0 to Y_2.

Because of the implications of shifts in consumer confidence for business-cycle fluctuations, government officials, along with business people, watch the consumer confidence measures to maintain a sense of what is happening in the typical household. The two best-known surveys, the Michigan and Conference Board surveys, ask questions like: "Six months from now do you think business conditions will be better, the same, or worse?" "Would you say that you are better off or worse off financially than you were a year ago?" The answers to these questions and others are used as inputs in constructing an index of consumer confidence, so that the press typically only reports how the overall index changes rather than responses to any particular question.

Although the popular consumer confidence indexes fluctuate up and down every month, researchers have found that the monthly fluctuations are not very useful in predicting consumption or GDP. In fact, as the article states, the different surveys may sometimes give conflicting signals regarding changes in consumer confidence. But major shifts in the indexes or several months of rising or falling indexes may provide an early signal of forthcoming changes in consumption and GDP.

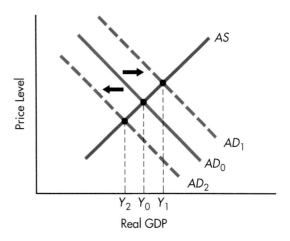

Copyright © by Houghton Mifflin Company. All rights reserved.

10

Aggregate Expenditures

FUNDAMENTAL QUESTIONS

1. How are consumption and saving related?

2. What are the determinants of consumption?

3. What are the determinants of investment?

4. What are the determinants of government spending?

5. What are the determinants of net exports?

6. What is the aggregate expenditures function?

Copyright © by Houghton Mifflin Company. All rights reserved.

To understand why real GDP, unemployment, and inflation rise and fall over time, we must know what causes the aggregate demand and aggregate supply curves to shift. We cannot understand why the U.S. economy has experienced ten recessions since 1945 or why the 1980s witnessed the longest peacetime business-cycle expansion in modern times unless we understand why the AD and AS curves shift. In this chapter, we examine in more detail the demand side of the economy.

Chapter 9 discussed how the price level affects aggregate expenditures through the interest rate, international trade, and wealth effects. This chapter examines in greater detail the nonprice determinants of spending and shifts in aggregate demand and assumes the price level is fixed. This assumption means the aggregate supply curve is a horizontal line at the fixed-price level. This approach was used by John Maynard Keynes, who analyzed the macro economy during the Great Depression. A fixed-price level, as shown in Figure 1, suggests a situation in which unemployment and excess capacity exist. Firms can hire from this pool of unemployed labor and increase their output at no extra cost and without any pressure on the price level. It is not surprising that Keynes would rely on such a model at a time when he was surrounded by mass unemployment. He was more interested in the determination of income and output than in the problem of inflation.

With a horizontal AS curve, as shown in Figure 1, the location of the AD curve will determine the equilibrium level of real GDP, Y_e. If we understand what determines aggregate demand—consumption, investment, government spending, and net exports—we will understand what determines real GDP.

We begin our detailed examination of aggregate expenditures by discussing consumption, which accounts for approximately 68 percent of total expenditures in the U.S. economy. We then look at investment (15 percent of total expenditures), government spending (18 percent of total expenditures), and net exports (recently, a small negative percentage of total expenditures). ■

1. CONSUMPTION AND SAVING

Households can do three things with their income. They can spend it for the consumption of goods and services, they can save it, or they can pay taxes.

Copyright © by Houghton Mifflin Company. All rights reserved.

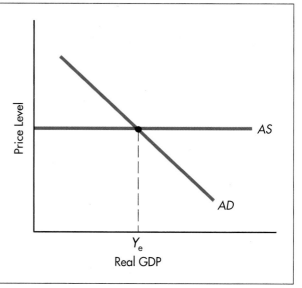

Figure 1
The Fixed-Price Keynesian Model
The Keynesian assumption that the price level is fixed requires a horizontal aggregate supply curve. In this case, aggregate demand will determine the equilibrium level of real GDP.

Copyright © by Houghton Mifflin Company. All rights reserved.

How are consumption and saving related?

Disposable income is what is left after taxes have been paid. It is the sum of consumption and saving:

$$\text{Disposable income} = \text{consumption} + \text{saving}$$

or

$$Yd = C + S$$

Disposable income is the income that households actually have available for spending after taxes. Whatever disposable income is not spent is saved.

Why are we talking about saving, which is not a component of total spending, in a chapter that sets out to discuss the components of total spending? Saving is simply "not consuming"; it is impossible to separate the incentives to save from the incentives to consume.

1.a. Saving and Savings

Saving occurs over a unit of time; it is a flow concept.

Savings are an amount accumulated at a point in time; they are a stock concept.

Before we go on, it is necessary to understand the difference between *saving* and *savings. Saving* occurs over a unit of time—a week, a month, a year. For instance, you might save $10 a week or $40 a month. Saving is a *flow* concept. *Savings* are an amount accumulated at a particular point in time—today, December 31, your sixty-fifth birthday. For example, you might have savings of $2,500 on December 31. Savings are a *stock* concept.

Like saving, GDP and its components are flow concepts. They are measured by the year or quarter of the year. Consumption, investment, government spending, and net exports are also flows. Each of them is an amount spent over a period of time.

1.b. The Consumption and Saving Functions

The primary determinant of the level of consumption over any given period is the level of disposable income. The higher disposable income, the more households are willing and able to spend. This relationship between disposable

Figure 2
Consumption and Saving in a Hypothetical Economy

Figure 2(a) shows that consumption is a positive function of disposable income: it goes up as disposable income rises. The line labeled $C = Yd$ forms a 45-degree angle at the origin. It shows all points where consumption equals disposable income. The point at which the consumption function (line C) crosses the 45-degree line—where disposable income measures $100—is the point at which consumption equals disposable income. At lower levels of disposable income, consumption is greater than disposable income; at higher levels, consumption is less than disposable income. Figure 2(b) shows the saving function. Saving equals disposable income minus consumption. When consumption equals disposable income, saving is 0. At higher levels of disposable income, we find positive saving; at lower levels, we find negative saving, or dissaving.

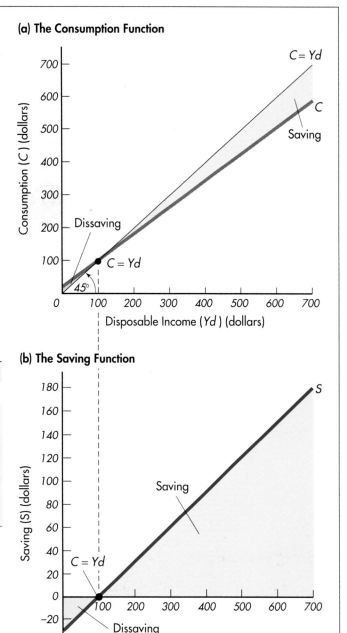

Disposable Income (Yd)	Consumption (C)	Saving (S)
$ 0	$ 30	$- 30
100	100	0
200	170	30
300	240	60
400	310	90
500	380	120
600	450	150
700	520	180

consumption function:
the relationship between disposable income and consumption

income and consumption is called the **consumption function.** To focus on the relationship between income and consumption, we draw a graph, Figure 2, with income on the horizontal axis and consumption on the vertical axis. Figure 2(a) shows a hypothetical consumption function. In this economy, when disposable income is zero, consumption is $30. As disposable income rises, consumption rises. For instance, when disposable income is $100, consumption is $100.

Copyright © by Houghton Mifflin Company. All rights reserved.

Consumption spending is the largest component of aggregate expenditures. Households in Grenada come to the produce market shown here to purchase food. Their expenditures on food will be counted in the consumption and GDP of Grenada. If the households decide to save less and spend more, then, other things being equal, the higher consumption will raise the GDP of Grenada.

We use C to represent consumption and Yd to represent disposable income. The line labeled C in Figure 2(a) is the consumption function: it represents the relationship between disposable income and consumption. The other line in the figure creates a 45-degree angle with either axis. (A 45-degree line makes a graph easier to read because every point on the line represents the same value on both axes.) In Figure 2(a), the 45-degree line shows all the points where consumption equals disposable income.

The level of disposable income at which all disposable income is being spent occurs at the point where the consumption function (line C) crosses the 45-degree line. In the graph, C equals Yd when disposable income is $100. Consumers save a fraction of any disposable income above $100. You can see this in the graph. Saving occurs at any level of disposable income at which the consumption function lies below the 45-degree line (at which consumption is less than disposable income). The amount of saving is measured by the vertical distance between the 45-degree line and the consumption function. If disposable income is $600, consumption is $450 and saving is $150.

saving function:
the relationship between disposable income and saving

The **saving function** is the relationship between disposable income and saving. Figure 2(b) plots the saving function (S). When the level of disposable income is at $100, consumption equals disposable income, so saving is zero. As disposable income increases beyond $100, saving goes up. In Figure 2(a), saving is the vertical distance between the 45-degree line and the consumption function. In Figure 2(b), we can read the level of saving directly from the saving function.

Notice that at relatively low levels of disposable income, consumption exceeds disposable income. How can consumption be greater than disposable income? When a household spends more than it earns in income, the house-

Copyright © by Houghton Mifflin Company. All rights reserved.

Copyright © by Houghton Mifflin Company. All rights reserved.

dissaving:
spending financed by borrowing
or using savings

hold must finance the spending above income by borrowing or using savings. This is called **dissaving.** In Figure 2(a), dissaving occurs at levels of disposable income between 0 and $100, where the consumption function lies above the 45-degree line. Dissaving, like saving, is measured by the vertical distance between the 45-degree line and the consumption function, but dissaving occurs when the consumption function lies *above* the 45-degree line. In Figure 2(b), dissaving occurs where the saving function (line *S*) lies below the disposable income axis, at disposable income levels between zero and $100. For example, when disposable income is $0, dissaving (negative saving) is –$30.

Both the consumption function and the saving function have positive slopes: as disposable income rises, consumption and saving increase. Consumption and saving, then, are positive functions of disposable income. Notice that when disposable income equals zero, consumption is still positive.

autonomous consumption:
consumption that is independent
of income

There is a level of consumption, called **autonomous consumption**, that does not depend on income. (*Autonomous* here means "independent of income.") In Figure 2(a), consumption equals $30 when disposable income equals zero. This $30 is autonomous consumption; it does not depend on income but will vary with the nonincome determinants of consumption that will soon be introduced. The intercept of the consumption function (the value of *C* when *Yd* equals zero) measures the amount of autonomous consumption. The intercept in Figure 2(a) is $30, which means that autonomous consumption in this example is $30.

1.c. Marginal Propensity to Consume and Save

**marginal propensity to
consume (*MPC*):**
change in consumption as a proportion of the change in disposable income

Total consumption equals autonomous consumption plus the spending that depends on income. As disposable income rises, consumption rises. This relationship between *change* in disposable income and *change* in consumption is the **marginal propensity to consume (*MPC*)**. The *MPC* measures change in consumption as a proportion of the change in disposable income:

$$MPC = \frac{\text{change in consumption}}{\text{change in disposable income}}$$

In Table 1, columns 1 and 2 list the consumption function data used in Figure 2. The marginal propensity to consume is shown in column 4. In our example, each time that disposable income changes by $100, consumption changes by $70. This means that consumers spend 70 percent of any extra income they receive.

$$MPC = \frac{\$70}{\$100}$$

$$= .70$$

**marginal propensity to save
(*MPS*):**
change in saving as a proportion
of the change in disposable
income

The *MPC* tells us how much consumption changes when income changes. The **marginal propensity to save (*MPS*)** defines the relationship between change in saving and change in disposable income. It is the change in saving divided by the change in disposable income:

$$MPS = \frac{\text{change in saving}}{\text{change in disposable income}}$$

TABLE 1
Marginal Propensity to Consume and Save

Disposable Income (Yd)	Consumption (C)	Saving (S)	Marginal Propensity to Consume (MPC)	Marginal Propensity to Save (MPS)
0	$ 30	$−30	—	—
$100	100	0	.70	.30
200	170	30	.70	.30
300	240	60	.70	.30
400	310	90	.70	.30
500	380	120	.70	.30
600	450	150	.70	.30
700	520	180	.70	.30

The *MPS* in Table 1 is a constant 30 percent at all levels of income. Each time that disposable income changes by $100, saving changes by $30:

$$MPS = \frac{\$30}{\$100}$$

$$= .30$$

The *MPC* and the *MPS* will always be constant at all levels of disposable income in our examples.

Since disposable income will be either consumed or saved, the marginal propensity to consume plus the marginal propensity to save must total 1:

$$MPC + MPS = 1$$

The percentage of additional income that is not consumed must be saved. If consumers spend 70 percent of any extra income, they save 30 percent of that income.

The slope of the consumption function is the same as the MPC; the slope of the saving function is the same as the MPS.

The *MPC* and the *MPS* determine the rate of consumption and saving as disposable income changes. The *MPC* is the slope of the consumption function; the *MPS* is the slope of the saving function. Remember that the slope of a line measures change along the vertical axis that corresponds to change along the horizontal axis; the rise over the run (see the Appendix to Chapter 1). In the case of the consumption function, the slope is the change in consumption (the change on the vertical axis) divided by the change in disposable income (the change on the horizontal axis):

$$\text{Slope of consumption function} = \frac{\text{change in consumption}}{\text{change in disposable income}}$$

$$= MPC$$

The higher the *MPC*, the greater the fraction of any additional disposable income consumers will spend. At .70, consumers spend 70 percent of any change in disposable income; at an *MPC* of .85, consumers want to spend 85 percent of any change in disposable income. The size of the *MPC* shows up graphically as the steepness of the consumption function. The consumption

Copyright © by Houghton Mifflin Company. All rights reserved.

function with an *MPC* of .85 is a steeper line than the one drawn in Figure 2(a). In general, the steeper the consumption function, the larger the *MPC*. If the *MPC* is less than .70, the consumption function would be flatter than the one in the figure.

The slope of the saving function is the *MPS*:

$$\text{Slope of saving function} = \frac{\text{change in saving}}{\text{change in disposable income}}$$

$$= MPS$$

In general, the steeper the saving function, the greater the slope and the greater the *MPS*.

Figure 3(a) shows three consumption functions. Since all three functions have the same intercept, autonomous consumption is the same for all. But each consumption function in Figure 3(a) has a different slope. C_1 has an *MPC* of .70. A larger *MPC*, .80, produces a steeper function (line C_2). A smaller *MPC*, .60, produces a flatter function (line C_3). The saving functions that correspond to these consumption functions are shown in Figure 3(b). Function S_1, with an *MPS* of .30, corresponds to consumption function C_1, with an *MPC* of .70 (remember: $MPS = 1 - MPC$). Function S_2 corresponds to C_2, and S_3 corresponds to C_3. The higher the *MPC* (the steeper the consumption function), the lower the *MPS* (the flatter the saving function). If people spend a greater fraction of extra income, they save a smaller fraction.

1.d. Average Propensity to Consume and Save

Suppose our interest is not the proportion of change in disposable income that is consumed or saved, but the proportion of disposable income that is consumed or saved. For this we must know the average propensity to consume and the average propensity to save.

average propensity to consume (*APC*):
the proportion of disposable income spent for consumption

The **average propensity to consume (*APC*)** is the proportion of disposable income spent for consumption:

$$APC = \frac{\text{consumption}}{\text{disposable income}}$$

or

$$APC = \frac{C}{Yd}$$

average propensity to save (*APS*):
the proportion of disposable income saved

The **average propensity to save (*APS*)** is the proportion of disposable income that is saved:

$$APS = \frac{\text{saving}}{\text{disposable income}}$$

or

$$APS = \frac{S}{Yd}$$

Table 2 uses the consumption and saving data plotted in Figure 2. The *APC* and *APS* are shown in columns 4 and 5. When disposable income is $100, consumption is also $100, so the ratio of consumption to disposable income (*C/Yd*) equals 1 ($100/$100). At this point, saving equals 0, so the ratio of saving to disposable income (*S/Yd*) also equals 0 (0/$100). We really do not

Copyright © by Houghton Mifflin Company. All rights reserved.

Figure 3
Marginal Propensity to Consume and Save
The *MPC* is the slope of the consumption function. The greater the *MPC*, the steeper the consumption function. The *MPS* is the slope of the saving function. The greater the *MPS*, the steeper the saving function. Because the sum of the *MPC* and the *MPS* is 1, the greater the *MPC*, the smaller the *MPS*. The steeper the consumption function, then, the flatter the saving function.

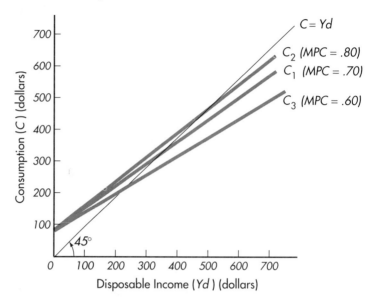

(a) Three Consumption Functions

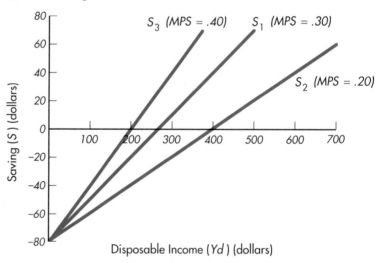

(b) Three Saving Functions

have to compute the *APS* because we already know the *APC*. There are only two things to do with disposable income: spend it or save it. The percentage of income spent plus the percentage saved must add up to 100 percent of disposable income. This means that

$$APC + APS = 1$$

If the *APC* equals 1, then the *APS* must equal 0.

When disposable income equals $600, consumption equals $450, so the *APC* equals .75 ($450/$600) and the *APS* equals .25 ($150/$600). As always, the *APC* plus the *APS* equals 1. If households are spending 75 percent of their disposable income, they must be saving 25 percent.

Copyright © by Houghton Mifflin Company. All rights reserved.

TABLE 2
Average Propensity to Consume and Save

Disposable Income (Yd)	Consumption (C)	Saving (S)	Average Propensity to Consume (APC)	Average Propensity to Save (APS)
$ 0	$ 30	$−30	—	—
100	100	0	1.00	0
200	170	30	.85	.15
300	240	60	.80	.20
400	310	90	.78	.22
500	380	120	.76	.24
600	450	150	.75	.25
700	520	180	.74	.26

Notice in Table 2 how the *APC* falls as disposable income rises. This is because households spend just a part of any change in income. In Figure 2(a), the consumption function rises more slowly than the 45-degree line. (Remember that consumption equals disposable income along the 45-degree line.) The consumption function tells us, then, that consumption rises as disposable income rises, but not by as much as income rises. Because households spend a smaller fraction of disposable income as that income rises, they must be saving a larger fraction. You can see this in Table 2, where the *APS* rises as disposable income rises. At low levels of income, the *APS* is negative, a product of dissaving (we are dividing negative saving by disposable income). As disposable income rises, saving rises as a percentage of disposable income, which means that the *APS* is increasing.

1.e. Determinants of Consumption

What are the determinants of consumption?

Disposable income is an important determinant of household spending. But disposable income is not the only factor that influences consumption. Wealth, expectations, demographics, and taxation (taxation effects will be considered in Chapter 12) are other determinants of consumption.

1.e.1. Disposable Income Household income is the primary determinant of consumption, which is why the consumption function is drawn with disposable income on the horizontal axis. Household income usually is measured as current disposable income. By *current* we mean income that is received in the current period—the current period could be today, this month, this year, whatever period we are discussing. Past income and future income certainly can affect household spending, but their effect is through household wealth or expectations, not income. Disposable income is after-tax income.

The two-dimensional graphs we have been using relate consumption only to current disposable income. A change in consumption caused by a change in disposable income is shown by *movement along* the consumption function. The effects of other variables are shown by *shifting* the intercept of the consumption function up and down as the values of these other variables change. All variables *except* disposable income change *autonomous* consumption.

Copyright © by Houghton Mifflin Company. All rights reserved.

Copyright © by Houghton Mifflin Company. All rights reserved.

Figure 4
Autonomous Shifts in Consumption and Saving
Autonomous consumption is the amount of consumption that exists when income is 0. It is the intercept of the consumption function. The shift from C to C_1 is an autonomous increase in consumption of $40; it moves the intercept of the consumption function from $60 to $100. The shift from C to C_2 is an autonomous decrease in consumption of $40; it moves the intercept of the consumption function from $60 to $20. Autonomous saving is the amount of saving that exists when real GDP is 0. This is the intercept of the saving function. The shift from S to S_1 is an autonomous decrease in saving of $40; it moves the intercept of the saving function from −$60 to −$100. The shift from S to S_2 is an autonomous increase in saving of $40; it moves the intercept of the saving function from −$60 to −$20. Because disposable income minus consumption equals saving, an autonomous increase in consumption is associated with an autonomous decrease in saving, and an autonomous decrease in consumption is associated with an autonomous increase in saving.

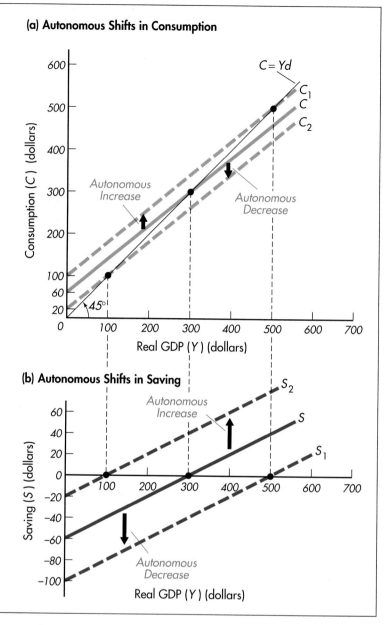

(a) Autonomous Shifts in Consumption

(b) Autonomous Shifts in Saving

Changes in taxes will affect disposable income. *If we assume that there are no taxes, then* Yd *equals* Y, *and consumption (and other expenditures) may be drawn as a function of real GDP rather than disposable income.* Chapter 12 is devoted to an analysis of government fiscal policy, including taxation. As a result, we put off our discussion of tax effects until then, which allows us to simplify our analysis of aggregate expenditures. The discussion of the components of aggregate expenditures in the remainder of this chapter and in later chapters will be related graphically to pretax real GDP rather than to disposable income.

wealth:
the value of all assets owned by a household

1.e.2. Wealth Wealth is the value of all the assets owned by a household. Wealth is a stock variable; it includes homes, cars, checking and savings accounts, and stocks and bonds, as well as the value of income expected in the future. As household wealth increases, households have more resources available for spending so consumption increases at every level of real GDP. You can see this in Figure 4(a) as a shift of the consumption function from C to C_1. The autonomous increase in consumption shifts the intercept of the consumption function from $60 to $100, so consumption increases by $40 at every level of real GDP. If households spend more of their current income as wealth increases, they save less. You can see this as the downward shift of the saving function in Figure 4(b), from S to S_1. The higher level of wealth has households more willing to dissave at each income level than before. Dissaving now occurs at any level of income below $500.

A decrease in wealth has just the opposite effect. For instance, during the 1990–1991 recession, property values declined in most areas of the United States. Household wealth declined as the value of real estate fell, and spending fell as a result. Here you would see an autonomous drop in consumption, like the shift from C to C_2, and an autonomous increase in saving, like the shift from S to S_2. Now at every level of real GDP, households spend $40 less than before and save $40 more. The intercept of the consumption function is $20, not $60, and the intercept of the saving function is -20, not -60. The new consumption function parallels the old one; the curves are the same vertical distance apart at every level of income. So consumption is $40 lower at every level of income. Similarly, the saving functions are parallel because saving is $40 greater at every level of real GDP along S_2 compared to S.

1.e.3. Expectations

Another important determinant of consumption is consumer expectations about future income, prices, and wealth. When consumers expect a recession, when they are worried about losing jobs or cutbacks in hours worked, they tend to spend less and save more. This means an autonomous decrease in consumption and increase in saving, like the shift from C to C_2 and S to S_2 in Figure 4. Conversely, when consumers are optimistic, we find an autonomous increase in consumption and decrease in saving, like the shift from C to C_1 and S to S_1 in Figure 4.

Expectations are subjective opinions; they are difficult to observe and measure. This creates problems for economists looking to analyze the effect of expectations on consumption. The Conference Board surveys households to construct its *Consumer Confidence Index,* a measure of consumer opinion regarding the outlook for the economy. Economists follow the index in order to predict how consumer spending will change. Since consumption is the largest component of GDP, changes in consumption have important implications for business cycles.

Clearly the Consumer Confidence Index is not always a reliable indicator of expansion or recession. Still economists' increasing use of this and other measures to better understand fluctuations in consumption underscores the importance of consumer expectations in the economy (see the Economic Insight "Permanent Income, Life Cycles, and Consumption").

1.e.4. Demographics

Other things being equal, economists expect the level of consumption to rise with increases in population. The focus here is on both the number of people in the economy and the composition of that population. The size of the population affects the position of the consumption function; the age of the population affects the slope of the consumption function. The greater the size of the population, other things equal, the higher the intercept of the consumption function. With regard to the effect of age composition on the economy, young households typically are accumulating durable consumer goods (refrigerators, washing machines, automobiles); they have higher *MPCs* than older households.

Copyright © by Houghton Mifflin Company. All rights reserved.

RECAP

1. It is impossible to separate incentives to save from incentives to consume.

2. Saving is a flow; savings is a stock.

3. Dissaving is spending financed by borrowing or using savings.

4. The marginal propensity to consume measures change in consumption as a proportion of change in disposable income.

5. The marginal propensity to save measures change in saving as a proportion of change in disposable income.

6. The *MPC* plus the *MPS* must equal 1.

7. Change in the *MPC* changes the slope of the consumption function; change in the *MPS* changes the slope of the saving function.

8. The average propensity to consume measures that portion of disposable income spent for consumption.

9. The average propensity to save measures that portion of disposable income saved.

10. The *APC* and the *APS* must equal 1.

11. The determinants of consumption include income, wealth, expectations, demographics, and taxation.

12. A change in consumption caused by a change in disposable income is shown by movement along the consumption function.

13. Changes in wealth, expectations, or population change autonomous consumption, which is shown as a shift of the consumption function.

2. INVESTMENT

Investment is business spending on capital goods and inventories. It is the most variable component of total spending. In this section we look at the determinants of investment and see why investment changes so much over the business cycle.

2.a. Autonomous Investment

In order to simplify our analysis of real GDP in the next chapter, we assume that investment is autonomous, that it is independent of current real GDP. This does not mean that we assume investment is fixed at a constant amount. There are several factors that cause investment to change, but we assume that current real GDP is not one of them.

As a function of real GDP, autonomous investment is drawn as a horizontal line. This means that investment remains constant as real GDP changes. In Figure 5, the investment function (the horizontal line labeled I) indicates that investment equals $50 at every level of real GDP. As the determinants of investment change, the investment function shifts autonomously. As investment increases, the function shifts upward (for example, from I to I_1); as investment decreases, the function shifts downward (from I to I_2).

Copyright © by Houghton Mifflin Company. All rights reserved.

Figure 5
Investment as a Function of Income
Investment is assumed to be autonomous. Because it is independent of current real GDP, it is drawn as a horizontal line. An autonomous increase in investment shifts the function upward, from I to I_1. An increase could be the product of lower interest rates, optimism in business about future sales and revenues, technological change, an investment tax credit that lowers the cost of capital goods, or a need to expand capacity because of a lack of available productive resources. An autonomous decrease in investment moves the function down, from I to I_2. The same factors that cause investment to rise can also cause it to fall as they move in the opposite direction.

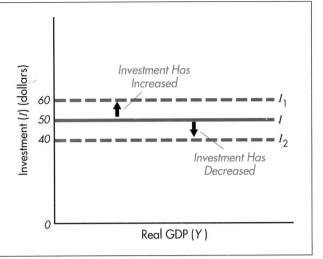

2.b. Determinants of Investment

What are the determinants of investment?

Investment is business spending on capital goods and inventories. Capital goods are the buildings and equipment businesses need to produce their products. Inventories are final goods that have not been sold. Inventories can be planned or unplanned. For example, in the fall a retail department store wants to have enough sizes and styles of the new clothing lines to attract customers. Without a good-sized inventory, sales will suffer. The goods it buys are *planned* inventory, based on expected sales. But come February, the store wants to have as few fall clothes left unsold as possible. Goods not sold at this stage are *unplanned* inventory. They are a sign that sales were not as good as expected and that too much was produced last year.

Both types of inventories—planned and unplanned—are called investment. But only planned investment—capital purchases plus planned inventories—combine with planned consumer, government, and foreign-sector spending to determine the equilibrium level of aggregate expenditures, as we will see in the next chapter. Unplanned investment and unwanted inventories do not affect the equilibrium. They are simply the leftovers of what has recently gone on in the economy. What economists are interested in are the determinants of planned investment.

2.b.1. The Interest Rate Business investment is made in the hopes of earning profits. The greater the expected profit, the greater is investment. A primary determinant of whether or not an investment opportunity will be profitable is the rate of interest. The interest rate is the cost of borrowed funds. Much of business spending is financed by borrowing. As the rate of interest goes up, fewer investment projects offer enough profit to warrant their undertaking. In other words, the higher the interest rate, the lower the rate of investment. As the interest rate falls, opportunities for greater profits increase and investment rises.

Let's look at a simple example. A firm can acquire a machine for $100 that will yield $120 in output. Whether or not the firm is willing to undertake the investment depends on whether it will earn a sufficient return on its investment. The return from an investment is the profit from an investment divided by its cost.

Copyright © by Houghton Mifflin Company. All rights reserved.

Permanent Income, Life Cycles, and Consumption

Studies of the consumption function over a long period of time find a function like the one labeled C_L in the graph. This function has a marginal propensity to consume of .90 and an intercept of 0. Consumption functions studied over a shorter period of time have lower *MPCs* and positive intercepts, like function C_S in the graph, with an *MPC* of .60. How do we reconcile these two functions?

Economists offer two related explanations for the difference between long-run and short-run consumption behavior: the permanent income hypothesis and the life-cycle hypothesis. The basic idea is that people consume based on their idea of what their long-run or permanent level of income is. A substantial increase in income this month does not affect consumption much in the short run unless it is perceived as a permanent increase.

Let's use point 1 on the graph as our starting point. Here disposable income is $50,000 and consumption is $45,000. Now suppose household income rises to $60,000. Initially consumption increases by 60 percent, the short-run *MPC*. The household moves from point 1 to point 2 along the short-run consumption function (C_S). The short-run consumption function has a lower *MPC* than the long-run consumption function because households do not completely adjust their spending and saving habits to short-run fluctuations in income. Once the household is convinced that $60,000 is a permanent level of income, it moves

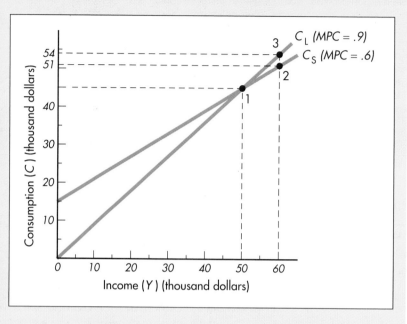

from point 2 to point 3 along the long-run consumption function. At point 3, consumption has increased by 90 percent, the long-run *MPC*. In the long run, households adjust fully to changes in income; in the short run, a fluctuation in income does not cause as large a fluctuation in consumption.

When income falls below the permanent income level, the household is willing to dissave or borrow to support its normal level of consumption. When income rises above the permanent income level, the household saves at a higher rate than the long-run *MPS*. The lower *MPC* in the short run works to smooth out consumption in the long run. The household does not adjust current consumption to every

up and down movement in household income.

To maintain a steady rate of consumption over time, households follow a pattern of saving over the life cycle. Saving is low when current income is low relative to permanent income (during school years, periods of unemployment, or retirement). Saving is high when current income is high relative to the lifetime average, typically during middle age.

In the long run, households adjust fully to changes in income. In the short run, in order to smooth consumption over time, they do not. This explains both the difference between the long-run and short-run consumption functions and the stability of consumption over time.

Copyright © by Houghton Mifflin Company. All rights reserved.

If the firm has to borrow $100 for the investment, it will have to pay interest to the lender. Suppose the lender charges 10 percent interest. The firm will have to pay 10 percent of $100, or $10 interest. This raises the cost of the investment to $110, the $100 cost of the machine plus the $10 interest. The firm's return from the investment is 9 percent:

$$\text{Return on investment} = \frac{(\$120 - \$110)}{\$110}$$

$$= .09$$

As the interest rate rises, the firm's cost of borrowing also rises and the return on investment falls. When the interest rate is 20 percent, the firm must pay $20 in interest, so the total cost of the investment is $120. Here the return is 0 ([$120 − $120]/$120). The higher interest rate reduces the return on the investment and discourages investment spending.

As the interest rate falls, the firm's cost of borrowing falls and the return from the investment rises. If the interest rate is 5 percent, the firm must pay $5 in interest. The total cost of the investment is $105, and the return is 14 percent ([$120 − $105]/$105). The lower interest rate increases the return from the investment and encourages investment spending.

2.b.2. Profit Expectations   Firms undertake investment in the expectation of earning a profit. Obviously, they cannot know exactly how much profit they will earn. So they use forecasts of revenues and costs to decide on an appropriate level of investment. It is their *expected* rate of return that actually determines their level of investment.

Many factors affect expectations of profit and, therefore, change the level of investment. Among them are new firms entering the market; political change; new laws, taxes, or subsidies from government; and the overall economic health of the country or world as measured by gross domestic product.

2.b.3. Other Determinants of Investment   Everything that might affect a firm's expected rate of return determines its level of investment. But three factors—technological change, the cost of capital goods, and capacity utilization—warrant special attention.

Technological Change   Technological change is often a driving force behind new investment. New products or processes can be crucial to remaining competitive in an industry. The computer industry, for example, is driven by technological change. As faster and larger-capacity memory chips are developed, computer manufacturers must utilize them in order to stay competitive.

The impact of technology on investment spending is not new. For example, the invention of the cotton gin stimulated investment spending in the early 1800s, and the introduction of the gasoline-powered tractor in 1905 created an agricultural investment boom in the early 1900s. More recently, the development of integrated circuits stimulated investment spending in the electronics industry.

One measure of the importance of technology is commitment to research and development. Data on spending for research and development across U.S. industries and across countries are listed in Table 3. The industries listed in the table are those that rely on innovation and the development of new technologies to remain competitive. Research and development is a multi-billion-dollar commitment for these industries. The data on the four industrial countries indicate that these countries spend roughly the same percentage of

Copyright © by Houghton Mifflin Company. All rights reserved.

Technological progress results from research and development efforts. The photo illustrates the ongoing efforts in the athletic shoe industry to provide technological advances in shoe design through research. In this case, electrodes and reflectors are attached to a subject's leg and foot to allow Reebok researchers to closely monitor the effects of shoe design on running performance. In the event of a major modification of shoe design, competitors would adapt their designs to compete with the innovator. In this manner, research and development expenditures may stimulate investment spending throughout an industry or economy.

TABLE 3
Research and Development Expenditures

In Selected U.S. Industries, 1994

Industry	Expenditures (millions of dollars)	Expenditures as Percentage of Sales	Number of Researchers
Aircraft and Missiles	14,260	13.8	65,700
Electrical Equipment	15,338	5.9	101,000
Chemicals and Allied Products	15,381	5.3	92,300

As a Percentage of GDP, Selected Years, 1965–1994

Year	United States	France	Germany	Japan
1965	2.8	2.0	1.7	1.5
1968	2.8	2.1	2.0	1.6
1971	2.4	1.9	2.2	1.9
1974	2.2	1.8	2.1	2.0
1977	2.2	1.8	2.1	1.9
1980	2.3	1.8	2.4	2.2
1983	2.6	2.2	2.5	2.6
1985	2.8	2.3	2.7	2.9
1988	2.8	2.3	2.8	2.9
1991	2.7	2.4	2.8	3.0
1994	2.5	2.4	2.3	2.7

Source: U.S. Bureau of the Census, *Statistical Abstract of the United States,* 1997.

Copyright © by Houghton Mifflin Company. All rights reserved.

GDP on research and development. The most obvious trend is the increase in Japanese spending since the mid-1960s. As Japan has grown to be an industrial giant, the role of technological innovation has become increasingly important there.

A commitment to research and development is a sign of the technological progress that marks the industrial nation. The countries listed in Table 3, along with other industrial nations, are the countries where new technology generally originates. New technology developed in any country tends to stimulate investment spending across all nations as firms in similar industries are forced to adopt new production methods to keep up with their competition.

Cost of Capital Goods   The cost of capital goods also affects investment spending. As capital goods become more expensive, the rate of return from investment in them drops and the amount of investment falls. One factor that can cause the cost of capital goods to change sharply is government tax policy. The U.S. government has imposed and then removed investment tax credits several times in the past. These credits allow firms to deduct part of the cost of investment from their tax bill. When the cost of investment drops, investment increases. When the cost of investment increases, the level of investment falls.

Capacity Utilization   If its existing capital stock is being used heavily, a firm has an incentive to buy more. But if much of its capital stock stands idle, the firm has little incentive to increase that stock. Economists sometimes refer to the productive capacity of the economy as the amount of output that can be produced by businesses. In fact the Federal Reserve constructs a measure of capacity utilization that indicates how close the economy is to capacity output.

Figure 6 plots the rate of capacity utilization in the U.S. economy. During this time, U.S. industry operated at a high rate of 88.4 percent of capacity in 1973 and at a low rate of 74.6 percent of capacity in the recession year of 1975. We never expect to see 100 percent of capacity utilized for the same reasons that we never expect zero unemployment. There are always capital goods that are temporarily unused, as in the case of frictional unemployment of labor, and there are always capital goods that are obsolete because of technological change, similar to the case of structural unemployment of labor.

When the economy is utilizing its capacity at a high rate, there is pressure to increase the production of capital goods and expand productive capacity. When capacity utilization is low—when factories and machines sit idle—investment tends to fall.

2.c. Volatility

We said that investment is the most variable component of total spending. What role do the determinants of investment play in that volatility?

Interest rates fluctuate widely. They are much more variable than income. Interest rates are a very important determinant of investment. Clearly the fact that they are so variable contributes to the variability of investment.

Expectations are subjective judgments about the future. Expectations can and often do change suddenly with new information. A rumor of a technological breakthrough, a speech by the president or a powerful member of Congress, even a revised weather forecast can cause firms to reexamine their

Copyright © by Houghton Mifflin Company. All rights reserved.

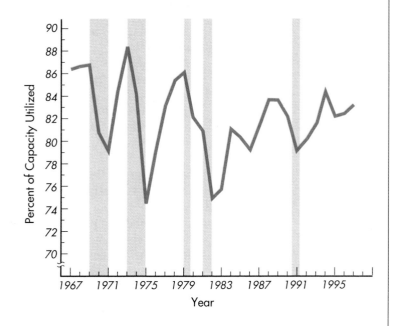

Figure 6
Capacity Utilization Rates for Total U.S. Industry
The Federal Reserve estimates the rate at which capacity is utilized in U.S. industry. The higher the rate, the greater the pressure for investment to expand productive capacity.

thinking about the expected profitability of an investment. In developing economies, the protection of private property rights can have a large impact on investment spending. If a business expects a change in government policy to increase the likelihood of the government's expropriating its property, obviously it is not going to undertake new investments. Conversely, if a firm believes that the government will protect private property and encourage the accumulation of wealth, it will increase its investment spending. The fact that expectations are subject to large and frequent swings contributes to the volatility of investment.

Technological change proceeds very unevenly, making it difficult to forecast. Historically we find large increases in investment when a new technology is first developed and decreases in investment after the new technology is in place. This causes investment to move up and down unevenly through time.

Changes in tax policy occur infrequently, but they can create large incentives to invest or not to invest. U.S. tax laws have swung back and forth on whether or not to offer an investment tax credit. A credit was first introduced in 1962. It was repealed in 1969, then readopted in 1971, and later revised in 1975, 1976, and 1981. In 1986, the investment tax credit was repealed again. Each of these changes had an impact on the cost of capital goods and contributed to the volatility of investment.

Finally, investment generally rises and falls with the rate of capacity utilization over the business cycle. As capacity utilization rises, some firms must add more factories and machines in order to continue increasing output and avoid reaching their maximum output level. As capacity utilization fluctuates, so will investment.

Copyright © by Houghton Mifflin Company. All rights reserved.

RECAP

1. As a function of real GDP, autonomous investment is drawn as a horizontal line.

2. The primary determinants of investment are the interest rate and profit expectations. Technological change, the cost of capital goods, and the rate of capacity utilization have an enormous impact on those expectations.

3. Investment fluctuates widely over the business cycle because the determinants of investment are so variable.

3. GOVERNMENT SPENDING

What are the determinants of government spending?

Government spending on goods and services is the second largest component of aggregate expenditures in the United States. In later chapters we examine the behavior of government in detail. Here we focus on how the government sector fits into the aggregate expenditures–income relationship. We assume that government spending is set by government authorities at whatever level they choose, independent of current income. In other words, we assume that government spending, like investment, is autonomous.

Figure 7 depicts government expenditures as a function of real GDP. The function, labeled G, is a horizontal line. If government officials increase government expenditures, the function shifts upward, parallel to the original curve by an amount equal to the increase in expenditures (for example, from G to G_1). If government expenditures are reduced, the function shifts downward by an amount equal to the drop in expenditures (for example, from G to G_2).

Copyright © by Houghton Mifflin Company. All rights reserved.

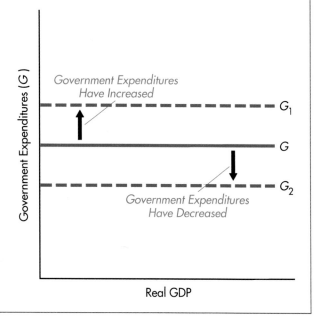

Figure 7
Government Expenditures as a Function of Real GDP
Government spending is assumed to be autonomous and set by government policy. The government spending function is the horizontal line labeled G. Autonomous increases in government spending move the function upward (for example, from G to G_1); decreases move the function downward (for example, from G to G_2).

4. NET EXPORTS

The last component of aggregate expenditures is net exports, spending in the international sector. Net exports equal a country's exports of goods and services (what it sells to the rest of the world) minus its imports of goods and services (what it buys from the rest of the world). When net exports are positive, there is a surplus on the merchandise and services accounts. When net exports are negative, there is a deficit. The United States has had a net exports deficit since 1975. This is a relatively new phenomenon: the country had run surpluses throughout the post–World War II era.

4.a. Exports

We assume that exports are autonomous. There are many factors that determine the actual value of exports, among them foreign income, tastes, prices, government trade restrictions, and exchange rates. But we assume that exports are not affected by current domestic income. You see this in the second column of Table 4, where exports are $50 at each level of real GDP.

As foreign income increases, foreign consumption rises—including consumption of goods produced in other countries—so domestic exports increase at every level of domestic real GDP. Decreases in foreign income lower domestic exports at every level of domestic real GDP. Similarly, changes in tastes or government restrictions on international trade or exchange rates can cause the level of exports to shift autonomously. When tastes favor domestic goods, exports go up. When tastes change, exports go down. When foreign governments impose restrictions on international trade, domestic exports fall. When restrictions are lowered, exports rise. Finally, as discussed in Chapter 7, when the domestic currency depreciates on the foreign exchange market (making domestic goods cheaper in foreign countries), exports rise. When the domestic currency appreciates on the foreign exchange market (making domestic goods more expensive in foreign countries), exports fall.

4.b. Imports

Domestic purchases from the rest of the world (imports) are also determined by tastes, trade restrictions, and exchange rates. Here domestic income

TABLE 4
Hypothetical Export and Import Schedule

Real GDP	Exports	Imports	Net Exports
$ 0	$50	$ 0	$50
100	50	10	40
200	50	20	30
300	50	30	20
400	50	40	10
500	50	50	0
600	50	60	− 10
700	50	70	− 20

Copyright © by Houghton Mifflin Company. All rights reserved.

plays a role too. The greater domestic real GDP, the greater domestic imports. The import data in Table 4 show imports increasing with real GDP. When real GDP is 0, autonomous imports equal $0. As real GDP increases, imports increase.

We measure the sensitivity of changes in imports to changes in real GDP by the marginal propensity to import. **The marginal propensity to import (*MPI*)** is the proportion of any extra income spent on imports.

marginal propensity to import (*MPI*):
change in imports as a proportion of change in income

$$MPI = \frac{\text{change in imports}}{\text{change in income}}$$

In Table 4, the *MPI* is .10, or 10 percent. Every time income changes by $100, imports change by $10.

How do other factors—tastes, government trade restrictions, and exchange rates—affect imports? When domestic tastes favor foreign goods, imports rise. When they do not, imports fall. When the domestic government tightens restrictions on international trade, domestic imports fall. When those restrictions are loosened, imports rise. Finally, when the domestic currency depreciates on the foreign exchange market (making foreign goods more expensive to domestic residents), imports fall. And when the domestic currency appreciates on the foreign exchange market (lowering the price of foreign goods), imports rise.

4.c. The Net Export Function

The higher domestic income, the lower net exports.

In our hypothetical economy in Table 4, net exports are listed in the last column. They are the difference between exports and imports. Because imports rise with domestic income, the higher that income, the lower net exports.

The net exports function, labeled *X*, is shown in Figure 8. The downward slope of the function (given by the *MPI*) indicates that net exports fall as real GDP increases. Net exports are the only component of aggregate expenditures that can take on a negative value (saving can be negative, but it is not part of spending). Negative net exports mean that the domestic economy is importing more than it exports. The net exports function shifts with changes in foreign income, prices, tastes, government trade restrictions, and exchange rates. For example, as foreign income increases, domestic exports increase and the net exports function shifts upward.

RECAP

1. Net exports equal a country's exports minus its imports.
2. Exports are determined by foreign income, tastes, government trade restrictions, and exchange rates; they are independent of domestic real GDP.
3. Imports are a positive function of domestic real·GDP; they also depend on tastes, domestic government trade restrictions, and exchange rates.
4. The marginal propensity to import measures change in imports as a proportion of the change in domestic income.
5. Net exports fall as domestic real GDP rises.

Copyright © by Houghton Mifflin Company. All rights reserved.

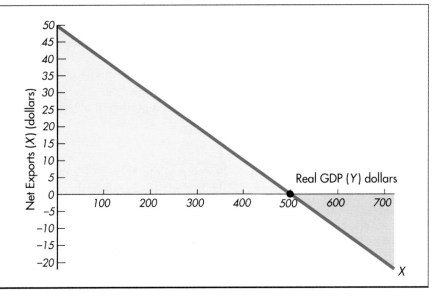

Figure 8
Net Exports as a Function of Real GDP
The net exports function is the downward-sloping line labeled *X*. Because exports are autonomous and imports increase with income, net exports fall as domestic real GDP rises. Notice that net exports can be positive or negative.

5. THE AGGREGATE EXPENDITURES FUNCTION

Copyright © by Houghton Mifflin Company. All rights reserved.

The aggregate, or total, expenditures function is the sum of the individual functions for each component of planned spending. Aggregate expenditures (*AE*) equal consumption (*C*), plus investment (*I*), plus government spending (*G*), plus net exports (*X*):

$$AE = C + I + G + X$$

5.a. Aggregate Expenditures Table and Function

The table in Figure 9 lists aggregate expenditures data for a hypothetical economy. Real GDP is in the first column; the individual components of aggregate expenditures are in columns 2 through 5. Aggregate expenditures, listed in column 6, is the sum of the components at each level of income.

The aggregate expenditures function (*AE*) can be derived graphically by summing the individual expenditure functions (Figure 9) in a vertical direction. We begin with the consumption function (*C*) and then add autonomous investment, $50, to the consumption function at every level of income to arrive at the *C* + *I* function. To this we add constant government spending, $70, at every level of income to find the *C* + *I* + *G* function. Finally, we add the net exports function to find *C* + *I* + *G* + *X*, or the *AE* function.

Notice that the *C*, *C* + *I*, and *C* + *I* + *G* functions are all parallel. They all have the same slope, that determined by the *MPC*. This is because *I* and *G* are autonomous. The *AE* function has a smaller slope than the other functions because the slope of the net exports function is negative. By adding the *X* function to the *C* + *I* + *G* function, we are decreasing the slope of the *AE* function; the *C* + *I* + *G* + *X* function has a smaller, flatter slope than the *C* + *I* + *G* function.

The *X* function increases spending for levels of real GDP below $500 and decreases spending for levels of real GDP above $500. At $500, net exports

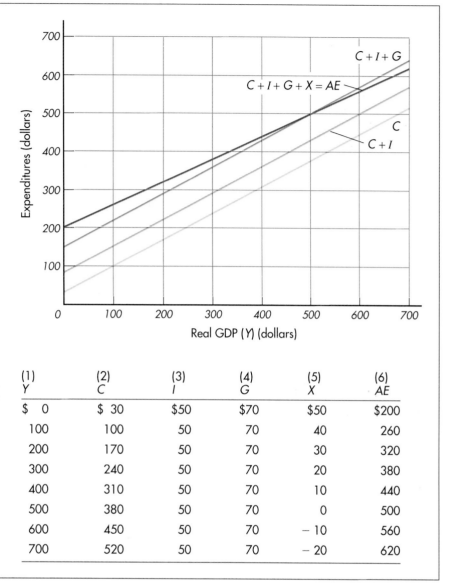

Figure 9
The Aggregate Expenditures Function
To find the aggregate expenditures function, we begin with the consumption function (labeled *C*) and add the investment function (*I*), to create the *C* + *I* function. We then add the government spending function (*G*) to find the *C* + *I* + *G* function. Notice that the *C*, *C* + *I*, and *C* + *I* + *G* functions are all parallel. They have the same slope because investment and government spending are assumed to be autonomous. Because *I* and *G* do not change with income, the slope of the *C* + *I* and *C* + *I* + *G* functions equals the slope of the consumption function (the *MPC*). Net exports are added to the *C* + *I* + *G* function to find the aggregate expenditures function, *C* + *I* + *G* + *X*. The aggregate expenditures function has a smaller slope than the other functions because the slope of the net exports function is negative.

(1) Y	(2) C	(3) I	(4) G	(5) X	(6) AE
$ 0	$ 30	$50	$70	$50	$200
100	100	50	70	40	260
200	170	50	70	30	320
300	240	50	70	20	380
400	310	50	70	10	440
500	380	50	70	0	500
600	450	50	70	− 10	560
700	520	50	70	− 20	620

equal 0 (see column 5). Because domestic imports increase as domestic income increases, net exports fall as income rises. At incomes above $500, net exports are negative, so aggregate expenditures are less than *C* + *I* + *G*.

5.b. The Next Step

Though we have also been using "aggregate demand" to refer to total spending, you can see from Figure 9 that the aggregate expenditures line slopes up while the aggregate demand curve you saw in Figure 1 slopes down. In the next chapter we will explore the formal relationship between these two related concepts, when we go about determining the equilibrium level of real GDP using the *AE* function.

The concept of macroeconomic equilibrium points out the key role aggregate expenditures play in determining output and income. As you will see, the

Copyright © by Houghton Mifflin Company. All rights reserved.

equilibrium level of real GDP is that level toward which the economy automatically tends to move. Once that equilibrium is established, there is no tendency for real GDP to change unless a change in autonomous expenditures occurs. If aggregate expenditures rise, then the equilibrium level of real GDP rises. If aggregate expenditures fall, then the equilibrium level of real GDP falls. Such shifts in the *AE* function are associated with shifts in *C, I, G,* or *X*.

RECAP

1. Aggregate expenditures are the sum of planned consumption, planned investment, planned government spending, and planned net exports at every level of real GDP.

2. Assuming that *I* and *G* are autonomous, the *C, C + I,* and *C + I + G* functions are parallel lines.

3. Net exports increase aggregate expenditures at relatively low levels of domestic real GDP and decrease aggregate expenditures at relatively high levels of domestic real GDP.

SUMMARY

How are consumption and saving related?

1. Consumption and saving are the components of disposable income; they are determined by the same variables. §1

2. Dissaving occurs when consumption exceeds income. §1.b

3. The marginal propensity to consume (*MPC*) is change in consumption divided by change in disposable income; the marginal propensity to save (*MPS*) is change in saving divided by change in disposable income. §1.c

4. The average propensity to consume (*APC*) is consumption divided by disposable income; the average propensity to save (*APS*) is saving divided by disposable income. §1.d

What are the determinants of consumption?

5. The determinants of consumption are income, wealth, expectations, demographics, and taxation. §1.e.1, 1.e.2, 1.e.3, 1.e.4

What are the determinants of investment?

6. Investment is assumed to be autonomous, independent of current income. §2.a

7. The determinants of investment are the interest rate, profit expectations, technological change, the cost of capital goods, and the rate at which capacity is utilized. §2.b.1, 2.b.2, 2.b.3

8. Firms use the expected return on investment to determine the expected profitability of an investment project. §2.b.1

9. Investment is highly variable over the business cycle because the determinants of investment are themselves so variable. §2.c

What are the determinants of government spending?

10. Government spending is set by government authorities at whatever level they choose. §3

What are the determinants of net exports?

11. Net exports are the difference between what a country exports and what it imports; both exports and imports are a product of foreign or domestic income, tastes, foreign and domestic government trade restrictions, and exchange rates. §4.a, 4.b

Copyright © by Houghton Mifflin Company. All rights reserved.

12. Because imports rise with domestic income, the higher that income, the lower net exports. §4.c

What is the aggregate expenditures function?

13. The aggregate expenditures function is the sum of the individual functions for each component of spending. §5

14. The slope of the aggregate expenditures function is flatter than that of the consumption function because it includes the net exports function, which is negative. §5.a

KEY TERMS

consumption function §1.b

saving function §1.b

dissaving §1.b

autonomous consumption §1.b

marginal propensity to consume (*MPC*) §1.c

marginal propensity to save (*MPS*) §1.c

average propensity to consume (*APC*) §1.d

average propensity to save (*APS*) §1.d

wealth §1.e.2

marginal propensity to import (*MPI*) §4.b

EXERCISES

1. Why do we study the consumption and saving functions together?

2. Explain the difference between a flow and a stock. Classify each of the following as a stock or flow: income, wealth, saving, savings, consumption, investment, government expenditures, net exports, GDP.

3. Fill in the blanks in the following table:

Income	Consumption	Saving	MPC	MPS	APC	APS
$1,000	$ 400	_____			__	.60
2,000	900	$1,100	__	__	__	__
3,000	1,400	_____	__	.50	__	__
4,000	_____	2,100	__	__	__	__

4. Why is consumption so much more stable over the business cycle than investment? In your answer, discuss household behavior as well as business behavior.

5. Assuming investment is autonomous, draw an investment function with income on the horizontal axis. Show how the function shifts if:

   a. The interest rate falls.

   b. An investment tax credit is repealed by Congress.

   c. A new president is expected to be a strong advocate of probusiness policies.

   d. There is a great deal of excess capacity in the economy.

6. Use the following table to answer these questions:

Y	C	I	G	X
$ 500	$500	$10	$20	$60
600	590	10	20	40
700	680	10	20	20
800	770	10	20	0
900	860	10	20	−20
1,000	950	10	20	−40

   a. What is the *MPC*?

   b. What is the *MPS*?

   c. What is the *MPI*?

   d. What is the level of aggregate expenditures at each level of income?

   e. Graph the aggregate expenditures function.

Copyright © by Houghton Mifflin Company. All rights reserved.

7. Based on the table in exercise 6, what is the linear equation for each of the following functions?

    a. Consumption

    b. Investment

    c. Net exports

    d. Aggregate expenditures

8. Is the *AE* function the same thing as a demand curve? Why or why not?

9. What is the level of saving if:

    a. Disposable income is $500 and consumption is $450?

    b. Disposable income is $1,200 and the *APS* is .9?

    c. The *MPC* equals .9, disposable income rises from $800 to $900, and saving is originally $120 when income equals $800?

10. What is the marginal propensity to consume if:

    a. Consumption increases by $75 when disposable income rises by $100?

    b. Consumption falls by $50 when disposable income falls by $100?

    c. Saving equals $20 when disposable income equals $100 and saving equals $40 when disposable income equals $300?

11. How can the *APC* fall as income rises if the *MPC* is constant?

12. Why would economies with older populations tend to have greater slopes of the consumption function?

13. Draw a diagram and illustrate the effects of the following on the net exports function for the United States:

    a. The French government imposes restrictions on French imports of U.S. goods.

    b. U.S. national income rises.

    c. Foreign income falls.

    d. The dollar depreciates on the foreign exchange market.

14. Why is the slope of the $C + I + G$ function different from the slope of the $C + I + G + X$ function?

15. Suppose the consumption function is $C = \$200 + 0.8Y$.

    a. What is the amount of autonomous consumption?

    b. What is the marginal propensity to consume?

    c. What would consumption equal when real GDP equals $1,000?

Copyright © by Houghton Mifflin Company. All rights reserved.

INTERNET EXERCISE

Section 4.c of this chapter informs us that net exports are the only component of aggregate expenditures that can be negative (when imports exceed exports). In recent years, the United States is well known to have run large net export deficits. However, has this always been true? To investigate this issue, go to the Boyes/Melvin web site at **http://www/hmco.com/college/** and click on the internet exercise link for this chapter. Now answer the questions that appear on the web page.

Copyright © by Houghton Mifflin Company. All rights reserved.

U.S. Trade Deficit with China Widens; Record Gap Shows up As Summit Nears

WASHINGTON—America's monthly trade deficit ballooned to $10.4 billion as imports of toys and Christmas decorations pushed the trade gap with China to an all-time high just before the U.S.-China summit.

The widening deficit in August, reported on Tuesday, was the worst showing in seven months. It came at an inopportune time for President Clinton, who is trying to sell a reluctant Congress on the virtues of free trade while also preparing for the state visit next week of Chinese President Jiang Zemin. . . .

The U.S. appetite for imports from all countries hit a new record in August. On the export side, sales of commercial jetliners, normally a bright spot in the trade picture, fell by $888 million from July.

For the first eight months of 1997, the total trade deficit is running at an annual rate of $114.5 billion, even worse than the eight-year high of $111 billion in 1996.

The White House sought to play down the higher overall deficit, arguing that it comes at a time when the United States' economy is outperforming those of its major trading partners.

"The strength of the U.S. economy makes it possible for the U.S. consumer to buy more from abroad," said presidential spokesman Mike McCurry.

Clinton met with congressional leaders Tuesday in his continued efforts to lobby for the "fast track" authority he needs to negotiate new free trade agreements. McCurry said the administration remained convinced that the path to future prosperity lies in reducing foreign trade barriers.

But critics contend that Clinton's trade policies have failed to keep the deficit from rising every year he has been in office, at a cost of thousands of American jobs lost to low-wage competitors.

The trade deficit with Japan in August narrowed for the first time since May, falling to $4.5 billion, but it is still running 17 percent ahead of a year ago. That reversal after two years of narrow deficits was one of the factors that led to the dramatic show-down last week between the United States and Japan over port practices.

America's deficit with its biggest trade partner, Canada, grew 20 percent from July to $2.6 billion in August, while the imbalance with Mexico rose 0.5 percent to $992 million.

Overall, U.S. exports of goods and services rose 0.2 percent to $77.96 billion. Sales of American farm products were up 11.2 percent to $4.26 billion, the first improvement this year.

Overall imports of goods and services increased 0.6 percent to a record $88.32 billion. The volume of imported crude oil hit an all-time high of 282.5 million barrels, with the price per barrel rising slightly to $16.94, compared to $16.50 in July.

Source "U.S. Trade Deficit with China Widens; Record Gap Shows up As Summit Nears," by Martin Crutsinger. Appeared in *The Houston Chronicle*, October 22, 1997. Reprinted with the permission of Associated Press.

Copyright © by Houghton Mifflin Company. All rights reserved.

The Houston Chronicle/October 22, 1997

COMMENTARY

In this chapter, we saw how net exports contribute to aggregate expenditures. Merchandise exports bring money from the rest of the world, and higher net exports mean greater aggregate expenditures. Merchandise imports involve outflows of money to foreign countries, and lower net exports mean lower aggregate expenditures.

We saw in the chapter that higher domestic real GDP leads to higher imports and lower net exports. This article points out that the U.S. net export deficit is a symptom of a stronger U.S. economy as the "strength of the U.S. economy makes it possible for the U.S. consumer to buy more from abroad." As a result of the effect of net exports on aggregate expenditures, we often hear arguments for policy aimed at increasing exports and decreasing imports. Domestic residents are often resentful of foreign producers and blame foreign competitors for job losses in the home country. However, we must consider the circumstances and then ask if a policy aimed at increasing the national trade surplus (or decreasing the deficit) is really desirable.

Since one country's export is another's import, it is impossible for everyone to have surpluses—on a worldwide basis the total value of exports equals the total value of imports. If someone must always have a trade deficit when others have trade surpluses, is it necessarily true that surpluses are good and deficits bad so that one country benefits at another's expense? In a sense, imports should be preferred to exports since exports represent goods no longer available for domestic consumption that will be consumed by foreign importers. In later chapters you will learn that the benefits of free international trade include more efficient production and increased consumption. Furthermore, if trade among nations is voluntary, it is difficult to argue that deficit countries are harmed while surplus countries benefit from trade.

In general, it is not obvious whether a country is better or worse off running merchandise surpluses rather than deficits. Consider the following simple example of a world with two countries, R and P. Country R is a rich creditor country that is growing rapidly and has a net exports deficit. Country P is a poor debtor country that is growing slowly and has positive net exports. Should we prefer living conditions in P to R based solely on the knowledge that P has a net exports surplus and R has a net exports deficit? Although this is indeed a simplistic example, there are real-world analogues of rich creditor countries with international trade deficits and poor debtor nations with international trade surpluses. The point is that you cannot analyze the balance of payments apart from other economic considerations. Deficits are not inherently bad, nor are surpluses necessarily good.

Copyright © by Houghton Mifflin Company. All rights reserved.

10

An Algebraic Model of Aggregate Expenditures

Aggregate expenditures (AE) equal consumption (C) plus investment (I) plus government spending (G) plus net exports (X). If we can develop an equation for each component of spending, we can put them together in a single model.

Consumption The consumption function can be written in general form as

$$C = C^a + cYd$$

where C^a is autonomous consumption and c is the *MPC*. The consumption function for the data in Chapter 10 is

$$C = \$30 + .70Yd \text{ as shown in Figure 1.}$$

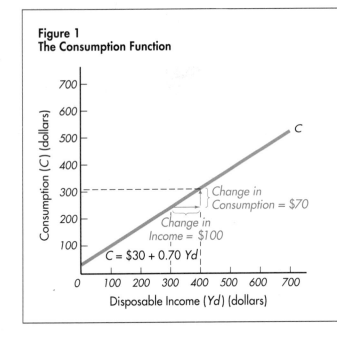

Figure 1
The Consumption Function

$C = \$30 + 0.70\,Yd$

Change in Consumption = $70
Change in Income = $100

Consumption (C) (dollars)

Disposable Income (Yd) (dollars)

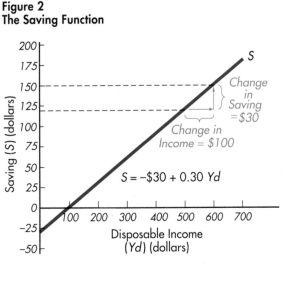

Figure 2
The Saving Function

$S = -\$30 + 0.30\,Yd$

Change in Saving = $30
Change in Income = $100

Saving (S) (dollars)

Disposable Income (Yd) (dollars)

Copyright © by Houghton Mifflin Company. All rights reserved.

Saving The corresponding saving function is

$$S = -\$30 + .30Yd \text{ as illustrated in Figure 2.}$$

Investment Investment is autonomous at I^a, which is equal to $50.

Government Spending Government spending is autonomous at G^a, which is equal to $70.

Net Exports Exports are autonomous at EX^a and equal to $50. Imports are given by the function

$$IM = IM^a + imY$$

where im is the *MPI*. Here, then,

$$IM = \$0 + .10Y$$

Net exports equal exports minus imports, or

$$X = \$50 - \$0 - .10Y$$

$$= \$50 - .10Y$$

as shown in Figure 3.

Aggregate Expenditures Summing the functions for the four components (and ignoring taxes, so that Yd equals Y) gives

$$AE = C^a + cY + I^a + G^a + EX^a - IM^a - imY$$

$$= \$30 + .70Y + \$50 + \$70 + \$50 - \$0 - .10Y$$

$$= \$200 + .60Y$$

as shown in Figure 4.

In the Appendix to Chapter 11 we use the algebraic model of aggregate expenditures presented here to solve for the equilibrium level of real GDP.

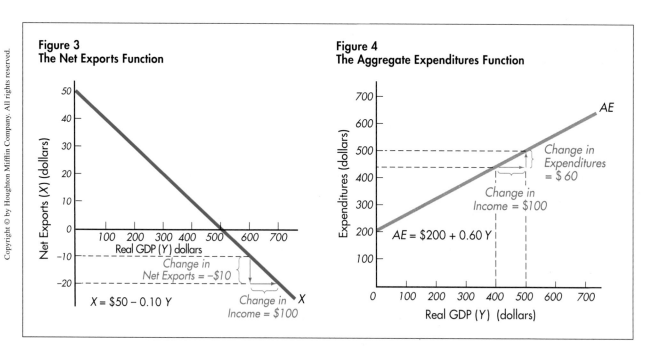

Figure 3
The Net Exports Function

Figure 4
The Aggregate Expenditures Function

Copyright © by Houghton Mifflin Company. All rights reserved.

11

Income and Expenditures Equilibrium

FUNDAMENTAL QUESTIONS

1. What does equilibrium mean in macroeconomics?

2. How do aggregate expenditures affect income or real GDP?

3. What are the leakages from and injections to spending?

4. Why does equilibrium real GDP change by a multiple of a change in autonomous expenditures?

5. What is the spending multiplier?

6. What is the relationship between the GDP gap and the recessionary gap?

7. How does international trade affect the size of the multiplier?

8. Why does the aggregate expenditures curve shift with changes in the price level?

Copyright © by Houghton Mifflin Company. All rights reserved.

Preview

What determines the level of income and expenditures, or real GDP? In Chapter 9 we used aggregate demand and aggregate supply to answer this question. Then in Chapter 10 we developed the components of aggregate expenditures in more detail to provide the foundation for an additional approach to answering the question "What determines the level of real GDP?" If you know the answer to this question, you are well on your way to understanding business cycles. Sometimes real GDP is growing and jobs are relatively easy to find; at other times real GDP is falling and large numbers of people are out of work. Macroeconomists use several models to analyze the causes of business cycles. Underlying all of the models is the concept of macroeconomic equilibrium.

Equilibrium here means what it did when we talked about supply and demand: a point of balance, a point from which there is no tendency to move. In macroeconomics, equilibrium is the level of income and expenditures that the economy tends to move toward and remain at until autonomous spending changes.

Economists have not always agreed on how an economy reaches equilibrium and on the forces that move an economy from one equilibrium to another. This last issue formed the basis of economic debate during the Great Depression of the 1930s. Before the 1930s, economists generally believed that the economy always was at or moving toward an equilibrium consistent with a high level of employed resources. The British economist John Maynard Keynes did not agree. He believed that an economy could come to rest at a level of real GDP that is too low to provide employment for all those who desired it. He also believed that certain actions are necessary to ensure that the economy rises to a level of real GDP consistent with a high level of employment. In particular, Keynes argued that government must intervene in a big way in the economy (see the Economic Insight "John Maynard Keynes").

To understand the debate that began during the 1930s and continues on various fronts today, it is necessary to understand the Keynesian view of how equilibrium real GDP is determined. This is our focus here. We have seen in Chapter 9 that the aggregate demand and supply model of macroeconomic equilibrium allowed the price level to fluctuate as the equilibrium level of real GDP changed. The Keynesian income-expenditures model assumes that the price level is fixed. It emphasizes aggregate expenditures without explicit consideration of the supply side of the economy. This is why we

Copyright © by Houghton Mifflin Company. All rights reserved.

ECONOMIC INSIGHT

John Maynard Keynes

John Maynard Keynes (pronounced "canes") is considered by many to be the greatest economist of the twentieth century. His major work, *The General Theory of Employment, Interest, and Money,* had a profound impact on macroeconomics, on both thought and policy. Keynes was born in Cambridge, England, on June 5, 1883. He studied economics at Cambridge University, where he became a lecturer in economics in 1908. During World War I, Keynes worked for the British treasury. At the end of the war, he was the treasury's representative at the Versailles Peace Conference. He resigned from the

British delegation at the conference to protest the harsh terms being imposed on the defeated countries. His resignation and publication of the *Economic Consequences of the Peace* (1919) made him an international celebrity.

In 1936, Keynes published *The General Theory.* It was a time of world recession (it has been estimated that around one-quarter of the U.S. labor force was unemployed at the height of the Depression), and policymakers were searching for ways to explain the persistent unemployment. In the book, Keynes suggested that an economy could come to equi-

librium at less than potential GDP. More important, he argued that government policy could be altered to end recession. His analysis emphasized aggregate expenditures. If private expenditures were not sufficient to create equilibrium at potential GDP, government expenditures could be increased to stimulate income and output. This was a startling concept. Most economists of the time believed that government should not take an active role in the economy. With his *General Theory,* Keynes started a "revolution" in macroeconomics.

considered the components of spending in detail in Chapter 10—to provide a foundation for the analysis in this chapter. The Keynesian model may be viewed as a special fixed-price case of the aggregate demand and aggregate supply model. In later chapters we examine the relationship between equilibrium and the level of employed resources, and the effect of government policy on both of these elements. ∎

1. EQUILIBRIUM INCOME AND EXPENDITURES

What does equilibrium mean in macroeconomics?

Equilibrium is a point from which there is no tendency to move. People do not change their behavior when everything is consistent with what they expect. However, when plans and reality do not match, people adjust their behavior to make them match. Determining a nation's equilibrium level of income and expenditures is the process of defining the level of income and expenditures at which plans and reality are the same.

1.a. Expenditures and Income

How do aggregate expenditures affect income or real GDP?

We use the aggregate expenditures function described at the end of Chapter 10 to demonstrate how equilibrium is determined. Keep in mind that the aggregate expenditures function represents *planned* expenditures at different levels of income or real GDP. We focus on planned expenditures because they represent the amount households, firms, government, and the foreign sector expect to spend.

Copyright © by Houghton Mifflin Company. All rights reserved.

Actual expenditures always equal income and output because they reflect changes in inventories. That is, inventories automatically raise or lower investment expenditures so that actual spending equals income, which equals output, which equals real GDP. However, aggregate expenditures (which are planned spending) may not equal real GDP. What happens when planned spending and real GDP are not equal? When planned spending on goods and services *exceeds* the current value of output, the production of goods and services increases. Because output equals income, the level of real GDP also increases. This is the situation for all income levels below $500 in Figure 1. At these levels, total spending is greater than real GDP, which means that more goods and services are being purchased than are being produced. The only way this can happen is for goods produced in the past to be sold. When planned spending is greater than real GDP, business inventories fall. The change in inventories offsets the excess of planned expenditures over real GDP, so that actual expenditures (including the unplanned change in inventories) equal real GDP. You can see this in column 7 of the table in Figure 1,

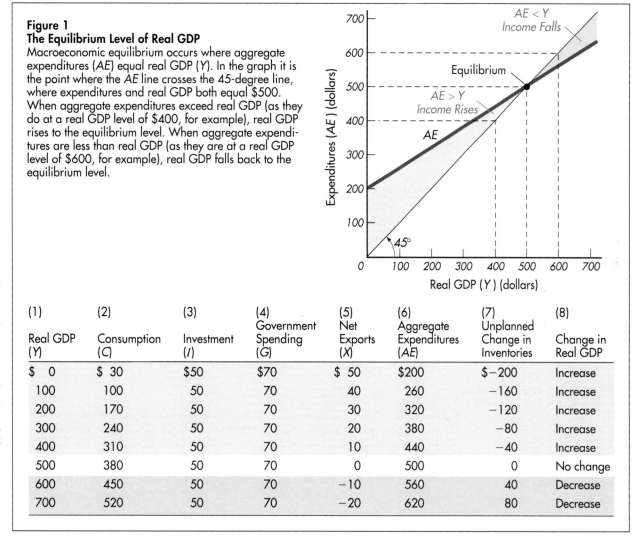

Figure 1
The Equilibrium Level of Real GDP
Macroeconomic equilibrium occurs where aggregate expenditures (*AE*) equal real GDP (*Y*). In the graph it is the point where the *AE* line crosses the 45-degree line, where expenditures and real GDP both equal $500. When aggregate expenditures exceed real GDP (as they do at a real GDP level of $400, for example), real GDP rises to the equilibrium level. When aggregate expenditures are less than real GDP (as they are at a real GDP level of $600, for example), real GDP falls back to the equilibrium level.

(1) Real GDP (Y)	(2) Consumption (C)	(3) Investment (I)	(4) Government Spending (G)	(5) Net Exports (X)	(6) Aggregate Expenditures (AE)	(7) Unplanned Change in Inventories	(8) Change in Real GDP
$ 0	$ 30	$50	$70	$ 50	$200	$−200	Increase
100	100	50	70	40	260	−160	Increase
200	170	50	70	30	320	−120	Increase
300	240	50	70	20	380	−80	Increase
400	310	50	70	10	440	−40	Increase
500	380	50	70	0	500	0	No change
600	450	50	70	−10	560	40	Decrease
700	520	50	70	−20	620	80	Decrease

Copyright © by Houghton Mifflin Company. All rights reserved.

where the change in inventories offsets the excess of aggregate expenditures over real GDP (the difference between columns 6 and 1).

What happens when inventories fall? As inventories fall, manufacturers increase production to meet the demand for products. The increased production raises the level of real GDP. *When aggregate expenditures exceed real GDP, real GDP rises.*

When aggregate expenditures exceed real GDP, real GDP rises.

At real GDP levels above $500 in the table, aggregate expenditures are less than income. As a result, inventories are accumulating above planned levels—more goods and services are being produced than are being purchased. As inventories rise, businesses begin to reduce the quantity of output they produce. The unplanned increase in inventories is counted as a form of investment spending, so that actual expenditures equal real GDP. For example, when real GDP is $600, aggregate expenditures are only $560. The $40 of produced goods that are not sold are measured as inventory investment. The $560 of aggregate expenditures plus the $40 of unplanned inventories equal $600, the level of real GDP. As inventories increase, firms cut production, which causes real GDP to fall. *When aggregate expenditures are less than real GDP, real GDP falls.*

When aggregate expenditures are less than real GDP, real GDP falls.

There is only one level of real GDP in the table in Figure 1 where real GDP does not change. When real GDP is $500, aggregate expenditures equal $500. The equilibrium level of real GDP (or output) is that point at which aggregate expenditures equal real GDP (or output).

The equilibrium level of real GDP is where aggregate expenditures equal real GDP.

When aggregate expenditures equal real GDP, planned spending equals the output produced and the income generated from producing that output. As long as planned spending is consistent with real GDP, real GDP does not change. But if planned spending is higher or lower than real GDP, real GDP does change. Equilibrium is that point at which planned spending and real GDP are equal.

The graph in Figure 1 illustrates equilibrium. The 45-degree line shows all possible points where aggregate expenditures (measured on the vertical axis) equal real GDP (measured on the horizontal axis). The equilibrium level of real GDP, then, is simply the point where the aggregate expenditures line (*AE*) crosses the 45-degree line. In the figure, equilibrium occurs where real GDP and expenditures are $500.

When the *AE* curve lies above the 45-degree line—for example, at a real GDP level of $400—aggregate expenditures are greater than real GDP. What happens? Real GDP rises to the equilibrium level, where it tends to stay. When the *AE* curve lies below the 45-degree line—at a real GDP level of $600, for example—aggregate expenditures are less than real GDP, which pushes real GDP down. Once real GDP falls to the equilibrium level ($500 in our example), it tends to stay there.

1.b. Leakages and Injections

Equilibrium can be determined by using aggregate expenditures and real GDP, which represents income. Another way to determine equilibrium involves leakages from and injections into the income stream, the circular flow of income and expenditures.

What are the leakages from and injections to spending?

Leakages reduce autonomous aggregate expenditures. There are three leakages in the stream from domestic income to spending: saving, taxes, and imports.

Copyright © by Houghton Mifflin Company. All rights reserved.

ECONOMIC INSIGHT

The Paradox of Thrift

People generally believe that saving is good and that more saving is better. However, if every family increased its saving, the result could be less income for the economy as a whole. In fact, increased saving could actually lower savings for all households.

An increase in saving may provide an example of a *paradox of thrift*. A *paradox* is a true proposition that seems to contradict common beliefs. We believe that we will be better off by increased saving, but in the aggregate, increased saving could cause the economy to be worse off. The paradox of thrift is a *fallacy of composition*: the assumption that what is true of a part is true of the whole. It often is unsafe to generalize from what is true at the micro level to what is true at the macro level.

The graph illustrates the effect of higher saving. Initial equilibrium occurs where the $S_1 + T + IM$ curve intersects the $I + G + EX$ curve, at an income of $500. Suppose saving increases by $20 at every level of income. The $S_1 + T + IM$ curve shifts up to the

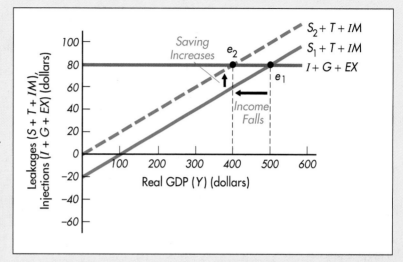

$S_2 + T + IM$ curve. A new equilibrium is established at an income level of $400. The higher rate of saving causes equilibrium income to fall by $100.

Notice that the graph is drawn with a constant $I + G + EX$ line. If investment increases along with saving, equilibrium income would not necessarily fall. In fact, because saving is necessary before there can be any investment, we would expect a greater demand for

investment funds to induce higher saving. If increased saving is used to fund investment expenditures, the economy should grow over time to higher and higher levels of income. Only if the increased saving is not injected back into the economy is there a paradox of thrift. The fact that governments do not discourage saving suggests that the paradox of thrift generally is not a real-world problem.

Saving, taxes, and imports are leakages that reduce autonomous aggregate expenditures.

■ The more households save, the less they spend. An increase in autonomous saving means a decrease in autonomous consumption, which could cause the equilibrium level of real GDP to fall (see the Economic Insight "The Paradox of Thrift").

■ Taxes are an involuntary reduction in consumption. The government transfers income away from households. Higher taxes lower autonomous consumption, in the process lowering autonomous aggregate expenditures and the equilibrium level of real GDP.

Investment, government spending, and exports are injections that increase autonomous aggregate expenditures.

■ Imports are expenditures for foreign goods and services. They reduce expenditures on domestic goods and services. An autonomous increase in imports reduces net exports, causing autonomous aggregate expenditures and the equilibrium level of real GDP to fall.

Copyright © by Houghton Mifflin Company. All rights reserved.

For equilibrium to occur, these leakages must be offset by corresponding *injections* of spending into the domestic economy, through investment, government spending, and exports.

- Household saving generates funds that businesses can borrow and spend for investment purposes.
- The taxes collected by government are used to finance government purchases of goods and services.
- Exports bring foreign expenditures into the domestic economy.

There is no reason to expect that each injection matches its corresponding leakage—that investment equals saving, that government spending equals taxes, or that exports equal imports. But for equilibrium to occur, total injections must equal total leakages.

Figure 2 shows how leakages and injections determine the equilibrium level of real GDP. Column 5 of the table lists the total leakages from aggregate expenditures: saving (S) plus taxes (T) plus imports (IM). Saving and imports both increase when real GDP increases. We assume that there are no taxes so the total amount of leakages ($S + T + IM$) increases as real GDP increases.

The equilibrium level of real GDP occurs where leakages equal injections.

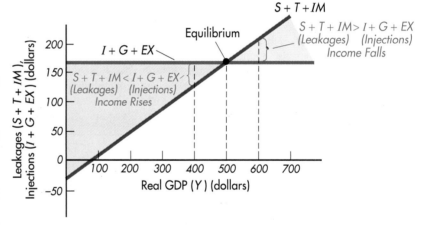

Figure 2
Leakages, Injections, and Equilibrium Income
Leakages equal saving (S), taxes (T), and imports (IM). Injections equal investment (I), government spending (G), and exports (EX). Equilibrium is that point where leakages equal injections. In the graph, equilibrium is the point at which the $S + T + IM$ curve intersects the $I + G + EX$ curve, where real GDP (Y) equals $500. At lower levels of income, injections exceed leakages, so Y rises. At higher levels of income, leakages exceed injections, so Y falls.

(1) Real GDP (Y)	(2) Saving (S)	(3) Taxes (T)	(4) Imports (IM)	(5) Leakages ($S + T + IM$)	(6) Investment (I)	(7) Government Spending (G)	(8) Exports (EX)	(9) Injections ($I + G + EX$)	(10) Change in Real GDP
$ 0	$−30	$0	$ 0	$−30	$50	$70	$50	$170	Increase
100	0	0	10	10	50	70	50	170	Increase
200	30	0	20	50	50	70	50	170	Increase
300	60	0	30	90	50	70	50	170	Increase
400	90	0	40	130	50	70	50	170	Increase
500	120	0	50	170	50	70	50	170	No change
600	150	0	60	210	50	70	50	170	Decrease
700	180	0	70	250	50	70	50	170	Decrease

Copyright © by Houghton Mifflin Company. All rights reserved.

Column 9 lists the injections at alternative income levels. Because investment (I), government spending (G), and exports (EX) are all autonomous, total injections ($I + G + EX$) are constant at all levels of real GDP.

To determine the equilibrium level of real GDP, we compare leakages with injections. When injections exceed leakages, planned spending is greater than current income or output, so real GDP rises. In the table in Figure 2, this occurs for levels of real GDP under $500, so real GDP increases if under $500 (see the last column). When leakages exceed injections, planned spending is less than current real GDP, so real GDP falls. In Figure 2, at all levels of real GDP above $500, real GDP falls. Only when leakages equal injections is the equilibrium level of real GDP established. When real GDP equals $500, both leakages and injections equal $170, so there is no pressure for real GDP to change. The equilibrium level of real GDP occurs where leakages ($S + T + IM$) equal injections ($I + G + EX$).

Figure 2 shows the interaction of leakages and injections graphically. The equilibrium point is where the $S + T + IM$ and $I + G + EX$ curves intersect, at a real GDP level of $500. At higher levels of real GDP, leakages are greater than injections (the $S + T + IM$ curve lies above the $I + G + EX$ curve). When leakages are greater than injections, real GDP falls to the equilibrium point. At lower levels of income, injections are greater than leakages (the $I + G + EX$ curve lies above the $S + T + IM$ curve). Here real GDP rises until it reaches $500. Only at $500 is there no pressure for real GDP to change.

If you compare Figures 1 and 2, you can see that it does not matter whether we use aggregate expenditures or leakages and injections—the equilibrium level of real GDP is the same.

RECAP

1. Equilibrium is a point from which there is no tendency to move.
2. When aggregate expenditures exceed real GDP, real GDP rises.
3. When aggregate expenditures are less than real GDP, real GDP falls.
4. Saving, taxes, and imports are leakages of planned spending from domestic aggregate expenditures.
5. Investment, government spending, and exports are injections of planned spending into domestic aggregate expenditures.
6. Equilibrium occurs at the level of real GDP at which aggregate expenditures equal real GDP, and leakages equal injections.

2. CHANGES IN EQUILIBRIUM INCOME AND EXPENDITURES

Why does equilibrium real GDP change by a multiple of a change in autonomous expenditures?

Equilibrium is a point from which there is no tendency to move. But in fact the equilibrium level of real GDP does move. In the last section we described how aggregate expenditures push real GDP representing the economy's income and output up or down toward their level of equilibrium. Here we examine how changes in autonomous expenditures affect equilibrium. This becomes very important in understanding macroeconomic policy, the kinds of things government can do to control the business cycle.

Copyright © by Houghton Mifflin Company. All rights reserved.

2.a. The Spending Multiplier

What is the spending
multiplier?

*Any change in autonomous
expenditures is multiplied into
a larger change in equilibrium
real GDP.*

Remember that equilibrium is that point where aggregate expenditures equal real GDP. If we increase autonomous expenditures, then we raise the equilibrium level of real GDP. But by how much? It seems logical to expect a 1 to 1 ratio: if autonomous spending increases by a dollar, equilibrium real GDP should increase by a dollar. Actually, equilibrium real GDP increases by *more* than a dollar. The change in autonomous expenditures is *multiplied* into a larger change in the equilibrium level of real GDP.

In Chapter 6 we used a circular flow diagram to show the relationship of expenditures to income. In that diagram we saw how one sector's expenditures become another sector's income. This concept helps explain the effect of a change in autonomous expenditures on the equilibrium level of income or real GDP. If A's autonomous spending increases, then B's income rises. Then B spends part of that income in the domestic economy (the rest is saved or used to buy foreign goods), generating new income for C. In turn C spends part of that income in the domestic economy, generating new income for D. And the rounds of increased spending and income continue. All of this is the

TABLE 1
The Spending Multiplier Effect

	(1) Change in Income	(2) Change in Domestic Expenditures	(3) Change in Saving	(4) Change in Imports
Round 1	$20	$12	$ 6	$2
Round 2	12	7.20	3.60	1.20
Round 3	7.20	4.32	2.16	0.72
Round 4	4.32	2.59	1.30	0.43
	.	.	.	.
	.	.	.	.
	.	.	.	.
Totals	$50	$30	$15	$5

$$\text{Column 2} = \text{column 1} \times (MPC - MPI)$$

$$\text{Column 3} = \text{column 1} \times MPS$$

$$\text{Column 4} = \text{column 1} \times MPI$$

$$\text{Multiplier} = \frac{1}{MPS + MPI}$$

$$= \frac{1}{.30 + .10}$$

$$= \frac{1}{.40}$$

$$= 2.5$$

Copyright © by Houghton Mifflin Company. All rights reserved.

product of A's initial autonomous increase in spending. And each round of increased spending and income affects the equilibrium level of income or real GDP.

Let's look at an example, using Table 1. Suppose government spending goes up $20 to improve public parks. What happens to the equilibrium level of income? The autonomous increase in government spending increases the income of park employees by $20. As their income increases, so does the consumption of park employees. For example, let's say they spend more money on hamburgers. In the process, they are increasing the income of the hamburger producers, who in turn increase their consumption.

Table 1 shows how a single change in spending generates further changes. Round 1 is the initial increase in government spending to improve public parks. That $20 expenditure increases the income of park employees by $20 (column 1). As income increases, those components of aggregate expenditures that depend on current income—consumption and net exports—also increase by some fraction of the $20.

Consumption changes by the marginal propensity to consume multiplied by the change in income; imports change by the marginal propensity to import multiplied by the change in income. To find the total effect of the initial change in spending, we must know the fraction of any change in income that is spent in the domestic economy. In the hypothetical economy we have been using, the *MPC* is .70 and the *MPI* is .10. This means that for each $1 of new income, consumption rises by $.70 and imports rise by $.10. Spending on *domestic* goods and services, then, rises by $.60. Because consumption is spending on domestic goods and services, and imports are spending on foreign goods and services, the percentage of a change in income that is spent domestically is the difference between the *MPC* and the *MPI*. If the *MPC* equals .70 and the *MPI* equals .10, then 60 percent of any change in domestic income (*MPC* − *MPI* = .60) is spent on domestic goods and services.

The percentage of a change in income that is spent domestically is the difference between the MPC and the MPI.

In round 1 of Table 1, the initial increase in income of $20 induces an increase in spending on domestic goods and services of $12 (.60 × $20). Out of the $20, $6 is saved because the marginal propensity to save is .30 (1 − *MPC*). The other $2 is spent on imports (*MPI* = .10). The park employees receive $20 more income. They spend $12 on hamburgers at a local restaurant; they save $6; and they spend $2 on imported beer.

Only $12 of the workers' new income is spent on goods produced in the domestic economy, hamburgers. That $12 becomes income to the restaurant's employees and owner. When their income increases by $12, they spend 60 percent of that income ($7.20) on domestic goods (round 2, column 2). The rest of the income is saved and spent on imports.

Each time income increases, expenditures increase. But the increase is smaller and smaller each new round of spending. Why? Because 30 percent of each change in income is saved and another 10 percent is spent on imports. These are leakages out of the income stream. This means just 60 percent of the change in income is spent and passed on to others in the domestic economy as income in the next round.

To find the total effect of the initial change in spending of $20, we could keep on computing the change in income and spending round after round, and then sum the total of all rounds. The change in income and spending never reaches zero, but becomes infinitely small.

Copyright © by Houghton Mifflin Company. All rights reserved.

spending multiplier:
a measure of the change in equilibrium income or real GDP produced by a change in autonomous expenditures

Fortunately, we do not have to compute each round-by-round increase in spending to find the total increase. If we know the percentage of additional income that "leaks" from domestic consumption at each round, we can determine the total change in income or real GDP by finding its reciprocal. This measure is called the **spending multiplier.** The leakages are that portion of the change in income that is saved (the *MPS*) and that proportion of the change in income that is spent on imports (the *MPI*).

$$\text{Multiplier} = \frac{1}{\text{leakages}}$$

$$= \frac{1}{MPS + MPI}$$

When the *MPS* is .30 and the *MPI* is .10, the multiplier equals 2.5 (1/.4). An initial change in expenditures of $20 results in a total change in real GDP of $50, 2.5 times the original change in expenditures. The greater the leakages, the smaller the multiplier. When the *MPS* equals .35 and the *MPI* equals .15, the multiplier equals 2 (1/.50). The multiplier is smaller here because less new income is being spent in the domestic economy. The more people save, the smaller the expansionary effect on income of a change in spending. And the more people spend on imports, the smaller the expansionary effect on income of a change in spending. Notice that the multiplier would be larger in a *closed economy*, an economy that does not trade with the rest of the world. In that economy, because the *MPI* equals zero, the spending multiplier is simply equal to the reciprocal of the *MPS*.

2.b. The Spending Multiplier and Equilibrium

The spending multiplier is an extremely useful concept. It allows us to calculate how a change in autonomous expenditures affects real GDP. To better understand how changes in spending can bring about changes in equilibrium income or real GDP, let's modify the example we used in Figure 1. In the table in Figure 3 we have increased government spending to $110. The autonomous increase in government spending raises aggregate expenditures by $40 at every level of income. Aggregate expenditures now equal real GDP at $600. The increase in government spending of $40 yields an increase in equilibrium real GDP of $100.

The graph in Figure 3 illustrates the multiplier effect and shows the change in equilibrium income when spending increases by $40. The original aggregate expenditures curve, AE_1, intersects the 45-degree line at a real GDP level of $500. A spending increase of $40 at every level of real GDP creates a new aggregate expenditures curve, AE_2, which lies $40 above the original curve. AE_2 is parallel to AE_1 because the increase is in autonomous spending. The new curve, AE_2, intersects the 45-degree line at an income of $600.

In Chapter 8 we introduced the concept of the natural rate of unemployment—the unemployment rate that exists in the absence of cyclical unemployment. When the economy operates at the natural rate of unemployment, the corresponding level of output (and income) is called potential real GDP. However, equilibrium does not necessarily occur at potential real GDP. Equilibrium is any level of real GDP at which planned expenditures equal real GDP. Suppose that equilibrium real GDP is not at the level of potential

Copyright © by Houghton Mifflin Company. All rights reserved.

Figure 3
A Change in Equilibrium Expenditures and Income

A change in aggregate expenditures (AE) causes a change in equilibrium real GDP (Y). Initially equilibrium is $500, the point at which the AE_1 curve intersects the 45-degree line. If autonomous expenditures increase by $40, the aggregate expenditures curve shifts up to AE_2. The new curve intersects the 45-degree line at a new equilibrium level of real GDP, $600. An increase in autonomous expenditures of $40, then, causes equilibrium real GDP to increase by $100.

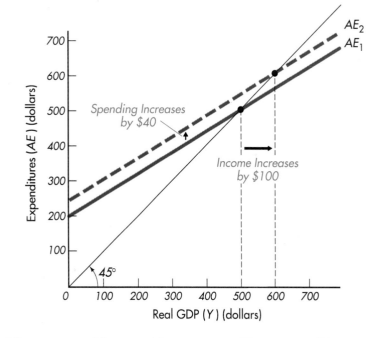

(1) Real GDP (Y)	(2) Consumption (C)	(3) Investment (I)	(4) Government Spending (G)	(5) Net Exports (X)	(6) Aggregate Expenditures (AE)	(7) Unplanned Change in Inventories	(8) Change in Real GDP
$ 0	$ 30	$50	$110	$ 50	$240	$−240	Increase
100	100	50	110	40	300	−200	Increase
200	170	50	110	30	360	−160	Increase
300	240	50	110	20	440	−120	Increase
400	310	50	110	10	480	−80	Increase
500	380	50	110	0	540	−40	Increase
600	450	50	110	−10	600	0	No change
700	520	50	110	−20	660	40	Decrease

Copyright © by Houghton Mifflin Company. All rights reserved.

What is the relationship between the GDP gap and the recessionary gap?

real GDP and that government policymakers make the achievement of potential real GDP an important goal. In this case, government policy is addressed to closing the *GDP gap*, the difference between potential real GDP and actual real GDP. The nature of that policy depends on the value of the multiplier.

If we know the size of the GDP gap and we know the size of the spending multiplier, we can determine how much spending needs to change to yield equilibrium at potential real GDP. Remember that the GDP gap equals potential real GDP minus actual real GDP:

GDP gap = potential real GDP − actual real GDP

When real GDP is less than potential real GDP, the GDP gap is the amount the GDP must rise to reach its potential. Suppose potential real GDP is $500, but the economy is in equilibrium at $300. GDP must rise by $200 to reach

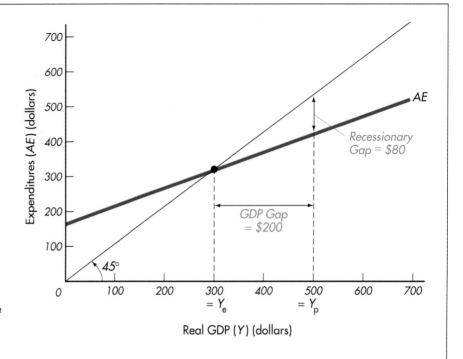

Figure 4
The GDP Gap and the Recessionary Gap
In the graph, the GDP gap is $200, the difference between potential real GDP (Y_p) of $500 and equilibrium real GDP (Y_e) of $300. The GDP gap tells us that equilibrium real GDP must rise by $200 to reach equilibrium at the potential level of real GDP. The recessionary gap indicates the amount that autonomous expenditures must rise to close the GDP gap. The recessionary gap is the vertical distance between the 45-degree line and the AE curve at the potential level of real GDP, or $80. If autonomous expenditures are increased by $80, the AE curve moves up, intersecting with the 45-degree line at $500.

recessionary gap:
the increase in expenditures required to reach potential GDP

The recessionary gap is the vertical distance between the aggregate expenditures curve and the 45-degree line at the potential level of real GDP.

potential real GDP. How much must spending rise? If we know the size of the spending multiplier, we simply divide the spending multiplier into the GDP gap to determine how much spending must rise to achieve equilibrium at potential real GDP. This required change in spending is called the **recessionary gap**:

$$\text{Recessionary gap} = \frac{\text{GDP gap}}{\text{spending multiplier}}$$

Figure 4 shows an economy in which equilibrium real GDP (Y_e) is less than potential real GDP (Y_p). The difference between the two—the GDP gap—is $200. It is the *horizontal* distance between equilibrium real GDP and potential real GDP. The amount that spending must rise in order for real GDP to reach a new equilibrium level of $500 is measured by the recessionary gap. The recessionary gap is the *vertical* distance between the aggregate expenditures curve and the 45-degree line at the potential real GDP level.

The recessionary gap in Figure 4 is $80:

$$\text{Recessionary gap} = \frac{\$200}{2.5}$$

$$= \$80$$

With a spending multiplier of 2.5, if aggregate expenditures rise by $80, equilibrium income rises by the $200 necessary to close the GDP gap. Government policy may be addressed to closing the gap, as an increase in government expenditures of $80 would move the economy to the potential level of real GDP in this example.

Copyright © by Houghton Mifflin Company. All rights reserved.

2.c. Real-World Complications

Our definition of the spending multiplier,

$$\frac{1}{MPS + MPI}$$

is a simplification of reality. Often other factors besides the *MPS* and *MPI* determine the actual multiplier in an economy. If prices rise when spending increases, the spending multiplier will not be as large as shown here. Also, taxes (which are ignored until Chapter 12, on fiscal policy) will reduce the size of the multiplier. Another factor is the treatment of imports. We have assumed that whatever is spent on imports is permanently lost to the domestic economy. For a country whose imports are a small fraction of the exports of its trading partners, this is a realistic assumption. But for a country whose imports are very important in determining the volume of exports of the rest of the world, this simple spending multiplier understates the true multiplier effect. To see why, let's examine how U.S. imports affect income in the rest of the world.

2.c.1. Foreign Repercussions of Domestic Imports
When a resident of the United States buys goods from another country, that purchase becomes income to foreign residents. If Mike in Miami buys coral jewelry from Victor in the Dominican Republic, Mike's purchase increases Victor's income. So the import of jewelry into the United States increases income in the Dominican Republic.

How does international trade affect the size of the multiplier?

Imports purchased by one country can have a large effect on the level of income in other countries. For instance, Canada and Mexico are very dependent on sales to the United States since about 80 percent of their exports goes to the United States. South Africa, on the other hand, sells about 5 percent of its total exports to U.S. buyers. If U.S. imports from South Africa doubled, the effect on total South African exports and income would be small. But if imports from Canada or Mexico doubled, the effect on those countries' exports and income would be substantial.

Imports from the United States play a key role in determining the real GDP of its major trading partners. This is important because foreign income is a determinant of U.S. exports. As that income rises, U.S. exports rise (see Chapter 10). That is, foreign imports increase with foreign income, and some of those imports come from the United States. And, of course, when foreign spending on U.S. goods increases, national income in the United States rises.

The simple spending multiplier understates the true multiplier effects of increases in autonomous expenditures because of the foreign repercussions of domestic spending. Some spending on imports comes back to the domestic economy in the form of exports. This means the chain of spending can be different from that assumed in the simple spending multiplier. Figure 5 illustrates the difference.

Figure 5(a) shows the sequence of spending when there are no foreign repercussions from domestic imports. In this case, domestic spending rises, which causes domestic income or real GDP to rise. Higher domestic real GDP leads to increased spending on imports as well as further increases in domestic spending, which induce further increases in real GDP, and so on, as the multiplier process works itself out. Notice, however, that the imports are simply a leakage from the spending stream.

Copyright © by Houghton Mifflin Company. All rights reserved.

Figure 5
The Sequence of Expenditures

If there are no foreign repercussions from changes in domestic income or real GDP, the simple spending multiplier holds. Increases in domestic spending increase domestic income or real GDP, which causes domestic spending—including spending on foreign goods—to rise further. Here higher expenditures on domestic imports do not have any effect on domestic exports to foreign countries.

If there are foreign repercussions from changes in domestic real GDP, the simple spending multiplier underestimates the actual effect of a change in autonomous expenditures on the equilibrium level of real GDP. As part (b) shows, increases in domestic spending increase domestic income or real GDP, which causes domestic spending—including spending on foreign goods—to rise further. Here higher spending on foreign goods causes foreign real GDP to rise, and with it, spending on domestic exports. Higher domestic exports stimulate domestic real GDP further. The actual multiplier effect of an increase in domestic spending, then, is larger than it is when domestic imports have no effect on domestic exports.

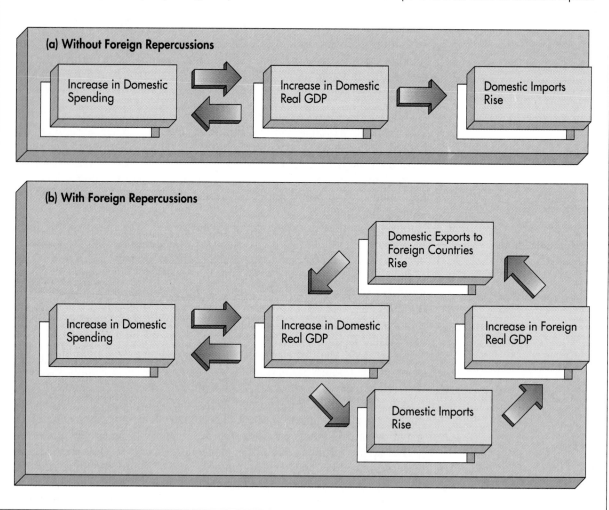

In Figure 5(b), the sequence of expenditures includes the foreign repercussions of domestic imports. As before, increases in domestic spending cause domestic income or real GDP to rise, which in turn leads to more domestic spending as well as greater domestic imports. Now, however, the greater imports increase foreign income or real GDP, which increases foreign imports of goods produced in the domestic economy. As domestic exports rise, domestic real GDP rises.

Copyright © by Houghton Mifflin Company. All rights reserved.

TABLE 2
Spending Multiplier Estimates

Multiplier Effects of U.S. Government Spending Increases

Country	Multiplier*
United States	2.0
Canada	.5
Germany	.2
Japan	.7
United Kingdom	.2

Multiplier Effects in the U.S. of Foreign Government Spending Increases

Country	Multiplier*
Canada	.2
Germany	.1
Japan	.1
United Kingdom	.1

*Based on first year after increase in spending.

Source: Hali J. Edison, Jaime R. Marquez, and Ralph W. Tryon, *The Structure and Properties of the FRB Multicountry Model*, International Finance Discussion Paper, no. 293 (Washington, D.C.: Board of Governors of the Federal Reserve System, 1986).

The diagrams in Figure 5 show why the multiplier effect is higher with foreign repercussions than without. Rather than complicate the multiplier definition, we continue to use the simple spending multiplier. But remember that (holding prices constant and ignoring taxes) our definition underestimates the true magnitude of the multiplier's effects in open economies. In fact, the foreign repercussions of domestic imports help explain the similarity in business cycles across countries. When the United States is booming, the economies of other countries that depend on exports to the U.S. market also boom. When the United States is in recession, income in these other countries tends to fall.

2.c.2. Multiplier Estimates Many private and public organizations have developed models that are used to analyze current economic developments and to forecast future ones. A large number of these models include foreign repercussions. From these models we get a sense of just how much the simple multiplier underestimates the true multiplier. Table 2 reports multiplier estimates from one well-known model that incorporates foreign repercussions. The numbers listed in the table are the multiplier effects after one year. Because of further rounds of spending in later years, the actual multipliers are larger than those reported in the table.

The first section of the table gives the multiplier effects of an increase in U.S. government spending. The U.S. effect is a multiplier of 2. This means that if autonomous government expenditures increased by $25, U.S. equilibrium national income would be $50 higher after one year.

The income of the other countries in the first part of the table is increased by higher spending in the United States because some of that spending is on imports into the United States. The spending multipliers for these countries

Copyright © by Houghton Mifflin Company. All rights reserved.

range from .7 for Japan to .2 for Germany and the United Kingdom. If U.S. autonomous government expenditures go up $25, U.K. equilibrium national income would be $5 (.2 × $25) higher after one year. Over time, as income in these foreign countries rises, their spending on U.S. goods and services increases. And as U.S. exports increase, so does U.S. income.

The second part of the table shows the sensitivity of U.S. income to changes in foreign government spending. The largest multiplier is only .2, in the case of Canada. If autonomous government spending increases by $25 in Canada, U.S. equilibrium national income would be $5 higher after one year. Clearly, U.S. spending increases have a much larger effect on foreign income than foreign spending increases have on U.S. income. The reason for this is the vast size of the domestic market in the United States relative to that in other countries.

The multiplier examples we use in this chapter show autonomous government spending changing. It is important to realize that the multiplier effects apply to any change in autonomous expenditures in any sector of the economy.

RECAP

1. Any change in autonomous expenditures is multiplied into a larger change in the equilibrium level of real GDP.

2. The multiplier measures the change in equilibrium real GDP produced by a change in autonomous spending.

3. The multiplier equals

$$\frac{1}{\text{Leakages}} = \frac{1}{MPS + MPI}$$

4. The recessionary gap is the amount spending must increase to achieve equilibrium at potential real GDP; graphically, it is measured by the vertical distance between the 45-degree line and the aggregate expenditures curve at potential real GDP.

5. The true spending multiplier is larger than the simple spending multiplier ($1/[MPS + MPI]$) because of the foreign repercussions of domestic spending. Price changes and taxes cause the simple spending multiplier to overestimate the true multiplier.

3. AGGREGATE EXPENDITURES AND AGGREGATE DEMAND

The approach to macroeconomic equilibrium presented in this chapter focuses on aggregate expenditures and income. It is called the *Keynesian model*. This model of the economy can be very useful in explaining some real-world events, but it suffers from a serious drawback: the model assumes that the supply of goods and services in the economy always adjusts to aggregate expenditures, that there is no need for price changes. The Keynesian model is a *fixed-price model*.

In the real world, we find that shortages of goods and services often are met by rising prices, not just increased production. We also find that when supply increases in the face of relatively constant demand, prices may fall. In other words, prices as well as production adjust to differences between demand and

Copyright © by Houghton Mifflin Company. All rights reserved.

supply. We introduced price as a component of macroeconomic equilibrium in Chapter 9, in the aggregate demand and supply model. You may recall that aggregate expenditures represent demand when the price level is constant. This can be demonstrated by using the income and expenditures approach developed in this chapter to derive the aggregate demand curve that was introduced in Chapter 9.

3.a. Aggregate Expenditures and Changing Price Levels

Why does the aggregate expenditures curve shift with changes in the price level?

As discussed in Chapter 9, the *AE* curve will shift with changes in the price level because of the wealth effect, interest rate effect, and international trade effect. Wealth is one of the nonincome determinants of consumption. Households hold part of their wealth in financial assets like money and bonds. As the price level falls, the purchasing power of money rises and aggregate expenditures increase. As the price level rises, the purchasing power of money falls and aggregate expenditures fall.

The interest rate is a determinant of investment spending. As the price level changes, interest rates may change as households and business firms change their demand for money. The change in interest rates will then affect investment spending. For instance, when the price level rises, more money is needed to buy any given quantity of goods and services. To acquire more money, households and firms sell their nonmonetary financial assets like bonds. The increased supply of bonds will tend to raise interest rates to attract buyers. The higher interest rates will tend to lower investment spending and aggregate expenditures. Conversely, a lower price level will tend to be associated with lower interest rates, greater investment spending, and greater aggregate expenditures.

Net exports may change, causing aggregate expenditures to change, when the domestic price level changes. If domestic prices rise while foreign prices and the exchange rate are constant, then domestic goods become more expensive relative to foreign goods, and net exports and aggregate expenditures tend to fall. If domestic prices fall while foreign prices and the exchange rate are constant, then domestic goods become cheaper relative to foreign goods, and net exports and aggregate expenditures tend to rise.

3.b. Deriving the Aggregate Demand Curve

The aggregate demand curve (*AD*) shows how the equilibrium level of expenditures changes as the price level changes. In other words, the curve shows the amount people spend at different price levels. Let's use the example of Figure 6 to show how aggregate demand is derived from the shifting aggregate expenditures curve (*AE*).

The aggregate demand curve is derived from the *AE* curve. Part (a) of Figure 6 shows three *AE* curves, each drawn for a different price level. Suppose that the initial equilibrium occurs at point *A* on curve AE_0 with prices at P_0. At this point, equilibrium real GDP and expenditures are $500. If prices fall to P_1, the *AE* curve shifts up to AE_1. Here equilibrium is at point *C*, where real GDP equals $700. If prices rise from P_0 to P_2, the *AE* curve falls to AE_2. Here equilibrium is at point *B*, where real GDP equals $300.

In part (b) of Figure 6, price level is plotted on the vertical axis and real GDP is plotted on the horizontal axis. A price level change here means that, on average, all prices in the economy change. The negative slope of the

Copyright © by Houghton Mifflin Company. All rights reserved.

aggregate demand curve results from the effect of changing prices on wealth, interest rates, and international trade. If you move vertically down from points *A, B,* and *C* in the top figure, you find corresponding points along the aggregate demand curve in the lower figure. The *AD* curve shows all of the combinations of price levels and corresponding equilibrium levels of real GDP and aggregate expenditures.

3.c. A Fixed-Price *AD-AS* Model

The Keynesian model is a fixed-price model.

The Keynesian model of fixed-price equilibrium may be considered a special case of the aggregate demand and aggregate supply equilibrium. We can define a horizontal segment of the aggregate supply curve as the Keynesian

Figure 6
Aggregate Expenditures and Aggregate Demand
Part (a) shows how changes in the price level cause the *AE* curve to shift. The initial curve, AE_0, is drawn at the initial level of prices, P_0. On this curve, the equilibrium level of aggregate expenditures (where expenditures equal real GDP) is $500. If the price level falls to P_1, autonomous expenditures increase, shifting the curve up to AE_1 and moving the equilibrium level of aggregate expenditures to $700. If the price level rises to P_2, autonomous expenditures fall, shifting the curve down to AE_2 and moving the equilibrium level of aggregate expenditures to $300.

The aggregate demand curve (*AD*) in part (b) is derived from the aggregate expenditures curves. The *AD* curve shows the equilibrium level of aggregate expenditures at different price levels. At price level P_0, equilibrium aggregate expenditures are $500; at P_1, $700; and at P_2, $300.

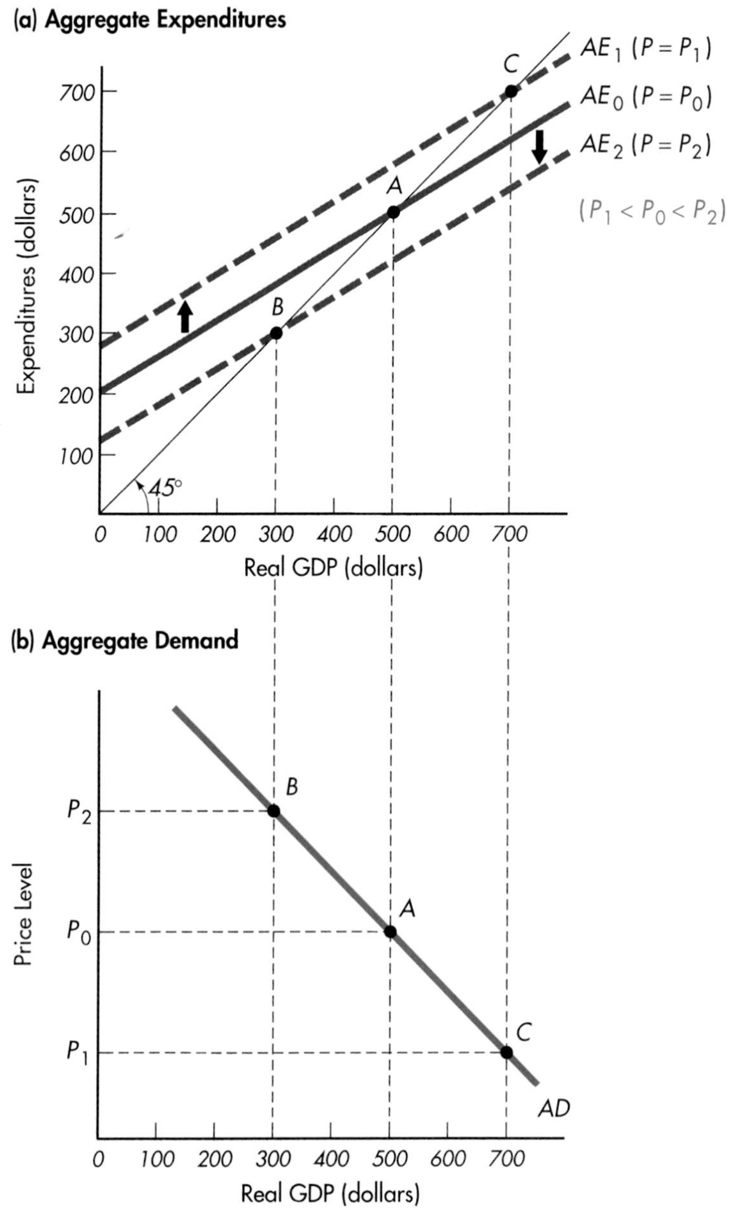

(a) Aggregate Expenditures

(b) Aggregate Demand

Copyright © by Houghton Mifflin Company. All rights reserved.

region of the curve. This represents an economy with substantial unemployment and excess capacity where real GDP and output may be increased without pressure on the price level. Figure 7 illustrates this case.

In Figure 7, the aggregate supply curve is horizontal at price level P_e. Throughout the range of the AS curve, the price level is fixed. Suppose aggregate expenditures increase due to some reason other than a price-level change. For instance, consumers could expect future incomes to rise so they increase consumption now, or business firms expect sales to rise in the future so they increase investment spending now, or government spending rises to improve the national highway system, or foreign prices rise so that net exports increase. If aggregate expenditures rise due to other than a domestic price-level change, then the aggregate demand curve shifts to the right like the shift from AD_1 to AD_2 in Figure 7. This increase in AD causes real GDP to rise to Y_2 yet the price level remains fixed at P_e.

Because the fixed-price model of macroeconomic equilibrium requires a horizontal AS curve, many economists believe that this model is too restrictive and not representative of the modern economy. As a result, we will generally see the AD-AS model using upward-sloping AS curves so that price as well as real GDP fluctuates with shifts in aggregate demand.

RECAP

1. As the price level rises (falls), aggregate expenditures fall (rise).
2. Aggregate demand is the equilibrium aggregate expenditures at alternative price levels.
3. The Keynesian fixed-price model is represented by a horizontal aggregate supply curve.

Figure 7
A Fixed-Price *AD-AS* Model
If the *AS* curve is horizontal, then shifts in the *AD* curve will have no effect on the equilibrium level of prices but will change the equilibrium level of real GDP.

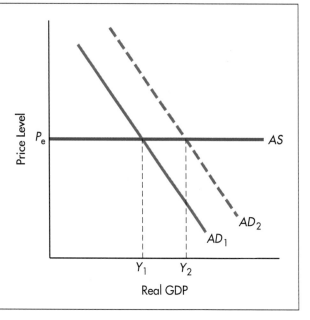

Copyright © by Houghton Mifflin Company. All rights reserved.

SUMMARY

▬ What does equilibrium mean in macro-economics?

1. Macroeconomic equilibrium is that point where aggregate expenditures equal real GDP. §1.a

▬ How do aggregate expenditures affect income or real GDP?

2. When aggregate expenditures exceed income or real GDP, real GDP rises; when they are less than real GDP, real GDP falls. §1.a

▬ What are the leakages from and injections to spending?

3. Leakages are saving, taxes, and imports; injections are investment, government spending, and exports. §1.b

4. Equilibrium real GDP occurs where leakages equal injections. §1.b

▬ Why does equilibrium real GDP change by a multiple of a change in autonomous expenditures?

5. The effect of a change in autonomous spending is multiplied by a spiral of increased spending and income. §2.a

▬ What is the spending multiplier?

6. The spending multiplier equals the reciprocal of the sum of the *MPS* and the *MPI*. §2.a

▬ What is the relationship between the GDP gap and the recessionary gap?

7. The recessionary gap is the amount autonomous expenditures must change to eliminate the GDP gap and reach potential GDP. §2.b

▬ How does international trade affect the size of the spending multiplier?

8. The actual spending multiplier may be larger than the reciprocal of the sum of the *MPS* and the *MPI* because of the foreign repercussions of changes in domestic spending. §2.c.1

▬ Why does the aggregate expenditures curve shift with changes in the price level?

9. The *AE* curve shifts with changes in the price level because of the wealth effect, interest rate effect, and international trade effect. §3.a

10. The Keynesian model of fixed-price equilibrium is a special case of the *AD* and *AS* equilibrium. §3.c

KEY TERMS

spending multiplier §2.a
recessionary gap §2.b

EXERCISES

1. Explain the role of inventories in keeping actual expenditures equal to real GDP.

2. Rework Figure 1 assuming a closed economy (net exports equal zero at all levels of income). What is the equilibrium level of real GDP? What is the spending multiplier?

3. Draw a graph representing a hypothetical economy. Carefully label the two axes, the $S + T + IM$ curve, the $I + G + EX$ curve, and the equilibrium level of real GDP. Illustrate the effect of an increase in the level of autonomous saving.

4. Given the following information, what is the spending multiplier in each case?
   a. $MPC = .90, MPI = .10$
   b. $MPC = .90, MPI = .30$
   c. $MPC = .80, MPI = .30$
   d. $MPC = .90, MPI = 0$

5. Draw a graph representing a hypothetical economy in a recession. Carefully label the two axes, the 45-degree line, the *AE* curve, and the equilibrium level of real GDP. Indicate and label the GDP gap and the recessionary gap.

Copyright © by Houghton Mifflin Company. All rights reserved.

6. Explain the effect of foreign repercussions on the value of the spending multiplier.

7. Suppose the *MPC* is .80, the *MPI* is .10, and the income tax rate is 10 percent. What is the multiplier in this economy?

Use the following table information to answer questions 8–15:

Y	C	I	G	X
$100	$120	$20	$30	$ 10
300	300	20	30	−10
500	480	20	30	−30
700	660	20	30	−50

8. The *MPC* equals?

9. The *MPI* equals?

10. The *MPS* equals?

11. The multiplier equals?

12. What is the equilibrium level of real GDP?

13. What is the value of autonomous consumption?

14. If government spending increases by $20, what is the new equilibrium level of real GDP?

15. What is the equation for the consumption, net exports, and aggregate expenditures functions?

16. Derive the aggregate demand curve from an aggregate expenditures diagram. Explain how aggregate demand relates to aggregate expenditures.

▯ INTERNET EXERCISE

In section 2.c of this chapter we learned how a change in U.S. income could affect other countries through U.S. imports. This occurs because a change in U.S. imports causes net exports to change in other countries. However, this effect should differ considerably depending on the magnitude of trade between the United States and different countries and how big this trade is relative to the countries' incomes. One approach to predicting which countries would be more sensitive to changes in U.S. income would be to examine the size of the countries' exports to the United States as a fraction of their GDP. To do so, go to the Boyes/Melvin web site at **http://www.hmco.com/college/** and click on the internet exercise link for this chapter. Now answer the questions that appear on the web page.

Copyright © by Houghton Mifflin Company. All rights reserved.

Economy May Catch Chill

Canada's economic boom could turn to bust next year.

While 1995 may be the economy's best year since 1988, more and more forecasters think that will be reversed abruptly next year as Canada's dominant export market catches a chill.

"A sharp slowdown in the U.S. is likely to have a crushing impact on Canada," said Paul Summerville, chief economist at Richardson Greenshields of Canada Ltd., in his latest forecast.

"A high price will be paid for Canada's overwhelming dependence in this cycle on the above-potential performance of the U.S. economy."

Ted Carmichael, senior economist at Morgan Bank of Canada, added, "Canada has lagged the U.S. recovery, its growth has been driven primarily by exports and business investment, and business investment is largely in the export-oriented industries."

But unlike Canada, the U.S. is growing beyond its capacity. The Federal Reserve Board's determination to change that threatens the underpinnings of Canadian growth, Carmichael said.

Consensus forecasts are for real gross domestic product in Canada to grow by 3.8 percent this year and 3.2 percent in 1996, down from 1994's 4.3 percent increase. But Summerville and Carmichael are more pessimistic, predicting a sharp slowing to about 2 percent in 1996.

This would make the year a "soft landing" or "growth recession," rather than an outright recession, in which GDP actually shrinks.

Having struggled out of recession only two years ago, Canada should by most measures have at least one or two more years of strong, non-inflationary growth ahead. But the current economic expansion differs significantly from its predecessors in its dependence on exports to the U.S., which have risen to 34 percent of GDP from 22 percent in 1990.

Almost one-third of the increase in real output in the past three years has come from our trade surplus. But Carmichael thinks export growth will slide from its blistering 13 percent annual pace of 1993-1995 to just 4 percent next year, reversing the rise in the surplus and making trade a drag on growth.

If U.S. demand for Canadian products drops abruptly, there is little else to take up the slack. Government spending is shrinking, consumer spending remains subdued, construction has been depressed by high mortgage rates, and business investment is closely linked to export sales.

"As the U.S. slows down, which is what the Fed says it will do, and Canadian exports by definition slow down, can Canada make the transition . . . to growing autonomously and independently of the U.S.?" asked Summerville.

"My answer is 'No'."

Forecasters who still see Canada's GDP growing by more than 3 percent next year are generally more optimistic about household consumption picking up.

While a soft landing is not a recession, it means the economy grows less than its long-term potential rate of about 3 percent, below which unemployment tends to rise. Carmichael sees the jobless rate falling to 8.6 percent by the end of this year, but rising to 9 percent over the following nine months.

In fact, economists say such a soft landing is welcome because it contains inflation early enough to give the expansion a second leg.

In postwar history, the U.S. has had nine recessions, but only two soft landings, in 1966 and 1986, said David Wyss, research director at DRI/McGraw Hill in Lexington, Mass. In the 1960s and 1980s, "you had two cycles divided by a growth recession, instead of a real recession."

Ironically, the probability of a real recession rises with the strength of the U.S. economy because this increases the risk the Fed's tightening will overshoot, said Wyss.

"I don't think the Fed has made a mistake yet that will cause a recession, but we're getting nervous," he added. . . .

Source: "Economy May Catch Chill," by Greg Ip. Appeared in *The Financial Post*, February 9, 1995, p. 1. Reprinted with permission.

Copyright © by Houghton Mifflin Company. All rights reserved.

The Financial Post/February 9, 1995

COMMENTARY

This article re-emphasizes a main point made in this chaper: countries are linked internationally, so that aggregate expenditure shifts in one country will have an impact on other nations. When other countries, like Canada, buy goods from the United States, the purchases increase U.S. GDP since net exports is one of the components of GDP. Remembering that net exports increase with a country's GDP, we should expect net exports to vary over the business cycle. Since Canadian imports vary with Canadian GDP, a recession in Canada tends to reduce U.S. exports, leading to lower GDP in the United States. Conversely, when the Canadian economy is booming, U.S. exports to Canada will rise and stimulate GDP growth in the United States.

The United States buys about 80 percent of Canadian exports but only about 8 percent of German exports. As a result, we would expect the business cycles of Canada and the United States to be much more similar than that of the United States and Germany. A recession in the United States would be more likely to cause a recession in Canada than Germany.

The United States had a recession in 1990 and 1991. Did the economies of the major trading partners of the United States have recessions around this time? There was a recession in Canada that roughly coincided with the U.S. recession. However, real GDP continued to grow in Germany until the fourth quarter of 1991. These numbers reflect the fact that the Canadian economy is much more integrated with the United States than the economy of Germany.

We should also expect Mexico to be greatly affected by U.S. business cycles since about 85 percent of Mexican exports go to the United States. Australia, South Africa, Sweden, and Turkey are likely to have business cycles that are more independent of U.S. influences since their exports to the U.S. as a share of their total exports is less than 10 percent.

The international links between countries should grow over time as restrictions on international trade are removed and transportation and communication costs continue to fall. The future may be one in which national business cycles are increasingly interdependent and such interdependences will have to be given greater emphasis in national policymaking.

Copyright © by Houghton Mifflin Company. All rights reserved.

11

An Algebraic Model of Income and Expenditures Equilibrium

Continuing the example we began in the Appendix to Chapter 10, if we know the equations for each component of aggregate expenditures (AE), we can solve for the equilibrium level of real GDP (Y) for the economy represented in Figure 1:

$$C = \$30 + .70Y$$

$$I = \$50$$

$$G = \$70$$

$$X = \$50 - .10Y$$

Summing these components, we can find the aggregate expenditures function:

$$AE = \$30 + .70Y + \$50 + \$70 + \$50 - .10Y$$

$$= \$200 + .60Y$$

Given the AE function, we can solve for the equilibrium level of Y where

$$Y = AE$$

$$= \$200 + .60Y$$

$$Y - .60Y = \$200$$

$$.40Y = \$200$$

$$.40Y/.40 = \$200/.40$$

$$Y = \$500$$

Copyright © by Houghton Mifflin Company. All rights reserved.

The Spending Multiplier　It is also possible to solve for the spending multiplier algebraically. We start by writing the general equations for each function where C^a, I^a, G^a, EX^a, and IM^a represent autonomous consumption, investment, government spending, exports, and imports, respectively, and where c represents the *MPC* and *im* represents the *MPI*:

$$C = C^a + cY$$

$$I = I^a$$

$$G = G^a$$

$$X = EX^a - IM^a - imY$$

Now we sum the individual equations for the components of aggregate expenditures to get the aggregate expenditures function:

$$AE = C + I + G + X$$

$$= C^a + cY + I^a + G^a + EX^a - IM^a - imY$$

$$= (C^a + I^a + G^a + EX^a - IM^a) + cY - imY$$

We know that aggregate expenditures equal income. So

$$Y = (C^a + I^a + G^a + EX^a - IM^a) + cY - imY$$

Solving for Y, we first gather all of the terms involving Y on the left side of the equation:

$$Y[1 - (c - im)] = C^a + I^a + G^a + EX^a - IM^a$$

Next we divide each side of the equation by $[1 - (c - im)]$ to get an equation for Y:

$$Y = \frac{1}{1 - (c - im)}(C^a + I^a + G^a + EX^a - IM^a)$$

A change in autonomous expenditures causes Y to change by

$$\frac{1}{1 - (c - im)}$$

times the change in expenditures. Because c is the *MPC* and *im* is the *MPI*, the multiplier can be written

$$\frac{1}{1 - (MPC - MPI)}$$

or, since $1 - MPC = MPS$, then $1 - (MPC - MPI) = MPS + MPI$, and the multiplier equals

$$\frac{1}{MPS + MPI}$$

Copyright © by Houghton Mifflin Company. All rights reserved.

Copyright © by Houghton Mifflin Company. All rights reserved.

III

Macroeconomic Policy

Copyright © by Houghton Mifflin Company. All rights reserved.

12

Fiscal Policy

FUNDAMENTAL QUESTIONS

1. How can fiscal policy eliminate a GDP gap?

2. How has U.S. fiscal policy changed over time?

3. What are the effects of budget deficits?

4. How does fiscal policy differ across countries?

Copyright © by Houghton Mifflin Company. All rights reserved.

Macroeconomics plays a key role in national politics. When Jimmy Carter ran for the presidency against Gerald Ford in 1976, he created a "misery index" to measure the state of the economy. The index was the sum of the inflation rate and the unemployment rate, and Carter showed that it had risen during Ford's term in office. When Ronald Reagan challenged Carter in 1980, he used the misery index to show that inflation and unemployment had gone up during the Carter years. The implication is that presidents are responsible for the condition of the economy. If the inflation rate or the unemployment rate is relatively high coming into an election year, incumbent presidents are open to criticism by their opponents. For instance, many people believe that George Bush was defeated by Bill Clinton in 1992 because of the recession that began in 1990—a recession that was not announced as having ended in March 1991 until after the election. Clinton's 1992 campaign made economic growth a focus of its attacks on Bush, and his 1996 campaign emphasized the strength of the economy.

Preview

In 1996, a healthy economy helped Clinton defeat Bob Dole. This was more than just campaign rhetoric, however. By law the government *is* responsible for the macroeconomic health of the nation. The Employment Act of 1946 states:

> It is the continuing policy and responsibility of the Federal Government to use all practical means consistent with its needs and obligations and other essential considerations of national policy to coordinate and utilize all its plans, functions, and resources for the purpose of creating and maintaining, in a manner calculated to foster and promote free competitive enterprise and the general welfare conditions under which there will be afforded useful employment opportunities, including self-employment for those able, willing, and seeking to work, and to promote maximum employment, production, and purchasing power.

Fiscal policy is one tool that government uses to guide the economy along an expansionary path. In this chapter we examine the role of fiscal policy—government spending and taxation—in determining the equilibrium level of income. Then we review the budget process and the history of fiscal policy in the United States. Finally we describe the difference in fiscal policy between industrial and developing countries. ■

Copyright © by Houghton Mifflin Company. All rights reserved.

1. FISCAL POLICY AND AGGREGATE DEMAND

The GDP gap is the difference between potential real GDP and the equilibrium level of real GDP. If the government wants to close the GDP gap so that the equilibrium level of real GDP reaches its potential, it must use fiscal policy to alter aggregate expenditures and cause the aggregate demand curve to shift.

Fiscal policy is the government's policy with respect to spending and taxation. Since aggregate demand includes consumption, investment, net exports, and government spending, government spending on goods and services affects the level of aggregate demand directly. Taxes affect aggregate demand indirectly by changing the disposable income of households, which alters consumption.

1.a. Shifting the Aggregate Demand Curve

By varying the level of government spending, policymakers can affect the level of real GDP.

Changes in government spending and taxes shift the aggregate demand curve. Remember that the aggregate demand curve represents combinations of equilibrium aggregate expenditures and alternative price levels. An increase in government spending or a decrease in taxes raises the level of expenditures at every level of prices and moves the aggregate demand curve to the right.

Figure 1 shows an increase in aggregate demand that would result from an increase in government spending or a decrease in taxes. Only if the aggregate supply curve is horizontal do prices remain fixed as aggregate demand increases. In Figure 1(a), equilibrium occurs along the horizontal segment (the Keynesian region) of the AS curve. If government spending increases and the price level remains constant, aggregate demand shifts from AD to AD_1; it increases by the horizontal distance from point A to point B. Once aggregate demand shifts, the AD_1 and AS curves intersect at potential real GDP, Y_p.

But Figure 1(a) is not realistic. The AS curve is not likely to be horizontal all the way to the level of potential real GDP; it should begin sloping up well before Y_p. And once the economy reaches the capacity level of output, the AS curve should become a vertical line, as shown in Figure 1(b).

If the AS curve slopes up before reaching the potential real GDP level, as it does in part (b) of the figure, expenditures have to go up by more than the amount suggested in part (a) for the economy to reach Y_p. Why? Because when prices rise, the effect of spending on real GDP is reduced. This effect is shown in Figure 1(b). To increase the equilibrium level of real GDP from Y_e to Y_p, aggregate demand must shift by the amount from point A to C, a larger increase than that shown in Figure 1(a), where the price level is fixed.

1.b. Multiplier Effects

Changes in government spending may have an effect on real GDP that is a multiple of the original change in government spending; a $1 change in government spending may increase real GDP by more than $1. This is because the original $1 of expenditure is spent over and over again in the economy as it passes from person to person. The government spending multiplier measures the multiple by which an increase in government spending increases real GDP. Similarly, a change in taxes may have an effect on real GDP that is a

Copyright © by Houghton Mifflin Company. All rights reserved.

Figure 1
Eliminating the Recessionary Gap: Higher Prices Mean Greater Spending

When aggregate demand increases from AD to AD_1 in Figure 1(a), equilibrium real GDP increases by the full amount of the shift in demand. This is because the aggregate supply curve is horizontal over the area of the shift in aggregate demand. In Figure 1(b), in order for equilibrium real GDP to rise from Y_e to Y_p, aggregate demand must shift by more than it does in part (a). In reality, the aggregate supply curve begins to slope up before potential real GDP (Y_p) is reached, as shown in part (b) of the figure.

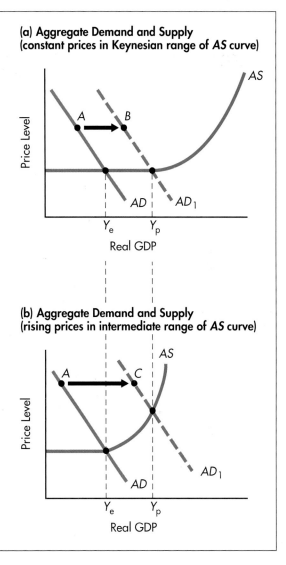

(a) Aggregate Demand and Supply (constant prices in Keynesian range of *AS* curve)

(b) Aggregate Demand and Supply (rising prices in intermediate range of *AS* curve)

Copyright © by Houghton Mifflin Company. All rights reserved.

If the price level rises as real GDP increases, the multiplier effects of any given change in aggregate expenditures are smaller than they would be if the price level remains constant.

multiple of the original change in taxes. (The appendix to this chapter provides an algebraic analysis of the government spending and tax multipliers.)

If the price level rises as real GDP increases, the multiplier effects of any given change in aggregate demand are smaller than they would be if the price level remains constant. In addition to changes in the price level modifying the effect of government spending and taxes on real GDP, there are other factors that affect how much real GDP will change following a change in government spending. One such factor is how the government pays for, or finances, its spending.

Government spending must be financed by some combination of taxing, borrowing, or creating money:

$$\text{Government spending} = \text{taxes} + \text{change in government debt} + \text{change in government-issued money}$$

In Chapter 14 we discuss the effect of financing government spending by creating money. As you will see, this source of government financing is relied on heavily in some developing countries. Here we talk about the financing problem relevant for industrial countries: how taxes and government debt can modify the expansionary effect of government spending on national income.

1.c. Government Spending Financed by Tax Increases

Suppose that government spending rises by $100 billion and that this expenditure is financed by a tax increase of $100 billion. Such a "balanced-budget" change in fiscal policy will cause equilibrium real GDP to rise. This is because government spending increases aggregate expenditures directly, but higher taxes lower aggregate expenditures indirectly through consumption spending. For instance, if taxes increase $100, consumers will not cut their spending by $100, but by some fraction, say 9/10, of the increase. If consumers spend 90 percent of a change in their disposable income, then a tax increase of $100 would lower consumption by $90. So the net effect of raising government spending and taxes by the same amount is an increase in aggregate demand, illustrated in Figure 2 as the shift from AD to AD_1. However, it may be incorrect to assume that the only thing that changes is aggregate demand. An increase in taxes may also affect aggregate supply.

Aggregate supply measures the output that producers offer for sale at different levels of prices. When taxes go up, workers have less incentive to work because their after-tax income is lower. The cost of taking a day off or extending a vacation for a few extra days is less than it is when taxes are lower and after-tax income is higher. When taxes go up, then, output can fall, causing the aggregate supply curve to shift to the left. Such supply-side effects of taxes have been emphasized by the so-called supply-side

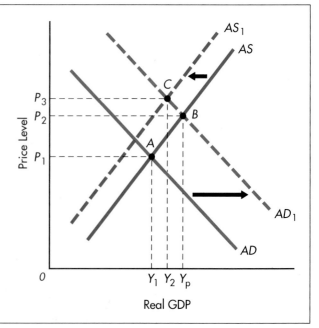

Figure 2
The Effect of Taxation on Aggregate Supply
An increase in government spending shifts the aggregate demand curve from AD to AD_1, moving equilibrium from point A to point B, and equilibrium real GDP from Y_1 to Y_p. If higher taxes reduce the incentive to work, aggregate supply could fall from AS to AS_1, moving equilibrium to point C and equilibrium real GDP to Y_2, a level below potential real GDP.

Copyright © by Houghton Mifflin Company. All rights reserved.

Part III / Macroeconomic Policy

Much of government expenditures is unrelated to current economic conditions. For instance, the provision of national defense, a legal system, and police and fire protection are all cases where government expenditures would not typically fluctuate with the business cycle. This Canadian mountie serving in Banff National Park in Alberta is employed through booms and recessions in the Canadian economy. Although macroeconomists focus typically on the discretionary elements of fiscal policy that may be altered to combat business cycles, the nondiscretionary elements account for the bulk of governments' budgets.

Copyright © by Houghton Mifflin Company. All rights reserved.

economists, as discussed in the Economic Insight "Supply-Side Economics and the Laffer Curve."

Figure 2 shows the possible effects of an increase in government spending financed by taxes. The economy is initially in equilibrium at point A, with prices at P_1 and real GDP at Y_1. The increase in government spending shifts the aggregate demand curve from AD to AD_1. If this was the only change, the economy would be in equilibrium at point B. But if the increase in taxes reduces output, the aggregate supply curve moves back from AS to AS_1, and output does not expand all the way to Y_p. The decrease in aggregate supply creates a new equilibrium at point C. Here real GDP is at Y_2 (less than Y_p) and the price level is P_3 (higher than P_2).

The standard analysis of government spending and taxation assumes that aggregate supply is not affected by the change in fiscal policy, leading us to expect a greater change in real GDP than may actually occur. If tax changes do affect aggregate supply, the expansionary effects of government spending financed by tax increases are moderated. The actual magnitude of the effect is the subject of debate among economists. Most argue that the evidence in the United States indicates that tax increases have a fairly small effect on aggregate supply.

1.d. Government Spending Financed by Borrowing

The standard multiplier analysis of government spending does not differentiate among the different methods of financing that spending. Yet you just saw how taxation can offset at least part of the expansionary effect of higher government spending. Borrowing to finance government spending can also limit the increase in aggregate demand.

A government borrows funds by selling bonds to the public. These bonds represent debt that must be repaid at a future date. Debt is, in a way, a kind of

Supply-Side Economics and the Laffer Curve

The large budget deficits incurred by the U.S. government in the 1980s were in part a product of lower tax rates engineered by the Reagan administration. President Reagan's economic team took office in January 1981 apparently believing that lower taxes would stimulate the supply of goods and services to a level that would raise tax revenues even though tax rates as a percentage of income had been cut. These arguments were repeated in 1995 by members of Congress pushing for tax-rate cuts. This emphasis on greater incentives to produce created by lower taxes has come to be known as *supply-side economics.*

The most widely publicized element of supply-side economics was the *Laffer curve.* The curve is drawn with the tax rate on the vertical axis and tax revenue on the horizontal axis. When the rate of taxation is zero, there is no tax revenue. As the tax rate increases, tax revenue increases up to a point. The assumption here is that there is some rate of taxation that is so high that it discourages productive activity. Once this rate is reached, tax revenue begins to fall as the rate of taxation goes up. In the graph, tax revenue is maximized at

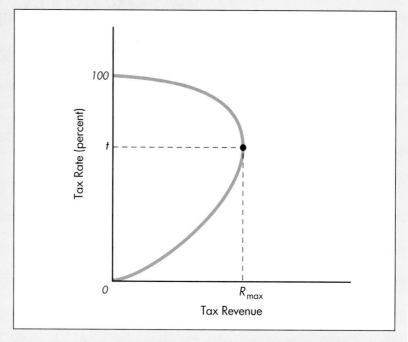

R_{max} with a tax rate of t percent. Any increase in the rate of taxation above t percent produces lower tax revenues. In the extreme case—a 100 percent tax rate—no one is willing to work because the government taxes away all income.

Critics of the supply-side tax cuts proposed by the Reagan administration argued that lower taxes would increase the budget deficit. Supply-side advocates insisted that

if the United States was in the backward-bending region of the Laffer curve (above t percent in the graph), tax cuts would actually raise, not lower, tax revenue. The evidence following the tax cuts indicates that the tax cuts did, however, contribute to a larger budget deficit, implying that the U.S. was not on the backward-bending portion of the Laffer curve.

Copyright © by Houghton Mifflin Company. All rights reserved.

substitute for current taxes. Instead of increasing current taxes to finance higher spending, the government borrows the savings of households and businesses. Of course the debt will mature and have to be repaid. This means that taxes will have to be higher in the future in order to provide the government with the funds to pay off the debt.

Current government borrowing, then, implies higher future taxes. This can limit the expansionary effect of increased government spending. If households and businesses take higher future taxes into account, they tend to save more today so that they will be able to pay those taxes in the future. And as saving today increases, consumption today falls.

The idea that current government borrowing can reduce current nongovernment expenditures was suggested originally by the early nineteenth-century English economist David Ricardo. Ricardo recognized that government borrowing could function like increased current taxes, reducing current household and business expenditures. *Ricardian equivalence* is the principle that government spending activities financed by taxation or borrowing have the same effect on the economy. If Ricardian equivalence holds, it doesn't matter whether the government raises taxes or borrows more to finance increased spending. The effect is the same: private-sector spending falls by the same amount today, and this drop in private spending will, at least partially, offset the expansionary effect of government spending on real GDP. Just how much private spending drops (and how far to the left the aggregate demand curve shifts) depends on the degree to which current saving increases in response to expected higher taxes. The less that people respond to the future tax liabilities arising from current government debt, the smaller the reduction in private spending.

There is substantial disagreement among economists over the extent to which current government borrowing acts like an increase in taxes. Some argue that it makes no difference whether the government raises current taxes or borrows. Others insist that the public does not base current spending on future tax liabilities. If the first group is correct, we would expect government spending financed by borrowing to have a smaller effect than if the second group is correct. Research on the issue continues, with most economists questioning the relevance of Ricardian equivalence and a small but influential group arguing its importance.

Copyright © by Houghton Mifflin Company. All rights reserved.

Ricardian equivalence holds if taxation and government borrowing both have the same effect on spending in the private sector.

1.e. Crowding Out

crowding out:
a drop in consumption or investment spending caused by government spending

Expansionary fiscal policy can crowd out private-sector spending; that is, an increase in government spending can reduce consumption and investment. **Crowding out** is usually discussed in the context of government spending financed by borrowing rather than by taxing. Though we have just seen how future taxes can cause consumption to fall today, investment can also be affected. Increases in government borrowing drive up interest rates. As interest rates go up, investment falls. This sort of indirect crowding out works through the bond market. The U.S. government borrows by selling Treasury bonds or bills. Because the government is not a profit-making institution, it does not have to earn a profitable return from the money it raises by selling bonds. A corporation does, however. When interest rates rise, fewer corporations offer new bonds to raise investment funds because the cost of repaying the bond debt may exceed the rate of return on the investment.

Crowding out, like Ricardian equivalence, is important in principle, but economists have never demonstrated conclusively that its effects can substantially alter spending in the private sector. Still you should be aware of the possibility to understand the potential shortcomings of changes in government spending and taxation.

RECAP

1. Fiscal policy refers to government spending and taxation.

2. By increasing spending or cutting taxes, a government can close the GDP gap.

3. If government spending and taxes increase by the same amount, equilibrium real GDP rises.

4. If a tax increase affects aggregate supply, then a balanced-budget change in fiscal policy will have a smaller expansionary effect on equilibrium real GDP than otherwise.

5. Current government borrowing reduces current spending in the private sector if people increase current saving in order to pay future tax liabilities.

6. Ricardian equivalence holds when taxation and government borrowing have the same effect on current spending in the private sector.

7. Increased government borrowing can crowd private borrowers out of the bond market so that investment falls.

2. FISCAL POLICY IN THE UNITED STATES

How has U.S. fiscal policy changed over time?

Our discussion of fiscal policy assumes that policy is made at the federal level. In the modern economy this is a reasonable assumption. This was not the case before the 1930s, however. Before the Depression, the federal government limited its activities largely to national defense and foreign policy, and left other areas of government policy to the individual states. With the growth of the importance of the federal government in fiscal policy has come a growth in the role of the federal budget process.

2.a. The Budget Process

Fiscal policy in the United States is the product of a complex process that involves both the executive and legislative branches of government (Figure 3). The fiscal year for the U.S. government begins October 1 of one year and ends September 30 of the next. The budget process begins each spring, when the president directs the federal agencies to prepare their budgets for the fiscal year that starts almost eighteen months later. The agencies submit their budget requests to the Office of Management and Budget (OMB) by early September. The OMB reviews and modifies each agency's request and consolidates all of the proposals into a budget that the president presents to Congress in January.

Once Congress receives the president's budget, the Congressional Budget Office (CBO) studies it and committees modify it before funds are appropriated. The budget is evaluated in Budget Committee hearings in both the House of Representatives and the Senate. In addition, the CBO reports to Congress on the validity of the economic assumptions made in the president's budget. A budget resolution is passed by April 15 that sets out major expenditures and estimated revenues. (Revenues are estimated because future tax payments can never be known exactly.) The resolution is followed by *recon-*

Copyright © by Houghton Mifflin Company. All rights reserved.

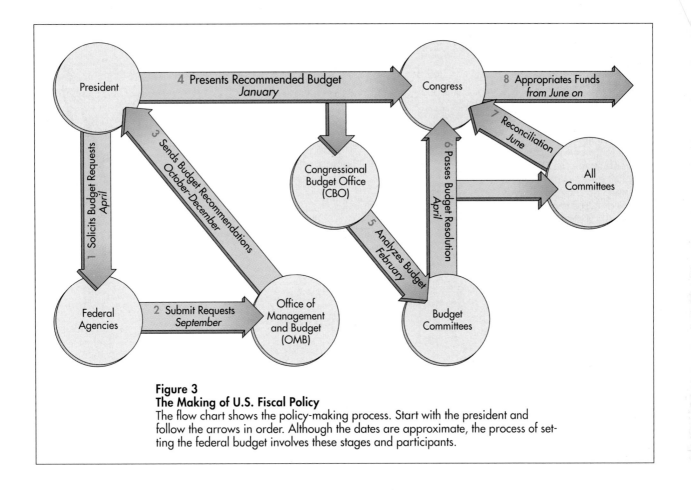

Figure 3
The Making of U.S. Fiscal Policy
The flow chart shows the policy-making process. Start with the president and
follow the arrows in order. Although the dates are approximate, the process of setting the federal budget involves these stages and participants.

ciliation, a process in which each committee of Congress must coordinate relevant tax and spending decisions. Once the reconciliation process is completed, funds are appropriated. The process is supposed to end before
Congress recesses for the summer, at the end of June. When talking about the
federal budget, the monetary amounts of various categories of expenditures
are so huge that they are often difficult to comprehend. But if one were to
divide up the annual budget by the number of individual taxpayers, you'd
come up with an average individual statement that might make more sense, as
shown in the Economic Insight "The Taxpayer's Federal Government Credit
Card Statement."

The federal budget is determined as much by politics as economics.
Politicians respond to different groups of voters by supporting different government programs regardless of the needed fiscal policy. It is the political
response to constituents that tends to drive up federal budget deficits (the difference between government expenditures and tax revenues), not the need for
expansionary fiscal policy. As a result, deficits have become commonplace.

2.b. The Historical Record

The U.S. government has grown dramatically since the early part of the century. Figure 4 shows federal revenues and expenditures over time. Figure 5

Copyright © by Houghton Mifflin Company. All rights reserved.

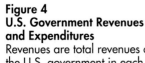

Figure 4
U.S. Government Revenues and Expenditures
Revenues are total revenues of the U.S. government in each fiscal year. Expenditures are total spending of the U.S. government in each fiscal year. The difference between the two curves equals the U.S. budget deficit (when expenditures exceed revenues) or surplus (when revenues exceed expenditures). Source: *Economic Report of the President, 1997.*

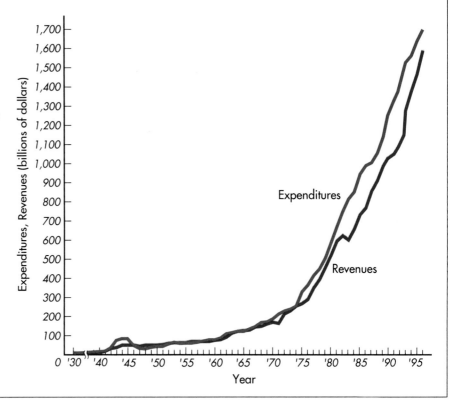

places the growth of government in perspective by plotting U.S. government spending as a percentage of gross domestic product over time. Before the Great Depression, federal spending was approximately 3 percent of the GDP; by the end of the Depression, it had risen to almost 10 percent. The ratio of spending to GDP reached its peak during World War II, when federal

Figure 5
U.S. Government Expenditures as a Percentage of Gross Domestic Product
U.S. federal government spending as a percentage of the GDP reached a high of 45 percent in 1943 and 1944. Discounting wartime spending and cutbacks after the war, you can see the upward trend in U.S. government spending, which has constituted a larger and larger share of the GDP over time.

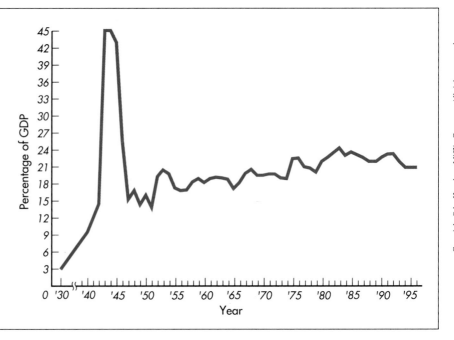

Copyright © by Houghton Mifflin Company. All rights reserved.

The Taxpayer's Federal Government Credit Card Statement

Suppose the U.S. government's expenditures and revenues were accounted for annually to each individual income tax payer like a credit card statement. For 1997, the statement would look like the table to the right.

Statement for 1997 budget year		
Previous balance (your average taxpayer share of the beginning-of-year national debt)		$45,170.01
New purchases during the year (your average taxpayer share)		
Social security	$3,217.09	
National defense	2,327.81	
Income security	2,083.70	
Medicare	1,691.37	
Commerce and housing credit	−78.47	
Health	1,115.95	
Education, training, and employment	444.64	
Veterans' benefits and services	348.74	
Transportation	340.02	
Natural resources and environment	200.52	
Science, space, and technology	148.21	
International affairs	130.78	
Agriculture	87.18	
Administration of justice	183.09	
General government	113.34	
Community and regional development	113.34	
Energy	17.43	
Payments received—Thank you (your average taxpayer share)		
Individual income taxes		$ 5,867.48
Corporate income taxes		1,534.44
Social security taxes		4,673.06
Other		1,054.93
Finance charge (your average taxpayer share of net interest on the national debt)	$2,153.44	
New balance due (your average taxpayer share of the end-of-year national debt)		$47,541.41

Copyright © by Houghton Mifflin Company. All rights reserved.

spending hit 45 percent of the GDP. After the war, the ratio fell dramatically and then slowly increased to a little more than 20 percent today.

Fiscal policy has two components: discretionary fiscal policy and automatic stabilizers. **Discretionary fiscal policy** refers to changes in government spending and taxation aimed at achieving a policy goal. **Automatic stabilizers** are elements of fiscal policy that automatically change in value as national income changes. Figures 4 and 5 suggest that government spending is dominated by growth over time. But there is no indication here of discretionary changes in fiscal policy, changes in government spending and taxation aimed at meeting specific policy goals. Perhaps a better way to evaluate the fiscal policy record is in terms of the budget deficit. Government expenditures can rise, but the effect on aggregate demand could be offset by a simultaneous increase in taxes, so that there is no expansionary effect on the equilibrium level of national income. By looking at the deficit, we see the combined spending and tax policy results that are missing if only government expenditures are considered.

Figure 6 illustrates the pattern of the U.S. federal deficit and the deficit as a percentage of GDP over time. Part (a) shows that the United States ran close to a balanced budget for much of the 1950s and 1960s. There were large deficits associated with financing World War II, and then large deficits resulting from fiscal policy decisions in the 1970s, 1980s, and 1990s. Figure 6(b) shows that the deficit as a percentage of GDP was much larger during World War II than in recent years.

The deficit increase in the mid-1970s was a product of a recession that cut the growth of tax revenues. Historically, aside from wartime, budget deficits

discretionary fiscal policy:
changes in government spending and taxation aimed at achieving a policy goal

automatic stabilizer:
an element of fiscal policy that changes automatically as income changes

---

Figure 6
The U.S. Deficit
As part (a) shows, since 1940 the U.S. government has rarely shown a surplus. For much of the 1950s and 1960s, the United States was close to a balanced budget.

Part (b) shows the federal deficit as a percentage of GDP. The deficits during the 1950s and 1960s generally were small. The early 1980s were a time of rapid growth in the federal budget deficit, and this is reflected in the growth of the deficit as a percentage of GDP.

(a) Federal Surplus (+) or Deficit (–)

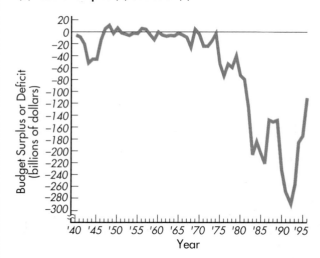

(b) Federal Deficit as a Percent of GDP (absolute value of deficit)

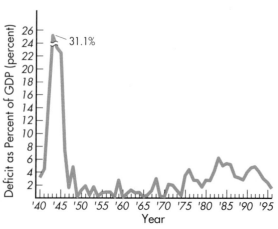

Copyright © by Houghton Mifflin Company. All rights reserved.

increase the most during recessions. When real GDP falls, tax revenues go down and government spending on unemployment and welfare benefits goes up. These are examples of automatic stabilizers in action. As income falls, taxes fall and personal benefit payments rise to partially offset the effect of the drop in income. The rapid growth of the deficit in the 1980s involved more than the recessions in 1980 and 1982, however. The economy grew rapidly after the 1982 recession ended, but so did the fiscal deficit. The increase in the deficit was the product of a rapid increase in government spending to fund new programs and enlarge existing programs while taxes were held constant. In the late 1990s the deficit decreased. This was the result of surprisingly large tax revenue gains, generated by strong economic growth, combined with only moderate government spending increases.

2.c. Deficits and the National Debt

What are the effects of budget deficits?

The recent increase in the federal deficit has led many observers to question whether a deficit can harm the economy. Figure 6 shows how the fiscal deficit has changed over time. One major implication of a large deficit is the resulting increase in the national debt, the total stock of government bonds outstanding. Table 1 lists data on the debt of the United States. Notice that the total debt doubled between 1981 ($994.8 billion) and 1986 ($2,120.6 billion). Column 3 shows debt as a percentage of GDP. In recent years, the debt has been rising as a percent of GDP. During World War II, the debt was greater than the GDP for five years. Despite the talk of "unprecedented" federal deficits in recent years, clearly the ratio of the debt to GDP was by no means unprecedented.

We have not yet answered the question of whether deficits are bad. To do so, we have to consider their potential effects.

2.c.1. Deficits, Interest Rates, and Investment
Because government deficits mean government borrowing and debt, many economists argue that deficits raise interest rates. Increased government borrowing raises interest rates, which in turn can depress investment. (Remember that as interest rates rise, the rate of return on investment drops, along with the incentive to invest.) What happens when government borrowing crowds out private investment? Lower investment means fewer capital goods in the future. So deficits lower the level of output in the economy both today and in the future. In this sense, deficits are potentially bad.

Through their effect on investment, deficits can lower the level of output in the economy.

2.c.2. Deficits and International Trade
If government deficits raise real interest rates (the nominal interest rate minus the expected inflation rate), they also may have an effect on international trade. A higher real return on U.S. securities makes those securities more attractive to foreign investors. As the foreign demand for U.S. securities increases, so does the demand for U.S. dollars in exchange for Japanese yen, British pounds, and other foreign currencies. As the demand for dollars increases, the dollar *appreciates* in value on the foreign exchange market. This means that the dollar becomes more expensive to foreigners while foreign currency becomes cheaper to U.S. residents. This kind of change in the exchange rate encourages U.S. residents to buy more foreign goods, and foreign residents to buy fewer U.S. goods. Ultimately, then, as deficits and government debt increase, U.S. net exports fall. Many economists believe that the growing fiscal deficits of the 1980s were responsible for the record decline in U.S. net exports during that period.

Copyright © by Houghton Mifflin Company. All rights reserved.

TABLE 1
Debt of the U.S. Government (dollar amounts in billions)

(1) Year	(2) Total Debt	(3) Debt/GDP (percent)	(4) Net Interest	(5) Interest/Government Spending (percent)
1958	$ 279.7	63	$ 5.6	6.8
1960	290.5	57	6.9	7.5
1962	302.9	55	6.9	6.5
1964	316.1	50	8.2	6.9
1966	328.5	44	9.4	7.0
1968	368.7	43	11.1	6.2
1970	380.9	39	14.4	7.4
1972	435.9	38	15.5	6.7
1974	483.9	34	21.4	8.0
1976	629.0	37	26.7	7.3
1978	776.6	36	35.4	7.9
1980	909.1	34	52.5	9.1
1981	994.8	34	68.8	10.5
1982	1,137.3	36	85.0	11.6
1983	1,371.7	41	89.8	11.2
1984	1,564.7	42	111.1	13.2
1985	1,817.5	46	129.5	13.6
1986	2,120.6	50	136.0	13.7
1987	2,396.1	53	138.7	13.8
1988	2,601.3	54	151.8	14.3
1989	2,868.0	55	169.3	14.8
1990	3,206.6	56	184.2	14.7
1991	3,598.5	61	194.5	14.7
1992	4,002.1	65	199.4	14.4
1993	4,351.4	67	198.8	14.1
1994	4,643.7	68	203.0	13.9
1995	4,921.0	69	232.2	15.3
1996	5,181.9	69	241.1	15.5
1997	5,453.7	69	247.4	15.2

Copyright © by Houghton Mifflin Company. All rights reserved.

The U.S. federal budget deficit rose from $73.8 billion in 1980 to $212.3 billion in 1985. During this time, the dollar appreciated in value from 1.95 German marks per dollar to 3.32 marks per dollar and from 203 Japanese yen per dollar to 260 yen per dollar. These changes in the dollar exchange rate caused U.S. goods to rise in price to foreign buyers. For instance, a $1,000 IBM personal computer would sell for 1,950 German marks at the exchange rate of 1.95 marks per dollar. But at the rate of 3.32 marks per dollar, the $1,000 computer would sell for 3,320 marks. Furthermore, foreign currencies became cheaper to U.S. residents, making foreign goods cheaper in dollars. In 1980, one German mark sold for $.51. In 1985, one mark sold for $.30. At these prices, a Volkswagen wheel that sells for 100 marks would have changed in dollar price from $51 to $30 as the exchange rate changed. The combination of the dollar price of U.S. imports falling and the foreign currency price of U.S. exports rising caused U.S. net exports to fall dramatically at the same time that the fiscal deficit rose dramatically. Such foreign trade effects are another potentially bad effect of deficits.

2.c.3. Interest Payments on the National Debt

The national debt is the stock of government bonds outstanding. It is the product of past and current budget deficits. As the size of the debt increases, the interest that must be paid on the debt tends to rise. Column 4 of Table 1 lists the amount of interest paid on the debt; column 5 lists the interest as a percentage of government expenditures. The numbers in both columns have risen steadily over time and only recently started to level off. The federal government has been paying a higher dollar amount of interest each year. When the dollar amount of interest paid is rising as a percentage of total government expenditures, means that interest payments are rising faster than total government spending.

The steady increase in the interest cost of the national debt is an aspect of fiscal deficits that worries some people. However, to the extent that U.S. citizens hold government bonds, we owe the debt to ourselves. The tax liability of funding the interest payments is offset by the interest income bondholders earn. In this case there is no net change in national wealth when the national debt changes.

Of course, we do not owe the national debt just to ourselves. The United States is the world's largest national financial market, and many U.S. securities, including government bonds, are held by foreign residents. In the late 1990s, foreign holdings of the U.S. national debt amounted to about 30 percent of the outstanding debt. Because the tax liability for paying the interest on the debt falls on U.S. taxpayers, the greater the payments made to foreigners, the lower the wealth of U.S. residents, other things being equal.

Other things are not equal, however. To understand the real impact of foreign holdings on the economy, we have to evaluate what the economy would have been like if the debt had not been sold to foreign investors. If the foreign savings placed in U.S. bonds allowed the United States to increase investment and its productive capacity beyond what would have been possible in the absence of foreign lending, then the country could very well be better off for selling government bonds to foreigners. The presence of foreign funds may keep interest rates lower than they would otherwise be, preventing the substantial crowding out associated with an increase in the national debt.

So while deficits are potentially bad due to the crowding out of investment, larger trade deficits with the rest of the world, and greater interest costs of the debt, we cannot generally say that all deficits are bad. It depends on what benefit the deficit provides. If the deficit spending allowed for greater productivity than would have occurred otherwise, the benefits may outweigh the costs.

2.d. Automatic Stabilizers

We have largely been talking about discretionary fiscal policy, the changes in government spending and taxing that policymakers make consciously. *Automatic stabilizers* are the elements of fiscal policy that change automatically as income changes. Automatic stabilizers partially offset changes in income: as income falls, automatic stabilizers increase spending; as income rises, automatic stabilizers decrease spending. Any program that responds to

Copyright © by Houghton Mifflin Company. All rights reserved.

fluctuations in the business cycle in a way that moderates the effect of those fluctuations is an automatic stabilizer. Examples are progressive income taxes and transfer payments.

In our examples of tax changes, we have been using *lump-sum taxes*—taxes that are a flat dollar amount regardless of income. However, income taxes are determined as a percentage of income. In the United States, the federal income tax is a **progressive tax**: as income rises, so does the rate of taxation. A person with a very low income pays no income tax, while a person with a high income can pay more than a third of that income in taxes. Countries use different rates of taxation on income. Taxes can be *regressive* (the tax rate falls as income rises) or *proportional* (the tax rate is constant as income rises). But most countries, including the United States, use a progressive tax, the percentage of income paid as taxes rising with taxable income.

Progressive income taxes act as an automatic stabilizer. As income falls, so does the average tax rate. Suppose a household earning $60,000 must pay 30 percent of its income ($18,000) in taxes, leaving 70 percent of its income ($42,000) for spending. If that household's income drops to $40,000 and the tax rate falls to 25 percent, the household has 75 percent of its income ($30,000) available for spending. But if the tax rate is 30 percent at all levels of income, the household earning $40,000 would have only 70 percent of its income ($28,000) to spend. By allowing a greater percentage of earned income to be spent, progressive taxes help offset the effect of lower income on spending.

A **transfer payment** is a payment to one person that is funded by taxing others. Food stamps, welfare benefits, and unemployment benefits are all government transfer payments: current taxpayers provide the funds to pay those who qualify for the programs. Transfer payments that use income to establish eligibility act as automatic stabilizers. In a recession, as income falls, more people qualify for food stamps or welfare benefits, raising the level of transfer payments.

Unemployment insurance is also an automatic stabilizer. As unemployment rises, more workers receive unemployment benefits. Unemployment benefits tend to rise in a recession and fall during an expansion. This countercyclical pattern of benefit payments offsets the effect of business cycle fluctuations on consumption.

RECAP

1. Fiscal policy in the United States is a product of the budget process.

2. Federal spending in the United States has grown rapidly over time, from just 3 percent of the GDP before the Great Depression to approximately 24 percent of the GDP in the early 1990s.

3. Government budget deficits can hurt the economy through their effect on interest rates and private investment, net exports, and the tax burden on current and future taxpayers.

4. Automatic stabilizers are government programs that are already in place and that respond automatically to fluctuations in the business cycle, moderating the effect of those fluctuations.

progressive tax:
a tax whose rate rises as income rises

transfer payment:
a payment to one person that is funded by taxing others

Copyright © by Houghton Mifflin Company. All rights reserved.

3. FISCAL POLICY IN DIFFERENT COUNTRIES

A country's fiscal policy reflects its philosophy toward government spending and taxation. In this section we present comparative data that demonstrate the variety of fiscal policies in the world.

3.a. Government Spending

How does fiscal policy differ across countries?

Government spending has grown over time as a fraction of GNP in all industrial countries.

Our discussion to this point has centered on U.S. fiscal policy. But fiscal policy and the role of government in the economy can be very different across countries. Government has played an increasingly larger role in the major industrial countries over time. Table 2 shows how government spending has gone up as a percentage of output in five industrial nations. In every case, government spending accounted for a larger percentage of output in 1994 than it did 100 years earlier. For instance, in 1880, government spending was only 10 percent of the GNP in the United Kingdom. By 1929 it had risen to 24 percent; and by 1994, to 40 percent.

Historically in industrial countries, the growth of government spending has been matched by growth in revenues. But in the 1960s, government spending began to grow faster than revenues, creating increasingly larger debtor nations.

Developing countries have not shown the uniform growth in government spending found in industrial countries. In fact, in some developing countries (for instance, Chile, the Dominican Republic, and Peru), government spending was a smaller percentage of GDP in 1994 than it was twenty years earlier. And we find a greater variation in the role of government in developing countries.

One important difference between the typical developed country and the typical developing country is that government plays a larger role in investment spending in the developing country. One reason for this difference is that state-owned enterprises account for a larger percentage of economic activity in developing countries than they do in developed countries. Also, developing countries usually rely more on government than the private sector

TABLE 2
Share of Government Spending in GNP in Selected Industrial Countries, 1880, 1929, and 1994 (percent)

Year	France	Germany	Sweden	United Kingdom	United States
1880	15	10*	6	10	8
1929	19	31	8	24	10
1994	45	32	50	40	22

*1881

Source: From WORLD DEVELOPMENT REPORT 1996 by World Bank. Copyright © 1996 by The International Bank for Reconstruction and Development/The World Bank. Used by permission of Oxford University Press, Inc.

Copyright © by Houghton Mifflin Company. All rights reserved.

to build their infrastructure—schools, roads, hospitals—than do developed countries.

How a government spends its money is a function of its income. Here we find differences not only between industrial and developing countries but also among developing countries. Figure 7 divides developing countries into low-income (the poorest) and middle-income (not as poor) groups. It clearly illustrates the relative importance of social welfare spending in industrial and developing countries. Although standards of living are lowest in the poorest countries, these countries do not have the resources to spend on social services (education, health, housing, social security, welfare). The industrial countries, on average, spend 58 percent of their budgets on social programs. Middle-income developing countries spend 39 percent of their budgets on social programs. Low-income countries spend only 24 percent of their budgets on these programs.

The labor forces in industrial countries are much better educated than those in developing countries. Figure 8 shows why. The figure measures the cost of educating a student for a year as a percentage of per capita GDP. On average it costs 49 percent of per capita GDP to educate a college student in an industrial country. It costs 370 percent of per capita GDP to provide a year of college education in the average developing country. In the poorest region of the world, sub-Saharan Africa, a year of college costs 800 percent of per capita GDP. Governments in the poorest countries simply cannot afford to provide a comprehensive system of higher education.

Figure 7
Central Government Spending by Functional Category
The charts show the pattern of government spending in industrial countries, middle-income developing countries, and low-income developing countries. Social programs (education, health, and housing, social security, and welfare) account for 58 percent of federal government expenditures in industrial countries, but only 39 percent in middle-income countries and 24 percent in low-income countries. Source: World Bank, *World Development Report, 1994.*

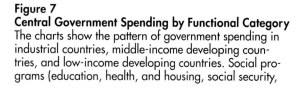

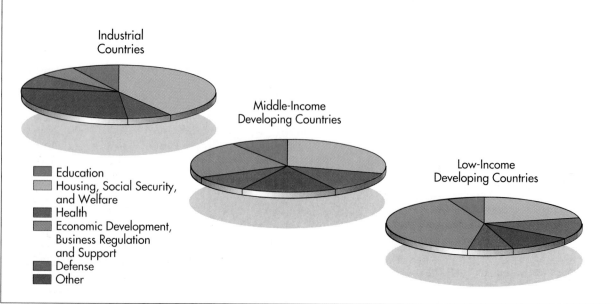

Industrial
Countries

Middle-Income
Developing Countries

Low-Income
Developing Countries

■ Education
▨ Housing, Social Security, and Welfare
■ Health
▦ Economic Development, Business Regulation and Support
■ Defense
■ Other

Copyright © by Houghton Mifflin Company. All rights reserved.

3.b. Taxation

There are two different types of taxes: *direct taxes* (on individuals and firms) and *indirect taxes* (on goods and services). Figure 9 compares the importance of different sources of central government tax revenue across industrial and developing countries. The most obvious difference is that personal income taxes are much more important in industrial countries than in developing countries. Why? Because personal taxes are hard to collect in agricultural nations, where a large percentage of household production is for personal consumption. Taxes on businesses are easier to collect, and thus are more important in developing countries.

That industrial countries are better able to afford social programs is reflected in the great disparity in social security taxes between industrial countries and developing countries. With so many workers living near the subsistence level in the poorest countries, their governments simply cannot tax workers for retirement and health security programs.

Figure 9 also shows that taxes on international trade are very important in developing countries. Because goods arriving or leaving a country must pass through customs inspection, export and import taxes are relatively easy to collect compared to income taxes. In general, developing countries depend more heavily on indirect taxes on goods and services than do developed countries.

value-added tax (VAT):
a general sales tax collected at each stage of production

Figure 9 lists "goods and services" taxes. Of these, 65 percent are **value-added (VAT) taxes** for industrial countries, while 61 percent of developing country commodity taxes come from value-added taxes. A value-added tax is an indirect tax imposed on each sale at each stage of production. Each seller from the first stage of production on collects the VAT from the buyer, and then deducts any VATs it has paid in buying its inputs. The difference is remitted to the government. From time to time, Congress has debated the merits of a VAT in the United States, but has never approved this kind of tax.

Copyright © by Houghton Mifflin Company. All rights reserved.

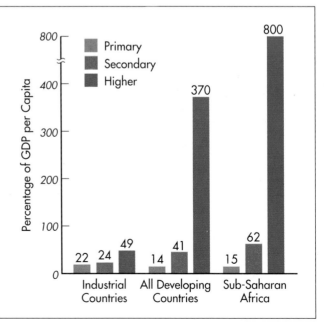

Figure 8
Cost per Student of Public Education as a Percentage of GDP per Capita in Three Country Groups
Industrial countries have much better educated populations than do poor countries. One reason is the higher cost of education in poor countries in terms of percentage of per capita GDP. A year of college education for one student costs an average of 49 percent of per capita GDP in industrial countries; it costs 370 percent on average in developing countries. In the poorest region in the world, sub-Saharan Africa, one year of higher education costs 800 percent of per capita GDP. Source: From WORLD DEVELOPMENT REPORT *1988* by World Bank. Copyright © 1988 by The International Bank for Reconstruction and Development/The World Bank. Used by permission of Oxford University Press, Inc.

**Figure 9
Central Government Tax
Composition by Income
Group**
When we group countries by
income level, the importance of
different sources of tax
revenue is obvious. Domestic
income taxes account for
roughly a third of government
revenue in industrial and
middle-income developing
countries and a quarter of government revenue in developing
countries. However, personal
income taxes are most important in industrial countries,
while business income taxes
are most important in developing countries. Social security
taxes are a major source of
government revenue in industrial countries; they are less
important in developing countries, which cannot afford
social programs. International
trade taxes represent just 3
percent of tax revenues in
industrial countries; developing
countries rely heavily on these
taxes. Source: From
Government Finance Statistics,
1992. Reprinted by permission
of International Monetary
Fund.

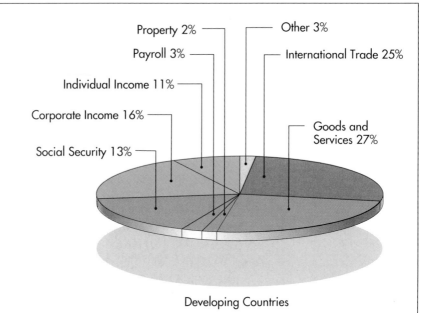

Developing Countries

Property 2%
Payroll 3%
Individual Income 11%
Corporate Income 16%
Social Security 13%
Other 3%
International Trade 25%
Goods and Services 27%

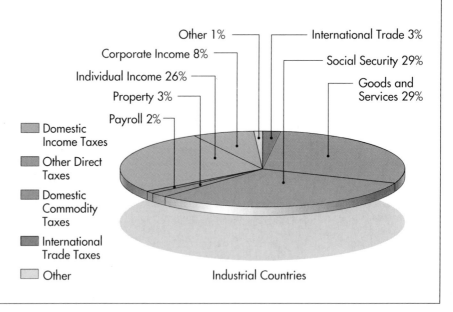

Other 1%
Corporate Income 8%
Individual Income 26%
Property 3%
Payroll 2%
International Trade 3%
Social Security 29%
Goods and Services 29%

Domestic Income Taxes

Other Direct Taxes

Domestic Commodity Taxes

International Trade Taxes

Other

Industrial Countries

Copyright © by Houghton Mifflin Company. All rights reserved.

RECAP

1. Over time, government spending has become more important in indus-
    trial countries.

2. Governments in developing countries typically play a larger role in investment spending in their economies than do the governments of developed countries.

3. Developing countries depend more on indirect taxes on goods and services as a source of revenue than on direct taxes on individuals and businesses.

4. Value-added taxes are general sales taxes that are collected at every stage of production.

SUMMARY

▰▰▰ How can fiscal policy eliminate a GDP gap?

1. A GDP gap can be closed by increasing government spending or by cutting taxes. §1

2. Government spending affects aggregate expenditures directly; taxes affect aggregate expenditures indirectly, through their effect on consumption. §1

3. Aggregate expenditures must rise to bring equilibrium real GDP up to potential real GDP—to eliminate the GDP gap. §1

4. An increase in government spending matched by an increase in taxes raises equilibrium spending and real GDP. §1.c

5. If the public expects to pay higher taxes as a result of government borrowing, then the expansionary effects of government deficits may be reduced. §1.c.

6. Government borrowing can crowd out private spending by raising interest rates and reducing investments. §1.e

▰▰▰ How has U.S. fiscal policy changed over time?

7. Fiscal policy in the United States is a product of the budget process. §2.a

8. Federal government spending in the United States has increased from just 3 percent of the

GDP before the Great Depression to a little more than 20 percent of the GDP today. §2.b

9. Fiscal policy has two components: discretionary fiscal policy and automatic stabilizers. §2.b

▰▰▰ What are the effects of budget deficits?

10. Budget deficits, through their effects on interest rates, international trade, and the national debt, can reduce investment, output, net exports, and national wealth. §2.c.1, 2.c.2, 2.c.3

11. Progressive taxes and transfer payments are automatic stabilizers, elements of fiscal policy that change automatically as national income changes. §2.d

▰▰▰ How does fiscal policy differ across countries?

12. Industrial countries spend a much larger percentage of their government budget for social programs than do developing countries. §3.a

13. Industrial countries depend more on direct taxes and less on indirect taxes than do developing countries. §3.b

KEY TERMS

crowding out §1.e

discretionary fiscal policy §2.b

automatic stabilizer §2.b

progressive tax §2.d

transfer payment §2.d

value-added tax (VAT) §3.b

Copyright © by Houghton Mifflin Company. All rights reserved.

EXERCISES

1. What is the role of aggregate demand in eliminating the GDP gap? How does the slope of the *AS* curve affect the fiscal policy actions necessary to eliminate the GDP gap?

2. Briefly describe the process of setting the federal budget in the United States. What is the time lag between the start of the process and the point at which the money is actually spent?

3. In what ways are government deficits harmful to the economy?

4. Define and give three examples of automatic stabilizers.

5. Briefly describe the major differences between fiscal policy in industrial countries and that in developing countries.

6. Why will real GDP tend to rise when government spending and taxes rise by the same amount?

7. How can a larger government fiscal deficit cause a larger international trade deficit?

8. Why do government budget deficits grow during recessions?

9. Taxes can be progressive, regressive, or proportional. Define each, and briefly offer an argument for why income taxes are usually progressive.

The following questions are based on the appendix to this chapter.

Answer questions 10–13 on the basis of the following information. Assume that equilibrium real GDP

is $800 billion, potential real GDP is $900 billion, the *MPC* is .80, and the *MPI* is .40.

10. What is the size of the GDP gap?

11. How much must government spending increase to eliminate the GDP gap?

12. How much must taxes fall to eliminate the GDP gap?

13. If government spending and taxes both change by the same amount, how much must they change to eliminate the recessionary gap?

14. Suppose the *MPC* is .90 and the *MPI* is .10. If government expenditures go up $100 billion while taxes fall $10 billion, what happens to the equilibrium level of real GDP?

Use the following equations to answer questions 15–17.

$$C = \$100 + .8Y$$

$$I = \$200$$

$$G = \$250$$

$$X = \$100 - .2Y$$

15. What is the equilibrium level of real GDP?

16. What is the new equilibrium level of real GDP if government spending increases by $100?

17. What is the new equilibrium level of real GDP if government spending and taxes both increase by $100?

Copyright © by Houghton Mifflin Company. All rights reserved.

INTERNET EXERCISE

Section 3.b discussed how different governments raise revenue. To see how the U.S. government raises its revenue, go to the Boyes/Melvin web site at **http://www.hmco.com/college/** and click on the internet exercise link for this chapter. Now answer the questions that appear on the web page.

Copyright © by Houghton Mifflin Company. All rights reserved.

Think of the Federal Budget as a Little Like Air

CLEVELAND—Think of the federal budget deficit as a little like air.

You can't see it, feel it or hold it in your hand. But it's all around you. And it affects every economic breath you take.

"A deficit has to be covered in one of two ways," explained David Bowers, professor of banking and finance at Case Western Reserve University. "The government either borrows the money from the public or it prints the money. That's the only two choices it has. One gives you higher interest rates. The other gives you higher inflation."

Right now, most economists believe, the deficit's biggest impact is on interest rates. And that determines what we pay for loans. Loans to buy cars or houses. To start or expand businesses.

Frank Clayton feels the pinch. He runs a small, but thriving, wholesale business on Cleveland's southeast side. Like a lot of other entrepreneurs, Clayton occasionally has to go to the bank for a line of credit to keep his operation growing.

And when he does, the frugal, hands-on boss of Central Electric Supply must bid for money against Uncle Sam, that mother of all spendthrifts. Uncle Sam needs to borrow an extra $300 billion or so every year. He also can pay whatever interest is required to get the cash because taxpayers like you pick up the tab.

So Uncle Sam gets what he needs. Frank Clayton and everybody else get what's left—at the prices Uncle Sam set. It's the old law of supply and demand.

"The deficit makes it harder to get the capital because the government competes with you for what's available," Clayton said the other day. "That means the cost of the money just gets higher and higher."

Or at least higher than it ought to be. . . .

Kenneth T. Mayland, senior vice president and chief economist at Society Bank, cautions that hypotheticals about how the economy might look if the budget were balanced tend to ignore the costs of reaching that fiscal promised land.

"Part of the mechanism that results in lower rates puts some people out of work," said Mayland. "Raising taxes $300 billion is going to put some people out of work. Same with cutting government spending. Keep in mind that government spending is somebody's income."

Source: "Think of the Federal Budget as a Little Like Air," by Joe Frolik. Appeared in *The Plain Dealer*, February 28, 1993, p. 8A. Reprinted with permission from the *Plain Dealer*, ©1993. All rights reserved.

Copyright © by Houghton Mifflin Company. All rights reserved.

The Plain Dealer (Cleveland)/February 28, 1993

COMMENTARY

Although the extent, causes, and political impact of the massive budget deficit have been extensively covered by the media, there has been relatively less reporting on the deficit's precise effects on the economy. An implicit message in many reports is that budget deficits are harmful. Other reports suggest that budget deficits are either helpful (at least in moderation) or have no effect. Careful economic reasoning provides us with insight into the consequences of the budget deficit for the U.S. economy.

You may have heard arguments concerning the effects of the budget deficit that proceed by means of an analogy between the government's budget and a family's budget. Just as a family cannot spend more than it earns, so the argument goes, the government cannot follow this practice without bringing itself to ruin. The problem with this analogy is that the government has the ability to raise money through taxes and bond sales, options not open to a family.

A more appropriate analogy is to compare the government's budget to that of a large corporation. Large corporations run persistent deficits that are never paid back. Instead, when corporate debt comes due, the corporations "roll over" their debt by selling new debt. Corporations are able to do this because they use their debt to finance investment that enables them to increase their worth. To the extent that the government is investing in projects like road repairs and building the nation's infrastructure, it is increasing the productive capacity of the economy, which widens the tax base and increases potential future tax receipts.

There are, of course, legitimate problems associated with the budget deficit. The government has two options if it cannot pay for its expenditures with tax receipts. One method of financing the budget deficit is by printing money. This is an unattractive option because it leads to inflation. Another method is to borrow funds by selling government bonds. A problem with this option is that the government must compete for scarce loanable funds and, unless saving increases at the same time, interest rates rise and government borrowing "crowds out" private investment. In the article, the owner of Central Electric Supply in Cleveland complains about how government borrowing makes it harder for him to borrow to finance the growth of his company. If this is a problem throughout the economy, it results in a lower capital stock and diminished prospects for future economic growth.

Although everyone complains about the harmful effects of the budget deficit, cutting the deficit is politically difficult. As the banker quoted in the article says, "Government spending is somebody's income." Cutting spending means hurting someone, which politicians are hesitant to do. The deficit could also be cut by raising taxes, but that means less private spending and angry taxpayers—not an easy political solution. As a result, it is reasonable to expect tax increases generally to be modest. As we saw in the late 1990s, reduced growth of government spending coupled with a growing economy generates tax revenue increases, and if government spending grows slower than tax revenue, deficits fall.

Copyright © by Houghton Mifflin Company. All rights reserved.

12

An Algebraic Examination of the Balanced-Budget Change in Fiscal Policy

What would happen if government spending and taxes went up by the same amount? We can analyze such a change by expanding the analysis begun in the Appendix to Chapter 11.

The spending multiplier is the simple multiplier defined in Chapter 11:

$$\text{Spending multiplier} = \frac{1}{MPS + MPI}$$

In the Chapter 11 example, because the *MPS* equals .30 and the *MPI* equals .10, the spending multiplier equals 2.5:

$$\text{Spending multiplier} = \frac{1}{MPS + MPI} = \frac{1}{.30 + .10}$$

$$= \frac{1}{.40} = 2.5$$

When government spending increases by \$20, the equilibrium level of real GDP increases by 2.5 times \$20, or \$50.

We also can define a tax multiplier, a measure of the effect of a change in taxes on equilibrium real GDP. Because a percentage of any change in income is saved and spent on imports, we know that a tax cut increases expenditures by less than the amount of the cut. The percentage of the tax cut that actually is spent is the marginal propensity to consume (*MPC*) less the *MPI*. If consumers save 30 percent of any extra income, they spend 70 percent, the *MPC*. But the domestic economy does not realize 70 percent of the extra income because 10 percent of the extra income is spent on imports. The percentage of any extra income that actually is spent at home is the *MPC* minus the *MPI*. In our example, 60 percent (.70 − .10) of any extra income is spent in the domestic economy.

Copyright © by Houghton Mifflin Company. All rights reserved.

With this information, we can define the tax multiplier like this:

$$\text{Tax multiplier} = -(MPC - MPI)\,\frac{1}{MPS + MPI}$$

In our example, the tax multiplier is −1.5:

$$\text{Tax multiplier} = -(.70 - .10)\,\frac{1}{.30 + .10}$$

$$= -(.60)\,(2.5) = -1.5$$

A tax cut increases equilibrium real GDP by 1.5 times the amount of the cut. Notice that the tax multiplier is always a *negative* number because a change in taxes moves income and expenditures in the opposite direction. Higher taxes lower income and expenditures; lower taxes raise income and expenditures.

Now that we have reviewed the spending and tax multipliers, we can examine the effect of a balanced-budget change in fiscal policy where government spending and taxes change by the same amount. To simplify the analysis, we assume that taxes are lump-sum taxes (taxpayers must pay a certain amount of dollars as tax) rather than income taxes (where the tax rises with income). We can use the algebraic model presented in the Appendix to Chapter 11 to illustrate the effect of a balanced-budget change in government spending. Here are the model equations:

$$C = \$30 + .70Y$$

$$I = \$50$$

$$G = \$70$$

$$X = \$50 - .10Y$$

Solving for the equilibrium level of Y (as we did in the Appendix to Chapter 11), Y equals \$500 where Y equals aggregate expenditures.

Now suppose that G increases by \$10 and that this increase is funded by taxes of \$10. The increase in G changes autonomous government spending to \$80. The increase in taxes affects the autonomous levels of C and X. The new model equations are

$$C = \$30 + .70(Y - \$10) = \$23 + .70Y$$

$$X = \$50 - .10(Y - \$10) = \$51 - .10Y$$

Using the new G, C, and X functions, we can find the new equilibrium level of real GDP by setting Y equal to AE $(C + I + G + X)$:

$$Y = C + I + G + X$$

$$Y = \$23 + .70Y + \$50 + \$80 + \$51 - .10Y$$

$$Y = \$204 + .60Y$$

$$Y - .60Y = \$204$$

$$.40Y = \$204$$

$$Y = \$510$$

Increasing government spending and taxes by \$10 each raises the equilibrium level of real GDP by \$10. A balanced-budget increase in G increases Y by the change in G. If government spending and taxes both fall by the same amount, then real GDP will also fall by an amount equal to the change in government spending and taxes.

Copyright © by Houghton Mifflin Company. All rights reserved.

13

Money and Banking

FUNDAMENTAL QUESTIONS

1. What is money?

2. How is the U.S. money supply defined?

3. How do countries pay for international transactions?

4. Why are banks considered intermediaries?

5. How does international banking differ from domestic banking?

6. How do banks create money?

Copyright © by Houghton Mifflin Company. All rights reserved.

U p to this point, we have been talking about aggregate expenditures, aggregate demand and supply, and fiscal policy without explicitly discussing money. Yet money is used by every sector of the economy in all nations and plays a crucial role in every economy. In this chapter we discuss what money is, how the quantity of money is determined, and the role of banks in determining this quantity. In the next chapter, we examine the role of money in the aggregate demand and supply model.

As you will see in the next two chapters, the quantity of money has a major impact on interest rates, inflation, and the amount of spending in the economy. Money is, then, important for macroeconomic policy making, and government officials use both monetary and fiscal policy to influence the equilibrium level of real GDP and prices.

Preview

Banks and the banking system also play key roles, both at home and abroad, in the determination of the amount of money in circulation and the movement of money between nations. After we define money and its functions, we look at the banking system. We begin with banking in the United States, and then discuss international banking. Someone once joked that banks follow the rule of 3-6-3. They borrow at 3 percent interest, lend at 6 percent interest, and close at 3 P.M. If those days ever existed, clearly they do not today. The banking industry in the United States and the rest of the world has undergone tremendous change in recent years. New technology and government deregulation are allowing banks to respond to changing economic conditions in ways that were unthinkable only a few years ago, and these changes have had dramatic effects on the economy. ∎

1. WHAT IS MONEY?

Copyright © by Houghton Mifflin Company. All rights reserved.

What is money?

money:
anything that is generally acceptable to sellers in exchange for goods and services

Money is anything that is generally acceptable to sellers in exchange for goods and services. The cash in your wallet can be used to buy groceries or a movie ticket. You simply present your cash to the cashier, who readily accepts it. If you want to use your car to buy groceries or a movie ticket, the exchange is more complicated. You would probably have to sell the car before you could use it to buy other goods and services. Cars are seldom exchanged directly for goods and services (except for other cars). Because

liquid asset:
an asset that can easily be
exchanged for goods and
services

cars are not a generally acceptable means of paying for other goods and services, we don't consider them to be money.

Money is the most liquid asset. A **liquid asset** is an asset that can easily be exchanged for goods and services. Cash is a liquid asset; a car is not. How liquid must an asset be before we consider it money? To answer this question, we must first consider the functions of money.

1.a. Functions of Money

Money serves four basic functions: it is a *medium of exchange,* a *unit of account,* a *store of value,* and a *standard of deferred payment.* Not all monies serve all of these functions equally well, as will be apparent in the following discussion. But to be money, an item must perform enough of these functions to induce people to use it.

1.a.1. Medium of Exchange   Money is a medium of exchange; it is used in exchange for goods and services. Sellers willingly accept money in payment for the products and services they produce. Without money, we would have to resort to *barter,* the direct exchange of goods and services for other goods and services.

For a barter system to work, there must be a *double coincidence of wants.* Suppose Bill is a carpenter and Jane is a plumber. In a monetary economy, when Bill needs plumbing repairs in his home, he simply pays Jane for the repairs using money. Because everyone wants money, money is an acceptable means of payment. In a barter economy, Bill must offer his services as a carpenter in exchange for Jane's work. If Jane does not want any carpentry work done, Bill and Jane cannot enter into a mutually beneficial transaction. Bill has to find a person who can do what he wants and also wants what he can do—there must be a double coincidence of wants.

The use of money as a medium of exchange lowers transaction costs.

The example of Bill and Jane illustrates the fact that barter is a lot less efficient than using money. This means that the cost of a transaction in a barter economy is higher than the cost of a transaction in a monetary economy. The use of money as a medium of exchange lowers transaction costs.

The people of Yap Island highly value and thus accept as their medium of exchange giant stones. But in most cultures, money must be portable in order to be an effective medium of exchange—a property the stone money of Yap Island clearly lacks. Another important property of money is *divisibility.* Money must be measurable in both small units (for low-value goods and services) and large units (for high-value goods and services). Yap stone money is not divisible, so it is not a good medium of exchange for the majority of goods bought and sold.

1.a.2. Unit of Account   Money is a unit of account: We price goods and services in terms of money. This common unit of measurement allows us to compare relative values easily. If whole-wheat bread sells for a dollar a loaf and white bread sells for 50 cents, we know that whole-wheat bread is twice as expensive as white bread.

The use of money as a unit of account lowers information costs.

Using money as a unit of account is efficient. It reduces the costs of gathering information on what things are worth. The use of money as a unit of account lowers information costs relative to barter. In a barter economy, people constantly have to evaluate the worth of the goods and services being offered. When money prices are placed on goods and services, their relative value is obvious.

Copyright © by Houghton Mifflin Company. All rights reserved.

1.a.3. Store of Value

Money functions as a store of value or purchasing power. If you are paid today, you do not have to hurry out to spend your money. It will still have value next week or next month. Some monies retain their value better than others. In colonial New England, fish and furs both served as money. But because fish does not store as well as furs, its usefulness as a store of value was limited. An important property of a money is its *durability*, its ability to retain its value over time.

Inflation plays a major role in determining the effectiveness of a money as a store of value. The higher the rate of inflation, the faster the purchasing power of money falls. In high-inflation countries, workers spend their pay as fast as possible because the purchasing power of their money is falling rapidly. It makes no sense to hold on to a money that is quickly losing value. In countries where the domestic money does not serve as a good store of value, it ceases to fulfill this function of money and people begin to use something else as money, like the currency of another nation. For instance, U.S. dollars have long been a favorite store of value in Latin American countries that have experienced high inflation. This phenomenon—**currency substitution**—has been documented in Argentina, Bolivia, Mexico, and other countries during times of high inflation.

currency substitution:
the use of foreign money as a substitute for domestic money when the domestic economy has a high rate of inflation

1.a.4. Standard of Deferred Payment

Finally, money is a standard of deferred payment. Debt obligations are written in terms of money values. If you have a credit card bill that is due in 90 days, the value you owe is stated in monetary units—for example, dollars in the United States and yen in Japan. We use money values to state amounts of debt and use money to pay our debts.

We should make a distinction here between money and credit. Money is what we use to pay for goods and services. **Credit** is available savings that are lent to borrowers to spend. If you use your Visa or MasterCard to buy a shirt, you are not buying the shirt with your money. You are taking out a loan from the bank that issued the credit card in order to buy the shirt. Credit and money are different. Money is an asset, something you own. Credit is *debt*, something you owe.

credit:
available savings that are lent to borrowers to spend

1.b. The U.S. Money Supply

How is the U.S. money supply defined?

The quantity of money available for spending is an important determinant of many key macroeconomic variables, since changes in the money supply affect interest rates, inflation, and other indicators of economic health. When economists measure the money supply, they measure spendable assets. Identifying those assets, however, can be difficult. Although it would seem that *all* bank deposits are money, some bank deposits are held for spending while others are held for saving. In defining the money supply, then, economists must differentiate among assets on the basis of their liquidity and the likelihood of their being used for spending.

The problem of distinguishing among assets has produced several definitions of the money supply: M1, M2, and M3. Economists and policymakers use all three definitions to evaluate the availability of funds for spending. Although economists have tried to identify a single measure that best influences the business cycle and changes in interest rates and inflation, research indicates that different definitions work better to explain changes in macroeconomic variables at different times.

Copyright © by Houghton Mifflin Company. All rights reserved.

M1 money supply:
financial assets that are the most liquid

transactions account:
a checking account at a bank or other financial institution that can be drawn on to make payments

1.b.1. M1 Money Supply

The narrowest and most liquid measure of the money supply is the **M1 money supply,** the financial assets that are immediately available for spending. This definition emphasizes the use of money as a medium of exchange. The M1 money supply consists of currency, travelers' checks, demand deposits, and other checkable deposits. Demand and other checkable deposits are **transactions accounts**; they can be used to make direct payments to a third party.

Surveys find that families use their main checking account for about 40 percent of purchases. (The *main checking account* is the one a household uses most frequently.) Cash transactions account for about 35 percent of purchases. Other checking accounts are used for about 10 percent of expenditures.

The components of the M1 money supply are used for about 85 percent of family purchases. This is one reason why the M1 money supply may be a useful variable in formulating macroeconomic policy.

- *Currency* includes coins and paper money in circulation (in the hands of the public). In 1998, currency represented 39 percent of the M1 money supply. A common misconception about currency today is that it is backed by gold or silver. This is not true. There is nothing backing the U.S. dollar except the confidence of the public. This kind of monetary system is called a *fiduciary monetary system.* Fiduciary comes from the Latin *fiducia,* which means "trust." Our monetary system is based on trust. As long as we believe that our money is an acceptable form of payment for goods and services, the system works. It is not necessary for money to be backed by any precious object. As long as people believe that a money has value, it will serve as money.

  The United States has not always operated under a fiduciary monetary system. At one time the U.S. government issued gold and silver coins and paper money that could be exchanged for silver. In 1967, Congress authorized the U.S. Treasury to stop redeeming "silver certificate" paper money for silver. Coins with an intrinsic value are known as *commodity money*; they have value as a commodity in addition to their face value. The problem with commodity money is that as the value of the commodity increases, the money stops being circulated. People hoard coins when their commodity value exceeds their face value. For example, no one would take an old $20 gold piece to the grocery store to buy $20 worth of groceries because the gold is worth much more than $20 today.

  The tendency to hoard money as its commodity value increases is called *Gresham's Law*. Thomas Gresham was a successful businessman and financial adviser to Queen Elizabeth I. He insisted that if two coins have the same face value but different intrinsic values—perhaps one is silver and the other brass—the cheaper coin will be used in exchange while the more expensive coin will be hoarded. People sometimes state Gresham's Law as "bad money drives out good money," meaning that the money with the low commodity value will be used in exchange while the money with the high commodity value will be driven out of hand-to-hand use and be hoarded.[1]

According to Gresham's Law, bad money drives out good money.

[1]Actually, Gresham was not the first to recognize that bad money drives out good money. A fourteenth-century French theologian, Nicholas Oresme, made the same argument in his book *A Treatise on the Origin, Nature, Law, and Alterations of Money,* written almost 200 years before Gresham was born.

Copyright © by Houghton Mifflin Company. All rights reserved.

- *Travelers' checks* Outstanding U.S. dollar-denominated travelers' checks issued by nonbank institutions are counted as part of the M1 money supply. There are several nonbank issuers, among them American Express and Cook's. (Travelers' checks issued by banks are included in demand deposits. When a bank issues its own travelers' checks, it deposits the amount paid by the purchaser in a special account that is used to redeem the checks. Because this amount is counted as part of demand deposits, it is not counted again as part of outstanding travelers' checks.) Travelers' checks accounted for less than 1 percent of the M1 money supply in 1998.

- *Demand deposits* Demand deposits are checking account deposits at a commercial bank. These deposits pay no interest. They are called *demand deposits* because the bank must pay the amount of the check immediately on the demand of the depositor. Demand deposits accounted for 37 percent of the M1 money supply in 1998.

- *Other checkable deposits* Until the 1980s, demand deposits were the only kind of checking account. Today there are many different kinds of checking accounts, known as *other checkable deposits (OCDs)*. OCDs are accounts at financial institutions that pay interest and give the depositor check-writing privileges. Among the OCDs included in the M1 money supply are the following:

  Negotiable orders of withdrawal (NOW) accounts are interest-bearing checking accounts offered by savings and loan institutions.

  Automatic transfer system (ATS) accounts are accounts at commercial banks that combine an interest-bearing savings account with a non-interest-bearing checking account. The depositor keeps a small balance in the checking account; anytime the checking account balance is overdrawn, funds automatically are transferred from the savings account.

  Credit union share draft accounts are interest-bearing checking accounts that credit unions offer their members.

  Demand deposits at mutual savings banks are checking account deposits at nonprofit savings and loan organizations. Any profits after operating expenses have been paid may be distributed to depositors.

1.b.2. M2 Money Supply The components of the M1 money supply are the most liquid assets, the assets most likely to be used for transactions. M2 is a broader definition of the money supply that includes assets in somewhat less liquid forms. The M2 money supply includes the M1 money supply plus savings and small-denomination time deposits, and balances in retail money market mutual funds.

- *Savings deposits* are accounts at banks and savings and loan associations that earn interest but offer no check-writing privileges.

- *Small-denomination time deposits* are often called *certificates of deposit*. Funds in these accounts must be deposited for a specified period of time. (*Small* means less than $100,000.)

- *Retail money market mutual fund balances* combine the deposits of many individuals and invest them in government Treasury bills and other short-term securities. Many money market mutual funds grant check-writing privileges but limit the size and number of checks.

Copyright © by Houghton Mifflin Company. All rights reserved.

1.b.3. M3 Money Supply
The M3 money supply equals the M2 money supply plus *large time deposits* (deposits in amounts of $100,000 or more), *repurchase agreements, Eurodollar deposits*, and *institution-only money market mutual fund balances* (that do not include the balances of individuals). These additional assets are less liquid than those found in the M1 or M2 money supply. Figure 1 summarizes the three definitions of the money supply.

■ *A repurchase agreement (RP)* is an agreement between a bank and a customer under which the customer buys U.S. government securities from the bank one day and then sells them back to the bank later at a price that includes the interest earned overnight. Overnight RPs are used by firms that have excess cash one day that may be needed the next.

■ *Eurodollar deposits* are deposits denominated in dollars but held outside the U.S. domestic bank industry.

1.c. Global Money

How do countries pay for international transactions?

So far we have discussed the money supply in a domestic context. Just as the United States uses dollars as its domestic money, every nation has its own monetary unit of account. Japan has the yen, Mexico the peso, Canada the Canadian dollar, and so on. Since each nation uses a different money, how do countries pay for transactions that involve residents of other countries? As you saw in Chapter 7, the foreign exchange market links national monies together, so that transactions can be made across national borders. If Sears in the United States buys a home entertainment system from Sony in Japan, Sears can exchange dollars for yen in order to pay Sony in yen. The exchange rate between the dollar and yen determines how many dollars are needed to purchase the required number of yen. For instance, if Sony wants 1,000,000 yen for the component and the exchange rate is ¥100 = $1, Sears needs $10,000 (1,000,000/100) to buy the yen.

Sales contracts between developed countries usually are written (invoiced) in the national currency of the exporter. To complete the transaction, the importer buys the exporter's currency on the foreign exchange market. Trade between developing and developed nations typically is invoiced in the currency of the developed country, whether the developed country is the exporter or importer because the currency of the developed country is usually more stable and more widely traded on the foreign exchange market than the currency of the developing country. As a result, the currencies of the major developed countries tend to dominate the international medium-of-exchange and unit-of-account functions of money.

The currencies of the major developed countries tend to dominate the international medium-of-exchange and unit-of-account functions of money.

international reserve asset:
an asset used to settle debts between governments

international reserve currency:
a currency held by a government to settle international debts

1.c.1. International Reserve Currencies
Governments hold monies as a temporary store of value until money is needed to settle international debts. At one time gold was the primary **international reserve asset,** an asset used to settle debts between governments. Although gold still serves as an international reserve asset, its role is unimportant relative to that of currencies. Today national currencies function as international reserves. The currencies that are held for this purpose are called **international reserve currencies**.

Copyright © by Houghton Mifflin Company. All rights reserved.

Copyright © by Houghton Mifflin Company. All rights reserved.

Figure 1
The U.S. Money Supply:
M1, M2, M3 (billions
of dollars)

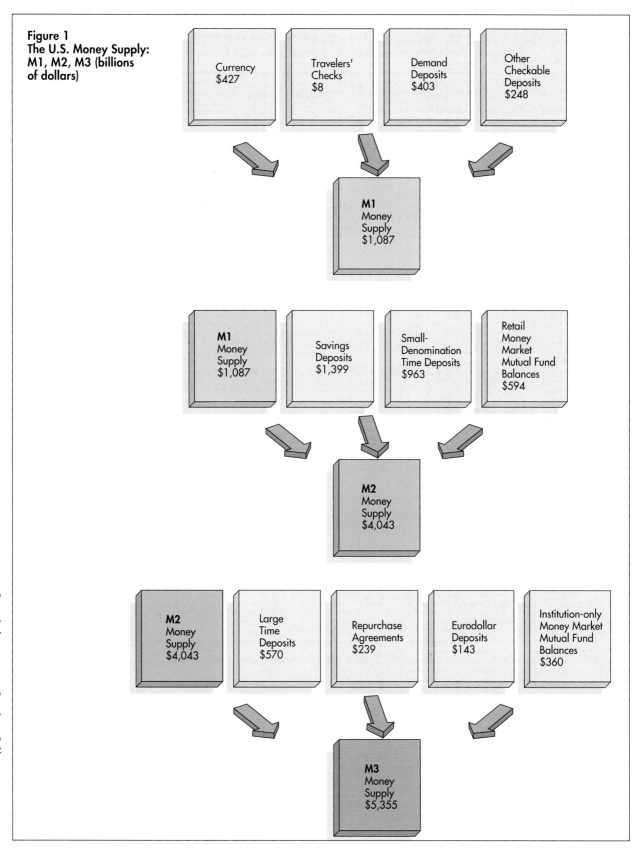

TABLE 1
International reserve currencies (percentage shares of national currencies in total official holdings of foreign exchange)

Year	U.S. Dollar	Pound Sterling	Deutsche Mark	French Franc	Japanese Yen	Swiss Franc	Netherlands Guilder	ECUs	Unspecified Currencies
1976	78.8	1.0	8.7	1.5	1.9	2.1	0.8	—	5.2
1980	56.6	2.5	12.8	1.5	3.7	2.8	1.1	16.4	2.7
1990	49.6	3.1	18.7	2.0	8.6	1.5	1.1	8.2	7.2
1996	58.9	3.4	13.6	1.6	6.0	0.7	0.3	5.9	9.5

Source: International Monetary Fund, *Annual Report*.

Table 1 shows the importance of the major international reserve currencies over time. In the mid-1970s, the U.S. dollar comprised almost 80 percent of international reserve holdings. By 1990 its share had fallen to less than 50 percent, but the share has risen again recently.

1.c.2. Composite Currencies   The industrial nations of western Europe introduced a new unit of currency, the **European currency unit (ECU)**, in March 1979. These nations use ECUs to settle debts between them. The ECU is a **composite currency**; its value is an average of the values of several different national currencies: the Austrian schilling, the Belgian franc, the Danish krone, the Finnish markkaa, the French franc, the German mark, the Greek drachma, the Irish pound, the Italian lira, the Luxembourg franc, the Netherlands guilder, the Spanish peseta, and the Portuguese escudo (the U.K. pound was withdrawn from the system in September 1992). The European Monetary System, an organization made up of the participating nations, determines the amount of each currency that is used to make up the ECU and regularly publishes its value.

The ECU is not an actual money but an accounting entry transferred between two parties. However, there will soon be an actual money, *the euro,* which will replace the ECU and circulate throughout the member countries as a European money. Ultimately, each country will eliminate its national money and adopt the euro as its money.

Another composite currency used in international financial transactions is the **special drawing right (SDR)**. The value of the SDR is an average of the values of the currencies of the five major industrial countries: the U.S. dollar, the French franc, the German mark, the Japanese yen, and the U.K. pound. This currency was created in 1970 by the International Monetary Fund, an international organization that oversees the monetary relationships among countries. SDRs, like ECUs, are an international reserve asset; they are used to settle international debts by transferring governments' accounts held at the International Monetary Fund. We discuss the SDR and the role of the International Monetary Fund in later chapters.

European currency unit (ECU):
a unit of account used by western European nations as their official reserve asset

composite currency:
an artificial unit of account that is an average of the values of several national currencies

special drawing right (SDR):
a composite currency whose value is the average of the value of the U.S. dollar, the French franc, the German mark, the Japanese yen, and the U.K. pound

Copyright © by Houghton Mifflin Company. All rights reserved.

RECAP

1. Money is the most liquid asset.

2. Money serves as a medium of exchange, a unit of account, a store of value, and a standard of deferred payment.

3. The use of money lowers transaction and information costs relative to barter.

4. To be used as money, an asset should be portable, divisible, and durable.

5. The M1 money supply is the most liquid definition of money and equals the sum of currency, travelers' checks, demand deposits, and other checkable deposits.

6. The M2 money supply equals the sum of the M1 money supply, savings and small-denomination time deposits, and retail money market mutual fund balances.

7. The M3 money supply equals the sum of the M2 money supply, large time deposits, repurchase agreements, Eurodollar deposits, and institution-only money market mutual fund balances.

8. International reserve currencies are held by governments to settle international debts.

9. ECUs and SDRs are composite currencies; their value is an average of the values of several national currencies.

2. BANKING

Commercial banks are financial institutions that offer deposits on which checks can be written. In the United States and most other countries, commercial banks are privately owned. *Thrift institutions* are financial institutions that historically offered just savings accounts, not checking accounts. Savings and loan associations, credit unions, and mutual savings banks are all thrift institutions. Prior to 1980, the differences between commercial banks and thrift institutions were much greater than they are today. For example, only commercial banks could offer checking accounts, and those accounts earned no interest. The law also regulated maximum interest rates. In 1980 Congress passed the Depository Institutions Deregulation and Monetary Control Act, in part to stimulate competition among financial institutions. Now thrift institutions and even brokerage houses offer many of the same services as commercial banks.

2.a. Financial Intermediaries

Why are banks considered intermediaries?

Both commercial banks and thrift institutions are *financial intermediaries,* middlemen between savers and borrowers. Banks accept deposits from individuals and firms, then use those deposits to make loans to individuals and firms. The borrowers are likely to be different individuals or firms from the depositors, although it is not uncommon for a household or business to be both a depositor and a borrower at the same institution. Of course, depositors and borrowers have very different interests. For instance, depositors typically prefer short-term deposits; they don't want to tie their money up for a long time. Borrowers, on the other hand, usually want more time for repayment.

Copyright © by Houghton Mifflin Company. All rights reserved.

Banks typically package short-term deposits into longer-term loans. To function as intermediaries, banks must serve the interests of both depositors and borrowers.

A bank is willing to serve as an intermediary because it hopes to earn a profit from this activity. It pays a lower interest rate on deposits than it charges on loans; the difference is a source of profit for the bank. Islamic banks are prohibited by holy law from charging interest on loans; thus they use a different system for making a profit (see the Economic Insight "Islamic Banking").

2.b. U.S. Banking

2.b.1. Current Structure   Banking in the United States went through many changes in the 1980s. The Depository Institutions Deregulation and Monetary Control Act narrowed the distinction between commercial banks and thrift institutions. The act also narrowed the distinctions among commercial banks. If you add together all the pieces of the pie chart in Figure 2, you see that there were 66,767 banking offices operating in the United States at the end of 1996. Roughly half these offices were operated by *national banks*, banks chartered by the federal government; the other half, by *state banks*, banks chartered under state laws. Before the deregulation act was passed, the regulations placed on national banks were more stringent than the regulations placed on state banks. The deregulation act made the regulations affecting state and national banks more equal.

Another change that has taken place in the U.S. bank market is the growth of interstate banking. Historically, banks were allowed to operate in just one state. In some states, banks could operate in only one location. This is known as *unit banking*. Today there are still many unit banks, but these are typically small community banks. Figure 2 shows that at the end of 1996 less than half of all state banks (2,457) and national banks (821) operated as unit banks; the rest operated 26,450 state branch offices and 30,809 national branch offices.

Over time, legal barriers have been reduced so that today almost all states permit entry to banks located out of state. In the future, banking is likely to be

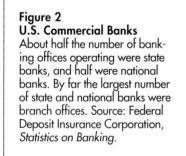

Figure 2
U.S. Commercial Banks
About half the number of banking offices operating were state banks, and half were national banks. By far the largest number of state and national banks were branch offices. Source: Federal Deposit Insurance Corporation, *Statistics on Banking.*

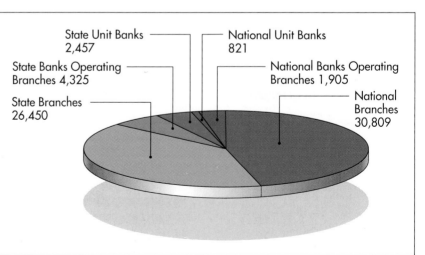

State Unit Banks 2,457

State Banks Operating Branches 4,325

State Branches 26,450

National Unit Banks 821

National Banks Operating Branches 1,905

National Branches 30,809

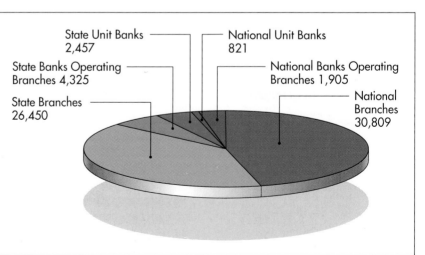

Copyright © by Houghton Mifflin Company. All rights reserved.

Islamic Banking

According to the Muslim holy book, the Koran, Islamic law prohibits interest charges on loans. Banks that operate under Islamic law still act as intermediaries between borrowers and lenders. However, they do not charge interest on loans or pay interest on deposits. Instead they take a pre-determined percentage of the borrowing firm's profits until the loan is repaid, then share those profits with depositors.

Since the mid-1970s, over a hundred Islamic banks have opened, most in Arab nations. Deposits in these banks have grown rapidly. In fact, in some banks deposits have grown faster than good loan opportunities, forcing the banks to

refuse new deposits until their loan portfolio could grow to match available deposits. One bank in Bahrain claimed that over 60 percent of deposits during its first two years in operation were made by people who had never made a bank deposit before.

In addition to profit-sharing deposits, Islamic banks typically offer checking accounts, travelers' checks, and trade-related services on a fee basis. The return on profit-sharing deposits has fluctuated with regional economic conditions. In the late 1970s and early 1980s, when oil prices were high, returns were higher than they were in the mid-1980s, when oil prices were depressed.

Because the growth of deposits has usually exceeded the growth of local investment opportunities, Islamic banks have been lending money to traditional banks, to fund investments that satisfy the moral and commercial needs of both, such as lending to private firms. These funds cannot be used to invest in interest-bearing securities or in firms that deal in alcohol, pork, gambling, or arms. The growth of mutually profitable investment opportunities suggests that Islamic banks are meeting both the dictates of Muslim depositors and the profitability requirements of modern banking.

done on a national rather than a local scale. The growth of automated teller machines (ATMs) is a big step in this direction. ATM networks give bank customers access to services over a much wider geographic area than any single bank's branches cover. These international networks allow a bank customer from Dallas to withdraw cash in Seattle, Zurich, or almost anywhere in the world. Today more than one-fourth of ATM transactions occur at banks that are not the customer's own bank.

2.b.2. Bank Failures
Banking in the United States has had a colorful history of booms and panics. Banking is like any other business. Banks that are poorly managed can fail; banks that are properly managed tend to prosper. Regional economic conditions are also very important. In the mid-1980s, hundreds of banks in states with large oil industries, like Texas and Oklahoma, and farming states, like Kansas and Nebraska, could not collect many of their loans due to falling oil and agricultural prices. Those states that are heavily dependent on the oil industry and farming had significantly more banks fail than did other states. The problem was not so much bad management as it was a matter of unexpectedly bad business conditions. The lesson here is simple: commercial banks, like other profit-making enterprises, are not exempt from failure.

A bank panic occurs when depositors become frightened and rush to withdraw their funds.

Federal Deposit Insurance Corporation (FDIC): a federal agency that insures deposits in commercial banks

At one time a bank panic could close a bank. A bank panic occurs when depositors, fearing a bank's closing, rush to withdraw their funds. Banks keep only a fraction of their deposits on reserve, so bank panics often result in bank closings as depositors try to withdraw more money than the banks have on a given day. In the United States today, this is no longer true. The **Federal Deposit Insurance Corporation (FDIC)** was created in 1933. The FDIC is

Copyright © by Houghton Mifflin Company. All rights reserved.

a federal agency that insures bank deposits in commercial banks so that depositors do not lose their deposits when a bank fails. Figure 3 shows the number of failed banks and the number without deposit insurance. In the 1930s, many of the banks that failed were not insured by the FDIC. In this environment, it made sense for depositors to worry about losing their money. In the 1980s, the number of bank failures increased dramatically, but none of the failed banks were uninsured. Deposits in those banks were protected by the federal government. Even though large banks have failed in recent times, the depositors have not lost their deposits.

2.c. International Banking

How does international banking differ from domestic banking?

Large banks today are truly transnational enterprises. International banks, like domestic banks, act as financial intermediaries, but they operate in a different legal environment. The laws regulating domestic banking in each nation are typically very restrictive, yet many nations allow international banking to operate largely unregulated. Because they are not hampered by regulations, international banks typically can offer depositors and borrowers better terms than could be negotiated at a domestic bank.

2.c.1. Eurocurrency Market

Eurocurrency market (offshore banking):
the market for deposits and loans generally denominated in a currency other than the currency of the country in which the transaction occurs

Because of the competitive interest rates offered on loans and deposits, there is a large market for deposits and loans at international banks. For instance, a bank in London, Tokyo, or the Bahamas may accept deposits and make loans denominated in U.S. dollars. The international deposit and loan market often is called the **Eurocurrency market,** or **offshore banking.** In the Eurocurrency market, the currency used in a banking transaction generally is not the domestic currency of the country in which the bank is located. (The prefix *Euro* is misleading here. Although the market originated in Europe, today the market is global and operates with different foreign currencies; it is in no way limited to European currencies or European banks.)

In those countries that allow offshore banking, we find two sets of banking rules: restrictive regulations for banking in the domestic market and little or no regulation of offshore-banking activities. Domestic banks are required

Copyright © by Houghton Mifflin Company. All rights reserved.

Figure 3
Number of Failed and Uninsured Banks
The number of banks that went out of business in the 1980s was the highest it had been since the Depression. Unlike the banks that failed in the 1930s, the banks that closed in the 1980s were covered by deposit insurance, so depositors did not lose their money. Source: Federal Deposit Insurance Corporation.

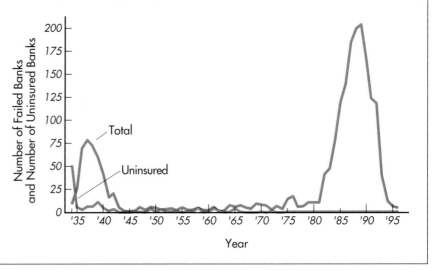

to hold reserves against deposits and to carry deposit insurance; and they often face government-mandated credit or interest rate restrictions. The Eurocurrency market operates with few or no costly restrictions, and international banks generally pay lower taxes than domestic banks. Because offshore banks operate with lower costs, they are able to offer better terms to their customers than domestic banks.

Figure 4 compares U.S. domestic deposit and loan rates with Eurodollar deposit and loan rates. (A U.S. dollar-denominated deposit outside the domestic U.S. banking industry is called a *Eurodollar deposit;* a U.S. dollar-denominated loan outside the domestic U.S. banking industry is called a *Eurodollar loan.*)

Offshore banks are able to offer a higher rate on dollar deposits and a lower rate on dollar loans than their domestic competitors. Without these differences, the Eurodollar market probably would not exist because Eurodollar transactions are riskier than domestic transactions in the United States, due to the lack of government regulation and deposit insurance.

There are always risks involved in international banking. Funds are subject to control both by the country in which the bank is located and the country in whose currency the deposit or loan is denominated. Suppose a Canadian firm wants to withdraw funds from a U.S. dollar-denominated bank deposit in Hong Kong. The transaction is subject to control in Hong Kong. For example, the government may not allow foreign exchange to leave the country freely. It is also subject to U.S. control. If the United States reduces its outflow of dollars, for instance, the Hong Kong bank may have difficulty paying the Canadian firm with U.S. dollars.

The Eurocurrency market exists for all of the major international currencies, but the value of activity in Eurodollars dwarfs the rest. Eurodollars account for about 60 percent of deposit and loan activity in the Eurocurrency market. This emphasizes the important role the U.S. dollar plays in global finance. Even deposits and loans that do not involve a U.S. lender or borrower often are denominated in U.S. dollars.

Copyright © by Houghton Mifflin Company. All rights reserved.

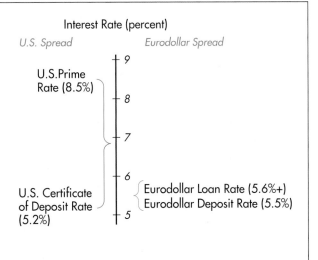

Figure 4
U.S. and Eurodollar Interest Rate Spreads
The U.S. deposit rate is the average rate paid on certificates of deposit by major New York banks. The U.S. loan rate is the *prime rate*, the rate banks charge their best corporate customers. The Eurodollar deposit rate is the rate offered on three-month deposits. The Eurodollar loan rate is the *London interbank offer rate*, the rate London banks charge for interbank deposits. The interest rate for nonbank borrowers will include an additional amount based on the creditworthiness of the borrower.

The *spread* is the difference between the interest rate for a deposit and the interest rate on a loan. Eurodollar spreads are narrower than U.S. spreads. This means that Eurodollar deposits offer a higher interest rate than U.S. bank deposits and that Eurodollar loans charge a lower interest rate than U.S. bank loans. Source: *The Wall Street Journal*, January 22, 1998, p. C28.

2.c.2. International Banking Facilities The term *offshore banking* is somewhat misleading in the United States today. Prior to December 1981, U.S. banks were forced to process international deposits and loans through their offshore branches. Many of the branches in places like the Cayman Islands and the Bahamas were little more than "shells," small offices with a telephone. Yet these branches allowed U.S. banks to avoid the reserve requirements and interest rate regulations that restricted domestic banking activities.

In December 1981, the Federal Reserve Board legalized **international banking facilities (IBFs),** allowing domestic banks to take part in international banking on U.S. soil. IBFs are not a physical entity; they are a bookkeeping system set up in existing bank offices to record international banking transactions. IBFs can receive deposits from and make loans to nonresidents of the United States or other IBFs. These deposits and loans must be kept separate from other transactions because IBFs are not subject to the reserve requirements, interest rate regulations, or FDIC deposit insurance premiums that apply to domestic U.S. banking.

The goal of the IBF plan was to allow banking offices in the United States to compete with offshore banks without having to use offshore banking offices. The location of IBFs reflects the location of banking activity in general. It is not surprising that 47 percent of IBFs are located in New York State, the financial center of the country. New York also receives over 75 percent of IBF deposits.

international banking facility (IBF):
a division of a U.S. bank that is allowed to receive deposits from and make loans to nonresidents of the United States without the restrictions that apply to domestic U.S. banks

RECAP

1. The Depository Institutions Deregulation and Monetary Control Act (1980) eliminated many of the differences between commercial banks and thrift institutions.
2. Banks are financial intermediaries.
3. The deregulation act also eliminated many of the differences between national and state banks.
4. Since the FDIC began insuring bank deposits in commercial banks, bank panics are no longer a threat to the banking system.
5. The international deposit and loan market is called the Eurocurrency market, or offshore banking.
6. With the legalization in 1981 of international banking facilities, the Federal Reserve allowed international banking activities on U.S. soil.

3. BANKS AND THE MONEY SUPPLY

How do banks create money?

fractional reserve banking system:
a system in which banks keep less than 100 percent of the deposits available for withdrawal

Banks create money by lending money. They take deposits, then lend a portion of those deposits in order to earn interest income. The portion of deposits that banks keep on hand is a *reserve* to meet the demand for withdrawals. In a **fractional reserve banking system,** banks keep less than 100 percent of their deposits on reserve. If all banks hold 10 percent of their deposits as a reserve, for example, then 90 percent of their deposits are available for loans. When they loan these deposits, money is created.

Copyright © by Houghton Mifflin Company. All rights reserved.

3.a. Deposits and Loans

Figure 5 shows a simple balance sheet for First National Bank. A *balance sheet* is a financial statement that records a firm's assets (what the firm owns) and liabilities (what the firm owes). The bank has cash assets ($100,000) and loan assets ($900,000). The deposits placed in the bank ($1,000,000) are a liability (they are an asset of the depositors).[2] Total assets always equal total liabilities on a balance sheet.

Banks keep a percentage of their deposits on reserve. In the United States the reserve requirement is set by the Federal Reserve Board (which will be discussed in detail in the next chapter). Banks can keep more than the minimum reserve if they choose. Let's assume that the reserve requirement is set at 10 percent and that banks always hold actual reserves equal to 10 percent of deposits. With deposits of $1,000,000, the bank must keep $100,000 (.10 × $1,000,000) in cash reserves held in its vault. This $100,000 is the bank's **required reserves,** as the Federal Reserve requires the banks to keep 10 percent of deposits on reserve. This is exactly what First National Bank has on hand in Figure 5. Any cash held in excess of $100,000 would represent **excess reserves.** Excess reserves can be loaned by the bank. A bank is *loaned up* when it has zero excess reserves. Because its total reserves equal its required reserves, First National Bank has no excess reserves and is loaned up.

required reserves:
the cash reserves (a percentage of deposits) a bank must keep on hand

excess reserves:
the cash reserves beyond those required, which can be loaned

$$\text{Excess reserves} = \text{total reserves} - \text{required reserves}$$
$$= \$100,000 - \$100,000$$
$$= 0$$

The bank cannot make any new loans.

What happens if the bank receives a new deposit of $100,000? Figure 6 shows the bank's balance sheet right after the deposit is made. Its cash reserves are now $200,000, its deposits $1,100,000. With the additional deposit, the bank's total reserves equal $200,000. Its required reserves are $110,000 (.10 × $1,100,000). So its excess reserves are $90,000 ($200,000 − $110,000). Since a bank can lend its excess reserves, First National Bank can loan an additional $90,000.

---

[2]In our simplified balance sheet, we assume there is no net worth, or owner's equity. Net worth is the value of the owner's claim on the firm (the owner's equity) and is found as the difference between the value of assets and nonequity liabilities.

Figure 5
First National Bank Balance Sheet, Initial Position
The bank has cash totaling $100,000 and loans totaling $900,000, for total assets of $1,000,000. Deposits of $1,000,000 make up its total liabilities. With a reserve requirement of 10 percent, the bank must hold required reserves of 10 percent of its deposits, or $100,000. Because the bank is holding cash of $100,000, its total reserves equal its required reserves. Because it has no excess reserves, the bank cannot make new loans.

First National Bank

Assets		Liabilities	
Cash	$100,000	Deposits	$1,000,000
Loans	900,000		
Total	$1,000,000	Total	$1,000,000

Total reserves = $100,000
Required reserves = 0.1 ($1,000,000) = $100,000
Excess reserves = 0

Copyright © by Houghton Mifflin Company. All rights reserved.

Copyright © by Houghton Mifflin Company. All rights reserved.

Figure 6
First National Bank Balance Sheet After $100,000 Deposit

A $100,000 deposit increases the bank's cash reserves to $200,000 and deposits to $1,100,000. The bank must hold 10 percent of deposits, $110,000, on reserve. The difference between total reserves ($200,000) and required reserves ($110,000) is excess reserves ($90,000). The bank now has $90,000 available for lending.

First National Bank

Assets		Liabilities	
Cash	$200,000	Deposits	$1,100,000
Loans	900,000		
Total	$1,100,000	Total	$1,100,000

Total reserves = $200,000
Required reserves = 0.1 ($1,100,000) = $110,000
Excess reserves = $90,000

Suppose the bank lends someone $90,000 by depositing $90,000 in the borrower's First National account. At the time the loan is made, the money supply increases by the amount of the loan, $90,000. By making the loan, the bank has increased the money supply. But this is not the end of the story. The borrower spends the $90,000, and it winds up being deposited in the Second National Bank.

Figure 7 shows the balance sheets of both banks after the loan is made and the money is spent and deposited at Second National Bank. First National Bank now has loans of $990,000 and no excess reserves (the required reserves of $110,000 equal total reserves). So First National Bank can make no more loans until a new deposit is made. Second National Bank has a new deposit of $90,000 (to simplify the analysis, we assume that this is the first transaction at Second National Bank). Its required reserves are 10 percent of $90,000, or $9,000. With total reserves of $90,000, Second National Bank has excess reserves of $81,000. It can make loans up to $81,000.

Notice what has happened to the banks' deposits as a result of the initial $100,000 deposit in First National Bank. Deposits at First National Bank have increased by $100,000. Second National Bank has a new deposit of $90,000, and the loans it makes will increase the money supply even more. Table 2 shows how the initial deposit of $100,000 is multiplied through the banking system. Each time a new loan is made, the money is spent and redeposited in the banking system. But each bank keeps 10 percent of the deposit on reserve, lending only 90 percent. So the amount of money loaned decreases by 10 percent each time it goes through another bank. If we carried the calculations out, you would see that the total increase in deposits associated with the initial $100,000 deposit is $1,000,000. Required reserves would increase by $100,000, and new loans would increase by $900,000.

3.b. Deposit Expansion Multiplier

Rather than calculate the excess reserves at each bank, as we did in Table 2, we can use a simple formula to find the maximum increase in deposits given a new deposit. The **deposit expansion multiplier** equals the reciprocal of the reserve requirement:

deposit expansion multiplier: the reciprocal of the reserve requirement

$$\text{Deposit expansion multiplier} = \frac{1}{\text{reserve requirement}}$$

Figure 7
Balance Sheets After a $90,000 Loan Made by First National Bank Is Spent and Deposited at Second National Bank

Once First National Bank makes the $90,000 loan, its cash reserves fall to $110,000 and its loans increase to $990,000. At this point the bank's total reserves ($110,000) equal its required reserves (10 percent of deposits). Because it has no excess reserves, the bank cannot make new loans.

Second National Bank receives a deposit of $90,000. It must hold 10 percent, or $9,000, on reserve. Its excess reserves equal total reserves ($90,000) minus required reserves ($9,000), or $81,000. Second National Bank can make a maximum loan of $81,000.

First National Bank

Assets		Liabilities	
Cash	$110,000	Deposits	$1,100,000
Loans	990,000		
Total	$1,100,000	Total	$1,100,000

Total reserves = $110,000
Required reserves = 0.1 ($1,100,000) = $110,000
Excess reserves = 0

Second National Bank

Assets		Liabilities	
Cash	$90,000	Deposits	$90,000
Total	$90,000	Total	$90,000

Total reserves = $90,000
Required reserves = 0.1 ($90,000) = $9,000
Excess reserves = $81,000

In our example, the reserve requirement is 10 percent, or .10. So the deposit expansion multiplier equals 1/.10, or 10. An initial increase in deposits of $100,000 expands deposits in the banking system by 10 times $100,000, or $1,000,000. The maximum increase in the money supply is found by multiplying the deposit expansion multiplier by the amount of the new deposit. With no new deposits, the banking system can increase the money supply only by the multiplier times excess reserves:

Deposit expansion multiplier × excess reserves
= maximum increase in money supply

TABLE 2
The Effect on Bank Deposits of an Initial Bank Deposit of $100,000

Bank	New Deposit	Required Reserves	Excess Reserves (new loans)
First National	$ 100,000	$ 10,000	$ 90,000
Second National	90,000	9,000	81,000
Third National	81,000	8,100	72,900
Fourth National	72,900	7,290	65,610
Fifth National	65,610	6,561	59,049
Sixth National	59,049	5,905	53,144
⋮	⋮	⋮	⋮
Total	$1,000,000	$100,000	$900,000

Copyright © by Houghton Mifflin Company. All rights reserved.

The deposit expansion multiplier indicates the *maximum* possible change in total deposits when a new deposit is made. For the effect to be that large, all excess reserves must be loaned out and all of the money that is deposited must stay in the banking system.

If banks hold more reserves than the minimum required, they lend a smaller fraction of any new deposits, which reduces the effect of the deposit expansion multiplier. For instance, if the reserve requirement is 10 percent, we know that the deposit expansion multiplier is 10. If a bank chooses to hold 20 percent of its deposits on reserve, the deposit expansion multiplier equals 5 (1/.20).

If money (currency and coin) is withdrawn from the banking system and kept as cash, deposits and bank reserves are smaller and less money exists to loan out. This *currency drain*—removal of money—reduces the deposit expansion multiplier. The greater the currency drain, the smaller the multiplier. There is always some currency drain as people carry currency to pay for day-to-day transactions. However, during historical periods of bank panic where people lost confidence in banks, large currency withdrawals contributed to declines in money supply.

A single bank increases the money supply by lending its excess reserves; the banking system increases the money supply by the deposit expansion multiplier times the excess reserves of the system.

Remember that the deposit expansion multiplier measures the *maximum* expansion of the money supply by the banking system. Any single bank can lend only its excess reserves, but the whole banking system can expand the money supply by a multiple of the initial excess reserves. Thus the banking system as a whole can increase the money supply by the deposit expansion multiplier times the excess reserves of the system. The initial bank is limited to its initial loan; the banking system generates loan after loan based on that initial loan. A new deposit can increase the money supply by the deposit expansion multiplier times the new deposit.

In the next chapter we discuss how changes in the reserve requirement affect the money supply and the economy. This area of policy making is controlled by the Federal Reserve.

RECAP

1. The fractional reserve banking system allows banks to expand the money supply by making loans.

2. Banks must keep a fraction of their deposits on reserve; their excess reserves are available for lending.

3. The deposit expansion multiplier measures the maximum increase in the money supply given a new deposit; it is the reciprocal of the reserve requirement.

4. A single bank increases the money supply by lending its excess reserves.

5. The banking system can increase the money supply by the deposit expansion multiplier times the excess reserves in the banking system.

SUMMARY

■■ What is money?

1. Money is anything that is generally acceptable to sellers in exchange for goods and services. §1

2. Money serves as a medium of exchange, a unit of account, a store of value, and a standard of deferred payment. §1.a

3. Money, because it is more efficient than barter, lowers transaction costs. §1.a.1

Copyright © by Houghton Mifflin Company. All rights reserved.

4. Money should be portable, divisible, and durable. §1.a.1, 1.a.3

How is the U.S. money supply defined?

5. There are three definitions of money based on its liquidity. §1.b

6. The M1 money supply equals the sum of currency plus travelers' checks plus demand deposits plus other checkable deposits. §1.b.1

7. The M2 money supply equals the M1 money supply plus savings and small-denomination time deposits, and retail money market mutual fund balances. §1.b.2

8. The M3 money supply equals the M2 money supply plus large time deposits, repurchase agreements, Eurodollar deposits, and institution-only money market mutual fund balances. §1.b.3

How do countries pay for international transactions?

9. Using the foreign exchange market, governments (along with individuals and firms) are able to convert national currencies to pay for trade. §1.c

10. The U.S. dollar is the world's major international reserve currency. §1.c.1

11. The European currency unit (ECU) is a composite currency whose value is an average of the values of several western European currencies. §1.c.2

Why are banks considered intermediaries?

12. Banks serve as middlemen between savers and borrowers. §2.a

How does international banking differ from domestic banking?

13. Domestic banking in most nations is strictly regulated; international banking is not. §2.c

14. The Eurocurrency market is the international deposit and loan market. §2.c.1

15. International banking facilities (IBFs) allow U.S. domestic banks to carry on international banking activities on U.S. soil. §2.c.2

How do banks create money?

16. Banks can make loans up to the amount of their excess reserves, their total reserves minus their required reserves. §3.a

17. The deposit expansion multiplier is the reciprocal of the reserve requirement. §3.b

18. A single bank expands the money supply by lending its excess reserves. §3.b

19. The banking system can increase the money supply by the deposit expansion multiplier times the excess reserves in the system. §3.b

KEY TERMS

money §1

liquid asset §1

currency substitution §1.a.3

credit §1.a.4

M1 money supply §1.b.1

transactions account §1.b.1

international reserve asset §1.c.1

international reserve currency §1.c.1

European currency unit (ECU) §1.c.2

composite currency §1.c.2

special drawing right (SDR) §1.c.2

Federal Deposit Insurance Corporation (FDIC) §2.b.2

Eurocurrency market (offshore banking) §2.c.1

international banking facility (IBF) §2.c.2

fractional reserve banking system §3

required reserves §3.a

excess reserves §3.a

deposit expansion multiplier §3.b

Copyright © by Houghton Mifflin Company. All rights reserved.

EXERCISES

1. Describe the four functions of money using the U.S. dollar to provide an example of how dollars serve each function.

2. Discuss how the following would serve the functions of money.

   a. Gold

   b. Yap stone money

   c. Cigarettes

   d. Diamonds

3. What is a financial intermediary? Give an example of how your bank or credit union serves as a financial intermediary between you and the rest of the economy.

4. What is the Eurocurrency market, and how is banking in the Eurocurrency market different from domestic banking?

5. What are IBFs? Why do you think they were legalized?

6. First Bank has cash reserves of $200,000, loans of $800,000, and deposits of $1,000,000.

   a. Prepare a balance sheet for the bank.

   b. If the bank maintains a reserve requirement of 12 percent, what is the largest loan it can make?

   c. What is the maximum amount the money supply can be increased as a result of First Bank's new loan?

7. Yesterday bank A had no excess reserves. Today it received a new deposit of $5,000.

   a. If the bank maintains a reserve requirement of 2 percent, what is the maximum loan bank A can make?

   b. What is the maximum amount the money supply can be increased as a result of bank A's new loan?

8. "M2 is a better definition of the money supply than M1." Agree or disagree with this statement. In your argument, clearly state the criteria on which you are basing your decision.

9. The deposit expansion multiplier measures the maximum possible expansion of the money supply in the banking system. What factors could cause the actual expansion of the money supply to differ from that given by the deposit expansion multiplier?

10. What is liquidity? Rank the following assets in order of their liquidity: $10 bill, personal check for $20, savings account with $400 in it, stereo, car, house, travelers' check.

Use the following table on the components of money in a hypothetical economy to answer questions 11–13.

Money Component	Amount
Travelers' checks	$ 100
Currency	2,000
Small-denomination time deposits	3,500
Repurchase agreements	2,000
Demand deposits	5,000
Other checkable deposits	9,000
U.S. Treasury bonds	25,000
Large-denomination time deposits	8,000
Retail money market mutual funds	7,500

11. What is the value of M1 in the above table?

12. What is the value of M2 in the above table?

13. What is the value of M3 in the above table?

14. The deposit expansion multiplier has been defined as the reciprocal of the reserve requirement. Suppose that banks must hold 10 percent of their deposits in reserve. However, banks also lose 10 percent of their deposits through cash drains out of the banking system.

   a. What would the deposit expansion multiplier be if there were no cash drain?

   b. With the cash drain, what is the value of the deposit expansion multiplier?

Copyright © by Houghton Mifflin Company. All rights reserved.

INTERNET EXERCISE

Section 2.b of this chapter indicated that banks, like all other businesses, sometimes fail due to bad management or unexpectedly bad performance of certain key industries to which a bank has committed many loans. To see the recent experience of failed banks in the United States, go to the Boyes/Melvin web site at http://www.hmco.com/college/ and click on the internet exercise link for this chapter. Now answer the questions that appear on the web page.

Copyright © by Houghton Mifflin Company. All rights reserved.

The World Still Loves the Dollar

For the band of traders who peddle souvenirs to tourists taking in the sweeping view of the Russian capital near Moscow State University, there is one preferred currency for doing business: the U.S. dollar. Even the local police like their bribes in greenbacks.

Half a world away in the Cambodian capital, Phnom Penh, foreigners entering the country must pay for an entry visa, a hotel taxi and the hotel itself in a single currency: the U.S. dollar.

In Hamburg, Germany, a local trader buys oil from a Dutch company and ships it to Switzerland. The transaction is completed in a single currency: the U.S. dollar.

"It's the global currency," says Peter Stroink, a spokesman for Royal Dutch Shell in Rotterdam, the Netherlands. "That's the tradition, that's the reality." . . .

■ Cash. The U.S. Federal Reserve Board has found a steady increase in demand for cash dollars abroad since the early 1960s. In 1991, the latest year for which the Fed has figures, there were nearly twice as many greenbacks floating around outside the United States as there were within the 50 states.

Seven of every 10 $100 bills in circulation were estimated to be physically outside the United States in 1991, and Fed officials believe the share is higher today. "There's a large potential market out there, with the Russian appetite for dollars unslaked and the Chinese looming over the horizon," said Richard Porter, a Fed economist.

While America's position as the world's leading trading nation certainly helps keep the dollar popular, the American currency is also easy to use.

Like a bottle of Coke or a pair of Levi's, the dollar is instantly recognizable. Unlike those of other major currencies such as the yen, the mark and the Swiss franc, all dollar denominations are the same size, shape and color. What's more, U.S. paper money has not changed in more than half a century. . . .

The Russian language probably has more words for the dollar than for the ruble: baksi (bucks), zelyonyiye (green), kapusta (cabbage), krop (dill), zelon (green herbs) and even just green in accented English.

"There's no currency here more widely accepted than American dollars," said Igor Doronin, chief adviser of the Moscow Interbank Currency Exchange. "Just try to use Swiss francs or Japanese yen here. No one will take them. No one knows what they are."

The story is similar almost everywhere.

In Rio de Janeiro: "When people come from Europe or Asia or other countries, they don't bring their money; they bring dollars because they know they can get a better exchange rate," said Fabio Mamedio, whose downtown Rio travel agencies have changed money for years. "If they bring yen or francs, I charge them an extra 10% because there's no demand for it.". . .

A standing joke in Warsaw holds that the only similarity between the United States and Communist-era Poland was that a dollar could buy anything in either country, while the Polish zloty was worthless in both.

Although the post-Communist zloty has become a currency of genuine value, the dollar remains king in Poland. Buy a foreign car in Warsaw and the price is in dollars. . . .

In July, Brazil introduced a new currency, the real, and pegged its value to that of the U.S. dollar. That brought inflation down to about 2% in August from the 50% rate in June, the last month of the cruzeiro.

But the public remains understandably jittery. Rosanna Gois, an administrative assistant at a Sao Paulo architectural firm, is just one of many Brazilians who are not quite ready to declare the government's new economic plan a success and give up their caches of dollars.

"These plans come and go," she said. "But I know that the dollar is always going to be there." . . .

Source: "The World Still Loves the Dollar," by Tyler Marshall. From *Los Angeles Times*, October 9, 1994, p. A1. Copyright © 1994, *Los Angeles Times*. Reprinted by permission.

Los Angeles Times/October 9, 1994

Copyright © by Houghton Mifflin Company. All rights reserved.

COMMENTARY

There is considerable evidence that U.S. dollars are held in large amounts in many developing countries. Residents of these countries hold dollars because their domestic inflation rate is (or has been) very high, and by holding dollars they can avoid the rapid erosion of purchasing power that is associated with holding domestic currency. This "dollarization" of a country begins with people holding dollars as savings rather than domestic currency (the store-of value function of money). But if high inflation continues, dollars, rather than domestic currency, come to be used in day-to-day transactions as the medium of exchange. The article notes that even taxi drivers in Cambodia want dollars. In the late 1980s, as the Polish economy became heavily dollarized, a common joke in Poland was: "What do America and Poland have in common? In America, you can buy everything for dollars and nothing for zlotys [the Polish currency]. In Poland, it is exactly the same."

One implication of the demand for dollars in developing countries is that dollar currency leaves the United States. This currency drain will affect the size of the deposit expansion multiplier. In the chapter, the deposit expansion multiplier was defined as:

$$\text{Deposit expansion multiplier} = \frac{1}{\text{reserve requirement}}$$

This definition was based on the assumption that when a bank receives a deposit, all of the deposit will be loaned except for the fraction the bank is required to keep by the legal reserve requirement set by the Federal Reserve. With a currency drain, some of the deposit is withdrawn from the banking system as cash. As a result, the deposit expansion multiplier is now:

$$\text{Deposit expansion multiplier} = \frac{1}{(\text{reserve requirement} + \text{currency drain})}$$

For instance, if the reserve requirement equals 10 percent, our original definition of the deposit expansion multiplier would have a multiplier equal to $1/.10 = 10$. But if people withdraw 10 percent of their deposits as cash, then the 10 percent currency drain is added to the 10 percent reserve requirement to yield a deposit expansion multiplier of $1/.20 = 5$. So the larger the currency drain, the smaller the money-creating potential of the banking system.

An additional interesting aspect of the foreign demand for dollars is the *seigniorage*, or revenue earned by the government from creating money. If it costs about 7 cents to print a dollar bill but the exchange value is a dollar's worth of goods and services, then the government earns about 93 cents for each dollar put in circulation. If foreigners hold U.S. currency, then the government earns a profit from providing a stable-valued dollar that people want to hold. However, we should not overestimate the value of this in terms of the U.S. government budget. Even if all the new currency issued by the U.S. government flowed out to the rest of the world, the seigniorage earned by the United States over the past decade would have averaged less than 1.7 percent of federal government revenue. This is most certainly an overestimate of the actual seigniorage return to the United States since only a fraction of U.S. currency actually leaves the country. Given the relatively insignificant revenue earned from seigniorage, it is not surprising that U.S. policy with regard to the dollarization of developing countries has largely been one of disinterest.

Copyright © by Houghton Mifflin Company. All rights reserved.

14

Monetary Policy

FUNDAMENTAL QUESTIONS

1. What does the Federal Reserve do?

2. How is monetary policy set?

3. What are the tools of monetary policy?

4. What role do central banks play in the foreign exchange market?

5. What are the determinants of the demand for money?

6. How does monetary policy affect the equilibrium level of real GDP?

Copyright © by Houghton Mifflin Company. All rights reserved.

I n the previous chapter, we saw how banks "create" money by making loans. However, that money must get into the system to begin with. Most of us never think about how money enters the economy. All we worry about is having money available when we need it. But there is a government body that controls the U.S. money supply, and in this chapter we will learn about this agency—the Federal Reserve system and the Board of Governors that oversees monetary policy.

Preview

The amount of money available for spending by individuals or businesses affects prices, interest rates, foreign exchange rates, and the level of income in the economy. Thus, having control of the money supply gives the Federal Reserve powerful influence over these important economic variables. As we learned in Chapter 12, fiscal policy, or the control of government spending and taxes, is one of two ways by which government can change the equilibrium level of real GDP. Monetary policy as carried out by the Federal Reserve is the other mechanism through which attempts are made to manage the economy. In this chapter we will also explore the tools of monetary policy and see how changes in the money supply affect the equilibrium level of real GDP. ■

Copyright © by Houghton Mifflin Company. All rights reserved.

1. THE FEDERAL RESERVE SYSTEM

The Federal Reserve is the central bank of the United States. A *central bank* performs several functions: accepting deposits from and making loans to commercial banks, acting as a banker for the federal government, and controlling the money supply. We discuss these functions in greater detail below, but first we look at the structure of the Federal Reserve System, or the Fed.

1.a. Structure of the Fed

What does the Federal Reserve do?

Congress created the Federal Reserve System in 1913, with the Federal Reserve Act. Bank panics and failures had convinced lawmakers that the United States needed an agency to control the money supply and make loans to commercial banks when those banks found themselves without sufficient reserves. Because Americans tended to distrust large banking interests, Congress called for a decentralized central bank. The Federal Reserve System divides the nation into twelve districts, each with its own Federal Reserve bank (Figure 1).

Figure 1
The Federal Reserve System

The Federal Reserve System divides the country into twelve districts. Each district has its own Federal Reserve bank, headquarters for Fed operations in that district.

For example, the First District bank is in Boston; the Twelfth is in San Francisco. There are also branch banks in Los Angeles, Miami, and other cities. Source: *Federal Reserve Bulletin* (Washington, D.C.).

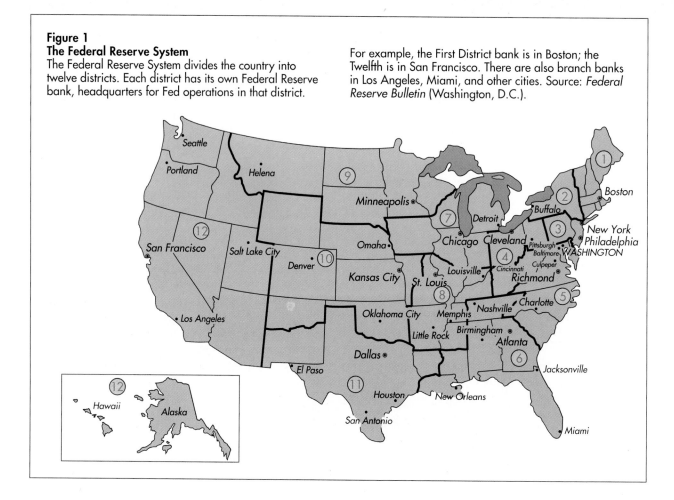

1.a.1. Board of Governors Although Congress created a decentralized system so that each district bank would represent the special interests of its own region, in practice the Fed is much more centralized than its creators intended. Monetary policy is largely set by the Board of Governors in Washington, D.C. This board is made up of seven members, who are appointed by the president and confirmed by the Senate.

The most visible and powerful member of the board is the chairman. In fact the chairman of the Board of Governors has been called *the second most powerful person in the United States.* This individual serves as a leader and spokesperson for the board, and typically exercises more authority in determining the course of monetary policy than do the other governors.

The chairman is appointed by the president to a four-year term. In recent years most chairmen have been reappointed to an additional term (Table 1). The governors serve fourteen-year terms, the terms staggered so that every two years a new position comes up for appointment. This system allows continuity in the policy-making process and is intended to place the board above politics. Congress created the Fed as an independent agency: monetary policy is supposed to be formulated independent of Congress and the president. Of course, this is impossible in practice because the president appoints and the Senate approves the members of the board. But because the governors serve fourteen-year terms, they outlast the president who appointed them.

Copyright © by Houghton Mifflin Company. All rights reserved.

TABLE 1
Recent Chairmen of the Federal Reserve Board

Name	Age at Appointment	Term Begins	Term Ends	Years of Tenure
William McChesney Martin	44	4/2/51	1/31/70	18.8
Arthur Burns	65	1/31/70	2/1/78	8.0
G. William Miller	52	3/8/78	8/6/79	1.4
Paul Volcker	51	8/6/79	8/5/87	8.0
Alan Greenspan	61	8/11/87		

1.a.2. District Banks Each of the Fed's twelve district banks is formally directed by a nine-person board of directors. Three directors represent commercial banks in the district, and three represent nonbanking business interests. These six individuals are elected by the Federal Reserve System member banks in the district. The three remaining directors are appointed by the Fed's Board of Governors. District bank directors are not involved in the day-to-day operations of the district banks, but they meet regularly to oversee bank operations. They also choose the president of the bank. The president, who is in charge of operations, participates in monetary policy making with the Board of Governors in Washington, D.C.

1.a.3. The Federal Open Market Committee The **Federal Open Market Committee (FOMC)** is the official policy-making body of the Federal Reserve System. The committee is made up of the seven members of the Board of Governors plus five of the twelve district bank presidents. All of the district bank presidents, except for the president of the Federal Reserve Bank of New York, take turns serving on the FOMC. Because the New York Fed actually carries out monetary policy, that bank's president is always on the committee. In section 2 we talk more about the FOMC's role and the tactics it uses.

Federal Open Market Committee (FOMC):
the official policy-making body of the Federal Reserve System

1.b. Functions of the Fed

The Federal Reserve System offers banking services to the banking community and the U.S. Treasury, and supervises the nation's banking system. The Fed also regulates the U.S. money supply.

1.b.1. Banking Services and Supervision The Fed provides several basic services to the banking community: it supplies currency to banks, holds their reserves, and clears checks. The Fed supplies U.S. currency (Federal Reserve notes) to the banking community through its twelve district banks. (See the Economic Insight "What's on a Dollar Bill?") Commercial banks in each district also hold reserves in the form of deposits at their district bank. In addition, the Fed makes loans to banks. In this sense, the Fed is a *banker's bank.* And the Fed clears checks, transferring funds to the banks where checks are deposited from the banks on which the checks are drawn.

The Fed also supervises the nation's banks, ensuring that they operate in a sound and prudent manner. And it acts as the banker for the U.S. government, selling U.S. government securities for the U.S. Treasury.

Copyright © by Houghton Mifflin Company. All rights reserved.

What's on a Dollar Bill?

The figure shows both sides of a dollar bill. We've numbered several elements for identification.

1. Currency is issued by the Federal Reserve System. The top of a dollar bill used to say "SILVER CERTIFICATE" where it now says "FEDERAL RESERVE NOTE." Silver certificates could be exchanged for silver dollars or silver bullion at the U.S. Treasury until 1967, when Congress authorized the Treasury to stop redeeming silver certificates.

2. Every dollar bill indicates which Federal Reserve bank issued it. The stamp with the *F* in the middle reads "FEDERAL RESERVE BANK OF ATLANTA GEORGIA." *F* is the sixth letter of the alphabet, and the Atlanta Fed is headquarters for the sixth Federal Reserve District. Also the serial number begins with an *F*. Finally, there is a number 6 in each corner, again indicating that the bill was issued by the Sixth District bank.

3. The dollar is the legal money of the United States. Debts and tax obligations can be legally discharged with dollars.

4. *D231* is the number of the engraving plate used to print this dollar bill.

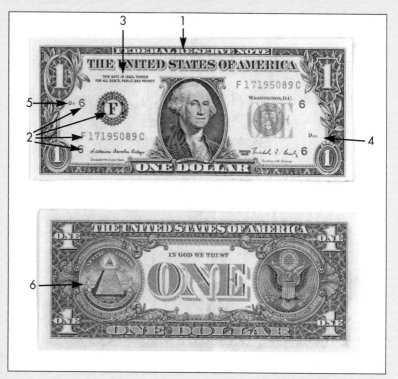

5. *D2*, which stands for row D, column 2, is the position on the sheet where this dollar was printed. Money is printed in large sheets, which are then cut to make individual bills.

6. There are several interesting features in the great seal. ANNUIT COEPTIS means "He has favored our undertakings." The eye represents an all-seeing deity. The pyramid stands for strength. NOVUS ORDO SECLORUM means a "new order of the ages." The Roman numerals at the bottom of the pyramid equal 1776.

Copyright © by Houghton Mifflin Company. All rights reserved.

1.b.2. Controlling the Money Supply All of the functions the Federal Reserve carries out are important, but none is more important than managing the nation's money supply. Before 1913 when the Fed was created, the money supply did not change to meet fluctuations in the demand for money. These fluctuations can stem from changes in income or seasonal patterns of demand. For example, every year during the Christmas season, the demand for currency rises because people carry more money to buy gifts. During the holiday season, the Fed increases the supply of currency to meet the demand for cash withdrawals from banks. After the holiday season, the demand for currency drops and the public deposits currency in banks, which then return the currency to the Fed.

The Fed controls the money supply to achieve the policy goals set by the FOMC. It does this largely through its ability to influence bank reserves and the money-creating power of commercial banks that we talked about in Chapter 13.

RECAP

1. As the central bank of the United States, the Federal Reserve accepts deposits from and makes loans to commercial banks, acts as a banker for the federal government, and controls the money supply.
2. The Federal Reserve system is made up of twelve district banks and the Board of Governors in Washington, D.C.
3. The most visible and powerful member of the Board of Governors is the chairman.
4. The governors are appointed by the president and confirmed by the Senate to serve fourteen-year terms.
5. Monetary policy is made by the Federal Open Market Committee, whose members include the seven governors and five district bank presidents.
6. The Fed provides currency, holds reserves, clears checks, and supervises commercial banks.
7. The most important function the Fed performs is controlling the U.S. money supply.

2. IMPLEMENTING MONETARY POLICY

How is monetary policy set?

Changes in the amount of money in an economy affect the inflation rate, the interest rate, and the equilibrium level of national income. Throughout history, monetary policy has made currencies worthless and toppled governments. This is why controlling the money supply is so important.

2.a. Policy Goals

The objective of monetary policy is economic growth with stable prices.

The ultimate goal of monetary policy is much like that of fiscal policy: economic growth with stable prices. *Economic growth* means greater output; *stable prices* means a low, steady rate of inflation.

2.a.1. Intermediate Targets The Fed does not control gross domestic product or the price level directly. Instead it controls the money supply, which in turn affects GDP and the level of prices. The money supply, or the growth of the money supply, is an **intermediate target,** an objective that helps the Fed achieve its ultimate policy objective—economic growth with stable prices.

intermediate target:
an objective used to achieve some ultimate policy goal

Using the growth of the money supply as an intermediate target assumes there is a fairly stable relationship between changes in money and changes in income and prices. The bases for this assumption are the equation of

Copyright © by Houghton Mifflin Company. All rights reserved.

The chairman of the Federal Reserve Board of Governors is sometimes referred to as the second most powerful person in the United States. At the time this book was written, Alan Greenspan was the Fed chairman. His leadership of the Fed has important implications for money and credit conditions in the United States.

equation of exchange:
an equation that relates the quantity of money to nominal GDP

exchange and the quantity theory of money. The **equation of exchange** is a definition that relates the quantity of money to nominal GDP:

$$MV = PQ$$

where

M = the quantity of money

V = the velocity of money

P = the price level

Q = the quantity of output, like real income or real GDP

This equation is true by definition: money times the velocity of money will always be equal to nominal GDP.

In Chapter 13 we said there are several definitions of the money supply: M1, M2, and M3. The **velocity of money** is the average number of times each dollar is spent on final goods and services in a year. If P is the price level and Q is real GDP (the quantity of goods and services produced in the economy), then PQ equals nominal GDP. If

velocity of money:
the average number of times each dollar is spent on final goods and services in a year

then

$$MV = PQ$$

$$V = \frac{PQ}{M}$$

Suppose the price level is 2 and real GDP is $500; PQ, or nominal GDP, is $1,000. If the money supply is $200, then velocity is 5 ($1,000/$200). A velocity of 5 means that each dollar must be spent an average of 5 times during the year if a money supply of $200 is going to support the purchase of $1,000 worth of new goods and services.

quantity theory of money:
with constant velocity, changes in the quantity of money change nominal GDP

The **quantity theory of money** uses the equation of exchange to relate changes in the money supply to changes in prices and output. If the money supply (M) increases and velocity (V) is constant, then nominal GDP (PQ) must increase. If the economy is operating at maximum capacity (producing at the maximum level of Q), an increase in M causes an increase in P. And if there is substantial unemployment so that Q can increase, the increase in M may mean a higher price level (P) as well as higher real GDP (Q).

Copyright © by Houghton Mifflin Company. All rights reserved.

The Fed attempts to set money growth targets that are consistent with rising output and low inflation. In terms of the quantity theory of money, the Fed wants to increase M at a rate that supports steadily rising Q with slow and steady increases in P. The assumption that there is a reasonably stable relationship among M, P, and Q is what motivates the Fed to use money supply growth rates as an intermediate target to achieve its ultimate goal—higher Q with slow increases in P.

The FOMC defines upper and lower bounds to describe its intermediate targets—the range in which it wants the money supply to grow. Figure 2 shows the ranges and the actual growth of the M2 money supply for recent years. In 1991 and 1992, the targeted growth of the M2 money supply was between 2.5 and 6.5 percent then it dropped to 2 to 6 percent in 1993 and to 1 to 5 percent in 1994. The upper and lower lines at these growth rates create a cone that represents the region of growth targeted by the Fed. The upper part of the cone is the highest growth rate of 5 percent and the lower part of the cone is the lowest growth rate of 1 percent. The heavy line plots the actual path of the M2 money supply in each year. If the M2 money supply grew at a rate of 5 percent over the year 1994, the heavy line would be up at the top of the cone. If it grew at 1 percent, the heavy line would be at the bottom of the cone—as it was. By specifying a range of growth rather than a single rate of growth, the Fed gives itself more room to maneuver in dealing with unexpected events that might make managing the money supply difficult.

From the late 1950s to the mid-1970s, the velocity of the M1 money supply grew at a steady pace, from 3.5 in 1959 to 5.5 in 1975. Knowing that V was growing at a steady pace, the Fed was able to set a target growth rate for the M1 money supply, confident that it would produce a fairly predictable growth in nominal GDP. But when velocity is not constant, there can be problems

Copyright © by Houghton Mifflin Company. All rights reserved.

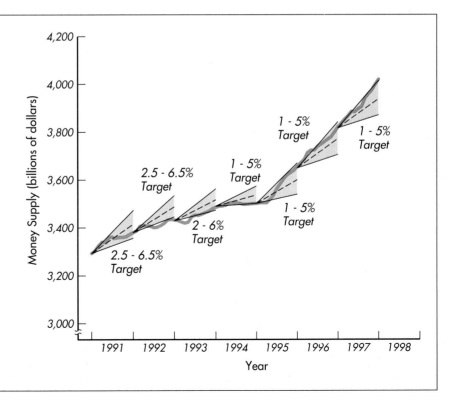

Figure 2
Targeted Versus Actual Growth in the M2 Money Supply
The Fed defines targeted growth in the money supply in terms of upper and lower bounds. These bounds define a region of acceptable growth shaped like a cone.

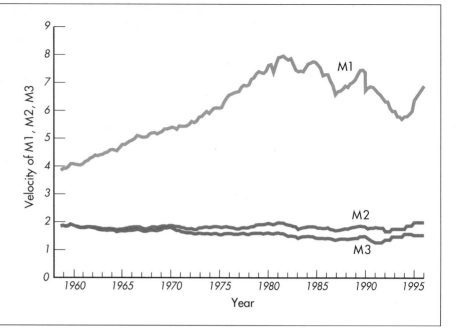

Figure 3
Velocity of the M1, M2, and M3 Money Supplies
The velocity of money is the ratio of nominal gross domestic product to the money supply. The narrower the definition of money, the higher its velocity. So M1, the narrowest definition, has a higher velocity than M2 or M3. In recent years, the velocity of M1 has been much less stable than the velocity of the broader money definitions.

using money growth rates as an intermediate target. This is exactly what happened in the late 1970s and early 1980s. Figure 3 plots the velocity of the M1, M2, and M3 money supplies from 1959 to 1996. Although the M2 and M3 velocities continued to indicate a stable pattern of growth, M1 velocity behaved erratically. With the breakdown of the relationship between the M1 money supply and GDP, the Fed shifted its emphasis from the M1 money supply, concentrating instead on achieving targeted growth in the M2 and M3 money supplies.

Economists are still debating the reason for the fluctuations in the velocity of the M1 money supply. Some argue that new deposits and innovations in banking led to fluctuations in the money held in traditional demand deposits as bank customers switched to different types of financial assets. These changes would affect the M1 supply because its definition is so narrow. They would not affect the M2 and M3 supplies because their broader definitions include many of the new types of financial products available to the public.

In addition to targeting money growth, the Fed monitors other key variables that are used to indicate the future course of the economy. These include commodity prices, interest rates, and foreign exchange rates. The Fed may not set formal targets for all of them, but it considers them in setting policy.

2.b. Operating Procedures

FOMC directive:
instructions issued by the FOMC to the Federal Reserve Bank of New York to implement monetary policy

What are the tools of monetary policy?

The FOMC sets monetary targets and then implements them through the Federal Reserve Bank of New York. The mechanism for translating policy into action is an **FOMC directive.** Each directive outlines the conduct of monetary policy over the six- to eight-week period until the FOMC meets again to adjust monetary targets and specify policy tools.

2.b.1. Tools of Monetary Policy The Fed controls the money supply by changing bank reserves. There are three tools the Fed can use to change reserves: the *reserve requirement,* the *discount rate,* and *open market opera-*

Copyright © by Houghton Mifflin Company. All rights reserved.

tions. In the last chapter, you saw that banks can expand the money supply by a multiple of their excess reserves—the deposit expansion multiplier, the reciprocal of the reserve requirement.

Reserve Requirement The Fed requires banks to hold a fraction of their transaction deposits on reserve. This fraction is the reserve requirement. *Transaction deposits* are checking accounts and other deposits that can be used to pay third parties. Large banks hold a greater percentage of deposits in reserve than do small banks (the reserve requirement increases from 3 to 10 percent for deposits in excess of $54 million).

Remember from Chapter 13 that required reserves are the dollar amount of reserves that a bank must hold to meet its reserve requirement. There are two ways in which required reserves may be held: vault cash at the bank or a deposit in the Fed. The sum of a bank's *vault cash* (coin and currency in the bank's vault) and deposit in the Fed is called its **legal reserves.** When legal reserves equal required reserves, the bank has no excess reserves and can make no new loans. When legal reserves exceed required reserves, the bank has excess reserves available for lending.

Copyright © by Houghton Mifflin Company. All rights reserved.

legal reserves:
the cash a bank holds in its vault plus its deposit in the Fed

As bank excess reserves change, the lending and money-creating potential of the banking system changes. One way the Fed can alter excess reserves is by changing the reserve requirement. If it lowers the reserve requirement, a portion of what was previously required reserves becomes excess reserves, which can be used to make loans and expand the money supply. A lower reserve requirement also increases the deposit expansion multiplier. By raising the reserve requirement, the Fed reduces the money-creating potential of the banking system and tends to reduce the money supply. A higher reserve requirement also lowers the deposit expansion multiplier.

Consider the example in Table 2. If First National Bank's balance sheet shows vault cash of $100,000 and a deposit in the Fed of $200,000, the bank has legal reserves of $300,000. The amount of money that the bank can lend is determined by its excess reserves. Excess reserves (ER) equal legal reserves (LR) minus required reserves (RR):

$$ER = LR - RR$$

If the reserve requirement (r) is 10 percent (.10), the bank must keep 10 percent of its deposits (D) as required reserves:

$$RR = rD$$
$$= .10(\$1,000,000)$$
$$= \$100,000$$

In this case, the bank has excess reserves of $200,000 ($300,000 − $100,000). The bank can make a maximum loan of $200,000. The banking system can expand the money supply by the deposit expansion multiplier ($1/r$) times the excess reserves of the bank, or $2,000,000 ($1/.10 \times $200,000).

If the reserve requirement goes up to 20 percent (.20), required reserves are 20 percent of $1,000,000, or $200,000. Excess reserves are now $100,000, which is the maximum loan the bank can make. The banking system can expand the money supply by $500,000:

$$\frac{1}{.20}(\$100,000) = 5(\$100,000)$$
$$= \$500,000$$

By raising the reserve requirement, the Fed can reduce the money-creating potential of the banking system and the money supply. And by lowering the

TABLE 2
The Effect of a Change in the Reserve Requirement

Balance Sheet of First National Bank			
Assets		**Liabilities**	
Vault cash	$ 100,000	Deposits	$1,000,000
Deposit in Fed	200,000		
Loans	700,000		
Total	$1,000,000	Total	$1,000,000

Legal reserves (LR) equal vault cash plus the deposit in the Fed, or $300,000:

$LR = \$100,000 + \$200,000$
$\quad = \$300,000$

Excess reserves (ER) equal legal reserves minus required reserves (RR):

$ER = LR - RR$

Required reserves equal the reserve requirement (r) times deposits (D):

$RR = rD$

If the reserve requirement is 10 percent:

$RR = (.10)(\$1,000,000)$
$\quad = \$100,000$

$ER = \$300,000 - \$100,000$
$\quad = \$200,000$

First National Bank can make a maximum loan of $200,000.

The banking system can expand the money supply by the deposit expansion multiplier ($1/r$) times the excess reserves of the bank or $2,000,000:

$(1/.10)(\$200,000) = 10(\$200,000)$
$\qquad\qquad\qquad = \$2,000,000$

If the reserve requirement is 20 percent:

$RR = (.20)(\$1,000,000)$
$\quad = \$200,000$

$ER = \$300,000 - \$200,000$
$\quad = \$100,000$

First National Bank can make a maximum loan of $100,000.

The banking system can expand the money supply by the deposit expansion multiplier ($1/r$) times the excess reserves of the bank or $500,000:

$(1/.20)(\$100,000) = 5(\$100,000)$
$\qquad\qquad\qquad = \$500,000$

reserve requirement, the Fed can increase the money-creating potential of the banking system and the money supply.

Discount Rate   If a bank needs more reserves in order to make new loans, it typically borrows from other banks in the federal funds market. The market is called the *federal funds market* because the funds are being loaned from one commercial bank's excess reserves on deposit with the Federal Reserve to another commercial bank's deposit account at the Fed. For instance, if the

Copyright © by Houghton Mifflin Company. All rights reserved.

TABLE 3
Federal Reserve Discount Rates

Date	Discount Rate (percent)	Date	Discount Rate (percent)
January 9, 1978	6.50	October 12, 1982	9.50
May 11, 1978	7.00	November 22, 1982	9.00
July 3, 1978	7.25	December 15, 1982	8.50
August 21, 1978	7.75	April 9, 1984	9.00
September 22, 1978	8.00	November 21, 1984	8.50
October 16, 1978	8.50	December 24, 1984	8.00
November 1, 1978	9.50	May 20, 1985	7.50
July 20, 1979	10.00	March 7, 1986	7.00
August 17, 1979	10.50	April 21, 1986	6.50
September 19, 1979	11.00	July 11, 1986	6.00
October 8, 1979	12.00	August 21, 1986	5.50
February 15, 1980	13.00	September 4, 1987	6.00
May 30, 1980	12.00	August 9, 1988	6.50
June 13, 1980	11.00	February 24, 1989	7.00
July 28, 1980	10.00	December 19, 1990	6.50
September 26, 1980	11.00	February 1, 1991	6.00
November 17, 1980	12.00	April 30, 1991	5.50
December 5, 1980	13.00	September 13, 1991	5.00
May 5, 1981	14.00	November 6, 1991	4.50
November 2, 1981	13.00	December 20, 1991	3.50
December 4, 1981	12.00	July 2, 1992	3.00
July 20, 1982	11.50	May 17, 1994	3.50
August 2, 1982	11.50	August 16, 1994	4.00
August 16, 1982	10.50	November 15, 1994	4.75
August 27, 1982	10.00	February 1, 1995	5.25
		January 31, 1996	5.00

Source: Federal Reserve.

Copyright © by Houghton Mifflin Company. All rights reserved.

federal funds rate:
the interest rate a bank charges when it lends excess reserves to another bank

discount rate:
the interest rate the Fed charges commercial banks when they borrow from it

First National Bank has excess reserves of $1 million, it can lend the excess to the Second National Bank. When a bank borrows in the federal funds market, it pays a rate of interest called the **federal funds rate**.

At times, however, banks borrow directly from the Fed, although the Fed restricts access to such funds. The **discount rate** is the rate of interest the Fed charges banks. (In other countries, the rate of interest the central bank charges commercial banks is often called the *bank rate*.) Another way the Fed controls the level of bank reserves and the money supply is by changing the discount rate.

When the Fed raises the discount rate, it raises the cost of borrowing reserves, reducing the amount of reserves borrowed. Lower levels of reserves limit bank lending and the expansion of the money supply. When the Fed lowers the discount rate, it lowers the cost of borrowing reserves, increasing the amount of borrowing. As bank reserves increase, so do loans and the money supply.

The discount rate is relatively stable. Although other interest rates can fluctuate daily, the discount rate usually remains fixed for months at a time. Table 3 lists the discount rate over recent years. The most the rate has been changed in a year has been seven times.

Open Market Operations The major tool of monetary policy is the Fed's **open market operations**, the buying and selling of U.S. government bonds. Suppose the FOMC wants to increase bank reserves to stimulate the growth of money. The committee issues a directive to the bond-trading desk at the Federal Reserve Bank of New York to buy bonds. The bonds are purchased from private bond dealers. The dealers are paid with checks drawn on the Federal Reserve, which then are deposited in the dealers' accounts at commercial banks. What happens? As bank deposits and reserves increase, banks are able to make new loans, which in turn expand the money supply through the deposit expansion multiplier process.

If the Fed wants to decrease the money supply, it sells bonds. Private bond dealers pay for the bonds with checks drawn on commercial banks. Commercial bank deposits and reserves drop, and the money supply decreases through the deposit expansion multiplier process.

Its open market operations allow the Fed to control the money supply. To increase the money supply, the Fed buys U.S. government bonds. To decrease the money supply, it sells U.S. government bonds. The effect of selling these bonds, however, varies according to whether or not there are excess reserves in the banking system. If there are excess reserves, the money supply does not necessarily decrease when the Fed sells bonds. The open market sale may simply reduce the level of excess reserves, reducing the rate at which the money supply increases.

Table 4 shows how open market operations change bank reserves and illustrates the money-creating power of the banking system. First National Bank's initial balance sheet shows excess reserves of $100,000 with a 20 percent reserve requirement. Therefore the bank can make a maximum loan of $100,000. Based on the bank's reserve position, the banking system can increase the money supply by a maximum of $500,000.

If the Fed purchases $100,000 worth of bonds from a private dealer, who deposits the $100,000 in an account at First National Bank, the excess reserves of First National Bank increase to $180,000. These reserves can generate a maximum increase in the money supply of $900,000. The open market purchase increases the excess reserves of the banking system, stimulating the growth of money and, eventually, nominal GDP.

What happens when an open market sale takes place? If the Fed sells $100,000 worth of bonds to a private bond dealer, the dealer pays for the bonds using a check drawn on First National Bank. First National's deposits drop from $1,000,000 to $900,000, and its legal reserves drop from $300,000 to $200,000. With excess reserves of $20,000, the banking system can increase the money supply by only $100,000. The open market sale reduces the money-creating potential of the banking system from $500,000 initially to $100,000.

2.b.2. FOMC Directives

When it sets monetary policy, the FOMC begins with its *ultimate goal*: economic growth at stable prices. It defines that goal in terms of GDP. Then it works backwards to identify its *intermediate target*, the rate at which the money supply must grow to achieve the wanted growth in GDP. Then it must decide how to achieve its intermediate target. In Figure 4, as is usually the case in real life, the Fed uses open market operations. But to know whether it should buy or sell bonds, the FOMC must have some indication of whether the money supply is growing too fast or too slow. The com-

open market operations:
the buying and selling of government bonds by the Fed to control bank reserves and the money supply

To increase the money supply, the Fed buys U.S. government bonds. To decrease the money supply, it sells U.S. government bonds.

Copyright © by Houghton Mifflin Company. All rights reserved.

TABLE 4
The Effect of an Open Market Operation

Balance Sheet of First National Bank			
Assets		**Liabilities**	
Vault cash	$ 100,000	Deposits	$1,000,000
Deposit in Fed	200,000		
Loans	700,000		
Total	$1,000,000	Total	$1,000,000

Initially legal reserves (LR) equal vault cash plus the deposit in the Fed, or $300,000:

$LR = \$100,000 + \$200,000$
$\quad = \$300,000$

If the reserve requirement (r) is 20 percent (.20), required reserves (RR) equal $200,000:

$.20(\$1,000,000) = \$200,000$

Excess reserves (ER), then, equal $100,000 ($300,000 − $200,000). The bank can make a maximum loan of $100,000. The banking system can expand the money supply by the deposit expansion multiplier ($1/r$) times the excess reserves of the bank, or $500,000:

$(1/.20)(\$100,000) = 5(\$100,000)$
$\qquad\qquad\qquad = \$500,000$

Open market purchase:

The Fed purchases $100,000 worth of bonds from a dealer, who deposits the $100,000 in an account at First National. At this point the bank has legal reserves of $400,000, required reserves of $220,000, and excess reserves of $180,000. It can make a maximum loan of $180,000, which can expand the money supply by $900,000 [(1/.20)($180,000)].

Open market sale:

The Fed sells $100,000 worth of bonds to a dealer, who pays with a check drawn on an account at First National. At this point, the bank has legal reserves of $200,000, required reserves of $180,000 (its deposits now equal $900,000), and excess reserves of $20,000. It can make a maximum loan of $20,000, which can expand the money supply by $100,000 [(1/.20)($20,000)].

mittee relies on a *short-run operating target* for this information. The short-run target indicates how the money supply should change. Both the quantity of excess reserves in the banking system and the federal funds rate can serve as short-run operating targets.

The FOMC carries out its policies through directives to the bond-trading desk at the Federal Reserve Bank of New York. The directives specify a short-run operating target that the trading desk must use in its day-to-day operations. When the FOMC first began setting intermediate monetary targets

Copyright © by Houghton Mifflin Company. All rights reserved.

Figure 4
Monetary Policy: Tools, Targets, and Goals
The Fed primarily uses open market operations to implement monetary policy. The decision to buy or sell bonds is based on a short-run operating target, like the level of reserves held by commercial banks. The short-run operating target is set to achieve an intermediate target, a certain level of money supply. The intermediate target is set to achieve the ultimate goal, a certain level of gross domestic product.

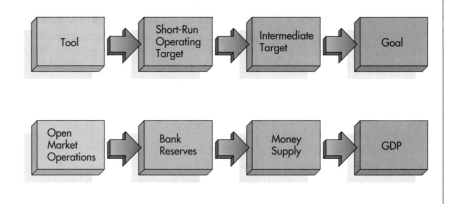

in 1970, it attempted to prescribe very specific target ranges for the federal funds interest rate. The committee chose the federal funds rate as the short-run target because it believed the rate was the best indicator of the status of reserves. Because the federal funds rate is the interest rate one bank charges another when the second bank borrows reserves from the first, the federal funds rate rises when there are few excess reserves and falls when the banking system has a large amount of excess reserves. The Fed believed that if the federal funds rate rose above the FOMC's target, it would indicate that there were not enough reserves in the banking system, that the money supply was not growing fast enough. The bond-trading desk would then purchase bonds from bond dealers.

In the 1970s, the federal funds rate target worked well to stabilize interest rates. However, the money supply fluctuated a great deal more than the FOMC wanted. For example, when people were spending at a rapid pace and so borrowing increasing amounts of money, the banking system's reserves fell and the federal funds rate rose. The rising rate signaled the trading desk to purchase bonds and increase reserves. These reserves were immediately lent, and the money supply grew more quickly. As long as the federal funds rate continued to go up, new reserves were being pumped into the banking system and the money supply grew faster and faster. Conversely, when people were not spending and excess reserves accumulated, the trading desk sold bonds, the money supply fell and continued to fall as long as the federal funds rate was below the target range. By the fall of 1979, the FOMC had decided that it needed a better indicator of money supply growth for its short-run operating target. The committee chose bank reserves. FOMC directives now phrase their short-run operating targets in terms of the level of bank reserves.

The nature of the Fed's policy regarding reserve targeting has changed over time. In addition, the Fed takes other factors into account. For example, FOMC directives still cite a desired level for the federal funds rate. The directives also cite real GDP growth, the rate of inflation, and the foreign exchange value of the dollar, factors that could affect the FOMC-targeted bank reserves.

Copyright © by Houghton Mifflin Company. All rights reserved.

Figure 5
The Dollar-Yen Foreign Exchange Market
The demand is the demand for dollars arising out of the Japanese demand for U.S. goods and services. The supply is the supply of dollars arising out of the U.S. demand for Japanese goods and services. Initially, the equilibrium exchange rate is at the intersection of the demand curve (D_1) and the supply curve (S_1), where the exchange rate is ¥100 = $1. An increase in the U.S. demand for Japanese goods increases S_1 to S_2 and pushes the equilibrium exchange rate down to point B, where ¥90 = $1. If the Fed's target exchange rate is ¥100 = $1, the Fed must intervene, buying dollars in the foreign exchange market. This increases demand to D_2 and raises the equilibrium exchange rate to point C, where ¥100 = $1.

2.c. Foreign Exchange Market Intervention

Copyright © by Houghton Mifflin Company. All rights reserved.

What role do central banks play in the foreign exchange market?

foreign exchange market intervention:
the buying and selling of foreign exchange by a central bank to move exchange rates up or down to a targeted level

In the mid-1980s, conditions in the foreign exchange market took on a high priority in FOMC directives, which continues to this day. There was concern that the value of the dollar in relation to other currencies was contributing to a large U.S. international trade deficit. Furthermore, the governments of the major industrial countries decided to work together to maintain more stable exchange rates. This meant that the Federal Reserve and the central banks of the other developed countries had to devote more attention to maintaining exchange rates within a certain target band of values, much as the federal funds rate had been targeted in the 1970s.

2.c.1. Mechanics of Intervention   **Foreign exchange market intervention** is the buying and selling of foreign exchange by a central bank in order to move exchange rates up or down. We can use a simple supply and demand diagram to illustrate the role of intervention. Figure 5 shows the U.S. dollar–Japanese yen exchange market. The demand curve is the demand for dollars produced by the demand for U.S. goods and financial assets. The supply curve is the supply of dollars generated by U.S. residents' demand for the products and financial assets of other countries. Here, the supply of dollars to the dollar-yen market comes from the U.S. demand to buy Japanese products.

The initial equilibrium exchange rate is at point A, where the demand curve (D_1) and the supply curve (S_1) intersect. At point A, the exchange rate is ¥100 = $1, and Q_1 dollars are exchanged for yen. Suppose that over time, U.S. residents buy more from Japan than Japanese residents buy from the United States. As the supply of dollars increases in relation to the demand for dollars, equilibrium shifts to point B. At point B, Q_2 dollars are exchanged at a rate of ¥90 = $1. The dollar has *depreciated* against the yen, or, conversely, the yen has *appreciated* against the dollar.

When the dollar depreciates, U.S. goods are cheaper to Japanese buyers (it takes fewer yen to buy each dollar). The depreciated dollar stimulates U.S. exports to Japan. It also raises the price of Japanese goods to U.S. buyers, reducing U.S. imports from Japan. Rather than allow exchange rates to change, with the subsequent changes in trade, central banks often seek to maintain fixed exchange rates because of international agreements or desired trade in goods or financial assets.

Suppose the Fed sets a target range for the dollar at a minimum exchange rate of ¥100 = $1. If the exchange rate falls below the minimum, the Fed must intervene in the foreign exchange market to increase the value of the dollar. In Figure 5, you can see that the only way to increase the dollar's value is to increase the demand for dollars. The Fed intervenes in the foreign exchange market by buying dollars in exchange for yen. It uses its holdings of Japanese yen to purchase $Q_3 - Q_1$ dollars, shifting the demand curve to D_2. Now equilibrium is at point C, where Q_3 dollars are exchanged at the rate of ¥100 = $1.

The kind of intervention shown in Figure 5 is only temporary because the Fed has a limited supply of yen. Under another intervention plan, the Bank of Japan would support the ¥100 = $1 exchange rate by using yen to buy dollars. The Bank of Japan could carry on this kind of policy indefinitely because it has the power to create yen. A third alternative is *coordinated intervention,* in which both the Fed and the Bank of Japan sell yen in exchange for dollars to support the minimum yen-dollar exchange rate.

Coordinated intervention involves more than one central bank in attempts to shift the equilibrium exchange rate.

2.c.2. Effects of Intervention   Intervention can be used to shift the demand and supply for currency and thereby change the exchange rate. Foreign exchange market intervention also has effects on the money supply. If the Federal Reserve wanted to increase the dollar price of the French franc, it would create dollars to purchase francs. Thus when foreign exchange market intervention involves the use of domestic currency to buy foreign currency, it increases the domestic money supply. The expansionary effect of this intervention can be offset by a domestic open market operation, in a process called **sterilization.** If the Fed creates dollars to buy French francs, for example, it increases the money supply, as we have just seen. To reduce the money supply, the Fed can direct an open market bond sale. The bond sale sterilizes the effect of the intervention on the domestic money supply.

sterilization:
the use of domestic open market operations to offset the effects of a foreign exchange market intervention on the domestic money supply

RECAP

1. The ultimate goal of monetary policy is economic growth with stable prices.
2. The Fed controls GDP indirectly, through its control of the money supply.
3. The equation of exchange (MV = PQ) relates the quantity of money to nominal GDP.
4. The quantity theory of money states that with constant velocity, changes in the quantity of money change nominal GDP.
5. Every six to eight weeks, the Federal Open Market Committee issues a directive to the Federal Reserve Bank of New York that defines the FOMC's monetary targets and policy tools.
6. The Fed controls the nation's money supply by changing bank excess reserves.

Copyright © by Houghton Mifflin Company. All rights reserved.

7. The tools of monetary policy are reserve requirements, the discount rate, and open market operations.

8. The money supply tends to increase (decrease) as the reserve requirement falls (rises), the discount rate falls (rises), and the Fed buys (sells) bonds.

9. Each FOMC directive defines its short-run operating target in terms of bank reserves, but also considers the federal funds rate, the growth of real GDP, the rate of inflation, and the foreign exchange rate of the dollar.

10. Foreign exchange market intervention is the buying and selling of foreign exchange by a central bank to achieve a targeted exchange rate.

11. Sterilization is the use of domestic open market operations to offset the money supply effects of foreign exchange market intervention.

3. MONETARY POLICY AND EQUILIBRIUM INCOME

To see how changes in the money supply affect the equilibrium level of real GDP, we incorporate monetary policy into the aggregate demand and supply model. The first step in understanding monetary policy is understanding the demand for money. If you know what determines money demand, you can see how monetary policy is used to shift aggregate demand and change the equilibrium level of real GDP.

3.a. Money Demand

What are the determinants of the demand for money?

transactions demand for money:
the demand to hold money to buy goods and services

Why do you hold money? What does it do for you? What determines how much money you will hold? These questions are addressed in this section. Wanting to hold more money is not the same as wanting more income. You can decide to carry more cash or keep more dollars in your checking account even though your income has not changed. The quantity of dollars you want to hold is your demand for money. By summing the quantity of money demanded by each individual, we can find the money demand for the entire economy. Once we understand what determines money demand, we can put that demand together with the money supply and examine how money influences the interest rate and the equilibrium level of income.

In Chapter 13 we discussed the functions of money, that is, what money is used for. People use money as a unit of account, a medium of exchange, a store of value, and a standard of deferred payment. These last functions help explain the demand for money.

People use money for transactions, to buy goods and services. The **transactions demand for money** is a demand to hold money in order to spend it on goods and services. Holding money in your pocket or checking account is a demand for money. Spending money is not demanding it; by spending it you are getting rid of it.

If your boss paid you the same instant that you wanted to buy something, the timing of your receipts and expenditures would match perfectly. You would not have to hold money for transactions. But because receipts typically occur much less often than expenditures, money is necessary to cover transactions between paychecks.

Copyright © by Houghton Mifflin Company. All rights reserved.

**precautionary demand
for money:**
the demand for money to cover
unplanned transactions or
emergencies

**speculative demand
for money:**
the demand for money created
by uncertainty about the value
of other assets

People also hold money to take care of emergencies. The **precautionary demand for money** exists because emergencies happen. People never know when an unexpected expense will crop up or when actual expenditures will exceed planned expenditures. So they hold money as a precaution.

Finally, there is a **speculative demand for money,** a demand created by uncertainty about the value of other assets. This demand exists because money is the most liquid store of value. If you want to buy a stock, but you believe the price is going to fall in the next few days, you hold the money until you are ready to buy the stock.

The speculative demand for money is not necessarily tied to a particular use of funds. People hold money because they expect the price of any asset to fall. Holding money is less risky than buying the asset today if the price of the asset seems likely to fall. For example, suppose you buy and sell fine art. The price of art fluctuates over time. You try to buy when prices are low and sell when prices are high. If you expect prices to fall in the short term, you hold money rather than art until the prices do fall. Then you use money to buy art for resale when the prices go up again.

3.a.1. The Money Demand Function If you understand why people hold money, you can understand what changes the amount of money they hold. As you've just seen, people hold money in order to: (1) carry out transactions (transactions demand), (2) be prepared for emergencies (precautionary demand), and (3) speculate on purchases of various assets (speculative demand). The interest rate and nominal income (income measured in current dollars) influence how much money people hold in order to carry out these three activities.

The Interest Rate There is an inverse relationship between the interest rate and the quantity of money demanded (see Figure 6). The interest rate is the *opportunity cost* of holding money. If you bury a thousand dollar bills in your

The interest rate is the opportunity cost of holding money.

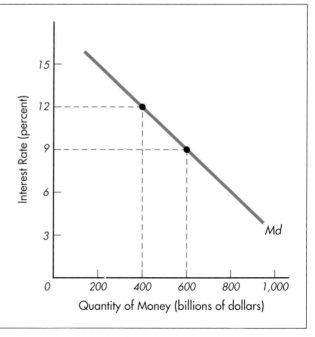

**Figure 6
The Money Demand Function**
Money demand (*Md*) is a negative function of the rate of interest. The interest rate is the opportunity cost of holding money. The higher the interest rate, the lower the quantity of money demanded. At an interest rate of 9 percent, the quantity of money demanded is $600 billion. At an interest rate of 12 percent, the quantity of money demanded falls to $400 billion.

Copyright © by Houghton Mifflin Company. All rights reserved.

backyard, that currency is earning no interest—you are forgoing the interest. At a low interest rate, the cost of forgone interest is small. At a higher interest rate, however, the cost of holding wealth in the form of money means giving up more interest. The higher the rate of interest, the greater the interest forgone by holding money, so the less money held. The costs of holding money limit the amount of money held.

Some components of the money supply pay interest to the depositor. Here the opportunity cost of holding money is the difference between the interest rate on a bond or some other nonmonetary asset and the interest rate on money. If a bond pays 9 percent interest a year and a bank deposit pays 5 percent, the opportunity cost of holding the deposit is 4 percent.

Figure 6 shows a money demand function where the demand for money depends on the interest rate. The downward slope of the money demand curve (Md) shows the inverse relation between the interest rate and the quantity of money demanded. For instance, at an interest rate of 12 percent, the quantity of money demanded is $400 billion. If the interest rate falls to 9 percent, the quantity of money demanded increases to $600 billion.

Nominal Income   The demand for money also depends on nominal income. Money demand varies directly with nominal income because as income increases, more transactions are carried out and more money is required for those transactions.

The transactions demand for money rises with nominal income.

The greater nominal income, the greater the demand for money. This is true whether the increase in nominal income is a product of a higher price level or an increase in real income. Both generate a greater dollar volume of transactions. If the prices of all goods increase, then more money must be used to purchase goods and services. And as real income increases, more goods and services are being produced and sold and living standards rise, which means more money is being demanded to execute the higher level of transactions.

A change in nominal income changes the demand for money at any given interest rate. Figure 7 shows the effect of changes in nominal income on the

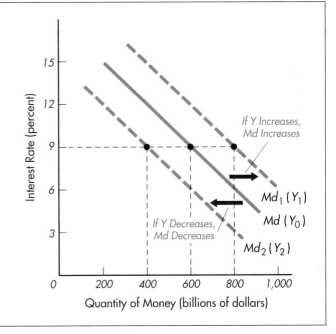

Figure 7
The Effect of a Change in Income on Money Demand
A change in real GDP, whatever the interest rate, shifts the money demand curve. Initially real GDP is Y_0; the money demand curve at that level of income is Md. At an interest rate of 9 percent, the quantity of money demanded is $600 billion. If income increases to Y_1, the money demand shifts to Md_1. Here $800 billion is demanded at 9 percent. If income falls to Y_2, the money demand curve falls to Md_2, where $400 billion is demanded at 9 percent.

Copyright © by Houghton Mifflin Company. All rights reserved.

Figure 8
The Money Supply Function
The money supply function is a vertical line. This indicates that the Fed can choose any money supply it wants independent of the interest rate (and real GDP). In the figure, the money supply is set at $600 billion at all interest rates. The Fed can increase or decrease the money supply, shifting the curve to the right or left, but the curve remains vertical.

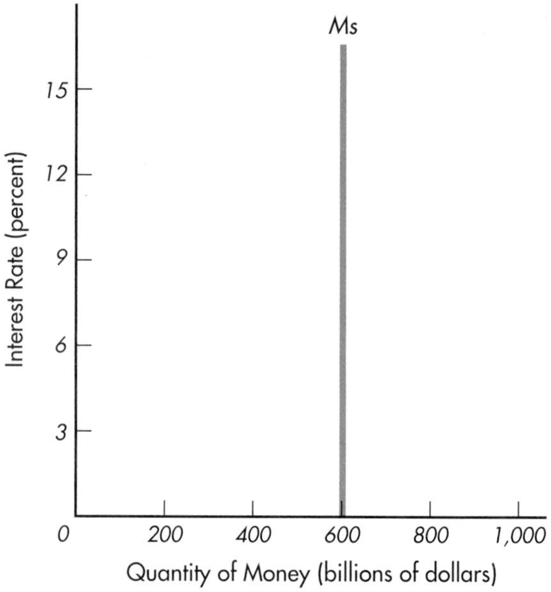

money demand curve. If income rises from Y_0 to Y_1, money demand increases from *Md* to Md_1. If income falls from Y_0 to Y_2, money demand falls from *Md* to Md_2. When the money demand function shifts from *Md* to Md_1, the quantity of money demanded at an interest rate of 9 percent increases from $600 billion to $800 billion. When the money demand function shifts from *Md* to Md_2, the quantity of money demanded at 9 percent interest falls from $600 billion to $400 billion.

3.a.2. The Money Supply Function The Federal Reserve is responsible for setting the money supply. The fact that the Fed can choose the money supply means that the money supply function is independent of the current interest rate and income. Figure 8 illustrates the money supply function (*Ms*). In the figure, the money supply is $600 billion at all interest rate levels. If the Fed increases the money supply, the vertical money supply function shifts to the right. If the Fed decreases the money supply, the function shifts to the left.

3.a.3. Equilibrium in the Money Market To find the equilibrium interest rate and quantity of money, we have to combine the money demand and money supply functions in one diagram. Figure 9 graphs equilibrium in the money market. Equilibrium, point *e*, is at the intersection of the money demand and money supply functions. In the figure the equilibrium interest rate is 9 percent and the quantity of money is $600 billion.

What forces work to ensure that the economy tends toward the equilibrium rate of interest? Let's look at Figure 9 again to understand what happens if the interest rate is not at equilibrium. If the interest rate falls below 9 percent, there will be an excess demand for money. People will want more money than

Copyright © by Houghton Mifflin Company. All rights reserved.

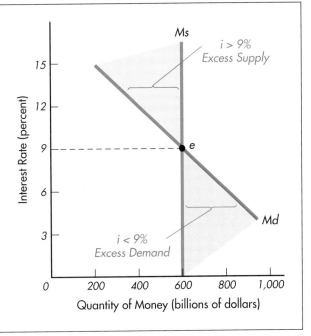

Figure 9
Equilibrium in the Money Market
Equilibrium is at point *e*, where the money demand and money supply curves intersect. At equilibrium, the interest rate is 9 percent and the money supply is $600 billion. An interest rate above 9 percent would create an excess supply of money because the quantity of money demanded falls as the interest rate rises. An interest rate below 9 percent would create an excess demand for money because the quantity of money demanded rises as the interest rate falls.

Copyright © by Houghton Mifflin Company. All rights reserved.

the Fed is supplying. But because the supply of money does not change, the demand for more money just forces the interest rate to rise. How? Suppose people try to increase their money holdings by converting bonds and other nonmonetary assets into money. As bonds and other nonmonetary assets are sold for money, the interest rate goes up.

To understand the connection between the rate of interest and buying and selling bonds, you must realize that the current interest rate (yield) on a bond is determined by the bond price:

$$\text{Current interest rate} = \frac{\text{annual interest payment}}{\text{bond price}}$$

The numerator, the annual interest payment, is fixed for the life of the bond. The denominator, the bond price, fluctuates with supply and demand. As the bond price changes, the interest rate changes.

Suppose a bond pays $100 a year in interest and sells for $1,000. The interest rate is 10 percent ($100/$1,000). If the supply of bonds increases because people want to convert bonds to money, the price of bonds falls. Suppose the price drops to $800. At that price the interest rate equals 12.5 percent ($100/$800). This is the mechanism by which an excess demand for money changes the interest rate. As the interest rate goes up, the excess demand for money disappears.

Just the opposite occurs at interest rates above equilibrium. In Figure 9, any rate of interest above 9 percent creates an excess supply of money. Now people are holding more of their wealth in the form of money than they would like. What happens? They want to convert some of their money balances into nonmonetary assets, like bonds. As the demand for bonds rises, bond prices increase. And as bond prices go up, interest rates fall. This drop in interest rates restores equilibrium in the money market.

Figure 10
Monetary Policy and Equilibrium Income
The three diagrams show the sequence of events by which a change in the money supply affects the equilibrium level of real GDP. In part (a), the money supply increases, low-ering the equilibrium interest rate. In part (b), the lower interest rate pushes the equilibrium level of investment up. In part (c), the increase in investment increases aggregate demand and equilibrium real GDP.

(a) Money Supply Increases and Interest Rate Falls

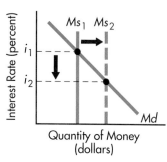

Quantity of Money
(dollars)

(b) Investment Spending Increases

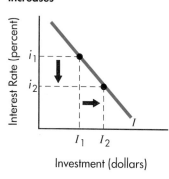

Investment (dollars)

(c) Aggregate Demand and Equilibrium Income Increase

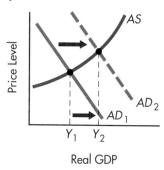

Real GDP

3.b. Money and Equilibrium Income

How does monetary policy affect the equilibrium level of real GDP?

Now we are ready to relate monetary policy to the equilibrium level of real GDP. We use Figure 10 to show how a change in the money supply affects real GDP. In part (a), as the money supply increases from Ms_1 to Ms_2, the equilibrium rate of interest falls from i_1 to i_2.

Remember that investment (business spending on capital goods) declines as the rate of interest increases. The interest rate is the cost of borrowed funds. As the interest rate rises, the return on investment falls and with it the level of investment. As the interest rate falls, the return on investment rises and with it the level of investment. In part (a) of Figure 10, the interest rate falls. In part (b) of the figure you can see the effect of the lower interest rate on investment spending. As the interest rate falls from i_1 to i_2, investment increases from I_1 to I_2.

Figure 10(c) is the aggregate demand and supply equilibrium diagram. When investment spending increases, aggregate expenditures are higher at every price level, so the aggregate demand curve shifts to the right, from AD_1 to AD_2. The increase in aggregate demand increases equilibrium income from Y_1 to Y_2.

How does monetary policy affect equilibrium income? As the money supply increases, the equilibrium interest rate falls. As the interest rate falls, the equilibrium level of investment rises. Increased investment increases aggregate demand and equilibrium income. A decrease in the money supply works in reverse: as the interest rate rises, investment falls; as investment falls, aggregate demand and equilibrium income go down.

The mechanism we have just described is an oversimplification because the only element of aggregate expenditures that changes in this model is investment. But an excess demand for or supply of money involves more than simply selling or buying bonds. An excess supply of money probably would be reflected in increased consumption as well. If households are holding more

An excess supply of (demand for) money can increase (decrease) consumption as well as investment.

Copyright © by Houghton Mifflin Company. All rights reserved.

money than they want to hold, they buy not only bonds but also goods and services so that consumption increases. If they are holding less money than they want to hold, they will sell bonds and consume less. So the effect of monetary policy on aggregate demand is a product of a change in both investment and consumption. We discuss this in Chapter 15, where we also examine the important role expected policy changes can play.

RECAP

1. The transactions demand for money is a demand to hold money to buy goods and services.
2. The precautionary demand for money exists because all expenditures cannot be planned.
3. The speculative demand for money is created by uncertainty about the value of other assets.
4. There is an inverse relationship between the interest rate and the quantity of money demanded.
5. The greater nominal income, the greater the demand for money.
6. Because the Federal Reserve sets the money supply, the money supply function is independent of the interest rate and nominal income.
7. The current yield on a bond equals the annual interest payment divided by the price of the bond.
8. An increase in the money supply lowers the interest rate, which raises the level of investment, which in turn increases aggregate demand and equilibrium income. A decrease in the money supply works in reverse.

SUMMARY

▪ What does the Federal Reserve do?

1. The Federal Reserve is the central bank of the United States. §1
2. The Federal Reserve System is operated by twelve district banks and a Board of Governors in Washington, D.C. §1.a
3. The Fed services and supervises the banking system, acts as the banker of the U.S. Treasury, and controls the money supply. §1.b

▪ How is monetary policy set?

4. The Fed controls nominal GDP indirectly by controlling the quantity of money in the nation's economy. §2.a.1
5. The Fed uses the growth of the money supply as an intermediate target to help it achieve its ultimate goal—economic growth with stable prices. §2.a.1

▪ What are the tools of monetary policy?

6. The three tools of monetary policy are the reserve requirement, the discount rate, and open market operations. §2.b.1
7. The Fed buys bonds to increase the money supply and sells bonds to decrease the money supply. §2.b.1
8. The Federal Open Market Committee (FOMC) issues directives to the Federal Reserve Bank of New York outlining the conduct of monetary policy. §2.b.2

▪ What role do central banks play in the foreign exchange market?

9. Central banks intervene in the foreign exchange market when it is necessary to maintain a targeted exchange rate. §2.c

Copyright © by Houghton Mifflin Company. All rights reserved.

What are the determinants of the demand for money?

10. The demand for money stems from the need to buy goods and services, to prepare for emergencies, and to retain a store of value. §3.a

11. There is an inverse relationship between the quantity of money demanded and the interest rate. §3.a.1

12. The greater nominal income, the greater the demand for money. §3.a.1

13. Because the Fed sets the money supply, the money supply function is independent of the interest rate and real GDP. §3.a.2

How does monetary policy affect the equilibrium level of real GDP?

14. By altering the money supply, the Fed changes the interest rate and the level of investment, shifting aggregate demand and the equilibrium level of real GDP. §3.b

KEY TERMS

Federal Open Market Committee (FOMC) §1.a.3
intermediate target §2.a.1
equation of exchange §2.a.1
velocity of money §2.a.1
quantity theory of money §2.a.1
FOMC directive §2.b
legal reserves §2.b.1
federal funds rate §2.b.1

discount rate §2.b.1
open market operations §2.b.1
foreign exchange market intervention §2.c.1
sterilization §2.c.2
transactions demand for money §3.a
precautionary demand for money §3.a
speculative demand for money §3.a

EXERCISES

1. The Federal Reserve System divides the nation into twelve districts.

   a. List the twelve cities where the district banks are located.

   b. Which Federal Reserve district do you live in?

2. Briefly describe the functions the Fed performs for the banking community. In what sense is the Fed a banker's bank?

3. Draw a graph showing equilibrium in the money market. Carefully label all curves and axes and explain why the curves have the slopes they do.

4. Using the graph you prepared for exercise 3, illustrate and explain what happens when the Fed decreases the money supply.

5. When the Fed decreases the money supply, the equilibrium level of income changes. Illustrate and explain how.

6. Describe the quantity theory of money, defining each variable. Explain how changes in the money supply can affect real GDP and the price level. Under what circumstances could an increase in the money supply have *no* effect on nominal GDP?

7. There are several tools the Fed uses to implement monetary policy.

   a. Briefly describe these tools.

   b. Explain how the Fed would use each tool in order to increase the money supply.

8. First Bank has total deposits of $2,000,000 and legal reserves of $220,000.

   a. If the reserve requirement is 10 percent, what is the maximum loan that First Bank can make, and what is the maximum increase in the money supply based on First Bank's reserve position?

Copyright © by Houghton Mifflin Company. All rights reserved.

b. If the reserve requirement is changed to 5 percent, how much can First Bank lend, and how much can the money supply be expanded?

9. Suppose you are a member of the FOMC and the U.S. economy is entering a recession. Write a directive to the New York Fed about the conduct of monetary policy over the next two months. Your directive should address targets for the rate of growth of the M2 and M3 money supplies, the federal funds rate, the rate of inflation, and the foreign exchange value of the dollar versus the Japanese yen and German mark. You may refer to the *Federal Reserve Bulletin* for examples, since this publication reports FOMC directives.

10. Suppose the Fed has a target range for the yen-dollar exchange rate. How would it keep the exchange rate within the target range if free market forces push the exchange rate out of the range? Use a graph to help explain your answer.

11. Why do you demand money? What determines how much money you keep in your pocket, purse, or bank accounts?

12. What is the current yield on a bond? Why do interest rates change when bond prices change?

13. If the Fed increases the money supply, what will happen to each of the following (other things being equal)?
   a. Interest rates
   b. Money demand
   c. Investment spending
   d. Aggregate demand
   e. The equilibrium level of national income

14. It is sometimes said that the Federal Reserve System is a nonpolitical agency. In what sense is this true? Why might you doubt that politics don't affect Fed decisions?

15. Suppose the banking system has vault cash of $1,000, deposits at the Fed of $2,000, and demand deposits of $10,000.

   a. If the reserve requirement is 20 percent, what is the maximum potential increase in the money supply given the banks' reserve position?

   b. If the Fed now purchases $500 worth of government bonds from private bond dealers, what are excess reserves of the banking system? (Assume that the bond dealers deposit the $500 in demand deposits.) How much can the banking system increase the money supply given the new reserve position?

🖥 INTERNET EXERCISE

In section 2.b of this chapter we learned that the FOMC meetings produce a directive as a guideline for the course of monetary policy over the near future. To explore current FOMC policy go to the Boyes/Melvin web site at http://www.hmco.com/college/ and click on the internet exercise link for this chapter. Now answer the questions that appear on the web page.

Copyright © by Houghton Mifflin Company. All rights reserved.

Greenspan and Fed Act Prudently in Raising Rates to Guard Against Inflation

. . . I spent the late 1960s and all of the '70s covering the inflationary explosion that slashed the value of the dollar by half in less than a dozen years.

I watched as the politicians and the bureaucrats, including the Federal Reserve Board, dithered over escalating prices without having the guts to take decisive action. . . .

In 1973, for example, inflation was running at little more than 3 percent. By 1974 it had nearly tripled to 8.7 percent and a year later it blossomed to 12.3 percent. . . .

Despite the absence of serious inflationary pressures, however, Greenspan appropriately cautioned Congress early last week that waiting until the economy starts to overheat would only mean harsher control measures later on.

"By the time inflation pressures are evident, many imbalances that are costly to rectify have already developed, and only harsh monetary therapy can restore the financial stability necessary to sustain growth," Greenspan said in testimony before the Joint Economic Committee. In fact, he noted, there has been some recent upward pressure on a number of industrial materials.

Once again, I offer a bit of history to illustrate his point about how virulent the inflation bug can be, particularly if you mix politics too richly into the economic model.

Consider: Despite the inflationary pressures that remained when he took office, President Jimmy Carter was reluctant to mount a strong anti-inflation program lest it interfere with his commitment to lower the unemployment rate. The result was an inflation-fighting strategy described by Carter's disenchanted Treasury Secretary W. Michael Blumenthal as one that aimed to battle inflation without offending any special interest group "or affecting any natural constituency of the Democratic Party."

The upshot: Carter worked the unemployment rate down from 7.7 percent in 1976 to 5.8 percent in 1979—but at fearful cost on the inflation front. The CPI, which rose 4.9 percent in 1976, soared above 13 percent in 1979 and remained at more than 12 percent in 1980. At that rate, prices will double in little more than five years.

When the Federal Reserve finally got around to taking action in 1980 it required back-to-back recessions—and unemployment rates approaching 10 percent in 1981–82—to damp the inflationary fires. . . .

As history clearly shows us—and as Greenspan obviously knows—a little inflation can easily erupt into both a lot of inflation and much higher unemployment.

Source: "Greenspan and Fed Act Prudently in Raising Rates to Guard Against Inflation," by Dick Youngblood. Appeared in *Minneapolis Star Tribune*, February 9, 1994, p. 2D. Reprinted by permission.

Copyright © by Houghton Mifflin Company. All rights reserved.

Minneapolis Star Tribune/February 9, 1994

COMMENTARY

The Board of Governors of the Federal Reserve System sets the monetary policy for the country. If the Fed believes that economic growth is too fast and inflation is likely to rise, then it tries to reduce aggregate demand by decreasing money growth. As we learned in this chapter, when the Fed decreases the money supply, interest rates rise, aggregate demand falls, and real GDP growth falls.

The article discusses the controversy over Federal Reserve interest rate increases in 1994 that were aimed at fighting inflation. The controversy arose because the inflation rate had been quite low and many people wondered why the Fed was fighting inflation when there was no apparent inflation problem. The reporter reviewed some historical circumstances where he believed that the Fed waited too long to react to rising inflation and, as a result, the contractionary monetary policy needed to end the inflation was much more severe than would have occurred if the Fed had acted sooner to stop the rising inflation.

One problem with such historical analyses is that we can look back and see the mistakes made with the advantage of full information of the circumstances that existed at that time and later. However, the policymakers do not have this same information at the time they must make policy decisions. For instance, the consumer price index is available with a one-month lag, so our knowledge of inflation is always running a month behind the actual economy. GDP is even worse. GDP data are available quarterly and we do not find out about GDP until well after a quarter ends, and even then there are often substantial revisions to the numbers occurring many months after a quarter. The point is simply that the Federal Reserve (and other policymaking institutions) must formulate policy today based on less than complete knowledge of the *current* situation and the policy must be addressed at their best guess of the *future* situation.

For these reasons, policymakers often find themselves the target of critics who dispute the current and future outlook on inflation and other key economic variables. Even though the inflation rate in 1994 was quite low and had been low for several years, the Fed was worried that several indicators of the future course of inflation (like some commodity prices) signaled rising inflation. By acting to reduce the inflationary pressures in the economy before inflation actually rose, the Fed hoped to avoid any significant increase in inflation. The passing of time reveals that the Fed policy in 1994 was successful in preventing rising inflation.

Copyright © by Houghton Mifflin Company. All rights reserved.

15

Macroeconomic Policy: Tradeoffs, Expectations, Credibility, and Sources of Business Cycles

FUNDAMENTAL QUESTIONS

1. Is there a tradeoff between inflation and the unemployment rate?

2. How does the tradeoff between inflation and the unemployment rate vary from the short to the long run?

3. What is the relationship between unexpected inflation and the unemployment rate?

4. How are macroeconomic expectations formed?

5. What makes government policies credible?

6. Are business cycles related to political elections?

7. How do real shocks to the economy affect business cycles?

8. How is inflationary monetary policy related to government fiscal policy?

Copyright © by Houghton Mifflin Company. All rights reserved.

Copyright © by Houghton Mifflin Company. All rights reserved.

Macroeconomics is a dynamic discipline. Monetary and fiscal policies change over time. And so does our understanding of those policies. Economists debate the nature of business cycles—what causes them and what, if anything, government can do about them. Some economists argue that policies that lower the unemployment rate tend to raise the rate of inflation. Others insist that only unexpected inflation can influence real GDP and employment. If the latter economists are right, does government always have to surprise the public in order to improve economic conditions?

Some economists claim that politicians manipulate the business cycle to increase their chances of reelection. If they are right, we should expect economic growth just before national elections. But what happens after the elections? What are the long-term effects of political business cycles? Because of these issues, the material in this chapter should be considered somewhat controversial. In Chapter 16 we will examine the controversies in more detail, and it will be more apparent where the sources of controversy lie. ■

1. THE PHILLIPS CURVE

In 1958 a New Zealand economist, A. W. Phillips, published a study of the relationship between the unemployment rate and the rate of change in wages in England. He found that over the period from 1826 to 1957 there had been an inverse relationship between the unemployment rate and the rate of change in wages: the unemployment rate fell in years when there were relatively large increases in wages and rose in years when wages increased relatively little. Phillips's study started other economists searching for similar relationships in other countries. In those studies, it became common to substitute the rate of inflation for the rate of change in wages.

Early studies in the United States found an inverse relationship between inflation and the unemployment rate. The graph that illustrates this relationship is called a **Phillips curve**. Figure 1 shows a Phillips curve for the United States in the 1960s. Over this period, lower inflation rates were associated with higher unemployment rates, as shown by the downward-sloping curve.

The slope of the curve in Figure 1 depicts an inverse relationship between the rate of inflation and the unemployment rate: As the inflation rate falls, the unemployment rate rises. In 1969 the inflation rate was relatively high, at 5.5

Phillips curve:
a graph that illustrates the relationship between inflation and the unemployment rate

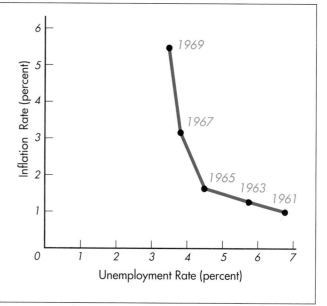

Figure 1
A Phillips Curve, United States, 1961–1969
In the 1960s, as the rate of inflation rose, the unemployment rate fell. This inverse relationship suggests a tradeoff between the rate of inflation and the unemployment rate. Source: *Economic Report of the President, 1995* (Washington, D.C.: U.S. Government Printing Office, 1995).

percent, while the unemployment rate was relatively low, at 3.5 percent. In 1967 an inflation rate of 3.1 percent was consistent with an unemployment rate of 3.8 percent; and in 1961, 1 percent inflation occurred with 6.7 percent unemployment.

The downward-sloping Phillips curve seems to indicate a tradeoff between unemployment and inflation. A country could have a lower unemployment rate by accepting higher inflation, or a lower rate of inflation by accepting higher unemployment. Certainly this was the case in the United States in the 1960s. But is the curve depicted in Figure 1 representative of the tradeoff over long periods of time?

1.a. An Inflation-Unemployment Tradeoff?

Is there a tradeoff between inflation and the unemployment rate?

Figure 2 shows unemployment and inflation rates in the United States for several years from 1955 to 1995. The points in the figure do not lie along a downward-sloping curve like the one shown in Figure 1. For example, in 1955 the unemployment rate was 4.4 percent and the inflation rate was −.4 percent. In 1960 the unemployment rate was 5.5 percent and the inflation rate was 1.7 percent. Both unemployment and inflation rates had increased since 1955. Moving through time, you can see that the inflation rate tended to increase along with the unemployment rate through the 1960s and 1970s. By 1980, the unemployment rate was 7.1 percent and the inflation rate was 13.5 percent.

The scattered points in Figure 2 show no evidence of a tradeoff between unemployment and inflation. A downward-sloping Phillips curve does not seem to exist over the long term.

1.b. Short-Run Versus Long-Run Tradeoffs

Most economists believe that the downward-sloping Phillips curve and the tradeoff it implies between inflation and unemployment are short-term phe-

Copyright © by Houghton Mifflin Company. All rights reserved.

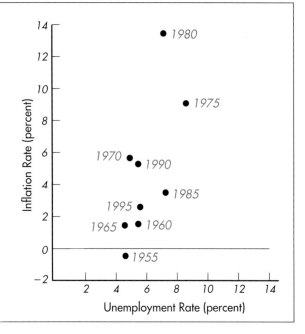

Figure 2
Unemployment and Inflation in the United States, 1955–1995
The data on inflation and unemployment rates in the United States between 1955 and 1995 show no particular relationship between inflation and unemployment over the long run. There is no evidence here of a downward-sloping Phillips curve. Source: *Economic Report of the President, 1997.*

How does the tradeoff between inflation and the unemployment rate vary from the short to the long run?

The data indicate that the Phillips curve may have shifted out in the 1960s and 1970s and shifted in during the 1980s.

Copyright © by Houghton Mifflin Company. All rights reserved.

nomena. Think of a series of Phillips curves, one for each of the points in Figure 2. From 1955 to 1980, the curves shifted out to the right. In the early 1980s, they shifted in to the left.

Figure 3 shows a series of Phillips curves that could account for the data in Figure 2. At any point in time, a downward-sloping Phillips curve indicates a tradeoff between inflation and unemployment. Many economists believe that this kind of tradeoff is just a short-term phenomenon. Over time, the Phillips curve shifts so that the short-run tradeoff between inflation and unemployment disappears in the long run.

On the early 1960s curve in Figure 3, 5 percent unemployment is consistent with 2 percent inflation. By the early 1970s, the curve had shifted up. Here 5 percent unemployment is associated with 6 percent inflation. On the late 1970s curve, 5 percent unemployment is consistent with 10 percent inflation. For more than two decades, the tradeoff between inflation and unemployment worsened as the Phillips curves shifted up, so that higher and higher inflation rates were associated with any given level of unemployment. Then in the 1980s, the tradeoff seemed to improve as the Phillips curve shifted down. On the late 1980s curve, 5 percent unemployment is consistent with 4 percent inflation.

The Phillips curves in Figure 3 represent changes that took place over time in the United States. We cannot be sure of the actual shape of a Phillips curve at any time, but an outward shift of the curve in the 1960s and 1970s and an inward shift during the 1980s are consistent with the data. Later in this chapter we describe how changing government policy and the public's expectations about that policy may have shifted aggregate demand and aggregate supply and produced these shifts in the Phillips curves.

Figure 3
The Shifting Phillips Curve

We can reconcile the long-run data on unemployment and inflation with the downward-sloping Phillips curve by using a series of Phillips curves. (In effect, we treat the long run as a series of short-run curves.) The Phillips curve for the early 1960s shows 5 percent unemployment and 2 percent inflation. Over time, the short-run curve shifted out to the right. The early 1970s curve shows 5 percent unemployment and 6 percent inflation. And the short-run curve for the late 1970s shows 5 percent unemployment and 10 percent inflation. In the early 1980s, the short-run Phillips curve began to shift down toward the origin. By the late 1980s, 5 percent unemployment was consistent with 4 percent inflation.

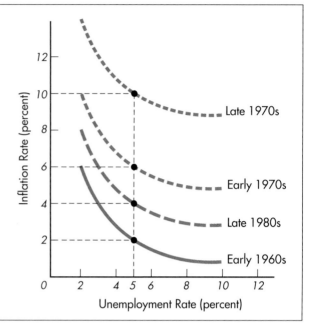

1.b.1. In the Short Run Figure 4 uses the aggregate demand and supply analysis we developed in Chapter 9 to explain the Phillips curve. Initially the economy is operating at point 1 in both diagrams. In part (a), the aggregate demand curve (AD_1) and aggregate supply curve (AS_1) intersect at price level P_1 and real GDP level Y_p, the level of potential real GDP. Remember that potential real GDP is the level of income and output generated at the natural rate of unemployment, the unemployment rate that exists in the absence of cyclical unemployment. In part (b), point 1 lies on Phillips curve I, where the inflation rate is 3 percent and the unemployment rate is 5 percent. We assume that the 5 percent unemployment rate at the level of potential real GDP is the natural rate of unemployment (U_n). A discussion of the natural rate of unemployment and its determinants is given in the Economic Insight "The Natural Rate of Unemployment."

What happens when aggregate demand goes up from AD_1 to AD_2? A new equilibrium is established along the short-run aggregate supply curve (AS_1) at point 2. Here the price level (P_2) is higher, as is the level of real GDP (Y_2). In part (b), the increase in price and income is reflected in the movement along Phillips curve I to point 2. At point 2, the inflation rate is 6 percent and the unemployment rate is 3 percent. The increase in expenditures raises the inflation rate and lowers the unemployment rate (because national output has surpassed potential output).

Notice that there appears to be a tradeoff between inflation and unemployment on Phillips curve I. The increase in spending increases output and stimulates employment, so that the unemployment rate falls. And the higher spending pushes the rate of inflation up. But this tradeoff is only temporary. Point 2 in both diagrams is only a short-run equilibrium.

1.b.2. In the Long Run As we discussed in Chapter 9, the short-run aggregate supply curve shifts over time as production costs rise in response to higher prices. Once the aggregate supply curve shifts to AS_2, long-run equilib-

Copyright © by Houghton Mifflin Company. All rights reserved.

Figure 4
Aggregate Demand and Supply and the Phillips Curve
The movement from point 1 to point 2 to point 3 traces the adjustment of the economy to an increase in aggregate demand. Point 1 is initial equilibrium in both diagrams. At this point potential real GDP is Y_p and the price level is P_1 in the aggregate demand and supply diagram, and the inflation rate is 3 percent with an unemployment rate of 5 percent (the natural rate) along short-run curve I in the Phillips curve diagram.

If the aggregate demand curve shifts from AD_1 to AD_2, equilibrium real GDP goes up to Y_2 and the price level rises to P_2 in the aggregate demand and supply diagram. The increase in aggregate demand pushes the inflation rate up to 6 percent and the unemployment rate down to 3 percent along Phillips curve I. The movement from point

1 to point 2 along the curve indicates a tradeoff between inflation and the unemployment rate.

Over time the AS curve shifts in response to rising production costs at the higher rate of inflation. Along AS_2, equilibrium is at point 3, where real GDP falls back to Y_p and the price level rises to P_3. As we move from point 2 to point 3 in part (b), we shift to short-run Phillips curve II. Here the inflation rate remains high (at 6 percent), while the unemployment rate goes back up to 5 percent, the rate consistent with production at Y_p. In the long run, then, there is no tradeoff between inflation and unemployment. The vertical long-run aggregate supply curve at the potential level of real GDP is associated with the vertical long-run Phillips curve at the natural rate of unemployment.

(a) Aggregate Demand and Supply

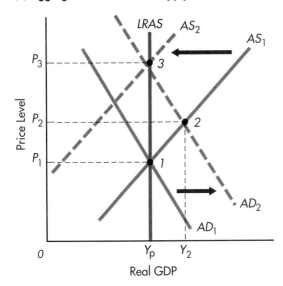

(b) Phillips Curve

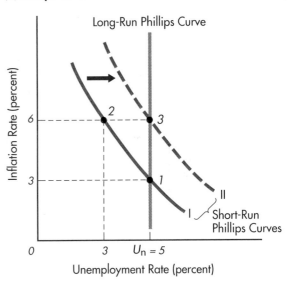

Copyright © by Houghton Mifflin Company. All rights reserved.

rium occurs at point 3, where AS_2 intersects AD_2. Here, the price level is P_3 and real GDP returns to its potential level, Y_p.

The shift in aggregate supply lowers real GDP. As income falls, the unemployment rate goes up. The decrease in aggregate supply is reflected in the movement from point 2 on Phillips curve I to point 3 on Phillips curve II. As real GDP returns to its potential level (Y_p), unemployment returns to the natural rate (U_n), 5 percent. In the long run, as the economy adjusts to an increase in aggregate demand and expectations adjust to the new inflation rate, there is a period in which real GDP falls and the price level rises.

Over time there is no relationship between the price level and the level of real GDP. You can see this in the aggregate demand and supply diagram. Points 1 and 3 both lie along the long-run aggregate supply curve (*LRAS*) at potential real GDP. The *LRAS* curve has its analogue in the long-run Phillips curve, a vertical line at the natural rate of unemployment. Points 1 and 3 both lie along this curve.

The long-run Phillips curve is a vertical line at the natural rate of unemployment.

The Natural Rate of Unemployment

The natural rate of unemployment is defined as the unemployment rate that exists in the absence of cyclical unemployment. As we discussed in Chapter 8, the natural rate of unemployment reflects the normal amount of frictional unemployment (people temporarily between jobs), structural unemployment (people who lost jobs because of technological change), and seasonal unemployment (people who lost jobs because the jobs are available only at certain times of the year). What factors determine the normal amount of frictional and structural unemployment?

One of the most important factors is demographic change. As the age, gender, and racial makeup of the labor force changes, the natural rate of unemployment also changes. For instance, when the baby boom generation entered the labor force, the natural rate of unemployment increased because new workers typically have the highest unemployment rates. Between 1956 and 1979, the proportion of young adults (ages sixteen to twenty-four) in the labor force increased, increasing the nat-

ural rate of unemployment. Since 1979, the fraction of young adults in the labor force has fallen, tending to lower the natural rate of unemployment.

In addition to the composition of the labor force, several other factors affect the natural rate of unemployment:

- In the early 1990s, structural changes in the economy, such as the shift from manufacturing to service jobs and the "downsizing" and restructuring of firms throughout the economy contributed to a higher natural rate of unemployment. Related to these structural changes is a decline in the demand for low-skilled workers so that rising unemployment is overwhelmingly concentrated among workers with limited education and skills.

- Increases in the legal minimum wage tend to raise the natural rate of unemployment. When the government mandates that employers pay some workers a higher wage than a freely competitive labor market would pay, fewer workers are employed.

- The more generous the unemployment benefits, the higher the natural rate of unemployment. Increased benefits reduce the cost of being out of work and allow unemployed workers to take their time finding a new job.

- Income taxes can also affect the natural rate of unemployment. Higher taxes mean that workers keep less of their earned income and so have less incentive to work.

The effect of these factors on the unemployment rate is complex, so it is difficult to state what the natural rate of unemployment is exactly. But as these factors change over time, the natural rate of unemployment also changes.

One last thing. It is not clear that minimizing the natural rate of unemployment is a universal goal. Minimum wages, unemployment benefits, and taxes have other important implications besides their effect on the natural rate of unemployment. We cannot expect these variables to be set solely in terms of their effect on unemployment.

Copyright © by Houghton Mifflin Company. All rights reserved.

RECAP

1. The Phillips curve shows an inverse relationship between inflation and unemployment.

2. The downward slope of the Phillips curve indicates a tradeoff between inflation and unemployment.

3. Over the long run that tradeoff disappears.

4. The long-run Phillips curve is a vertical line at the natural rate of unemployment, analogous to the long-run aggregate supply curve at potential real GDP.

2. THE ROLE OF EXPECTATIONS

The data and analysis in the previous section indicate that there is no long-run tradeoff between inflation and unemployment. But they do not explain the movement of the Phillips curve in the 1960s, 1970s, and 1980s. To understand why the short-run curve shifts, you must understand the role that unexpected inflation plays in the economy.

2.a. Expected Versus Unexpected Inflation

What is the relationship between unexpected inflation and the unemployment rate?

Figure 5 shows two short-run Phillips curves like those in Figure 4. Each curve is drawn for a particular expected rate of inflation. Curve I shows the tradeoff between inflation and unemployment when the inflation rate is expected to be 3 percent. If the actual rate of inflation (measured along the vertical axis) is 3 percent, the economy is operating at point 1, with an unemployment rate of 5 percent (the natural rate). If the inflation rate unexpectedly increases to 6 percent, the economy moves from point 1 to point 2 along Phillips curve I. Obviously, unexpected inflation can affect the unemployment rate. There are three factors at work here: wage expectations, inventory fluctuations, and wage contracts.

2.a.1. Wage Expectations and Unemployment
Unemployed workers who are looking for a job choose a **reservation wage**, the minimum wage they are willing to accept. They continue to look for work until they receive an offer that equals or exceeds their reservation wage.

reservation wage:
the minimum wage a worker is willing to accept

Wages are not the only factor that workers take into consideration before accepting a job offer. A firm that offers good working conditions and fringe benefits can pay a lower wage than a firm that does not offer these advantages. But other things being equal, workers choose higher wages over lower wages. We simplify our analysis here by assuming that the only variable that affects the unemployed worker who is looking for a job is the reservation wage.

Copyright © by Houghton Mifflin Company. All rights reserved.

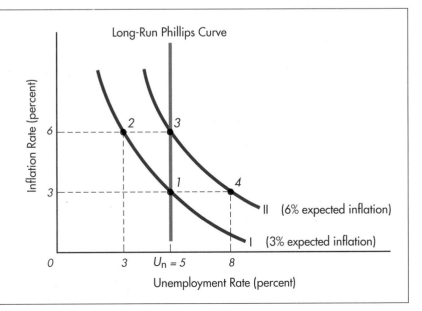

Figure 5
Expectations and the Phillips Curve
Short-run Phillips curve I shows the tradeoff between inflation and the unemployment rate as long as people expect 3 percent inflation. When the actual rate of inflation is 3 percent, the rate of unemployment (U_n) is 5 percent (point 1). Short-run Phillips curve II shows the tradeoff as long as people expect 6 percent inflation. When the actual rate of inflation is 6 percent, the unemployment rate is 5 percent (point 3).

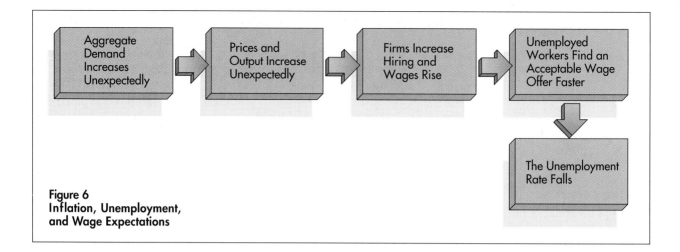

Figure 6
Inflation, Unemployment, and Wage Expectations

The link between unexpected inflation and the unemployment rate stems from the fact that wage offers are surprisingly high when the rate of inflation is surprisingly high. An unexpected increase in inflation means that prices are higher than anticipated, as are nominal income and wages. If aggregate demand increases unexpectedly, then, prices, output, employment, and wages go up. Unemployed workers with a constant reservation wage find it easier to obtain a satisfactory wage offer during a period when wages are rising faster than the workers expected. This means that more unemployed workers find jobs, and they find those jobs quicker than they do in a period when the rate of inflation is expected. So the unemployment rate falls during a period of unexpectedly high inflation (Figure 6).

Consider an example. Suppose an accountant named Jason decides that he must find a job that pays at least $105 a day. Jason's reservation wage is $105. Furthermore, Jason expects prices and wages to be fairly stable across the economy; he expects no inflation. Jason looks for a job and finds that the jobs he qualifies for are only offering wages of $100 a day. Because his job offers are all paying less than his reservation wage, he keeps on looking. Let's say that aggregate demand rises unexpectedly. Firms increase production and raise prices. To hire more workers, they increase the wages they offer. Suppose wages go up 5 percent. Now the jobs that Jason qualifies for are offering 5 percent higher wages, $105 a day instead of $100 a day. At this higher wage rate, Jason quickly accepts a job and starts working. This example explains why the move from point 1 to point 2 in Figure 5 occurs.

The short-run Phillips curve assumes a constant *expected* rate of inflation. It also assumes that every unemployed worker who is looking for a job has a constant reservation wage. When inflation rises unexpectedly, then, wages rise faster than expected and the unemployment rate falls. The element of "surprise" is critical here. If the increase in inflation is *expected*, unemployed workers who are looking for a job will revise their reservation wage to match the expected change in the level of prices. If reservation wages go up with the rate of inflation, there is no tradeoff between inflation and the unemployment rate. Higher inflation is associated with the original unemployment rate.

Let's go back to Jason, the accountant who wants a job that pays $105 a day. Previously we said that if wages increased to $105 unexpectedly because

If the reservation wage goes up with the rate of inflation, there is no tradeoff between inflation and the unemployment rate.

Copyright © by Houghton Mifflin Company. All rights reserved.

of an increase in aggregate demand, he would quickly find an acceptable job. However, if Jason knows that the price level is going to go up 5 percent, then he knows that a wage increase from $100 to $105 is not a real wage increase because he needs $105 in order to buy what $100 would buy before. The *nominal wage* is the number of dollars earned; the *real wage* is the purchasing power of those dollars. If the nominal wage increases 5 percent at the same time that prices have gone up 5 percent, it takes 5 percent more money to buy the same goods and services. The real wage has not changed. What happens? Jason revises his reservation wage to account for the higher price level. If he wants a 5 percent higher real wage, his reservation wage goes up to $110.25 (5 percent more than $105). Now if employers offer him $105, he refuses and keeps searching.

In Figure 5, an expected increase in inflation moves us from point 1 on curve I to point 3 on curve II. When increased inflation is expected, the reservation wage reflects the higher rate of inflation and there is no tradeoff between inflation and the unemployment rate. Instead the economy moves along the long-run Phillips curve, with unemployment at its natural rate. The clockwise movement from point 1 to point 2 to point 3 is the pattern that follows an unexpected increase in aggregate demand.

What if the inflation rate is lower than expected? Here we find a reservation wage that reflects higher expected inflation. This means that those people who are looking for jobs are going to have a difficult time finding acceptable wage offers, the number of unemployed workers is going to increase, and the unemployment rate is going to rise. This sequence is shown in Figure 5, as the economy moves from point 3 to point 4. When the actual inflation rate is 6 percent and the expected inflation rate is also 6 percent, the economy is operating at the natural rate of unemployment. When the inflation rate falls to 3 percent but workers still expect 6 percent inflation, the unemployment rate rises (at point 4 along curve II). Eventually, if the inflation rate remains at 3 percent, workers adjust their expectations to the lower rate and the economy moves to point 1 on curve I. The short-run effect of unexpected *disinflation* is rising unemployment. Over time the short-run increase in the unemployment rate is eliminated.

As long as the actual rate of inflation equals the expected rate, the economy remains at the natural rate of unemployment. The tradeoff between inflation and the unemployment rate comes from unexpected inflation.

2.a.2. Inventory Fluctuations and Unemployment
Businesses hold inventories based on what they expect their sales to be. When aggregate demand is greater than expected, inventories fall below targeted levels. To restore inventories to the levels wanted, production is increased. Increased production leads to increased employment. If aggregate demand is lower than expected, inventories rise above targeted levels. To reduce inventories, production is cut back and workers are laid off from their jobs until sales have lowered unwanted inventories. Once production increases, employment rises again.

Inventory, production, and employment all play a part in the Phillips curve analysis (Figure 7). Expected sales and inventory levels are based on an expected level of aggregate demand. If aggregate demand is greater than expected, inventories fall and prices rise on the remaining goods in stock. With the unexpected increase in inflation, the unemployment rate falls as businesses hire more workers to increase output to offset falling inventories.

As long as the actual rate of inflation equals the expected rate, the economy operates at the natural rate of unemployment.

When aggregate demand is higher than expected, inventories are lower than expected and prices are higher than expected, so the unemployment rate falls. When aggregate demand is lower than expected, inventories are higher than expected and prices are lower than expected, so the unemployment rate rises.

Copyright © by Houghton Mifflin Company. All rights reserved.

Figure 7
Inflation, Unemployment, and Inventories

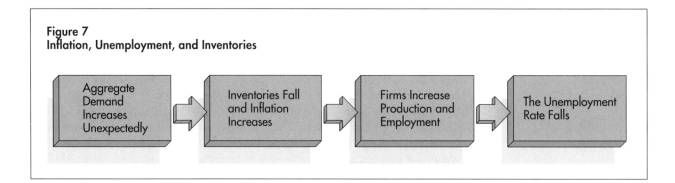

This sequence represents movement along a short-run Phillips curve because there is a tradeoff between inflation and the unemployment rate. We find the same tradeoff if aggregate demand is lower than expected. Here inventories increase and prices are lower than anticipated. With the unexpected decrease in inflation, the unemployment rate goes up as workers are laid off to reduce output until inventory levels fall.

2.a.3. Wage Contracts and Unemployment   Another factor that explains the short-run tradeoff between inflation and unemployment is labor contracts that fix wages for an extended period of time. When an existing contract expires, management must renegotiate with labor. A firm facing lower demand for its products may negotiate lower wages in order to keep as many workers employed as before. If the demand for a firm's products falls while a wage contract is in force, the firm must maintain wages, which means it is going to have to lay off workers.

For example, a pizza restaurant with $1,000 a day in revenues employs 4 workers at $40 a day each. The firm's total labor costs are $160 a day. Suppose revenues fall to $500 a day. If the firm wants to cut its labor costs in half, to $80, it has two choices: it can maintain wages at $40 a day and lay off 2 workers, or it can lower wages to $20 a day and keep all 4 workers. If the restaurant has a contract with the employees that sets wages at $40 a day, it must lay off 2 workers.

If demand increases while a wage contract is in force, a business hires more workers at the fixed wage. Once the contract expires, the firm's workers will negotiate higher wages, to reflect increased demand. For instance, suppose prices in the economy, including the price of pizzas, go up 10 percent. If the pizza restaurant can raise its prices 10 percent and sell as many pizzas as before (because the price of every other food also has gone up 10 percent), its daily revenues increase from $1,000 to $1,100. If the restaurant has a labor contract that fixes wages at $40 a day, its profits are going to go up, reflecting the higher price of pizzas. With its increased profits, the restaurant may be willing to hire more workers. Once the labor contract expires, the workers ask for a 10 percent wage increase to match the price level increase. If wages go up to $44 a day (10 percent higher than $40), the firm cannot hire more workers because wages have gone up in proportion to the increase in prices. If the costs of doing business rise at the same rate as prices, both profits and employment remain the same.

In the national economy, wage contracts are staggered; they expire at different times. Each year only 30 to 40 percent of all contracts expire across the

Copyright © by Houghton Mifflin Company. All rights reserved.

Copyright © by Houghton Mifflin Company. All rights reserved.

Figure 8
Inflation, Unemployment, and Wage Controls

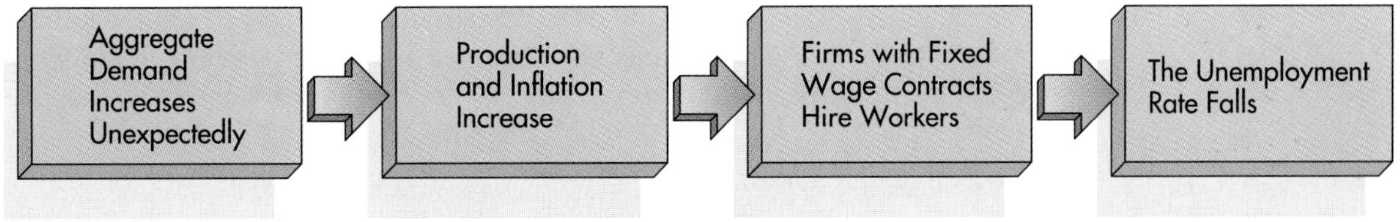

entire economy. As economic conditions change, firms with expiring wage contracts can adjust *wages* to those conditions; firms with existing contracts must adjust *employment* to those conditions.

How do long-term wage contracts tie in with the Phillips curve analysis? The expected rate of inflation is based on expected aggregate demand and reflected in the wage that is agreed on in the contract. When the actual rate of inflation equals the expected rate, businesses retain the same number of workers they had planned on when they signed the contract. For the economy overall, when actual and expected inflation rates are the same, the economy is operating at the natural rate of unemployment. That is, businesses are not hiring new workers because of an unexpected increase in aggregate demand, and they are not laying off workers because of an unexpected decrease in aggregate demand.

When aggregate demand is higher than expected, those firms with unexpired wage contracts hire more workers at the fixed wage, reducing unemployment (Figure 8). Those firms with expiring contracts have to offer higher wages in order to maintain the existing level of employment at the new demand condition. When aggregate demand is lower than expected, those firms with unexpired contracts have to lay off workers because they cannot lower the wage, while those firms with expiring contracts negotiate lower wages in order to keep their workers.

Wage contracts force businesses to adjust employment rather than wages in response to an unexpected change in aggregate demand.

If wages were always flexible, unexpected changes in aggregate demand might be reflected largely in *wage* rather than *employment* adjustments. Wage contracts force businesses to adjust employment when aggregate demand changes unexpectedly.

2.b. Forming Expectations

How are macroeconomic expectations formed?

Expectations play a key role in explaining the short-run Phillips curve, the tradeoff between inflation and the unemployment rate. How are these expectations formed?

adaptive expectation:
an expectation formed on the basis of information collected in the past

2.b.1. Adaptive Expectations Expectations can be formed solely on the basis of experience. **Adaptive expectations** are expectations that are determined by what has happened in the recent past.

People learn from their experiences. For example, suppose the inflation rate has been 3 percent for the past few years. Based on past experience, then, people expect the inflation rate in the future to remain at 3 percent. If the Federal Reserve increases the growth of the money supply to a rate that produces 6 percent inflation, the public will be surprised by the higher rate of inflation. This unexpected inflation creates a short-run tradeoff between inflation and the unemployment rate along a short-run Phillips curve. Over time, if the inflation rate remains at 6 percent, the public will learn that the 3 percent rate is too low and will adapt its expectations to the actual, higher inflation rate. Once public expectations have adapted to the new rate of inflation, the economy returns to the natural rate of unemployment along the long-run Phillips curve.

2.b.2. Rational Expectations

Many economists believe that adaptive expectations are too narrow. If people look only at past information, they are ignoring what could be important information in the current period. **Rational expectations** are based on all available relevant information.

We are not saying that people have to know everything in order to form expectations. Rational expectations require only that people consider the information they believe to be relevant. This information includes their past experience along with what is currently happening and what they expect to happen in the future. For instance, in forming expectations about inflation, people consider rates in the recent past, current policy, and anticipated shifts in aggregate demand and supply that could affect the future rate of inflation.

If the inflation rate has been 3 percent over the past few years, adaptive expectations suggest that the future inflation rate will be 3 percent. No other information is considered. Rational expectations are based on more than the historical rate. Suppose the Fed announces a new policy that everyone believes will increase inflation in the future. With rational expectations the effect of this announcement will be considered. Here, when the actual rate of inflation turns out to be more than 3 percent, there is no short-run tradeoff between inflation and the unemployment rate. The economy moves directly along the long-run Phillips curve to the higher inflation rate, while unemployment remains at the natural rate.

If we believe that people have rational expectations, we do not expect them to make the same mistakes over and over. We expect them to learn and react quickly to new information.

rational expectation:
an expectation that is formed using all available relevant information

RECAP

1. Wage expectations, inventory fluctuations, and wage contracts help explain the short-run tradeoff between inflation and the unemployment rate.

2. The reservation wage is the minimum wage a worker is willing to accept.

3. Because wage expectations reflect expected inflation, when the inflation rate is surprisingly high, unemployed workers find jobs faster and the unemployment rate falls.

4. Unexpected increases in aggregate demand lower inventories and raise prices. To increase output (to replenish shrinking inventories), businesses hire more workers, which reduces the unemployment rate.

5. When aggregate demand is higher than expected, those businesses with wage contracts hire more workers at the fixed wage, lowering unemployment.

6. If wages were always flexible, unexpected changes in aggregate demand

Copyright © by Houghton Mifflin Company. All rights reserved.

would be reflected in wage adjustments rather than employment adjustments.

7. Adaptive expectations are formed on the basis of information about the past.

8. Rational expectations are formed using all available relevant information.

3. CREDIBILITY AND TIME INCONSISTENCY

The rate of inflation is a product of growth in the money supply. That growth is controlled by the country's central bank. If the Federal Reserve follows a policy of rapidly increasing the money supply, one consequence is rapid inflation. If it follows a policy of slow growth, it keeps inflation down.

To help the public predict the future course of monetary policy, Congress passed the Federal Reserve Reform Act (1977) and the Full Employment and Balanced Growth Act (1978). The Full Employment Act requires that the chairman of the Board of Governors of the Federal Reserve System testify before Congress annually, presenting the Fed's targets for money growth along with other policy plans.

Of course, the Fed's plans are only plans. There is no requirement that the central bank actually follow the plans announced to Congress. During the course of the year, the Fed may decide that a new policy is necessary in light of economic developments. Changing conditions mean that plans can be **time inconsistent**. A plan is time inconsistent when it is changed over time in response to changed conditions.

time inconsistent:
a characteristic of a policy or plan that changes over time in response to changing conditions

3.a. The Policymaker's Problem

Time inconsistency gives the Fed a credibility problem and the public the problem of guessing where monetary policy and the inflation rate are actually heading.

Figure 9 shows an example of how announced monetary policy can turn out to be time inconsistent. The Fed, like all central banks, always announces that it plans to follow a low-money-growth policy to promote a low rate of inflation. (It is unlikely that a central bank would ever state that it intends to follow an inflationary monetary policy.) Yet we know that the world often is characterized by higher rates of inflation. Because the actual inflation rate often ends up being higher than the intended inflation rate, low-inflation plans often are time inconsistent.

In Figure 9, labor contracts are signed following the central bank's announcement. The contracts call for either low wage increases or high wage increases. If everyone believes that the money supply is going to grow at the announced low rate, then the low-wage contracts are signed. However, if there is reason to believe that the announced policy is time inconsistent, the high-wage contracts are signed.

Over time, the central bank either follows the announced low-money-growth policy or implements a high-money-growth policy. If the low-wage contract is in force and the central bank follows the low-money-growth policy, the actual inflation rate will match the low rate that people expected and the unemployment rate will equal the natural rate. If the central bank follows

Copyright © by Houghton Mifflin Company. All rights reserved.

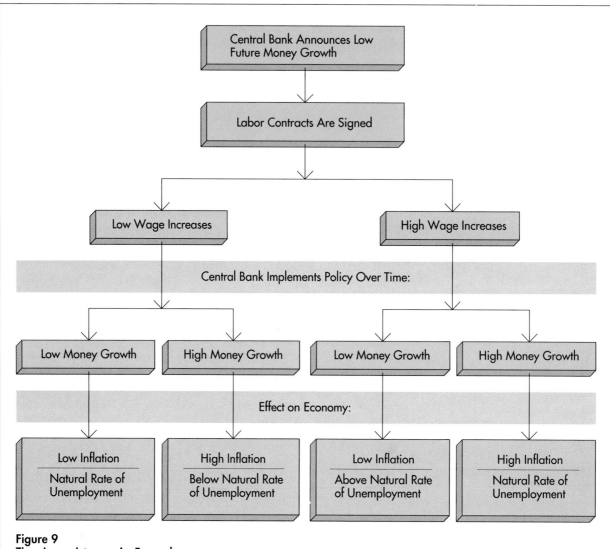

Figure 9
Time Inconsistency: An Example
Regardless of which labor contract is signed, the central bank achieves the lowest
unemployment rate by following the high-money-growth policy—the opposite of its
announced policy.

a high-money-growth policy, the rate of inflation will be higher than expected
and the unemployment rate will fall below the natural rate.

If the high-wage contract is in force and the low-money-growth policy is
followed, the inflation rate will be lower than expected and the unemployment
rate will exceed the natural rate. If the high-money-growth policy is followed,
the inflation rate will be as expected and the unemployment rate will be at the
natural rate.

Look what happens to unemployment. Regardless of which labor contract is
signed, if the central bank wants to keep unemployment as low as possible, it
must deviate from its announced plan. The plan turns out to be time inconsis-

Copyright © by Houghton Mifflin Company. All rights reserved.

tent. Because the public knows that unemployment, like the rate of inflation, is a factor in the Fed's policymaking, the central bank's announced plan is not credible.

3.b. Credibility

What makes government policies credible?

If the public does not believe the low-money-growth plans of the central bank, high-wage contracts will always be signed, and the central bank will always have to follow a high-money-growth policy to maintain the natural rate of unemployment. This cycle creates an economy where high inflation persists year after year. If the central bank always followed its announced plan of low money growth and low inflation, the public would believe the plan, low-wage contracts would always be signed, and the natural rate of unemployment would exist at the low rate of inflation. In either case, high or low inflation, if the inflation rate is expected, the unemployment rate does not change. If the central bank eliminates the goal of reducing unemployment below the natural rate, the problem of inflation disappears. However, the public must be convinced that the central bank intends to pursue low money growth in the long run, avoiding the temptation to reduce the unemployment rate in the short run.

How does the central bank achieve credibility? One way is to fix the growth rate of the money supply by law. Congress could pass a law requiring that the Fed maintain a growth rate of, say, 3 to 5 percent a year. There would be problems defining the money supply, but this kind of law would give the Fed's policies credibility.

Another way for the Fed to establish credibility is to create incentives for monetary authorities to take a long-term view of monetary policy. In the long run, the economy is better off if policymakers do not try to exploit the short-run tradeoff between inflation and the unemployment rate. The central bank can achieve a lower rate of inflation at the natural rate of unemployment by avoiding unexpected increases in the rate at which money and inflation grow.

Reputation is a key factor here. If the central bank considers the effects of its actual policy on public expectations, it will find it easier to achieve low inflation by establishing a reputation for low-inflation policies. A central bank with a reputation for time-consistent plans will find labor contracts calling for low wage increases because people believe that the bank is going to follow its announced plans and generate a low rate of inflation. In other words, by maintaining a reputation for following through on announced policy, the Fed can earn the public confidence necessary to produce a low rate of inflation in the long run.

RECAP

1. A plan is time inconsistent when it changes over time in response to changing conditions.
2. If the public believes that an announced policy is time inconsistent, policymakers have a credibility problem that can limit the success of their plans.
3. Credibility can be achieved by fixing the growth rate of the money supply by law or by creating incentives for policymakers to follow through on announced plans.

Copyright © by Houghton Mifflin Company. All rights reserved.

4. SOURCES OF BUSINESS CYCLES

In Chapter 12 we examined the effect of fiscal policy on the equilibrium level of real GDP. Changes in government spending and taxes can expand or contract the economy. In Chapter 14 we described how monetary policy affects the equilibrium level of real GDP. Changes in the money supply also produce booms and recessions. Besides the policy-induced sources of business cycles covered in earlier chapters, there are other sources of economic fluctuations that economists have studied. One is the election campaign of incumbent politicians, and when a business cycle results from this action it is called a *political business cycle*. Macroeconomic policy may be used to promote the reelection of incumbent politicians. We also examine another source of business cycles that is not related to discretionary policy actions, the *real business cycle*.

4.a. The Political Business Cycle

Are business cycles related to political elections?

If a short-run tradeoff exists between inflation and unemployment, an incumbent administration could stimulate the economy just before an election to lower the unemployment rate, making voters happy and increasing the probability of reelection. Of course, after the election, the long-run adjustment to the expansionary policy would lead to higher inflation and move unemployment back to the natural rate.

Figure 10 illustrates the pattern. Before the election, the economy is initially at point 1 in parts (a) and (b). The incumbent administration stimulates the economy by increasing government spending or increasing the growth of the money supply. Aggregate demand shifts from AD_1 to AD_2 in part (a). In the short run, the increase in aggregate demand is unexpected, so the economy moves along the initial aggregate supply curve (AS_1) to point 2. This movement is reflected in part (b) of the figure, in the movement from point 1 to point 2 along short-run Phillips curve I. The pre-election expansionary policy increases real GDP and lowers the unemployment rate. Once the public adjusts its expectations to the higher inflation rate, the economy experiences a recession. Real GDP falls back to its potential level (Y_p) and the unemployment rate goes back up to the natural rate (U_n), as shown by the movement from point 2 to point 3 in both parts of the figure.

An unexpected increase in government spending or money growth temporarily stimulates the economy. If an election comes during the period of expansion, higher incomes and lower unemployment may increase support for the incumbent administration. The long-run adjustment back to potential real GDP and the natural rate of unemployment comes after the election.

Economists do not agree on whether a political business cycle exists in the United States. But they do agree that an effort to exploit the short-run tradeoff between inflation and the unemployment rate would shift the short-run Phillips curve out as shown in part (b) of Figure 10.

The evidence of a political business cycle is not clear. If government macroeconomic policy is designed to stimulate the economy before elections and to bear the costs of rising unemployment and inflation after elections, we should see recessions regularly following national elections. Table 1 lists the presidential elections since 1948 along with the recessions that followed

Copyright © by Houghton Mifflin Company. All rights reserved.

Figure 10
The Political Business Cycle
Before the election, the government stimulates the economy, unexpectedly increasing aggregate demand. The economy moves from point 1 to point 2, pushing equilibrium real GDP above Y_p (part [a]) and the unemployment rate below U_n (part [b]). The incumbent politicians hope that rising incomes and lower unemployment will translate into votes. After the election comes adjustment to the higher aggregate demand, as the economy moves from point 2 to point 3. The aggregate supply curve shifts to the left, and equilibrium real GDP falls back to Y_p. Unemployment goes back up to U_n, and the rate of inflation rises.

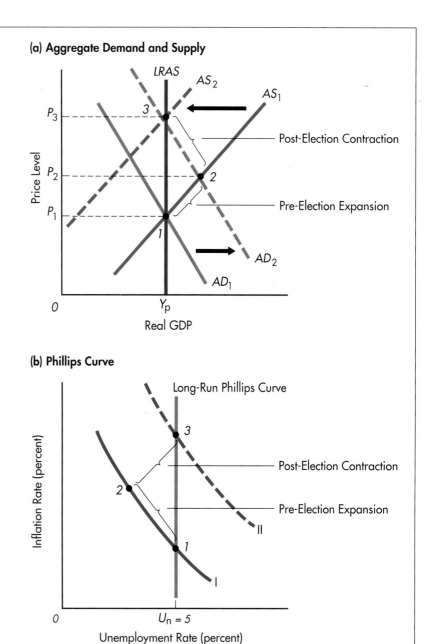

(a) Aggregate Demand and Supply

(b) Phillips Curve

them. In five cases, a recession occurred the year after an election. A recession began before President Kennedy's election, and there was no recession during the Johnson and second Reagan administrations. Of course, just because recessions do not follow every election, there is no guarantee that some business cycles have not stemmed from political manipulation. If a short-run Phillips curve exists, the potential for a political business cycle exists as long as the public does not expect the government to stimulate the economy before elections.

Copyright © by Houghton Mifflin Company. All rights reserved.

TABLE 1
Presidential Elections and U.S. Recessions, 1948–1996

Presidential Election (Winner)	*Next Recession*
November 1948 (Truman)	November 1948–October 1949
November 1952 (Eisenhower)	June 1953–May 1954
November 1956 (Eisenhower)	June 1957–April 1958
November 1960 (Kennedy)	April 1960–February 1961
November 1964 (Johnson)	
November 1968 (Nixon)	October 1969–November 1970
November 1972 (Nixon)	December 1973–March 1975
November 1976 (Carter)	January 1980–July 1980
November 1980 (Reagan)	May 1981–November 1982
November 1984 (Reagan)	
November 1988 (Bush)	July 1990–March 1991
November 1992 (Clinton)	
November 1996 (Clinton)	

4.b. Real Business Cycles

shock:
an unexpected change in a variable

In recent years economists have paid increasing attention to real **shocks**— unexpected changes—in the economy as a source of business cycles. Many believe that it is not only fiscal or monetary policy that triggers expansion or contraction in the economy, but technological change, change in tastes, labor strikes, weather, or other real changes. A real business cycle is one that is generated by a change in one of those real variables.

Interest in the real business cycle was stimulated by the oil price shocks in the early 1970s and the important role they played in triggering the recession of 1973–1975. At that time, many economists were focusing on the role of unexpected changes in monetary policy in generating business cycles. They argued that these kinds of policy changes (changes in a nominal variable, the money supply) were responsible for the shifts in aggregate demand that led to expansions and contractions. When OPEC raised oil prices, it caused major shifts in aggregate supply. Higher oil prices in 1973 and 1974, and in 1979 and 1980, reduced aggregate supply, pushing the equilibrium level of real GDP down. Lower oil prices in 1986 raised aggregate supply and equilibrium real GDP.

How do real shocks to the economy affect business cycles?

An economywide real shock, like a substantial change in the price of oil, can affect output and employment across all sectors of the economy. Even an industry-specific shock can generate a recession or expansion in the entire economy if the industry produces a product used by a substantial number of other industries. For example, a labor strike in the steel industry would have major recessionary implications for the economy as a whole. If the output of steel fell, the price of steel would be bid up by all the industries that use steel as an input. This would shift the short-run aggregate supply curve to the left, as shown in part (a) of Figure 11, and would move equilibrium real GDP from Y_1 down to Y_2.

Real shocks can also have expansionary effects on the economy. Suppose that the weather is particularly good one year and that harvests are surpris-

Copyright © by Houghton Mifflin Company. All rights reserved.

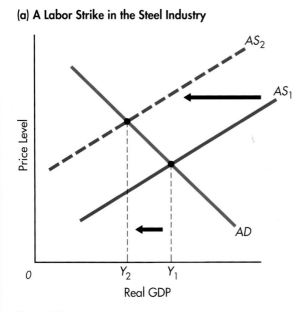

(a) A Labor Strike in the Steel Industry

Price Level

AS_2

AS_1

AD

0 Y_2 Y_1

Real GDP

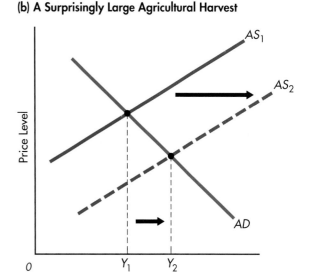

(b) A Surprisingly Large Agricultural Harvest

Price Level

AS_1

AS_2

AD

0 Y_1 Y_2

Real GDP

Figure 11
The Impact of Real Shocks on Equilibrium Real GDP
A labor strike in a key industry can shift the aggregate supply curve to the left, like the shift from AS_1 to AS_2. This pushes equilibrium real GDP down from Y_1 to Y_2.
   If good weather leads to a banner harvest, the aggre-

gate supply curve shifts to the right, like the shift from AS_1 to AS_2, raising equilibrium real GDP from Y_1 to Y_2.

A business cycle can be the product of discretionary government policy or of real shocks that occur independent of government actions.

ingly large. What happens? The price of food, cotton, and other agricultural output tends to fall, and the short-run aggregate supply curve shifts to the right, as shown in Figure 11(b), raising equilibrium real GDP from Y_1 to Y_2.

Real business cycles explain why national output can expand or contract in the absence of a discretionary macroeconomic policy that would shift aggregate demand. To fully understand business cycles, we must consider both policy-induced changes in real GDP, as covered in Chapters 12 and 14, and real shocks that occur independent of government actions.

RECAP

1. The political business cycle is a short-term expansion stimulated by an administration before an election to earn votes. After the election comes the long-term adjustment (rising unemployment and inflation).

2. A real business cycle is an expansion and contraction caused by a change in tastes or technology, strikes, weather, or other real factors.

5. THE LINK BETWEEN MONETARY AND FISCAL POLICIES

In earlier chapters we have described how monetary and fiscal policies determine the equilibrium level of prices and national income. In our discussions

Copyright © by Houghton Mifflin Company. All rights reserved.

Those who were around in the 1970s can remember the long lines and shortages at gas stations and the rapid increase in the price of oil that resulted from the oil embargo imposed by the Organization of Petroleum Exporting Countries. There was another effect of the oil price shock—the aggregate supply curve in the United States and other oil-importing nations shifted to the left, lowering the equilibrium level of real GDP while raising the price level. Such "real" sources of business cycles can explain why national output can rise or fall in the absence of any discretionary government macroeconomic policy.

we have talked about monetary policy and fiscal policy individually. Here we consider the relationship between them.

In some countries, monetary and fiscal policies are carried out by a single central authority. Even in the United States, where the Federal Reserve was created as an independent agency, monetary policy and fiscal policy are always related. The actions of the central bank have an impact on the proper role for fiscal policy, and the actions of fiscal policymakers have an impact on the proper role for monetary policy.

For example, suppose the central bank follows a monetary policy that raises interest rates. That policy raises the interest cost of new government debt, in the process increasing government expenditures. On the other hand, a fiscal policy that generates large fiscal deficits could contribute to higher interest rates. If the central bank has targeted an interest rate that lies below the current rate, the central bank could be drawn into an expansionary monetary policy. This interdependence between monetary and fiscal policy is important to policymakers as well as to business people and others who seek to understand current economic developments.

5.a. The Government Budget Constraint

How is inflationary monetary policy related to government fiscal policy?

The *government budget constraint* clarifies the relationship between monetary and fiscal policies:

$$G = T + B + \Delta M$$

where

G = government spending

T = tax revenue

Copyright © by Houghton Mifflin Company. All rights reserved.

$$B = \text{government borrowing}$$

$$\Delta M = \text{the change in the money supply}[1]$$

The government budget constraint always holds because there are only three ways for the government to finance its spending: by taxing, by borrowing, and by creating money.

We can rewrite the government budget constraint with the change in M on the left-hand side of the equation:

$$\Delta M = (G - T) - B$$

In this form you can see that the change in government-issued money equals the government fiscal deficit $(G - T)$ minus borrowing. This equation is always true. A government that has the ability to borrow at reasonable costs will not have the incentive to create rapid money growth and the consequent inflation that results in order to finance its budget deficit.

5.b. Monetary Reforms

In the United States and other industrial nations, monetary and fiscal policies are conducted by separate, independent agencies. Fiscal authorities (Congress and the president in the U.S.) cannot impose monetary policy on the central bank. But in typical developing countries, monetary and fiscal policies are controlled by a central political authority. Here monetary policy is often an extension of fiscal policy. Fiscal policy can impose an inflationary burden on monetary policy. If a country is running a large fiscal deficit, and much of this deficit cannot be financed by government borrowing, monetary authorities must create money to finance the deficit.

Using money to finance fiscal deficits has produced very rapid rates of inflation in several countries. As prices reach astronomical levels, currency must be issued with very large face values. For instance, when Bolivia faced a sharp drop in the availability of willing lenders in the mid-1980s, the government began to create money to finance its fiscal deficit. As the money supply increased in relation to the output of goods and services, prices rose. In 1985 the government was creating money so fast that the rate of inflation reached 8,170 percent. Lunch in a La Paz hotel could cost 10 million Bolivian pesos. You can imagine the problem of counting money and recording money values with cash registers and calculators. As the rate of inflation increased, Bolivians had to carry stacks of currency to pay for goods and services. Eventually the government issued a 1 million peso note, then 5 million and 10 million peso notes.

This extremely high inflation, or hyperinflation, ended when a new government introduced its economic program in August 1985. The program reduced government spending dramatically, which slowed the growth of the fiscal deficit. At the same time, a monetary reform was introduced. A **monetary reform** is a new monetary policy that includes the introduction of a new

monetary reform:
a new monetary policy that includes the introduction of a new monetary unit

Copyright © by Houghton Mifflin Company. All rights reserved.

---

[1]The M in the government budget constraint is government-issued money (usually called *base money*, or *high-powered money*). It is easiest to think of this kind of money as currency, although in practice base money includes more than currency.

Some aspects of the macro-economy are beyond the control of the government. This photo depicts the damage done in Kobe, Japan following an earthquake. Natural disasters, such as earthquakes or bad weather, sometimes play a role in determining the price level and national output in the short run. A major earthquake will lower national output and raise the price level. However, such effects should be important only in the short run as other determinants of the equilibrium price level and real GDP will dominate the forces of nature in normal times.

The introduction of a new monetary unit without a change in fiscal policy has no lasting effect on the rate of inflation.

monetary unit. The central bank of Bolivia announced that it would restrict money creation and introduced a new currency, the boliviano. It set 1 boliviano equal to 1 million Bolivian pesos.

The new monetary unit, the boliviano, did not lower prices; it lowered the units in which prices were quoted. Lunch now cost 10 bolivianos instead of 10 million pesos. More important, the rate of inflation dropped abruptly.

Did the new unit of currency end the hyperinflation? No. The rate of inflation dropped because the new fiscal policy controls introduced by the government relieved the pressure on the central bank to create money in order to finance government spending. Remember the government budget constraint. The only way to reduce the amount of money being created is to reduce the fiscal deficit $(G - T)$ minus borrowing (B). Once fiscal policy is under control, monetary reform is possible. If a government introduces a new monetary unit without changing its fiscal policy, the monetary unit by itself has no lasting effect on the rate of inflation.

Table 2 lists monetary reforms enacted in recent years. Argentina had a monetary reform in June 1983. Yet by June 1985, another reform was needed. The inflationary problems Argentina faced could not be solved just by issuing a new unit of currency. Fiscal reform also was needed, and none was made. In any circumstances of inflationary monetary policy, monetary reform by itself is not enough. It must be coupled with a reduction in the fiscal deficit or an increase in government borrowing to produce a permanent change in the rate of inflation.

Monetary policy is tied to fiscal policy through the government budget constraint. Although money creation is not an important source of deficit financing in developed countries, it has been and still is a significant source of revenue for developing countries, where taxes are difficult to collect and borrowing is limited.

Copyright © by Houghton Mifflin Company. All rights reserved.

TABLE 2
Recent Monetary Reforms

Country	Old Currency	New Currency	Date of Change	Nature of Change
Argentina	Peso	Peso Argentino	June 1983	1 peso argentino = 10,000 pesos
	Peso Argentino	Austral	June 1985	1 austral = 1,000 pesos argentino
	Austral	Peso Argentino	January 1992	1 peso argentino = 10,000 australes
Bolivia	Peso	Boliviano	January 1987	1 boliviano = 1,000,000 pesos
Brazil	Cruzeiro	Cruzado	February 1986	1 cruzado = 1,000 cruzeiros
	Cruzado	New cruzado	January 1989	1 new cruzado = 1,000 cruzados
	New cruzado	Cruzeiro	March 1990	1 cruzeiro = 1 new cruzado
Chile	Peso	Escudo	January 1969	1 escudo = 1,000 pesos
	Escudo	Peso	September 1975	1 peso = 1,000 escudos
Israel	Pound	Shekel	February 1980	1 shekel = 10 pounds
	Old shekel	New shekel	September 1985	1 new shekel = 1,000 old shekels
Mexico	Peso	New peso	January 1993	1 new peso = 1,000 pesos
Peru	Sol	Inti	February 1985	1 inti = 1,000 soles
	Inti	New sol	July 1991	1 new sol = 1,000,000 intis
Poland	Zloty	New zloty	January 1995	1 new zloty = 10,000 zlotys
Uruguay	Old peso	New peso	July 1975	1 new peso = 1,000 old pesos

RECAP

1. The government budget constraint (G = T + B + ΔM) defines the relationship between fiscal and monetary policies.

2. The implications of fiscal policy for the growth of the money supply can be seen by rewriting the government budget constraint this way:

$$\Delta M = (G - T) - B.$$

3. A monetary reform is a new monetary policy that includes the introduction of a new unit of currency.

4. A government can end an inflationary monetary policy only with a fiscal reform that lowers the fiscal deficit $(G - T)$ minus borrowing (B).

Copyright © by Houghton Mifflin Company. All rights reserved.

SUMMARY

■ **Is there a tradeoff between inflation and the unemployment rate?**

1. The Phillips curve shows the relationship between inflation and the unemployment rate. §1

■ **How does the tradeoff between inflation and the unemployment rate vary from the short to the long run?**

2. In the long run, there is no tradeoff between inflation and the unemployment rate. §1.b

3. The long-run Phillips curve is a vertical line at the natural rate of unemployment. §1.b.2

■ **What is the relationship between unexpected inflation and the unemployment rate?**

4. Unexpected inflation can affect the unemployment rate through wage expectations, inventory fluctuations, and wage contracts. §2.a, 2.a.1, 2.a.2, 2.a.3

■ **How are macroeconomic expectations formed?**

5. Adaptive expectations are formed on the basis of past experience; rational expectations are formed on the basis of all available relevant information. §2.b.1, 2.b.2

■ **What makes government policies credible?**

6. A policy is credible only if it is time consistent. §3.b

■ **Are business cycles related to political elections?**

7. A political business cycle is created by politicians who want to improve their chances of reelection by stimulating the economy just before an election. §4.a

■ **How do real shocks to the economy affect business cycles?**

8. Real business cycles are a product of unexpected change in technology, weather, or some other real variable. §4.b

■ **How is inflationary monetary policy related to government fiscal policy?**

9. The government budget constraint defines the relationship between monetary and fiscal policies. §5.a

10. When government-issued money is used to finance fiscal deficits, inflationary monetary policy can be a product of fiscal policy. §5.b

KEY TERMS

Phillips curve §1
reservation wage §2.a.1
adaptive expectation §2.b.1
rational expectation §2.b.2

time inconsistent §3
shock §4.b
monetary reform §5.b

Copyright © by Houghton Mifflin Company. All rights reserved.

EXERCISES

1. What is the difference between the short-run Phillips curve and the long-run Phillips curve? Use an aggregate supply and demand diagram to explain why there is a difference between them.

2. Give two reasons why there may be a short-run tradeoff between unexpected inflation and the unemployment rate.

3. "Unexpected increases in the money supply cause clockwise movements in the Phillips curve diagram; unexpected decreases in the money supply cause counterclockwise movements in the Phillips curve diagram." Evaluate this statement using a graph to illustrate your answer.

4. Economists have identified two kinds of macroeconomic expectations.

   a. Define them.

b. What are the implications for macro-economic policy of these two forms of expectations?

5. Write down the government budget constraint and explain how it can be used to understand the relationship between fiscal and monetary policies.

6. Using the government budget constraint, explain

   a. why some countries experience hyper-inflation.

   b. how fiscal policy must change in order to implement a noninflationary monetary policy.

7. Parents, like governments, establish credibility by seeing to it that their "policies" (the rules they outline for their children) are time consistent. Analyze the potential for time consistency of these rules:

   a. If you don't eat the squash, you'll go to bed 30 minutes early tonight!

   b. If you get any grades below a C, you won't be allowed to watch television on school nights!

   c. If you don't go to my alma mater, I won't pay for your college education!

   d. If you marry that disgusting person, I'll disinherit you!

8. Suppose an economy has witnessed an 8 percent rate of growth in its money supply and prices over the last few years. How do you think the public will respond to an announced plan to increase the money supply by 4 percent over the next year if:

   a. the central bank has a reputation for always meeting its announced policy goals.

b. the central bank rarely does what it says it will do.

9. What are the implications for the timing of business-cycle fluctuations over the years if all business cycles are:

   a. manipulated by incumbent administrations?

   b. a product of real shocks to the economy?

10. Suppose the Federal Reserve System was abolished and the Congress assumed responsibility for monetary policy along with fiscal policy. What potential harm to the economy could result from such a change?

11. Suppose tax revenues equal $100 billion, government spending equals $130 billion, and the government borrows $25 billion. How much do you expect the money supply to increase given the government budget constraint?

12. If the government budget deficit equals $220 billion and the money supply increases by $100 billion, how much must the government borrow?

13. Discuss how each of the following sources of real business cycles would affect the economy.

   a. Farmers go on strike for six months.

   b. Oil prices fall substantially.

   c. Particularly favorable weather increases agricultural output nationwide.

14. Using an aggregate demand and aggregate supply diagram, illustrate and explain how a political business cycle is created.

15. Use a Phillips curve diagram to illustrate and explain how a political business cycle is created.

 ## INTERNET EXERCISE

In section 1 of this chapter we explored the possibility of a tradeoff between inflation and unemployment. A key element of discussion was the "natural rate of unemployment", the unemployment rate that would exist in the absence of any cyclical unemployment. An alternate concept relating inflation and unemployment rate is the *NAIRU*, the "nonac-celerating-inflation rate of unemployment." To understand the NAIRU, we can go to the Boyes/Melvin web site at **http://www.hmco.com/college/** and click on the internet exercise link for this chapter. Now answer the questions that appear on the web page.

Copyright © by Houghton Mifflin Company. All rights reserved.

Greenspan Grilled:
Congress Questions Inflation, Rates, Dollar

Greenspan: "Some critics of our latest policy actions have noted that we [raised short-term interest rates] even though inflation had not picked up. That observation is accurate. . . . To be successful, we must implement the necessary monetary policy adjustments well in advance of the potential emergence of inflationary pressures, so as to forestall their actual occurrence. . . . If we are successful in our current endeavors, there will not be an increase in overall inflation. . . .

Rep. Barney Frank, D-Mass.: "One of the predictions we had last year was that to the extent that we did raise taxes . . . [on] a fairly small percentage of upper-income people. . . . that would have a very negative effect on employment. . . . Did we have a very negative effect on employment?"

Greenspan: "In the short run the answer is no. . . . The problem, however, with taxation is I think you can't really determine the extent to which the impact of taxation has an effect on the economy except in retrospect over a number of years. So I would say that the effect of raising marginal tax rates is the type of thing which you don't see immediately."

Rep. Martin Sabo, D-Minn.: "Are long-term interest rates too high for the realities of our economy?"

Greenspan: "Absolutely. In the context of the longer-term outlook, I think that the inflation premium is too high, that nominal long-term rates for the long run are higher than they should be, and that if we can credibly hold inflation increasingly toward a path of stable prices, I think with time we will find that that inflation premium will fall significantly, and I think that will be much to the benefit of the economy because . . . real interest rates in the long end of the market will also decline, since one must presume that inflation instabilities create a higher real rate than would otherwise be the case, and it is the real rate which is crucial to long-term growth." . . .

Rep. Christopher Cox, R-Calif.: "In light of Woodward's book [*The Agenda*], and in light of some of the Clinton administration media spinners to make the Fed the scapegoat for foiling the Clinton plans . . . should we be concerned about these reports? Has the long-term institutional relationship between the Fed and the executive branch been compromised?"

Greenspan: "I don't know what to make of this. First we are perceived to be under the thumb of the executive branch, then we are running the executive branch. . . . What actually happens and what should happen is that there should be a coordinated policy between the central bank and the executive branch, because there is one economy and there is one government. There is, nonetheless, a very crucial issue that the Federal Reserve has to be independent in its actions and as an institution, because if the Federal Reserve's independence is in any way compromised, it undercuts our capability of protecting the value of the currency. I know of nothing which has undercut the independence of the Federal Reserve, and I see nothing which, in my judgment, will do the same."

Source: Copyright © 1994, *USA Today*. Reprinted with permission.

Copyright © by Houghton Mifflin Company. All rights reserved.

USA Today/June 23, 1994

COMMENTARY

Macroeconomic policy in the United States is determined by Congress, the presidential administration, and the Federal Reserve. The article reports testimony of Federal Reserve Chairman Alan Greenspan before the United States Congress in June 1994 that highlights some of the issues raised in this chapter.

The role of Federal Reserve policy credibility is highlighted in Representative Sabo's question: "Are long-term interest rates too high for the realities of our economy?" Greenspan replied that he thinks the inflation premium is too high and nominal interest rates should fall if the Fed *credibly* maintains low inflation policies. Remember that the nominal interest rate is equal to the real interest rate plus the expected inflation rate. At the time of this testimony, long-term interest rates were around 7½ percent on government bonds, and inflation was around 3 percent. The actual real interest rate was, therefore, about 4½ percent. Greenspan argued that the expected inflation rate would fall over time if the Fed continued to follow low inflation policies so that the "inflation premium" in long-term interest rates will fall. By early 1998, the inflation rate was still around 3 percent but long-term interest rates on government bonds were about 6 percent. So the "inflation premium" had, indeed, fallen to where the actual real interest rate was about 3 percent.

This is where the credibility of policy is impor-tant. Inflation expectations are based on more than the current rate of inflation. The expected future Fed policy is an important determinant of inflation expectations, and only by following policies believed to be credible and time consistent can the Fed lower long-term interest rates.

A second key point brought out in the testimony is the link between fiscal and monetary policy. Representative Cox asks a question that many people were wondering about at this time: were the Federal Reserve and the Clinton administration working too closely together and compromising the independence of the Fed? Greenspan stated that the Fed's independence had never been threatened but that coordination of monetary and fiscal policy was desirable. Greenspan had pushed hard for the federal government to reduce the deficit spending due to his belief that large budget deficits made it difficult to keep interest rates low. The logic here is that the government must borrow to finance the budget deficit, and large government borrowing pushes up interest rates. The Clinton administration was pressuring the Fed to hold interest rates as low as possible, but the Fed can do this only by following credible low inflation policies. The administration can contribute to lower interest rates by cutting the budget deficit. This is an example of how monetary and fiscal policy can be coordinated to achieve a policy goal.

Copyright © by Houghton Mifflin Company. All rights reserved.

16

Macroeconomic Viewpoints: New Keynesian, Monetarist, and New Classical

FUNDAMENTAL QUESTIONS

1. What do Keynesian economists believe about macroeconomic policy?

2. What role do monetarists believe the government should play in the economy?

3. What is new classical economics?

4. How do theories of economics change over time?

Copyright © by Houghton Mifflin Company. All rights reserved.

E conomists do not all agree on macroeconomic policy. Sometimes disagreements are due to normative differences, or differences in personal values, regarding what the truly pressing needs are that should be addressed. Other disagreements are based on different views of how the economy operates and what determines the equilibrium level of real GDP.

It would be very easy to classify economists, to call them liberals or conservatives, for example. But an economist who believes the government should not intervene in social decisions (abortion, censorship) may favor an active role for government in economic decisions (trade protection, unemployment insurance, welfare benefits). Another economist may support an active role for government in regulating the social behavior of individuals, yet believe that government should allow free markets to operate without interference.

In this chapter, an overview of important differences among schools of macroeconomic thought is presented. Most economists probably do not align themselves solely with any one theory of macroeconomics, choosing instead pieces of various schools of thought. But the three approaches we discuss in this chapter—Keynesian, monetarist, and new classical—have had enormous impact on macroeconomic thinking and policy. ■

Preview

Copyright © by Houghton Mifflin Company. All rights reserved.

What do Keynesian economists believe about macroeconomic policy?

1. KEYNESIAN ECONOMICS

Keynesian macroeconomics (named after the English economist John Maynard Keynes) dominated the economics profession from the 1940s through the 1960s. Some economists today refer to themselves as "new Keynesians." The common thread that pervades Keynesian economics is an emphasis on the inflexibility of wages and prices. This leads many Keynesians to recommend an activist government macroeconomic policy aimed at achieving a satisfactory rate of economic growth.

1.a. The Keynesian Model

The Keynesian model of macroeconomic equilibrium assumes that prices are constant and that changes in aggregate expenditures determine equilibrium real GDP. In an aggregate demand and supply analysis, the simple Keynesian model looks like the graph in Figure 1. The aggregate supply curve is a horizontal line at a fixed level of prices, P_1. Changes in aggregate demand, such

Figure 1
The Fixed-Price Keynesian Model
In the simple Keynesian model, prices are fixed at P_1 by the horizontal aggregate supply curve, so that changes in aggregate demand determine equilibrium real GDP.

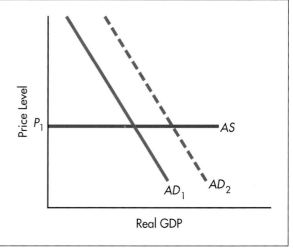

as from AD_1 to AD_2, cause changes in real GDP with no change in the price level.

Figure 1 reflects the traditional Keynesian emphasis on aggregate demand as a determinant of equilibrium real GDP. But no economist today would argue that the aggregate supply curve is always horizontal at every level of real GDP. More representative of Keynesian economics today is the aggregate supply curve shown in Figure 2. At low levels of real GDP, the curve is flat. In this region (the Keynesian region), increases in aggregate demand are associated with increases in output but not increases in prices. This flat region of the aggregate supply curve reflects the Keynesian belief that inflation is not a problem when unemployment is high. As the level of real GDP increases, and more and more industries reach their capacity level of output, the aggregate supply curve grows steeper.

Figure 2
The Modern Keynesian Model
Modern Keynesians typically believe that the aggregate supply curve is horizontal only at relatively low levels of real GDP. As real GDP increases, more and more industries reach their capacity level of output and the aggregate supply curve becomes steeper.

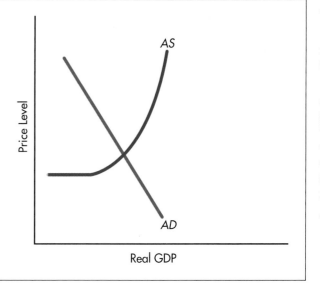

Copyright © by Houghton Mifflin Company. All rights reserved.

Keynesian economics:
a school of thought that emphasizes the role government plays in stabilizing the economy by managing aggregate demand

The economic theories John Maynard Keynes proposed in the 1930s have given way to new theories. Today **Keynesian economics** focuses on the role the government plays in stabilizing the economy by managing aggregate demand. *New Keynesians* believe that wages and prices are not flexible in the short run. They use their analysis of business behavior to explain the Keynesian region on the aggregate supply curve of Figure 2. They believe that the economy is not always in equilibrium. For instance, if the demand for labor falls, we would expect the equilibrium price of labor (the wage) to fall and, because fewer people want to work at a lower wage, the number of people employed to fall. New Keynesians argue that wages do not tend to fall, because firms choose to lay off workers rather than decrease wages. Businesses retain high wages for their remaining employees in order to maintain morale and productivity. As a result, wages are quite rigid. This wage rigidity is reflected in price rigidity in goods markets according to new Keynesian economics.

New Keynesian macroeconomists argue that wages and prices are not flexible in the short run.

1.b. The Policymakers' Role

Keynesians believe the government must take an active role in the economy to restore equilibrium. Traditional Keynesians identified the private sector as an important source of shifts in aggregate demand. For example, they argued that investment is susceptible to sudden changes. If business spending falls, the argument continued, monetary and fiscal policies should be used to stimulate spending and offset the drop in business spending. Government intervention is necessary to offset private-sector shifts in aggregate demand and avoid recession. And if private spending increases, creating inflationary pressure, then monetary and fiscal policies should restrain spending, again to offset private-sector shifts in aggregate demand.

New Keynesian macroeconomics does not focus on fluctuations in aggregate demand as the primary source of the problems facing policymakers. Keynesian economists realize that aggregate supply shocks can be substantial. But whatever the source of the instability—aggregate demand or aggregate supply—they emphasize active government policy to return the economy to equilibrium.

RECAP

1. Keynesian economists today reject the simple fixed-price model in favor of a model in which the aggregate supply curve is relatively flat at low levels of real GDP, sloping upward as real GDP approaches its potential level.

2. Keynesians believe that the tendency for the economy to experience disequilibrium in labor and goods markets forces the government to intervene in the economy.

2. MONETARIST ECONOMICS

monetarist economics:
a school of thought that emphasizes the role changes in the money supply play in determining equilibrium real GDP and price level

The Keynesian view dominated macroeconomics in the 1940s, 1950s, and most of the 1960s. In the late 1960s and the 1970s, Keynesian economics faced a challenge from **monetarist economics,** a school of thought that

Copyright © by Houghton Mifflin Company. All rights reserved.

emphasizes the role changes in the money supply play in determining equilibrium real GDP and prices. The leading monetarist, Milton Friedman, had been developing monetarist theory since the 1940s, but it took several decades before his ideas became popular. In part the shift was a product of the forcefulness of Friedman's arguments, but the relatively poor macroeconomic performance of the United States in the 1970s probably contributed to a growing disenchantment with Keynesian economics, creating an environment ripe for new ideas. The Economic Insight "Milton Friedman" describes how Friedman's monetarist theories became popular.

2.a. The Monetarist Model

Monetarists focus on the role of the money supply in determining the equilibrium level of real GDP and prices. In Chapter 14 we discussed monetary policy and equilibrium income. We showed that monetary policy is linked to changes in the equilibrium level of real GDP through changes in investment (and consumption). Keynesians traditionally assumed that monetary policy affects aggregate demand by changing the interest rate and, consequently, investment spending. Monetarists believe that changes in the money supply have broad effects on expenditures through both investment and consumption. An increase in the money supply pushes aggregate demand up by increasing both business and household spending, and raises the equilibrium level of real GDP. A decrease in the money supply does the opposite.

Monetarists believe that accelerating inflation is a product of efforts to increase real GDP through expansionary monetary policy.

Monetarists believe that changes in monetary policy (or fiscal policy, for that matter) have only a short-term effect on real GDP. In the long run, they expect real GDP to be at a level consistent with the natural rate of unemployment. As a result, the long-run effect of a change in the money supply is fully reflected in a change in the price level. Attempts to exploit the short-run effects of expansionary monetary policy produce an inflationary spiral, in which the level of GDP increases temporarily, then falls back to the potential level while prices rise. This is the rightward shift of the Phillips curve we described in Chapter 15.

2.b. The Policymakers' Role

What role do monetarists believe the government should play in the economy?

Unlike Keynesian economists, monetarists do not believe that the economy is subject to a disequilibrium that must be offset by government action. Most monetarists believe that the economy tends toward equilibrium at the level of potential real GDP. Their faith in the free market (price) sytem leads them to favor minimal government intervention.

Monetarists often argue that government policy heightens the effects of the business cycle. This is especially true of monetary policy. To prove their point, monetarists link changes in the growth of the money supply to business-cycle fluctuations. Specifically, they suggest that periods of relatively fast money growth are followed by booms and inflation, and that periods of relatively slow money growth are followed by recessions.

Figure 3 shows the rate at which the money supply, consumer prices, and real GDP grew in the United States in recent years. The inflation rate (consumer prices) seems to follow changes in the growth rate of the money supply with a lag of one or two years; GDP typically follows a change in the growth rate of the money supply by a year. The links between money growth and

Copyright © by Houghton Mifflin Company. All rights reserved.

Copyright © by Houghton Mifflin Company. All rights reserved.

Figure 3
The Growth Rate of the Money Supply, Consumer Prices, and Real GDP, United States
In general, the inflation rate follows the rate at which the money supply grows with a lag of one or two years. Growth in real GDP follows growth in the money supply with a lag of about one year. Source: *Economic Report of the President, 1997.* (Washington, D.C.: U.S. Government Printing Office, 1997).

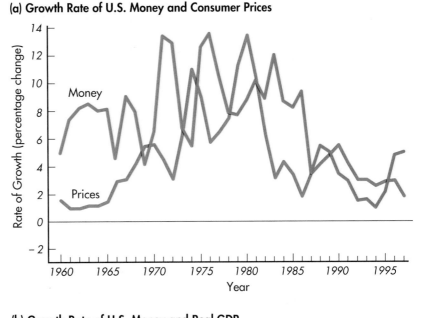

(a) Growth Rate of U.S. Money and Consumer Prices

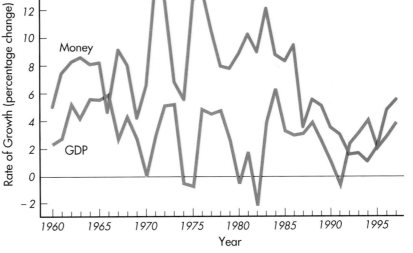

(b) Growth Rate of U.S. Money and Real GDP

Economic policy operates with a long and variable lag.

inflation, and money growth and GDP, are by no means perfect. Sometimes there seem to be closer relationships than at other times. This makes it difficult to predict the effect of a particular change in monetary policy on prices or real GDP. In addition, a number of other variables influence GDP.

Monetarists favor nonactivist government policy because they believe that the government's attempts to make the economy better off by aiming monetary and fiscal policies at low inflation and low unemployment often make things worse. Why? Because economic policy, which is very powerful, operates with a long and variable lag. First, policymakers have to recognize that a problem exists. This is the *recognition lag.* Then they must formulate an

Milton Friedman

Milton Friedman is widely considered to be the father of monetarism. Born in 1912 in New York City, Friedman spent most of his career at the University of Chicago. Early in his professional life, he recognized the importance of developing economics as an empirical science—that is, using data to test the applicability of economic theory.

In 1957, Friedman published *A Theory of the Consumption Function*. In the book he discussed the importance of *permanent income*, rather than current income, in understanding consumer spending. His analysis of consumption won widespread acclaim, an acclaim that would be a long time coming for his work relating monetary policy to real output and prices.

In the 1950s, Keynesian theory dominated economics. Most macroeconomists believed that the supply of money in the economy was of little importance. In 1963, with the publication of *A Monetary History of the United States, 1867–1960* (coauthored with Anna Schwartz of the National Bureau of Economic Research), Friedman focused attention on the monetarist argument. Still Keynesian economics dominated scholarly and policy debate.

In the late 1960s and early 1970s, the rate of inflation and unemployment simultaneously increased. This was a situation that Keynesian economics could not explain. The timing was right for a new theory of macroeconomic behavior, and monetarism, with Milton Friedman its most influential advocate, grew in popularity. The new stature of monetarism was clearly visible in 1979, when the Fed adopted a monetarist approach to targeting the money supply.

In 1976, Milton Friedman was awarded the Nobel Prize for economics. By this time he had become a public figure. He wrote a column for *Newsweek* from 1966 to 1984 and in 1980 developed a popular public television series, "Free to Choose," based on his book of the same title. Through the popular media, Friedman became the most effective and well-known supporter of free markets in the United States and much of the rest of the world. Many would argue that only Keynes has had as much influence on scholarly literature and public policy in economics as Milton Friedman.

appropriate policy. This is the *reaction lag.* Then the effects of the policy must work through the economy. This is the *effect lag.*

When the Federal Reserve changes the rate of growth of the money supply, real GDP and inflation do not change immediately. In fact, studies show that as much as two years can pass between a change in policy and the effect of that change on real GDP. This means that when policymakers institute a change targeted at a particular level of real GDP or rate of inflation, the effect of the policy is not felt for a long time. And it is possible that the economy could be facing an entirely different set of problems in a year or two than those policymakers are addressing today. But today's policy will still have effects next year, and those effects may aggravate next year's problems.

Because of the long and variable lag in the effect of fiscal and monetary policies, monetarists argue that policymakers should set policy according to rules that do not change from month to month or even year to year. What kinds of rules? A fiscal policy rule might be to balance the budget annually; a monetary policy rule might be to require that the money supply grow at a fixed rate over time. These kinds of rules restrict policymakers from formulating discretionary policy. Monetarists believe that by reducing discretionary shifts in policy, economic growth is steadier than it is when government consciously sets out to achieve full employment and low inflation.

Copyright © by Houghton Mifflin Company. All rights reserved.

RECAP

1. Monetarists emphasize the role changes in the money supply play in determining equilibrium real GDP and the level of prices.

2. Monetarists do not believe that the economy is subject to disequilibrium in the labor and goods markets or that government should take an active role in the economy.

3. Because economic policy operates with a long and variable lag, attempts by government to stabilize the economy may, in fact, make matters worse.

4. Monetarists believe that formal rules should govern economic policy-making.

3. NEW CLASSICAL ECONOMICS

In the 1970s an alternative to Keynesian and monetarist economics was developed: new classical economics. But before we discuss the new classical theory, let's look at the old one.

classical economics:
a school of thought that assumes that real GDP is determined by aggregate supply, while the equilibrium price level is determined by aggregate demand

Classical economics is the theory that was popular before Keynes changed the face of economics in the 1930s. According to classical economics, real GDP is determined by aggregate supply, while the equilibrium price level is determined by aggregate demand. Figure 4, the classical aggregate demand and supply diagram, shows the classical economist's view of the world. The vertical aggregate supply curve means that the equilibrium level of output (income) is a product only of the determinants of aggregate supply: the price of resources, technology, and expectations (see Chapter 9).

Copyright © by Houghton Mifflin Company. All rights reserved.

Figure 4
The Classical Model
The vertical aggregate supply curve indicates that equilibrium national income is determined strictly by the determinants of aggregate supply.

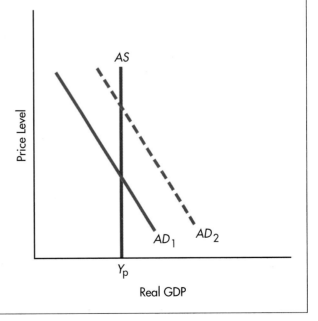

If the aggregate supply curve is vertical, then changes in aggregate demand, such as from AD_1 to AD_2, change only the price level; they do not affect the equilibrium level of output. Classical economics assumes that prices and wages are perfectly flexible. This rules out contracts that fix prices or wages for periods of time. It also rules out the possibility that people are not aware of all prices and wages. They know when prices have gone up and ask for wage increases to compensate.

Keynesians and monetarists would argue that information about the economy, including prices and wages, is not perfect. When workers and businesses negotiate wages, they may not know what current prices are, but they certainly do not know what future prices will be. Furthermore, many labor contracts fix wages for long periods of time. This means that wages are not flexible, that they cannot adjust to new price levels.

3.a. The New Classical Model

new classical economics:
a school of thought that holds that changes in real GDP are a product of unexpected changes in the level of prices

What is new classical economics?

New classical economics was a response to the problems of meeting economic policy goals in the 1970s. New classical economists questioned some of the assumptions on which Keynesian economics was based. For instance, new classical economists believe wages are flexible, while both traditional Keynesian and new Keynesian economists assume wages can be fixed in the short run.

New classical economics does not assume that people know everything that is happening, as the old theory did. People make mistakes because their expectations of prices or some other critical variable are different from the future reality. New classical economists emphasize rational expectations. As defined in Chapter 15, *rational expectations* are based on all available relevant information. This was a new way of thinking about expectations. Earlier theories assumed that people formed adaptive expectations—that their expectations were based only on their past experience. With rational expectations, people learn not only from their past experience but also from any other information that helps them predict the future.

Suppose the chairman of the Federal Reserve Board announces a new monetary policy. Price-level expectations that are formed rationally take this announcement into consideration; those formed adaptively do not. It is much easier for policymakers to make unexpected changes in policy if expectations are formed adaptively rather than rationally.

Another element of new classical economics is the belief that markets are in equilibrium. Keynesian economics argues that disequilibrium in markets demands government intervention. For instance, Keynesian economists define a recession as a disequilibrium in the labor market—a surplus of labor—that requires expansionary government policy. New classical economists believe that because real wages are lower during a recession, people are more willing to substitute nonlabor activities (going back to school, early retirement, work at home, or leisure) for work. As the economy recovers and wages go up, people substitute away from nonlabor activities toward more working hours. The substitution of labor for leisure and leisure for labor, over time, suggests that much of observed unemployment is voluntary in the sense that those who are unemployed choose not to take a job at a wage below their reservation wage (see Chapter 15).

Copyright © by Houghton Mifflin Company. All rights reserved.

3.b. The Policymakers' Role

New classical economics emphasizes expectations. Its basic tenet is that changes in monetary policy can change the equilibrium level of real GDP only if those changes are *unexpected*. Fiscal policy can change equilibrium real GDP only if it *unexpectedly* changes the level of prices or one of the determinants of aggregate supply.

Figure 5 (which is the same as Figure 4 in Chapter 15) illustrates the new classical view of the effect of an unexpected increase in the money supply. Suppose initially the expected rate of inflation is 3 percent and the actual rate of inflation is also 3 percent. The economy is operating at point 1 in part (b), the Phillips curve diagram, with unemployment at 5 percent, which is assumed to be the natural rate of unemployment. At the natural rate of unemployment, the economy is producing the potential level of real GDP (Y_p), at price level P_1. If the central bank unexpectedly increases the money supply, pushing the inflation rate up from 3 percent to 6 percent, the economy moves from point 1

Figure 5
New Classical Economics
New classical economists believe that government-induced shifts in aggregate demand affect real GDP only if they are unexpected. In part (a), the economy initially is operating at point 1, with real GDP at Y_p, the potential level. An unexpected increase in aggregate demand shifts the economy to point 2, where both real GDP (Y_2) and prices (P_2) are higher. Over time, as sellers adjust to higher prices and costs of doing business, aggregate supply shifts from AS_1 to AS_2. This shift moves the economy to point 3. Here GDP is back at the potential level, and prices are even higher. In the long run, an increase in aggregate demand does not increase output. The long-run aggregate supply curve (*LRAS*) is a vertical line at the potential level of real GDP.

In part (b), if the expected rate of inflation is 3 percent and actual inflation is 3 percent, the economy is operating at point 1, at the natural rate of unemployment (U_n). If aggregate demand increases, there is an unexpected increase in inflation from 3 percent to 6 percent. This moves the economy from point 1 to point 2 along short-run Phillips curve I. Here the unemployment rate is 3 percent. As people learn to expect 6 percent inflation, they adjust to the higher rate and the economy moves back to the natural rate of unemployment, at point 3. If the increase in inflation is expected, then the economy moves from point 1 to point 3 directly with no temporary decrease in the unemployment rate.

(a) Aggregate Demand and Supply

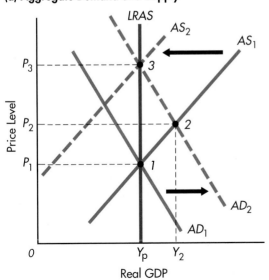

(b) Phillips Curve

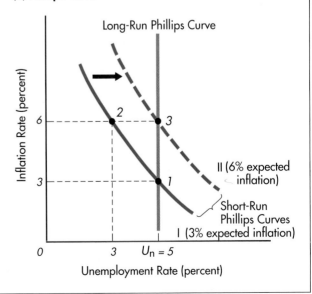

Copyright © by Houghton Mifflin Company. All rights reserved.

to point 2 along short-run Phillips curve I, which is based on 3 percent expected inflation. The unemployment rate is now 3 percent, which is less than the natural rate. In part (a), real GDP rises above potential income to Y_2.

Over time, people come to expect 6 percent inflation. They adjust to the higher inflation rate, and the economy moves back to the natural rate of unemployment. At the expected rate of inflation, 6 percent, the economy is operating at point 3 on short-run Phillips curve II. As the expected rate of inflation increases from 3 percent to 6 percent, workers negotiate higher wages and the aggregate supply curve shifts to the left, from AS1 to AS2. A new equilibrium exists at point 3 in the aggregate demand and supply diagram, and real GDP drops back to its potential level.

The analysis changes dramatically if the change in the money supply is expected. Now the economy moves not from point 1 to point 2 to point 3 but from point 1 directly to point 3. This is because the shift from point 1 to point 2 is temporary, based on unexpected inflation. If the inflation is expected, the economy is on short-run Phillips curve II, where inflation is 6 percent, unemployment is at the natural rate, and real GDP is at the potential level.

The lesson of new classical economics for policymakers is that managing aggregate demand has an effect on real GDP only if change is unexpected. Any predictable policy simply affects prices. As a result, new classical economists argue that monetary and fiscal policies should be aimed at maintaining a low, stable rate of inflation and should not attempt to alter real national income and unemployment. This brings new classical economists close to the monetarists, who would choose policy rules over discretionary policy.

New classical economists believe that wages and prices are flexible and that people form expectations rationally, so that only unexpected changes in the price level can affect real GDP.

RECAP

1. New classical economics holds that wages are flexible and that expectations are formed rationally, so that only unexpected changes in prices have an effect on real GDP.

2. New classical economists believe that markets are always in equilibrium.

3. According to new classical economic theory, any predictable macroeconomic policy has an effect only on prices.

4. New classical economists argue that monetary and fiscal policies should try to achieve a low, stable rate of inflation rather than changes in real GDP or unemployment.

4. COMPARISON AND INFLUENCE

How do theories of economics change over time?

The three theories of macroeconomics we have been talking about are often treated as though they are different in every way. Yet at times they overlap and even share conclusions. Moreover, as we mentioned at the beginning of the chapter, it is an oversimplification to categorize economists by a single school of thought. Many if not most economists do not classify themselves by economic theory. Typically they take elements of each so that their approach to macroeconomics is more a synthesis of the various theories than strict adherence to any one theory.

Macroeconomic theories have developed over time in response to the economy's performance and the shortcomings of existing theories. Keynesian economics became popular in the 1930s because classical economics did not

Copyright © by Houghton Mifflin Company. All rights reserved.

TABLE 1
Major Approaches to Macroeconomic Policy

Approach	Major Source of Problems	Proper Role for Government
New Keynesian	Disequilibrium in private labor and goods markets	Active management of monetary and fiscal policies to restore equilibrium
Monetarist	Government's discretionary policies increase and decrease aggregate demand	Follow fixed rules for money growth and minimize fiscal policy shocks
New classical	Government policies have effect on real GDP only if unexpected, yet government tries to manipulate aggregate demand	Follow predictable monetary and fiscal policies for long-run stability

explain or help resolve the Great Depression. Monetarist economics offered an explanation for rising unemployment and rising inflation in the United States in the 1960s and 1970s. New classical economics suggested an alternative explanation for rising unemployment and inflation that the static Phillips curve analysis used by traditional Keynesians could not explain. Each of these theories, then, was developed or became popular because an existing theory did not answer pressing new questions.

All of these theories have influenced government policy. A by-product of Keynes's work in the 1930s was the wide acceptance and practice of activist government fiscal policy. Monetarist influence was dramatically apparent in the change in monetary policy announced by the Federal Reserve in 1979. Monetarists had criticized the Fed's policy of targeting interest rates. They argued that money-growth targets would stabilize income and prices. In October 1979, Chairman Paul Volcker announced that the Fed would concentrate more on achieving money-growth targets and less on controlling interest rates. This change in policy reflected the Fed's concern over rising inflation and the belief that the monetarists were right, that a low rate of money growth would bring about a low rate of inflation. The new policy led to an abrupt drop in the rate of inflation, from more than 13 percent in 1979 to less than 4 percent in 1982.

The new classical economists' emphasis on expectations calls for more information from policymakers to allow private citizens to incorporate government plans in their outlook for the future. The Federal Reserve Reform Act (1977) and the Full Employment and Balanced Growth Act (1978) require the Board of Governors to report to Congress semiannually on its goals and money targets for the next twelve months. New classical economists also believe that only credible government policies can affect expectations. In the last chapter we discussed the time consistency of plans. For plans to be credible, to influence private expectations, they must be time consistent.

Table 1 summarizes the three approaches to macroeconomics, describing the major source of problems facing policymakers and the proper role of government policy according to each view. Only Keynesian economics supports an active role for government; the other two theories suggest that government should not intervene in the economy.

Copyright © by Houghton Mifflin Company. All rights reserved.

RECAP

1. Different economic theories developed over time as changing economic conditions pointed out the shortcomings of existing theories.
2. Keynesian, monetarist, and new classical economics have each influenced macroeconomic policy.
3. Only Keynesian economists believe that government should actively intervene to stabilize the economy.

SUMMARY

1. All economists do not agree on the determinants of economic equilibrium or the appropriate role of government policy. § Preview

■■■ What do Keynesian economists believe about macroeconomic policy?

2. Keynesian economists believe the government should take an active role in stabilizing the economy by managing aggregate demand. §1.a

■■■ What role do monetarists believe the government should play in the economy?

3. Monetarists do not believe that the economy is subject to serious disequilibrium, which means they favor minimal government intervention in the economy. §2.b

4. Monetarists believe that a government that takes an active role in the economy may do more harm than good because economic policy operates with a long and variable lag. §2.b

■■■ What is new classical economics?

5. New classical economics holds that only unexpected changes in policy can influence real GDP, so government policy should target a low, stable rate of inflation. §3.b

■■■ How do theories of economics change over time?

6. New economic theories are a response to changing economic conditions that point out the shortcomings of existing theories. §4

KEY TERMS

Keynesian economics §1.a
monetarist economics §2

classical economics §3
new classical economics §3.a

EXERCISES

1. What is the difference between traditional Keynesian and new Keynesian economics?
2. Why does monetary policy operate with a long and variable lag? Give an example to illustrate your explanation.
3. What is the difference between old classical and new classical economics?
4. Draw an aggregate demand and supply diagram for each theory of macroeconomics. Use the diagrams to explain how the government can influence equilibrium real GDP and prices.

5. What, if any, similarities are there among the theories of economics discussed in this chapter regarding the use of fiscal and monetary policies to stimulate real GDP?
6. If unexpected increases in the growth rate of the money supply can increase real GDP, why doesn't the Fed follow a policy of unexpectedly increasing the money supply to increase the growth of real GDP?
7. "The popular macroeconomic theories have evolved over time as economic conditions

Copyright © by Houghton Mifflin Company. All rights reserved.

have changed to reveal shortcomings of existing theory." Evaluate this quote in terms of the emergence of the three theories discussed in this chapter.

For questions 8–15, tell which school of thought would be most likely associated with the following quotes:

8. "Changes in prices and wages are too slow to support the new classical assumption of persistent macroeconomic equilibrium."

9. "The best monetary policy is to keep the money supply growing at a slow and steady rate."

10. "Frictional unemployment is a result of workers voluntarily substituting leisure for labor when wages fall."

11. "A change in the money supply will affect GDP after a long and variable lag, so it is difficult to predict the effects of money on output."

12. "Government policymakers should use fiscal policy to adjust aggregate demand in response to aggregate supply shocks."

13. "The economy is subject to recurring disequilibrium in labor and goods markets, so government can serve a useful function of helping the economy adjust to equilibrium."

14. "Since the aggregate supply curve is horizontal, aggregate demand will determine the equilibrium level of real GDP."

15. "If everyone believed that the monetary authority was going to cut the inflation rate from 6 percent to 3 percent, such a reduction in inflation could be achieved without any significant increase in unemployment."

▣ INTERNET EXERCISE

In section 2.b of this chapter we saw plots of money growth and real GDP for the United States that suggested that changes in real GDP growth seemed to lag behind changes in money supply growth by about one year. Let's see whether money growth and real GDP growth have a similiar relationship in a small developing country like the Philippines. To access data for the Philippines, go to the Boyes/Melvin web site at http://www.hmco.com/college/ and click on the internet exercise link for this chapter. Now answer the questions that appear on the web page.

Copyright © by Houghton Mifflin Company. All rights reserved.

Sun is Finally Setting on Economic Conservatism

KEYNES famously remarked that what mattered in politics was not vested interests, but what he termed the "gradual encroachment of the ideas" that are the world's true rulers. "Practical men," he wrote, "who believe themselves to be quite exempt from intellectual influences, are usually the slave of some defunct economist." It may take time, but it is the ideas that count. . . .

There has been a chipping away at the edifice put in place over the 1970s as the then "New Right" developed its now familiar arsenal of ideas and policies: that inflation was solely a monetary phenomenon, that price stability was the necessary and sufficient condition for growth, that unemployment arises because of blockages in the labour market. Ronald Reagan and Margaret Thatcher brilliantly exploited the tide; the rest is history.

But over the past 10 years a new generation of economists, almost entirely American, has been attacking those precepts— and over the past two months, there have been the first signs that their ideas have begun to move the hitherto highly conservative policy consensus. It was evident last week in Washington, where the U.S. central bank—the Federal Reserve Board—refused to raise interest rates despite a powerful monetarist case that it should; and where the International Monetary Fund, in its annual World Economic Outlook, raised doubts that the correct approach to lowering inflation is to focus solely on the growth of the money supply and that the costs of raising interest rates too aggressively and pre-emptively can be disregarded. . . .

The battle of ideas is being engaged at the highest level. For example, every year the world's central bankers, the guardians of financial orthodoxy, meet in August for an informal conference at Jackson Hole, Wyoming. But this year was different. Instead of the usual consensus that nothing took precedence over price stability and rolling back the state, there was a heated discussion over whether lower inflation was the ultimate lodestar of policy—prompted by a technical, but nonetheless politically important paper, by among others, one of the ringleaders of the "New Keynesian" fightback— George Akerlof.

Akerlof has been questioning for some years the extent to which it is reasonable to assume—as free-market economists do—that we all behave rationally when confronted with price signals in markets, and particularly if the consequences are painful. For example, a business under pressure and needing to cut wages by 3 percent will find it much easier to get agreement from its workforce if it offers a wage increase of 2 percent against a background of 5 percent inflation, rather than a wage cut of 3 percent if prices are stable. It is the same 3 percent cut in real wages in both cases; but one is more acceptable than another. . . .

. . . if Akerlof is right, then the secret of America's job creation record may lie as much in its reliable 3 percent inflation rate, allowing real wage flexibility, as in its famed hire and fire, deregulated labour markets. . . .

It is this line of argument that is influencing the Federal Reserve. If the old rules had held, there is little doubt that last week U.S. interest rates would have risen. Unemployment is well-below its "natural rate," growth is clipping along and credit growth accelerating. But with inflation steady at around 3 percent, the balance of argument was to keep the momentum of the economy going. The "natural rate" of unemployment was too uncertain to block the case for going for still more growth and employment. . . .

Source: "Sun is Finally Setting on Economic Conservatism", from *The Observer*, September 29, 1996, p. 24. Copyright © 1996 by *The Observer*. Reprinted by permission.

Copyright © by Houghton Mifflin Company. All rights reserved

The Observer/ **September 29, 1996**

COMMENTARY

Macroeconomics has always been a lively field, filled with controversy over the proper approach to modeling the economy, the correct interpretation of experience, and the role government policy can and should play. Indeed, debate in macroeconomics is as old as the field itself. The views of John Maynard Keynes, the founder of macroeconomics, were challenged by his colleague at Cambridge University, Arthur Pigou. This debate focused on the importance of the "real balance effect," whereby a fall in the price level raises real money balances (or the purchasing power of the money supply), increases wealth, and thus increases consumption. Like most debates in macroeconomics, this was more than an ivory-tower exercise since the real balance effect provides a channel for the economy to bring itself out of a slump without government intervention.

The debate between the Keynesians and the monetarists dominated the macroeconomic discourse of the 1950s and 1960s. During this period, those who identified themselves as Keynesians gave primacy to the role of fiscal policy and to the issue of unemployment; these economists had great faith in the ability of the government to fine-tune the economy through the proper application of policy, thereby ensuring stability and growth. Keynesians of this vintage also believed that changes in the money supply had little effect on the economy. In contrast, monetarists were very concerned about inflation, which they believed to be a purely monetary phenomenon. These economists also doubted that active government intervention could stabilize the economy, for they believed that policy operated only with long and variable lags. Today, you will often hear people refer to Clinton's advisers as "Keynesians." Although none of these economists would neces-

sarily subscribe to the philosophy of John Maynard Keynes, the term is popularly assigned to macroeconomists who emphasize that free markets don't always provide the best solutions, so there is a needed role for government activism to ensure that the economy provides for growth with low inflation.

New Keynesian economists (including Clinton's economic team) take issue with the monetarist and new classical approach to macroeconomics, which is characterized by well-functioning markets, the efficient use of information, and the consequent ineffectiveness of government policy. In criticizing the new classical approach, Keynesian economists consider why prices may be sticky and may not clear markets, why people may not be able to use information efficiently, and thus how government policy affects the economy.

The passing of time is often associated with changes in economic philosophy. As this article makes clear, in recent years major institutions were more sympathetic toward the activist economic policy approaches generally associated with Keynesian economics.

Although outside observers may view the debate within macroeconomics as evidence of confusion, a more accurate appraisal is that the debate is a healthy intellectual response to a world in which few things are certain and much is unknown—and perhaps unknowable. That there are differences between New Keynesians and other schools of thought masks the fact that there is a great deal of consensus about a number of issues in macroeconomics. This consensus is a product of lessons learned from past debates. In a similar fashion, the controversies of today will yield tomorrow's consensus, and our knowledge of the real workings of the economy will grow.

Copyright © by Houghton Mifflin Company. All rights reserved.

17

Macroeconomic Links Between Countries

Copyright © by Houghton Mifflin Company. All rights reserved.

FUNDAMENTAL QUESTIONS

1. How does a change in the exchange rate affect the prices of goods traded between countries?

2. Why don't similar goods sell for the same price all over the world?

3. What is the relationship between inflation and changes in the exchange rate?

4. How do we find the domestic currency return on a foreign bond?

5. What is the relationship between domestic and foreign interest rates and changes in the exchange rate?

6. Why don't similar financial assets yield the same return all over the world?

7. How does fiscal policy affect exchange rates?

8. How does monetary policy affect exchange rates?

9. What can countries gain by coordinating their macroeconomic policies?

In every chapter we have talked about the international aspects of the topics discussed. But we have yet to consider explicitly how individual economies are linked together in a global economy. At a basic level, the economic ties between nations are much like the economic ties between any two markets in different locations. For example, when Mazda introduced the Miata sports car to the United States, there were not enough cars to meet the initial demand. So car dealers began charging thousands of dollars more than the $13,000 sticker price. In some states the cars sold for almost double the sticker price; in others the surcharge was relatively small. In California the price reached approximately $25,000; in Michigan, about $15,000. What happened? Enterprising individuals were buying Miatas in Michigan and reselling them in California. This purchase and resale activity eventually raised the price of the car in Michigan and lowered the price in California until the price in California exceeded the Michigan price only by an amount equal to shipping and other transaction costs.

The California and Michigan markets were linked by **arbitrage**, the act of buying in a market where the price is low and selling the same product in a market where the price is high to profit from the price differential. Arbitrageurs equalize prices in different markets. When they buy in the low-price market, prices there go up. And when they sell in the high-price market, prices there fall.

We are talking about California and Michigan and the market for sports cars. But we could be talking about Japan and Canada and the market for sulfur, or about Israel and Brazil and the market for diamonds, or about any number of different trading partners and goods. Arbitrage produces similar prices for similar goods and generates similar returns on similar financial assets wherever they are traded. Arbitrage links economies to each other.

In this chapter we discuss the ties among national economies. Our discussion applies to **open economies**, economies that trade goods, services, and financial assets with the rest of the world. Economies that are open will be sensitive to prices and interest rates in other countries and to changes in international economic conditions in general. A closed economy is isolated economically from the rest of the world; it does not trade with other nations. Although no economy is absolutely closed, there are different degrees of openness. Table 1 ranks eighteen countries in order of the value of international

Copyright © by Houghton Mifflin Company. All rights reserved.

arbitrage:
buying in a market where the price is low and selling the same product in a market where the price is high to profit from the price differential

open economy:
an economy that trades goods, services, and financial assets with the rest of the world

Preview

TABLE 1
**A Sample of Countries Ranked in Order of Importance of
International Trade**

Country	(Exports + Imports) /GDP	Country	(Exports + Imports) /GDP
Malaysia	1.58	Kenya	.55
Jamaica	.79	Austria	.53
Thailand	.70	United Kingdom	.47
Sri Lanka	.68	Germany	.41
Philippines	.65	Australia	.32
Sweden	.61	United States	.19
Israel	.55	Japan	.17

trade as a fraction of gross domestic product. We must be careful, however, in considering such measures as indications of how countries differ in terms of their openness. Nations with a large domestic market in relation to the value of international trade, like the United States, are generally open to international trade but the size of the domestic economy results in international trade being a relatively small share of GDP. Nations where the value of international trade is large in relation to the size of the domestic market, like Malaysia and Jamaica, will have larger trade shares, as reported in the table. ■

1. PRICES AND EXCHANGE RATES

Copyright © by Houghton Mifflin Company. All rights reserved.

> How does a change in the exchange rate affect the prices of goods traded between countries?

An exchange rate, as you learned in Chapters 3 and 7, is the price of one money in terms of another. The exchange rate doesn't enter into the purchase and sale of Miatas in Michigan and California because each state uses the U.S. dollar. But for goods and services traded across national borders, the exchange rate is an important part of the total price. In later chapters we discuss some of the ways nations restrict free trade in their currencies, the ways they "manage" exchange rates. Here we assume that currencies are traded freely for each other and that foreign exchange markets respond to supply and demand without government intervention.

Let's look at an example. A U.S. wine importer purchases 1,000,000 French francs (FF1,000,000) worth of wine from France. The importer demands francs in order to pay the French wine seller. Suppose the initial equilibrium exchange rate is $.15 = FF1. At this rate, the U.S. importer needs 1,000,000 francs at $.15 apiece, or $150,000:

$$\$.15 \times 1,000,000 = \$150,000$$

1.a. Appreciation and Depreciation

When the exchange rate between two currencies changes, we say that one currency *depreciates* while the other *appreciates*. Suppose the exchange rate goes from $.15 = FF1 to $.20 = FF1. The French franc is now worth $.20

instead of $.15. The dollar has depreciated in value in relation to the franc; dollars are worth less in terms of francs. At the new equilibrium exchange rate, the U.S. importer needs $200,000 ($.20 × 1,000,000) to buy FF1,000,000 worth of wine.

Instead of saying that the dollar has depreciated against the franc, we can say that the franc has *appreciated* against the dollar. If the dollar is depreciating against the franc, the franc must be appreciating against the dollar. Whichever way we describe the change in the exchange rate, the result is that francs are now worth more in terms of dollars. The price of a franc has gone from $.15 to $.20.

As exchange rates change, the prices of goods and services traded in international markets also change. Suppose the dollar appreciates against the franc. This means that a franc costs fewer dollars; it also means that French goods cost U.S. buyers less. If the exchange rate falls to $.10 = FF1, then FF1,000,000 costs $100,000 ($.10 × 1,000,000). The French wine has become less expensive to the U.S. importer.

- When the domestic (home) currency *depreciates*, foreign goods become *more expensive* to domestic buyers.
- When the domestic currency *appreciates*, foreign goods become *less expensive* to domestic buyers.

Let's look at the problem from the French side. When the dollar price of the franc rises, the franc price of the dollar falls; and when the dollar price of the franc falls, the franc price of the dollar rises. If the dollar price of the franc ($/FF) is originally $.15, the franc price of the dollar (FF/$) is the reciprocal (1/.15), or FF6.67. If the dollar depreciates against the franc to $.20, then the franc appreciates against the dollar to 1/.20, or FF5. As the franc appreciates, U.S. goods become less expensive to French buyers. If the dollar appreciates against the franc to $.10, then the franc depreciates against the dollar to 1/.10, or FF10. As the franc depreciates, U.S. goods become more expensive to French buyers.

When the dollar depreciates, U.S. goods become less expensive to foreign buyers; as the dollar appreciates, those goods become more expensive.

- When the domestic currency *depreciates,* domestic goods become *less expensive* to foreign buyers.
- When the domestic currency *appreciates,* domestic goods become *more expensive* to foreign buyers.

The exchange rate is just one determinant of the demand for goods and services. Income, tastes, the prices of substitutes and complements, expectations, and the exchange rate all determine the demand for U.S. wheat, for example. As the dollar depreciates in relation to other currencies, the demand for U.S. wheat increases (along with foreign demand for all other U.S. goods) even if all the other determinants do not change. Conversely, as the dollar appreciates, the demand for U.S. wheat falls (along with foreign demand for all other U.S. goods) even if all the other determinants do not change.

1.b. Purchasing Power Parity

Within a country, where prices are quoted in terms of a single currency, all we need to know is the price in the domestic currency of an item in two different locations to determine where our money buys more. If Joe's bookstore charges $20 for a book and Pete's bookstore charges $40 for the same

Copyright © by Houghton Mifflin Company. All rights reserved.

book, the purchasing power of our money is twice as great at Joe's as it is at Pete's.

International comparisons of prices must be made using exchange rates because different countries use different monies. Once we cross national borders, prices are quoted in different currencies. Suppose Joe's bookstore in New York City charges $20 for a book and Pierre's bookstore in Paris charges FF40. To compare the prices, we must know the exchange rate between dollars and francs.

If we find that goods sell for the same price in different markets, our money has the same purchasing power in those markets, which means that we have **purchasing power parity (PPP)**. PPP reflects a relationship among the domestic price level, the exchange rate, and the foreign price level:

$$P = EP^F$$

where

P = the domestic price

E = the exchange rate (units of domestic currency per unit of foreign currency)

P^F = the foreign price

If the dollar-franc exchange rate is .50 ($.50 = FF1), then a book priced at FF40 in Pierre's store in Paris costs the same as a book priced at $20 in Joe's store in New York:

$$P = EP^F$$
$$= \$.50 \times 40$$
$$= \$20$$

The domestic price (we are assuming that the U.S. dollar is the domestic currency) equals the exchange rate times the foreign price. Because the dollar price of the book in Paris is $20 and the price in the United States is $20, PPP holds. The purchasing power (value) of the dollar is the same in both places.

Realistically, similar goods don't always sell for the same price everywhere. Actually they don't even sell for the same price within a country. If the same textbook is priced differently at different bookstores, it is unrealistic to expect the price of the book to be identical worldwide. There are several reasons why PPP does not hold. The most important are that goods are not identical, that information is costly, that shipping costs affect prices, and that tariffs and legal restrictions on trade affect prices. If these factors did not exist, we would expect that anytime a price was lower in one market than in another, arbitrageurs would buy in the low-price market (pushing prices up) and simultaneously sell in the high-price market (pushing prices down). This arbitrage activity would ensure that PPP holds.

Goods are not identical   We would expect PPP to hold for identical goods, but few goods sold around the world are exactly the same in every country. Even goods that are identical and transportable may sell for much different prices in different countries. For instance, a recent survey indicated that a Big Mac hamburger in Paris costs $3.04; a Big Mac in Hong Kong is just $1.28. Why? This is where the costs of information, shipping costs, and tariffs and legal restrictions come into play.

purchasing power parity (PPP):
the condition under which monies have the same purchasing power in different markets

To determine the domestic currency value of a foreign currency price, multiply the exchange rate by the foreign price.

Why don't similar goods sell for the same price all over the world?

Copyright © by Houghton Mifflin Company. All rights reserved.

Information is costly People do not know everything about everything. To learn about the quality or prices of a product offered by different stores takes time and effort. It is in this sense that information is costly. Goods may thus sell for different prices in different countries in part because of information costs. When we pay $3.04 for a Big Mac in Paris, we may not know that a Big Mac is selling for $1.28 in Hong Kong. Furthermore, the price in Hong Kong may be irrelevant to our decision to buy a Big Mac in Paris. The Big Mac is such a small part of our total budget that it would not be worth our time to find out what the item costs in other countries. However, for automobiles and other expensive items, international price differences may determine where goods are bought. When prices are high, the value of information about differences in international prices may be worth the cost of obtaining that information.

Shipping costs alter prices It is costly to ship goods from one country to another. Shipping costs are reflected in price differentials across countries. If prices differ by no more than the costs of shipping, then it is not profitable to buy in the cheap country and sell in the more expensive country. The price difference simply reflects the cost of moving the goods.

Tariffs and legal restrictions on trade affect prices No country permits the free movement of all goods and services across its borders. Nations erect barriers to international trade for different reasons. These barriers may take the form of a *tariff*, a tax on goods that are traded internationally. Prices may differ across countries because of different tariff structures. Other barriers to trade place limits on the quantity of a good that can be bought or sold, or simply prohibit the import of some goods. All of these restrictions on the free movement of goods and services contribute to different prices for the same good in different countries. Big Macs cost more in countries with high tariffs on beef imports than they do in countries that allow beef to move freely into them.

Arbitrage, the act of profiting from international price differences, brings prices closer together. If there were no information costs, shipping costs, or tariffs, PPP would hold for similar goods.

Even though PPP does not hold for most goods, it is a useful concept. It points out an important link between national economies. Exchange rates tend to change as prices change in the direction suggested by PPP. In the next section we describe the impact of purchasing power parity on the relationship between inflation and exchange rates.

1.c. Inflation and Exchange Rate Changes

What is the relationship between inflation and changes in the exchange rate?

The idea of purchasing power parity reflects a tendency for exchange rates to adjust to offset price-level differences in different currencies. Goods tend to sell for equal prices all over the world. Price differences are smaller the more similar the goods being sold in different countries, the easier it is to gather information about prices, the lower the shipping costs, and the less restrictive the government barriers to trade. Even if PPP does not hold exactly, we expect the exchange rate to change in a manner roughly consistent with PPP. Because we measure price-level changes by inflation rates, we can relate changes in exchange rates to inflation differentials between countries.

To see how inflation differences are reflected in exchange rates, let's go back to the book selling for $20 in New York and FF40 in Paris. When the

Copyright © by Houghton Mifflin Company. All rights reserved.

exchange rate is $.50 = FF1, FF40 equals $20, so PPP holds. Now suppose that there is 100 percent inflation in France and zero inflation in the United States. If all prices double in France, the book sells for FF80. With no inflation in the United States, the book still sells for $20 in the United States.

How much must the exchange rate change to maintain PPP? We can find out by rewriting the PPP equation this way:

$$E = \frac{P}{P^F}$$

The exchange rate consistent with PPP equals the ratio of the domestic price to the foreign price. If the book sells for $20 in New York and FF80 in Paris, then the PPP exchange rate is (20/80), or 0.25. Notice what's happened. Because the price level in France doubled while the price level in the United States was constant, the dollar price of the franc was halved. Generally the dollar appreciates against currencies that have a higher inflation rate than the dollar and depreciates against currencies that have a lower inflation rate due to PPP pressures.

Generally the dollar appreciates against currencies that have a higher inflation rate than the dollar and depreciates against currencies with a lower inflation rate.

RECAP

1. When the exchange rate between two currencies changes, one currency depreciates while the other appreciates.

2. Purchasing power parity means that money has the same purchasing power in different markets.

3. Similar goods do not sell for the same price all over the world because goods are not identical, information is costly, shipping costs affect prices, and tariffs and legal restrictions on international trade affect prices.

4. The exchange rate tends to change to offset differences in the rate of inflation between two countries.

2. INTEREST RATES AND EXCHANGE RATES

Exchange rates are used to compare international prices of goods and services. They are also used to compare the return on foreign currency-denominated stocks and bonds to the return on domestic assets. For example, suppose you have a choice of buying a U.S. or a U.K. bond. The U.S. bond is denominated in dollars and pays 15 percent interest; the U.K. bond is denominated in British pounds and pays 10 percent interest. Because you are a U.S. resident and ultimately want dollars for household spending, you must compare the dollar return from holding each bond.

2.a. The Domestic Currency Return from Foreign Bonds

When deciding whether to buy a bond denominated in the domestic currency or in a foreign currency, the buyer must take expected changes in the exchange rate into account.

The U.S. bond is denominated in dollars, so the 15 percent interest is a dollar return. The U.K. bond, on the other hand, promises to pay 10 percent in terms of British pounds. If you buy the U.K. bond, you exchange dollars for pounds at the time the bond is purchased. When the bond matures, you exchange the principal and interest (the proceeds), trading pounds for dollars. If the exchange rate remains the same, the return on the U.K. bond is 10 percent.

Copyright © by Houghton Mifflin Company. All rights reserved.

But if the exchange rate changes between the time you buy the bond and the time it matures, your return in dollars may be more or less than 10 percent.

Figure 1 shows what happens when a U.S. resident buys a one-year U.K. bond. Suppose the exchange rate is $2 = £1 when the bond is purchased, and the bond sells for £1. The U.S. resident needs $2 to buy the bond. A year later the bond matures. The bondholder receives the principal of £1 plus 10 percent interest (£.10). Now the U.S. resident wants to convert the pounds into dollars. If the exchange rate has gone up from $2 = £1 to $2.10 = £1, the £1.10 proceeds from the bond are converted into dollars at the rate of 2.10 dollars per pound. The *dollar value* of the proceeds is $2.31 (the exchange rate [2.10] multiplied by the pound proceeds [£1.10]). The *dollar return* from the U.K. bond is the percentage difference between the dollar proceeds received after one year, and the initial dollar amount invested, approximately 15 percent:

$$\text{Dollar return} = \frac{\$2.31 - \$2}{\$2}$$

$$= \frac{\$.31}{\$2}$$

$$= .15$$

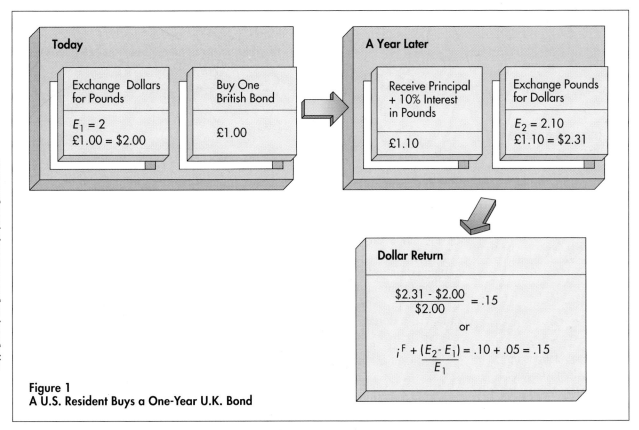

Figure 1
A U.S. Resident Buys a One-Year U.K. Bond

Copyright © by Houghton Mifflin Company. All rights reserved.

We can also determine the dollar return from the U.K. bond by adding the U.K. interest rate to the percentage change in the exchange rate. The percentage change in the exchange rate is 5 percent:

$$\text{Percentage change in exchange rate} = \frac{\$2.10 - \$2}{\$2}$$

$$= \frac{\$.10}{\$2}$$

$$= .05$$

The dollar return from the U.K. bond equals the 10 percent interest paid in British pounds plus the 5 percent change in the exchange rate, or 15 percent.

In our example, the pound appreciates against the dollar. When the pound increases in value, foreign residents holding pound-denominated bonds earn a higher return on those bonds than the pound interest rate. If the pound depreciates against the dollar, so that the pounds received at maturity are worth less than the pounds originally purchased, then the dollar return from the U.K. bond is lower than the interest rate on the bond. If the pound depreciates 5 percent, the dollar return is just 5 percent (the interest rate [10 percent] *minus* the exchange rate change [5 percent]).

We calculate the domestic currency return from a foreign bond by adding the foreign interest rate (i^F) plus the percentage change in the exchange rate ($[E_2 - E_1]/E_1$), where E_2 is the dollar price of a unit of foreign currency next period when the bond matures and E_1 is the exchange rate in the current period when the bond is purchased:

$$\text{Domestic currency return} = \text{foreign interest rate}$$
$$+ \text{percentage change in exchange rate}$$

$$= i^F + \frac{E_2 - E_1}{E_1}$$

How do we find the domestic currency return on a foreign bond?

2.b. Interest Rate Parity

interest rate parity (IRP): the condition under which similar financial assets have the same interest rate when measured in the same currency

Because U.S. residents can hold U.S. bonds, U.K. bonds, or the bonds or other securities of any country they choose, they compare the returns from the different alternatives when deciding what assets to buy. Foreign investors do the same thing. One product of the process is a close relationship among international interest rates. Specifically, the return, or interest rate, tends to be the same on similar bonds when returns are measured in terms of the domestic currency. This is called **interest rate parity (IRP)**.

Interest rate parity is the financial-asset version of purchasing power parity. Similar financial assets have the same percentage return when that return is computed in terms of one currency. Interest rate parity defines a relationship among the domestic interest rate, the foreign interest rate, and the expected change in the exchange rate:

$$\text{Domestic interest rate} = \text{foreign interest rate}$$
$$+ \text{expected change in exchange rate}$$

In our example, the U.S. bond pays 15 percent interest; the U.K. bond offers 10 percent interest in pounds. If the pound is expected to appreciate 5 percent, the U.K. bond offers U.S. residents an expected dollar return of 15

What is the relationship between domestic and foreign interest rates and changes in the exchange rate?

Copyright © by Houghton Mifflin Company. All rights reserved.

percent. Interest rate parity holds in this case. The domestic interest rate is 15 percent, which equals the foreign interest rate (10 percent) plus the expected change in the exchange rate (5 percent).

Interest rate parity is the product of arbitrage in financial markets. If U.S. bonds and U.K. bonds are similar in every respect except the currency used to pay the principal and interest, then they should yield similar returns to bond-holders. If U.S. investors can earn a higher return from buying U.K. bonds, they are going to buy more U.K. bonds and fewer U.S. bonds. This tends to raise the price of U.K. bonds, pushing U.K. interest rates down. At the same time, the price of U.S. bonds drops, raising U.S. interest rates. The initial higher return on U.K. bonds and resulting greater demand for U.K. bonds increases the demand for pounds, increasing the value of the pound versus the dollar today. As the pound appreciates today, if investors expect the same future exchange rate as they did before the current appreciation, the expected appreciation over the future falls. The change in the exchange rate and inter-est rates equalizes the expected dollar return from holding a U.S. bond or a U.K. bond. U.K. bonds originally offered a higher return than U.S. bonds, but the increase in demand for U.K. bonds relative to U.S. bonds lowers U.K. interest rates and the expected appreciation of the pound so that the bond returns are equalized.

2.c. Deviations from Interest Rate Parity

Interest rate parity does not hold for all financial assets. Like PPP, which applies only to similar goods, IRP applies only to similar assets. We do not expect the interest rate on a 90-day U.S. Treasury bill to equal the dollar return on a one-year U.K. Treasury bill because the maturity dates are differ-ent, 90 days versus a year. Financial assets with different terms to maturity typically pay different interest rates. We also do not expect different kinds of assets to offer the same return. A 90-day Japanese yen bank deposit in a Tokyo bank should not offer the same dollar return as a 90-day U.S. Treasury bill. The bank deposit and the Treasury bill are different assets.

Even with what seem to be similar assets, we can find deviations from interest rate parity. For instance, a 90-day peso certificate of deposit in a Mexico City bank does not offer a U.S. resident the same dollar return as a 90-day certificate of deposit denominated in U.S. dollars in a New York City bank. The reasons for the difference include government controls, political risk, and taxes.

Why don't similar financial assets yield the same return all over the world?

capital controls:
quotas or other forms of government-imposed controls on the flow of money between countries

Government controls   Certain government controls erect barriers to the free flow of money between countries. These controls can take the form of quotas on the amount of foreign exchange that can be bought or sold, high reserve requirements on foreign-owned bank deposits, or other controls designed to change the pattern in which financial assets flow between countries. These controls are called **capital controls**, where *capital* means "financial capital," not a resource used in producing other goods and services (the usual macro-economic sense of the word).

Political risk   Political risk is the risk associated with holding a financial asset issued in a foreign country. This risk arises from uncertainty. In 1982 the Mexican government imposed capital controls that restricted the flow of foreign exchange out of Mexico. U.S. residents who owned bank deposits or

Copyright © by Houghton Mifflin Company. All rights reserved.

risk premium:
the extra return required to offset the higher risk associated
with investing in a foreign asset

other financial assets in Mexico found that the controls substantially reduced the return on their assets. If U.S. residents believe that a foreign government may impose restrictions that reduce the return on assets issued in that country, those foreign-issued assets must offer a higher return than that offered on similar domestic assets. That extra return is called a **risk premium**. A risk premium offsets the higher risk associated with buying a foreign asset.

If political risk exists, IRP does not hold because the return on the foreign asset exceeds the return on the domestic asset by the amount of the risk premium.

Taxes Taxes also can account for deviations from IRP. Tax rates affect after-tax returns on investments. Different countries have different tax rates, so the same financial asset can yield a different before-tax return for residents of different countries. Because nominal interest rates (the rates observed in the market) are quoted without regard to taxes, some apparent deviations from IRP are only before-tax deviations. After taxes are taken into account, similar assets should yield a similar return in the absence of capital controls and political risk.

If there are no government controls, political risk, or different tax rates, IRP should hold exactly for financial assets that differ only in the currency of denomination. This is evident from the many studies of interest rate parity performed by economists.

RECAP

1. The domestic currency return from a foreign bond equals the foreign interest rate plus the percentage change in the exchange rate.

2. Interest rate parity exists when similar financial assets have the same interest rate when measured in the same currency, or when the domestic interest rate equals the foreign interest rate plus the expected change in the exchange rate.

3. Deviations from interest rate parity are a product of government controls, political risk, and different tax structures.

3. POLICY EFFECTS

The government budget constraint described in Chapter 15 links fiscal and monetary policies. It states that government spending is financed by taxes, borrowing, and changes in the money supply. This means that when government spending exceeds tax revenues, the budget deficit must be financed by borrowing or issuing money. Both methods of financing can affect exchange rates and interest rates. Here we look first at borrowing; then we turn to monetary policy and changes in the money supply.

3.a. Government Borrowing

An increase in government borrowing increases the supply of government bonds. As the supply of bonds increases with a given demand, bond prices fall and interest rates go up. The higher interest rate will induce people to willingly hold the greater bond supply. In Chapter 14 we defined the current interest rate (yield) this way:

Copyright © by Houghton Mifflin Company. All rights reserved.

Part III / Macroeconomic Policy

$$\text{Current interest rate} = \frac{\text{annual interest payment}}{\text{bond price}}$$

Because the annual interest payment is fixed, only the bond price changes. As the price of a bond increases, the interest rate falls; and as the price falls, the interest rate rises.

Let's continue with our bond example to illustrate the probable effect of financing an increased budget deficit by borrowing. Initially the U.S. bond interest rate is 15 percent, the U.K. bond interest rate is 10 percent, and the expected change in the exchange rate is 5 percent. Remember that when interest rate parity holds, the domestic interest rate equals the foreign interest rate plus the expected change in the exchange rate.

$$i_\$ = i_\pounds + \frac{E_2 - E_1}{E_1}$$

In our example, interest rate parity holds:

$$i_\$ = .10 + \frac{\$2.10 - \$2}{\$2}$$

$$= .10 + \frac{\$.10}{\$2}$$

$$= .10 + .05 = .15$$

Copyright © by Houghton Mifflin Company. All rights reserved.

How does fiscal policy affect exchange rates?

Suppose that to finance its higher deficit, the government increases the supply of bonds, pushing the interest rate on U.S. bonds up to 20 percent. The higher rate of interest attracts foreign investors, who demand dollars to purchase U.S. bonds. As the demand for dollars increases, the dollar appreciates. Let's say the dollar appreciates today to $1.91 per pound. If the future expected exchange rate is still $2.10 = £1, the expected change in the exchange rate is approximately 10 percent:

$$\frac{E_2 - E_1}{E_1} = \frac{\$2.10 - \$1.91}{\$1.91}$$

$$= \frac{\$.19}{\$1.91} = .10$$

Notice that the interest-rate-parity equation holds true:

$$i_\$ = i_\pounds + \frac{E_2 - E_1}{E_1}$$

$$= .10 + .10 = .20$$

Fiscal policy affects the exchange rate by changing interest rates, which changes the foreign demand for bonds.

Borrowing to finance the higher budget deficit raises the interest rate in the United States and causes the dollar to appreciate against foreign currencies.

The appreciation of the dollar also affects the international trade of goods and services. As the dollar appreciates on the foreign exchange market, U.S. goods become more expensive to foreign buyers and foreign goods become less expensive to U.S. buyers. What happens? U.S. exports decrease and U.S. imports increase. The foreign demand for U.S. bonds created by borrowing to finance the higher budget deficit pushes U.S. net exports down (Figure 2). A change in policy that lowers the budget deficit (reducing government borrowing) has the opposite effect.

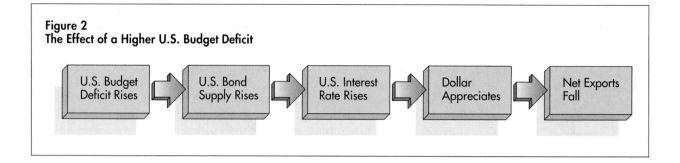

Figure 2
The Effect of a Higher U.S. Budget Deficit

| U.S. Budget Deficit Rises | ⇨ | U.S. Bond Supply Rises | ⇨ | U.S. Interest Rate Rises | ⇨ | Dollar Appreciates | ⇨ | Net Exports Fall |

3.b. Monetary Policy

How does monetary policy affect exchange rates?

In Chapter 8 we said that the actual interest rate observed in the economy, the *nominal interest rate,* has two components: the real interest rate and the rate of inflation. Of course, at the time a bond is purchased, no one knows what the actual rate of inflation is going to be over the life of the bond. This means the expected rate of inflation, not the actual rate of inflation, is reflected in the nominal interest rate:

Nominal interest rate = real interest rate + expected inflation

The greater the rate at which money grows, the greater the expected rate of inflation and the higher the nominal interest rate. So the process of financing government budget deficits by creating money pushes nominal interest rates up.

In the last section we saw that government borrowing to finance budget deficits also raises the nominal interest rate, but there the increase was a product of an increase in the real interest rate. The government must offer higher real interest rates on government bonds to induce domestic and foreign residents to buy the greater quantity of bonds supplied. In the case of monetary policy, higher nominal interest rates are a product of higher expected inflation; the real interest rate does not change.

As the nominal interest rate on domestic bonds increases, the exchange rate must change in order to maintain IRP. Let's go back to our example, in which the U.S. interest rate is 15 percent, the U.K. interest rate is 10 percent, the expected future exchange rate is $2.10 = £1, and the current exchange rate is $2 = £1. Interest rate parity holds because the dollar interest rate equals the foreign interest rate plus the expected change in the exchange rate:

$$i_\$ = i_£ + \frac{E_2 - E_1}{E_1}$$

$$= .10 + \frac{\$2.10 - \$2}{\$2} = .10 + \frac{\$.10}{\$2}$$

$$= .10 + .05 = .15$$

The dollar is expected to depreciate against the pound (or the pound is expected to appreciate against the dollar) by 5 percent, so the U.K. interest rate (10 percent) plus the higher value of U.K. currency (5 percent) equals the U.S. interest rate (15 percent).

Suppose the United States adopts an inflationary monetary policy, pushing the U.S. interest rate up to 20 percent. If the U.K. interest rate is still 10 percent, the dollar must depreciate by 10 percent for the expected return on

If one country has a higher rate of money growth than another country, the currency of the country with the higher rate of money growth tends to depreciate against the currency of the country with the lower rate of money growth.

Copyright © by Houghton Mifflin Company. All rights reserved.

International trade links the economies of nations together. Even countries as different as the United States and India will be increasingly interdependent economically as trade between the two nations grows. The photo shows large rolls of textiles from India being offloaded from a barge in Houston, Texas. These textiles will compete with U.S.-produced textiles so that the price of textiles in India has an effect on the prices charged by textile firms in the United States. Trade between nations also links business cycles. For example, a recession in the United States that reduces U.S. imports from India will reduce the real GDP of India.

holding a U.K. bond to equal the return on holding a U.S. bond. The dollar depreciates because the inflation rate in the United States is expected to be higher than that in the United Kingdom.

When a nation is expected to have higher inflation because of some new policy, people want to hold less of that nation's currency. If a new monetary policy raises the expected inflation rate in the United States, the nominal interest rate goes up. The higher expected inflation also has people selling dollars on the foreign exchange market, causing the dollar to depreciate. So higher nominal U.S. interest rates caused by greater expected U.S. inflation are associated with dollar depreciation. Continuing with our example, the U.S. interest rate is now 20 percent, the U.K. interest rate is 10 percent, and the exchange rate is $2.10 = £1. With the higher expected inflation and higher interest rate in the United States, the dollar is expected to depreciate to 2.31 dollars per pound in one year. Interest rate parity still holds:

$$i_\$ = i_£ + \frac{E_2 - E_1}{E_1}$$

$$= .10 + \frac{\$2.31 - \$2.10}{\$2.10} = .10 + \frac{\$.21}{\$2.10}$$

$$= .10 + .10 = .20$$

The depreciation of the dollar has no effect on international trade if the depreciation simply offsets rising prices in the United States. Here purchasing power parity holds: the relative prices of goods in each country stay the same. Even though prices in the United States are rising faster, the depreciation of the dollar lowers the cost of dollars to foreigners, compensating for the higher dollar price of goods. U.S. goods continue to sell for the same foreign currency price they did before the change in monetary policy. So there is no incentive to alter the quantities of goods bought and sold internationally.

If the growth of the money supply slows, other things being equal, the expected inflation rate falls. As a result, the nominal interest rate falls and the

Copyright © by Houghton Mifflin Company. All rights reserved.

domestic currency appreciates. Assuming that appreciation maintains purchasing power parity, the monetary policy has no effect on international trade and investment.

3.c. Linking IRP and PPP

As you have just seen, changes in government policy can affect both the exchange rate and the price level. Both PPP and IRP are relevant to the analysis. In fact now we can link the two together to demonstrate the relationship among inflation differentials between countries, interest rate differentials between countries, and expected changes in exchange rates.

IRP holds when the domestic interest rate equals the foreign interest rate plus the expected change in the exchange rate:

$$i = i_F + \frac{E_2 - E_1}{E_1}$$

We can rewrite the equation with the interest differential (the difference between the domestic and foreign interest rates) equal to the expected change in the exchange rate:

$$\frac{E_2 - E_1}{E_1} = i - i_F$$

PPP holds when the change in the exchange rate equals the inflation differential between countries. Inflation is the percentage change in the price level:

$$\text{Inflation} = \frac{P_2 - P_1}{P_1}$$

So PPP holds when

$$\frac{E_2 - E_1}{E_1} = \frac{P_2 - P_1}{P_1} - \frac{P_2^F - P_1^F}{P_1^F}$$

Let's use the data from our bond example to illustrate the link between IRP and PPP. Initially the U.S. interest rate is 15 percent and the U.K. interest rate is 10 percent. For IRP to hold, the dollar is expected to depreciate against the pound by 5 percent:

$$i_\$ - i_£ = \frac{E_2 - E_1}{E_1}$$

$$.15 - .10 = .05$$

If IRP and PPP hold, the expected change in the exchange rate equals the interest differential between domestic and foreign bonds, which equals the expected inflation differential between the domestic and foreign countries.

For PPP to hold, the expected change in the exchange rate must match the expected inflation differential between the United States and the United Kingdom (assuming the expected U.S. inflation rate is 12 percent and the expected U.K. inflation rate is 7 percent):

$$\frac{E_2 - E_1}{E_1} = \frac{P_2^\$ - P_1^\$}{P_1^\$} - \frac{P_2^£ - P_1^£}{P_1^£}$$

$$.05 = .12 - .07$$

By combining the IRP and PPP conditions, we can see that a change in government policy is reflected in a new interest differential, a new expected change in the exchange rate, and a new expected inflation differential.

Copyright © by Houghton Mifflin Company. All rights reserved.

RECAP

1. An increase in U.S. government spending financed by borrowing tends to raise the real interest rate in the United States and cause the dollar to appreciate.

2. Changes in the rate of growth of the money supply tend to change the exchange rate but may not affect international trade if PPP holds.

3. If PPP and IRP both hold, then the expected change in the exchange rate equals the interest differential between domestic and foreign bonds, which equals the expected inflation differential between the domestic and foreign countries.

4. INTERNATIONAL POLICY COORDINATION

Economies are linked globally by trade in goods, services, and financial assets. This means the policies of one nation can have important implications for other nations. One way this happens is because of the foreign repercussions of domestic spending. That is, some spending on imports comes back to the domestic economy in the form of exports. An increase in U.S. government expenditures increases U.S. real GDP. As income increases, U.S. imports increase, pushing foreign income up. As foreign income rises, so do foreign imports of goods produced in the United States. Ultimately, then, U.S. income rises by more than it would if based on only the domestic increase in spending. Since one country's economic policy can cause changes that affect other nations, there are potential gains from having economic policy formulated with a view toward the international effects.

Because countries are linked through their trade in goods, services, and financial assets, business cycles tend to follow similar trends across countries. When the U.S. economy is booming, income in countries that depend on exports to the U.S. market increases. When the United States is in a recession, income in other countries tends to fall. Because the nations of the world are linked by their common interests in trade, every country's domestic macroeconomic policy affects more than its domestic economy. And because every country has the potential to affect the economies of other nations, setting macroeconomic policy cooperatively may improve overall macroeconomic performance.

Macroeconomic policy in the United States traditionally has been formulated with little attention to the rest of the world. But in recent years, the potential gains from coordinating economic policies across countries have become increasingly apparent. Large fluctuations in exchange rates and net exports in the 1980s showed the interdependencies among nations. Over time, technological improvements in transportation and communication have created opportunities for substitution in international goods and services markets.

To coordinate economic policies, governments must communicate. Senior economic officials of the leading industrial countries come together regularly at meetings of the International Monetary Fund (IMF) and the Organization for Economic Cooperation and Development (OECD). Since 1975 the leaders of the seven largest industrial nations have held annual

Copyright © by Houghton Mifflin Company. All rights reserved.

The G7 countries are Canada, France, Germany, Italy, Japan, the United Kingdom, and the United States.

economic summit meetings. These seven nations (Canada, France, Germany, Italy, Japan, the United Kingdom, and the United States), known as the *Group of 7 (G7)* countries, have made a commitment to monitor one another's economic policies.

4.a. Potential Gains

What can countries gain by coordinating their macroeconomic policies?

Coordination among countries can take several directions. Countries can coordinate their goals, targeting inflation or unemployment, for example. They also can coordinate their information, exchanging forecasts of key macroeconomic variables based on their economic plans. Finally, they can coordinate the policymaking and implementation processes. The potential gains of coordination are a product of the form that coordination takes.

Setting joint goals could induce policy changes that make those goals attainable. For example, let's say that all countries set a goal of reducing the unemployment rate. To meet that goal, the countries would have to set expansionary monetary or fiscal policies. Even if the countries do not explicitly discuss their future policies, the goals they set guide those policies. Of course, this assumes that policymakers target the agreed-on goals when they formulate their domestic economic policy.

The coordination of information regarding the current state of the economy and forecasts of future changes can take place both informally and through formal meetings of key policymakers. Central bank and treasury staff members may regularly talk to compare notes on the world economy.

Coordination of the policymaking process offers the hope of making every country better off. For instance, since the mid-1980s, the United States has experienced a large international trade deficit, while Japan and Germany have had trade surpluses. At several international conferences, leading policymakers have proposed that the United States reduce its fiscal deficit to reduce domestic spending and improve its international balance of trade. Simultaneously, Japan and Germany were going to increase their fiscal deficits to stimulate spending in those countries in order to increase their imports from the United States and to avoid recessions if exports to the United States fell.

The proposed fiscal policy has proven difficult to implement, but future policy actions may very well reflect this kind of multinational decision making. For example, suppose the United States wants to stimulate the domestic economy but is concerned about increasing its international trade deficit (rising income increases imports). If U.S. expansionary policies could be coordinated with expansionary policies in other large countries, so that income rises in all the countries simultaneously, the balance of trade might not change even though all the countries are increasing their real GDP. This is a potential benefit of international cooperation: by acting together, nations can achieve better outcomes than would be possible if they acted individually.

4.b. Obstacles

Obviously, international coordination of macroeconomic policy makes sense. In practice, however, several problems stand in the way of designing and implementing economic policy across countries. First, countries may not

Copyright © by Houghton Mifflin Company. All rights reserved.

agree on goals. Some countries may be willing to exploit the short-run trade-off between inflation and the unemployment rate, while other countries may choose to follow passive policies, refusing to manipulate aggregate demand. In addition, the politicians who are involved in international agreements tend to make policies aimed at short-term political gains rather than long-term economic stability.

Second, even if countries can agree on goals, they may disagree on the current economic situation. GDP and other key macroeconomic variables are measured with a lag and are often revised substantially after their values are initially announced. At any point in time, policymakers cannot be sure whether the economy is expanding or contracting. Eventually, as official data are collected, the economic health of the nation is known, but only several months later. This means that the economic policymakers of the major developed countries could disagree on an appropriate course of action because they do not agree on current economic conditions.

Consider an example. In 1994, the Federal Reserve declared that inflation was Public Enemy Number One. So the Fed implemented a restrictive economic policy of raising interest rates aimed at slowing the growth of aggregate demand. As the Fed raised interest rates repeatedly during the year, some economists and politicians in the United States as well as abroad argued that there was no inflation problem and the Fed might create a recession by raising interest rates. Other economists believed that inflationary pressures were building and the Fed was wisely fighting these pressures. In retrospect, we can look back at the record since 1994 and see that no recession occurred and inflation remained low. However, we cannot be sure that what happened may not have been a result of Fed actions. Another example arises out of the dollar depreciation of early 1995. As the dollar fell in value against the yen and mark, Japanese officials argued that the United States should take action to support the dollar while U.S. officials tended to state that while they were surprised at the falling dollar, they did not feel a need to actively change U.S. policy with the aim of increasing the value of the dollar. Such disagreements are commonplace and to be expected in a world where economic policy is made by politicians and is compounded by the fact that good economists often disagree about the proper role of government policy.

Even if countries can agree on goals and current conditions, they still may disagree on appropriate policy because they adhere to different theories of macroeconomics. Some policymakers believe that a new Keynesian fixed-price model (with a horizontal aggregate supply curve) best describes current economic conditions, and that by increasing aggregate demand they can increase output and employment. Others believe that the new classical model (in which the aggregate supply curve is vertical in the presence of expected policy changes) best describes the current economic situation and that increasing aggregate demand in a predictable way has no effect on output and employment but causes the price level to rise. These very basic disagreements make it difficult to reach a consensus on economic policy.

These obstacles may make it impossible to coordinate international economic policy. But at least international economic meetings and discussions help each country understand the views of other nations and the likely course of policy in the rest of the world. This sharing of information allows each nation to formulate its own policy in light of what policy in the rest of the world is likely to be.

Copyright © by Houghton Mifflin Company. All rights reserved.

RECAP

1. Because every country has the potential to affect the economies of other nations, coordinating macroeconomic policy may improve overall economic performance.

2. Coordination here means setting joint goals, exchanging information, and forming and executing policy cooperatively.

3. Obstacles to the international coordination of economic policy are disagreements over goals, current economic conditions, and macroeconomic theory.

SUMMARY

1. Arbitrage equalizes the prices of similar goods in different markets. § Preview

2. An open economy trades goods, services, and financial assets with the rest of the world. § Preview

▓▓▓ How does a change in the exchange rate affect the prices of goods traded between countries?

3. When the domestic currency depreciates against other currencies, foreign goods become more expensive to domestic buyers and domestic goods become less expensive to foreign buyers. §1.a

4. When the domestic currency appreciates against other currencies, foreign goods become less expensive to domestic buyers and domestic goods become more expensive to foreign buyers. §1.a

5. Purchasing power parity exists when monies have the same value in different markets. §1.b

▓▓▓ Why don't similar goods sell for the same price all over the world?

6. Deviations from PPP arise because goods are not identical in different countries, information is costly, shipping costs affect prices, and tariffs and restrictions on trade affect prices. §1.b

▓▓▓ What is the relationship between inflation and changes in the exchange rate?

7. Exchange rates tend to change to offset inflation differentials between countries. §1.c

▓▓▓ How do we find the domestic currency return on a foreign bond?

8. The domestic currency return from holding a foreign bond equals the foreign interest rate plus the percentage change in the exchange rate. §2.a

▓▓▓ What is the relationship between domestic and foreign interest rates and changes in the exchange rate?

9. Interest rate parity exists when the domestic interest rate equals the foreign interest rate plus the expected change in the exchange rate, so that similar financial assets yield the same return when measured in the same currency. §2.b

▓▓▓ Why don't similar financial assets yield the same return all over the world?

10. Deviations from IRP are a product of government controls, political risk, and taxes. §2.c

▓▓▓ How does fiscal policy affect exchange rates?

11. Financing a government budget deficit by selling bonds (borrowing) tends to raise domestic interest rates, which attracts foreign investors and causes the domestic currency to appreciate. Ultimately, increased government borrowing tends to reduce net exports. §3.a

▓▓▓ How does monetary policy affect exchange rates?

12. Higher expected inflation, a product of increasing the rate at which the money supply

Copyright © by Houghton Mifflin Company. All rights reserved.

grows, tends to increase nominal interest rates. The domestic currency depreciates to offset rising prices but has no effect on net exports. §3.b

13. If IRP and PPP hold, the expected change in the exchange rate equals the interest differential between domestic and foreign bonds, which equals the expected inflation differential between the domestic and foreign economies. §3.c

What can countries gain by coordinating their macroeconomic policies?

14. By coordinating macroeconomic policies, the goals of those policies become more attain-able, nations have greater access to economic information, and the results of those policies are improved. §4.a

15. Obstacles to the international coordination of macroeconomic policy are disagreements over policy goals, the current economic situation, and macroeconomic theory. §4.b

KEY TERMS

arbitrage § Preview
open economy § Preview
purchasing power parity (PPP) §1.b

interest rate parity (IRP) §2.b
capital controls §2.c
risk premium §2.c

EXERCISES

1. Find the U.S. dollar value of each of the following currencies at the given exchange rates:

   a. $1 = C$1.20 (Canadian dollars)

   b. $1 = ¥140 (Japanese yen)

   c. $1 = FL2 (Netherlands guilder)

   d. $1 = SKr6 (Swedish krona)

   e. $1 = SF1.5 (Swiss franc)

2. You are a U.S. importer who buys goods from many different countries. How many U.S. dollars do you need to settle each of the following invoices?

   a. 1,000,000 Australian dollars for wool blankets (exchange rate: A$1 = $.769)

   b. 500,000 British pounds for dishes (exchange rate: £1 = $1.5855)

   c. 100,000 Indian rupees for baskets (exchange rate: Rs1 = $.0602)

   d. 150 million Japanese yen for stereo components (exchange rate: ¥1 = $.0069)

   e. 825,000 German marks for wine (exchange rate: DM1 = $.5515)

3. What is the dollar value of the invoices in exercise 2 if the dollar

   a. depreciates 10 percent against the Australian dollar?

   b. appreciates 10 percent against the British pound?

   c. depreciates 10 percent against the Indian rupee?

   d. appreciates 20 percent against the Japanese yen?

   e. depreciates 100 percent against the German mark?

4. Explain purchasing power parity and why it does not hold perfectly in the real world.

5. Write an equation that describes purchasing power parity and explain the equation.

6. Write an equation that describes interest rate parity and explain the equation.

Copyright © by Houghton Mifflin Company. All rights reserved.

7. Use the equation in exercise 6 to describe the effects of an increase in domestic government spending financed by

   a. borrowing

   b. money creation

8. If the interest rate on one-year government bonds is 5 percent in Germany and 8 percent in the United States, what do you think is expected to happen to the dollar value of the mark? Explain your answer.

9. Suppose that on January 1 the yen price of the dollar is 100. Over the year, the Japanese inflation rate is 5 percent and the U.S. inflation rate is 10 percent. If the exchange rate is $1 = ¥110$ at the end of the year, relative to PPP, does the yen appear to be overvalued, undervalued, or at the PPP level? Explain your answer.

10. In 1960 a U.S. dollar sold for 620 Italian lire. If PPP held in 1960, what would the PPP value of the exchange rate have been in 1987 if Italian prices rose 12 times and U.S. prices rose 4 times between 1960 and 1987?

11. Suppose a personal computer sold for $1,500 in Los Angeles and $1,700 in San Francisco. How would arbitrage operate to keep the prices of the computer in the two cities from moving too far apart?

12. If the U.S. dollar depreciates against the German mark, what will be the economic consequences for U.S. residents?

13. If the price of a pound of salmon is $5 in Seattle, Washington, and the exchange rate between U.S. and Canadian dollars is $.80 = C$1.00$, then what would the Canadian dollar price of salmon have to be in Vancouver, British Columbia, in order for PPP to hold?

14. Suppose at the beginning of the year a best-selling CD sells for FF60 in Paris, France, and DM20 in Hanover, Germany, and PPP holds. Over the year, there is an inflation rate of 33 percent in France and no inflation in Germany. What exchange rate would maintain PPP at the end of the year?

15. Suppose a U.S. investor buys a one-year German bond with a face value of DM10,000 that has a 10 percent annual interest rate. How many dollars will a U.S. investor receive at maturity if the exchange rate is $.40 = DM1.00$?

Copyright © by Houghton Mifflin Company. All rights reserved.

☐ INTERNET EXERCISES

In Section 4 of this chapter we learned how countries can potentially improve economic outcomes through international policy coordination. One organization that aids the process of policy coordination is the Organization for Economic Cooperation and Development (OECD). To learn more about the OECD and its activities, go to the Boyes/Melvin web site at **http://www.hmco.com/college/** and click on the internet exercise link for this chapter. Now answer the questions that appear on the web page.

Copyright © by Houghton Mifflin Company. All rights reserved.

Expats' Currency Conundrum/American Investors Try to Predict Future of the Dollar

Americans living and working in Japan are taking the dollar's tumble against the yen personally.

Foreign-exchange loss has become a big concern among expats, whether they are paid in yen or dollars. "I've been telling my clients to hold onto their yen, but now I would start encouraging people to switch to dollars, says Karen Wenk-Jordan, a former New York resident who runs a financial-services company in Tokyo.

Bob Davis, a management consultant for McKinsey and Co., and a native of Western Springs, Ill., converted a portion of his yen savings two weeks ago at 98 yen, then converted more this week at 94.

"I was doing local certificates of deposits here in Japan that have 1.8% interest, which is all you get. Now I've exchanged everything I had in yen to dollars and have almost no yen," says Davis.

He invested 5% in a U.S. money market fund, 25% in bond mutual funds and the remaining 70% in three different types of stock mutual funds. To move money swiftly, many expats in Japan hold both a yen and foreign-currency account.

Citibank, the only American retail bank in Japan, offers a multimoney account in which clients can hold up to 14 currencies. Transfers can be made instantly over the phone.

"Foreign exchange is our forte," says Susan Nakano, who moved from Hawaii to Tokyo to run the bank's expatriate services. But the multimoney account earns only 0.75% interest, and the yen savings account is even less at 0.25%.

"It's pitiful," says Christine Davis, an English school teacher from Putnam, Conn., who has a yen savings account with Citibank. "The bank charges you $10 a month if you have less than $3,000 in your account."

Banks in Japan offer meager returns on fixed-term deposits as well. "I never recommend holding dollars in Japan because interest rates are so low," says Wenk-Jordan.

"If the person is going home in a couple of years, I suggest keeping dollars in the USA. But expats who plan to be away for a long time should think about moving their money offshore."

Hong Kong is a popular choice. Wenk-Jordan says the Hong Kong Shanghai Bank's multimoney account offers a higher interest rate than banks in Japan and the minimum deposit is only $250.

Other personal investors who want to keep some savings in yen, purchase money management funds—equivalent to money market funds in the USA. Japan's major securities companies sell them in the equivalent of $1,000 units.

But money managers warn that brokerages usually refuse clients who do not read Japanese because of contract liabilities.

Wiring money to a bank account in a home country probably is the easiest investment strategy; Americans paid in yen benefit from both the foreign exchange rate and the high U.S. interest rates.

Finally, expats planning to return to their home country should keep their old bank account and credit card in order to maintain their credit rating.

"Lenders get uncomfortable when they see a dormant period in a person's credit profile," Wenk-Jordan says. "One way to get around this is to occasionally charge up about $500 then pay it off over a period of four or five months. That way you establish a history of payments and reliability."

Source: Copyright© 1995, USA TODAY. Reprinted with permission.

USA Today/March 10, 1995

Copyright © by Houghton Mifflin Company. All rights reserved.

COMMENTARY

This article points out the real-world fact of exchange rate uncertainty and the costs it can impose on even thoughtful investors. We are told that Karen Wenk-Jordan, who runs a financial services company in Tokyo, was advising her clients to switch their savings from yen to dollars in the second week of 1995. Bob Davis did just this, converting a portion of his yen savings into dollars at an exchange rate of 98 yen per dollar. Why the switch from yen to dollars? Because the yen interest rate was very low, only 1.8 percent on the yen certificates of deposit (CDs) that Davis held. At this time, dollar CDs in the United States were offering around 6 percent interest. Since 6 percent is greater than 1.8 percent, it seems clear that one should invest in dollar CDs rather than yen.

However, things are not this simple. Only 2 weeks after this article was written, the dollar dropped in value against the yen by a surprisingly large amount. By early April, instead of 98 yen per dollar, the exchange rate was 83 yen per dollar. We can estimate the cost to an investor of switching from yen to dollar CDs prior to the dollar depreciation. For example, suppose Bob Davis has ¥1,000,000 to invest at the beginning of 1995 when the dollar is worth 98 yen. If he buys a yen CD paying 1.8 percent per year in interest, then after 3 months (a quarter of a year) he will have ¥1,004,500. If instead he converts his yen to dollars at the beginning of the year, he will have ¥1,000,000/98 = $10,204 to invest in U.S. CDs. If these CDs earn 6 percent interest, then after a quar-

ter of a year, he will have $10,357. However, when the dollars are converted back into yen at the new exchange rate he ends up with $10,357 × 83 = ¥859,636. Because of the dollar depreciation, he ends up with fewer yen than he started with.

Since international investing involves more than one currency, it is not enough to just compare interest rates. Exchange rate changes will also have an impact on the returns investors earn. The fact that the yen deposits were offering a lower interest rate than dollar deposits, suggests that people believe that the dollar will depreciate against the yen so that the higher dollar interest rate, at least partially, compensates for the falling value of the currency. If investors did not expect the dollar to depreciate, then no one would buy yen deposits offering a lower interest rate as everyone would want the higher interest rate dollar deposits.

The bottom line is that the interest differential between yen and dollar CDs reflects the expected change in the exchange rate. Once expected exchange rate changes are considered, investors will not all agree that the higher interest rate CD is the preferred investment. Since Karen Wenk-Jordan and Bob Davis thought the higher interest rates on U.S. CDs were attractive, they must have expected no significant change in the yen/dollar exchange rate. The surprising (to them) dollar depreciation cost Mr. Davis and Ms. Wenk-Jordan's other clients a substantial loss. The lesson is that both exchange rates and interest rates must be considered when making international investment decisions.

Copyright © by Houghton Mifflin Company. All rights reserved.

Copyright © by Houghton Mifflin Company. All rights reserved.

etween 1967 and 1996 real GDP grew at an average annual rate of 2.9 percent across all industrial countries. Over this same time period, Japanese real GDP grew at an average annual rate of 4.4 percent while U.S. real GDP grew at an average annual rate of only 2.5 percent. Why has Japanese real GDP grown at a faster rate in recent decades than U.S. real GDP? Is it because Japanese workers are more diligent or more highly motivated than U.S. workers? Is it because Japanese students study more and so are better educated than U.S. students? Is it because Japanese firms are more concerned with developing new products and new production techniques than U.S. firms? Understanding why and how economic growth happens is a very important part of macroeconomics.

Preview

Although much of macroeconomics is aimed at understanding business cycles —recurring periods of prosperity and recession—the fact is that over the long run, most economies do grow wealthier. The long-run trend of real GDP in the United States and most other countries is positive. Yet the rate at which real GDP grows is very different across countries. Why? What factors cause economies to grow and living standards to rise?

In this chapter we focus on the long-term picture. We begin by defining economic growth and discussing its importance. Then we examine the determinants of economic growth, to understand what accounts for the different rates of growth across countries. ∎

1. DEFINING ECONOMIC GROWTH

What do we mean by economic growth? Economists use two measures of growth—real GDP and per capita real GDP—to compare how economies grow over time.

1.a. Real GDP

What is economic growth?

economic growth:
an increase in real GDP

Basically, **economic growth** is an increase in real GDP. As more goods and services are produced, the real GDP increases and people are able to consume more.

To calculate the percentage change in real GDP over a year, we simply divide the change in GDP by the value of GDP at the beginning of the year,

Copyright © by Houghton Mifflin Company. All rights reserved.

and then multiply the quotient by 100. For instance, the real GDP of Singapore was approximately 109,787 million Singapore dollars in 1996 and approximately 102,299 million in 1995. So the economy grew 7.3 percent in 1996:

$$\text{Percentage change in real GDP} = \frac{\text{change over year}}{\text{beginning value}} \times 100$$

$$= \frac{109{,}787 - 102{,}299}{102{,}299} \times 100$$

$$= .073 \times 100$$

$$= 7.3$$

1.a.1. Compound Growth
From 1980 to 1995, the industrial countries of the world showed an average annual growth rate of real GDP of 2.4 percent. Over the same period, the average annual growth rate of real GDP for low-income developing countries was 4.2 percent. The difference between a growth rate of 2.4 percent and one of 4.2 percent may not seem substantial, but in fact it is. Growth is compounded over time. This means that any given rate of growth is applied every year to a growing base of real GDP, so any difference is magnified over time.

Small changes in rates of growth produce big changes in real GDP over a period of many years.

Figure 1 shows the effects of compounding growth rates. The upper line in the figure represents the path of real GDP if the economy grows at a rate of 4.2 percent a year. The lower line shows real GDP growing at a rate of 2.4 percent a year.

Suppose in each case the economy originally is producing a real GDP of $1 billion. After five years, there is not much difference: a GDP of $1.13 billion at 2.4 percent growth versus $1.23 billion at 4.2 percent growth. The effect of compounding becomes more visible over long periods of time. After

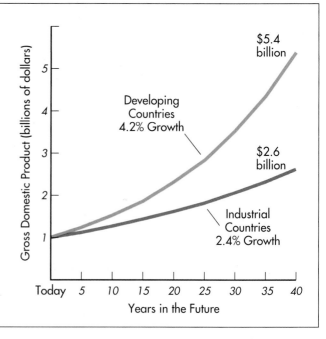

Figure 1
Comparing GDP Growth Rates of 2.4% and 4.2%
Between 1980 and 1995, real GDP in the industrial countries grew at an average annual rate of 2.4 percent, while real GDP in developing countries grew at an average annual rate of 4.2 percent. The difference seems small, but the graph shows how even a small difference is compounded over time, producing a substantial difference in real GDP.

Copyright © by Houghton Mifflin Company. All rights reserved.

40 years, the difference between 2.4 and 4.2 percent growth, a seemingly small difference, represents a huge difference in output. A 2.4 percent rate of growth yields an output of $2.6 billion; at 4.2 percent, output is $5.4 billion. After 40 years, the level of output is twice as large at the higher growth rate.

1.a.2. The Rule of 72 Compound growth explains why countries are so concerned about maintaining positive high rates of growth. If growth is maintained at a constant rate, we can estimate the number of years required for output to double by using the **rule of 72**. If we divide 72 by the growth rate, we find the approximate time it takes for any value to double.

rule of 72:
the number of years required for an amount to double in value is 72 divided by the annual rate of growth

Suppose you deposit $100 in a bank account that pays a constant 6 percent annual interest. If you allow the interest to accumulate over time, the amount of money in the account grows at a rate of 6 percent. At this rate of interest, the rule of 72 tells us that your account will have a value of approximately $200 (double its initial value) after 12 years:

$$\frac{72}{6} = 12$$

The interest rate gives the rate of growth of the amount deposited if earned interest is allowed to accumulate in the account. If the interest rate is 3 percent, the amount would double in 24 (72/3) years.

The rule of 72 applies to any value. If real GDP is growing at a rate of 6 percent a year, then real GDP doubles every 12 years. At a 3 percent annual rate, real GDP doubles every 24 years.

Table 1 lists the average annual rate of growth of GDP between 1980 and 1996 and approximate doubling times for five countries. The countries listed range from a high growth rate of 8.7 percent in Korea to a low rate of 2.5 percent in the United States. If these growth rates are maintained over time, it would take just 8 years for GDP in Korea to double and 29 years for the GDP in the United States to double.

TABLE 1
GDP Growth Rates and Doubling Times

Country	Average Annual Growth Rate (percent)*	Doubling Time (years)
Korea	8.7	8
Bangladesh	4.3	17
Japan	3.4	21
Australia	3.2	22
United States	2.5	29

*Average annual growth rates from 1980 to 1996.

Source: Data are from International Monetary Fund, *International Financial Statistics Yearbook*, (Washington, D.C., 1997).

Copyright © by Houghton Mifflin Company. All rights reserved.

1.b. Per Capita Real GDP

Economic growth is sometimes defined as an increase in per capita real GDP.

per capita real GDP: real GDP divided by the population

We've defined economic growth as an increase in real GDP. But, if growth is supposed to be associated with higher standards of living, our definition may be misleading. A country could show positive growth in real GDP, but if the population is growing at an even higher rate, output per person can actually fall. Economists, therefore, often adjust the growth rate of output for changes in population. **Per capita real GDP** is real GDP divided by the population. If we define economic growth as rising per capita real GDP, then growth requires a nation's output of goods and services to increase faster than its population.

The World Bank computes per capita GNP for countries as an indicator of economic development. You may recall from Chapter 6 that GNP equals GDP plus net factor income from abroad. From 1985 to 1995, per capita real GNP grew at an average annual rate of 3.8 percent in low-income developing countries and 1.9 percent in industrial countries. The difference in per capita real GNP growth between low-income developing and industrial countries is much smaller than the difference in real GDP growth. The difference in growth rates between the level of output and per capita output points out the danger of just looking at real GDP as an indicator of change in the economic well-being of the citizens in developing countries. Population growth rates are considerably higher in developing countries than they are in industrial countries, so real GDP must grow at a faster rate in developing countries than it does in industrial countries just to maintain a similar growth rate in per capita real GDP.

1.c. The Problems with Definitions of Growth

Economic growth is considered to be good because it allows people to have a higher standard of living, to have more material goods. But an increase in real GDP or per capita real GDP does not tell us whether the average citizen is better off. One problem is that these measures say nothing about how income is distributed. The national economy may be growing, yet the poor may be staying poor while the rich get richer.

We thus have to be careful about using per capita real GDP as an indicator of the standard of living. Table 2 shows why. The table lists historical data on the percentage share of household income in Sri Lanka by income groups. In 1969–1970, the poorest 20 percent of households received 7.5 percent of the nation's total income; the next 20 percent received 11.7 percent; the third 20 percent received 15.7 percent; 21.7 percent went to the next group; and, finally, the wealthiest 20 percent of households received 43.4 percent.

Although per capita real GDP did grow in Sri Lanka from 1970 to 1990, we cannot say that all households benefited from that growth. Between 1969–1970 and 1980–1981, the share of household income going to each of the four poorest groups of households in Sri Lanka fell. Only the wealthiest group, which already had a disproportionate share of real GDP, saw that share increase. So from 1970 to 1980, it is not clear that the poorest groups benefited from GDP growth. However, between 1980–1981 and 1990, the share of household income going to the poorest groups increased, so that they were more likely to benefit from GDP growth.

Copyright © by Houghton Mifflin Company. All rights reserved.

TABLE 2
Income Distribution, Sri Lanka

	Percentage Share of Household Income Going to				
	Lowest 20 Percent	Second 20 Percent	Third 20 Percent	Fourth 20 Percent	Highest 20 Percent
1969–1970	7.5	11.7	15.7	21.7	43.4
1980–1981	5.8	10.1	14.1	20.3	49.8
1990	8.9	13.1	16.9	21.7	39.3

Source: Data are from World Bank, *World Development Report* (Washington, D.C., 1988), p. 272, and 1997, p. 222.

The lesson here is simple. Economic growth may benefit some groups more than others. And it is entirely possible that despite national economic growth, some groups can be worse off than they were before. Clearly, per capita real GDP or real GDP does not accurately measure the standard of living for all of a nation's citizens.

Another reason real GDP or per capita real GDP is misleading is that it says nothing about the quality of life. People have nonmonetary needs—they care about personal freedom, the environment, their leisure time. If a rising per capita GDP goes hand in hand with a repressive political regime or rapidly deteriorating environmental quality, people are not going to feel better off. By the same token, a country could have no economic growth, yet reduce the hours worked each week. More leisure time could make workers feel better off, even though per capita GDP has not changed.

Per capita real GDP is a questionable indicator of the typical citizen's standard of living or quality of life.

Once again, be careful in interpreting per capita GDP. Don't allow it to represent more than it does. Per capita GDP is simply a measure of the output produced divided by the population. It is a useful measure of economic activity in a country, but it is a questionable measure of the typical citizen's standard of living or quality of life.

RECAP

1. Economic growth is an increase in real GDP.
2. Because growth is compounded over time, small differences in rates of growth are magnified over time.
3. For any constant rate of growth, the time required for real GDP to double is 72 divided by the annual growth rate.
4. Per capita real GDP is real GDP divided by the population.
5. Per capita real GDP says nothing about the distribution of income in a country or the nonmonetary quality of life.

Copyright © by Houghton Mifflin Company. All rights reserved.

2. THE DETERMINANTS OF GROWTH

How are economic growth
rates determined?

*Economic growth raises the
potential level of real GDP, shifting the long-run aggregate supply curve to the right.*

The long-run aggregate supply curve is a vertical line at the potential level of
real GDP (Y_{p_1}). As the economy grows, the potential output of the economy
rises. Figure 2 shows the increase in potential output as a rightward shift in
the long-run aggregate supply curve. The higher the rate of growth, the far-
ther the aggregate supply curve moves to the right. To illustrate several years'
growth, we would show several curves shifting to the right.

To find the determinants of economic growth, we must turn to the determinants of aggregate supply. In Chapter 9, we identified three determinants of
aggregate supply: resource prices, technology, and expectations. Changes in
expectations can shift the aggregate supply curve, but changing expectations
are not a basis for long-run growth in the sense of continuous rightward
movements in aggregate supply. The long-run growth of the economy rests on
growth in productive resources (labor, capital, and land) and technological
advances.

2.a. Labor

Economic growth depends on the size and quality of the labor force. The size
of the labor force is a function of the size of the working-age population (sixteen and older in the United States) and the percentage of that population
in the labor force. The labor force typically grows more rapidly in developing countries than in industrial countries because birthrates are higher
in developing countries. Figure 3 shows the annual growth rates of the
population for selected developing and industrial countries, as well as
average growth rates for all developing countries and all industrial
countries. Between 1990 and 1995, the population grew at an average annual

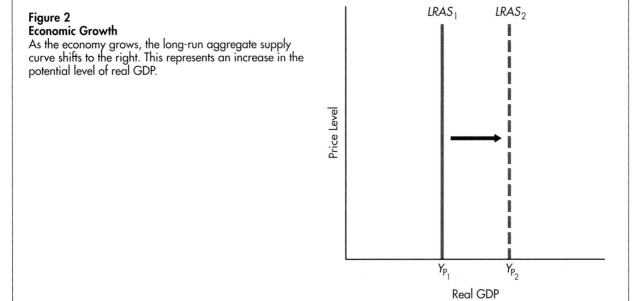

Figure 2
Economic Growth
As the economy grows, the long-run aggregate supply
curve shifts to the right. This represents an increase in the
potential level of real GDP.

Copyright © by Houghton Mifflin Company. All rights reserved.

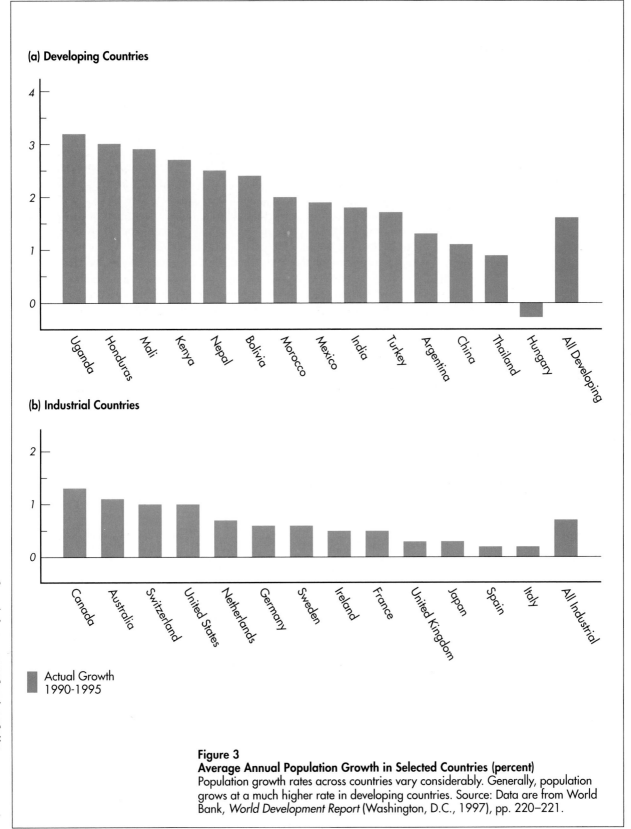

(a) Developing Countries

(b) Industrial Countries

Actual Growth
1990-1995

Figure 3
Average Annual Population Growth in Selected Countries (percent)
Population growth rates across countries vary considerably. Generally, population
grows at a much higher rate in developing countries. Source: Data are from World
Bank, *World Development Report* (Washington, D.C., 1997), pp. 220–221.

Copyright © by Houghton Mifflin Company. All rights reserved.

rate of 1.6 percent in developing countries and 0.7 percent in industrial countries.

Based solely on growth in the labor force, it seems that developing countries are growing faster than industrial countries. But the size of the labor force is not all that matters; changes in productivity can compensate for lower growth in the labor force, as we discuss in section 3.

The U.S. labor force has changed considerably in recent decades. The most notable event of the post–World War II period was the baby boom. The children born between the late 1940s and the early 1960s made up more than a third of the total U.S. population in the early 1960s and have significantly altered the age structure of the population. In 1950 the largest percentage of males and females in the population was in the category of young children. By 1970 the largest percentage of the U.S. population was in the five- to twenty-nine-year range. By 1980 this bulge in the age distribution had moved to the twenty- to forty-four-year range, where it remains today. Over time the bulge will be moving to older ranges of the population.

The initial pressure of the baby boom fell on school systems faced with rapidly expanding enrollments. Over time, as these children aged and entered the labor market, they had a large impact on potential output. The U.S. labor force grew at an average rate of about 2.5 percent a year in the 1970s, approximately twice the rate of growth experienced in the 1950s. The growth of the labor force slowed in the 1980s and 1990s, as the baby boom population aged. Based on the size of the labor force, the 1970s should have been a time of greater economic growth than the 1950s, 1960s, or 1980s and 1990s. It was not. More important than the size of the labor force is its productivity.

2.b. Capital

Labor is combined with capital to produce goods and services. A rapidly growing labor force by itself is no guarantee of economic growth. Workers need machines, tools, and factories to work. If a country has lots of workers but few machines, then the typical worker cannot be very productive. Capital is a critical resource in growing economies.

The ability of a country to invest in capital goods is tied to its ability to save. A lack of current saving can be offset by borrowing, but the availability of borrowing is limited by the prospects for future saving. Debt incurred today must be repaid by not consuming all output in the future. If lenders believe that a nation is going to consume all of its output in the future, they do not make loans today.

The lower the standard of living in a country, the harder it is to forgo current consumption in order to save. It is difficult for a population living at or near subsistence level to do without current consumption. This in large part explains the low level of saving in the poorest countries.

2.c. Land

Abundant natural resources are not a necessary condition for economic growth.

Land surface, water, forests, minerals, and other natural resources are called *land*. Land can be combined with labor and capital to produce goods and services. Abundant natural resources can contribute to economic growth, but natural resources alone do not generate growth. Several developing countries, like Argentina and Brazil, are relatively rich in natural resources but have not

Copyright © by Houghton Mifflin Company. All rights reserved.

been very successful in exploiting these resources to produce goods and services. Japan, on the other hand, has relatively few natural resources but has shown dramatic economic growth in recent decades. The experience of Japan makes it clear that abundant natural resources are not a necessary condition for economic growth.

2.d. Technology

technology:
ways of combining resources to produce output

Technological advances allow the production of more output from a given amount of resources.

A key determinant of economic growth is **technology**, ways of combining resources to produce goods and services. New management techniques, scientific discoveries, and other innovations improve technology. Technological advances allow the production of more output from a given amount of resources. This means that technological progress accelerates economic growth for any given rate of growth in the labor force and the capital stock.

Technological change depends on the scientific community. The more educated a population, the greater its potential for technological advances. Industrial countries have better-educated populations than do developing countries. Education gives industrial countries a substantial advantage over developing countries in creating and implementing innovations. In addition, the richest industrial countries traditionally have spent 2 to 3 percent of their GNP on research and development, an investment developing countries cannot afford. The greater the funding for research and development, the greater the likelihood of technological advances.

Impeded by low levels of education and limited funds for research and development, the developing countries lag behind the industrial countries in developing and implementing new technology. Typically these countries follow the lead of the industrial world, adopting new technology developed in that world once it is affordable and feasible, given their capital and labor

It is no longer accurate to consider all developing countries as possessing only large quantities of low-skilled workers. Some countries have produced a significant number of well-trained workers who are employed in modern, high-tech industries.

Copyright © by Houghton Mifflin Company. All rights reserved.

resources. In the next chapter we discuss the role of foreign aid, including technological assistance, in promoting economic growth in developing countries.

RECAP

1. Economic growth raises the potential level of real GDP, shifting the long-run aggregate supply curve to the right.
2. The long-run growth of the economy is a product of growth in labor, capital, and natural resources, and advances in technology.
3. The size of the labor force is determined by the working-age population and the percentage of that population in the labor force.
4. The post–World War II baby boom has created a bulge in the age distribution of the U.S. population.
5. Growth in capital stock is tied to current and future saving.
6. Abundant natural resources contribute to economic growth but are not essential to that growth.
7. Technology is the way that resources are combined to produce output.
8. Hampered by low levels of education and limited financial resources, developing countries lag behind the industrial nations in developing and implementing new technology.

3. PRODUCTIVITY

What is productivity?

total factor productivity (TFP):
the ratio of the economy's output to its stock of labor and capital

In the last section we described how output depends on resource inputs like labor and capital. One way to assess the contribution a resource makes to output is its productivity. *Productivity* is the ratio of output produced to the amount of input. We could measure the productivity of a single resource—say labor or capital—or the overall productivity of all resources. **Total factor productivity (TFP)** is the term economists use to describe the overall productivity of an economy. It is the ratio of the economy's output to its stock of labor and capital.

3.a. Productivity and Economic Growth

Economic growth depends on both the growth of resources and technological progress. Advances in technology allow resources to be more productive. If the quantity of resources is growing and each resource is more productive, then output grows even faster than the quantity of resources. Economic growth, then, is the sum of the growth rate of total factor productivity and the growth rate of resources:

Economic growth = growth rate of *TFP* + growth rate of resources

The amount that output grows because the labor force is growing depends on how much labor contributes to the production of output. Similarly, the amount that output grows because capital is growing depends on how much capital contributes to the production of output. To relate the growth of labor

Copyright © by Houghton Mifflin Company. All rights reserved.

and capital to the growth of output (we assume no change in natural resources), then, the growth of labor and the growth of capital must be multiplied by their relative contributions to the production of output. The most straightforward way to measure those contributions is to use the share of real GDP received by each resource. For instance, in the United States, labor receives about 70 percent (.70) of real GDP and capital receives about 30 percent (.30). So we can determine the growth of output by using this formula:

$$\%\Delta Y = \%\Delta TFP + .70(\%\Delta L) + .30(\%\Delta K)$$

where

$$\%\Delta = \text{percentage change in}$$

$$Y = \text{real GDP}$$

$$TFP = \text{total factor productivity}$$

$$L = \text{size of the labor force}$$

$$K = \text{capital stock}$$

The equation shows how economic growth depends on changes in productivity ($\%\Delta TFP$) as well as changes in resources ($\%\Delta L$ and $\%\Delta K$). Even if labor (L) and capital stock (K) are constant, technological innovation would generate economic growth through changes in total factor productivity (TFP).

For example, suppose TFP is growing at a rate of 2 percent a year. Then, even with labor and capital stock held constant, the economy grows at a rate of 2 percent a year. If labor and capital stock also grow at a rate of 2 percent a year, output grows by the sum of the growth rates of all three components (TFP, .70 times labor growth, and .30 times the capital stock growth), or 4 percent.

How do we account for differences in growth rates across countries? Because almost all countries have experienced growth in the labor force, percentage increases in labor forces have generally supported economic growth. But growth in the capital stock has been steadier in the industrial countries than in the developing countries, so differences in capital growth rates may explain some of the differences in economic growth across countries. Yet differences in resource growth rates alone cannot explain the major differences we find across countries. In recent years, those differences seem to be related to productivity. In the United States, for example, there is concern that productivity has been growing too slowly. We use the recent history of U.S. productivity growth to illustrate the determinants of total factor productivity and to show how changes in these determinants affect a country's economic growth.

3.b. The U.S. Productivity Slowdown

Why has U.S. productivity changed?

Productivity in the United States became a major topic of discussion in the late 1970s as the growth of total factor productivity fell dramatically. From 1948 to 1965, TFP grew at an annual average rate of 2.02 percent. In the 1970s, TFP growth averaged 0.7 percent per year; in the 1980s, 0.6 percent; and in the early 1990s, 0.8 percent. If the pre-1965 rate of growth had been maintained, output in the United States would be an estimated 39 percent

Copyright © by Houghton Mifflin Company. All rights reserved.

higher today than it actually is. What happened? What caused this dramatic change in productivity?

Several factors may be at work here. They include a drop in the quality of the U.S. labor force, fewer technological innovations, higher energy prices, and a shift from manufacturing to service industries.

3.b.1. Labor Quality
Labor productivity is measured as output per hour of labor. Figure 4 shows how the productivity of labor changed in the United States between 1960 and 1996. Although changes in the productivity of labor can stem from technological innovation and changes in the capital stock, we focus here on changes in the quality of labor. These changes may be a product of the level and quality of education in the United States, demographic change, and changing attitudes toward work.

Education level
The average level of education in the United States has gone up over time. Table 3 lists three measures of education level. The first, median school years completed, increased from 8.6 years in 1940 to 12.9 years in 1996. In the same period, the percentage of adults with at least a high school education rose from 24.5 to 81.7, and the percentage of those with a college education rose from 4.6 to 23.6. The figures seem to indicate that the level of education is not responsible for the slowdown in U.S. productivity.

Quality of education
Some economists argue that it is not the level of education but the quality of education that has declined in the United States. They point to the change in college entrance examination scores to support their thinking. For instance, students born in 1945 who took their SATs in 1963 scored an average of 566 on the verbal test and 530 on the math test. Students born in 1962 and tested in 1980 scored an average of 502 on the verbal test and an average of 492 on the math. Figure 5 shows the drop in test scores from the 1960s to the 1990s.

Test scores started to drop in 1967. This decline may have had a significant effect on the productivity of the nation by the early 1970s, as this group of students entered the labor market. By the mid-1980s, test scores started to rise again, signaling a turnaround in the quality of education. By the early 1990s,

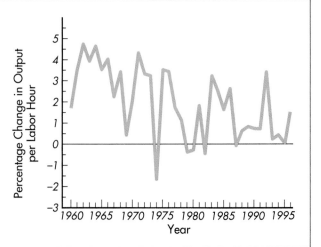

Figure 4
Percentage Change in Output per Hour of Labor, United States
Output per labor hour is a measure of productivity. The graph shows the percentage change in productivity. Notice the large fluctuations from one year to the next.
Source: Bureau of Labor Statistics.

Copyright © by Houghton Mifflin Company. All rights reserved.

TABLE 3
The Average Level of Education, United States, 1940–1996*

	1940	1950	1960	1970	1980	1990	1996
Median school years completed	8.6	9.3	10.6	12.1	12.5	12.7	12.9
People with at least a high school education (percent)	24.5	34.3	41.1	52.3	66.5	76.9	81.7
People with at least four years of college (percent)	4.6	6.2	7.7	10.7	16.2	21.1	23.6

*People 25 years of age and over.

Source: U.S. Department of Commerce, *Statistical Abstract of the United States, 1997.*

this change is consistent with the increase in the productivity of labor that has occurred.

Demographic change   Changes in the size and composition of the population have an impact on the labor market. As the baby boom generation entered the labor force in the late 1960s and early 1970s, a large pool of inexperienced, unskilled workers was created. The average quality of the labor force may have fallen at this time, as reflected in some large drops in output per hour of labor. In the 1980s, the baby boom segment of the labor force had more experience, skills, and education, thus pushing the quality of the labor force up.

Copyright © by Houghton Mifflin Company. All rights reserved.

Figure 5
Average Scholastic Aptitude Test (SAT) Scores
Both the math and verbal scores on the SAT fell between the late 1960s and early 1980s. This trend may have reflected a decline in the average quality of education or of students taking the test. Source: U.S. Department of Commerce, *Statistical Abstract of the United States, 1997.*

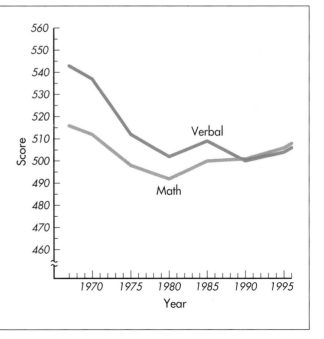

Another important demographic change that has affected the quality of the labor force is the participation rates of women. As more and more women entered the labor force in the 1980s, the pool of untrained workers increased, probably reducing the average quality of labor. Over time, as female participation rates stabilize, the average quality of labor should rise as the skills and experience of female workers rise.

Finally, the 1970s and 1980s saw a change in the pattern of U.S. immigration. Although many highly skilled professionals immigrate to the United States as part of the "brain drain" from developing countries, recent immigrants, both legal and illegal, have generally added to the supply of unskilled labor and reduced the average quality of the labor force.

Attitudes toward work Some economists argue that the slowdown in productivity in the United States reflects a loss of traditional values. They assert that education and hard work are not as important to Americans as they once were. As a result, the level of effort in school and on the job has fallen, and so has the quality of labor. One product of this thinking is an interest in Japanese culture.

Japan has experienced a dramatic increase in labor productivity since the early 1970s, growing substantially faster than other industrial countries. Many analysts have studied the Japanese economy to understand the source of this growth. One important finding apart from the issue of labor quality is that Japan has a relatively high saving rate, which allows a relatively high rate of growth of capital goods. The popular press in the United States regularly reports on the diligence of Japanese students and the dedication of Japanese workers. Many believe that this effort accounts for the different rates of productivity growth in Japan and the United States. They argue that Americans should rethink their values, focusing on productivity. Unfortunately, things like diligence and dedication are difficult to identify and measure. If in fact a change in attitudes about work has lowered the level of effort U.S. workers are willing to expend, then the quality of labor has fallen.

3.b.2. Technological Innovation New technology alters total factor productivity. Innovations increase productivity, so when productivity falls, it is natural to look at technological developments to see whether they are a factor in the change. Like diligence and dedication, the pace of technological innovation is difficult to measure. Expenditures on research and development are related to the discovery of new knowledge, but actual changes in technology do not proceed as evenly as those expenditures. We expect a long lag between funding and operating a laboratory and the discovery of useful technology. Still, a decline in spending on research and development may indicate less of a commitment to increasing productivity.

Figure 6 shows how real expenditures on research and development have changed in the United States over recent decades. Notice that these expenditures grew at a relatively rapid rate in the early 1960s and 1980s, but grew at a relatively slow rate (they actually fell in five separate years) in the late 1960s, early 1970s, late 1980s, and early 1990s. The period of falling expenditures in the 1960s and 1970s may have been a contributing factor in the U.S. productivity slump.

Some economists look at the record of new patents as an indicator of technological progress. A **paten**t is a document issued by the government that gives an inventor the legal right to develop and profit from an invention.

patent:
a legal document that gives an inventor the legal rights to an invention

Copyright © by Houghton Mifflin Company. All rights reserved.

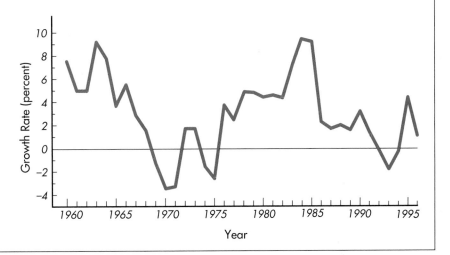

Figure 6
Annual Percentage Change in Real Spending on Research and Development in the United States
Expenditures on research and development reflect a country's commitment to developing new technology. Expenditures in the United States grew rapidly in the early 1960s and 1980s but grew slowly (and in some years fell) in the late 1960s, the 1970s, and early 1990s.
Source: U.S. Department of Commerce, *Statistical Abstract of the United States, 1997.*

Individuals and business firms seek patents to protect themselves from those who would copy their innovations.

The number of patents issued to U.S. firms serves as a crude measure of technological innovation. Figure 7 shows that the number of patents issued peaked in 1971 and then began to fall. This pattern is consistent with the idea that a decline in technological innovation was responsible for the decline in U.S. productivity in the 1970s. The recent resurgence in patent activity may indicate increases in productivity in years to come.

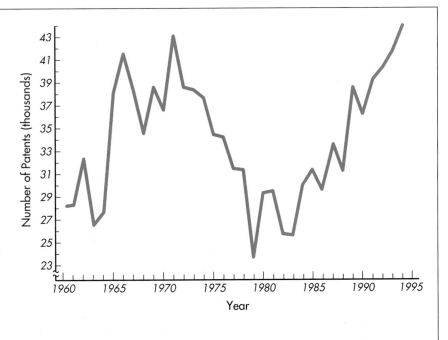

Figure 7
Number of Patents Issued to U.S. Corporations
The number of patents issued is a rough indicator of technological progress. From a peak in 1971, the number of patents issued in the United States fell. Some economists argue that this decline in patent activity signals a slower rate of technological progress that could be related to the slowdown in U.S. productivity. If so, then the recent resurgence in patents granted could signal greater productivity in the future.
Source: U.S. Department of Commerce, *Statistical Abstract of the United States, 1997.*

Copyright © by Houghton Mifflin Company. All rights reserved.

3.b.3. Other Factors
We have seen how changing labor quality and technological innovation are related to changes in productivity. Other reasons have been offered to explain the decline in the growth of U.S. productivity in the 1970s. We examine two of them: the increased cost of energy and the shift from a manufacturing- to a service-oriented economy.

Energy prices OPEC succeeded in raising the price of oil substantially in 1973, 1974, and 1979. The timing of the dramatic increase in oil prices coincided with the drop in productivity growth in the United States. A look back at Figure 4 shows that output per labor hour actually fell in 1974 and 1979. Higher energy prices due to restricted oil output should directly decrease aggregate supply because energy is an important input across industries. As the price of energy increases, the costs of production rise and aggregate supply decreases.

Higher energy prices can affect productivity through their impact on the capital stock. As energy prices go up, energy-inefficient capital goods become obsolete. Like any other decline in the value of the capital stock, this change reduces economic growth. Standard measures of capital stock do not account for energy obsolescence, so they suggest that total factor productivity fell in the 1970s. However, if the stock of usable capital actually did go down, it was the growth rate of capital, not *TFP*, that fell.

Manufacturing versus services The United States economy has, in recent decades, seen a shift away from manufacturing toward services. Some economists believe that productivity grows more slowly in service industries than in manufacturing, because of the less capital-intensive nature of providing services. Therefore, the movement into services reduces the overall growth rate of the economy.

Although a greater emphasis on service industries may explain a drop in productivity, we must be careful with this kind of generalization. In fact, labor productivity in communications and some other service industries has

Productivity changes in service industries are difficult to measure. For instance, this café in Paris offers food service to the public. How should we measure the productivity of the café? If the number of meals served per waiter increased, does this mean that productivity has increased? What if the café changed its menu from crepes to multi-course fine dining and the number of meals served per waiter dropped dramatically? This would not signal a drop in productivity but a change in the kind of service provided. Economists still debate the appropriate measurement of productivity in services.

Copyright © by Houghton Mifflin Company. All rights reserved.

grown faster than in manufacturing industries. Also, it is more difficult to measure changes in the quality of services than changes in the quality of goods. If prices in an industry rise with no change in the quantity of output, it makes sense to conclude that the real level of output in the industry has fallen. However, if prices have gone up because the quality of the service has increased, then output actually has changed. Suppose a hotel remodels its rooms. In effect it is improving the quality of its service. Increased prices here would reflect this change in output.

Service industries—fast-food restaurants, airlines, hotels, banks—are not all alike. One way service firms compete is on the basis of the quality of service they provide. Because productivity is measured by the amount of output per unit of input, if we don't adjust for quality changes, we may underestimate the amount of output and so underestimate the productivity of the industry. The issue of productivity measurement in the services industries is an important topic of discussion among economists today.

3.c. Growth and Development

Economic growth depends on the growth of productivity and resources. Productivity grows unevenly, and its rate of growth is reflected in economic growth. Although the labor force seems to grow faster in developing countries than in industrial countries, lower rates of saving have limited the growth of the capital stock in developing countries. Without capital, workers cannot be very productive. This means that the relatively high rate of growth in the labor force in the developing world does not translate into a high rate of economic growth. We use this information on economic growth in Chapter 19 to explain and analyze the strategies used by developing countries to stimulate output and increase standards of living.

RECAP

1. Productivity is the ratio of output produced to the amount of input.
2. Total factor productivity is the nation's real GDP (output) divided by its stock of labor and capital.
3. Economic growth is the sum of the growth of total factor productivity and the growth rate of resources (labor and capital).
4. The decline in U.S. productivity growth may be a product of a drop in the quality of the labor force, fewer technological innovations, higher energy prices, and a shift from manufacturing to service industries.

SUMMARY

▬▬▬ What is economic growth?

1. Economic growth is an increase in real GDP. §1.a

2. Economic growth is compounded over time. §1.a.1

3. Per capita real GDP is real GDP divided by the population. §1.b

4. The definitions of economic growth are misleading because they do not indicate anything about the distribution of income or the quality of life. §1.c

Copyright © by Houghton Mifflin Company. All rights reserved.

5. The growth of the economy is tied to the growth of productive resources and technological advances. §2

6. Because their populations tend to grow more rapidly, developing countries typically experience faster growth in the labor force than do industrial countries. §2.a

7. The inability to save limits the growth of capital stock in developing countries. §2.b

8. Abundant natural resources are not necessary for rapid economic growth. §2.c

9. Technology defines the ways in which resources can be combined to produce goods and services. §2.d

■■■ **What is productivity?**

10. Productivity is the ratio of output produced to the amount of input. §3

11. Total factor productivity is the overall productivity of an economy. §3

12. The percentage change in real GDP equals the percentage change in total factor productivity plus the percentage changes in labor and capital multiplied by the share of GDP taken by labor and capital. §3.a

■■■ **Why has U.S. productivity changed?**

13. The slowdown in U.S. productivity growth may be a product of a change in the quality of the labor force, fewer technological innovations, higher energy prices, and a shift away from manufacturing to service industries. §3.b

KEY TERMS

economic growth §1.a
rule of 72 §1.a.2
per capita real GDP §1.b

technology §2.d
total factor productivity (*TFP*) §3
patent §3.b.2

EXERCISES

1. Why is the growth of per capita real GDP a better measure of economic growth than the growth of real GDP?

2. What is the level of output after four years if initial output equals $1,000 and the economy grows at a rate of 10 percent a year?

3. Use the data in the following table to determine the average annual growth rate for each country in terms of real GDP growth and per capita real GDP growth (real GDP is in billions of units of domestic currency, and population is in millions of people). Which country grew at the fastest rate?

Country (currency)	1990		1996	
	Real GDP	Population	Real GDP	Population
Senegal (franc)	1,552	7.30	2,638	8.57
Spain (peseta)	50,145	38.84	54,708	39.27
Morocco (dirham)	212.85	24.49	248.62	27.62

Copyright © by Houghton Mifflin Company. All rights reserved.

4. Suppose labor's share of GDP is 70 percent and capital's is 30 percent, real GDP is growing at a rate of 4 percent a year, the labor force is growing at 2 percent, and the capital stock is growing at 3 percent. What is the growth rate of total factor productivity?

5. Suppose labor's share of GDP is 70 percent and capital's is 30 percent, total factor productivity is growing at an annual rate of 2 percent, the labor force is growing at a rate of 1 percent, and the capital stock is growing at a rate of 3 percent. What is the annual growth rate of real GDP?

6. Discuss the possible reasons for the slowdown in U.S. productivity growth and relate each reason to the equation for economic growth. (Does the growth of *TFP* or resources change?)

7. How did the post–World War II baby boom affect the growth of the U.S. labor force? What effect is this baby boom likely to have on the future U.S. labor force?

8. How do developing and industrial countries differ in their use of technological change, labor, capital, and natural resources to produce economic growth? Why do these differences exist?

9. How would an aging population affect economic growth?

10. If real GDP for Spain is 60,000 billion pesetas at the end of 1996 and 52,000 billion pesetas at the end of 1997, what is the annual rate of growth of the Spanish economy?

11. If Kenya's economy grows at a rate of 4 percent during 1998 and real GDP at the beginning of the year is 170,000 shillings, then what is real GDP at the end of the year?

12. Suppose a country has a real GDP equal to $1 billion today. If this economy grows at a rate of 10 percent a year, what will be the value of real GDP after five years?

13. Is the following statement true or false? Explain your answer. "Abundant natural resources are a necessary condition for economic growth."

14. What is the difference between total factor productivity and the productivity of labor? Why do you suppose that people often measure a nation's productivity using labor productivity only?

15. How would each of the following affect productivity in the United States?

    a. The quality of education increases in high schools.

    b. The number of patents issued falls significantly.

    c. A cutback in oil production by oil-exporting nations raises oil prices.

    d. A large number of unskilled immigrant laborers moves into the country.

![] INTERNET EXERCISE

In Section 3 of this chapter we learned that productivity is the ratio of output produced to the amount of input employed. Economists often like to think that market economies tend to have resources going to their most productive uses so that productivity is maximized. However, corrupt practices by government and business result in resource uses being determined by other than productivity so that a country's growth rate suffers. To see how countries differ in terms of the perceived level of corruption, go to the Boyes/Melvin web site at **http://www.hmco.com/college/** and click on the internet exercise link for this chapter. Now answer the questions that appear on the web page.

Copyright © by Houghton Mifflin Company. All rights reserved.

What's Up

WASHINGTON—The U.S. economy is growing faster than expected and inflation's slowing —even in service industries. Economists say that can only mean one thing: For the first time in decades worker productivity gains are accelerating.

Labor Department figures to be released today might obscure what's happening. The rise in U.S. worker productivity for last year's final quarter is expected to be revised lower to a 1.7 percent annual rate, down from an initial estimate of a 2.0 percent gain, according to economists surveyed by Bloomberg News.

This reduction doesn't mean American workers extended their coffee breaks, though. Overall growth for the quarter was slower than first thought, cutting into the output per worker hour. And worker productivity for the full year is still expected to increase 2.2 percent, up from a 1.7 percent gain in 1996 and the largest since 1992.

"Corporate earnings, through last year at least, continued to rise at a double-digit rate even though real wages rose at the fastest pace in 25 years," said Bruce Steinberg, chief economist at Merrill Lynch in New York "That combination was only possible because productivity growth was strong."

Moreover, consumer prices rose just 1.7 percent last year, even as wages rose and unemployment fell to a quarter-century low. Companies were able to pay more money to more workers because those new workers produced more than they cost.

The investments U.S. businesses are making in new technology are paying off, suggests Federal Reserve Board Chairman Alan Greenspan. As a result, over the last year or two the United States has witnessed a "notable pickup" in productivity, he said.

To Greenspan, "There is something different" going on in the U.S. economy.

And the productivity numbers confirm it. Worker output per hour—the common measure of productivity—rose an average 2.25 percent each quarter last year. That's close to the 2.6 percent average quarterly gains of the 1960s, and it reversed a long, slow decline, from an average 1.8 percent increase in the 1970s to 1.3 percent the first five years of this decade.

Those figures probably even understate the good news, given the country's metamorphosis into a service-based economy.

Greenspan, and most other economists, argue productivity gains are better than the government's official figures show, because it's hard to measure the output of lawyers, flight attendants, retail clerks and other service workers.

NationsBank Corp., for instance, currently has 7,000 ATMs, up from 3,929 in 1996 and 2,205 in 1995. The increase has helped speed transactions both for customers and the bank itself, said John Brennan, channel strategies and development executive at Charlotte, North Carolina-based NationsBank.

"Productivity for our customers has significantly improved, since they need to spend less time driving to a bank and waiting in a teller line," Brennan said.

Bank workers, meanwhile, are spending less time recording deposits, and more time on other services, such as explaining how customers can do their banking by personal computer, Brennan said. That should increase productivity further.

All of that is hard to quantify. Yet on the bottom line, NationsBank earnings rose 6.75 percent in 1997, helping push up its share price by 25 percent over the year.

Technology is playing a big role in increasing productivity in all industries. LTV Steel Corp. of Cleveland figures its productivity has risen 79 percent since 1986, when the company filed for bankruptcy protection. It emerged from bankruptcy in 1992 after closing older plants, dismissing thousands of workers and using the savings to invest in new technology.

Source: Appeared in *The Denver Post*. March 10, 1998. Reprinted by permission of The Associated Press.

The Denver Post/March 10, 1998

Copyright © by Houghton Mifflin Company. All rights reserved.

Copyright © by Houghton Mifflin Company. All rights reserved.

COMMENTARY

The accompanying figure illustrates how services (retail and wholesale sales, transportation, communications, finance, insurance, real estate, and other service industries) have grown as a fraction of GDP in the United States. As the figure shows, the shift from the production of goods to services is not new but has continued over recent decades. If services are becoming an increasingly important sector of the U.S. economy, and measurement of productivity in the services sector is subject to large error, it may be that actual productivity in the United States has grown faster than the BEA's figures indicate. In banking, where output is the service provided by tellers and loan officers, productivity has been measured by counting number of employees (on the theory that the busier the bank, the more employees needed). Banking is not alone in this. Other service industries have also estimated output by measuring the quantity of an input. However, if number of employees is used to measure output of an industry, then productivity will not grow *by definition*. If measured output rises right along with employment, then output per worker cannot change.

The compensation data offer a useful alternative to the measures of output constructed by the BEA. Although wages may rise for reasons other

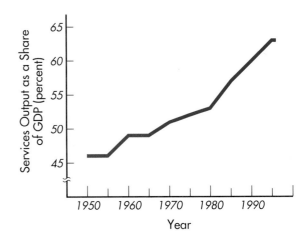

than productivity changes, the large differences between the compensation changes and BEA productivity measures should cause us to use great caution with the BEA estimates of productivity. The problem, of course, is that output in the services industry is essentially unmeasurable. As a result, we must resort to looking at related data to try to infer productivity changes. All of this should create a healthy skepticism regarding official productivity figures as services grow in importance. We should also expect to see further refinement in the way productivity is measured in service industries.

19

Development Economics

FUNDAMENTAL QUESTIONS

1. How is poverty measured?

2. Why are some countries poorer than others?

3. What strategies can a nation use to increase its economic growth?

4. How are savings in one nation used to speed development in other nations?

5. What microeconomic issues are involved in the transition from socialism?

6. What macroeconomic issues are involved in the transition from socialism?

Copyright © by Houghton Mifflin Company. All rights reserved.

Preview

There is an enormous difference between the standards of living in the poorest and richest countries in the world. In Mozambique the average life expectancy at birth is forty-seven years, almost thirty years less than in the United States. In Burma only an estimated 25 percent of the population has access to safe water. In Burundi only 23 percent of urban houses have electricity. And in Chad only 29 percent of students reach the sixth grade.

The plight of developing countries is our focus in this chapter. We begin by discussing the extent of poverty and how it is measured across countries. Then we turn to the reasons why developing countries are poor and look at strategies for stimulating growth and development. The reasons for poverty are many, and the remedies often are rooted more in politics than economics. Still, economics has much to say about how to improve the living standards of the world's poorest citizens. Finally we discuss the development problems of countries in the transition from socialism to capitalism. ■

Copyright © by Houghton Mifflin Company. All rights reserved.

1. THE DEVELOPING WORLD

Three-fourths of the world's population lives in developing countries. These countries are often called *less developed countries (LDCs)* or *Third World countries.* "First World" countries are the industrialized nations of Western Europe and North America, along with Australia, Japan, and New Zealand. Second World countries are (or were) the communist countries of Eastern Europe and the former Soviet Union. The Third World is made up of noncommunist developing countries, although people commonly use the term to refer to all developing countries.

The common link among developing countries is low per capita GNP or GDP, which implies a relatively low standard of living for the typical citizen. Otherwise the LDCs are a diverse group—their cultures, politics, even their geography varying enormously. Although we have used GDP throughout the text as the popular measure of a nation's output, in this chapter we frequently refer to GNP, as this is the measure used by the World Bank in classifying countries in terms of stage of development.

The developing countries are located primarily in South and East Asia, Africa, the Middle East, and Latin America (Figure 1). The total population of developing countries is over 4 billion people. Of this population, 27 percent

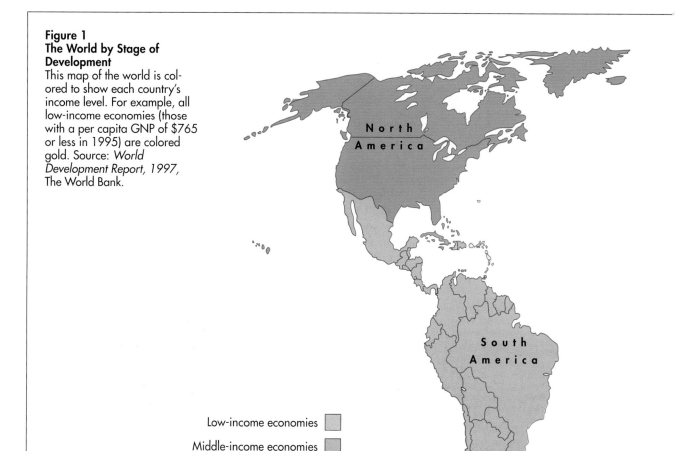

Figure 1
The World by Stage of Development
This map of the world is colored to show each country's income level. For example, all low-income economies (those with a per capita GNP of $765 or less in 1995) are colored gold. Source: *World Development Report, 1997,* The World Bank.

North America

South America

Low-income economies

Middle-income economies

High-income economies

Countries where data are not available

Copyright © by Houghton Mifflin Company. All rights reserved.

live in China and 20 percent live in India. The next largest concentration of people is in Indonesia (4 percent), followed by Brazil, Bangladesh, Nigeria, and Pakistan. Except for Latin America, where 40 percent of the population lives in cities, most Third World citizens live in rural areas and are largely dependent on agriculture.

1.a. Measuring Poverty

How is poverty measured?

Poverty is not easy to measure. Typically poverty is defined in an *absolute* sense: a family is poor if its income falls below a certain level. For example, the poverty level for a family of four in the United States in 1997 was an income of $16,404. The government sets the poverty level, basing it on the estimated cost of feeding a family a minimally adequate amount of food. Once the cost of an adequate diet is estimated, it is multiplied by 3 (the assumption is that one-third of income is spent on food) to determine the

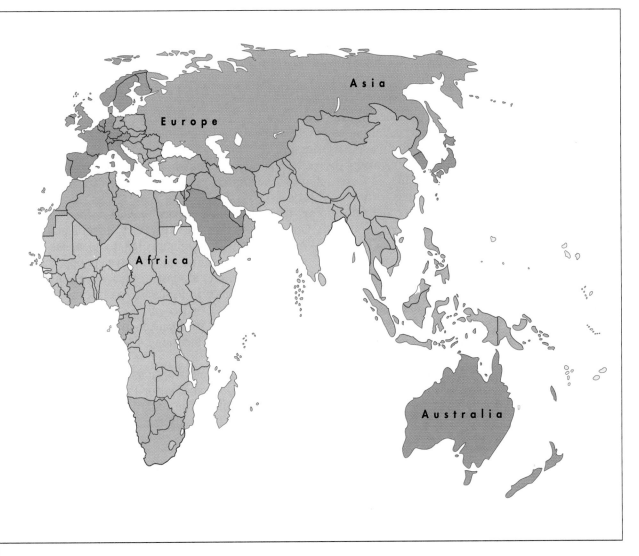

Copyright © by Houghton Mifflin Company. All rights reserved.

Poverty typically is defined in absolute terms.

poverty level income. The World Bank uses per capita GNP of less than $765 as its criterion of a low-income country. The countries in gold in Figure 1 meet this absolute definition of poverty.

Poverty is also a *relative* concept. Family income in relation to other incomes in the country or region is important in determining whether or not a family feels poor. The poverty level in the United States would represent a substantial increase in the living standard of most of the people in the world. Yet a poor family in the United States does not feel less poor because it has more money than the poor in other countries. In a nation where the median income of a family of four is more than $50,000, a family with an income of $16,404 clearly is disadvantaged.

Because poverty is also a relative concept, using a particular level of income to distinguish the poor from the not poor is often controversial. Besides the obvious problem of where to draw the poverty line, there is the more difficult problem of comparing poverty across countries with different currencies, customs, and living arrangements. Also, data are often limited and difficult to obtain because many of the poor in developing countries live in isolated areas. This makes it difficult to draw a comprehensive picture of the typical poor household in the Third World.

1.b. Basic Human Needs

Basic human needs are a minimal level of caloric intake, health care, clothing, and shelter.

Some economists and other social scientists, recognizing the limitations of an absolute definition of poverty (like the per capita GNP measure most commonly used), suggest using indicators of how basic human needs are being met. Although they disagree on an exact definition of *basic human needs,* the general idea is to set minimal levels of caloric intake, health care, clothing, and shelter.

Another alternative to per capita GNP is a physical *quality-of-life index* to evaluate living standards. One approach uses life expectancy, infant mortality, and literacy as indicators—a very narrow definition that ignores elements like justice, personal freedom, environmental quality, and employment opportunities. Nonetheless, these three indicators are, at least in theory, measures of social progress that allow meaningful comparisons across countries whatever their social or political orientation.

The United Nations maintains a Human Development Index (HDI) which measures a country's development in three dimensions: life expectancy, education, and per capita GDP.

Table 1 lists per capita GDP and the indicators of human development for selected countries. The table shows the actual data for the indicators along with the overall index value for each country. The countries are listed by per capita GDP, beginning with the smallest. Generally there is a strong positive

TABLE 1
Quality-of-Life Measures, Selected Countries

Country	Per Capita GDP*	Life Expectancy at Birth (years)	Literacy Rate†	Human Development Index
Ethiopia	427	48	35%	.24
Bangladesh	1,331	56	37	.37
India	1,348	61	51	.45
El Salvador	2,417	69	71	.59
China	2,604	69	81	.63
Philippines	2,681	67	94	.67
Namibia	4,027	56	40	.57
Turkey	5,193	68	82	.77
Mexico	7,384	72	89	.85
Greece	11,265	78	97	.92
United States	26,397	76	99	.94

*1994 data measured in terms of U.S. dollars.

†Percentage of the adult population that is literate.

Source: *United Nations Human Development Report, 1997* (New York, 1997).

Copyright © by Houghton Mifflin Company. All rights reserved.

relationship between per capita GDP and the quality-of-life index. But there are cases where higher per capita GDP does not mean lower quality of life. For instance, Namibia has a higher per capita GDP than El Salvador, China, or the Philippines, but the human development index is lower in Namibia than it is in the other three countries. Remember the limitations of per capita output: it is not a measure of everyone's standard of living in a particular country. However, as the table shows, it is a fairly reliable indicator of differences across countries in living standards. Ethiopia has the lowest per capita GDP and is clearly one of the world's poorest nations. Usually as per capita GDP increases, living standards increase as well.

Per capita GDP and quality-of-life indexes are not the only measures used to determine a country's level of economic development—we could consider the number of households with running water, televisions, or any other good that varies with living standards. Recognizing that there is no perfect measure of economic development, economists and other social scientists often use several indicators to assess economic progress.

RECAP

1. Usually poverty is defined in an absolute sense, as a specific level of family income or per capita GNP or GDP.
2. Within a country or region, poverty is a relative concept.
3. Human development indexes based on indicators of basic human needs are an alternative to per capita GDP for measuring economic development.

2. OBSTACLES TO GROWTH

Why are some countries poorer than others?

Every country is unique. Each nation's history, both political and cultural, helps economists understand why poor nations have not developed and what policies offer the best hope for their development. Generally the factors that impede development are political or social. The political factors include a lack of administrative skills, instability, corruption, and the ability of special interest groups to block changes in economic policy. The social obstacles include a lack of entrepreneurs and rapid population growth.

2.a. Political Obstacles

2.a.1. Lack of Administrative Skills Government support is essential to economic development. Whether support means allowing private enterprise to flourish and develop or actively managing the allocation of resources, a poorly organized or corrupt government can present an obstacle to economic growth. Some developing countries have suffered from well-meaning but inept government management. This is most obvious in countries with a long history of colonization. For example, when Zaire won independence from Belgium, few of its native citizens were college educated. Moreover, Belgians had run most of the important government offices. Independence brought a large group of inexperienced and unskilled workers to important positions of power. And at first there was a period of "learning by doing."

Copyright © by Houghton Mifflin Company. All rights reserved.

2.a.2. Political Instability and Risk

One of the most important functions a government performs in stimulating economic growth is providing a political environment that encourages saving and investment. People do not want to do business in an economy weakened by wars, demonstrations, or uncertainty. For instance, since becoming an independent nation in 1825, Bolivia has had more than 150 changes in government. This kind of instability forces citizens to take a short-run view of the economy. Long-term planning is impossible without knowing the attitudes and policies of the government that is going to be in power next year or even next month.

A country must be able to guarantee the rights of private property if it is going to create an environment that encourages private investment.

The key issue here is *property rights.* A country that guarantees the right of private property encourages private investment and development. Where ownership rights may be changed by revolution or political decree, there is little incentive for private investment and development. People do not start new businesses or build new factories if they believe that a change in government or a change in the political will of the current government could result in the confiscation of their property.

expropriation:
the government seizure of assets, typically without adequate compensation to the owners

This confiscation is called **expropriation.** Countries with a history of expropriating foreign-owned property without compensating the owners (paying them its market value) have difficulty encouraging foreign investment. An example is Uganda. In 1973 a successful revolution by Idi Amin was followed by the expropriation of over 500 foreign-owned (mostly British) firms. Foreign and domestic investment in Uganda fell dramatically as a result.

The loss of foreign investment is particularly important in developing countries. In Chapter 18 we pointed out that developing countries suffer from a lack of saving. If domestic residents are not able to save because they are living at or below subsistence level, foreign saving is a crucial source of investment. Without that investment, the economies of developing countries cannot grow.

2.a.3. Corruption

Corrupt practices by government officials have long reduced economic growth. Payment of money or gifts in order to receive a government service or benefit is quite widespread in many countries. Research shows that there is a definite negative relationship between the level of corruption in a country and both investment and growth.

Research also shows that corruption thrives in countries where government regulations create distortions between the economic outcomes that would exist with free markets and actual outcomes. For instance, a country where government permission is required to buy or sell foreign currency will have a thriving black market in foreign exchange in which the black market exchange rate of a U.S. dollar will cost much more domestic currency than the official rate offered by the government. This distortion allows government officials an opportunity for personal gain by providing access to the official rate.

Generally speaking, the more competitive a country's markets are, the fewer the opportunities for corruption. So policies aimed at reducing corruption typically involve reducing the discretion that public officials have in granting benefits or imposing costs on others. This may include greater transparency of government practices and the introduction of merit-based competition for government employment.

2.a.4. Good Economics as Bad Politics

Every Third World politician wants to maximize economic growth, all things being equal. But all things are rarely equal. Political pressures may force a government to work toward more immediate objectives than economic growth.

Copyright © by Houghton Mifflin Company. All rights reserved.

For example, maximizing growth may mean reducing the size of government in order to lower taxes and increase investment. However, in many developing countries, the strongest supporters of the political leaders are those working for the current government. Obviously it's not good political strategy to fire those workers. So the government stays overstaffed and inefficient, and the potential for economic growth falls. The governments in LDCs often subsidize purchases of food and other basic necessities. Reducing government expenditures and moving toward free market pricing of food, energy, and other items make good economic sense. But the citizens who depend on those subsidies are not going to be happy if they stop.

In 1977 the Egyptian government lowered its food subsidies in order to use those funds for development. What happened? There was widespread rioting that ended only when the government reinstituted the subsidies. In 1989, Venezuela lowered government subsidies on public transportation and petroleum products. Public transit fares went up 30 percent, to the equivalent of 7 U.S. cents, and gasoline prices went from 16 cents to 26 cents a gallon. (One official said that the prices were raised "from the cheapest in the world to the cheapest in the world."[1]) The resulting rioting in Caracas led to 50 deaths, over 500 injuries, and more than 1,000 arrests. Lowering government expenditures and reducing the role of government in the economy can be politically and physically dangerous.

What we are saying here is that seemingly good economics can make for bad politics. Because some group is going to be hurt in the short run by any change in policy aimed at increasing growth, there always is opposition to change. Often the continued rule of the existing regime depends on not alienating a certain group. Only a government stabilized by military force (a dictatorship), popular support (a democracy), or party support (a communist or socialist country) has the power to implement needed economic change. A government that lacks this power is handicapped by political constraints in its efforts to stimulate economic growth.

2.b. Social Obstacles

Cultural traditions and attitudes can work against economic development. In traditional societies, children follow in their parents' footsteps. If your father is a carpenter, there is a good chance that you will be a carpenter. Moreover, production is carried out in the same way generation after generation. For an economy to grow, it must be willing to change.

2.b.1. Lack of Entrepreneurs
A society that answers the questions What to produce? How to produce? and For whom to produce? by doing things as they were done by the previous generation lacks a key ingredient for economic growth: entrepreneurs. Entrepreneurs are risk-takers; they bring innovation and new technology into use. Understanding why some societies are better at producing entrepreneurs than others may help explain why some nations have remained poor while others have grown rapidly.

Copyright © by Houghton Mifflin Company. All rights reserved.

[1]See "Venezuela Rumblings: Riots and Debt Crisis," *New York Times,* March 2, 1989, p. A13.

Entrepreneurs are more likely to develop among minority groups that have been blocked from traditional high-paying jobs.

One theory is that entrepreneurs often come from *blocked minorities.* Some individuals in the traditional society are blocked from holding prestigious jobs or political office because of discrimination. This discrimination can be based on race, religion, or immigrant status. Because discrimination keeps them from the best traditional occupations, these minority groups can achieve wealth and status only through entrepreneurship. The Chinese in Southeast Asia, the Jews in Europe, and the Indians in Africa were all blocked minorities, forced to turn to entrepreneurship to advance themselves.

Immigrants provide a pool of entrepreneurs who have skills and knowledge that often are lacking in the developing country.

In developing countries, entrepreneurship tends to be concentrated among immigrants, who have skills and experience that do not exist in poor countries. Many leaders of industry in Latin America, for example, are Italian, German, Arab, or Basque immigrants or the descendants of immigrants; they are not part of the dominant Spanish or native Indian population. The success of these immigrants is less a product of their being discriminated against than of their expertise in commerce. They know the foreign suppliers of goods. They have business skills that are lacking in developing regions. And they have the traditions—among them, the work ethic—and training instilled in their home country.

Motivation also plays a role in the level of entrepreneurship that exists in developing countries. In some societies, traditional values may be an obstacle to development because they do not encourage high achievement. A good example is provided in the Economic Insight "Development and Cultural Values in Sub-Saharan Africa." Societies in which the culture supports individual achievement produce more entrepreneurs. It is difficult to identify the specific values in a society that account for a lack of motivation. In the past, researchers have pointed to factors that are not always valid across different societies. For instance, at one time many argued that the Protestant work ethic was responsible for the large number of entrepreneurs in the industrial world. According to this argument, some religions are more supportive of the accumulation of wealth than others. Today this argument is difficult to make because we find economic development in nations with vastly different cultures and religions.

2.b.2. Rapid Population Growth

Remember that per capita real GNP is real GNP divided by the population. Although labor is a factor of production, and labor force growth may increase output, when population rises faster than GNP, the standard of living of the average citizen does not improve. One very real problem for many developing countries is the growth of their population. With the exception of China and India (where population growth is controlled), population growth in the developing countries is proceeding at a pace that will double the Third World population every 25 years. In large part the rate at which the population of the Third World is growing is a product of lower death rates. Death rates have fallen, but birthrates have not.

Social scientists do not all agree on the effects of population growth on development. A growing labor force can serve as an important factor in increasing growth. But those who believe that population growth has a negative effect cite three reasons:

Capital shallowing Rapid population growth may reduce the amount of capital per worker, lowering the productivity of labor.

Age dependency Rapid population growth produces a large number of dependent children, whose consumption requirements lower the ability of the economy to save.

Copyright © by Houghton Mifflin Company. All rights reserved.

ECONOMIC INSIGHT

Development and Cultural Values in Sub-Saharan Africa

. . . Traditional development projects have erred by focusing unduly on technical prescriptions, ignoring the need to adapt development assistance to the local cultural environment. . . . The lack of success of most traditional approaches to institutional and public sector development in Africa clearly shows the limitations of the technological approach. . . . Western values are not always congruent with traditional incentives and behavioral patterns prevalent in most African countries. Self-reliance and self-interest tend to take a back seat to ethnicity and group loyalty. . . . Generally, the interest of the local and ethnic communities takes precedence over whatever the government may declare as national goals.

Typically, a higher value is placed on interpersonal relations and the timely execution of certain social and religious or mystic activities than on individual achievements. . . . The value of economic acts is measured in terms of their capacity to reinforce the bonds of the group.

Attitudes toward savings and investment

In Sub-Saharan Africa, it might well be said that, in general, the only riches are those shared with—and socially visible to—the community.

There is a social and mystical need for what westerners may call "wastefulness." . . . It is not uncommon for poor, malnourished farmers to give away vast quantities of foods on the occasion of marriages, circumcisions, or burials. . . . Excess income is distributed first to close members of the extended family, then to the neighbors, and then to the ethnic tribe. . . . Economic success in itself does not lead to upward social mobility. In fact, if achieved outside of the group, it may even lead to social ostracism. From the development perspective, the problem is that this tendency—attaching little value to the self-control needed for saving—runs counter to the prerequisites for promoting private investment and African entrepreneurship.

Attitude toward labor

The tendency to value group solidarity and socializing has generally led Africans to attach a high value to leisure and the attendant ability to engage in rituals, ceremonies, and social activities. . . . The high value Africans generally attach to leisure has often been misconstrued by outsiders as "laziness." Simply put, in Africa, these activities serve as a means of reinforcing social bonds, which are the foundation of its society. As a result, farmers tend to adopt innovations

only when the expected return on additional labor, measured in both social and economic terms, is likely to be substantially higher than what they are already receiving from the prevailing combination of leisure and productive activities.

A new vision of management

The reconciliation of these traditional values with the imperatives of economic efficiency and accumulation . . . is, therefore, crucial to economic development. . . . Other societies have successfully modernized without renouncing local customs, culture, or traditional values. Japan, the Republic of Korea, and Taiwan Province of China are examples of economies that have achieved high levels of modern production and advanced technology while maintaining their unique national traits. Their experience proves that acculturation is not a prerequisite to development, that whatever direction the development process may take, its success and sustainability will depend on how well it takes account of the needs and culture of the beneficiaries.

Source: "Development and Cultural Values in Sub-Saharan Africa," from Mamadou Dia, *Finance and Development*, December 1991, pp. 10–13. Reprinted with permission.

Copyright © by Houghton Mifflin Company. All rights reserved.

Investment diversion Rapid population growth shifts government expenditures from the country's infrastructure (roads, communication systems) to education and health care.

Population growth may have had a negative effect on development in many countries, but the magnitude of the effect is difficult to assess. And in some cases, population growth probably has stimulated development. For instance, the fact that children consume goods and services and thus lower the ability of a nation to save ignores the fact that the children grow up and become productive adults. Furthermore, any investment diversion from infrastructure to education and health care is not necessarily a loss, as education and health care will build up the productivity of the labor force. The harmful effect of population growth should be most pronounced in countries where usable land and water are relatively scarce. Although generalizations about acceptable levels of population growth do not fit all circumstances, the World Bank has stated that population growth rates above 2 percent a year act as a brake on economic development.

GNP can grow steadily year after year, but if the population grows at a faster rate, the standard of living of the average individual falls. The simple answer to reducing population growth seems to be education: programs that teach methods of birth control and family planning. But reducing birthrates is not simply a matter of education. People have to choose to limit the size of their families. It must be socially acceptable and economically advantageous for families to use birth control, and for many families it is neither.

Remember that what is good for society as a whole may not be good for the individual. Children are a source of labor in rural families and a support for parents in their old age. How many children are enough? That depends on the expected infant mortality rate. Although infant mortality rates in developing countries have fallen in recent years, they are still quite high relative to the developed countries. Families still tend to follow tradition, to keep having lots of children.

RECAP

1. In some countries, especially those that have been colonies, economic growth has been slow because government officials lack necessary skills.
2. Countries that are unable to protect the rights of private property have difficulty attracting investors.
3. Expropriation is the seizure by government of assets without adequate compensation.
4. Corruption in government reduces investment and growth.
5. Often government officials know the right economic policies to follow but are constrained by political considerations from implementing those policies.
6. Immigrants are often the entrepreneurs in developing countries.
7. Rapid population growth may slow development because of the effects of capital shallowing, age dependency, and investment diversion.

3. DEVELOPMENT STRATEGIES

What strategies can a nation use to increase its economic growth?

Different countries follow different strategies to stimulate economic development. There are two basic types of development strategies: inward oriented and outward oriented.

Copyright © by Houghton Mifflin Company. All rights reserved.

3.a. Inward-Oriented Strategies

primary product:
a product in the first stage of production, which often serves as an input in the production of another product

The typical developing country has a comparative advantage over other countries in the production of certain primary products. Having a comparative advantage means that a country has the lowest opportunity cost of producing a good. (We talked about comparative advantage in Chapter 2.) A **primary product** is a product in the first stage of production, which often serves as input in the production of some other good. Agricultural produce and minerals are examples of primary products. In the absence of a conscious government policy that directs production, we expect countries to concentrate on the production of that thing in which they have a comparative advantage. For example, we expect Cuba to focus on sugar production, Colombia to focus on coffee production, and the Ivory Coast to focus on cocoa production—each country selling its output of its primary product to the rest of the world.

Today many developing countries have shifted their resources away from producing primary products for export. Inward-oriented development strategies focus on production for the domestic market rather than exports of goods and services. For these countries, development means industrialization. The objective of this kind of inward-oriented strategy is **import substitution,** replacing imported manufactured goods with domestic goods.

import substitution:
the substitution of domestically produced manufactured goods for imported manufactured goods

Import-substitution policies dominate the strategies of the developing world. The basic idea is to identify domestic markets that are being supplied in large part by imports. Those markets that require a level of technology available to the domestic economy are candidates for import substitution. Industrialization goes hand in hand with tariffs or quotas on imports that protect the newly developing domestic industry from its more efficient foreign competition. As a result, production and international trade will not occur solely on the basis of comparative advantages but are affected primarily by these countries' import-substitution policy activities.

Because the domestic industry can survive only with protection from foreign competition, import-substitution policies typically raise the price of the domestically produced goods over the imported goods. In addition, quality may not be as good (at least at first) as the quality of the imported goods. Ideally, as the industry grows and becomes more experienced, price and quality become competitive with foreign goods. Once this happens, the import barriers are no longer needed, and the domestic industry may even become an export industry. Unfortunately, the ideal is seldom realized. The Third World is full of inefficient manufacturing companies that are unlikely ever to improve enough to be able to survive without protection from foreign competitors.

3.b. Outward-Oriented Strategies

The inward-oriented strategy of developing domestic industry to supply domestic markets is the most popular development strategy, but it is not the only one. A small group of countries (notably South Korea, Hong Kong, Singapore, and Taiwan) chose to focus on the growth of exports beginning in the 1960s. These countries follow an outward-oriented strategy, utilizing their most abundant resource to produce those products that they can produce better than others.

The abundant resource in these countries is labor, and the goods they produce are labor-intensive products. This kind of outward-oriented policy is

Copyright © by Houghton Mifflin Company. All rights reserved.

export substitution:
the use of resources to produce manufactured products for export rather than agricultural products for the domestic market

called **export substitution.** The countries use labor to produce manufactured goods for export rather than agricultural products for domestic use.

Outward-oriented development strategies are based on efficient, low-cost production. Their success depends on being able to compete effectively with producers in the rest of the world. Here most governments attempt to stimulate exports. This can mean subsidizing domestic producers to produce goods for export rather than for domestic consumption. International competition is often more intense than the competition at home—producers face stiffer price competition, higher quality standards, and greater marketing expertise in the global marketplace. This means domestic producers may have to be induced to compete internationally. Inducements can take the form of government assistance in international marketing, tax reductions, low-interest-rate loans, or cash payments.

The Hyundai shipyard in Korea is symbolic of the outward-oriented development strategy of Korea, one of the newly industrialized Asian nations. By emphasizing exports of manufactured products rather than producing substitutes for import goods from the industrial countries, Korea has developed rapidly. Korea is Asia's major shipbuilder and has achieved this success in other industries through aggressive competition in international goods markets.

Copyright © by Houghton Mifflin Company. All rights reserved.

Another inducement of sorts is to make domestic sales less attractive. This means implementing policies that are just the opposite of import substitution. The government reduces or eliminates domestic tariffs that keep domestic price levels above international levels. As profits from domestic sales fall, domestic industry turns to producing goods for export.

3.c. Comparing Strategies

Import-substitution policies are enacted in countries that believe industrialization is the key to economic development. In the 1950s and 1960s economists argued that specializing in the production and export of primary products does not encourage the rapid growth rates developing countries are looking for. This argument—the *deteriorating-terms-of-trade argument*—was based on the assumption that the real value of primary products would fall over time. If the prices of primary products fall in relation to the prices of manufactured products, then countries that export primary products and import manufactured goods find the cost of manufactured goods rising in terms of the primary products required to buy them. The amount of exports that must be exchanged for some quantity of imports is often called the **terms of trade.**

terms of trade:
the amount of exports that must be exchanged for some amount of imports

The deteriorating-terms-of-trade argument in the 1950s and 1960s led policymakers in developing countries to fear that the terms of trade would become increasingly unfavorable. One product of that fear was the choice of an inward-oriented strategy, a focus on domestic industrialization rather than production for export.

At the root of the pessimism about the export of primary products was the belief that technological change would slow the growth of demand for primary products over time. That theory ignored the fact that if the supply of natural resources is fixed, those resources could become more valuable over time, even if demand grows slowly or not at all. And if the real value of primary products does fall over time, it does not necessarily mean that inward-oriented policy is required. Critics of inward-oriented policies argue that nations should exploit their comparative advantage, that resources should be free to move to their highest-valued use. And they argue that market-driven resource allocation is unlikely to occur in an inward-oriented economy where government has imposed restrictions aimed at maximizing the rate of growth of industrial output.

Other economists believe that developing countries have unique problems that call for active government intervention and regulation of economic activity. These economists often favor inward-oriented strategies. They focus on the structure of developing countries in terms of uneven industrial development. Some countries have modern manufacturing industries paying relatively high wages that operate alongside traditional agricultural industries paying low wages. A single economy with industries at very different levels of development is called a **dual economy.** Some insist that in a dual economy, the markets for goods and resources do not work well. If resources could move freely between industries, then wages would not differ by the huge amounts observed in certain developing countries. Where markets are not functioning well, these economists support active government direction of the economy, believing that resources are unlikely to move freely to their highest-valued use if free markets are allowed.

dual economy:
an economy in which two sectors (typically manufacturing and agriculture) show very different levels of development

Copyright © by Houghton Mifflin Company. All rights reserved.

The growth rates of outward-oriented economies are significantly higher than the growth rates of inward-oriented economies.

The growth rates of the outward-oriented economies are significantly higher than the growth rates of the inward-oriented economies.[2] The success of the outward-oriented economies is likely to continue in light of a strong increase in saving in those economies. In 1963, domestic saving as a fraction of GDP was only 13 percent in the strongly outward-oriented economies. After more than two decades of economic growth driven by export-promotion policies, the rate of saving in these countries had increased to 31.4 percent of GDP. This high rate of saving increases investment expenditures, which increase the productivity of labor, further stimulating the growth of per capita real GDP.

Why are outward-oriented strategies more successful than inward-oriented strategies? The primary advantage of an outward orientation is the efficient utilization of resources. Import-substitution policies do not allocate resources on the basis of cost minimization. In addition, an outward-oriented strategy allows the economy to grow beyond the scale of the domestic market. Foreign demand creates additional markets for exports, beyond the domestic market.

RECAP

1. Inward-oriented strategies concentrate on building a domestic industrial sector.
2. Outward-oriented strategies utilize a country's comparative advantage in exporting.
3. The deteriorating-terms-of-trade argument has been used to justify import-substitution policies.
4. Evidence indicates that outward-oriented policies have been more successful than inward-oriented policies at generating economic growth.

4. FOREIGN INVESTMENT AND AID

How are savings in one nation used to speed development in other nations?

Developing countries rely on savings in the rest of the world to finance much of their investment needs. Foreign savings may come from industrial countries in many different ways. In this section we describe the ways that savings are transferred from industrial to developing countries and the benefits of foreign investment and aid to developing countries.

4.a. Foreign Savings Flows

Poor countries that are unable to save enough to invest in capital stock must rely on the savings of other countries to help them develop economically. Foreign savings come from private sources as well as official government sources.

Private sources of foreign savings can take the form of direct investment, portfolio investment, commercial bank loans, and trade credit. **Foreign direct investment** is the purchase of a physical operating unit, like a factory, or an

foreign direct investment: the purchase of a physical operating unit in a foreign country, or more than 10 percent ownership

---

[2]Nouriel Roubini and Xavier Sala-i-Martin found that the strongly outward-oriented countries had an annual growth rate 2.5 percentage points higher on average than that of the strongly inward-oriented countries. Source: "Trade Promotes Growth," *NBER Digest*, March 1992.

Copyright © by Houghton Mifflin Company. All rights reserved.

portfolio investment:
the purchase of securities

commercial bank loan:
a bank loan at market rates of interest, often involving a bank syndicate

trade credit:
the extension of a period of time before an importer must pay for goods or services purchased

ownership position in a foreign country that gives the domestic firm making the investment ownership of more than 10 percent of the foreign firm. This is different from **portfolio investment,** which is the purchase of securities, like stocks and bonds. In the case of direct investment, the foreign investor may actually operate the business. Portfolio investment helps finance a business, but host-country managers operate the firm; foreign investors simply hold pieces of paper that represent a share of the ownership or the debt of the firm. **Commercial bank loans** are loans made at market rates of interest to either foreign governments or business firms. These loans are often made by a *bank syndicate,* a group of several banks, to share the risk associated with lending to a single country. Finally, exporting firms and commercial banks offer **trade credit,** allowing importers a period of time before payment is due on the goods or services purchased. Extension of trade credit usually involves payment in thirty days (or some other term) after the goods are received.

Direct investment and bank lending have changed over time. In 1970, direct investment in developing countries was greater than bank loans. By the late 1970s and early 1980s, however, bank loans far exceeded direct investment. Bank lending gives the borrowing country greater flexibility in deciding how to use funds. Direct investment carries with it an element of foreign control over domestic resources. Nationalist sentiment combined with the fear of exploitation by foreign owners and managers led many developing countries to pass laws restricting direct investment. By the early 1990s, however, as more nations emphasized the development of free markets, direct investment was again growing in importance as a source of funds for developing countries.

4.b. Benefits of Foreign Investment

Not all developing countries discourage foreign direct investment. In fact many countries have benefited from foreign investment. Those benefits fall into three categories: new jobs, new technology, and foreign exchange earnings.

4.b.1. New Jobs
Foreign investment should stimulate growth and create new jobs in developing countries. But the number of new jobs created directly by foreign investment is often limited by the nature of the industries in which foreign investment is allowed.

Usually foreign investment is invited in capital-intensive industries, like chemicals or mineral extraction. Because capital goods are expensive and often require advanced technology to operate, foreign firms can build a capital-intensive industry faster than the developing country. One product of the emphasis on capital-intensive industries is that foreign investment often has little effect on employment in developing countries. A $.5-billion oil refinery may employ just a few hundred workers; yet the creation of these few hundred jobs, along with other expenditures by the refinery, will stimulate domestic income by raising incomes across the economy, through the multiplier effect.

4.b.2. Technology Transfer
In Chapter 18 we said that economic growth depends on the growth of resources and technological change. Most expenditures on research and development are made in the major industrial countries. These are also the countries that develop most of the innovations that make production more efficient. For the Third World country with limited scientific

Copyright © by Houghton Mifflin Company. All rights reserved.

Developing countries have become a global work force that competes with industrial countries for new firms and expansions of existing firms. The photo shows workers at a 3M plant in Bangalore, India, that makes tapes, chemicals, and electrical parts. Increasingly sophisticated production is being carried out in developing countries as firms in industrial nations tap the talent in low-wage nations. This global competition for jobs should lead to a convergence of wages over time as developing countries' wages rise closer to wages in industrial nations.

Copyright © by Houghton Mifflin Company. All rights reserved.

resources, the industrial nations are a critical source of information, technology, and expertise.

The ability of foreign firms to utilize modern technology in a developing country depends in part on having a supply of engineers and technical personnel in the host country. India and Mexico have a fairly large number of technical personnel, which means new technology can be adapted relatively quickly. Other countries, where a large fraction of the population has less than an elementary-level education, must train workers and then keep those workers from migrating to industrial countries, where their salaries are likely to be much higher.

4.b.3. Foreign Exchange Earnings Developing countries expect foreign investment to improve their balance of payments. The assumption is that the multinational firms located inside the developing country increase exports and thus generate greater foreign currency earnings that can be used for imports or for repaying foreign debt. But this scenario does not unfold if the foreign investment is used to produce goods primarily for domestic consumption. In fact, the presence of a foreign firm can create a larger deficit in the balance of payments if the firm sends profits back to its industrial country headquarters from the developing country and the value of those profits exceeds the value of foreign exchange earned by exports.

4.c. Foreign Aid

foreign aid:
gifts or low-cost loans made to developing countries from official sources

bilateral aid:
foreign aid that flows from one country to another

multilateral aid:
aid provided by international organizations supported by many nations

Official foreign savings are usually available as either outright gifts or low-interest-rate loans. These funds are called **foreign aid.** Large countries, like the United States, provide much more funding in terms of the dollar value of aid than do small countries. However, some small countries—for example, the Netherlands and Norway—commit a much larger percentage of their GNP to foreign aid.

Foreign aid itself can take the form of cash grants or transfers of goods or technology, with nothing given in return by the developing country. Often foreign aid is used to reward political allies, particularly when those allies hold a strategic military location. Examples of this politically inspired aid are the former Soviet support of Cuba and U.S. support of Turkey.

Foreign aid that flows from one country to another is called **bilateral aid.** Governments typically have an agency that coordinates and plans foreign aid programs and expenditures. The U.S. Agency for International Development (USAID) performs these functions in the United States. Most of the time bilateral aid is project oriented, given to fund a specific project (an educational facility, an irrigation project).

Food makes up a substantial portion of bilateral aid. After a bad harvest or a natural disaster (drought in the Sudan, floods in Bangladesh), major food-producing nations help feed the hungry. Egypt and Bangladesh were the leading recipients of food aid during the late 1980s. In the early 1990s, attention shifted to Somalia. The major recipients of food aid change over time, as nature and political events combine to change the pattern of hunger and need in the world.

The economics of food aid illustrates a major problem with many kinds of charity. Aid is intended to help those who need it without interfering with domestic production. But when food flows into a developing country, food prices tend to fall, pushing farm income down and discouraging local production. Ideally food aid should go to the very poor, who are less likely to have the income necessary to purchase domestic production anyway.

Foreign aid does not flow directly from the donors to the needy. It goes through the government of the recipient country. Here we find another problem: the inefficient and sometimes corrupt bureaucracies in recipient nations. There have been cases where recipient governments have sold products that were intended for free distribution to the poor. In other cases, food aid was not distributed because the recipient government had created the conditions leading to starvation. The U.S. intervention in Somalia in 1993 was aimed at helping food aid reach the starving population. In still other cases, a well-intentioned recipient government simply did not have the resources to distribute the aid, so the products ended up largely going to waste. One response to these problems is to rely on voluntary agencies to distribute aid. Another is to rely on multilateral agencies.

Multilateral aid is provided by international organizations that are supported by many nations. The largest and most important multilateral aid insti-

Copyright © by Houghton Mifflin Company. All rights reserved.

tution is the World Bank. The World Bank makes loans to developing countries at below-market rates of interest and oversees projects it has funded in developing countries. As an international organization, the World Bank is not controlled by any single country. This allows the organization to advise and help developing countries in a nonpolitical way that is usually not possible with bilateral aid.

RECAP

1. Private sources of foreign savings include direct investment, portfolio investment, commercial bank loans, and trade credit.
2. Developing countries can benefit from foreign investment through new jobs, the transfer of technology, and foreign exchange earnings.
3. Foreign aid involves gifts or low-cost loans made available to developing countries by official sources.
4. Foreign aid can be provided bilaterally or multilaterally.

5. ECONOMIES IN TRANSITION FROM SOCIALISM

As the world turned from the 1980s into the 1990s, the economies of the former Soviet Union and its eastern European satellites were leaving socialism behind and embracing capitalism as the road to future prosperity. The desire for change was motivated by low productivity and consumption, or as Soviet workers were fond of saying, "We pretend to work and the state pretends to pay us." The transition road has not been easy; it has proven much more difficult to make the transition from socialism than many thought in 1990.

An economy in transition poses special development problems as it moves from socialism, with widespread government ownership of productive resources and massive government intervention in economic decision-making, to a market-based economy, with an emphasis on private property and individual decision-making. Since much is still being learned and there is no clearly established "best way," we focus on certain fundamentals that are required for a successful transition.

5.a. Microeconomic Issues

What microeconomic issues are involved in the transition from socialism?

privatize:
to convert state-owned enterprises to private ownership

The transformation of a socialist economy into a capitalist economy requires the creation of markets. Resources that were formerly owned and allocated by government must be **privatized,** or converted from state ownership to private ownership. The state still has a role, since private property rights must be developed, recognized, and protected by government. Privately owned resources will then be allocated by the market system through prices set by supply and demand in a competitive environment with incomes that are based on productivity. Although it is easy to state where an economy should be in terms of free markets rather than central planning, getting there is easier said than done. The issue of privatization is the most obvious case.

5.a.1 Privatization Socialist economies are characterized by many state-owned enterprises (SOEs). These enterprises are frequently large, technologi-

Copyright © by Houghton Mifflin Company. All rights reserved.

The transition from socialism to capitalism should create a class of successful entrepreneurs. Here we see Jan Pazdera outside his photo and video store in the Czech Republic. First-wave entrepreneurs like Pazdera should provide useful models for the next generation of risk takers by efficiently providing the goods and services people want. The owners are rewarded with profits not legally obtainable by private citizens under socialism.

Copyright © by Houghton Mifflin Company. All rights reserved.

cally outdated, and unprofitable. The move to a market economy requires that these enterprises be privatized. How should SOEs be sold or otherwise converted to private ownership?

One alternative is to issue shares of ownership (like shares of stock) to existing workers and managers in an enterprise. This method has the advantage of simplicity—the new private owners are easy to identify, and ownership is easy to transfer. The disadvantage is that some SOEs may be uncompetitive in a capitalist environment so that ownership of such a firm is worthless, while other SOEs may be able to compete effectively so that ownership may have considerable value. This privatization system would reward and penalize the working population based on where they were previously assigned to work by the state rather than on the basis of individual investment and risk-taking. Moreover, a simple change of ownership may not change the manner in which the firm operates.

Another alternative is to issue shares of ownership randomly to the public in a kind of lottery. You may have an equal chance of becoming one of the owners of a steel mill, a shoe factory, or a farm. In a truly random assignment of ownership, everyone has an equal chance of receiving a profitable share. This scheme does away with the unfortunate circumstance associated with those who have the misfortune to be employed by the state in an unproductive job when shares are issued only to existing employees of each firm. A problem with this scheme is that those interested in, or knowledgeable about, a particular firm or industry would have no better chance to be involved in that industry than would those who had no interest.

Yet another alternative is to auction ownership of SOEs to the highest bidder. In addition to raising revenue for the state, this method is quite straightforward to carry out. A common argument against this method is that those with enough wealth to make winning bids are likely to be former Communist party leaders or individuals who traded on black markets under the socialist regime. Such people are not favorably viewed by the masses, and as a result, auctions are controversial.

The privatization method chosen by Czechoslovakia (before its split into two nations) was a coupon giveaway to millions of citizens, who then used the coupons to buy stock in SOEs. The goal of this kind of plan was to create a broad-based democratic capitalism with millions of citizens holding ownership positions in productive firms. An advantage of this plan is that the government does not have to find buyers willing to exchange real money for SOEs. Since many SOEs have a questionable initial money value, by granting ownership to a wide group of citizens, the state pushes the burden of managing relatively unproductive firms to the general public.

There is no universal approach to converting SOEs into privately owned firms. Each nation has taken the approach that best seems to fit its particular political and economic system. In all cases, it has been relatively easy to privatize small, profitable firms but much more difficult to privatize large unprofitable firms.

5.a.2. Price Reform
Under socialism, prices of goods and services are established by the state. These prices need not reflect economic costs or scarcity. But in a market-oriented economy, prices serve an important signaling role. If consumers want more of a good or service, its price rises, and that induces producers to offer more for sale. If consumer tastes change so that demand for a good or service falls, then the price should fall to induce producers to offer less for sale. If there is an excess supply of a good, its price falls, and that induces consumers to buy more. If there is an excess demand for a good, the price rises to induce consumers to buy less. A major problem with socialism is that prices are not free to serve this role of a signal to producers and consumers. Therefore, an important step in the transition from socialism to capitalism is the freeing of prices so that they may seek their free market levels.

A market system requires that prices be free to fluctuate to reflect supply and demand fluctuations.

Considering that there were around 25 million goods and services to be priced in the former Soviet Union, it was impossible for government officials to know and then plan a shift from the state-regulated price to the appropriate free market price for each item. However, there is a way to allow the correct prices to be set very quickly. There are prices existing for every good in the rest of the world. By opening the economy to competition from foreign countries, foreign trade will force the domestic prices to be comparable to foreign prices. Of course, the presence of tariffs or quotas on foreign goods will distort the price comparisons, but the lower the restrictions on trade, the more domestic prices will conform to prices in the rest of the world. For goods that are not traded internationally or for many services, foreign trade will not set a domestic price. In this case, the market may be allowed to adjust the price over time to the internal domestic pressures of supply and demand.

The normal response to a freeing of prices from state control is an increase in the availability of goods and services, although initially output may fall. However, the beneficial aspects of price reform require privatization of the economy. Price changes bring about profits and losses that induce profit-seeking producers to provide what buyers want. If production is still controlled by state-owned enterprises that have no profit incentive, then price reform will not have the desired effect of increasing output and efficiency.

Copyright © by Houghton Mifflin Company. All rights reserved.

It is important to realize that price reform has an initial shock effect on the economy. Prices under socialism are typically well below the true opportunity cost for most items considered to be necessities. Speaking of price reform in Bulgaria, the Bulgarian National Bank's chief economist said, "One no longer has to get up at four or five a.m. to line up for bread and milk. Items that in the past might not even be available when one finally reached the counter now are available, but at ten times higher prices." This is a source of political conflict in taking an economy on the transition path from socialism to capitalism. People have to learn the new rules of the game, and the lessons are often quite harsh to those who have lived under decades of socialism.

5.a.3. Social Safety Net

Moving from socialism to capitalism will harm many people during the transition period as enterprises are closed and unemployment increases at the same time that prices of many goods and services rise. As a result, it is critical to have a program in place to provide a minimal standard of living for all citizens in order to avoid massive political unrest. Under socialism, the state provided for health care and took care of the disabled, aged, and unemployed. Moreover, many goods such as housing and food were heavily subsidized. Such widespread subsidies were inefficient because they were provided to everyone, even to those who could afford to pay higher prices. It is politically necessary that government subsidies continue, but they should be focused on the most needy groups. Over time, as more and more of the economy is privatized, government programs will have to be financed by explicit taxation of workers and firms. In other cases, user charges will be introduced, a phenomenon much less common under socialism.

The abandonment of socialism was due to populist sentiment in Eastern Europe. The populations of these nations were tired of stagnant or declining standards of living and were ready for change. However, market-oriented economies operate in a democratic framework, and political unrest due to dissatisfaction with the operation of the economy can much more easily be demonstrated in a democratic setting than under the authoritarian rule of the

Copyright © by Houghton Mifflin Company. All rights reserved.

The transition from central planning to a market-based economy is creating opportunities for hard-working, enterprising individuals to earn a standard of living previously only available to high-ranking members of the socialist elite. This woman, Maria Grigoreyeva, is one of Russia's wealthiest. She is a visible result of the opportunities available to new business leaders in Eastern Europe. At the same time, there are large masses of people who have been disenfranchised by the termination of their jobs or income security that existed under socialism. A major problem during the early transition from socialism is providing a safety net to protect the disenfranchised.

centrally planned economy. A social safety net must be generous enough to buy time for the transition to capitalism to yield benefits for the majority of citizens. Otherwise, the movement toward capitalism may never survive the transition period.

5.b Macroeconomic Issues

What macroeconomic issues are involved in the transition from socialism?

Good macroeconomic policy is aimed at providing steady income growth with low inflation. This is true whether we are talking about the United States, Japan, or Russia. Good macroeconomic policy, then, requires limited use of government budget deficits and tight control over monetary and credit growth. Although these features of good macroeconomic policy are universal, there are some macro issues that are unique to the transition from socialism to capitalism.

5.b.1. Monetary Policy
Monetary policy in the transition economy must deal with issues not covered in the earlier monetary policy discussion of Chapter 14. When prices were strictly controlled in the earlier socialist regime, money could not be used to freely buy and sell goods as in market-oriented economies. As a result, the following special problems must be addressed as part of the transition from socialism to capitalism.

Monetary Overhang In many socialist countries, there is believed to be a substantial **monetary overhang**, which is the term used to describe the money that households have accumulated because there was nothing they could buy with it. With limited access to consumer goods, and subsidized housing, food, and health care, the typical household had savings in the form of money building up over time that they would not have had if they had access to more consumer goods. In early 1991, the monetary overhang in the (former) Soviet Union was estimated to be half of household savings deposits.

monetary overhang:
money accumulated by households because there was nothing available that they wanted to buy

The potential problem with a large monetary overhang is that inflation could result if goods become available to induce spending of the saved funds. How can the monetary overhang be eliminated? One way is for the state to decontrol prices suddenly and have prices rise sharply, thereby decreasing the purchasing power of the money held by households. The state basically imposes its own inflation tax on the purchasing power of the monetary overhang early in the transition period rather than let the households create their own inflation later in the transition period. This was the approach taken in Poland and Yugoslavia in 1989 and the Soviet Union in 1991. Of course, it is critical that the one-time inflation not turn into a prolonged inflation if the economy is to enjoy long-term prosperity. Unfortunately, the early record suggests that high inflation has been difficult to reduce once allowed to emerge.

An alternative way of reducing the monetary overhang is to privatize—sell state-owned property (like houses or land) to private households. Another alternative is to allow greater access to Western consumer goods so that households spend their excess money balances on such goods. Yet another alternative is to allow interest rates to rise on household savings accounts so that households willingly hold on to their accumulated money.

During the transition from socialism, monetary policy should be aimed at achieving a low and stable inflation rate.

Beyond the issue of monetary overhang, monetary policy will be primarily aimed at controlling inflation during the transition to capitalism. The early lesson of successful transition is that without low inflation, it is impossible to have the growth of saving and investment required for sustainable growth of

Copyright © by Houghton Mifflin Company. All rights reserved.

GDP. By maintaining a steady and low rate of inflation, a nation will also realize stable exchange rates, which will contribute to its speedy integration into trade with the rest of the world.

Currency Convertibility   Closely related to the issue of foreign trade and exchange rates is **currency convertibility.** The currency of the country must be freely convertible into other currencies if domestic prices are to be linked to (and disciplined by) foreign markets. One cannot compare the cost of a tractor in Romania with a tractor in Germany if the currency of Romania cannot be freely traded for the currency of Germany at a market-determined exchange rate.

currency convertibility:
the ease with which the domestic currency can be converted into foreign currency so foreign exchange rates can properly reflect the domestic currency value of foreign prices

Socialist countries traditionally did not permit free exchange of their currencies for other currencies. Government controls on foreign exchange trading allowed the government to fix an official exchange-rate value of the domestic currency that was often far from the true market value. As a result, international prices were unable to serve their purpose of increasing production of the goods a country could produce relatively cheaply and increasing imports of those goods that could be produced more cheaply in the rest of the world. For instance, if the true value of a Soviet ruble relative to the U.S. dollar was 30 rubles per dollar, yet the official exchange rate set by the Soviet Union was 3 rubles per dollar, then the ruble was officially overvalued. Suppose a computer monitor produced in the United States sold for $200. At the official exchange rate, the monitor was worth 600 rubles ($200 at 3 rubles per dollar). At the true market value of the currencies, the monitor was worth 6,000 rubles ($200 at 30 rubles per dollar). Since Soviet citizens were unable to buy foreign goods (all foreign trade was in the hands of the state), the official exchange rate was largely irrelevant. However, the absence of free trading in a ruble that was convertible into dollars meant that there was no way to identify which goods the Soviet Union could produce more cheaply than other nations. The absence of such relative cost information made specialization according to comparative advantage a difficult task. If a country cannot-determine which goods it can produce more cheaply than others, it will not know which goods it should specialize in.

Under socialism, with central planning of production, the absence of relative price information was not as critical a problem as it is with capitalism. When private decision-makers must decide which goods to produce, they must rely on relative prices to guide them. In international trade, this requires a currency that is convertible into other currencies at market-determined exchange rates.

Money and Credit   In industrial countries with well-developed financial markets, monetary policy is often aimed at changing interest rates in order to change aggregate demand. For instance, when the monetary authorities are concerned that inflation is a problem, money growth is slowed and interest rates tend to rise. The higher interest rates reduce investment and consumption spending and lower (or at least slow the growth of) aggregate demand, or total spending in the economy. In a socialist system just beginning the transformation toward capitalism, financial markets are generally undeveloped, since the state under socialism regulated interest rates and limited the saving and borrowing opportunities for citizens. Changes in the money supply may have little or no effect on interest rates. Therefore, the role of monetary policy in terms of money growth rates should be to maintain a low and steady rate of

Copyright © by Houghton Mifflin Company. All rights reserved.

inflation. Any other effects of money growth on the economy are likely to be of secondary importance until further development of the economy occurs.

Under socialism, credit was often extended to enterprises on the basis of political connections or central planner preferences. A market economy requires that credit occur on the basis of productive potential. Firms that offer good prospects of earning a sufficient profit to repay debts should receive greater credit access than firms that have little hope of competing profitably. The move toward a market economy must include the development of financial institutions like banks that are able to efficiently evaluate creditworthiness and allocate credit accordingly. The experience so far indicates that the development of the banking system requires a low and stable inflation rate. High inflation and uncertainty about future macroeconomic policy make it difficult for banks to evaluate the likely profitability of a firm and discourage lenders (as well as depositors) from committing funds for long periods.

5.b.2. Fiscal Policy   Reform of fiscal policy involves reducing government subsidies and reforming tax policy to avoid large budget deficits. Socialist countries have been characterized by subsidies to enterprises that produced a value of output less than the costs of production. Under a market system, firms that cannot operate at a profit should not be allowed to exist forever by continued subsidies from the government. It is for this reason that, as noted earlier, a safety net is necessary since lower subsidies lead to transitional unemployment.

A socialist government does not rely on explicit or direct taxes on the public since the state controls prices, wages, and production. By paying workers less than the value of their output, the state can extract the revenue needed to operate the government. However, once private ownership and free markets have replaced central planning, the activities of government must be financed by explicit taxes. Reforming countries are implementing income, value-added, and profit taxes to produce revenue for the remaining functions of government. Again, the goal should be to match government revenue and expenditures as closely as possible to avoid a large budget deficit.

The experience of transition economies in terms of implementing successful fiscal policies is quite mixed. Some countries, like Hungary, Poland, Albania, and Slovenia, have had some success in reducing fiscal deficits so that the incentive to finance deficits through money creation has been reduced. This has allowed these economies to free prices without the high inflation experienced by other transition economies. The evidence so far suggests that those countries that have had major political changes have had opportunities to take more aggressive steps in establishing sound fiscal policies than the economies in which many of the remnants of the old socialist regime still linger. If major sectors of the economy are still dependent on government subsidies, or influential politicians cling to their power by offering support to old, inefficient enterprises, then fiscal deficit reduction will be much more difficult than in an environment where the population has clearly rejected the old ways along with the old politicians.

One problem that seems pervasive in the transition economy is collecting taxes. The largest of the old state-owned enterprises typically provided the largest tax revenue for the government. In many cases, these are now declining sectors of the economy and contribute less and less tax revenue. The newly emerging private sector, which should experience the fastest growth, is where tax collection has proved difficult. The problems include political pres-

Copyright © by Houghton Mifflin Company. All rights reserved.

sures to provide tax exemptions or even ignore evasion of legally required taxes. The issue of tax collection will not be solved quickly, as the economies must computerize tax assessment and collection information to allow efficient monitoring of the system. The development and implementation of effective tax-collection agencies should take place over the next few years.

5.c. The Sequencing of Reforms

Considering all of the reforms necessary in the transition from socialism to capitalism, how should a country proceed? Are some measures needed before others can be undertaken? How rapidly should the changes be introduced? There are no certain answers to these questions, and there is an ongoing debate regarding the proper order of the reforms.

Some economists argue that all reforms should be undertaken simultaneously (or as nearly so as possible). Most tend to agree that macroeconomic stabilization is necessary for any serious conversion of the economy to a market system. Inflation must be stabilized at a reasonably low and steady rate, and the fiscal deficit must be brought to a level low enough to support a noninflationary monetary policy (so that the monetary authorities are not creating money to fund the budget deficit). Included in the macroeconomic stabilization is the development of a convertible currency.

Following the macroeconomic reform, micro reforms like privatization may proceed, along with the opening of the economy to foreign trade and competition. Then the foreign prices will guide the deregulation of industry in setting appropriate prices for domestic products. It is generally thought that the micro reforms are intertwined and support one another. In this case, they should be carried out simultaneously. Otherwise, each element will tend to be less effective than it otherwise would be. For instance, privately owned firms need deregulated prices and wages to respond to changing relative prices and produce what consumers want.

RECAP

1. The transition from socialism to capitalism requires that state-owned enterprises be privatized.
2. A market system requires that prices fluctuate freely to allow producers and consumers to make efficient production and consumption decisions.
3. Since the transition from socialism will create unemployment and lower incomes for many, the government must provide a social safety net.
4. Since households could not buy all of the consumer goods they wanted, socialist economies often had a monetary overhang of excess money holdings.
5. The convertibility of the domestic currency into foreign currencies is necessary to link the domestic country with prices in the rest of the world.
6. The transition economy will aim monetary policy at the creation of a low and stable rate of inflation.

Copyright © by Houghton Mifflin Company. All rights reserved.

7. Credit must be available to firms on the basis of potential profitability rather than political relationships in order to increase productivity.

8. Fiscal policy should be reformed to reduce subsidies from government to firms and also to collect explicit taxes.

9. Macroeconomic reform must provide a stable, low-inflation environment for microeconomic reform to succeed.

10. Since microeconomic reforms tend to reinforce one another, they should generally be carried out simultaneously.

SUMMARY

▨ How is poverty measured?

1. Poverty usually is defined in an absolute sense as the minimum income needed to purchase a minimal standard of living and is measured by per capita GNP or GDP. §1.a

2. Some economists and social scientists use a quality-of-life index to evaluate standards of living. §1.b

▨ Why are some countries poorer than others?

3. Both political obstacles (lack of skilled officials, instability, corruption, constraints imposed by special interest groups) and social obstacles (cultural attitudes that discourage entrepreneurial activity and encourage rapid population growth) limit economic growth in developing countries. §2.a, 2.b

▨ What strategies can a nation use to increase its economic growth?

4. Inward-oriented development strategies focus on developing a domestic manufacturing sector to produce goods that can substitute for imported manufactured goods. §3.a

5. Outward-oriented development strategies focus on producing manufactured goods for export. §3.b

6. The growth rates of outward-oriented economies are significantly higher than those of inward-oriented economies. §3.c

▨ How are savings in one nation used to speed development in other nations?

7. Private sources of foreign savings include direct investment, portfolio investment, commercial bank loans, and trade credit. §4.a

8. Foreign investment in developing countries can increase their economic growth by creating jobs, transferring modern technology, and stimulating exports to increase foreign exchange earnings. §4.b

9. Official gifts or low-cost loans made to developing countries by official sources are called foreign aid. §4.c

10. Foreign aid can be distributed bilaterally or multilaterally. §4.c

▨ What microeconomic issues are involved in the transition from socialism?

11. The move toward capitalism requires that state-owned enterprises be privatized. §5.a

12. Prices and incomes must be freed from state control if markets are to work efficiently. §5.a.2

13. Since many workers may be unemployed and incomes may fall during the transition, there must be a social safety net provided by the government. §5.a.3

▨ What macroeconomic issues are involved in the transition from socialism?

14. There may be a substantial monetary overhang as a result of limited opportunities to exchange money for goods under socialism. §5.b.1

15. Exchange rates can link economies together, but the currency must be freely convertible into other currencies if exchange rates are to indicate accurate price information. §5.b.1

16. Monetary policy should be aimed at providing a low and steady rate of inflation. §5.b.1

Copyright © by Houghton Mifflin Company. All rights reserved.

17. Credit must be allocated on the basis of productivity and profitability rather than political connections. §5.b.1

18. Fiscal policy must avoid large deficits and must raise explicit taxes. §5.b.2

19. Macroeconomic stabilization is generally necessary before microeconomic reforms are implemented. §5.c

KEY TERMS

expropriation §2.a.2

primary product §3.a

import substitution §3.a

export substitution §3.b

terms of trade §3.c

dual economy §3.c

foreign direct investment §4.a

portfolio investment §4.a

commercial bank loan §4.a

trade credit §4.a

foreign aid §4.c

bilateral aid §4.c

multilateral aid §4.c

privatize §5.a

monetary overhang §5.b.1

currency convertibility §5.b.1

EXERCISES

1. What are basic human needs? Can you list additional needs besides those considered in the chapter?

2. Per capita GNP or GDP is used as an absolute measure of poverty.

   a. What are some criticisms of using per capita GNP as a measure of standard of living?

   b. Do any of these criticisms also apply to a quality-of-life index?

3. In many developing countries there are economists and politicians who were educated in industrial countries. These individuals know the policies that would maximize the growth of their countries, but they do not implement them. Why not?

4. Suppose you are a benevolent dictator who can impose any policy you choose in your country. If your goal is to accelerate economic development, how would you respond to the following problems?

   a. Foreign firms are afraid to invest in your country because your predecessor expropriated many foreign-owned factories.

   b. There are few entrepreneurs in the country.

   c. The dominant domestic religion teaches that the accumulation of wealth is sinful.

   d. It is customary for families to have at least six children.

5. What effect does population growth have on economic development?

6. Why have most developing countries followed inward-oriented development strategies?

7. Why is an outward-oriented development strategy likely to allocate resources more efficiently than an inward-oriented strategy?

8. Who benefits from an import-substitution strategy? Who is harmed?

9. If poverty is a relative concept, why don't we define it in relative terms?

10. "The poor will always be with us." Does this statement have different meanings depending on whether poverty is interpreted as an absolute or relative concept?

11. How do traditional societies answer the questions What to produce? How to produce? and For whom to produce?

Copyright © by Houghton Mifflin Company. All rights reserved.

12. What are the most important sources of foreign savings for developing countries? Why don't developing countries save more so that they don't have to rely on foreign savings for investment?

13. Private foreign investment and foreign aid are sources of savings to developing countries. Yet each has been controversial at times. What are the potential negative effects of private foreign investment and foreign aid for developing countries?

14. Why do immigrants often play an important role in developing the economies of poor nations?

15. How does a nation go about instituting a policy of import substitution? What is a likely result of such a policy?

16. Discuss the alternative ways in which state-owned enterprises can be privatized.

17. One problem associated with the transition from socialism to capitalism is deregulating prices of goods and services. How can government officials find the appropriate prices to use when ending the government regulation of prices?

18. What is monetary overhang, and how can government eliminate it?

19. Suppose the official exchange rate is set by the government at 10 rubles per dollar. If the government does not allow its citizens to freely trade rubles for dollars, what is the use of such an exchange rate? How would currency convertibility change things?

20. What is the proper role of monetary policy during the transition from socialism to capitalism?

21. Is there any particular order in which the reforms needed in the transition from socialism to capitalism should occur? If so, discuss why.

22. The social safety net necessary for easing the transition from socialism will require the government to continue many of its health and public welfare policies to protect the unemployed from creating social and political unrest that threatens the transition. In what sense does the social safety net program also hinder the movement toward a market-based economy?

23. What is the proper role of fiscal policy during the transition from socialism to capitalism?

Copyright © by Houghton Mifflin Company. All rights reserved.

INTERNET EXERCISE

In section 1 of this chapter we learned of the problems associated with defining poverty. To see how different measures can give different rankings, we can examine some data from the United Nations by going to the Boyes/Melvin web site at **http://www.hmco.com/college/** and clicking on the internet exercise link for this chapter. Now answer the questions that appear on the web page.

Copyright © by Houghton Mifflin Company. All rights reserved.

We Need the Will to Feed the Hungry

The world now produces enough food to feed everyone, United Nations experts said recently. Tell that to the 13 million children below age five who die every year of hunger-related causes. Or to the 786 million chronically undernourished people in the developing world. In South Asia, an estimated two out of three children are underweight. And in sub-Saharan Africa, the number of underweight children actually increased during the past 20 years.

Yet the UN Food and Agriculture Organization calculates average food availability in the world rose from 2,290 calories per day per person in 1961 to 2,700 calories in 1990. What's going wrong?

The answer is no great mystery. Harvard economist Amartya Sen, for instance, points out that even the poorest governments can reduce the incidence of hunger if they are committed to the task. Hunger and malnutrition have almost been eradicated in Costa Rica. And since independence India has virtually eliminated the threat of famine.

A government's will to feed its people, however, is intimately linked to the nature of the government. Sen's work suggests that the more dictatorial the regime, the more prone the country is to famine. This is because such governments are unresponsive to the needs of their citizens: political elites are, after all, the last to starve.

Although its record for feeding its people has definitely improved, China experienced one of the worst famines of all time during the Great Leap Forward between 1958 and 1961. An estimated 30 million people died.

While famines often can be blamed on the political and economic failures of dictatorial governments, the rich, democratic nations are not entirely blameless.

The IMF and the World Bank encourage farmers in poor countries to shift from subsistence farming to cash crops worth next to nothing on world markets.

When crises erupt, privileged countries deliver tonnes of food aid from their overstocked shelves. Canada's specialty is wheat. But the beneficiaries of our largesse often have little reason to be grateful.

Sen's research indicates, for example, that famines are not necessarily the result of a decline in food production. During the famines in Bengal in 1943, in Ethiopia in 1973 and in Bangalesh in 1974, those countries produced at least as much food as in previous years. The famines occurred either because incomes fell or because food prices were pushed out of reach by a newly rich group which started demanding more to eat.

In their recent book *Hunger and Public Action,* Sen and Jean Dreze (formerly of the London School of Economics), observe that where a country's economic system is still functioning it often makes more sense to give people money to buy the local food that is available than to give them food aid. Local traders can deliver food more quickly and efficiently. And domestic agricultural production isn't destroyed.

Somalia, unfortunately, seems beyond such solutions. Famines came and went when dictators ran the country. But neither the government nor the economic system survived the latest crisis.

The Red Cross is now distributing seeds to Somalian farmers in an attempt to circumvent the looters who are after food. Until stability is restored, however, the relief camps are the only hope for thousands of starving people. This is no way to run a world.

Source: "We Need the Will to Feed the Hungry," *The Ottowa Citizen,* September 27, 1992, p. B1. Reprinted by permission.

Copyright © by Houghton Mifflin Company. All rights reserved.

The Ottowa Citizen/September 27, 1992

COMMENTARY

Though efforts to combat famines often take the form of food aid, famines do not necessarily imply a shortage of food. Instead, famines sometimes represent shortfalls in purchasing power of the poorest sectors of society. In many cases, grants of income are a better means of alleviating famines than grants of food.

We can understand this argument using demand and supply analysis. In the following two diagrams we represent the demand for food and the supply of food in a famine-stricken country receiving aid. In each diagram, the demand curve D_1 intersects the supply curve S_1 at an equilibrium quantity of food Q_1, which represents a subsistence level of food consumption. The equilibrium depicted in each graph is one in which, in the absence of aid, a famine would occur.

The first graph illustrates the effects of providing aid in the form of food. The food aid increases the available supply of food, which is shown by an outward shift of the supply curve to S_2. The effect of this aid is to increase the equilib-

rium quantity of food (Q_2) and lower the equilibrium price (P_2). The lower price of food will adversely affect the income of domestic producers. Domestic producers will thus attempt to grow other crops, or to search for sources of income other than growing food, if they cannot receive enough money for their produce. As the amount of domestic food production falls, a country becomes more dependent upon imports of food.

The second graph illustrates the effect of income aid for the famine-stricken country. The aid is depicted by a shift in the demand curve to D_2. As with food aid, this relief allows consumption to rise to a point above the subsistence level. The effects of this aid on domestic food producers, however, are quite different. The price of food rises, and thus domestic food producers are not hurt by the aid package. As a result, aid in the form of income does not cause disincentives for production. An increase in domestic food production also serves to make a country less dependent upon food imports.

Copyright © by Houghton Mifflin Company. All rights reserved.

Food Aid

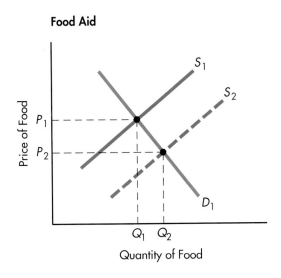

Income Aid

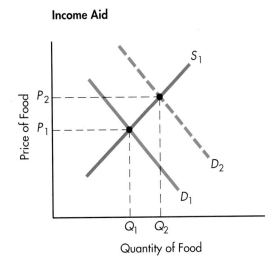

Copyright © by Houghton Mifflin Company. All rights reserved.

V

Issues in International Trade and Finance

Copyright © by Houghton Mifflin Company. All rights reserved.

20

World Trade Equilibrium

FUNDAMENTAL QUESTIONS

1. What are the prevailing patterns of trade between countries? What goods are traded?

2. What determines the goods a nation will export?

3. How are the equilibrium price and the quantity of goods traded determined?

4. What are the sources of comparative advantage?

Copyright © by Houghton Mifflin Company. All rights reserved.

Copyright © by Houghton Mifflin Company. All rights reserved.

T he United States's once-dominant position as an exporter of color television sets has since been claimed by nations like Japan and Taiwan. What caused this change? Is it because Japan specializes in the export of high-tech equipment? If countries tend to specialize in the export of particular kinds of goods, why does the United States import Heineken beer at the same time it exports Budweiser? This chapter will examine the volume of world trade and the nature of trade linkages between countries. As you saw in Chapter 2, trade occurs because of specialization in production. No single individual or country can produce everything better than others can. The result is specialization of production based on comparative advantage. Remember that comparative advantage is in turn based on relative opportunity costs: a country will specialize in the production of those goods for which its opportunity costs of production are lower than costs in other countries. Nations then trade what they produce in excess of their own consumption to acquire other things they want to consume. In this chapter, we will go a step further to discuss the sources of comparative advantage. We will look at why one country has a comparative advantage in, say, automobile production, while another country has a comparative advantage in wheat production.

The world equilibrium price and quantity traded are derived from individual countries' demand and supply curves. This relationship between the world trade equilibrium and individual country markets will be utilized in the chapter on "International Trade Restrictions" to discuss the ways that countries can interfere with free international trade to achieve their own economic or political goals. ∎

1. AN OVERVIEW OF WORLD TRADE

What are the prevailing patterns of trade between countries? What goods are traded?

Trade occurs because it makes people better off. International trade occurs because it makes people better off than they would be if they could consume only domestically produced products. Who trades with whom, and what sorts of goods are traded? These are the questions we first consider before investigating the underlying reasons for trade.

TABLE 1
The Direction of Trade
(in billions of dollars and percentages of world trade)

	Destination	
Origin	**Industrial Countries**	**Developing Countries**
Industrial countries	$2,435	$1,011
	47%	19%
Developing countries	$ 961	$770
	19%	15%

Source: *Direction of Trade Statistics Yearbook*, 1997, International Monetary Fund. Reprinted by permission of International Monetary Fund.

1.a. The Direction of Trade

Table 1 shows patterns of trade between two large groups of countries: the industrial countries and the developing countries. The industrial countries include all of Western Europe, Japan, Australia, New Zealand, Canada, and the United States. The developing countries are, essentially, the rest of the world. The table shows the dollar values and percentages of total trade between these groups of countries. The vertical column at the left lists the origin of exports, and the horizontal row at the top lists the destination of imports.

Trade between industrial countries accounts for the majority of international trade.

As Table 1 shows, trade between industrial countries accounts for the bulk of international trade. Trade between industrial countries is a little less than $2 trillion in value and amounts to 47 percent of world trade. Exports from industrial countries to developing countries represent 19 percent of total world trade. Exports from developing countries to industrial countries account for 19 percent of total trade, while exports from the developing countries to other developing countries currently represent only 15 percent of international trade.

Table 2 lists the major trading partners of selected countries and the percentage of total exports and imports accounted for by each country's top ten trading partners. For instance, 21 percent of U.S. exports went to Canada, and 14 percent of U.S. imports came from Japan. From a glance at the other countries listed in Table 2, it is clear that the United States is a major trading partner for many nations. This is true because of the size of the U.S. economy and the nation's relatively high level of income. It is also apparent that Canada and Mexico are very dependent on trade with the United States: about four-fifths of Canadian exports and 67 percent of its imports, and more than four-fifths of Mexican exports and over 70 percent of its imports involve the United States. The dollar value of trade among the three North American nations is shown in Figure 1.

Copyright © by Houghton Mifflin Company. All rights reserved.

1.b. What Goods Are Traded?

The volume of trade in motor vehicles exceeds that of any other good.

Because countries differ in their comparative advantages, they will tend to export different goods. Countries also have different tastes and technological needs, and thus tend to differ in what they will import. Some goods are more widely traded than others, as Table 3 shows. Motor vehicles is the most heavily traded good in the world, accounting for 5.17 percent of the total volume of world trade. Motor vehicles is followed by crude petroleum, motor vehicle parts, petroleum products, aircraft, and automatic data processing equipment. The top ten exported products, however, represent only 25 percent of world trade. The remaining 75 percent is distributed among a great variety of products. The importance of petroleum and motor vehicles in international trade should not obscure the fact that international trade involves all sorts of products from all over the world.

TABLE 2
Major Trading Partners of Selected Countries

United States

Exports		Imports	
Canada	21%	Canada	20%
Japan	11	Japan	14
Mexico	9	Mexico	9
U.K.	5	China	7
Germany	4	Germany	5

Canada

Exports		Imports	
U.S.	82%	U.S.	67%
Japan	4	Japan	5
U.K.	1	U.K.	3
Germany	1	China	2
China	1	Germany	2

Germany

Exports		Imports	
France	11%	France	11%
U.K.	8	Netherlands	9
U.S.	8	Italy	8
Italy	7	U.S.	7
Netherlands	7	U.K	7

Mexico

Exports		Imports	
U.S.	84%	U.S.	76%
Canada	1	Japan	4
Japan	1	Germany	4
Spain	1	Canada	2
Italy	1	Korea	1

Japan

Exports		Imports	
U.S.	28%	U.S.	23%
Korea	7	China	12
Hong Kong	6	Korea	5
China	5	Australia	4
Singapore	5	Indonesia	4

United Kingdom

Exports		Imports	
U.S.	12%	Germany	14%
Germany	11	U.S.	13
France	9	France	9
Netherlands	7	Netherlands	6
Belgium-Luxembourg	5	Japan	5

Source: Data for all countries from International Monetary Fund, *Direction of Trade Statistics Yearbook*, 1997.

Copyright © by Houghton Mifflin Company. All rights reserved.

Product Category	Value	Percentage of World Trade
Motor vehicles	$180,665	5.17%
Crude petroleum	174,847	5.00
Motor vehicle parts	88,062	2.52
Petroleum products	84,526	2.42
Aircraft	80,270	2.30
Data processing equipment	74,799	2.14
Special transactions	72,127	2.06
Transistors, valves, etc.	70,309	2.01
Telecom equipment, parts	65,005	1.86
ADP machine parts	56,051	1.60

Source: Data from United Nations Conference on Trade and Development: *Handbook of International Trade and Development Statistics, 1994* (TD/STAT.18), p. 172.

RECAP

1. Trade between industrial countries accounts for the bulk of international trade.

2. The most important trading partners of the United States are Canada and Japan.

3. Motor vehicles is the most heavily traded good in the world, in terms of value of exports.

4. World trade is distributed across a great variety of products.

Figure 1
Merchandise Trade Flows in North America (billions of dollars)
In 1996, the United States exported $132 billion worth of goods to Canada and imported $160 billion of goods from Canada. The same year, U.S. merchandise exports to Mexico were $57 billion, while merchandise imports from Mexico were $74 billion.
Source: *Direction of Trade Statistics Yearbook*, 1997, International Monetary Fund. Reprinted by permission of International Monetary Fund.

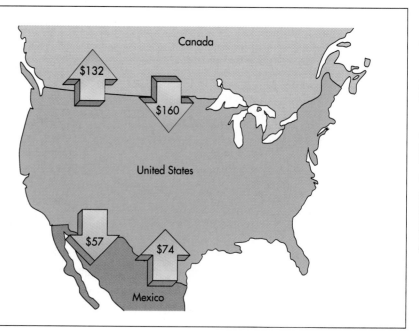

Copyright © by Houghton Mifflin Company. All rights reserved.

Comparative advantage is based on what a country can do relatively better than other countries. This photo shows a woman in Sri Lanka picking tea leaves. Sri Lanka is one of the few countries that export a significant amount of tea. Due to favorable growing conditions (a natural resource), these countries have a comparative advantage in tea production.

2. AN EXAMPLE OF INTERNATIONAL TRADE EQUILIBRIUM

The international economy is very complex. Each country has a unique pattern of trade, in terms both of trading partners and of goods traded. Some countries trade a great deal and others trade very little. We already know that countries specialize and trade according to comparative advantage, but what are the fundamental determinants of international trade that explain the pattern of comparative advantage?

The answer to this question will in turn provide a better understanding of some basic questions about how international trade functions: What goods will be traded? How much will be traded? What prices will prevail for traded goods?

2.a. Comparative Advantage

What determines the goods a nation will export?

absolute advantage:
an advantage derived from one country having a lower absolute input cost of producing a particular good than another country

Comparative advantage is found by comparing the relative costs of production in each country. We measure the cost of producing a particular good in two countries in terms of opportunity costs—what other goods must be given up in order to produce more of the good in question.

Table 4 presents a hypothetical example of two countries, the United States and India, that both produce two goods, wheat and cloth. The table lists the hours of labor required to produce 1 unit of each good. This example assumes that labor productivity differences alone determine comparative advantage. In the United States, 1 unit of wheat requires 3 hours of labor, and 1 unit of cloth requires 6 hours of labor. In India, 1 unit of wheat requires 6 hours of labor, and 1 unit of cloth requires 8 hours of labor.

The United States has an **absolute advantage**—a lower resource cost—in producing both wheat and cloth. Absolute advantage is determined by comparing the absolute cost in different countries of producing each good. Since it requires fewer hours of labor to produce either good in the United States

Copyright © by Houghton Mifflin Company. All rights reserved.

TABLE 4
An Example of Comparative Advantage

Labor Hours Required to Produce One Unit Each of Two Goods		
	U.S.	India
1 unit of wheat	3	6
1 unit of cloth	6	8

than in India, the United States is the more efficient producer of both goods in terms of the domestic labor hours required.

It might seem that since the United States is the more efficient producer of both goods, there would be no need for trade with India. But absolute advantage is not the critical consideration. What matters in determining the benefits of international trade is comparative advantage, as originally discussed in Chapter 2. To find the **comparative advantage**—the lower opportunity cost—we must compare the opportunity cost of producing each good in each country.

comparative advantage: an advantage derived from comparing the opportunity costs of production in two countries

The opportunity cost of producing wheat is what must be given up in cloth using the same resources, or number of labor hours. Look again at Table 4 to see the labor hours required for the production of wheat and cloth in the two countries. If the 3 labor hours it takes to produce wheat in the United States are devoted to cloth production, only 1/2 unit of cloth will result, since 6 labor hours are required to produce a full unit of cloth. The opportunity cost of producing wheat equals 3/6, or 1/2 unit of cloth:

$$\frac{\text{No. of labor hours to produce 1 unit of wheat}}{\text{No. of labor hours to produce 1 unit of cloth}} = \begin{array}{l}\text{opportunity cost of} \\ \text{producing 1 unit of wheat} \\ \text{(in terms of cloth given up)}\end{array}$$

$$3/6 = 1/2$$

Applying the same thinking to India, we find that devoting 6 hours of wheat production to the production of cloth yields 6/8, or 3/4 unit of cloth. The opportunity cost of producing 1 unit of wheat in India is 3/4 unit of cloth.

A comparison of the domestic opportunity costs in each country will reveal which one has the comparative advantage in producing each good. The U.S. opportunity cost of producing 1 unit of wheat is 1/2 unit of cloth; the Indian opportunity cost is 3/4 unit of cloth. Because the United States has a lower domestic opportunity cost, it has the comparative advantage in wheat production and will export wheat. Since wheat production costs are lower in the United States, India is better off trading for wheat rather than trying to produce it domestically.

The comparative advantage in cloth is found the same way. A unit of cloth requires 6 hours of labor in the United States. Since a unit of wheat requires 3 hours of labor, producing 1 more unit of cloth costs 2 units of wheat:

$$\frac{\text{No. of labor hours to produce 1 unit of cloth}}{\text{No. of labor hours to produce 1 unit of wheat}} = \begin{array}{l}\text{opportunity cost of} \\ \text{producing 1 unit of cloth} \\ \text{(in terms of wheat given up)}\end{array}$$

$$6/3 = 2$$

Copyright © by Houghton Mifflin Company. All rights reserved.

In India, 1 unit of cloth requires 8 hours of labor. Since 1 unit of wheat requires 6 hours of labor, shifting 8 hours of labor from wheat production to cloth production means an opportunity cost of 8/6, or 1 1/3 units of wheat for 1 unit of cloth. Comparing the U.S. opportunity cost of 2 units of wheat with the Indian opportunity cost of 1 1/3 units, we see that India has the comparative advantage in cloth production and will therefore export cloth. In this case, the United States is better off trading for cloth than producing it since India's costs of production are lower.

In international trade, as in other areas of economic decision-making, it is opportunity cost that matters—and opportunity costs are reflected in comparative advantage. Absolute advantage is irrelevant, because knowing the absolute number of labor hours required to produce a good does not tell us if we can benefit from trade. We benefit from trade if we are able to obtain a good from a foreign country by giving up less than we would have to give up to obtain the good at home. Because only opportunity cost can allow us to make such comparisons, international trade proceeds on the basis of comparative advantage.

Countries export goods in which they have a comparative advantage.

2.b. Terms of Trade

Based on comparative advantage, India will specialize in cloth production and the United States will specialize in wheat production. The two countries will then trade with each other to satisfy the domestic demand for both goods. International trade permits greater consumption than would be possible from domestic production alone. Since countries trade when they can obtain a good more cheaply from a foreign producer than they can at home, international trade allows all traders to consume more. This is evident when we examine the terms of trade.

terms of trade:
the amount of an exported good that must be given up to obtain one unit of an imported good

The **terms of trade** are the amount of an exported good that must be given up to obtain one unit of an imported good. The Economic Insight "The Dutch Disease" provides a popular example of a dramatic shift in the terms of trade. As you saw earlier, comparative advantage dictates that the United States will specialize in wheat production and export wheat to India in exchange for Indian cloth. But the amount of wheat that the United States will exchange for a unit of cloth is limited by the domestic tradeoffs. If a unit of cloth can be obtained domestically for 2 units of wheat, the United States will be willing to trade with India only if the terms of trade are less than 2 units of wheat for a unit of cloth.

India in turn will be willing to trade its cloth for U.S. wheat only if it can receive a better price than its domestic opportunity costs. Since a unit of cloth in India costs 1⅓ units of wheat, India will gain from trade if it can obtain more than 1⅓ units of wheat for its cloth.

The limits of the terms of trade are determined by the opportunity costs in each country:

1 unit of cloth for more than 1⅓ but less than 2 units of wheat

Within this range, the actual terms of trade will be decided by the bargaining power of the two countries. The closer the United States can come to giving up only 1⅓ units of wheat for cloth, the better the terms of trade for the United States. The closer India can come to receiving 2 units of wheat for its cloth, the better the terms of trade for India.

Copyright © by Houghton Mifflin Company. All rights reserved.

ECONOMIC INSIGHT

The Dutch Disease

The terms of trade are the amount of an export that must be given up for a certain quantity of an import. The price of an import will be equal to its price in the foreign country of origin multiplied by the exchange rate (the domestic-currency price of foreign currency). As the exchange rate changes, the terms of trade will change. This can have important consequences for international trade.

A problem can arise when one export industry in an economy is booming relative to others. In the 1970s, for instance, the Netherlands experienced a boom in its natural gas industry. The dramatic energy price increases of the 1970s resulted in large Dutch exports of natural gas. Increased demand for exports from the Netherlands caused the Dutch currency to appreciate, making Dutch goods more expensive for foreign buyers. This situation caused the terms of trade to worsen for the Netherlands. Although the natural gas sector boomed, Dutch manufacturing was finding it difficult to compete in the world market.

The phenomenon of a boom in one industry causing declines in the rest of the economy is popularly called the Dutch Disease. It is usually associated with dramatic increases in the demand for a primary commodity and can afflict any nation experiencing such a boom. For instance, a rapid rise in the demand for coffee could lead to a Dutch Disease problem for Colombia, where a coffee boom would be accompanied by decline in other sectors of the economy.

Though each country would like to push the other as close to the limits of the terms of trade as possible, any terms within the limits set by domestic opportunity costs will be mutually beneficial. Both countries benefit because they are able to consume goods at a cost less than their domestic opportunity costs. To illustrate the *gains from trade*, let us assume that the actual terms of trade are 1 unit of cloth for 1½ units of wheat.

Suppose the United States has 60 hours of labor, half of which goes to wheat production and the other half to cloth production. Since a unit of wheat requires 3 labor hours, 10 units of wheat are produced. Cloth requires 6 labor hours, so 5 units of cloth are produced. Without international trade, the United States can produce and consume 10 units of wheat and 5 units of cloth. If the United States, with its comparative advantage in wheat production, chooses to produce only wheat, it can use all 60 labor hours to produce 20 units. If the terms of trade are 1½ units of wheat per unit of cloth, the United States can keep 10 units of wheat and trade the other 10 for 6⅔ units of cloth (10 divided by 1½). By trading U.S. wheat for Indian cloth, the United States is able to consume more than it could without trade. With no trade, and half its labor hours devoted to each good, the United States could consume 10 units of wheat and 5 units of cloth. After trade, the United States consumes 10 units of wheat and 6⅔ units of cloth. By devoting all its labor hours to wheat production and trading wheat for cloth, the United States gains 1⅔ units of cloth. This is the gain from trade—an increase in consumption, as summarized in Table 5.

The gain from trade is increased consumption.

2.c. Export Supply and Import Demand

The preceding example suggests that countries all benefit from specialization and trade. Realistically, however, countries do not completely specialize.

Copyright © by Houghton Mifflin Company. All rights reserved.

TABLE 5
Hypothetical Example of U.S. Gains from Specialization and Trade

> **Without International Trade**
> 30 labor hours in wheat production: produce and consume 10 wheat
> 30 labor hours in cloth production: produce and consume 5 cloth
>
> **With Specialization and Trade**
> 60 labor hours in wheat production: produce 20 wheat and consume 10; trade 10 wheat for 6⅔ cloth
>
> **Before trade:** consume 10 wheat and 5 cloth
>
> **After trade:** consume 10 wheat and 6⅔ cloth;
> gain 1⅔ cloth by specialization and trade

Typically, domestic industries satisfy part of the domestic demand for goods that are also imported. To understand how the quantity of goods traded is determined, we must construct demand and supply curves for each country, and use them to create export supply and import demand curves.

The proportion of domestic demand for a good that is satisfied by domestic production and the proportion that will be satisfied by imports are determined by the domestic supply and demand curves and the international equilibrium price of a good. The international equilibrium price and quantity may be determined once we know the export supply and import demand curves for each country. These curves are derived from the domestic supply and demand in each country. Figure 2 illustrates the derivation of the export supply and import demand curves.

Figure 2(a) shows the domestic supply and demand curves for the U.S. wheat market. The domestic equilibrium price is $6 and the domestic equilibrium quantity is 200 million bushels. (The domestic "no-trade" equilibrium price is the price that exists prior to international trade.) A price above $6 will yield a U.S. wheat surplus. For instance, at a price of $9, the U.S. surplus will be 200 million bushels. A price below equilibrium will produce a wheat shortage: at a price of $3, the shortage will be 200 million bushels. The key point here is that the world price of a good may be quite different than the domestic "no-trade" equilibrium price. And once international trade occurs, the world price will prevail in the domestic economy.

If the world price of wheat is different than a country's domestic "no-trade" equilibrium price, the country will become an exporter or importer. For instance, if the world price is above the domestic "no-trade" equilibrium price, the domestic surplus can be exported to the rest of the world. Figure 2(b) shows the U.S. **export supply curve**. This curve illustrates the U.S. domestic surplus of wheat for prices above the domestic "no-trade" equilibrium price of $6. At a world price of $9, the United States would supply 200 million bushels of wheat to the rest of the world. The export supply is equal to the domestic surplus. The higher the world price above the domestic "no-trade" equilibrium, the greater the quantity of wheat exported by the United States.

export supply curve:
a curve showing the relationship between the world price of a good and the amount that a country will export

Copyright © by Houghton Mifflin Company. All rights reserved.

Figure 2
The Import Demand and Export Supply Curves

Figures 2(a) and 2(c) show the domestic demand and supply curves for wheat in the United States and India, respectively. The domestic "no-trade" equilibrium price is $6 in the United States and $12 in India. Any price above the domestic "no-trade" equilibrium prices will create domestic surpluses, which are reflected in the export supply curves in Figures 2(b) and 2(d). Any price below the domestic "no-trade" equilibrium prices will create domestic shortages, which are reflected in the import demand curves in Figures 2(b) and 2(d).

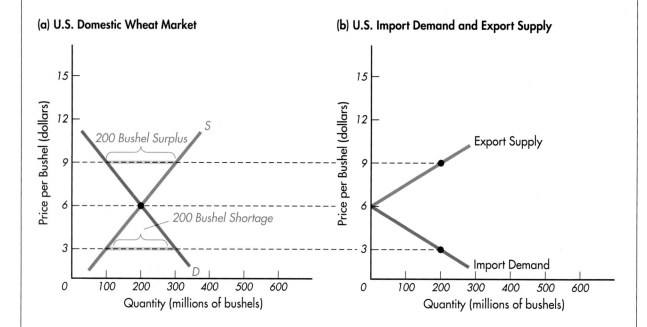

(a) U.S. Domestic Wheat Market

(b) U.S. Import Demand and Export Supply

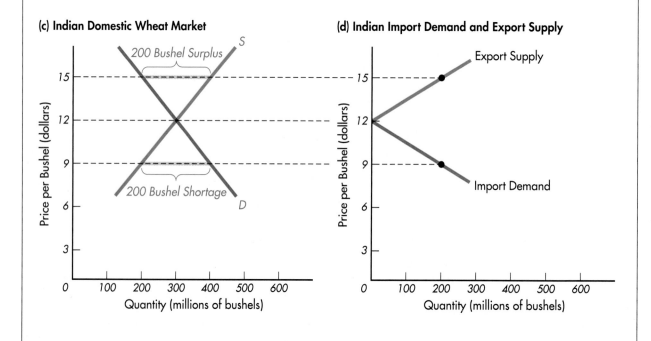

(c) Indian Domestic Wheat Market

(d) Indian Import Demand and Export Supply

Copyright © by Houghton Mifflin Company. All rights reserved.

import demand curve:
a curve showing the relationship between the world price of a good and the amount that a country will import

If the world price of wheat is below the domestic "no-trade" equilibrium price, the United States will import wheat. The **import demand curve** is the amount of the U.S. shortage at various prices below the "no-trade" equilibrium. In Figure 2(b), the import demand curve is a downward-sloping line, indicating that the lower the price below the domestic "no-trade" equilibrium of $6, the greater the quantity of wheat imported by the United States. At a price of $3, the United States will import 200 million bushels.

The domestic supply and demand curves and the export supply and import demand curves for India appear as parts (c) and (d) of Figure 2. The domestic "no-trade" equilibrium price in India is $12. At this price, India would neither import nor export any wheat because the domestic demand would be satisfied by domestic supply. The export supply curve for India is shown in Figure 2(d) as an upward-sloping line that measures the amount of the domestic surplus as the price level rises above the domestic "no-trade" equilibrium price of $12. According to Figure 2(c), if the world price of wheat is $15, the domestic surplus in India is equal to 200 million bushels. The corresponding point on the export supply curve indicates that, at a price of $15, 200 million bushels will be exported. The import demand curve for India reflects the domestic shortage at a price below the domestic "no-trade" equilibrium price. At $9, the domestic shortage is equal to 200 million bushels: the import demand curve indicates that, at $9, 200 million bushels will be imported.

2.d. The World Equilibrium Price and Quantity Traded

How are the equilibrium price and the quantity of goods traded determined?

The international equilibrium price of wheat and the quantity of wheat traded are found by combining the import demand and export supply curves for the United States and India, as in Figure 3. International equilibrium occurs if the quantity of imports demanded by one country is equal to the quantity of exports supplied by the other country. In Figure 3, this equilibrium occurs at the point labeled *e*. At this point, the import demand curve for India indicates that India wants to import 200 million bushels at a price of $9. The export

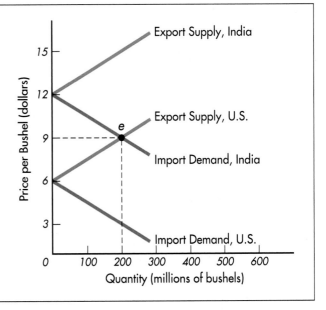

Figure 3
International Equilibrium Price and Quantity
The international equilibrium price is the price at which the export supply curve of the United States intersects with the import demand curve of India. At the equilibrium price of $9, the United States will export 200 million bushels to India.

Copyright © by Houghton Mifflin Company. All rights reserved.

International equilibrium occurs at the point where the quantity of imports demanded by one country is equal to the quantity of exports supplied by the other country.

supply curve for the United States indicates that the United States wants to export 200 million bushels at a price of $9. Only at $9 will the quantity of wheat demanded by the importing nation equal the quantity of wheat supplied by the exporting nation. So the equilibrium world price of wheat is $9 and the equilibrium quantity of wheat traded is 200 million bushels.

RECAP

1. Comparative advantage is based on the relative opportunity costs of producing goods in different countries.

2. A country has an absolute advantage when it can produce a good for a lower input cost than can other nations.

3. A country has a comparative advantage when the opportunity cost of producing a good, in terms of forgone output of other goods, is lower than that of other nations.

4. The terms of trade are the amount of an export good that must be given up to obtain one unit of an import good.

5. The limits of the terms of trade are determined by the domestic opportunity costs of production in each country.

6. The export supply and import demand curves measure the domestic surplus and shortage, respectively, at different world prices.

7. International equilibrium occurs at the point where one country's import demand curve intersects with the export supply curve of another country.

3. SOURCES OF COMPARATIVE ADVANTAGE

What are the sources of comparative advantage?

We know that countries specialize and trade in accordance with comparative advantage, but what gives a country a comparative advantage? Economists have suggested several theories of the source of comparative advantage. Let us review these theories.

3.a. Productivity Differences

The example of comparative advantage earlier in this chapter showed the United States to have a comparative advantage in wheat production and India to have a comparative advantage in cloth production. Comparative advantage was determined by differences in the labor hours required to produce each good. In this example, differences in the *productivity* of labor accounted for comparative advantage.

Comparative advantage due to productivity differences between countries is often called the Ricardian model of comparative advantage.

For over two hundred years, economists have argued that productivity differences account for comparative advantage. In fact, this theory of comparative advantage is often called the *Ricardian model*, after David Ricardo, a nineteenth-century English economist who explained and analyzed the idea of productivity-based comparative advantage. Variation in the productivity of labor can explain many observed trade patterns in the world.

Copyright © by Houghton Mifflin Company. All rights reserved.

Although we know that labor productivity differs across countries—and that this can help explain why countries produce the goods they do—there are factors other than labor productivity that determine comparative advantage. Furthermore, even if labor productivity were all that mattered, we would still want to know why some countries have more productive workers than others. The standard interpretation of the Ricardian model is that technological differences between countries account for differences in labor productivity. The countries with the most advanced technology would have a comparative advantage with regard to those goods that can be produced most efficiently with modern technology.

3.b. Factor Abundance

Goods differ in terms of the resources, or factors of production, required for their production. Countries differ in terms of the abundance of different factors of production: land, labor, capital, and entrepreneurial ability. It seems self-evident that countries would have an advantage in producing those goods that use relatively large amounts of their most abundant factor of production. Certainly countries with a relatively large amount of farmland would have a comparative advantage in agriculture, and countries with a relatively large amount of capital would tend to specialize in the production of manufactured goods.

Comparative advantage based on differences in the abundance of factors of production across countries is described in the Heckscher-Ohlin model.

The idea that comparative advantage is based on the relative abundance of factors of production is sometimes called the *Heckscher-Ohlin model*, after the two Swedish economists, Eli Heckscher and Bertil Ohlin, who developed the original argument. The original model assumed that countries possess only two factors of production: labor and capital. Thus, researchers have examined the labor and capital requirements of various industries to see whether labor-abundant countries export goods whose production is relatively labor-intensive, and capital-abundant countries export goods that are relatively capital-intensive. In many cases, factor abundance has served well as an explanation of observed trade patterns. However, there remain cases in which comparative advantage seems to run counter to the predictions of the factor-abundance theory. In response, economists have suggested other explanations for comparative advantage.

3.c. Other Theories of Comparative Advantage

New theories of comparative advantage have typically come about in an effort to explain the trade pattern in some narrow category of products. They are not intended to serve as general explanations of comparative advantage, as do factor abundance and productivity. These supplementary theories emphasize human skills, product cycles, and preferences.

Human skills This approach emphasizes differences across countries in the availability of skilled and unskilled labor. The basic idea is that countries with a relatively abundant stock of highly skilled labor will have a comparative advantage in producing goods that require relatively large amounts of skilled labor. This theory is similar to the factor-abundance theory, except that here the analysis rests on two segments (skilled and unskilled) of the labor factor.

The human-skills argument is consistent with the observation that most U.S. exports are produced in high-wage (skilled-labor) industries and most

Copyright © by Houghton Mifflin Company. All rights reserved.

U.S. imports are products produced in relatively low-wage industries. Since the United States has a well-educated labor force, relative to many other countries, we would expect the United States to have a comparative advantage in industries requiring a large amount of skilled labor. Developing countries would be expected to have a comparative advantage in industries requiring a relatively large amount of unskilled labor.

Product life cycles   This theory explains how comparative advantage in a specific good can shift over time from one country to another. This occurs because goods experience a *product life cycle*. At the outset, development and testing are required to conceptualize and design the product. For this reason, the early production will be undertaken by an innovative firm. Over time, however, a successful product tends to become standardized, in the sense that many manufacturers can produce it. The mature product may be produced by firms that do little or no research and development, specializing instead in copying successful products invented and developed by others.

The product-life-cycle theory is related to international comparative advantage in that a new product will be first produced and exported by the nation in which it was invented. As the product is exported elsewhere and foreign firms become familiar with it, the technology is copied in other countries by foreign firms seeking to produce a competing version. As the product matures, comparative advantage shifts away from the country of origin if other countries have lower manufacturing costs using the now-standardized technology.

The history of color television production shows how comparative advantage can shift over the product life cycle. Color television was invented in the United States, and U.S. firms initially produced and exported color TVs. Over time, as the technology of color television manufacturing became well known, countries like Japan and Taiwan came to dominate the business. Firms in these countries had a comparative advantage over U.S. firms in the manufacture of color televisions. Once the technology is widely available, countries with lower production costs, due to lower wages, can compete effectively against the higher-wage nation that developed the technology.

Preferences   The theories of comparative advantage we have looked at so far have all been based on supply factors. It may be, though, that the demand side of the market can explain some of the patterns observed in international trade. Seldom are different producers' goods exactly identical. Consumers may prefer the goods of one firm to those of another firm. Domestic firms usually produce goods to satisfy domestic consumers. But since different consumers have different preferences, some consumers will prefer goods produced by foreign firms. International trade allows consumers to expand their consumption opportunities.

Consumers who live in countries with similar levels of development can be expected to have similar consumption patterns. The consumption patterns of consumers in countries at much different levels of development are much less similar. This would suggest that firms in industrial countries will find a larger market for their goods in other industrial countries than in developing countries.

As you saw earlier in this chapter, industrial countries tend to trade with other industrial countries. This pattern runs counter to the factor-abundance

Manufactured goods have life cycles. At first they are produced by the firm that invented them. Later, they may be produced by firms in other countries that copy the technology of the innovator.

Copyright © by Houghton Mifflin Company. All rights reserved.

theory of comparative advantage, which would suggest that countries with the most dissimilar endowments of resources would find trade most beneficial. Yet rich countries, with large supplies of capital and skilled labor forces, trade more actively with other rich countries than they do with poor countries. Firms in industrial countries tend to produce goods that relatively wealthy consumers will buy. The key point here is that we do not live in a world based on simple comparative advantage, in which all cloth is identical, regardless of the producer. We inhabit a world of differentiated products, and consumers want choices between different brands or styles of a seemingly similar good.

intraindustry trade:
simultaneous import and export of goods in the same industry by a particular country

Another feature of international trade that may be explained by consumer preference is **intraindustry trade**, a circumstance in which a country both exports and imports goods in the same industry. The fact that the United States exports Budweiser beer and imports Heineken beer is not surprising when preferences are taken into account. Supply-side theories of comparative advantage rarely provide an explanation of intraindustry trade, since they would expect each country to export only those goods produced in industries in which a comparative advantage exists. Yet the real world is characterized by a great deal of intraindustry trade.

We have discussed several potential sources of comparative advantage: labor productivity, factor abundance, human skills, product cycles, and preferences. Each of these theories, summarized in Figure 4, has proven useful in understanding certain trade patterns. Each has also been shown to have limitations as a general theory applicable to all cases. Once again we are reminded that the world is a very complicated place. Theories are simpler than reality. Nevertheless, they help us to understand how comparative advantage arises.

RECAP

1. Comparative advantage can arise because of differences in labor productivity.
2. Countries differ in their resource endowments, and a given country may enjoy a comparative advantage in products that intensively use its most abundant factor of production.
3. Industrial countries may have a comparative advantage in products requiring a large amount of skilled labor. Developing countries may have a comparative advantage in products requiring a large amount of unskilled labor.
4. Comparative advantage in a new good initially resides in the country that invented the good. Over time, other nations learn the technology and may gain a comparative advantage in producing the good.
5. In some industries, consumer preferences for differentiated goods may explain international trade flows, including intraindustry trade.

Copyright © by Houghton Mifflin Company. All rights reserved.

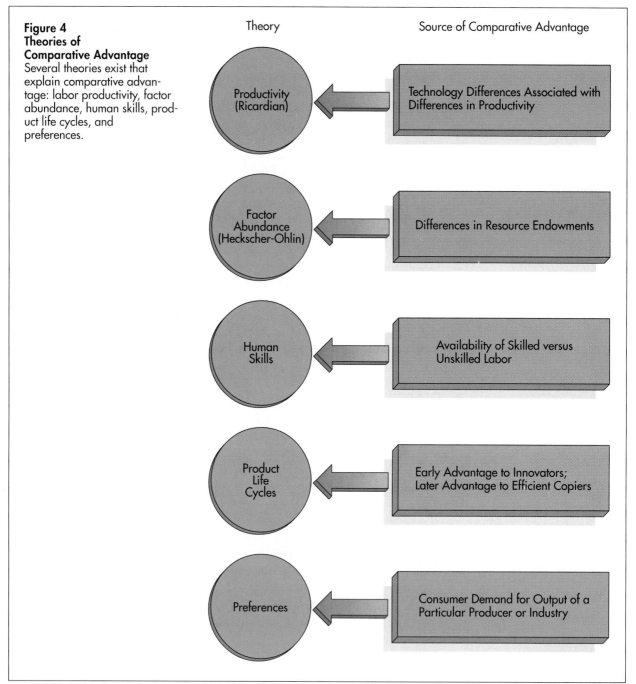

Figure 4
Theories of
Comparative Advantage
Several theories exist that explain comparative advantage: labor productivity, factor abundance, human skills, product life cycles, and preferences.

Theory | Source of Comparative Advantage

Productivity (Ricardian) ← Technology Differences Associated with Differences in Productivity

Factor Abundance (Heckscher-Ohlin) ← Differences in Resource Endowments

Human Skills ← Availability of Skilled versus Unskilled Labor

Product Life Cycles ← Early Advantage to Innovators; Later Advantage to Efficient Copiers

Preferences ← Consumer Demand for Output of a Particular Producer or Industry

Copyright © by Houghton Mifflin Company. All rights reserved.

SUMMARY

What are the prevailing patterns of trade between countries? What goods are traded?

1. International trade flows largely between industrial countries. §1.a

2. International trade involves many diverse products, but crude petroleum accounts for more than 5 percent of its total value. §1.b

███ What determines the goods a nation will export?

3. Comparative advantage is based on the opportunity costs of production. §2.a

4. Domestic opportunity costs determine the limits of the terms of trade between two countries—that is, the amount of exports that must be given up to obtain imports. §2.b

5. The export supply curve shows the domestic surplus and amount of exports available at alternative world prices. §2.c

6. The import demand curve shows the domestic shortage and amount of imports demanded at alternative world prices. §2.c

███ How are the equilibrium price and the quantity of goods traded determined?

7. The international equilibrium price and quantity of a good traded are determined by the intersection of the export supply of one country with the import demand of another country. §2.d

███ What are the sources of comparative advantage?

8. The productivity-differences and factor-abundance theories of comparative advantage are general theories that seek to explain patterns of international trade flow. §3.a, 3.b

9. Other theories of comparative advantage aimed at explaining trade in particular kinds of goods focus on human skills, product life cycles, and consumer preferences. §3.c

KEY TERMS

absolute advantage §2.a
comparative advantage §2.a
terms of trade §2.b

export supply curve §2.c
import demand curve §2.c
intraindustry trade §3.c

EXERCISES

1. Why must voluntary trade between two countries be mutually beneficial?

   Use the following table to answer questions 2–6.

   **Labor Hours Required to Produce
   One Unit of Each Good**

	Canada	*Japan*
Beef	2	4
Computers	6	5

2. Which country has the absolute advantage in beef production?

3. Which country has the absolute advantage in computer production?

4. Which country has the comparative advantage in beef production?

5. Which country has the comparative advantage in computer production?

Copyright © by Houghton Mifflin Company. All rights reserved.

6. What are the limits of the terms of trade? Specifically, when is Canada willing to trade with Japan, and when is Japan willing to trade with Canada?

7. Use the following supply and demand schedule for two countries to determine the international equilibrium price of shoes. How many shoes will be traded?

Demand and Supply of Shoes (1,000s)

	Mexico		Chile	
Price	Qty. Demanded	Qty. Supplied	Qty. Demanded	Qty. Supplied
$10	40	0	50	0
20	35	20	40	10
30	30	40	30	20
40	25	60	20	30
50	20	80	10	40

8. How would each of the following theories of comparative advantage explain the fact that the United States exports computers?

a. Productivity differences

b. Factor abundance

c. Human skills

d. Product life cycle

e. Preferences

9. Which of the theories of comparative advantage could explain why the United States exports computers to Japan at the same time that it imports computers from Japan? Explain.

10. Developing countries have complained that the terms of trade they face are unfavorable. If they voluntarily engage in international trade, what do you suppose they mean by "unfavorable terms of trade"?

11. If two countries reach equilibrium in their domestic markets at the same price, what can be said about their export supply and import demand curves and about the international trade equilibrium?

Copyright © by Houghton Mifflin Company. All rights reserved.

Section 1.b of this chapter presented data on the most important goods traded internationally. To see how the trade of the United States compares with the world's, go to the Boyes/Melvin web site at **http://www.hmco.com/college/** and click on the internet exercise link for this chapter. Now answer the questions that appear on the web page.

Copyright © by Houghton Mifflin Company. All rights reserved.

Stop U.S.-Japan Squabbling over Trade

The United States and Japan stand at the brink of another trade war. If the two governments can't agree by Wednesday on the specifics of an agreement reached in October, the United States could well begin a trade action that would limit Japan's access to the U.S. market.

These sanctions would disrupt Japanese-American trade, increase the price of imported Japanese goods and hurt U.S. consumers. If the agreement is reached, however, it will create more jobs there and help open closed Japanese markets.

At the heart of the dispute is foot-dragging by the Japanese on the import of flat glass from the United States and other countries. Japan is the second-largest flat-glass market in the world, consuming $4.5 billion worth of glass each year in homes, office buildings and autos.

U.S. glass manufacturers are the most efficient in the world and account for 20% to 30% of most markets. In the traditionally closed Japanese market, however, U.S.-based companies account for less than 1%.

That's because three major Japanese glass producers have such close ties with distributors that it is virtually impossible for U.S. manufacturers to bring their product to market. Government-imposed barriers are not the problem. Foreigners are shut out by the government's toleration of anti-competitive practices.

To their credit, the Bush and Clinton administrations have worked diligently to open Japanese markets to our products. The office of U.S. Trade Representative Mickey Kantor has been seeking to erode the effect of these traditional relationships.

While opening the flat-glass market won't erase the $60 billion-per-year U.S.-Japan trade imbalance, it is a step in the right direction.

If Japan imports more glass, our company alone is likely to hire more than 300 additional employees. Our suppliers could add as many as 700 more. Plants from Fullerton and Fresno, Calif., to Corsicana, Texas, Richburg, S.C., and even Thailand will gear up. In return, the Japanese construction industry will get a wider choice of quality products at lower costs.

Some urge Washington to focus instead on broader reforms of the Japanese economy. Rather than push for reforms in sectors such as flat glass, computer chips or telephones, these critics want the United States to demand that Japan take steps in areas such as deregulation and tax policy that would affect its entire economy.

We strongly believe the sector-by-sector approach is working and should be continued. It recognizes the unique complexities of Japan's marketplace and the particular needs of its producers and consumers. Each successful agreement creates new pressure in Japan to open other markets.

If agreement cannot be reached, there will be heavy pressure on the Clinton administration to use U.S. trade laws to take stronger action, possibly retaliating against Japanese imports. This would be a shame in light of the mutual benefits that a more open Japanese market would bring.

Source: "Stop U.S.-Japan Squabbling over Trade," Ralph Gerson, *USA Today*, December 5, 1994, p. 12A. Reprinted by permission of Ralph Gerson, Executive Vice President of Guardian Industries Corp., Auburn Hills, Michigan.

Copyright © by Houghton Mifflin Company. All rights reserved.

COMMENTARY

There is no lack of stories in the American media on the threat of Japanese economic domination. As this article indicates, many people see the solution coming from more open Japanese markets and point to the large U.S. trade deficit with Japan as evidence that a problem exists.

However, the bilateral trade accounts provide little, if any, information on such issues. Indeed, it is easy to think of an example in which a country has a persistent trade deficit with one of its trading partners but has its overall trade account in balance. Suppose there are three countries that trade among themselves, which we will call countries A, B, and C. The people of each country produce only one type of good and consume only one other type of good. The people of country A produce apples and consume bananas, the people of country B produce bananas and consume cucumbers, and the people of country C produce cucumbers and consume apples. Even when the trade account of each country is balanced, each has a deficit with one of its trading partners and a surplus with the other. Furthermore, a larger trade deficit between countries A and B (with each country retaining balanced trade) implies that the people of country A are better off since they are consuming more. If the government of country A tried to impose a law forcing bilateral trade balance with country B, citizens of country A could not consume as many bananas as before and would be forced to attempt to sell apples to the uninterested citizens of country B.

This simple example demonstrates that the U.S. trade deficit with Japan should not in itself be a cause for concern, especially if the overall trade deficit is shrinking. The United States could have a persistent trade deficit with Japan and yet maintain an overall balanced trade account. In fact,

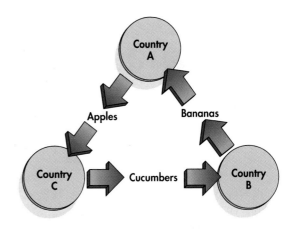

any country would be expected to have a trade deficit with some countries and a trade surplus with others. This reflects comparative advantage. Trade between countries makes both the exporting and the importing countries better off. Rather than point to the U.S. trade deficit with Japan as the problem, it is useful to have anecdotes like the one on the Japanese glass market to establish the existence of a problem. Clearly, U.S. glass producers would benefit from more open access to the Japanese market. Policymakers should be concerned with negotiating the removal of trade barriers rather than bilateral trade deficits.

This is not to say that concern about the overall trade deficit is not well founded. An overall trade deficit indicates that a country is consuming more than it is producing. At any particular time, a country may want to run a trade deficit or a trade surplus, depending on the circumstances it faces. But regardless of the overall trade account of a country, we should expect bilateral trade imbalances among trading partners.

Copyright © by Houghton Mifflin Company. All rights reserved.

21

International Trade Restrictions

1. Why do countries restrict international trade?

2. How do countries restrict the entry of foreign goods and promote the export of domestic goods?

3. What sorts of agreements do countries enter into to reduce barriers to international trade?

Copyright © by Houghton Mifflin Company. All rights reserved.

The Japanese government once announced that foreign-made skis would not be allowed into Japan because they were unsafe. Japanese ski manufacturers were active supporters of the ban. The U.S. government once imposed a tax of almost 50 percent on imports of motorcycles with engines larger than 700cc. The only U.S.-owned motorcycle manufacturer, Harley-Davidson, produced no motorcycles with engines smaller than 1,000cc and so did not care about the small-engine market. In the mid-1980s, Britain began replacing the distinctive red steel telephone booths that were used all through the country with new booths. Many U.S. residents were interested in buying an old British phone booth to use as a decorative novelty, so the phone booths were exported to the United States. However, when the phone booths arrived, the U.S. Customs Service impounded them because there was a limit on the amount of iron and steel products that could be exported from Britain to the United States. The phone booths would be allowed to enter the country only if British exports of some other iron and steel products were reduced. The British exporters protested the classification of the phone booths as iron and steel products and argued that they should be considered antiques (which have no import restrictions). The phone booths were not reclassified, so as a result, few have entered the United States, and prices of old British phone booths have been in the thousands of dollars. There are many examples of government policy influencing the prices and quantities of goods traded internationally.

International trade is rarely determined solely by comparative advantage and the free market forces of supply and demand. Governments often find that political pressures favor policies that at least partially offset the prevailing comparative advantages. Government policy aimed at influencing international trade flows is called **commercial policy**. This chapter first examines the arguments in support of commercial policy and then discusses the various tools of commercial policy employed by governments. ∎

commercial policy:
government policy that influences international trade flows

1. ARGUMENTS FOR PROTECTION

Why do countries restrict international trade?

Governments restrict foreign trade to protect domestic producers from foreign competition. In some cases the protection may be justified; in most cases it harms consumers. Of the arguments used to promote such protection, only a

Preview

Copyright © by Houghton Mifflin Company. All rights reserved.

few are valid. We will look first at arguments widely considered to have little or no merit, and then at those that may sometimes be valid.

International trade on the basis of comparative advantage maximizes world output and allows consumers access to better-quality products at lower prices than would be available in the domestic market alone. If trade is restricted, consumers pay higher prices for lower-quality goods, and world output declines. Protection from foreign competition imposes costs on the domestic economy as well as on foreign producers. When production does not proceed on the basis of comparative advantage, resources are not expended on their most efficient uses. Whenever government restrictions alter the pattern of trade, we should expect someone to benefit and someone else to suffer. Generally speaking, protection from foreign competition benefits domestic producers at the expense of domestic consumers.

Protection from foreign competition generally benefits domestic producers at the expense of domestic consumers.

1.a. Creation of Domestic Jobs

If foreign goods are kept out of the domestic economy, it is often argued, jobs will be created at home. This argument holds that domestic firms will produce the goods that otherwise would have been produced abroad, thus employing domestic workers instead of foreign workers. The weakness of this argument is that only the protected industry would benefit in terms of employment. Since domestic consumers will pay higher prices to buy the output of the protected industry, they will have less to spend on other goods and services, which could cause employment in other industries to drop. If other countries retaliate by restricting entry of U.S. exports, the output of U.S. firms that produce for export will fall as well. Typically, restrictions to "save domestic jobs" simply redistribute jobs by creating employment in the protected industry and reducing employment elsewhere.

Saving domestic jobs from foreign competition may cost domestic consumers more than it benefits the protected industries.

Table 1 shows estimates of consumer costs and producer gains associated with protection in certain U.S. industries. The first column lists the total cost to U.S. consumers, in terms of higher prices paid, for each industry. For instance, the consumer cost of protecting U.S. book manufacturing is $500 million. The second column lists the cost to consumers of saving one job in each industry (found by dividing the total consumer cost by the number of jobs saved by protection). In book manufacturing, each job saved costs U.S. consumers $100,000. The gain to U.S. producers appears in the third column. Government protection of book manufacturers allowed them to gain $305 million. This gain is less than the costs to consumers of $500 million.

Table 2 shows the annual cost to the United States of import restrictions in terms of reduced GDP as estimated by an agency of the U.S. government. The total estimated amount of $18,976 million means that U.S. GDP would be almost $19 billion higher without import restrictions.

Tables 1 and 2 demonstrate the very high cost per job saved by protection. If the costs to consumers are greater than the benefits to protected industries, you may wonder why government provides any protection aimed at saving jobs. The answer, in a word, is politics. Protection of book manufacturing means that all consumers pay a higher price for books. But the individual consumer does not know how much of the book's price is due to protection, and consumers rarely lobby their political representatives to eliminate protec-

Copyright © by Houghton Mifflin Company. All rights reserved.

TABLE 1
Benefits and Costs of Protection from Foreign Competition: Some U.S. Case Histories

Case	Consumer Losses		Producer Gains
	Totals (million dollars)	Per Job Saved[1] (dollars)	Totals (million dollars)
Manufacturing			
Book manufacturing	$ 500	$ 100,000	$ 305
Benzenoid chemicals	2,650	Over 1 million	2,250
Glassware	200	200,000	130
Rubber footwear	230	30,000	90
Ceramic articles	95	47,500	25
Ceramic tiles	116	135,000	62
Orange juice	525	240,000	390
Canned tuna	91	76,000	74
Textiles and apparel: Phase I	9,400	22,000	8,700
Textiles and apparel: Phase II	20,000	37,000	18,000
Textiles and apparel: Phase III	27,000	42,000	22,000
Carbon steel: Phase I	1,970	240,000	1,330
Carbon steel: Phase II	4,350	620,000	2,770
Carbon steel: Phase III	6,800	750,000	3,800
Ball bearings	45	90,000	21
Specialty steel	520	1,000,000	420
Nonrubber footwear	700	55,000	250
Color televisions	420	420,000	190
CB radios	55	93,000	14
Bolts, nuts, large screws	110	550,000	60
Prepared mushrooms	35	117,000	13
Automobiles	5,800	105,000	2,600
Motorcycles	104	150,000	67
Services			
Maritime industries	3,000	270,000	2,000
Agriculture and fisheries			
Sugar	930	60,000 (690/acre)	550
Dairy products	5,500	220,000 (1,800/cow)	5,000
Peanuts	170	1,000/acre	170
Meat	1,800	160,000 (225/head)	1,600
Fish	560	21,000	200
Mining			
Petroleum	6,900	160,000	4,800
Lead and zinc	67	30,000	46

[1]Unless otherwise specified, figures are per worker.

Sources: Cletus C. Coughlin, et al., "Protectionist Trade Policies: A Survey of Theory, Evidence, and Rationale," *Federal Reserve Bank of St. Louis Review* (January/February 1988), p. 18; and Gary Clyde Hufbauer et al., *Trade Protection in the United States: 31 Case Studies* (Washington, D.C.; Institute for International Economics, 1986).

Copyright © by Houghton Mifflin Company. All rights reserved.

TABLE 2
Annual Reduction in U.S. GDP Imposed by U.S. Import Restrictions

Sector	GDP Gain (million dollars)
Simultaneous liberalization of all restraints	18,976
Individual liberalization:	
Textiles and apparel	15,845
Maritime transport (Jones Act)	3,086
Dairy	847
Sugar	657
Peanuts	353
Meat	177
Nonrubber footwear	170
Watches, clocks, and parts	101
Ball and roller bearings, and parts	45
Pressed and blown glass	44
Costume jewelry and costume novelties	42
Machine tools	31
Cyclic organic crudes and intermediates	24
Frozen fruit, fruit juices, and vegetables	13
Ceramic wall and floor tile	12
Personal leather goods	7
Electronic capacitors	5
Leather gloves and mittens	2
China tableware	2

Source: *The Economic Effects of Significant U.S. Imports Restraints* (U.S. International Trade Commission, 1993), p. ix.

tion and reduce prices. Meanwhile, there is a great deal of pressure for protection. Employers and workers in the industry know the benefits of protection: higher prices for their output, higher profits for owners, and higher wages for workers. As a result, there will be active lobbying for protection against foreign competition.

1.b. Creation of a "Level Playing Field"

Special interest groups sometimes claim that other nations that export successfully to the home market have unfair advantages over domestic producers. Fairness, however, is often in the eye of the beholder. People who call for creating a "level playing field" believe that the domestic government should take steps to offset the perceived advantage of the foreign firm. They often claim that foreign firms have an unfair advantage because foreign workers are willing to work for very low wages. "Fair trade, not free trade" is the cry that this claim generates. But advocates of fair trade are really claiming that production in accordance with comparative advantage is unfair. This is clearly wrong. A country with relatively low wages is typically a country with an

Copyright © by Houghton Mifflin Company. All rights reserved.

abundance of low-skilled labor. Such a country will have a comparative advantage in products that use low-skilled labor most intensively. To create a "level playing field" by imposing restrictions that eliminate the comparative advantage of foreign firms will make domestic consumers worse off and undermine the basis for specialization and economic efficiency.

Some calls for "fair trade" are based on the notion of reciprocity. If a country imposes import restrictions on goods from a country that does not have similar restrictions, reciprocal tariffs and quotas may be called for in the latter country in order to stimulate a reduction of trade restrictions in the former country. For instance, it has been claimed that U.S. construction firms are discriminated against in Japan, because no U.S. firm has had a major construction project in Japan since the 1960s. Yet Japanese construction firms do billions of dollars' worth of business in the United States each year. Advocates of fair trade could argue that U.S. restrictions should be imposed on Japanese construction firms.

One danger of calls for fairness based on reciprocity is that calls for fair trade may be invoked in cases where, in fact, foreign restrictions on U.S. imports do not exist. For instance, suppose the U.S. auto industry wanted to restrict the entry of imported autos to help stimulate sales of domestically produced cars. One strategy might be to point out that U.S. auto sales abroad had fallen and to claim that this was due to unfair treatment of U.S. auto exports in other countries. Of course, there are many other possible reasons why foreign sales of U.S. autos might have fallen. But blaming foreign trade restrictions might win political support for restricting imports of foreign cars into the United States.

Calls for "fair trade" are typically aimed at imposing restrictions to match those imposed by other nations.

1.c. Government Revenue Creation

Developing countries often justify tariffs as an important source of government revenue.

Tariffs on trade generate government revenue. Industrial countries, which find income taxes easy to collect, rarely justify tariffs on the basis of the revenue they generate for government spending. But many developing countries find income taxes difficult to levy and collect, while tariffs are easy to collect. Customs agents can be positioned at ports of entry to examine all goods that enter and leave the country. The observability of trade flows makes tariffs a popular tax in developing countries, whose revenue requirements may provide a valid justification for their existence. Table 3 shows that tariffs account for a relatively large fraction of government revenue in many developing countries, and only a small fraction in industrial countries.

1.d. National Defense

Industries that are truly critical to the national defense should be protected from foreign competition if that is the only way to ensure their existence.

It has long been argued that industries crucial to the national defense, like shipbuilding, should be protected from foreign competition. Even though the United States does not have a comparative advantage in shipbuilding, a domestic shipbuilding industry is necessary since foreign-made ships may not be available during war. This is a valid argument as long as the protected industry is genuinely critical to the national defense. In some industries, like copper or other basic metals, it might make more sense to import the crucial products during peacetime and store them for use in the event of war; these products do not require domestic production to be useful. Care must be taken

Copyright © by Houghton Mifflin Company. All rights reserved.

TABLE 3
Tariffs as a Percentage of Total Government Revenue

Country	Tariffs as Percentage of Government Revenue
United Kingdom	0.1%
Japan	1.2
United States	1.5
Costa Rica	16.1
Ghana	31.2
Dominican Republic	44.2
Lesotho	55.1

Source: World Bank, *World Development Report*, 1997.

to ensure that the national-defense argument is not used to protect industries other than those truly crucial to the nation's defense.

1.e. Infant Industries

Countries sometimes justify protecting new industries that need time to become competitive with the rest of the world.

Nations are often inclined to protect new industries on the basis that the protection will give those industries adequate time to develop. New industries need time to establish themselves and to become efficient enough that their costs are no higher than those of their foreign rivals. An alternative to protecting young and/or critical domestic industries with tariffs and quotas is to subsidize them. Subsidies allow such firms to charge lower prices and to compete with more efficient foreign producers, while permitting consumers to pay the world price rather than the higher prices associated with tariffs or quotas on foreign goods.

Protecting an infant industry from foreign competition may make sense, but only until the industry matures. Once the industry achieves sufficient size, protection should be withdrawn, and the industry should be made to compete with its foreign counterparts. Unfortunately, such protection is rarely withdrawn, because the larger and more successful the industry becomes, the more political power it wields. In fact, if an infant industry truly has a good chance to become competitive and produce profitably once it is well established, it is not at all clear that government should even offer protection to reduce short-run losses. New firms typically incur losses, but they are only temporary if the firm is successful.

1.f. Strategic Trade Policy

strategic trade policy:
the use of trade restrictions or subsidies to allow domestic firms with decreasing costs to gain a greater share of the world market

There is another view of international trade that regards as misleading the description of comparative advantage presented in the previous chapter. According to this outlook, called **strategic trade policy,** international trade largely involves firms that pursue economies of scale—that is, firms that achieve lower costs per unit of production the more they produce. In contrast to the constant opportunity costs illustrated in the example of wheat and cloth in the chapter on "World Trade Equilibrium," opportunity costs in some

Copyright © by Houghton Mifflin Company. All rights reserved.

Copyright © by Houghton Mifflin Company. All rights reserved.

increasing-returns-to-scale industry:

an industry in which the costs of producing a unit of output fall as more output is produced

Government can use trade policy as a strategy to stimulate production by a domestic industry capable of achieving increasing returns to scale.

industries may fall with the level of output. Such **increasing-returns-to-scale industries** will tend to concentrate production in the hands of a few very large firms, rather than many competitive firms. Proponents of strategic trade policy contend that government can use tariffs or subsidies to allow domestic firms with decreasing costs an advantage over their foreign rivals.

A monopoly exists when there is only one producer in an industry, and no close substitutes for the product exist. If the average costs of production decline with increases in output, then the larger a firm is, the lower its per unit costs will be. One large producer will be more efficient than many small ones. A simple example of a natural-monopoly industry will indicate how strategic trade policy can make a country better off. Suppose that the production of buses is an industry characterized by increasing returns to scale and that there are only two firms capable of producing buses: Mercedes-Benz in Germany and General Motors in the United States. If both firms produce buses, their costs will be so high that both will experience losses. If only one of the two produces buses, however, it will be able to sell buses at home and abroad, creating a level of output that allows the firm to earn a profit.

Assume further that a monopoly producer will earn $100 million and that if both firms produce, they will each lose $5 million. Obviously, a firm that doesn't produce earns nothing. Which firm will produce? Because of the decreasing-cost nature of the industry, the firm that is the first to produce will realize lower costs and be able to preclude the other firm from entering the market. But strategic trade policy can alter the market in favor of the domestic firm.

Suppose Mercedes-Benz is the world's only producer of buses. General Motors does not produce them. The U.S. government could offer General Motors an $8 million subsidy to produce buses. General Motors would then enter the bus market, since the $8 million subsidy would more than offset the $5 million loss it would suffer by entering the market. Mercedes-Benz would sustain losses of $5 million once General Motors entered. Ultimately, Mercedes-Benz would stop producing buses to avoid the loss, and General Motors would have the entire market and earn $100 million plus the subsidy.

Strategic trade policy is aimed at offsetting the increasing-returns-to-scale advantage enjoyed by foreign producers and at stimulating production in domestic industries capable of realizing decreasing costs. One practical problem for government is the need to understand the technology of different industries and to forecast accurately the subsidy needed to induce domestic firms to produce new products. A second problem is the likelihood of retaliation by the foreign government. If the U.S. government subsidizes General Motors in its attack on the bus market, the German government is likely to subsidize Mercedes-Benz rather than lose the entire bus market to a U.S. producer. As a result, taxpayers in both nations will be subsidizing two firms, each producing too few buses to earn a profit.

RECAP

1. Government restrictions on foreign trade are usually aimed at protecting domestic producers from foreign competition.

2. Import restrictions may save domestic jobs, but the costs to consumers may be greater than the benefits to those who retain their jobs.

3. Advocates of "fair trade," or the creation of a "level playing field," call for import restrictions as a means of lowering foreign restrictions on markets for domestic exports.

4. Tariffs are an important source of revenue in many developing countries.

5. The national-defense argument in favor of trade restrictions is that protection from foreign competition is necessary to ensure that certain key defense-related industries continue to produce.

6. The infant-industries argument in favor of trade restriction is to allow a new industry a period of time in which to become competitive with its foreign counterparts.

7. Strategic trade policy is intended to provide domestic increasing-returns-to-scale industries an advantage over their foreign competitors.

2. TOOLS OF POLICY

How do countries restrict the entry of foreign goods and promote the export of domestic goods?

Commercial policy makes use of several tools, including tariffs, quotas, subsidies, and nontariff barriers like health and safety regulations that restrict the entry of foreign products. Since 1945, barriers to trade have been reduced. Much of the progress toward free trade may be linked to the *General Agreement on Tariffs and Trade*, or *GATT*, that began in 1947. In 1995, the *World Trade Organization (WTO)* was formed to incorporate the agreements under GATT into a formal permanent international organization that oversees world trade. The WTO has three objectives: to help global trade flow as freely as possible, to achieve reductions in trade restrictions gradually through negotiation, and to provide an impartial means of settling disputes. Nevertheless, restrictions on trade still exist, and this section will review the most commonly used restrictions.

2.a. Tariffs

tariff:
a tax on imports or exports

A **tariff** is a tax on imports or exports. Every country imposes tariffs on at least some imports. Some countries also impose tariffs on selected exports as a means of raising government revenue. Brazil, for instance, taxes coffee exports. The United States does not employ export tariffs, which are forbidden by the U.S. Constitution.

Tariffs are frequently imposed in order to protect domestic producers from foreign competition. The dangers of imposing tariffs are well illustrated in the Economic Insight "Smoot-Hawley Tariff." The effect of a tariff is illustrated in Figure 1, which shows the domestic market for oranges. Without international trade, the domestic equilibrium price, P_d, and quantity demanded, Q_d, are determined by the intersection of the domestic demand and supply curves. If the world price of oranges, P_w, is lower than the domestic equilibrium price, this country will import oranges. The quantity imported will be the difference between the quantity Q_1 produced domestically at a price of P_w and the quantity Q_2 demanded domestically at the world price of oranges.

Copyright © by Houghton Mifflin Company. All rights reserved.

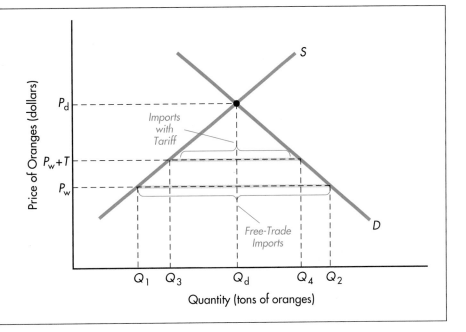

Figure 1
The Effects of a Tariff
The domestic equilibrium price and quantity with no trade are P_d and Q_d, respectively. The world price is P_w. With free trade, therefore, imports will equal $Q_2 - Q_1$. A tariff added to the world price reduces imports to $Q_4 - Q_3$.

Copyright © by Houghton Mifflin Company. All rights reserved.

When the world price of the traded good is lower than the domestic equilibrium price without international trade, free trade causes domestic production to fall and domestic consumption to rise. The domestic shortage at the world price is met by imports. Domestic consumers are better off, since they can buy more at a lower price. But domestic producers are worse off, since they now sell fewer oranges and receive a lower price.

Suppose a tariff of T (the dollar value of the tariff) is imposed on orange imports. The price paid by consumers is now $P_w + T$, rather than P_w. At this higher price, domestic producers will produce Q_3 and domestic consumers will purchase Q_4. The tariff has the effect of increasing domestic production and reducing domestic consumption, relative to the free trade equilibrium. Imports fall accordingly, from $Q_2 - Q_1$ to $Q_4 - Q_3$.

Domestic producers are better off, since the tariff has increased their sales of oranges and raised the price they receive. Domestic consumers pay higher prices for fewer oranges than they would with free trade, but they are still better off than they would be without trade. If the tariff had raised the price paid by consumers to P_d, there would be no trade, and the domestic equilibrium quantity, Q_d, would prevail.

The government earns revenue from imports of oranges. If each ton of oranges generates tariff revenue of T, the total tariff revenue to the government is found by multiplying the tariff by the quantity of oranges imported. In Figure 1, this amount is $T \times (Q_4 - Q_3)$. As the tariff changes, so does the quantity of imports and the government revenue.

Smoot-Hawley Tariff

Many economists believe that the Great Depression of the 1930s was at least partly due to the Smoot-Hawley Tariff Act, signed into law by President Herbert Hoover in 1930. Hoover had promised that, if elected, he would raise tariffs on agricultural products to raise U.S. farm income. Congress began work on the tariff increases in 1928. Congressman Willis Hawley and Senator Reed Smoot conducted the hearings.

In testimony before Congress, manufacturers and other special interest groups also sought protection from foreign competition. The resulting bill increased tariffs on over twelve thousand products. Tariffs reached their highest levels ever, about 60 percent of average import values. Only twice before in

U.S. history had tariffs approached the levels of the Smoot-Hawley era.

Before President Hoover signed the bill, thirty-eight foreign governments made formal protests, warning that they would retaliate with high tariffs on U.S. products. A petition signed by 1,028 economists warned of the harmful effects of the bill. Nevertheless, Hoover signed the bill into law.

World trade collapsed as other countries raised their tariffs in response. Between 1930 and 1931, U.S. imports fell 29 percent, but U.S. exports fell 33 percent. By 1933, world trade was about one-third of the 1929 level. As the level of trade fell, so did income and prices. In 1934, in an effort to correct the mistakes of Smoot-Hawley,

Congress passed the Reciprocal Trade Agreements Act, which allowed the president to lower U.S. tariffs in return for reductions in foreign tariffs on U.S. goods. This act ushered in the modern era of relatively low tariffs. In the United States today, tariffs are about 5 percent of the average value of imports.

Many economists believe the collapse of world trade and the Depression to be linked by a decrease in real income caused by abandoning production based on comparative advantage. Few economists argue that the Great Depression was caused solely by the Smoot-Hawley tariff, but the experience serves as a lesson to those who support higher tariffs to protect domestic producers.

2.b. Quotas

quantity quota:
a limit on the amount of a good that may be imported

value quota:
a limit on the monetary value of a good that may be imported

Quotas are limits on the quantity or value of goods imported and exported. A **quantity quota** restricts the physical amount of a good. For instance, through 1994 the United States allowed only 2.5 million tons of sugar to be imported. Even though the United States is not a competitive sugar producer compared to other nations like the Dominican Republic or Cuba, the quota allowed U.S. firms to produce about 6 percent of the world's sugar output. A **value quota** restricts the monetary value of a good that may be traded. Instead of a physical quota on sugar, the United States could have limited the dollar value of sugar imports.

Quotas are used to protect domestic producers from foreign competition. By restricting the amount of a good that may be imported, they increase its price and allow domestic producers to sell more at a higher price than they would with free trade. Figure 2 illustrates the effect of a quota on the domestic orange market. The domestic equilibrium supply and demand curves determine the equilibrium price and quantity without trade to be P_d and 250 tons, respectively. The world price of oranges is P_w. Since P_w lies below P_d, this country will import oranges. The quantity of imports is equal to the amount of the domestic shortage at P_w. The quantity demanded at P_w is 400 tons, and the quantity supplied domestically is 100 tons, so imports will equal 300 tons of oranges. With free trade, domestic producers sell 100 tons at a price of P_w.

Copyright © by Houghton Mifflin Company. All rights reserved.

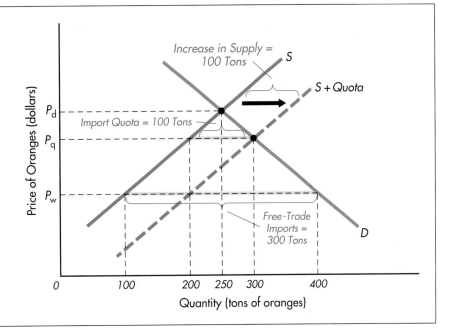

Figure 2
The Effects of a Quota
The domestic equilibrium price with no international trade is P_d. At this price, 250 tons of oranges would be produced and consumed at home. With free trade, the price is P_w and 300 tons will be imported. An import quota of 100 tons will cause the price to be P_q, where the domestic shortage equals the 100 tons allowed by the quota.

Copyright © by Houghton Mifflin Company. All rights reserved.

Voluntary export restraints are a substitute for quotas. They limit the amount exporters ship to an importing country.

But suppose domestic orange growers convince the government to restrict orange imports. The government then imposes a quota of 100 tons on imported oranges. The effect of the quota on consumers is to shift the supply curve to the right by the amount of the quota, 100 tons. Since the quota is less than the quantity of imports with free trade, the quantity of imports will equal the quota. The domestic equilibrium price with the quota occurs at the point where the domestic shortage equals the quota. At price P_q, the domestic quantity demanded (300 tons) is 100 tons more than the domestic quantity supplied (200 tons).

Quotas benefit domestic producers in the same way that tariffs do. Domestic producers receive a higher price (P_q instead of P_w) for a greater quantity (200 instead of 100) than they do under free trade. The effect on domestic consumers is also similar to that of a tariff: they pay a higher price for a smaller quantity than they would with free trade. A tariff generates government tax revenue; quotas do not (unless the government auctioned off the right to import under the quota). Furthermore, a tariff only raises the price of the product in the domestic market. Foreign producers receive the world price, P_w. With a quota, both domestic and foreign producers receive the higher price, P_q, for the goods sold in the domestic market. So foreign producers are hurt by the reduction in the quantity of imports permitted, but they do receive a higher price for the amount they sell.

In some cases, countries negotiate *voluntary export restraints* rather than imposing quotas. A voluntary export restraint limits the quantity of goods shipped from the exporting country to an importing country, so such restraints have the same practical effect as a quota. For instance, the United States has negotiated voluntary export restraints on Japanese auto exports to the United States. In 1992, the agreement allowed 1.65 million autos ranging from 480,000 Toyotas to 30,000 Suzukis. The Japanese Automobile Manufacturers Association monitors the exports for the Japanese government.

2.c. Other Barriers to Trade

Tariffs and quotas are not the only barriers to the free flow of goods across international borders. There are three additional sources of restrictions on free trade: subsidies, government procurement, and health and safety standards. Though often enacted for reasons other than protection from foreign competition, a careful analysis reveals their import-reducing effect.

Before discussing these three types of barriers, let us note the cultural or institutional barriers to trade that also exist in many countries. Such barriers may exist independently of any conscious government policy. For instance, Japan has frequently been criticized by U.S. officials for informal business practices that discriminate against foreigners. Under the Japanese distribution system, goods typically pass through several layers of middlemen before appearing in a retail store. A foreign firm faces the difficult task of gaining entry to this system to supply goods to the retailer. Furthermore, a foreigner cannot easily open a retail store. Japanese law requires a new retail firm to receive permission from other retailers in the area in order to open a business. A firm that lacks contacts and knowledge of the system cannot penetrate the Japanese market.

In the fall of 1989, the U.S. toy firm Toys "R" Us announced its intent to open several large discount toy stores in Japan. However, local toy stores in each area objected to having a Toys "R" Us store nearby. The U.S. government has argued that the laws favoring existing firms are an important factor in keeping Japan closed to foreign firms that would like to enter the Japanese market. Eventually, Toys "R" Us opened stores in Japan.

subsidies:
payments made by government to domestic firms to encourage exports

2.c.1. Subsidies

Subsidies are payments by a government to an exporter. Subsidies are paid to stimulate exports by allowing the exporter to charge a lower price. The amount of a subsidy is determined by the international price of a product relative to the domestic price in the absence of trade. Domestic consumers are harmed by subsidies in that their taxes finance the subsidies. Also, since the subsidy diverts resources from the domestic market toward export production, the increase in the supply of export goods could be associated with a decrease in the supply of domestic goods, causing domestic prices to rise.

Subsidies may take forms other than direct cash payments. These include tax reductions, low-interest loans, low-cost insurance, government-sponsored research funding, and other devices. The U.S. government subsidizes export activity through the U.S. Export-Import Bank, which provides loans and insurance to help U.S. exporters sell their goods to foreign buyers. Subsidies are more commonplace in Europe than in Japan or the United States.

2.c.2. Government Procurement

Governments are often required by law to buy only from local producers. In the United States, a "buy American" act passed in 1933 required U.S. government agencies to buy U.S. goods and services unless the domestic price was more than 12 percent above the foreign price. This kind of policy allows domestic firms to charge the government a higher price for their products than they charge consumers; the taxpayers bear the burden. The United States is by no means alone in the use of such policies. Many other nations also use such policies to create larger markets for domestic

Copyright © by Houghton Mifflin Company. All rights reserved.

goods. The World Trade Organization has a standing committee working to reduce discrimination against foreign producers and open government procurement practices to global competition.

2.c.3. Health and Safety Standards   Government serves as a guardian of the public health and welfare by requiring that products offered to the public be safe and fulfill the use for which they are intended. Government standards for products sold in the domestic marketplace can have the effect (intentional or not) of protecting domestic producers from foreign competition. These effects should be considered in evaluating the full impact of such standards.

As mentioned in the Preview, the government of Japan once threatened to prohibit foreign-made snow skis from entering the country for reasons of safety. Only Japanese-made skis were determined to be suitable for Japanese snow. Several Western European nations announced that U.S. beef would not be allowed into Europe because hormones approved by the U.S. government are fed to U.S. beef cattle. In the late 1960s, France required tractors sold there to have a maximum speed of 17 miles per hour; in Germany, the permissible speed was 13 mph, and in the Netherlands it was 10 mph. Tractors produced in one country had to be modified to meet the requirements of the other countries. Such modifications raise the price of goods and discourage international trade.

Product standards may not eliminate foreign competition, but standards different from those of the rest of the world do provide an element of protection to domestic firms.

RECAP

1. The World Trade Organization works to achieve reductions in trade barriers.
2. A tariff is a tax on imports or exports. Tariffs protect domestic firms by raising the prices of foreign goods.
3. Quotas are government-imposed limits on the quantity or value of an imported good. Quotas protect domestic firms by restricting the entry of foreign products to a level less than the quantity demanded.
4. Subsidies are payments by the government to domestic producers. Subsidies lower the price of domestic goods.
5. Governments are often required by law to buy only domestic products.
6. Health and safety standards can also be used to protect domestic firms.

3. PREFERENTIAL TRADE AGREEMENTS

What sorts of agreements do countries enter into to reduce barriers to international trade?

In an effort to stimulate international trade, groups of countries sometimes enter into agreements to abolish most barriers to trade among themselves. Such arrangements between countries are known as preferential trading

Copyright © by Houghton Mifflin Company. All rights reserved.

agreements. The European Union and the North American Free Trade Agreement (NAFTA) are examples of preferential trading agreements.

3.a. Free Trade Areas and Customs Unions

free trade area:
an organization of nations whose members have no trade barriers among themselves but are free to fashion their own trade policies toward nonmembers

customs union:
an organization of nations whose members have no trade barriers among themselves but impose common trade barriers on nonmembers

Two common forms of preferential trade agreements are **free trade areas** (FTAs) and **customs unions** (CUs). These two approaches differ with regard to treatment of countries outside the agreement. In an FTA, member countries eliminate trade barriers among themselves, but each member country chooses its own trade policies toward nonmember countries. Members of a CU agree to eliminate trade barriers among themselves and to maintain common trade barriers against nonmembers.

The best-known CU is the European Union (EU), formerly known as the European Economic Community (EEC), created in 1957 by France, West Germany, Italy, Belgium, the Netherlands, and Luxembourg. The United Kingdom, Ireland, and Denmark joined in 1973, followed by Greece in 1981 and Spain and Portugal in 1986. In 1992 the EEC was replaced by the EU with an agreement to create a single market for goods and services in Western Europe. Besides free trade in goods, European financial markets and institutions will eventually be able to operate across national boundaries. For instance, a bank in any EU country will be permitted to operate in any or all other EU countries.

In 1989, the United States and Canada negotiated a free trade area. The United States, Canada, and Mexico negotiated a free trade area in 1992 that became effective on January 1, 1994. Under NAFTA, tariffs are lowered on eight thousand different items, and each nation's financial market is opened to competition from the other two nations. NAFTA does not eliminate all barriers to trade among the three nations but is a significant step in that direction.

The North American Free Trade Agreement stimulates trade among Mexico, Canada, and the United States. In coming years, there will be more and more container ships from Mexico unloading their cargo at U.S. docks. This ship, *Mexicana,* tied up in Long Beach, California, is a sign of the times for U.S. ports. Similarly, freight from Canada and the United States will increase in volume at Mexican ports.

Copyright © by Houghton Mifflin Company. All rights reserved.

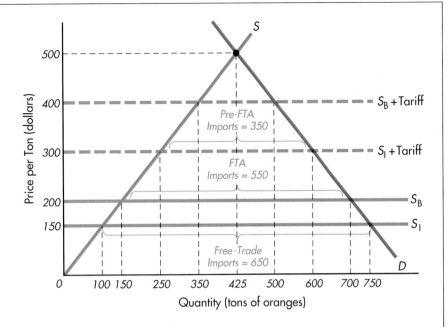

Figure 3
Trade Creation and
Trade Diversion with a
Free Trade Area
With no trade, the domestic equilibrium price is $500 and the equilibrium quantity is 425 tons. With free trade, the price is $150, and 650 tons would be imported, as indicated by the supply curve for Israel, S_I. A 100 percent tariff on imports would result in imports of 350 tons from Israel, according to the supply curve S_I + *Tariff*. A free trade agreement that eliminates tariffs on Brazilian oranges only would result in a new equilibrium price of $200 and imports of 550 tons from Brazil, according to supply curve S_B.

3.b. Trade Creation and Diversion

Free trade agreements provide for free trade among a group of countries, not worldwide. As a result, a customs union or free trade area may make a nation better off or worse off compared to the free trade equilibrium.

Figure 3 illustrates the effect of a free trade area. With no international trade, the U.S. supply and demand curves for oranges would result in an equilibrium price of $500 per ton and an equilibrium quantity of 425 tons. Suppose there are two other orange-producing countries, Israel and Brazil. Israel, the low-cost producer of oranges, is willing to sell all the oranges the United States can buy for $150 per ton, as represented by the horizontal supply curve S_I. Brazil will supply oranges for a price of $200 per ton, as represented by the horizontal supply curve S_B.

With free trade, the United States would import oranges from Israel. The quantity demanded at $150 is 750 tons, and the domestic quantity supplied at this price is 100 tons. The shortage of 650 tons is met by imports from Israel.

Now suppose a 100 percent tariff is imposed on orange imports. The price domestic consumers pay for foreign oranges is twice as high as before. For oranges from Israel the new price is $300, twice the old price of $150. The new supply curve for Israel is represented as S_I + *Tariff*. Oranges from Brazil now sell for $400, twice the old price of $200; the new supply curve for Brazil is shown as S_B + *Tariff*. After the 100 percent tariff is imposed, oranges are still imported from Israel. But at the new price of $300, the domestic quantity demanded is 600 tons and the domestic quantity supplied is 250 tons. Thus only 350 tons will be imported. The tariff reduces the volume of trade relative to the free trade equilibrium, at which 650 tons were imported.

Copyright © by Houghton Mifflin Company. All rights reserved.

Now suppose that the United States negotiates a free trade agreement with Brazil, eliminating tariffs on imports from Brazil. Israel is not a member of the free trade agreement, so imports from Israel are still covered by the 100 percent tariff. The relevant supply curve for Brazil is now S_B, so oranges may be imported from Brazil for $200, a lower price than Israel's price including the tariff. At a price of $200, the domestic quantity demanded is 700 tons and the domestic quantity supplied is 150 tons; 550 tons will be imported.

The effects of the free trade agreement are twofold. First, trade was diverted away from the lowest-cost producer, Israel, to the FTA partner, Brazil. This **trade diversion** effect of an FTA reduces worldwide economic efficiency, since production is diverted from the country with the comparative advantage. Oranges are not being produced as efficiently as possible. The other effect of the FTA is that the quantity of imports increases relative to the effect of a tariff applicable to all imports. Imports rise from 350 tons (the quantity imported from Israel with the tariff) to 550 tons. The FTA thus has a **trade creation** effect, resulting from the lower price available after the tariff reduction. Trade creation is a beneficial aspect of the FTA: the expansion of international trade allows this country to realize greater benefits from trade than would be possible without trade.

Countries form preferential trade agreements because they believe FTAs will make each member country better off. The member countries view the trade-creation effects of such agreements as benefiting their exporters by increasing exports to member countries and as benefiting consumers by making a wider variety of goods available at a lower price. From the point of view of the world as a whole, preferential trade agreements are more desirable the more they stimulate trade creation to allow the benefits of trade to be realized and the less they emphasize trade diversion, so that production occurs on the basis of comparative advantage. This principle suggests that the most successful FTAs or CUs are those that increase trade volume but do not change the patterns of trade in terms of who specializes and exports each good. In the case of Figure 3, a more successful FTA would reduce tariffs on Israeli as well as Brazilian oranges, so that oranges would be imported from the lowest-cost producer, Israel.

trade diversion:
an effect of a preferential trade agreement, reducing economic efficiency by shifting production to a higher-cost producer

trade creation:
an effect of a preferential trade agreement, allowing a country to obtain goods at a lower cost than is available at home

RECAP

1. Countries form preferential trade agreements in order to stimulate trade among themselves.

2. The most common forms of preferential trade agreement are free trade areas (FTAs) and customs unions (CUs).

3. Preferential trade agreements have a harmful trade-diversion effect when they cause production to shift from the nation with a comparative advantage to a higher-cost producer.

4. Preferential trade agreements have a beneficial trade-creation effect when they reduce prices for traded goods and stimulate the volume of international trade.

Copyright © by Houghton Mifflin Company. All rights reserved.

SUMMARY

Copyright © by Houghton Mifflin Company. All rights reserved.

▪ Why do countries restrict international trade?

1. Commercial policy is government policy that influences the direction and volume of international trade. §Preview

2. Protecting domestic producers from foreign competition usually imposes costs on domestic consumers. §1

3. Rationales for commercial policy include saving domestic jobs, creating a fair-trade relationship with other countries, raising tariff revenue, ensuring a domestic supply of key defense goods, allowing new industries a chance to become internationally competitive, and giving domestic industries with increasing returns to scale an advantage over foreign competitors. §1.a–1.f

▪ How do countries restrict the entry of foreign goods and promote the export of domestic goods?

4. Tariffs protect domestic industry by increasing the price of foreign goods. §2.a

5. Quotas protect domestic industry by limiting the quantity of foreign goods allowed into the country. §2.b

6. Subsidies allow relatively inefficient domestic producers to compete with foreign firms. §2.c.1

7. Government procurement practices and health and safety regulations can protect domestic industry from foreign competition. §2.c.2, 2.c.3

▪ What sorts of agreements do countries enter into to reduce barriers to international trade?

8. Free trade areas and customs unions are two types of preferential trade agreements that reduce trade restrictions among member countries. §3.a

9. Preferential trade agreements have harmful trade-diversion effects and beneficial trade-creation effects. §3.b

KEY TERMS

commercial policy §Preview

strategic trade policy §1.f

increasing-returns-to-scale industry §1.f

tariff §2.a

quantity quota §2.b

value quota §2.b

subsidies §2.c.1

free trade area §3.a

customs union §3.a

trade diversion §3.b

trade creation §3.b

EXERCISES

1. What are the potential benefits and costs of a commercial policy designed to pursue each of the following goals?

   a. Save domestic jobs

   b. Create a level playing field

   c. Increase government revenue

   d. Provide a strong national defense

   e. Protect an infant industry

   f. Stimulate exports of an industry with increasing returns to scale

2. For each of the goals listed in question 1, discuss what the appropriate commercial policy is likely to be (in terms of tariffs, quotas, subsidies, etc.).

3. Tariffs and quotas both raise the price of foreign goods to domestic consumers. What is the difference between the effects of a tariff and the effects of a quota on the following?

   a. The domestic government

   b. Foreign producers

   c. Domestic producers

4. Would trade-diversion and trade-creation effects occur if the whole world became a free trade area? Explain.

5. What is the difference between a customs union and a free trade area?

6. Draw a graph of the U.S. automobile market in which the domestic equilibrium price without trade is P_d and the equilibrium quantity is Q_d. Use this graph to illustrate and explain the effects of a tariff if the United States were an auto importer with free trade. Then use the graph to illustrate and explain the effects of a quota.

7. If commercial policy can benefit U.S. industry, why would any U.S. resident oppose such policies?

8. Suppose you were asked to assess U.S. commercial policy to determine whether the benefits of protection for U.S. industries are worth the costs. Do Tables 1 and 2 provide all the information you need? If not, what else would you want to know?

9. How would the effects of international trade on the domestic orange market change if the world price of oranges were above the domestic equilibrium price? Draw a graph to help explain your answer.

10. Suppose the world price of kiwi fruit is $20 per case and the U.S. equilibrium price with no international trade is $35 per case. If the U.S. government had previously banned the import of kiwi fruit but then imposed a tariff of $5 per case and allowed kiwi imports, what would happen to the equilibrium price and quantity of kiwi fruit consumed in the United States?

Copyright © by Houghton Mifflin Company. All rights reserved.

INTERNET EXERCISE

In the introduction to section 2 of this chapter the World Trade Organization (WTO) was introduced as an organization overseeing the global trading system with a goal of promoting free trade. To learn more about the WTO, go to the Boyes/Melvin web site at **http://www.hmco.com/college/** and click on the internet exercise link for this chapter. Now answer the questions that appear on the web page.

Copyright © by Houghton Mifflin Company. All rights reserved.

Imports and Competition in Domestic Markets

Foremost among the asserted benefits of reducing trade barriers is competition: firms that operate in an economy with relatively weak domestic competition are supposed to be forced by the onslaught of foreign goods to improve their quality and service and to keep costs and prices down. The benefits of trade liberalization are assumed to be particularly great in developing countries, where a relatively few firms may control a given industry. But while the theoretical benefits of freer trade are well understood, do businesses actually respond in that way? After studying the effects of trade liberalization in Turkey, NBER researcher James Levinsohn concludes that the answer is "yes."

Until 1984, the Turkish economy was highly protected against imports, with tariffs averaging 49 percent and an array of nontariff barriers including quotas, import licenses, and foreign exchange regulations. In 1984, however, tariffs were reduced to an average of 20 percent and restrictions on many types of imports were eliminated.... Levinsohn investigated the impact of this sweeping liberalization by using detailed data on individual firms from the Turkish manufacturing census. ...

Prior to the change in trade policy, Levinsohn finds, firms in six of the eleven industries studied were pricing at marginal cost, indicating a high level of competition. In three industries, companies were pricing above marginal cost, indicating the existence of imperfect competition, while in two industries, including the largely government-owned steel industry, firms were losing money on each unit of output. The 1984 trade liberalization reduced the level of protection enjoyed by nine of the eleven industries. In the three high-margin industries, miscellaneous chemicals, pottery, and electrical machinery, price markups declined as import competition increased. For two of the previously competitive industries, transport equipment and scientific equipment, the trade reform resulted in higher levels of import protection, and price mark-ups in those industries increased. Of the six previously competitive industries that had their protection reduced by the trade reform, three had lower markups and one was unchanged; one of the two industries in that category with higher mark-ups was the steel industry.

Levinsohn warns that the price markups reported by companies to census officials may not be completely accurate. Firms with high profits may be inclined to understate their revenues or overstate costs in case tax officials learn of their reports, while firms with losses may exit the industry and not report. Nonetheless, Levinsohn writes, the Turkish data indicate that imports increase competition and restrict the ability of domestic firms to exercise market power.

Source: From *NBER Digest*, July/August 1991. Used by permission of the National Bureau of Economic Research.

Copyright © by Houghton Mifflin Company. All rights reserved.

COMMENTARY

Copyright © by Houghton Mifflin Company. All rights reserved.

Consider the following hypothetical situation: The legislature of the state of Maine considers a tax to support the pineapple farmers of the state. Of course, Maine's climate is not conducive to growing pineapples, but it is possible, at great cost, to grow a few pineapples in greenhouses. The tax on pineapples brought into the state raises the price of Hawaiian pineapples by enough to make pineapples grown in Maine competitive. Thus Maine's pineapple industry is saved from competitors whose price reflects their unfair climactic advantage, though the consumers of the state must pay exorbitant prices for their pineapples.

This scenario, with its absurd distortion of the workings of the market, differs in degree but not in kind from the description of the effects of import competition in the accompanying article. The protectionist measure of imposing quotas or tariffs on imports saves jobs in the domestic import-competing industries, but at a great cost to consumers. It is estimated that the cost of protecting the U.S. domestic textile industry is $238 per family in the United States.

The effect of reducing domestic competition with quotas can be understood using supply and demand analysis. Let's analyze the case of quotas on textile imports into the United States. In the diagram, S_1 is the domestic supply of textiles, S_2 is the sum of the domestic supply and the foreign supply allowed in by the quotas, and D is the demand for textiles. Under the quota system, the price of textiles in the United States is represented by P_q and the quantity of textiles consumed is Q_q. If the quotas were removed, the price of textiles in the United States would equal the world price of P_w, and this lower price would be associated with an increase in the consumption of textiles to Q_w. The quota represents a cost to society in terms of a loss of consumer welfare as well as a loss from the inefficient use of resources in an industry in which this country has no com-

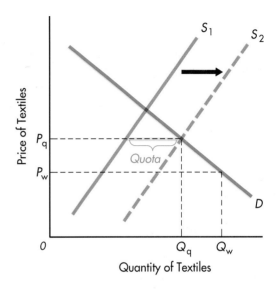

parative advantage, just as Maine has no comparative advantage in the production of pineapples.

Given the costs to society of these quotas, why is there such strong support for them in Congress? An important political aspect of protectionist policies is that their benefits are concentrated among a relatively small number of people while their costs are diffuse and spread across all consumers. Each individual import-competing producer faces very large losses from free trade while the cost to each consumer of a protectionist policy is less dramatic. It is also easier to organize a relatively small number of manufacturers than to mobilize a vast population of consumers. These factors explain the strong lobby for the protection of industries like textiles and the absence of a legislative lobby that operates specifically in the interest of textile consumers.

Industrial arguments for trade protection should be seen for what they are: an attempt by an industry to increase its profits at the expense of the general public.

22

Exchange-Rate Systems and Practices

FUNDAMENTAL QUESTIONS

1. How does a commodity standard fix exchange rates between countries?

2. What kinds of exchange-rate arrangements exist today?

3. How is equilibrium determined in the foreign exchange market?

4. How do fixed and floating exchange rates differ in their adjustment to shifts in supply and demand for currencies?

5. What are the advantages and disadvantages of fixed and floating exchange rates?

6. What determines the kind of exchange-rate system a country adopts?

Copyright © by Houghton Mifflin Company. All rights reserved.

E xchange-rate policy is an important element of macroeconomic policy. An exchange rate is the link between two nations' monies. The value of a U.S. dollar in terms of Japanese yen or German marks determines how many dollars a U.S. resident will need to buy goods priced in yen or marks. Thus changes in the exchange rate can have far-reaching implications. Exchange rates may be determined in free markets, or through government intervention in the foreign exchange market, or even by law.

In the early 1990s, one U.S. dollar was worth about 125 Japanese yen. By spring of 1995, the dollar was worth 83 yen. By early 1998, a dollar was worth 125 yen again. Why does the dollar fluctuate in value relative to the yen? What are the effects of such changes? Should governments permit exchange rates to change? What can governments do to discourage changing exchange rates? These are all important questions, which this chapter will help to answer.

Preview

This chapter begins with a review of the history of exchange-rate systems. Then follows an overview of exchange-rate practices in the world today and an analysis of the benefits and costs of alternative exchange-rate arrangements. Along the way, we will introduce terminology and institutions that play a major role in the evolution of exchange rates. ∎

1. PAST AND CURRENT EXCHANGE-RATE ARRANGEMENTS

1.a. The Gold Standard

How does a commodity standard fix exchange rates between countries?

gold standard:
a system whereby national currencies are fixed in terms of their value in gold, thus creating fixed exchange rates between currencies

In ancient times, government-produced monies were made of precious metals like gold. Later, when governments began to issue paper money, it was usually convertible into a fixed amount of gold. Ensuring the convertibility of paper money into gold was a way to maintain confidence in the currency's value, at home and abroad. If a unit of currency was worth a fixed amount of gold, its value could be stated in terms of its gold value. The countries that maintained a constant gold value for their currencies were said to be on a **gold standard.**

Some countries had backed their currencies with gold long before 1880; however, the practice became widespread around 1880, so economists typically date the beginning of the gold standard to this period. From roughly 1880 to 1914, currencies had fixed values in terms of gold. For instance, the

Copyright © by Houghton Mifflin Company. All rights reserved.

U.S. dollar's value was fixed at $20.67 per ounce of gold. Any other currency that was fixed in terms of gold also had a fixed exchange rate against the dollar. A simple example will illustrate how this works.

Suppose the price of an ounce of gold is $20 in the United States and £4 in the United Kingdom. The pound is worth five times the value of a dollar, since it takes five times as many dollars as pounds to buy one ounce of gold. Because one pound buys five times as much gold as one dollar, the exchange rate is £1 = $5. Since currency values are linked by gold values, as the supply of gold fluctuates, there will be pressure to alter prices of goods and services. The gold standard fixes only the current price of gold. As the stock of gold increases, everything else held constant, the gold and currency prices of goods and services will tend to rise (as would occur when the money supply increases).

A gold standard is only one possible *commodity money standard*. Any other highly valued commodity (silver, for instance) could serve as a standard linking monies in a fixed exchange-rate system.

The gold standard ended with the outbreak of World War I. War financing was partially funded by increases in the money supplies of the hostile nations. A gold standard would not permit such a rapid increase in the money supply unless the stock of gold increased dramatically, which it did not. As money supplies grew faster than gold supplies, the link between money and gold had to be broken. During the war years and the Great Depression of the 1930s, and on through World War II, there was no organized system for setting exchange rates. Foreign trade and investment shrunk as a result of the war, obviating the need for a well-functioning method of determining exchange rates.

A commodity money standard exists when exchange rates are fixed based on the values of different currencies in terms of some commodity.

1.b. The Bretton Woods System

The Bretton Woods agreement established a system of fixed exchange rates.

gold exchange standard:
an exchange-rate system in which each nation fixes the value of its currency in terms of gold but buys and sells the U.S. dollar rather than gold to maintain fixed exchange rates

reserve currency:
a currency that is used to settle international debts and is held by governments to use in foreign exchange market interventions

At the end of World War II, there was widespread political support for an exchange-rate system linking all monies in much the same way as the gold standard had. It was believed that a system of fixed exchange rates would promote the growth of world trade. In 1944, delegates from forty-four nations met in Bretton Woods, New Hampshire, to discuss the creation of such a system. The agreement reached at this conference has had a profound impact on the world.

The exchange-rate arrangement that emerged from the Bretton Woods conference is often called a **gold exchange standard**. Each country was to fix the value of its currency in terms of gold, just as it had under the gold standard. The U.S.-dollar price of gold, for instance, was $35 an ounce. However, there were fundamental differences between this system and the old gold standard. The U.S. dollar, rather than gold, served as the focal point of the system. Instead of buying and selling gold, countries bought and sold U.S. dollars to maintain a fixed exchange rate with the dollar. Since the United States was the major victor nation, its currency was the dominant world currency. The United States had the productive capacity to supply much-needed goods to the rest of the world, and these goods were priced in dollars.

The U.S. dollar was the **reserve currency** of the system. International debts were settled with dollars, and international trade contracts were often denominated in dollars. In effect, the world was on a dollar standard following World War II.

Copyright © by Houghton Mifflin Company. All rights reserved.

1.c. The International Monetary Fund and the World Bank

International Monetary Fund (IMF):
an international organization that supervises exchange-rate arrangements and lends money to member countries experiencing problems meeting their external financial obligations

World Bank:
an international organization that makes loans and provides technical expertise to developing countries

Two new organizations also emerged from the Bretton Woods conference: the International Monetary Fund and the World Bank. The **International Monetary Fund**, or **IMF**, was created to supervise the exchange-rate practices of member countries and to encourage the free convertibility of any national money into the monies of other countries. The IMF also lends money to countries that are experiencing problems meeting their international payment obligations. The funds available to the IMF come from the annual membership fees (called *quotas*) of the 178 member countries of the IMF. The U.S. quota, for instance, is almost $23 billion. (The term *quota* has a different meaning in this context than it does in international trade.)

The **World Bank** was created to help finance economic development in poor countries. It provides loans to developing countries at more favorable terms than are available from commercial lenders and also offers technical expertise. The World Bank obtains the funds it lends by selling bonds. It is one of the world's major borrowers. See the Economic Insight "The IMF and the World Bank" for an explanation of how these institutions work.

1.d. The Transition Years

foreign exchange market intervention:
buying or selling of currencies by a government or central bank to achieve a specified exchange rate

The Bretton Woods system of fixed exchange rates required countries to actively buy and sell dollars to maintain fixed exchange rates when the *free market equilibrium* in the foreign exchange market differed from the fixed rate. The free market equilibrium exchange rate is the rate that would be established in the absence of government intervention. Governmental buying and selling of currencies to achieve a target exchange rate is called **foreign exchange market intervention**. The effectiveness of such intervention was limited to situations in which free market pressure to deviate from the fixed exchange rate was temporary. For instance, suppose a country has a bad harvest and earns less foreign exchange than usual. This may only be a temporary situation if the next harvest is plentiful and the country resumes its typical export sales. During the period of reduced exports, it will be necessary for the government of this country to intervene to avoid a depreciation of its domestic currency. In the 1960s, however, there were several episodes of permanent rather than temporary changes that called for changes in exchange rates rather than government foreign exchange market intervention. The problems that arise in response to permanent pressures to change the exchange rate will be discussed further in section 2, when we analyze the benefits and costs of alternative exchange-rate systems.

devaluation:
a deliberate decrease in the official value of a currency

equilibrium exchange rates:
the exchange rates that are established in the absence of government foreign exchange market intervention

The Bretton Woods system officially dissolved in 1971, at a meeting of the finance ministers of the leading world powers at the Smithsonian Institution in Washington, D.C. The Smithsonian agreement changed the exchange rates set during the Bretton Woods era. One result was a **devaluation** of the U.S. dollar. (A currency is said to be devalued when its value is officially lowered.) The official dollar value of gold dropped from $35 an ounce to $38 an ounce.

Under the Smithsonian agreement, countries were to maintain fixed exchange rates at newly defined values. It soon became clear, however, that the new exchange rates were not **equilibrium exchange rates** that could be maintained without government intervention, and that government intervention could not maintain the disequilibrium fixed exchange rates forever. The

Copyright © by Houghton Mifflin Company. All rights reserved.

The IMF and the World Bank

The International Monetary Fund (IMF) and the World Bank were both created at the Bretton Woods conference in 1944. The IMF oversees the international monetary system, promoting stable exchange rates and macroeconomic policies. The World Bank promotes the economic development of the poor nations. Both organizations are owned and directed by their 181 member countries.

The IMF provides loans to nations having trouble repaying their foreign debts. Before the IMF lends any money, however, the borrower must agree to certain conditions. IMF *conditionality* usually requires that the country meet tar-gets for key macroeconomic variables like money-supply growth, inflation, tax collections, and subsidies. The conditions attached to IMF loans are aimed at promoting stable economic growth.

The World Bank assists developing countries by providing long-term financing for development projects and programs. The Bank also provides expertise in many areas in which poor nations lack expert knowledge: agriculture, medicine, construction, and education, as well as economics. The IMF primarily employs economists to carry out its mission.

The diversity of World Bank activities results in the employment of about 6,500 people. The IMF has a staff of approximately 1,700. Both organizations post employees around the world, but most work at the headquarters in Washington, D.C.

World Bank funds are largely acquired by borrowing on the international bond market. The IMF receives its funding from member-country subscription fees, called quotas. A member's quota determines its voting power in setting IMF policies. The United States, whose quota accounts for the largest fraction of the total, has the most votes.

U.S. dollar was devalued again in February 1973, when the dollar price of gold was raised to $42.22. This new exchange rate was still not an equilibrium rate, and in March 1973 the major industrial countries abandoned fixed exchange rates.

1.e. Floating Exchange Rates

What kinds of exchange-rate arrangements exist today?

In March 1973, the major industrial countries abandoned fixed exchange rates for floating rates.

managed floating exchange rates:
the system whereby central banks intervene in the floating foreign exchange market to influence exchange rates.

When fixed exchange rates were abandoned by the major industrial countries in March 1973, the world did not move to purely free-market-determined floating exchange rates. Under the system in existence since that time, the major industrial countries intervene to keep their currencies within acceptable ranges, while many smaller countries maintain fixed exchange rates.

The world today consists of some countries with fixed exchange rates, whose governments keep the exchange rates between two or more currencies constant over time; other countries with floating exchange rates, which shift on a daily basis according to the forces of supply and demand; and still others whose exchange-rate systems lie somewhere in between. Table 1, which lists the exchange-rate arrangements of over 180 countries, illustrates the diversity of exchange-rate arrangements currently in effect. We will focus here on the differences between fixed and floating exchange rates. All of the other exchange-rate arrangements listed in Table 1 are special versions of these two general exchange-rate systems.

As Table 1 shows, some countries maintain **managed floating exchange rates.** Although Table 1 lists countries like Japan and the United States as "independently floating," in fact their central banks, such as the Federal Reserve in the United States and the Bank of Japan in Japan, intervene from

Copyright © by Houghton Mifflin Company. All rights reserved.

TABLE 1
Exchange-Rate Arrangements[1]

		Currency Pegged to		
U.S. Dollar	**French Franc**	**Other Currency**	**SDR**	**Other Composite[2]**
Angola	Benin	Bhutan (Indian rupee)	Libya	Bangladesh
Antigua and Barbuda	Burkina Faso	Bosnia and Herzegovina (deutsche mark)	Myanmar	Botswana
Argentina	Cameroon			Burundi
Bahamas, The	C. African Rep.			Cape Verde
Barbados	Chad			Cyprus
Belize	Comoros	Brunei Darussalam (Singapore dollar)		Fiji
Djibouti	Congo, Rep. of			Iceland
Dominica	Côte d'Ivoire	Bulgaria (deutsche mark)		Jordan
Grenada	Equatorial Guinea			Kuwait
Iraq	Gabon	Estonia (deutsche mark)		Malta
Liberia	Guinea-Bissau	Kiribati (Australian dollar)		Morocco
Lithuania	Mali			Samoa
Marshall Islands	Niger			Seychelles
Micronesia, Fed. States of	Senegal	Lesotho (South African rand)		Slovak Republic
Nigeria	Togo	Namibia (South African rand)		Solomon Islands
Oman		Nepal (Indian rupee)		Tonga
Panama		San Marino (Italian lira)		Vanuatu
St. Kitts and Nevis		Swaziland (South African rand)		
St. Lucia				
St. Vincent and the Grenadines				
Syrian Arab Rep.				

[1]For members with dual or multiple exchange markets, the arrangement shown is that in the major market.
[2]Comprises currencies which are pegged to various "baskets" of currencies of the members' own choice, as distinct from the SDR basket.

(continued on p. 544)

Copyright © by Houghton Mifflin Company. All rights reserved.

TABLE 1
Exchange-Rate Arrangements (cont.)

	Flexibility Limited in Terms of a Single Currency or Group of Currencies			
Single Currency[3]	**Cooperative Arrangements[4]**			
Bahrain	Austria			
Qatar	Belgium			
Saudi Arabia	Denmark			
United Arab Emirates	Finland			
	France			
	Germany			
	Ireland			
	Italy			
	Luxembourg			
	Netherlands			
	Portugal			
	Spain			

More Flexible

Other Managed Floating		**Independently Floating**				
Algeria	Lao, P.D. Rep. of	Afghanistan, Islamic State of	Guinea	Moldova	South Africa
Belarus	Latvia	Albania	Guyana	Mongolia	Sweden
Brazil	Macedonia	Armenia	Haiti	Mozambique	Switzerland
Cambodia	Malaysia	Australia	India	New Zealand	Tajikistan
Chile	Maldives	Azerbaijan	Indonesia	Papua New Guinea	Tanzania
China, P.R.	Mauritius	Bolivia	Jamaica	Paraguay	Trinidad and Tobago
Colombia	Nicaragua	Canada	Japan	Peru	Uganda
Costa Rica	Norway	Congo, Dem. Rep.	Kazakhstan	Philippines	United Kingdom
Croatia	Pakistan	Ethiopia	Kenya	Romania	United States
Czech Republic	Poland	Gambia, The	Lebanon	Rwanda	Yemen
Dominican Republic	Russia	Ghana	Madagascar	Sao Tome and Principe	Zaire
Ecuador	Singapore	Guatemala	Malawi	Sierra Leone	Zambia
Egypt	Slovenia		Mauritania	Somalia	Zimbabwe
El Salvador	Sri Lanka		Mexico		
Eritrea	Sudan				
Georgia	Suriname				
Greece	Thailand				
Honduras	Tunisia				
Hungary	Turkmenistan				
Iran	Turkey				
Israel	Ukraine				
Korea	Uruguay				
Kyrgyz Rep.	Uzbekistan				
	Venezuela				
	Vietnam				

[3]Exchange rates of all currencies have shown limited flexibility in terms of the U.S. dollar.
[4]Refers to the cooperative arrangement maintained under the European Monetary System.
Source: International Monetary Fund, *International Financial Statistics* (Washington, D.C.; January 1998).

Copyright © by Houghton Mifflin Company. All rights reserved.

time to time in the foreign exchange market. Since exchange-rate variations can alter the prices of goods traded internationally, governments often attempt to push exchange rates to values consistent with some target value of international trade or investment. For example, on April 5, 1995, the U.S. Treasury and the Federal Reserve were concerned that the dollar had fallen in value too much, and investors were becoming concerned about the future stability of the currency. As a result, the Fed bought over $1 billion in exchange for German marks and Japanese yen. This intervention in the foreign exchange market caused the dollar to rise temporarily in value more than private-market pressures would have done.

Some countries, like Antigua, Barbuda and Benin, maintain a fixed value (or peg) relative to a single currency, such as the dollar or French franc. Fixed exchange rates are often called *pegged* exchange rates. Other countries, like Bangladesh, peg to a composite of currencies by setting the value of their currency at the average value of several foreign currencies.

Some currencies are pegged to the *SDR*, as you learned in the chapter on money and banking. The SDR, which stands for **special drawing right**, is an artificial unit of account. Its value is determined by combining the values of the U.S. dollar, German mark, Japanese yen, French franc, and British pound. A country that pegs to the SDR determines its currency's value in terms of an average of the five currencies that make up the SDR.

The column entitled "Cooperative Arrangements" in Table 1 lists the countries that belong to the **European Monetary System**, or **EMS**. These countries maintain fixed exchange rates against each other but allow their currencies to float jointly against the rest of the world. In other words, the values of currencies in the EMS all shift together relative to currencies outside the EMS.

Table 2 lists the end-of-year exchange rates for several currencies versus the U.S. dollar from the 1950s to the 1990s. For most of the currencies, there

Fixed (pegged) exchange rates are held constant over time.

special drawing right:
an artificial unit of account created by averaging the values of the U.S. dollar, German mark, Japanese yen, French franc, and British pound

European Monetary System (EMS):
an organization composed of Western European nations that maintain fixed exchange rates among themselves and floating exchange rates with the rest of the world

TABLE 2
Exchange Rates of Selected Countries (currency units per U.S. dollar)

Year	Canadian Dollar	Japanese Yen	French Franc	German Mark	Italian Lira	British Pound
1950	1.06	361	3.50	4.20	625	.36
1955	1.00	361	3.50	4.22	625	.36
1960	1.00	358	4.90	4.17	621	.36
1965	1.08	361	4.90	4.01	625	.36
1970	1.01	358	5.52	3.65	623	.42
1975	1.02	305	4.49	2.62	684	.50
1980	1.19	203	4.52	1.96	931	.42
1985	1.40	201	7.56	2.46	1,679	.69
1990	1.16	134	5.13	1.49	1,130	.52
1995	1.36	103	4.90	1.43	1,584	.65
1997	1.43	130	5.95	1.78	1,744	.60

Source: End-of-year exchange rates from International Monetary Fund, *International Financial Statistics*.

Copyright © by Houghton Mifflin Company. All rights reserved.

was little movement in the 1950s and 1960s, the era of the Bretton Woods agreement. In the early 1970s, exchange rates began to fluctuate. More recently, there has been considerable change in the foreign exchange value of a dollar, as Table 2 illustrates.

RECAP

1. Under a gold standard, each currency has a fixed value in terms of gold. This arrangement provides for fixed exchange rates between countries.

2. At the end of World War II, the Bretton Woods agreement established a new system of fixed exchange rates. Two new organizations—the International Monetary Fund (IMF) and the World Bank—also emerged from the Bretton Woods conference.

3. Fixed exchange rates are maintained by government intervention in the foreign exchange market; governments or central banks buy and sell currencies to keep the equilibrium exchange rate steady.

4. The governments of the major industrial countries adopted floating exchange rates in 1973. In fact, the prevailing system is characterized by "managed floating"—that is, by occasional government intervention rather than a pure free-market-determined exchange-rate system.

5. Some countries choose floating exchange rates; others peg their currencies to a single currency or a composite.

6. The European Monetary System maintains fixed exchange rates among several Western European currencies, which then float jointly against the rest of the world.

2. FIXED OR FLOATING EXCHANGE RATES

Is the United States better off today, with floating exchange rates, than it was with the fixed exchange rates of the post–World War II period? The choice of an exchange-rate system has multiple implications for the performance of a nation's economy and, therefore, for the conduct of macroeconomic policy. As is true of many policy issues in economics, economists often disagree about the merits of fixed versus flexible exchange rates. Let us look at the characteristics of the different exchange-rate systems.

2.a. Equilibrium in the Foreign Exchange Market

How is equilibrium determined in the foreign exchange market?

An exchange rate is the price of one money in terms of another. Equilibrium is determined by the supply of and demand for the two currencies in the foreign exchange market. Figure 1 contains two supply and demand diagrams for the U.S. dollar–French franc foreign exchange market. The downward-sloping demand curve indicates that the higher the dollar price of French francs, the fewer francs will be demanded. The upward-sloping supply curve indicates that the higher the dollar price of French francs, the more francs will be supplied.

In Figure 1(a), the initial equilibrium occurs at the point where the demand curve D_1 intersects the supply curve. At this point, the equilibrium

Copyright © by Houghton Mifflin Company. All rights reserved.

Figure 1
The Supply of and Demand for Foreign Exchange

This figure represents the foreign exchange market for francs traded for dollars. The demand curve for francs is based on the U.S. demand for French products, and the supply curve of francs is based on the French demand for U.S. products: an increase in demand for French wine causes demand for francs to increase from D_1 to D_2. This shift causes an increase from Q_1 to Q_2 in the equilibrium quantity of francs traded and causes the franc to appreciate to $.18 from the initial equilibrium exchange rate of $.15. A decrease in demand for French wine causes the demand for francs to fall from D_1 to D_3. This shift leads to a fall in the equilibrium quantity traded to Q_3 and a depreciation of the franc to $.12. If the French demand for U.S. tractors falls, fewer francs are supplied for exchange for dollars, as illustrated by the fall in supply from S_1 to S_3. This shift causes the franc to appreciate to $.18 and the equilibrium quantity of francs traded to fall to Q_3. If the French demand for U.S. tractors rises, then more francs are supplied for dollars and the supply curve increases from S_1 to S_2. This causes the franc to depreciate and the equilibrium quantity of francs traded to rise to Q_2.

(a) A Change in the U.S. Demand for French Wine

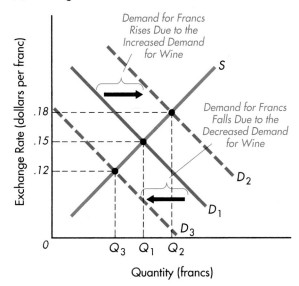

(b) A Change in the French Demand for U.S. Tractors

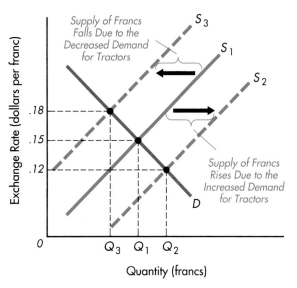

Copyright © by Houghton Mifflin Company. All rights reserved.

Equilibrium in the foreign exchange market occurs at the point where the foreign exchange demand and supply curves intersect.

exchange rate is $.15 (1 franc costs $.15) and the quantity of francs bought and sold is Q_1.

Suppose U.S. residents increase their demand for French wine. Because francs are needed to pay for the wine, the greater U.S. demand for French wine generates a greater demand for francs by U.S. citizens, who hold dollars. The demand curve in Figure 1(a) thus shifts from D_1 to D_2. This increased demand for francs causes the franc to appreciate relative to the dollar. The new exchange rate is $.18, and a greater quantity of francs, Q_2, is bought and sold.

If the U.S. demand for French wine falls, the demand for francs also falls, as illustrated by the shift from D_1 to D_3 in Figure 1(a). The decreased demand for francs causes the franc to depreciate relative to the dollar, so that the exchange rate falls to $.12.

So far, we have considered how shifts in the U.S. demand for French goods affect the dollar-franc exchange rate. We can also use the same supply and demand diagram to analyze how changes in the French demand for U.S. goods affect the equilibrium exchange rate. The supply of francs to the foreign exchange market originates with French residents who buy goods from the rest of the world. If a French importer buys a tractor from a U.S. firm, the importer must exchange francs for dollars to pay for the tractor. As French residents' demand for foreign goods and services rises and falls, the supply of francs to the foreign exchange market changes.

Suppose the French demand for U.S. tractors increases. This brings about a shift of the supply curve: as francs are exchanged for dollars to buy the U.S. tractors, the supply of francs increases. In Figure 1(b), the supply of francs curve shifts from S_1 to S_2. The greater supply of francs causes the franc to depreciate relative to the dollar, and the exchange rate falls from $.15 to $.12. If the French demand for U.S. tractors decreases, the supply of francs decreases from S_1 to S_3, and the franc appreciates to $.18.

Foreign exchange supply and demand curves are affected by changes in tastes and technology and by changing government policy. As demand and supply change, the equilibrium exchange rate changes. In fact, continuous shifts in supply and demand cause the exchange rate to change as often as every day, based on free market forces. Now let us consider how fixed exchange rates differ from floating exchange rates.

2.b. Adjustment Mechanisms Under Fixed and Flexible Exchange Rates

How do fixed and floating exchange rates differ in their adjustment to shifts in supply and demand for currencies?

Figure 2 shows the dollar-franc foreign exchange market. The exchange rate is the number of dollars required to buy one franc; the quantity is the quantity of francs bought and sold. Suppose that, initially, the equilibrium is at point A, with quantity Q_1 francs traded at $.15 per franc.

Suppose French wine becomes more popular in the United States, and the demand for francs increases from D_1 to D_2. With flexible exchange rates (as in Figure 1), a new equilibrium is established at point B. The exchange rate rises to $.18 per franc, and the quantity of francs bought and sold is Q_2.

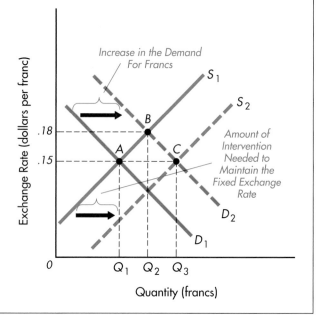

Figure 2
Foreign Exchange Market Equilibrium
Under Fixed and Flexible Exchange Rates
Initially, equilibrium is at point A; the exchange rate is $.15 and Q_1 francs are traded. An increase in demand for French wine causes the demand for francs to increase from D_1 to D_2. With flexible exchange rates, the franc appreciates in value to $.18 and Q_2 francs are traded; equilibrium is at point B. If the government is committed to maintaining a fixed exchange rate of $.15, the supply of francs must be increased to S_2 so that a new equilibrium can occur at point C. The government must intervene in the foreign exchange market and sell francs to shift the supply curve to S_2.

Copyright © by Houghton Mifflin Company. All rights reserved.

Copyright © by Houghton Mifflin Company. All rights reserved.

appreciate:
when the value of a currency increases under floating exchange rates—that is, exchange rates determined by supply and demand

depreciate:
when the value of a currency decreases under floating exchange rates

An increase in demand for a currency will cause an appreciation of its exchange rate, unless governments intervene in the foreign exchange market to increase the supply of that currency.

fundamental disequilibrium:
a permanent shift in the foreign-exchange-market supply and demand curves, such that the fixed exchange rate is no longer an equilibrium rate

speculators:
people who seek to profit from an expected shift in an exchange rate by selling the currency expected to depreciate and buying the currency expected to appreciate, then exchanging the appreciated currency for the depreciated currency after the exchange rate adjustment

The increased demand for francs has caused the franc to **appreciate** (rise in value against the dollar) and the dollar to **depreciate** (fall in value against the franc). This is an example of a freely floating exchange rate, determined by the free market forces of supply and demand.

Now suppose the Federal Reserve is committed to maintaining a fixed exchange rate of $.15 per franc. The increase in demand for francs causes a shortage of francs at the exchange rate of $.15. According to the new demand curve, D_2, the quantity of francs demanded at $.15 is Q_3. The quantity supplied is found on the original supply curve S_1, at Q_1. The only way to maintain the exchange rate of $.15 is for the Federal Reserve to supply francs to meet the shortage of $Q_3 - Q_1$. In other words, the Fed must sell $Q_3 - Q_1$ francs to shift the supply curve to S_2 and thus maintain the fixed exchange rate.

If the increased demand for francs is temporary, the Fed can continue to supply francs for the short time necessary. However, if the increased demand for francs is permanent, the Fed's intervention will eventually end when it runs out of francs. This situation—a permanent change in supply or demand—is referred to as a **fundamental disequilibrium**. The fixed exchange rate is no longer an equilibrium rate. Under the Bretton Woods agreement, a country was supposed to devalue its currency in such cases.

Suppose that the shift to D_2 in Figure 2 is permanent. In this case, the dollar should be devalued. A devaluation to $.18 per franc would restore equilibrium in the foreign exchange market without requiring further intervention by the government. Sometimes, however, governments try to maintain the old exchange rate ($.15 per franc, in this case) even though most people believe the shift in demand to be permanent. When this happens, **speculators** buy the currency that is in greater demand (francs, in our example) in anticipation of the eventual devaluation of the other currency (dollars, in Figure 2). A speculator who purchases francs for $.15 prior to the devaluation and sells them for $.18 after the devaluation earns $.03 per franc purchased—a 20 percent profit.

Speculation puts greater devaluation pressure on the dollar: the speculators sell dollars and buy francs, causing the demand for francs to increase even further. Such speculative activity contributed to the breakdown of the Bretton Woods system of fixed exchange rates. Several countries intervened to support exchange rates that were far out of line with free market forces. The longer a devaluation was put off, the more obvious it became that devaluation was forthcoming and the more speculators entered the market. In 1971 and 1973, speculators sold dollars for yen and German marks. They were betting that the dollar would be devalued; both times they were correct. The speculative activity of the early 1970s drew attention to the folly of efforts to maintain fixed exchange rates in the face of a change in the fundamental equilibrium exchange rate.

2.c. Constraints on Economic Policy

What are the advantages and disadvantages of fixed and floating exchange rates?

Fixed exchange rates can be maintained over time only between countries with similar economic policies and similar underlying economic conditions. As prices rise within a country, the domestic value of a unit of its currency falls, since the currency buys fewer goods and services. In the foreign exchange market too, the value of a unit of domestic currency falls, since it buys relatively fewer goods and services than the foreign currency does. A fixed exchange rate thus requires that the purchasing power of the two currencies change at roughly the same rate over time. Only if two nations have approximately the same inflation experience will they be able to maintain a fixed exchange rate. This condition was a frequent source of problems in the Bretton Woods era of fixed exchange rates. In the late 1960s, for instance, the U.S. government was following a more expansionary macroeconomic policy than was Germany. U.S. government expenditures on the war in Vietnam and domestic antipoverty initiatives led to inflationary pressures that were not matched in Germany. Between 1965 and 1970, price levels rose by 23.2 percent in the United States but only by 12.8 percent in Germany. Since the purchasing power of a dollar was falling faster than that of the mark, the fixed exchange rate could not be maintained. The dollar had to be devalued.

One of the advantages of floating exchange rates is that countries are free to pursue their own macroeconomic policies without worrying about maintaining an exchange-rate commitment. If U.S. policy produces a higher inflation rate than Japanese policy, the dollar will automatically depreciate in value against the yen. The United States can choose the macroeconomic policy it wants, independent of other nations, and let the exchange rate adjust if its inflation rate differs markedly from that of other nations. If the dollar were fixed in value relative to the yen, the two nations couldn't follow independent policies and expect to maintain the exchange rate.

It became obvious in the late 1960s that many governments considered other issues more important than maintenance of a fixed exchange rate. A nation that puts a high priority on reducing unemployment will typically stimulate the economy to try to increase income and create jobs. This initiative may cause the domestic inflation rate to rise and the domestic currency to depreciate relative to other currencies. If one goal or the other—lower unemployment or a fixed exchange rate—must be given up, it is likely that the exchange-rate goal will be sacrificed.

Floating exchange rates allow countries to formulate domestic economic policy solely in response to domestic issues; attention need not be paid to the exchange rate of the rest of the world. For residents of some countries, this freedom may be more of a problem than a benefit. The freedom to choose a rate of inflation and let the exchange rate adjust itself can have undesirable consequences in countries whose politicians, for whatever reason, follow highly inflationary policies. In these countries a fixed-exchange-rate system would impose discipline, since maintenance of the exchange rate would not permit policies that diverged sharply from those of its trading partner.

Floating exchange rates allow countries to formulate their macroeconomic policies independently of other nations. Fixed exchange rates require the economic policies of countries linked by the exchange rate to be similar.

RECAP

1. Under a fixed-exchange-rate system, governments must intervene in the foreign exchange market to maintain the exchange rate. A fundamental disequilibrium requires a currency devaluation.

2. Fixed exchange rates can be maintained only between countries with similar macroeconomic policies and similar underlying economic conditions.

3. Fixed exchange rates serve as a constraint on inflationary government policies.

Copyright © by Houghton Mifflin Company. All rights reserved.

3. THE CHOICE OF AN EXCHANGE-RATE SYSTEM

Different countries choose different exchange-rate arrangements. Why does the United States choose floating exchange rates while Barbados adopts a fixed exchange rate? Let us compare the characteristics of countries that choose to float with those of countries that choose to fix their exchange rates.

What determines the kind of exchange-rate system a country adopts?

3.a. Country Characteristics

The choice of an exchange-rate system is an important element of the macro-economic policy of any country. The choice seems to be related to country size, openness, inflation, and diversification of trade.

3.a.1. Size Large countries (measured by economic output or GDP) tend to be both independent and relatively unwilling to forgo domestic policy goals in order to maintain a fixed exchange rate. Because large countries have large domestic markets, international issues are less crucial to everyday business than they are in a small country.

3.a.2. Openness Closely related to size is the relative openness of the economy. By openness, we mean the degree to which the country depends on international trade. Because every country is involved in international trade, openness is very much a matter of degree. An **open economy**, according to economists, is one in which a relatively large fraction of the GDP is devoted to internationally tradable goods. In a closed economy, a relatively small fraction of the GDP is devoted to internationally tradable goods. The more open an economy, the greater the impact of variations in the exchange rate on the domestic economy. The more open the economy, therefore, the greater the tendency to establish fixed exchange rates.

open economy:
an economy in which a relatively large fraction of the GDP is devoted to internationally tradable goods

3.a.3. Inflation Countries whose policies produce inflation rates much higher or lower than those of other countries tend to choose floating exchange rates. A fixed exchange rate cannot be maintained when a country experiences inflation much different from that of the rest of the world.

3.a.4. Trade Diversification Countries that trade largely with a single foreign country tend to peg their currencies' value to that of the trading partner. For instance, South Africa accounts for the dominant share of the total trade of Swaziland. By pegging its currency, the lilangeni, to the South African rand, Swaziland enjoys more stable lilangeni prices of goods than it would with floating exchange rates. Trade with South Africa is such a dominant feature of the Swaziland economy that a fluctuating lilangeni price of the rand would be reflected in a fluctuating price level in Swaziland. If the lilangeni depreciated against the rand, the lilangeni prices of imports from South Africa would rise: this would bring about a rise in the Swaziland price level. Exchange-rate depreciation tends to affect the domestic price level in all countries, but the effect is magnified if a single foreign country accounts for much of a nation's trade. Countries with diversified trading patterns find fixed exchange rates less desirable, because price stability would prevail only in trade with a single country. With all other trading partners, prices would still fluctuate.

Table 3 summarizes the national characteristics associated with alternative exchange-rate systems. Many countries do not fit into the neat categorization of Table 3, but it is nonetheless useful for understanding the great majority of countries' choices.

Copyright © by Houghton Mifflin Company. All rights reserved.

TABLE 3
Characteristics of Countries with Fixed and Floating Exchange Rates

Fixed-Rate Countries	*Floating-Rate Countries*
Small size	Large size
Open economy	Closed economy
Harmonious inflation rate	Divergent inflation rate
Concentrated trade	Diversified trade

3.b. Multiple Exchange Rates

multiple exchange rates:
a system whereby a government fixes different exchange rates for different types of transactions

Most countries conduct all their foreign exchange transactions at a single exchange rate. For instance, if the dollar-pound exchange rate is $1.80, residents of the United States can purchase British pounds at $1.80, no matter what use they make of the pounds. However, some countries have **multiple exchange rates**—different exchange rates for different types of transactions. A typical arrangement is a dual exchange-rate system, consisting of a free-market-determined floating exchange rate for financial transactions and a fixed exchange rate that overvalues the domestic currency for transactions in goods and services. Some countries adopt even more elaborate arrangements, with special exchange rates for a variety of different transactions. For example, Venezuela once had a four-tier system. The central bank traded dollars for bolivars (Bs) at the following rates: sell dollars for Bs4.30 for interest payments on foreign debt; sell dollars for Bs6.00 for national petroleum and iron-ore companies; and sell dollars for Bs7.50 for other government agencies. All other transactions took place at the free market floating exchange rate of Bs14.40.

Countries with multiple exchange rates use them as an alternative to taxes and subsidies. Activities that the policymakers want to encourage are subsidized by allowing participants in them to buy foreign exchange at an artificially low price or sell foreign exchange at an artificially high price. Participants in activities that policymakers want to discourage are forced to pay an artificially high price to buy foreign exchange and an artificially low price to sell foreign exchange. For instance, firms that manufacture goods for export, but import some of the resources used in production, may be permitted to buy foreign exchange at an artificially low price. This allows them to pay a lower domestic-currency price for their imported resources and consequently to charge a lower price for their output, which increases exports. In Venezuela, as you just saw, petroleum companies could buy dollars from the Central Bank for Bs6.00 even though the free-market rate was Bs14.40. In order to encourage greater production and export of Venezuelan petroleum, the Central Bank subsidized the dollars the petroleum companies needed for imports.

In an effort to discourage imports, developing countries often charge an artificially high price for foreign exchange that will be used to import consumer goods. Such multiple-exchange-rate systems have the same effects as direct government subsidies to exporting manufacturers and taxes on the importation of consumer goods: exports are stimulated and consumer-goods imports are reduced.

Copyright © by Houghton Mifflin Company. All rights reserved.

Figure 3
Overvalued Exchange Rate
The official exchange rate is 150 pesos per dollar, while the free market equilibrium exchange rate is 200 pesos per dollar. Since the official peso price of a dollar is below the equilibrium, the peso is said to be overvalued.

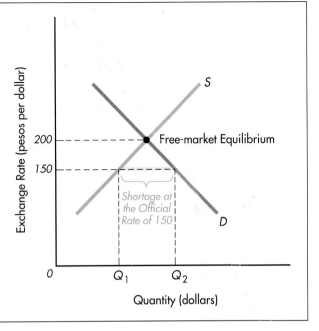

The IMF has tried to discourage multiple exchange rates, because they cause the domestic prices of internationally traded goods to differ from the international prices. The result is inefficient resource utilization in consumption and production, since domestic residents respond to the contrived relative prices rather than the true prices set on world markets. Monitoring and administering compliance with multiple exchange rates create additional costs, and people devote resources to avoiding the unfavorable aspects of multiple exchange rates (for example, by getting their transactions classified to the most favorable exchange rate).

3.c. Overvalued Exchange Rates

Developing countries often establish an official exchange rate—the exchange rate set by law—that differs from the equilibrium exchange rate. Figure 3 illustrates an overvalued exchange rate. Assume that a developing country whose currency is called the peso fixes an official peso-dollar exchange rate of 150 pesos per dollar, while the free market equilibrium exchange rate is 200 pesos per dollar. Since the official rate is less than the equilibrium rate, a dollar shortage results. Q_2 dollars are demanded at 150 pesos per dollar, but only Q_1 are supplied.

When the official peso-dollar rate is less than the free market rate, the peso is overvalued. To support the official rate, the country must impose tariffs or other restrictions on trade to reduce the demand for dollars. Overvaluing the domestic currency subsidizes favored activities or groups: if everyone had access to the official rate, there would be a dollar shortage. In addition to imposing quotas or tariffs on international trade in goods or financial assets, the country can use multiple exchange rates to ensure that only favored groups buy dollars at the official rate. In fact, a typical feature of multiple-exchange-rate regimes is the availability of an overvalued domestic-currency rate for favored transactions. Other residents are forced into the free market, where in this case they pay 200 pesos for their dollars.

Overvalued exchange rates are used to subsidize favored transactions.

Copyright © by Houghton Mifflin Company. All rights reserved.

RECAP

1. Countries with fixed exchange rates tend to be small, open economies with inflation rates similar to those of their trading partners. Their currencies are typically pegged to that of their main trading partner.

2. Some countries adopt multiple exchange rates for different kinds of transactions.

3. Multiple exchange rates resemble a system of subsidies for favored activities and taxes for activities that are discouraged.

4. An exchange rate is overvalued when the official domestic-currency price of foreign currency is lower than the equilibrium price.

SUMMARY

▬▬ How does a commodity standard fix exchange rates between countries?

1. Between 1880 and 1914, a gold standard provided for fixed exchange rates among countries. §1.a

2. The gold standard ended with World War I, and no established international monetary system replaced it until after World War II, when the Bretton Woods agreement created a fixed-exchange-rate system. §1.b

▬▬ What kinds of exchange-rate arrangements exist today?

3. Today some countries have fixed exchange rates, others have floating exchange rates, and still others have managed floats or other types of systems. §1.e

▬▬ How is equilibrium determined in the foreign exchange market?

4. Foreign-exchange-market equilibrium is determined by the intersection of the demand and supply curves for foreign exchange. §2.a

▬▬ How do fixed and floating exchange rates differ in their adjustment to shifts in supply and demand for currencies?

5. Under fixed exchange rates, central banks must intervene in the foreign exchange market to keep the exchange rate from shifting. §2.b

▬▬ What are the advantages and disadvantages of fixed and floating exchange rates?

6. Floating exchange rates permit countries to pursue independent economic policies. A fixed exchange rate requires a country to adopt policies similar to those of the country whose currency it pegs to. A fixed exchange rate may serve to prevent a country from pursuing inflationary policies. §2.c

▬▬ What determines the kind of exchange-rate system a country adopts?

7. The choice of an exchange-rate system is related to the size and openness of a country, its inflation experience, and the diversification of its international trade. §3.a

8. Multiple exchange rates are used to subsidize favored activities and raise costs for other activities. §3.b

KEY TERMS

gold standard §1.a

gold exchange standard §1.b

reserve currency §1.b

International Monetary Fund (IMF) §1.c

World Bank §1.c

foreign exchange market intervention §1.d

devaluation §1.d

equilibrium exchange rates §1.d

managed floating exchange rates §1.e

special drawing right §1.e

European Monetary System (EMS) §1.e

Copyright © by Houghton Mifflin Company. All rights reserved.

appreciate §2.b

depreciate §2.b

fundamental disequilibrium §2.b

speculators §2.b

open economy §3.a.2

multiple exchange rates §3.b

EXERCISES

1. Under a gold standard, if the price of an ounce of gold is 400 U.S. dollars and 500 Canadian dollars, what is the exchange rate between U.S. and Canadian dollars?

2. What were the three major results of the Bretton Woods conference?

3. What is the difference between the IMF and the World Bank?

4. How can Mexico fix the value of the peso relative to the dollar when the demand for and supply of dollars and pesos changes continuously? Illustrate your explanation with a graph.

5. Draw a foreign-exchange-market supply and demand diagram to show how the mark-dollar exchange rate is determined. Set the initial equilibrium at a rate of 1.5 marks per dollar.

6. Using the diagram in question 5, illustrate the effect of a change in tastes prompting German residents to buy more goods from the United States. If the exchange rate is floating, what will happen to the foreign-exchange-market equilibrium?

7. Using the diagram in question 5, illustrate the effect of the change in German tastes if exchange rates are fixed. What will happen to the foreign-exchange-market equilibrium?

8. When and why should exchange rates change under a fixed exchange-rate system?

9. Other things being equal, what kind of exchange-rate system would you expect each of the following countries to adopt?

   a. A small country that conducts all of its trade with the United States

   b. A country that has no international trade

   c. A country whose policies have led to a 300 percent annual rate of inflation

   d. A country that wants to offer exporters cheap access to the imported inputs they need but to discourage other domestic residents from importing goods

   e. A large country like the United States or Japan

10. Illustrate and explain the meaning and likely effects of an overvalued exchange rate.

11. The countries listed as pegging to the French franc in Table 1 have a characteristic in common that helps to explain why they maintain fixed exchange rates with the franc. Explain what that characteristic is.

12. Suppose you just returned home from a vacation in Mazatlán, Mexico, where you exchanged U.S. dollars for Mexican pesos. How did your trip to Mexico affect the supply and demand for dollars and the exchange rate (assume that all other things are equal)?

13. What does it mean to say that a currency appreciates or depreciates in value? Give an example of each and briefly mention what might cause such a change.

14. If you were an economic policy czar with total power to choose your country's economic policy, would you want a fixed or floating exchange rate for your currency? Why?

15. How does a currency speculator profit from exchange-rate changes? Give an example of a profitable speculation.

🖥 INTERNET EXERCISE

In section 1.e of this chapter we learned about the different exchange-rate arrangements existing in the world. To see current information on the choices of different countries, go to the Boyes/Melvin web site at http://www.hmco.com/college/ and click on the internet exercise link for this chapter. Now answer the questions that appear on the web page.

Copyright © by Houghton Mifflin Company. All rights reserved.

Germans Urge Delay of Euro Adoption: Economists Say Target Date of 1999 Won't Give Nations Enough Time to Fulfill Key Conditions to Ensure Success

Warning it is "too early" for a European common currency, more than 150 leading German economists yesterday called for the January 1999 adoption of the currency to be postponed for several years.

In a sharply worded petition published in the *Financial Times* and the *Frankfurter Allgemeine Zeitung*, the economists said proceeding on schedule will doom Europe's plans for monetary union to failure. Key conditions for success, like public debt reduction, have not been adequately met, the economists said.

"The current state of economic affairs is most unsuitable for starting monetary union," the economists wrote.

"The risks are too high," said one of the economists, Wim Kosters, in a telephone interview. "We have only one shot at economic union. The success of the euro is more important than the starting date."

The manifesto is the second effort to delay Europe's monetary union. Last month, four academics filed suit in Germany's highest court in hopes of stalling the introduction of the common currency, known as the euro. . . .

A common currency, agreed to by Europe's leaders in the 1992 Maastrict Treaty, was seen as a way to unite Europe into a forceful economic bloc to compete in today's global economy. To qualify, countries had to have their economic house in order, including running a budget deficit of less than 3 percent of gross domestic product.

Then, the greatest obstacle to a common currency was seen as public opinion. Few countries wanted to lose native currency.

Now, specialists warn, the obstacles are economic. Too many countries are dabbling in "creative accounting" in an effort to meet the economic union's criteria, they say.

Many countries, including Germany, will just be able to get their budget deficit down to 3 percent. But specialists say that target should be the limit, not the target. Budget deficits should now be closer to zero for the euro to stay sound. . . .

"The problem is not to meet the criteria now; the problem will be to keep the euro going," said Dr. Ernst Helmstaedter, a former economic advisor to Kohl, who was not among those who signed yesterday's petition.

Among the countries struggling to meet the criteria are those with the most vested in it: Germany and France. The two strong trade partners have been pushing for the euro's adoption since 1992.

But both countries are now reeling from double-digit unemployment and shaky economies. Outcry against the euro is strongest in Germany, as many here fear France and Germany are pushing the rest of Europe into economic union too quickly.

"We are witnessing the big policy makers in Europe risk the continent's biggest economic adventure of all time," said Wilhelm Noelling, the former president of the Central Bank Hamburg, one of the economists who filed the suit.

Source: "Germans Urge Delay of Euro Adoption: Economists Say Target Date of 1999 Won't Give Nations Enough Time to Fulfill Key Conditions to Ensure Success," by Elizabeth Neuffer, *The Boston Globe*, February 10, 1998. Reprinted by permission.

Copyright © by Houghton Mifflin Company. All rights reserved.

The Boston Globe/February 10, 1998

COMMENTARY

A fixed exchange-rate system represents an agreement among countries to convert their individual currencies from one to another at a given rate. The adoption of one money for Europe is the strongest possible commitment to fixed exchange rates among the EU countries. If every nation uses the same currency, the euro, then all would be linked to the same inflation rate and there would be no fluctuation of the value of the currency across the EU nations using the currency—just as each state in the United States uses the same money, the U.S. dollar. The adoption of a single currency requires that economic policies be similar across EU countries. This means that individual countries must subjugate their monetary policies to the goals of the European monetary and fiscal authority. If each nation insists on exercising its own monetary and fiscal policy and chooses different interest and inflation rates, there can never be one money.

A convergence in inflation rates is necessary for the smooth operation of any fixed exchange rate. Persistent inflation differentials across the members of a fixed exchange-rate system affect the competitiveness of each member's exports in the world market. Though a fixed exchange-rate system maintains stable *nominal exchange rates* (the rate observed in the foreign exchange market), the competitiveness of a currency is represented by the *real exchange rate*. The real exchange rate is the nominal exchange rate adjusted for the price level at home compared to the price level abroad. It is calculated as follows:

$$\text{Real exchange rate} = \frac{\begin{array}{c}\text{(nominal exchange rate}\\ \times \text{ foreign price level)}\end{array}}{\text{domestic price level}}$$

The disruptive changes in competitiveness caused by persistent inflation differentials require a realignment of a fixed exchange-rate system that adjusts nominal exchange rates to keep real exchange rates from drifting too far from their correct value. For instance, if the Italian price level starts to rise faster than German prices, Italian goods will be priced out of the German market unless the lira depreciates on the foreign exchange market. According to the equation just presented, if Italy is the domestic country and its price level rises, the real exchange rate falls and Italian goods are, therefore, relatively more expensive unless the nominal exchange rate rises to offset the higher domestic price level. The need for similar inflation rates within a fixed exchange-rate system indicates that a country could successfully join the fixed exchange-rate system or a region with one money only when its inflation rate fell to a level closer to that of other European countries.

The plan for a single currency hinges on the convergence of member country economic policies. To ensure convergence of their policies, each country is to meet the following criteria: the government budget deficit must not exceed 3 percent of GDP and government debt must not exceed 60 percent of GDP; the inflation rate must not exceed the average inflation of the three lowest inflation countries by more than 1.5 percentage points; and the long-term government bond interest rate must not exceed the average rate of the three lowest inflation countries by more than 2 percentage points. The article indicates that a large group of German economists thought that countries had not made sufficient progress toward these goals to warrent the move to the common euro currency. At the time of this article, February 1998, the start of the euro was scheduled for January 1, 1999. By the time you read this, you will know whether the European countries were able to execute the plan as scheduled.

Copyright © by Houghton Mifflin Company. All rights reserved.

Glossary

absolute advantage an advantage derived from one country having a lower absolute input cost of producing a particular good than another country (20)

adaptive expectation an expectation formed on the basis of information collected in the past (15)

aggregate demand curve a curve that shows the different equilibrium levels of expenditures at different price levels (9)

aggregate supply curve a curve that shows the amount of production at different price levels (9)

appreciate to increase the value of a currency under floating exchange rates—that is, exchange rates determined by supply and demand (22)

arbitrage buying in a market where the price is low and selling in a market where the price is high to profit from the price differential (17)

association as causation the mistaken assumption that because two events seem to occur together, one causes the other (1)

assumptions statements that are taken for granted without justification (1)

automatic stabilizer an element of fiscal policy that changes automatically as income changes (12)

autonomous consumption consumption that is independent of income (10)

average propensity to consume (APC) the proportion of disposable income spent for consumption (10)

average propensity to save (APS) the proportion of disposable income saved (10)

balance of payments a record of a country's trade in goods, services, and financial assets with the rest of the world (7)

balance of trade the balance on the merchandise account in the U.S. balance of payments (7)

barter the direct exchange of goods and services without the use of money (3)

base year the year against which other years are measured (6)

bilateral aid foreign aid that flows from one country to another (19)

budget deficit the shortage that results when government spending is greater than revenue (5)

budget surplus the excess that results when government spending is less than revenue (5)

business cycle the recurrent pattern of rising real GDP followed by falling real GDP (5, 8)

business firm a business organization controlled by a single management (4)

capital products such as machinery and equipment that are used in production (1)

capital account the record in the balance of payments of the flow of financial assets into and out of a country (7)

capital consumption allowance the estimated value of depreciation plus the value of accidental damage to capital stock (6)

capital control a government-imposed restriction on the free movement of financial assets between nations (17)

centrally planned economy an economic system in which the government determines what goods and services are produced and the prices at which they are sold (5)

ceteris paribus other things being equal, or everything else held constant (1)

chain-type real GDP the geometric mean of the growth rates found using beginning and ending year prices (6)

circular flow diagram a model showing the flow of output and income from one sector of the economy to another (4)

classical economics a school of thought that assumes that real national income is determined by aggregate supply, while the equilibrium price level is determined by aggregate demand (16)

coincident indicator a variable that changes at the same time that real output changes (8)

commercial bank loan a bank loan at market rates of interest, often involving a bank syndicate (19)

commercial policy government policy that influences international trade flows (21)

comparative advantage the ability to produce a good or service at a lower opportunity cost than someone else (2, 20)

complementary goods goods that are used together (as the price of one rises, the demand for the other falls) (3)

composite currency an artificial unit of account that is an average of the values of several national currencies (13)

consumer price index (CPI) a measure of the average price of goods and services purchased by the typical household (6)

consumer sovereignty the supreme authority of consumers to determine, by means of their purchases, what is produced (4)

consumption household spending (4)

consumption function the relationship between disposable income and consumption (10)

corporation a legal entity owned by shareholders whose liability for the firm's losses is limited to the value of the stock they own (4)

cost of living adjustment (COLA) an increase in wages that is designed to match increases in prices of items purchased by the typical household (6)

Copyright © by Houghton Mifflin Company. All rights reserved.

cost-push inflation inflation caused by rising costs of production (9)

credit available savings that are lent to borrowers to spend (13)

crowding out a drop in consumption or investment spending caused by government spending (12)

currency convertibility the ease with which the domestic currency can be converted into foreign currency so foreign exchange rates can properly reflect the domestic currency value of foreign prices (19)

currency substitution the use of foreign money as a substitute for domestic money when the domestic money has a high rate of inflation (13)

current account the sum of the merchandise, services, investment income, and unilateral transfers accounts in the balance of payments (7)

customs union an organization of nations whose members have no trade barriers among themselves but are free to fashion their own trade policies toward non-members (21)

deficit in a balance of payments account, the amount by which debits exceed credits (7)

demand the quantities of a well-defined commodity that consumers are willing and able to buy at each possible price during a given period of time, *ceteris paribus* (3)

demand curve a graph of a demand schedule that measures price on the vertical axis and quantity demanded on the horizontal axis (3)

demand-pull inflation inflation caused by increasing demand for output (9)

demand schedule a list or table of the prices and the corresponding quantities demanded of a particular good or service (3)

dependent variable the variable whose value depends on the value of the independent variable (1 App.)

deposit expansion multiplier the reciprocal of the reserve requirement (13)

depreciation (of capital) a reduction in the value of capital goods over time due to their use in production (6)

depreciate (a currency) a decrease in the value of a currency under floating exchange rates (22)

depression a severe, prolonged economic contraction (8)

determinants of demand factors other than the price of the good that influence demand—income, tastes, prices of related goods and services, expectations, and number of buyers (3)

determinants of supply factors other than the price of the good that influence supply—prices of resources, technology and productivity, expectations of producers, number of producers, and the prices of related goods and services (3)

devaluation a deliberate decrease in the official value of a currency (22)

direct or positive relationship the relationship that exists when the values of related variables move in the same direction (1 App.)

discount rate the interest rate the Fed charges commercial banks (14)

discouraged workers workers who have stopped looking for work because they believe no one will offer them a job (8)

discretionary fiscal policy changes in government spending and taxation aimed at achieving a policy goal (12)

disequilibrium a point at which quantity demanded and quantity supplied are not equal at a particular price (3)

disposable personal income (DPI) personal income minus personal taxes (6)

dissaving spending financed by borrowing or using savings (10)

double coincidence of wants the situation that exists when A has what B wants and B has what A wants (3)

double-entry bookkeeping a system of accounting in which every transaction is recorded in at least two accounts and in which the debit total must equal the credit total for the transaction as a whole (7)

dual economy an economy in which two sectors (typically manufacturing and agriculture) show very different levels of development (19)

economic bad any item for which we would pay to have less (1)

economic efficiency a situation where no one in society can be made better off without making someone else worse off (5)

economic good any good that is scarce (1)

economic growth an increase in real national income, usually measured as the percentage change in gross national product or gross domestic product per year (18)

equation of exchange an equation that relates the quantity of money to nominal GNP (14)

equilibrium the point at which quantity demanded and quantity supplied are equal at a particular price (3)

equilibrium exchange rates the exchange rates that are established in the absence of government foreign exchange market intervention (22)

Eurocurrency market the market for deposits and loans generally denominated in a currency other than the currency of the country in which the transaction occurs; also called offshore banking (13)

European Currency Unit (ECU) a unit of account used by western European nations as their official reserve asset (13)

European Monetary System (EMS) an organization composed of Western European nations that maintain fixed exchange rates among themselves and floating exchange rates with the rest of the world (22)

excess reserves the cash reserves beyond those required, which can be loaned (13)

exchange rate the price of one country's money in terms of another country's money (3, 7)

export substitution the use of labor to produce manufactured products for export rather than agricultural products for the domestic market (19)

export supply curve a curve showing the relationship between the world price of a good and the amount that a country will export (20)

exports products that a country sells to other countries (4)

expropriation a government seizure of assets, typically without adequate compensation to owners (19)

externalities costs or benefits of a transaction that are borne by someone not directly involved in the transaction (5)

fallacy of composition the mistaken assumption that what applies in the case of one applies to the case of many (1)

Copyright © by Houghton Mifflin Company. All rights reserved.

Federal Deposit Insurance Corporation (FDIC) a federal agency that insures deposits in commercial banks (13)

federal funds rate the interest rate a bank charges when it lends excess reserves to another bank (14)

Federal Open Market Committee (FOMC) the official policy-making body of the Federal Reserve System (14)

Federal Reserve the central bank of the United States (5)

financial capital the money used to purchase capital; stocks and bonds. (31)

financial intermediaries institutions that accept deposits from savers and make loans to borrowers (4)

fiscal policy policy directed toward government spending and taxation (5)

FOMC directive instructions issued by the FOMC to the Federal Reserve Bank of New York to implement monetary policy (14)

foreign aid gifts or low-cost loans made to developing countries from official sources (19)

foreign direct investment the purchase of a physical operating unit in a foreign country or more than ten percent investment (19)

foreign exchange foreign currency and bank deposits that are denominated in foreign money (7)

foreign exchange market a global market in which people trade one currency for another (7)

foreign exchange market intervention buying and selling of currencies by a government or central bank to achieve a specified exchange rate (14, 22)

fractional reserve banking system a system in which banks keep less than 100 percent of the deposits available for withdrawal (13)

free good a good for which there is no scarcity (1)

free ride the enjoyment of the benefits of a good by a producer or consumer without having to pay for it (5)

free trade area an organization of nations whose members have no trade barriers among themselves but are free to fashion their own trade policies toward non-members (21)

fundamental disequilibrium a permanent shift in the foreign-exchange-market supply and demand curves, such that the fixed exchange rate is no longer an equilibrium rate (22)

GDP price index a broad measure of the prices of goods and services included in the gross domestic product (6)

gold exchange standard an exchange-rate system in which each nation fixes the value of its currency in terms of gold, but buys and sells the U.S. dollar rather than gold to maintain fixed exchange rates (22)

gold standard a system whereby national currencies are fixed in terms of their value in gold, thus creating fixed exchange rates between currencies (22)

gross domestic product (GDP) the market value of all final goods and services produced in a year within a country (6)

gross investment total investment, including investment expenditures required to replace capital goods consumed in current production (6)

gross national production (GNP) gross domestic production plus receipts of factor income from the rest of the world minus payments of factor income to the rest of the world (6)

household one or more persons who occupy a unit of housing (4)

hyperinflation an extremely high rate of inflation (8)

import demand curve a curve showing the relationship between the world price of a good and the amount that a country will import (20)

import substitution the substitution of domestically produced manufactured goods for imported manufactured goods (19)

imports products that a country buys from other countries (4)

increasing-returns-to-scale industry an industry in which the costs of producing a unit of output fall as more output is produced (21)

independent variable the variable whose value does not depend on the value of other variables (1 App.)

indirect business tax a tax that is collected by businesses for a government agency (6)

inflation a sustained rise in the average level of prices (8)

interest rate effect a change in interest rates that causes investment and therefore aggregate expenditures to change as the level of prices changes (9)

interest rate parity (IRP) the condition under which similar financial assets have the same interest rate when measured in the same currency (17)

intermediate good a good that is used as an input in the production of final goods and services (6)

intermediate target an objective used to achieve some ultimate policy goal (14)

international banking facility (IBF) a division of a U.S. bank that is allowed to receive deposits from and make loans to nonresidents of the United States without the restrictions that apply to domestic U.S. banks (13)

International Monetary Fund (IMF) an international organization that supervises exchange-rate arrangements and lends money to member countries experiencing problems meeting their external financial obligations (22)

international reserve asset an asset used to settle debts between governments (13)

international reserve currency a currency held by a government to settle international debts (13)

international trade effect the change in aggregate expenditures resulting from a change in the domestic price level that changes the price of domestic goods in relation to foreign goods (9)

intraindustry trade simultaneous import and export of goods in the same industry by a particular country (21)

inventory the stock of unsold goods held by a firm (6)

inverse or negative relationship the relationship that exists when the values of related variables move in opposite directions (1 App.)

investment spending on capital goods to be used in producing goods and services (4)

Keynesian economics a school of thought that emphasizes the role government plays in stabilizing the economy by managing aggregate demand (16)

labor the physical and intellectual services of people, including the training, education, and abilities of the individuals in a society (1)

lagging indicator a variable that changes after real output changes (8)

Copyright © by Houghton Mifflin Company. All rights reserved.

land all natural resources, such as minerals, timber, and water, as well as the land itself (1)

law of demand as the price of a good or service rises (falls), the quantity of that good or service that people are willing and able to purchase during a particular period of time falls (rises), *ceteris paribus* (3)

law of supply as the price of a good or service that producers are willing and able to offer for sale during a particular period of time rises (falls), the quantity of that good or service supplied rises (falls), *ceteris paribus* (3)

leading indicator a variable that changes before real output changes (8)

legal reserves the cash a bank holds in its vault plus its deposit in the Fed (14)

liquid asset an asset that can easily be exchanged for goods and services (13)

long-run aggregate supply curve (LRAS) a vertical line at potential level of national income (9)

M1 money supply financial assets that are most liquid (13)

macroeconomics the study of the economy as a whole (1)

managed floating exchange rates the system whereby central banks intervene in the floating foreign-exchange market to influence exchange rates (22)

marginal benefit additional benefit (2)

marginal cost (MC) the additional costs of producing one more unit of output (2)

marginal opportunity cost the amount of one good or service that must be given up to obtain one additional unit of another good or service (2)

marginal propensity to consume (MPC) change in consumption as a proportion of change in disposable income (10)

marginal propensity to import (MPI) change in imports as a proportion of change in income (10)

marginal propensity to save (MPS) change in saving as a proportion of change in disposable income (10)

market a place or service that enables buyers and sellers to exchange goods and services (3)

market imperfection a lack of efficiency that results from imperfect information in the market place (5)

microeconomics the study of economics at the level of the individual (1)

monetarist economics a school of thought that emphasizes the role changes in the money supply play in determining equilibrium national income and price level (16)

monetary overhang money accumulated by households because there was nothing available that they wanted to buy (19)

monetary policy policy directed toward control of the money supply (5)

monetary reform a new monetary policy that includes the introduction of a new monetary unit (15)

money anything that is generally acceptable to sellers in exchange for goods and services (13)

money supply financial assets that are immediately available for spending (13)

monopoly a market structure in which there is a single supplier of a product (5)

multilateral aid aid provided by international organizations supported by many nations (19)

multinational business a firm that owns and operates producing units in foreign countries (4)

multiple exchange rates a system whereby a government fixes different exchange rates for different types of transactions (22)

national income (NI) net national product minus indirect business taxes (6)

national income accounting the process that summarizes the level of production in an economy over a specific period of time, typically a year (6)

natural rate of unemployment the unemployment rate that would exist in the absence of cyclical unemployment (8)

net exports exports minus imports (4)

net investment gross investment minus capital consumption allowance (6)

net national product (NNP) gross national product minus capital consumption allowance (6)

new classical economics a school of thought that holds that changes in real national income are a product of unexpected changes in the level of prices (16)

nominal GDP a measure of national output based on the current prices of goods and services (6)

nominal interest rate the observed interest rate in the market (8)

normative analysis analysis of what ought to be (1)

open economy an economy in which a relatively large fraction of the GDP is devoted to internationally tradable goods (17, 22)

open market operations the buying and selling of government bonds by the Fed to control bank reserves and the money supply (14)

opportunity costs the highest-valued alternative that must be forgone when a choice is made (2)

partnership a business with two or more owners who share the firm's profits and losses (4)

patent a legal document that gives an inventor the legal rights to an invention (18)

per capita real GDP real national income divided by the population (18)

personal income (PI) national income plus income currently received but not earned, minus income currently earned but not received (6)

Phillips curve a graph that illustrates the relationship between inflation and the unemployment rate (15)

portfolio investment the purchase of securities (19)

positive analysis analysis of what is (1)

potential real GDP the output produced at the natural rate of unemployment (8)

precautionary demand for money the demand for money to cover unplanned transactions or emergencies (14)

price ceiling a situation where the price is not allowed to rise above a certain level (3)

price floor a situation where the price is not allowed to decrease below a certain level (3)

price index a measure of the average price level in an economy (6)

primary product a product in the first stage of production, which often serves as input in the production of another product (19)

Copyright © by Houghton Mifflin Company. All rights reserved.

private property right   the limitation of ownership to an individual (5)

private sector   households, businesses, and the international sector (4)

privatize   transferring a publicly owned enterprise to a private ownership (19)

producer price index (PPI)   a measure of average prices received by producers (6)

production possibilities curve (PPC)   a graphical representation showing the maximum quantity of goods and services that can be produced using limited resources to the fullest extent possible (2)

productivity   the quantity of output produced per unit of resource (3)

progressive tax   a tax whose rate rises as income rises (12)

public choice   the use of economics to analyze the actions and inner workings of the public sector (5)

public goods   goods whose consumption cannot be limited only to the person who purchased the good (5)

public sector   the government (4)

purchasing power parity (PPP)   the condition under which monies have the same purchasing power in different markets (17)

quantity demanded   the amount of a product that people are willing and able to purchase at a specific price (3)

quantity quota   a limit on the amount of a good that may be imported (21)

quantity supplied   the amount sellers are willing and able to offer at a given price, during a given period of time, everything else held constant (3)

quantity theory of money   with constant velocity, changes in the quantity of money change nominal GDP (14)

rational expectation   an expectation that is formed using all available relevant information (15)

rational self-interest   the term economists use to describe how people make choices (1)

real GDP   a measure of the quantity of goods and services produced, adjusted for price changes (6)

real interest rate   the nominal interest rate minus the rate of inflation (8)

recession   a period in which real GDP falls (8)

recessionary gap   the increase in expenditures required to reach potential GDP (11)

relative price   the price of one good expressed in terms of another good (3)

rent seeking   the use of resources simply to transfer wealth from one group to another without increasing production or total wealth (5, 22)

required reserves   the cash reserves (a percentage of deposits) a bank must keep on hand or on deposit with the Federal Reserve (13)

reservation wage   the minimum wage a worker is willing to accept (15)

reserve currency   a currency that is used to settle international debts and is held by governments to use in foreign exchange market interventions (22)

resources   goods used to produce other goods, i.e., land, labor, capital, entrepreneurial ability (1)

risk premium   the extra return required to offset the higher risk associated with investing in a foreign asset (17)

rule of 72   the number of years required for an amount to double in value is 72 divided by the annual rate of growth (18)

saving function   the relationship between disposable income and saving (10)

scarcity   the shortage that exists when less of something is available than is wanted at a zero price (1)

scientific method   a manner of analyzing issues that involves five steps: recognition of the problem, assumptions, model building, predictions, tests of model (1)

shock   an unexpected change in a variable (15)

shortage   a quantity supplied that is smaller than the quantity demanded at a given price (3)

slope   the steepness of a curve, measured as the ratio of the rise to the run (1 App.)

sole proprietorship   a business owned by one person who receives all the profits and is responsible for all the debts incurred by the business (4)

special drawing right (SDR)   an artificial unit of account created by averaging the values of the U.S. dollar, German mark, Japanese yen, French franc, and British pound (13, 22)

speculative demand for money   the demand for money created by uncertainty about the value of other assets (14)

speculators   people who seek to profit from an expected shift in an exchange rate by selling the currency expected to depreciate and buying the currency expected to appreciate, then exchanging the appreciated currency for the depreciated currency after the rate adjustment (22)

spending multiplier   the reciprocal of the sum of the MPS and the MPI (11)

sterilization   the use of domestic open market operations to offset the effects of a foreign exchange market intervention on the domestic money supply (14)

strategic trade policy   the use of trade restrictions or subsidies to allow domestic firms with decreasing costs to gain a greater share of the world market (22)

subsidies   payments made by government to domestic firms to encourage exports (22)

substitute goods   goods that can be used in place of each other (as the price of one rises, the demand for the other rises) (3)

supply   the amount of a good or service that producers are willing and able to offer for sale at each possible price during a period of time, *ceteris paribus* (3)

supply curve   a graph of a supply schedule that measures price on the vertical axis and quantity supplied on the horizontal axis (3)

supply schedule   a list or table of prices and corresponding quantities supplied of a particular good or service (3)

surplus   a quantity supplied that is larger than the quantity demanded at a given price (3)

surplus (in a balance of payments account)   the amount by which credits exceed debits (7)

tariffs   taxes on imports or exports (21)

technical efficiency   producing at a point on the PPC (5)

technology   ways of combining resources to produce output (18)

terms of trade   the amount of exports that must be exchanged for some amount of imports (19, 20)

tests   trials or measurements used to determine whether a theory is consistent with the facts (1)

Copyright © by Houghton Mifflin Company. All rights reserved.

theory (or model) a simplified, logical story based on positive analysis that is used to explain an event (1)

time inconsistent a characteristic of a policy or plan that changes over time in response to changing conditions (15)

total factor productivity (TFP) the ratio of the economy's output to its stock of labor and capital (18)

trade creation an effect of a preferential trade agreement, allowing a country to obtain goods at a lower cost than is available at home (21)

trade credit the extension of a period of time before an importer must pay for goods or services purchased (19)

trade deficit exists when imports exceed exports (4)

trade diversion an effect of a preferential trade agreement, reducing economic efficiency by shifting production to a higher-cost producer (21)

trade off to give up one good or activity in order to obtain some good or activity (2)

trade surplus (deficit) exists when imports are less than exports (4)

transaction costs the costs involved in making an exchange (3)

transactions account a checking account at a bank or other financial institution that can be drawn on to make payments (13)

transactions demand for money the demand to hold money to buy goods and services (14)

transfer payment income transferred from one citizen, who is earning income, to another citizen (5, 6, 12)

underemployment the employment of workers in jobs that do not utilize their productive potential (8)

unemployment rate the percentage of the labor force that is not working (8)

value added the difference between the value of output and the value of the intermediate goods used in the production of that output (6)

value-added tax (VAT) a general sales tax collected at each stage of production (12)

value quota a limit on the monetary value of a good that may be imported (21)

velocity of money the average number of times each dollar is spent on final goods and services in a year (14)

wealth the value of all assets owned by a household (10)

wealth effect a change in the real value of wealth that causes spending to change when the price level changes (9)

World Bank an international organization that makes loans and provides technical expertise to developing countries (22)

Copyright © by Houghton Mifflin Company. All rights reserved.

Index

Copyright © by Houghton Mifflin Company. All rights reserved.

Copyright © by Houghton Mifflin Company. All rights reserved.

Customs unions (CUs), 530
Cyclical unemployment, 180, 181
Czech Republic
    economic development of, 479 (illus.)
    privatization in, 480

Debits, 162
Debt
    of developing countries, 97
    national, interest payments on, 303
    see also Government borrowing; Loans
Debtors, net, 165
Deficits
    balance of payments, 163
    budget, *see* Budget deficits
    trade, *see* Trade deficits
Demand, 53–61
    aggregate, *see* Aggregate demand *entries*
    changes in demand and changes in quantity demanded and, 57–59, 58 (fig.)
    determinants of, 54
    for imports, 502–503, 504 (fig.), 505
    international effect on, 59–60
    law of, 53–54
    shifts in, equilibrium price and, 70, 70 (fig.)
Demand curves, 54–55, 55 (fig.)
    for imports, 504 (fig.), 505
    individual and market, 55, 56 (fig.), 57
Demand deposits
    in money supply, 321
    at mutual savings banks, 321
Demand for money, 357–361
Demand-pull inflation, 191, 202
Demand schedule, 54
Demographics
    consumption and, 205, 239
    labor quality and, 451–452
Dependent variable, 20
Deposit(s)
    demand, *see* Demand deposits
    Eurodollar, 329
    fractional reserve banking system and, 331–332, 331–333 (fig.)
    savings, in money supply, 321
    time, small-denomination, in money supply, 321
    transaction, 349
Deposit expansion multiplier, 332–334, 333 (table)
Depository Institutions Deregulation and Monetary Control Act (1980), 325, 326
Depreciation, 140
    of currencies, 160, 414–415, 549
Depressions, 175
Deteriorating-terms-of-trade argument, 473
Determinants of demand, 54
Determinants of supply, 61–62
Devaluation, of currencies, 170–171, 541
Developing countries, 97
    basic human needs and, 464 (table), 464–465
    government spending in, 305–306, 307 (fig.)
    measuring poverty in, 462–464
    see also Economic development; *specific countries and regions*
Direct relationships, 20
Direct taxes, 307, 308 (fig.)
Discount rate, 350–353, 351 (table)
Discouraged workers, 178
Discretionary fiscal policy, 300
Disequilibrium, 68
    fundamental, 549
Disposable income
    consumption and, 237–238
    see also Consumption; Saving

Disposable personal income (DPI), 143
Dissaving, 233
District banks, of Federal Reserve System, 343
Dole, Bob, 289
Dollar
    appearance of, 344
    devaluation of, 541
    in international economy, 338–339
    value of, 539
Domestic jobs, as argument for trade protection, 518, 519–520 (table), 520
Domino's Pizza, 82, 84
Double coincidence of wants, 52
Double-entry bookkeeping, 162
DPI (disposable personal income), 143
Dual economies, 473
Durability, of money, 319
Dutch Disease, 502

Economic bads, 5
Economic Consequences of the Peace (Keynes), 262
Economic development, 460–487
    of economies in transition from socialism, *see* Socialist economies, transformation of
    foreign investment and aid and, 474–478
    obstacles to growth and, 465–470
    strategies for, 470–474
    see also Developing countries; *specific countries and regions*
Economic efficiency, 112–113
Economic goods, 4–5
Economic growth, 438–456
    per capita real GDP and, 442
    determinants of, 444 (fig.), 444–448
    development and, 455
    long-run aggregate supply shifts and, 220, 220 (fig.)
    problems with definitions of, 442–443, 443 (table)
    productivity and, *see* Productivity
    real GDP and, 439–441
Economies
    centrally planned, 122–123, 123 (fig.)
        see also Socialist economies, transformation of
    dual, 473
    open, 413–414, 414 (table), 551
    private sectors of, *see* Firms; Household(s); International sector; Private sectors
    public sectors of, *see* Government *entries*
    socialist, *see* Socialist economies, transformation of
ECU (European currency unit), 324
Education, labor quality and, 450–451, 451 (fig.), 451 (table)
EEC (European Economic Community), 530
Effect lag, 402
Efficiency
    economic, 112–113
    government as guardian of, 112–113
    productive (technical), 112
Egypt, economic development of, 467
Employment
    as argument for trade protection, 518, 519–520 (table), 520
    foreign direct investment and, 475
    full, 182
    see also Labor *entries*; Unemployment; Wage *entries*
EMS (European Monetary System), 545
Energy prices
    for gasoline, 16–17, 74
    U.S. productivity slowdown and, 454
England, *see* United Kingdom
Enterprises, *see* Firms
Entrepreneur(s), 92
    lack of, as obstacle to economic development, 467–468
Entrepreneurial ability, 92–93

Copyright © by Houghton Mifflin Company. All rights reserved.

Copyright © by Houghton Mifflin Company. All rights reserved.

Copyright © by Houghton Mifflin Company. All rights reserved.

Copyright © by Houghton Mifflin Company. All rights reserved.

of inflation, 192, 193 (table)
of market economies, 123 (fig.), 123–125
of research and development expenditures, 243, 244, 245
of unemployment rate, 185 (table), 185–186
International Monetary Fund (IMF), 427, 541, 542
International reserve assets, 322
International reserve currencies, 322, 324
International sector, 94–98
banking in, 328–330
in circular flow, 133, 134 (fig.)
dollar in, 338–339
interaction with households and firms, 101, 102 (fig.)
linkages in, 282–283
money in, 322, 324
spending by, 97–98, 98 (fig.), 99 (fig.)
supply and, 67, 68 (fig.)
types of countries and, 94–95 (fig.), 95–97
International trade, 495–511
budget deficits and, 301–303
comparative advantage and, see Comparative advantage
creation and diversion of, 531 (fig.), 531–532
direction of, 496, 496 (table), 497 (table), 498 (fig.)
diversification of, exchange rates and, 551, 552 (table)
equilibrium price and quantity traded and, 505 (fig.), 505–506
exchange rates and, see Exchange rates
export supply and import demand and, 502–503, 504 (fig.), 505
goods traded and, 497, 498 (table)
intraindustry, 509
preferential trade agreements and, 529–532
restriction of, see Trade restrictions
specialization and, see Comparative advantage; Specialization
terms of trade and, 473, 501–502, 503 (table)
see also Export entries; Import entries; Net export(s)
International trade effect, 209
Internet, 128–129
Intraindustry trade, 509
Inventory, 137
fluctuations in, unemployment and, 377–378, 378 (fig.)
planned and unplanned changes in, 137–138
Inverse relationships, 20
Investment, 93, 93 (fig.), 240–247
aggregate demand and, 205
autonomous, 240, 241 (fig.)
budget deficits and, 301
determinants of, 241–245
diversion of, population growth and, 469
factors affecting, 205
foreign, see Foreign direct investment
gross, 141–142
net, 142
volatility and, 245–246
Investment income account, balance of payments and, 163
Invisible hand, 85, 112
Inward-oriented strategies, for economic development, 471, 473–474
IRP, see Interest rate parity (IRP)
Islamic banking, 327
Israel, monetary reform in, 391 (table)
Itochu, 91 (table)

Japan, 96
business practices in, 528
economy of, 123 (fig.), 124–125
exchange rate of, 542, 544 (table)
safety standards of, 529
trade war with United States, 514–515
unemployment in, 185, 186

Keiretsu, 124
Kellogg, Will, 92
Keynes, John Maynard, 261, 262, 397

Keynesian economics, 397–399, 398 (fig.)
comparison with other theories, 406–408, 407 (table), 410–411
fixed-price model and, 276
income and expenditures equilibrium in, see Income and expenditures equilibrium
on policymakers' role, 399
Korea
economic development of, 472 (illus.)
U.S. trade with, 97 (illus.)
Kuwait, 96

Labor, 5, 6 (fig.), 7
economic growth and, 444, 445 (fig.), 446
quality of, U.S. productivity slowdown and, 450 (fig.), 450–452
see also Employment; Unemployment; Wage entries
Laffer curve, 294
Lagging indicators, 176–177, 177 (table)
Land, 5, 6 (fig.), 7
economic growth and, 446–447
Latin America
black market in foreign exchange in, 161
population of, 462
see also specific countries
Law of demand, 53–54
Law of supply, 61
LDCs (less developed countries), see Developing countries; specific countries and regions
Leading indicators, 176, 177 (table)
Leakages, 264–265, 266 (fig.)
Legal reserves, 349
Less developed countries (LDCs), see Developing countries; specific countries and regions
"Level playing field" argument, for trade protection, 520–521
Libya, 96
Life styles, permanent income and, 242
Line graphs, 18 (fig.), 18–19
Liquid assets, 318
Little Caesar's, 84
Living standards, see Economic development; Income distribution; Poverty
Loans
Eurodollar, 329
fractional reserve banking system and, 331–332, 331–333 (fig.)
see also Debt; Government borrowing
Long run, inflation-unemployment tradeoff in, 370–373, 372 (fig.)
Long-run aggregate supply curve (LRAS), 216, 217 (fig.), 218
Long-run equilibrium, 222–223
Los Angeles, air pollution in, 5
Low-income countries, 95–96
LRAS (long-run aggregate supply curve), 216, 217 (fig.), 218

McDonald's Corporation, 82, 90
Macroeconomic policy, 119–120, 368–392
international coordination of, 427–430
see also Banking; Federal Reserve System (Fed); Fiscal policy; Monetary policy; Money entries
Macroeconomics, 11
comparison of theories of, 406–408
see also Keynesian economics; Monetarist economics; New classical economics
Main checking account, 320
Managed floating exchange rates, 542, 545
Marginal benefits, 32
Marginal cost (MC), 32
Marginal opportunity costs, 36–38, 37 (fig.)
Marginal propensity to consume (MPC), 233, 234 (table), 234–235
permanent income and, 242
Marginal propensity to import (MPI), 249
Marginal propensity to save (MPS), 233–234, 234 (table), 235
permanent income and, 242

Copyright © by Houghton Mifflin Company. All rights reserved.

Copyright © by Houghton Mifflin Company. All rights reserved.

in gross domestic product, 139
resource allocation and, 82–85, 83 (fig.), 84 (fig.)
Profit-push pressures, 191
Progressive taxes, 304
Property rights
economic development and, 466
private, 115
Proportional taxes, 304
Protection, *see* Trade restrictions
Public choice, 117
Public choice theory of government, 116–117
Public goods, 114–115
free riders and, 115, 118–119
Public sector, 86
see also Government *entries*
Purchasing power, 187
Purchasing power parity (PPP), 415–417
interest rate parity and, 426

Quantity demanded, 53
changes in, 57–59, 58 (fig.)
Quantity quotas, 526
Quantity supplied, 61
changes in, 63, 65–67
Quantity theory of money, 346–347
Quotas
IMF, 541
import, 526–527, 527 (fig.)

Race, unemployment and, 183
Rational expectations, 380, 404
Rational self-interest, 7–8, 86
R&D, *see* Research and development (R&D)
Reaction lag, 402
Reagan, Ronald, 289
Real-balance effect, 207
Real business cycle, 386–387, 387 (fig.)
Real GDP, 144–146, 145 (fig.), 439–442
per capita, 442
growth in, *see* Economic growth
potential, 181
Real interest rate, 189
Real values, 207
Recession(s), 174
Recessionary gap, 272
Reciprocal exchange rates, 158
Reciprocal Trade Agreements Act (1934), 526
Recognition lag, 401–402
Reconciliation, 296–297
Reebok, 244 (illus.)
Regressive taxes, 304
Relative price, 52
Rent, 5, 6 (fig.), 7
in gross domestic product, 139
Rent controls, 72–74, 73 (fig.), 78–79
Rent seeking, 116
Repurchase agreements (RPs), 322
Research and development (R&D)
international comparison of spending on, 243, 244, 245
U.S. expenditures for, 452, 453 (fig.)
see also Technological advance
Reservation wage, 375–377, 376 (fig.)
Reserve(s), legal, 349
Reserve assets, international, 322
Reserve currencies, 540
international, 322, 324, 324 (table)
Reserve requirements, 349–350, 350 (table)
Resource(s), 5, 6 (fig.), 7
abundance of, comparative advantage and, 507

allocation of, profit and, 82–85, 83 (fig.), 84 (fig.)
flow of, 85
prices of, changes in supply and changes in quantity supplied and, 63, 65, 65 (fig.)
see also Capital; Entrepreneurial ability; Labor; Land
Resource prices
aggregate supply and, 218–219
changes in supply and changes in quantity supplied and, 63, 65, 65 (fig.)
Retail money market mutual fund balances, in money supply, 321
Revenue, government, as argument for trade protection, 521, 522 (table)
Ricardian equivalence, 295
Ricardian model, 506
Ricardo, David, 295, 506
Risk, political, deviations from interest rate parity and, 421–422
Risk premiums, 422
Royal Dutch/Shell Group, 91 (table)
RPs (repurchase agreements), 322
Rule of 72, 441, 441 (table)

Saudi Arabia, 96
Saving
average propensity to save and, 235–236, 237, 237 (table)
marginal propensity to save and, 233–234, 234 (table), 235, 242
savings versus, 230
Saving function, 232–233
Savings
foreign, flows of, 474–475
saving versus, 230
Savings deposits, in money supply, 321
Scarcity, 4
choices and, 7
Schwartz, Anna, 402
Scientific method, 9–11, 10 (fig.)
SDRs (special drawing rights), 324, 545
Seasonal unemployment, 180
Self-interest, rational, 7–8, 86
Services
shift toward, U.S. productivity slowdown and, 454–455, 458–459
see also Goods (goods and services)
Services account, balance of payments and, 163
Shipping costs, purchasing power parity and, 417
Shocks, 386–387, 387 (fig.)
Shortages, 68–69
Short run, inflation-unemployment tradeoff in, 370–373, 372 (fig.)
Short-run aggregate supply curve, 215 (fig.), 215–216
Short-run equilibrium, 221 (fig.), 221–222
Short-run operating targets, 353
Slopes, 25–27
equations and, 26–27
positive and negative, 25–26, 26 (fig.)
Small-denomination time deposits, in money supply, 321
Smith, Adam, 85, 86, 112
Smithsonian agreement, 541
Smoot, Reed, 526
Smoot-Hawley tariff, 526
Social factors, economic development and, 467–470
Socialist economies, transformation of, 478–486
macroeconomic issues for, 482–485
microeconomic issues for, 478–482
sequencing of reforms for, 485
Social programs, in former socialist economies, 481–482
SOEs, *see* State-owned enterprises (SOEs), privatization of
Sole proprietorships, 89
South Africa, exchange rate of, 551
Soviet Union, former
economy of, 122–123
see also specific states

Copyright © by Houghton Mifflin Company. All rights reserved.

Special drawing rights (SDRs), 324, 545
Specialization, 36–41
    comparative advantage and, *see* Comparative advantage
    marginal opportunity cost and, 36–38, 37 (fig.)
    where opportunity costs are lowest, 38–39
Speculative demand for money, 357
Speculators, 549
Spending, *see* Consumption; Expenditures; Government spending
Spending multiplier, 268 (table), 268–276
    equilibrium and, 270–272, 271 (fig.), 272 (fig.)
    estimates of, 275 (table), 275–276
    fiscal policy and, 290–292
Sri Lanka
    economic growth in, 442, 443 (table)
    tea exports of, 499 (illus.)
Standard of living, *see* Economic development; Income distribution;
    Poverty
State banks, 326
State-owned enterprises (SOEs), privatization of, in former socialist
    economies, 478–480
Statistical discrepancy account, 164–165
Sterilization, 356
Stock market, Super Bowl results for predicting, 11
Straight-line curves, 21
Strategic trade policy, 522–523
Structural unemployment, 180, 181, 198–199
Subsidies, to exporters, 528
Substitutes, prices of, 58
Sumimoto, 91 (table)
Supply, 61–67
    aggregate, *see* Aggregate supply *entries*
    changes in supply and changes in quantity supplied and, 63, 65–67
    determinants of, 61–62
    of exports, 502–503, 504 (fig.), 505
    international effects on, 67, 68 (fig.)
    law of, 61–62
    shifts in, equilibrium price and, 71, 71 (fig.)
Supply curve, 62 (fig.), 62–63
    for exports, 503, 504 (fig.)
    individual and market, 63, 64 (fig.)
Supply schedule, 62, 62 (fig.)
Supply-side economics, 294
Surpluses, 68
    balance of payments, 163
    budget, 121
    trade, 98
Swaziland, trade of, 551
Sweden
    economy of, 123 (fig.), 125
    unemployment in, 185

Tables, constructing graphs from, 22–24, 23 (fig.)
Tabloids, market for, 106–107
Taco Bell, 82
Tariffs, 524–525, 525 (fig.), 526
    purchasing power parity and, 417
Tastes, demand and, 57
Taxes
    consumption and, 205
    deviations from interest rate parity and, 422
    direct, 307, 308 (fig.)
    increases of, government spending financed by, 292 (fig.), 292–293
    indirect, 140–141, 307, 308 (fig.)
    international comparison of, 307, 308 (fig.)
    progressive, 304
    proportional, 304
    regressive, 304
    see also Fiscal policy
Technical efficiency, 112

Technological advance
    aggregate supply and, 219
    changes in supply and changes in quantity supplied and, 65 (fig.), 66
    economic growth and, 447–448
    investment and, 205, 243, 244 (table), 245
    U.S. productivity slowdown and, 452–453, 453 (fig.)
Technology transfer, foreign direct investment and, 475–476
Teenagers, unemployment among, 183
Terms of trade, 473, 501–502, 503 (table)
Tests, 11
TFP (total factor productivity), 448
Theories, 10
A Theory of the Consumption Function (Friedman), 402
Third World, *see* Developing countries; *specific countries and regions*
3M, 476 (illus.)
Thrift institutions, 325
Time deposits, small-denomination, in money supply, 321
Time inconsistency, 381–383, 382 (fig.)
Total factor productivity (TFP), 448
Toys "R" Us, 528
Trade
    balance of, 163
    international, *see* International trade
    specialization and, *see* Specialization
    see also Barter; Exchange
Trade creation, 531 (fig.), 531–532
Trade deficits, 98, 98 (fig.)
    U.S.-China, 256–257
Trade diversion, 531 (fig.), 531–532
Tradeoffs, 32
Trade restrictions, 516–533
    arguments for, 517–524
    government procurement, 528–529
    health and safety standards, 529
    purchasing power parity and, 417
    quotas, 526–527, 527 (fig.)
    subsidies, 528
    tariffs, 524–525, 525 (fig.), 526
Trade surpluses, 98
Transaction costs, 52
Transaction deposits, 349
Transactions accounts, 320
Transactions demand for money, 357
Transfer payments, 121, 143, 304
Travelers' checks, in money supply, 321
Trends, 175
Troughs, 175

Underemployment, 179
Underground economy, 179
Unemployment, 46–47, 177–186
    costs of, 181–183, 182 (fig.)
    cyclical, 180, 181
    defined, 178
    inventory fluctuations and, 377–378, 378 (fig.)
    measurement of, 178
    natural rate of, 374
    Phillips curve and, *see* Phillips curve
    record of, 183, 184 (table), 185 (table), 185–186
    seasonal, 180
    structural, 180, 181, 198–199
    wage contracts and, 378–379, 379 (fig.)
    wage expectations and, 375–377, 376 (fig.)
Unemployment rate, 178–179
    international comparison of, 185 (table), 185–186
    interpreting, 178–179
    natural, 181–183
Unilateral transfers account, balance of payments and, 163–164
Unit banking, 326

Copyright © by Houghton Mifflin Company. All rights reserved.

Copyright © by Houghton Mifflin Company. All rights reserved.